"We are pleased to witness publication of the
Ancient Christian Commentary on Scripture. It is most beneficial for us to learn
how the ancient Christians, especially the saints of the church
who proved through their lives their devotion to God and his Word, interpreted
Scripture. Let us heed the witness of those who have gone before us in the faith."

METROPOLITAN THEODOSIUS
Primate, Orthodox Church in America

"Across Christendom there has emerged a widespread interest
in early Christianity, both at the popular and scholarly level. . . .
Christians of all traditions stand to benefit from this project, especially clergy
and those who study the Bible. Moreover, it will allow us to see how our traditions are
both rooted in the scriptural interpretations of the church fathers while at
the same time seeing how we have developed new perspectives."

ALBERTO FERREIRO
Professor of History, Seattle Pacific University

"The Ancient Christian Commentary on Scripture fills a long overdue need for scholars and
students of the church fathers. . . . Such information will be of immeasurable
worth to those of us who have felt inundated by contemporary interpreters and novel theories
of the biblical text. We welcome some 'new' insight from the
ancient authors in the early centuries of the church."

H. WAYNE HOUSE
Professor of Theology and Law
Trinity University School of Law

Chronological snobbery—the assumption that our ancestors working without benefit of
computers have nothing to teach us—is exposed as nonsense by this magnificent
new series. Surfeited with knowledge but starved of wisdom, many of us are
more than ready to sit at table with our ancestors and listen to their holy
conversations on Scripture. I know I am.

EUGENE H. PETERSON
Professor Emeritus of Spiritual Theology
Regent College

"Few publishing projects have encouraged me as much as the recently announced Ancient Christian Commentary on Scripture with Dr. Thomas Oden serving as general editor. . . . How is it that so many of us who are dedicated to serve the Lord received seminary educations which omitted familiarity with such incredible students of the Scriptures as St. John Chrysostom, St. Athanasius the Great and St. John of Damascus? I am greatly anticipating the publication of this Commentary."

FR. PETER E. GILLQUIST
Director, Department of Missions and Evangelism
Antiochian Orthodox Christian Archdiocese of North America

"The Scriptures have been read with love and attention for nearly two thousand years, and listening to the voice of believers from previous centuries opens us to unexpected insight and deepened faith. Those who studied Scripture in the centuries closest to its writing, the centuries during and following persecution and martyrdom, speak with particular authority. The Ancient Christian Commentary on Scripture will bring to life the truth that we are invisibly surrounded by a 'great cloud of witnesses.'"

FREDERICA MATHEWES-GREEN
Commentator, National Public Radio

"For those who think that church history began around 1941 when their pastor was born, this Commentary will be a great surprise. Christians throughout the centuries have read the biblical text, nursed their spirits with it and then applied it to their lives. These commentaries reflect that the witness of the Holy Spirit was present in his church throughout the centuries. As a result, we can profit by allowing the ancient Christians to speak to us today."

HADDON ROBINSON
Harold John Ockenga Distinguished Professor of Preaching
Gordon-Conwell Theological Seminary

"All who are interested in the interpretation of the Bible will welcome the forthcoming multivolume series Ancient Christian Commentary on Scripture. Here the insights of scores of early church fathers will be assembled and made readily available for significant passages throughout the Bible and the Apocrypha. It is hard to think of a more worthy ecumenical project to be undertaken by the publisher."

BRUCE M. METZGER
Professor of New Testament, Emeritus
Princeton Theological Seminary

ANCIENT CHRISTIAN COMMENTARY ON SCRIPTURE

OLD TESTAMENT
X

ISAIAH 1-39

EDITED BY
STEVEN A. MCKINION

GENERAL EDITOR
THOMAS C. ODEN

InterVarsity Press
Downers Grove, Illinois

InterVarsity Press
P.O. Box 1400, Downers Grove, IL 60515-1426
World Wide Web: www.ivpress.com
E-mail: mail@ivpress.com

InterVarsity Press® is the book-publishing division of InterVarsity Christian Fellowship/USA®, a student movement active on campus at hundreds of universities, colleges and schools of nursing in the United States of America, and a member movement of the International Fellowship of Evangelical Students. For information about local and regional activities, write Public Relations Dept., InterVarsity Christian Fellowship/USA, 6400 Schroeder Rd., P.O. Box 7895, Madison, WI 53707-7895, or visit the IVCF website at <www.intervarsity.org>.

Cover photograph: Scala/Art Resource, New York. View of the apse. S. Vitale, Ravenna, Italy.
Spine photograph: Byzantine Collection, Dumbarton Oaks, Washington, D.C. Pendant cross (gold and enamel). Constantinople, late sixth century.

ISBN 0-8308-1480-9

Printed in the United States of America ∞

Library of Congress Cataloging-in-Publication Data

Isaiah 1-39/edited by Steven A. McKinion; general editor, Thomas C.
Oden
    p. cm.—(Ancient Christian commentary on Scripture. Old
Testament; 10) Includes bibliographical references and indexes.
  ISBN 0-8308-1480-9 (cloth: alk. paper)
  1. Bible. O.T. Isaiah I-XXXIX—Commentaries. I. McKinion, Steven A.
(Steven Alan) II. Oden, Thomas C. III. Series.
  BS1515.53.I63 2003
  224'.1077'09—dc22

2003016921

| P | 25 | 24 | 23 | 22 | 21 | 20 | 19 | 18 | 17 | 16 | 15 | 14 | 13 | 12 | 11 | 10 | 9 | 8 | 7 | 6 | 5 | 4 | 3 |
| Y | 25 | 24 | 23 | 22 | 21 | 20 | 19 | 18 | 17 | 16 | 15 | 14 | 13 | 12 | 11 | 10 | 09 | 08 | 07 | 06 | | | |

ANCIENT CHRISTIAN COMMENTARY
PROJECT RESEARCH TEAM

GENERAL EDITOR
Thomas C. Oden

ASSOCIATE EDITOR
Christopher A. Hall

OPERATIONS MANAGER
Joel Elowsky

TRANSLATIONS PROJECTS DIRECTOR
Joel Scandrett

RESEARCH AND ACQUISITIONS DIRECTOR
Michael Glerup

EDITORIAL SERVICES DIRECTOR
Warren Calhoun Robertson

ORIGINAL LANGUAGE VERSION DIRECTOR
Konstantin Gavrilkin

GRADUATE RESEARCH ASSISTANTS

Jeffrey Finch	*Sergey Kozin*
Steve Finlan	*Hsueh-Ming Liao*
Alexei Khamine	*Michael Nausner*
Vladimir Kharlamov	*Robert Paul Seesengood*
Susan Kipper	*Baek-Yong Sung*
	Elena Vishnevskaya

ADMINISTRATIVE ASSISTANT
Judy Cox

Contents

General Introduction

The Ancient Christian Commentary on Scripture has as its goal the revitalization of Christian teaching based on classical Christian exegesis, the intensified study of Scripture by lay persons who wish to think with the early church about the canonical text, and the stimulation of Christian historical, biblical, theological and pastoral scholars toward further inquiry into scriptural interpretation by ancient Christian writers.

The time frame of these documents spans seven centuries of exegesis, from Clement of Rome to John of Damascus, from the end of the New Testament era to A.D. 750, including the Venerable Bede.

Lay readers are asking how they might study sacred texts under the instruction of the great minds of the ancient church. This commentary has been intentionally prepared for a general lay audience of non-professionals who study the Bible regularly and who earnestly wish to have classic Christian observation on the text readily available to them. The series is targeted to anyone who wants to reflect and meditate with the early church about the plain sense, theological wisdom and moral meaning of particular Scripture texts.

A commentary dedicated to allowing ancient Christian exegetes to speak for themselves will refrain from the temptation to fixate endlessly upon contemporary criticism. Rather, it will stand ready to provide textual resources from a distinguished history of exegesis that has remained massively inaccessible and shockingly disregarded during the last century. We seek to make available to our present-day audiences the multicultural, multilingual, transgenerational resources of the early ecumenical Christian tradition.

Preaching at the end of the first millennium focused primarily on the text of Scripture as understood by the earlier esteemed tradition of comment, largely converging on those writers that best reflected classic Christian consensual thinking. Preaching at the end of the second millennium has reversed that pattern. It has so forgotten most of these classic comments that they are vexing to find anywhere, and even when located they are often available only in archaic editions and inadequate translations. The preached word in our time has remained largely bereft of previously influential patristic inspiration. Recent scholarship has so focused attention upon post-Enlightenment historical and literary methods that it has left this longing largely unattended and unserviced.

This series provides the pastor, exegete, student and lay reader with convenient means to see what Athanasius or John Chrysostom or the desert fathers and mothers had to say about a particular text for preaching, for study and for meditation. There is an emerging awareness among Catholic, Protestant and Orthodox laity that vital biblical preaching and spiritual formation need deeper grounding beyond the scope of the historical-critical orientations that have governed biblical studies in our day.

Hence this work is directed toward a much broader audience than the highly technical and specialized scholarly field of patristic studies. The audience is not limited to the university scholar concentrating on the study of the history of the transmission of the text or to those with highly focused philological interests in textual morphology or historical-critical issues. Though these are crucial concerns for specialists, they are not the paramount interests of this series.

This work is a Christian Talmud. The Talmud is a Jewish collection of rabbinic arguments and comments on the Mishnah, which epitomized the laws of the Torah. The Talmud originated in approximately the same period that the patristic writers were commenting on texts of the Christian tradition. Christians from the late patristic age through the medieval period had documents analogous to the Jewish Talmud and Midrash (Jewish commentaries) available to them in the *glossa ordinaria* and catena traditions, two forms of compiling extracts of patristic exegesis. In Talmudic fashion the sacred text of Christian Scripture was thus clarified and interpreted by the classic commentators.

The Ancient Christian Commentary on Scripture has venerable antecedents in medieval exegesis of both eastern and western traditions, as well as in the Reformation tradition. It offers for the first time in this century the earliest Christian comments and reflections on the Old and New Testaments to a modern audience. Intrinsically an ecumenical project, this series is designed to serve Protestant, Catholic and Orthodox lay, pastoral and scholarly audiences.

In cases where Greek, Latin, Syriac and Coptic texts have remained untranslated into English, we provide new translations. Wherever current English translations are already well rendered, they will be utilized, but if necessary their language will be brought up to date. We seek to present fresh dynamic equivalency translations of long-neglected texts which historically have been regarded as authoritative models of biblical interpretation.

These foundational sources are finding their way into many public libraries and into the core book collections of many pastors and lay persons. It is our intent and the publisher's commitment to keep the whole series in print for many years to come.

Thomas C. Oden
General Editor

A Guide to Using This Commentary

Several features have been incorporated into the design of this commentary. The following comments are intended to assist readers in making full use of this volume.

Pericopes of Scripture

The scriptural text has been divided into pericopes, or passages, usually several verses in length. Each of these pericopes is given a heading, which appears at the beginning of the pericope. For example, the first pericope in the commentary on Isaiah is "1:1-9 Rebellion Against God." This heading is followed by the Scripture passage quoted in the Revised Standard Version (RSV) across the full width of the page. The Scripture passage is provided for the convenience of readers, but it is also in keeping with medieval patristic commentaries, in which the citations of the Fathers were arranged around the text of Scripture.

Overviews

Following each pericope of text is an overview of the patristic comments on that pericope. The format of this overview varies within the volumes of this series, depending on the requirements of the specific book of Scripture. The function of the overview is to provide a brief summary of all the comments to follow. It tracks a reasonably cohesive thread of argument among patristic comments, even though they are derived from diverse sources and generations. Thus the summaries do not proceed chronologically or by verse sequence. Rather they seek to rehearse the overall course of the patristic comment on that pericope.

We do not assume that the commentators themselves anticipated or expressed a formally received cohesive argument but rather that the various arguments tend to flow in a plausible, recognizable pattern. Modern readers can thus glimpse aspects of continuity in the flow of diverse exegetical traditions representing various generations and geographical locations.

Topical Headings

An abundance of varied patristic comment is available for each pericope of these letters. For this reason we have broken the pericopes into two levels. First is the verse with its topical heading. The patristic comments are then focused on aspects of each verse, with topical headings summarizing the essence of the patristic comment by evoking a key phrase, metaphor or idea. This feature provides a bridge by which modern readers can enter into the heart of the patristic comment.

Identifying the Patristic Texts

Following the topical heading of each section of comment, the name of the patristic commentator is given. An English translation of the patristic comment is then provided. This is immediately followed by the title of the patristic work and the textual reference—either by book, section and subsection or by book-and-verse references. If the notation differs significantly between the English-language source footnoted and other sources, alternate references appear in parentheses. Some differences may also be due to variant biblical versification or chapter and verse numbering.

The Footnotes

Readers who wish to pursue a deeper investigation of the patristic works cited in this commentary will find the footnotes especially valuable. A footnote number directs the reader to the notes at the bottom of the right-hand column, where in addition to other notations (clarifications or biblical cross references) one will find information on English translations (where available) and standard original-language editions of the work cited. An abbreviated citation (normally citing the book, volume and page number) of the work is provided. A key to the abbreviations is provided on page xv. Where there is any serious ambiguity or textual problem in the selection, we have tried to reflect the best available textual tradition.

Where original language texts have remained untranslated into English, we provide new translations. Wherever current English translations are already well rendered, they are utilized, but where necessary they are stylistically updated. A single asterisk (*) indicates that a previous English translation has been updated to modern English or amended for easier reading. The double asterisk (**) indicates either that a new translation has been provided or that some extant translation has been significantly amended. We have standardized spellings and made grammatical variables uniform so that our English references will not reflect the odd spelling variables of the older English translations. For ease of reading we have in some cases edited out superfluous conjunctions.

For the convenience of computer database users the digital database references are provided to either the Thesaurus Linguae Graecae (Greek texts) or to the Cetedoc (Latin texts) in the appendix found on pages 267-75.

Abbreviations

ACW	Ancient Christian Writers: The Works of the Fathers in Translation. Mahwah, N.J.: Paulist, 1946-.
AF	J. B. Lightfoot and J. R. Harmer, trans. *The Apostolic Fathers.* Edited by M. W. Holmes, 2nd ed. Grand Rapids, Mich.: Baker, 1989.
AHSIS	Dana Miller, ed. *The Ascetical Homilies of Saint Isaac the Syrian.* Boston, Mass.: Holy Transfiguration Monastery, 1984.
ANF	A. Roberts and J. Donaldson, eds. Ante-Nicene Fathers. 10 vols. Buffalo, N.Y.: Christian Literature, 1885-1896. Reprint, Grand Rapids, Mich.: Eerdmans, 1951-1956; reprint, Peabody, Mass.: Hendrickson, 1994.
CCL	Corpus Christianorum. Series Latina. Turnhout, Belgium: Brepols, 1953-.
Comm	*Communio: International Catholic Review.* David L. Schindler, ed.
CS	Cistercian Studies. Kalamazoo, Mich.: Cistercian Publications, 1973-.
CSEL	Corpus Scriptorum Ecclesiasticorum Latinorum. Vienna, 1866-.
EBT	Theophylact. *The Explanation by Blessed Theophylact of the Holy Gospel According to St. Matthew.* Introduction by Fr. Christopher Stade. House Springs, Mo.: Chrysostom Press, 1992.
ECCI	M. J. Hollerich. *Eusebius of Caesarea's Commentary on Isaiah: Christian Exegesis in the Age of Constantine.* Oxford: Clarendon Press, 1999.
ECTD	C. McCarthy, trans. and ed. *Saint Ephrem's Commentary on Tatian's Diatessaron: An English Translation of Chester Beatty Syriac MS 709. Journal of Semitic Studies* Supplement 2. Oxford: Oxford University Press, 1993.
ESH	Ephrem the Syrian. *Hymns.* Translated and introduced by Kathleen E. McVey. Preface by John Meyendorff. Classics in Western Spirituality. New York: Paulist, 1989.
FC	Fathers of the Church: A New Translation. Washington, D.C.: Catholic University of America Press, 1947-.
HGE	*The Homilies of St. Gregory the Great on the Book of the Prophet Ezekiel.* Translated by Theodosia Gray. Etna, Calif.: Center for Traditionalist Orthodox Studies, 1990.
JCC	John Cassian. *Conferences.* Translated by Colm Luibheid. Classics of Western Spirituality. Mahwah, N.J.: Paulist, 1985.
JCD	*Jerome's Commentary on Daniel.* Translated by Gleason L. Archer Jr. Grand Rapids, Mich.: Baker, 1958.
LCC	J. Baillie et al., eds. The Library of Christian Classics. 26 vols. Philadelphia: Westminster Press, 1953-1966.
LCL	Loeb Classical Library. Cambridge, Mass.: Harvard University Press; London: Heinemann, 1912-.
LF	A Library of Fathers of the Holy Catholic Church Anterior to the Division of the East and West. Translated by members of the English Church. 44 vols. Oxford: John Henry Parker, 1800-1881.
MFC	Message of the Fathers of the Church. Edited by Thomas Halton. Collegeville, Minn.: Liturgical Press, 1983-.

NPNF	P. Schaff et al., eds. *A Select Library of the Nicene and Post-Nicene Fathers of the Christian Church.* 2 series (14 vols. each). Buffalo, N.Y.: Christian Literature, 1887-1894; Reprint, Grand Rapids, Mich.: Eerdmans, 1952-1956. Reprint, Peabody, Mass.: Hendrickson, 1994.
OFP	Origen. *On First Principles.* Translated by G. W. Butterworth. London: SPCK, 1936. Reprint, Gloucester, Mass.: Peter Smith, 1973.
OSW	*Origen: An Exhortation to Martyrdom, Prayer and Selected Writings.* Translated by Rowan A. Greer with preface by Hans Urs von Balthasar. Classics of Western Spirituality. New York: Paulist, 1979.
OWP	John Chrysostom. *On Wealth and Poverty.* Translated by Catharine P. Roth. New York: St. Vladimir's Seminary Press, 1984.
PDCW	*Pseudo-Dionysius: The Complete Works.* Translated by Colm Luibheid. Classics of Western Spirituality. New York: Paulist, 1987.
PG	J.-P. Migne, ed. Patrologiae cursus completus. Series Graeca. 166 vols. Paris: Migne, 1857-1886.
PL	J.-P. Migne, ed. Patrologiae cursus completus. Series Latina. 221 vols. Paris: Migne, 1844-1864.
POG	Eusebius. *The Proof of the Gospel.* 2 vols. Translated by W. J. Ferrar. London: SPCK, 1920. Reprint, Grand Rapids, Mich.: Baker, 1981.
SC	H. de Lubac, J. Daniélou et al., eds. Sources Chrétiennes. Paris: Éditions de Cerf, 1941-.
SCA	Alexander Kerrigan. *St. Cyril of Alexandria: Interpreter of the Old Testament.* Analecta Biblica 2. Rome: Pontoficio Istituto Biblico, 1952.
TASHT	Texts and Studies in the History of Theology. 7 vols. Edited by Mandelbachtal/Cambridge: 2000-.
TTH	G. Clark, M. Gibson and M. Whitby, eds. Translated Texts for Historians. Liverpool: Liverpool University Press, 1985-.
WSA	J. E. Rotelle, ed. *Works of St. Augustine: A Translation for the Twenty-First Century.* Hyde Park, N.Y.: New City Press, 1995.

Introduction to Isaiah 1-39

The book of Isaiah was a part of the Christian canon from the beginning. From the outset Christians accepted the Hebrew Bible as authoritative Scripture, made up of the Law, Prophets and Writings. Consequently, the earliest Christian writings quote Isaiah and frame the message of Jesus as the Messiah within the boundaries of the message of the Old Testament. Christians believe the prophetic announcement in Isaiah of the coming Messiah was fulfilled in the life and ministry of Jesus of Nazareth. The importance of Isaiah 1-39 for the Fathers was primarily its promise of the Savior.

Patristic writers expressed little concern over modern critical issues such as authorship. While they regarded the prophet Isaiah as the single author of the prophecy, of greater concern for them was the divine author behind the human one. They considered God to be the ultimate author of all Scripture, rendering the Christian interpreter responsible for discovering the divine meaning in the text. Consequently, the original setting of the prophecy or questions of multiple authorship, the use of existing sources by the author or redaction by a later writer were of little or no importance to the Fathers. Some readers may therefore be surprised at what one finds in the selections that follow. There is little emphasis on ancient Near Eastern customs and little effort to reconstruct the original historical context of the prophecy. For the writers in this volume, Scripture was not a compendium of Jewish history or even a textbook of Jewish theology but an announcement of the coming Messiah. This understanding of the Hebrew Bible meant that Christian interpreters looked for and believed they found the message of Jesus Christ throughout the Old Testament.

The Text of Isaiah
The book of Isaiah, like all but a few passages of the Old Testament, was written in Hebrew. Most patristic writers, however, read Isaiah in either Greek or Latin, though many of them demonstrated a knowledge of and interaction with a Hebrew text. The Greek text used was usually a translation of the Hebrew Bible produced by unknown Jewish translators in the third and second centuries before Christ. Due to a legendary tale regarding the independent work of seventy translators producing the exact same translation, this work came to be known as the Septuagint (LXX), from the Greek for seventy. In actuality, different parts of the Hebrew text were translated at various times, and these sections vary widely in style and accuracy. The Jewish scholars Aquila, Symmachus and Theodotion made three additional Greek translations of the Old Testament in the second century after Christ, as Christians contended the Septuagint was a Christian book. Patristic writers occasionally made reference to these editions. Origen of Alexandria gathered these four Greek translations along with a Hebrew text and a Greek transliteration of the Hebrew in a volume known as the Hexapla, a name derived from the six columns into which the volume was divided. In the Greek-speaking church, however, the Septuagint was largely believed to

be the inspired text and was the most widely used edition of the Old Testament.

As Latin became the language of the church in the West, there was need to translate the Bible into the vernacular. Passages from the Septuagint that had been rendered into Latin became widely used in the Western church. Eventually, sometime after the second century, these various Latin passages were gathered into one text, commonly called the Old Latin. In the fifth century Jerome translated the Old Testament into Latin from the Hebrew in an effort to produce a more accurate text. The Latin Vulgate, as it became known, eventually superseded the Old Latin as the official text of the Old Testament in the West. The Latin-speaking Fathers read Isaiah in either the Old Latin or the Vulgate.

Several Christian interpreters contended with Jewish interpreters over variant readings in the Old Testament. Often the controversy was over passages considered messianic by Christians. In Isaiah 7:14, for example, Jewish readers argued that the prophecy concerned a "young woman" who bore a child, while the Septuagint indicated that a "virgin" would conceive and bear a child. Christian writers including Justin Martyr, Eusebius of Caesarea and Jerome accused the Jewish interpreters of removing clearly messianic passages from the Old Testament, particularly those in Isaiah, making the prophecy an important battleground in Christian polemic against Judaism.

Patristic Commentary on Isaiah

Although there is a considerable number of quotations from and allusions to Isaiah in early Christian literature, there are only a few commentaries on the book. Eusebius of Caesarea, Jerome and Cyril of Alexandria all produced passage-by-passage commentaries on Isaiah. The three are remarkably similar in their interpretation of numerous passages. Cyril acknowledges the existence of and his use of other commentators in the preface to his commentary, certainly including Eusebius and Jerome. It is possible that although Cyril seems not to have been conversant in Latin he did have at his disposal translators who made Jerome's commentary available to him in a Greek translation. At least relevant passages would have been translated for him. Cyril's dependence on Eusebius and Jerome is, it seems, unmistakable.

John Chrysostom preached a series of homilies on Isaiah, although what remains covers only the first eight chapters of Isaiah. Chrysostom's interpretation of the first chapters of Isaiah is quite similar to that of Eusebius and Jerome. Like Chrysostom's other sets of homilies, these texts reflect a desire to explain the meaning of the passages for the edification of his congregation.

A commentary on Isaiah bearing the name of Basil of Caesarea has also come down to us. The authorship of the commentary, however, remains a source of scholarly contention. A recent English translation of the commentary by Nikolai Lipatov contends that the work is that of Basil, although the debate is not closed on the question of authorship. Despite this concern, the commentary is a rich exposition of Isaiah similar to that of other fourth- and fifth-century interpreters. Selections are here included under the name of Basil with the proviso that the authorship remains under dispute.

Theodoret of Cyr authored a substantial commentary on the Greek text of Isaiah. Although Theodoret and Cyril of Alexandria were opponents in the christological controversy of the fifth century, they were strikingly similar in their approach to and interpretation of Isaiah. The preface to Cyril's commentary begins in the same manner as that of Theodoret. Theodoret claims that the prophecy of Isaiah was to announce the coming of the Lord.[1] Cyril says, "The end of the Law and Prophets is Christ."[2] Theodoret states that the prophecy of Isaiah was also only to reveal the fate of Israel: Isaiah prophesies concerning Assyrian military operations against the Jews alongside the second coming of Christ. Cyril seeks first to explain the literal meaning of the text, which he does in one passage by surveying the lives and reigns of the kings mentioned in Isaiah 1. Theodoret explains to his readers that some of Isaiah's prophecies are clear, while others are figurative and require interpretation. Cyril says that proper interpretation of the book will consider the figurative character of the text and offer a full explanation of the meaning found within it. Throughout their respective commentaries the authors distinguish which passages were intended as a warning to Israel and which were intended to announce Christ.

Other Significant Sources

Besides line-by-line commentaries, there are numerous expositions of particular passages from Isaiah in dogmatic treatises, polemical works and homilies. Of particular importance are those patristic works directed against Judaism. In an effort to distance themselves from the Jewish faith, many patristic writers expounded the Old Testament's message concerning the Messiah, claiming that it was fulfilled in Jesus. These works are of great interest to the interpreter of Isaiah 1-39. Additionally, authors such as Augustine of Hippo, Gregory the Great and Bede the Venerable comment frequently on passages from Isaiah 1-39.

Selection Process and Criteria

While discovering patristic comment on Isaiah was an easy task, selecting the quotations to include was a difficult and sometimes frustrating process. Besides the line-by-line commentaries nearly every significant patristic writer commented on one or more important passages from Isaiah, particularly those cited in the New Testament. In determining which selections to include, I depended on the selection criteria for the ACCS project overall.

We have tried to represent fairly the major lines of thought in early Christian interpretation of Isaiah 1-39. In some places the consensual tradition has very little, if any, opposition. In other places the extant sources include several different accepted interpretations. In both instances we have sought to offer the reader an accurate portrayal of the state of patristic interpretation. We included selections from different periods of time and provenances to demonstrate instances of uniformity of interpretation. When significant difference of opinion existed, we have included the representative selections.

To determine which selections to include we kept in mind that the audience of this volume is first and foremost the community of faith. While the quotations provide the historian of exegesis or even the specialist in patristics a useful tool, we hope the church will be inspired by these voices from early Christianity. Our goal is that reading Isaiah 1-39 with the Fathers will enlighten readers and will inspire them to read the prophet closely and devotionally.

Our search for the patristic interpretation of Isaiah has been aided greatly by technology unavailable until recently. The Thesaurus Linguae Graecae and Latin Cetedoc tools were indispensable for the selec-

---

[1]*Commentary on Isaiah*, SC 1:138.
[2]PG 70:9A.

tion of texts. In addition, the commentaries of Isaiah in Migne or critical editions enabled us to locate many comments. Finally, immensely capable and helpful researchers at the ACCS project office searched existing patristic literature to discover quotations of and allusions to Isaiah in the Fathers.

Important Themes in Patristic Interpretation of Isaiah

The most important theme in the early Christian interpretation of Isaiah is messianic announcement. The prophecy of Isaiah occupied a central position in the early Christian proclamation of Jesus of Nazareth as the promised Messiah. Patristic writers followed the New Testament's understanding of the book as a prophetic announcement of the coming One who would save his people from their sins. Matthew introduces the forerunner to the Messiah, John the Baptist, by quoting from Isaiah.[3] Additionally, the Gospel writer explains the virgin birth of Jesus by appealing to Isaiah's prophecy of the virgin who would conceive and bear a son.[4] Jesus read from the book of Isaiah and announced that the promise was being fulfilled in the presence of those who listened to him.[5] In the wilderness Philip explained to the Ethiopian eunuch that Jesus was the fulfillment of the message of the prophet.[6] New Testament writers believed that the message of the gospel was inextricably linked to the message of Isaiah.

The Fathers followed the New Testament's interpretation of Isaiah as an announcement of the Messiah fulfilled in Jesus of Nazareth. Patristic writers focused considerable attention on Isaiah 7:14 and the announcement of the virgin who would bear a child. The Fathers were unanimous in their understanding of this passage as a prophecy concerning the virgin birth of the Savior. Several writers, such as Eusebius of Caesarea, Jerome and Justin Martyr, among others, dealt in detail with the question of whether the prophecy was intended to speak of Hezekiah's day. They were agreed in their belief that the text was intended to speak of the Messiah rather than premessianic events. Evidence for this view was the idea of a sign, along with the fact that neither Hezekiah nor any other child was called "God with us." In other words, were the birth of the Messiah to be like that of any other baby, rather than a virgin birth, how would the birth be significant?

There is also considerable treatment of the Hebrew word translated "virgin" in the Septuagint. The Fathers contended that Jewish opponents of Christianity had denied the prophecy of a virgin birth in order to discredit the claim that Jesus was the Messiah. They cited the text's promise that the event would be a sign as evidence for their contention. Were the Messiah to be born simply of a young woman, then how would that be a sign?

Another important element of the text was the name Immanuel. The Fathers recognized that Jesus' name was not Immanuel. However, they interpreted this part of the text as referring to what he would be called, not to what his name would be.

The other primary messianic locus for the Fathers was Isaiah 9:6-7. Patristic interpreters consistently identified Jesus with this text. Numerous authors explained each of the titles in the passage, referencing something about Christ's life and ministry that was associated with each. Variant readings of the text

---

[3]Mt 3:1-3, quoting Is 40:3.
[4]Mt 2:20-23, quoting Is 7:14.
[5]Lk 4:16-21.
[6]Acts 6.

offered different sets of titles, but they were all descriptive of Christ.

A second theme of the patristic interpretation of Isaiah 1-39 was Israel's rejection of the Messiah and consequent judgment by God. The warnings in Isaiah's prophecy about the overthrow of Jerusalem and the destruction of Israel by its enemies offered the Fathers what seemed to be a clear picture of God's rejection of the nation of Israel. According to the patristic understanding of Isaiah, Isaiah announced that when Messiah came, the Jews would not acknowledge him as the one sent from God.[7] While they had the Law and the Prophets to guide them to the Savior, because of their blindness they would reject him. Cyril of Alexandria claimed that they rejected him because they were tied to the laws of the Old Testament, refusing to see their purpose in leading Israel to the Messiah.[8]

The Fathers read Isaiah on two levels. First, the prophet warned the people not to fall into idolatry before the Messiah came. Constant calls to remember the law and to turn from sin were intended to remind Israel of the need to be faithful to God while awaiting Messiah's arrival. These warnings remained important for Christians as well, because they served to remind believers of the constant threat of idolatry. Second, the prophet announced the ultimate failure of Israel to remain faithful to God. Israel's refusal to receive the Messiah when he came would lead to its demise.

Along with Israel's loss of God's blessing because of their rejection of the Messiah, the Fathers also interpreted Isaiah to announce the extension of the blessing to the Gentiles. Matthew's Gospel had interpreted Isaiah 9:1-2 in the same manner.[9] God's blessing of the Gentiles was not based solely on the Jews' rejection of the Messiah. The promise to Abraham had included a promise to bless all nations. What followed from the failure of Israel to recognize their Messiah was the loss of a privileged status, not a simple transferal of God's blessing from one group to another, although this was the view of some writers.

Despite the refusal of the Jewish leaders to recognize Jesus as the promised Messiah, some of Israel would be saved, according to the patristic reading of Isaiah. Throughout Isaiah's prophecy there runs the theme of a remnant who will be spared. This remnant, according to the Fathers, were those from the Jews who did receive Jesus as the Christ, including the apostles, each of whom was Jewish. In other words, although Israel as a nation would forgo its claims to the blessing of God, those from Israel who received Jesus would become the remnant Isaiah had promised.

Elements of Patristic Hermeneutics

In this section I will only mention a few helpful elements of patristic hermeneutics. The reader is advised to consult the companion volume to the Ancient Christian Commentary on Scripture by Christopher Hall, *Reading Scripture with the Church Fathers*, which is a superb help to understanding how the Fathers read and interpreted the Bible.

Patristic exegesis of Scripture, particularly the Old Testament, is complex and difficult to categorize. The Fathers did not know the categories familiar to modern interpreters, nor did the Enlightenment or modernism influence them. Their interpretation of Scripture is precritical. Methods associated with mod-

---

[7]See Is 1:2.
[8]Cyril of Alexandria, *Commentary on Isaiah* (PG 70:960-61).
[9]Mt 4:15-16.

ern historical-critical exegesis are not found in patristic hermeneutics.

Scholars typically associate patristic interpreters with one of two schools of interpretation, Alexandrian and Antiochene. Alexandrian exegesis is commonly considered to emphasize allegorical or typological interpretation to the neglect of literal interpretation. Clement of Alexandria, Origen, Athanasius and Cyril of Alexandria are a few of the Fathers deemed to represent Alexandrian exegetes. Antiochene exegesis is considered by many to emphasize the literal meaning over the typological. Theodore of Mopsuestia, Theodoret and John Chrysostom represent Antiochene exegesis.

In recent years, however, several scholars have questioned the descriptions of these two categories. The older description of Alexandrian exegesis as allegorical and Antiochene exegesis as literal is simplistic and even misleading. As the selections that follow will demonstrate, many of the so-called Alexandrians insisted on the literal meaning of certain texts, while the so-called Antiochenes employed typological interpretation of others.

Although there were significant differences in exegetical method among the patristic writers, they operated from the same fundamental position with regard to the Old Testament: it announced Christ. As we have seen, Cyril of Alexandria and Theodoret of Cyr, representatives of the two schools of thought, each said precisely the same thing about the purpose of Isaiah and the remainder of the Law, the Prophets and the Writings. For the Fathers, Christ was the *skopos* ("aim," "object") of the Hebrew Scriptures. That is, the author's intention in writing the Old Testament was to announce the coming Messiah. Early Christian interpreters were nearly unanimous in this regard.[10]

The real difference between the Alexandrians and Antiochenes was not the nature of the Old Testament but the extent to which the interpreter could discover christological passages. The Alexandrians were christological maximalists while the Antiochenes were christological minimalists. In other words, it would perhaps be better to place the Fathers on a spectrum rather than into separate categories. At one end of the spectrum would be the view that every passage says something about Christ. At the other end would be the view that accepts only the most overtly messianic passage as properly referring to Jesus Christ. The vast majority of the interpreters cited in this volume would fall between these two extremes and far closer to one another in reality than only two categories allow.

Theodoret and Cyril represent this similarity. Both contend that Isaiah spoke of Christ. Both contend as well that some passages speak overtly and that others require interpretation. While they differ on the number of passages that do either, they still agree that Christ is the subject of the prophecy, as it exists in the Old Testament.

The Presentation of the Material

Selections from the patristic material have been presented in a manner that, it is hoped, will make the volume more readily usable to readers who wish to proceed through the volume in a linear fashion and to those who wish to consult the patristic comment about particular passages. For that reason, the quotations are divided according to the passage divisions in the Revised Standard Version. Occasionally there has been

---

[10]The best-known opponent of this view of the Hebrew Scriptures was Marcion, who claimed that the god of the Old Testament was not the same as the Father of Jesus Christ. Fundamentally, however, Christians agreed that Christ is the subject of the Scriptures.

need to alter the division, but most often the RSV divisions are followed.

The reader will immediately notice that the selections are identified by the patristic author and the source of the quotation. Readers who desire to look more closely at the immediate context of a given selection or who want to read more from a particular author will be able to identify easily the location of a given source. Sometimes the source was an existing English translation; in other instances we have rendered new English translations from the original languages.

Where contemporary translations were available, we chose, more often than not, to use what existed. On several occasions we used translations from the nineteenth-century Early Church Fathers series. However, we smoothed the English, particularly in de-archaizing the language, and often retranslated portions of the texts. The Ante-Nicene Fathers series and the two series of Nicene and Post-Nicene Fathers remain the most comprehensive collection of translated patristic materials and are still of use in reading the Fathers.

Each section begins with one-sentence overviews of the patristic commentary on the passage in question. These overviews are intended to help guide the reader's understanding of the selections and to provide a brief summary of the material that follows. By consulting the overviews the reader can gain an idea of the consistency or inconsistency of the interpretations that follow. One will quickly see the extent to which there might be uniformity or difference of opinion regarding a given passage.

Final Matters and Acknowledgments

Early Christian interpretation of the Bible offers the modern reader a treasure that is fascinating and inspiring. Many contemporary interpreters of the Bible will marvel at some of the conclusions ancient writers reached regarding the scriptural text. Those heavily influenced by the historical-critical approach to biblical exegesis may cringe at some of the comments. The reader should remember, however, that the Fathers approached Isaiah 1-39 as the living Word of God, a guide for belief and practice. It was not merely a source to be studied but also the Divine message to humanity concerning God's plan for his people.

I join the general editors of the Ancient Christian Commentary on Scripture in affirming contemporary value in reading the Bible alongside the Fathers. Perhaps it is we modern interpreters who have missed much of the message of Christ in the Bible in our never-ending effort to reconstruct the ancient Near Eastern context within which many of the events described in Scripture occurred. The patristic writers immersed themselves into the world within the Bible, not the world around it. This immersion was neither arbitrary nor illicit. Rather, early Christian interpreters of Scripture were convinced that the intent of the Hebrew Bible was to announce the coming Messiah; and that announcement was fulfilled in Jesus of Nazareth. For Christians the Old Testament, as it came to be called, was not a book of Jewish history or religion but a promise that was fulfilled in Jesus Christ.

It only remains that I express my deepest sense of gratitude to those who made this project possible. Tom Oden, general editor, deserves highest accolades for his vision of and commitment to the Ancient Christian Commentary on Scripture. Professor Oden and associate editor Christopher Hall have led the way for contemporary Christians to rediscover the vast treasures in patristic literature. Christians of all persuasions benefit from an ingestion of the Fathers, and the ACCS is helping make that possible. The ACCS staff has been superb, often going the second mile to help make this volume happen. Mike Glerup and Joel Elowsky in particular offered immeasurable assistance along the way. Other unnamed researchers searched for material that would allow readers to hear patristic writers speak once again. I am personally grateful to the Southeastern Baptist Theological Seminary for the time to work on this project. My secretary, Phyllis Keith, who typed most of the selections, now knows more about the ancient Christian understanding of Isaiah than she ever thought imaginable. Finally, my family has been indefatigably patient with me. My wife, Ginger, and children, Lachlan, Blakely and Harrison, have frequently wondered why Daddy was spending so much time with papers, books and a computer. My prayer is that this volume will help them, as well as the communion of the saints throughout the world, know better the Messiah Isaiah announced so long ago.

Steven A. McKinion
Wake Forest, North Carolina

1:1-9 REBELLION AGAINST GOD

¹*The vision of Isaiah the son of Amoz, which he saw concerning Judah and Jerusalem in the days of Uzziah, Jotham, Ahaz, and Hezekiah, kings of Judah.*

²*Hear, O heavens, and give ear, O earth;*
for the LORD *has spoken:*
"Sons have I reared and brought up,
but they have rebelled against me.
³*The ox knows its owner,*
and the ass its master's crib;
but Israel does not know,
my people does not understand."

⁴*Ah, sinful nation,*
a people laden with iniquity,
offspring of evildoers,
sons who deal corruptly!
They* have forsaken the LORD,
they have despised[†] the Holy One of
Israel,
they are utterly estranged.

⁵*Why will you still be smitten,*
that you continue to rebel?
The whole head is sick,
and the whole heart faint.

⁶*From the sole of the foot even to the head,*
there is no soundness in it,
but bruises and sores
and bleeding wounds;
they are not pressed out, or bound up,
or softened with oil.[‡]

⁷*Your country lies desolate,*
your cities are burned with fire;
in your very presence
aliens devour your land;
it is desolate, as overthrown by
aliens.
⁸*And the daughter of Zion is left*
like a booth in a vineyard,
like a lodge in a cucumber field,
like a besieged city.

⁹*If the* LORD *of hosts*
had not left us a few survivors,
we should have been like Sodom,
and become like Gomorrah.

*LXX *you* †LXX *provoked* ‡LXX *It is not possible to apply an ointment or oil or bandages*

OVERVIEW: Christian interpreters should seek the spiritual meaning of the text (CYRIL OF ALEXANDRIA). God speaks directly to the prophets through visions (BASIL). Isaiah's vision is of future events (EUSEBIUS). Isaiah should be viewed as an evangelist rather than a prophet. Christians interpret the truth of history in a spiritual manner (JEROME).

Isaiah calls on heaven and earth as witnesses to Judah's rebellion (CHRYSOSTOM). All of humanity was created with the ability to receive God (ORIGEN). God is our Father, and we should recognize him as such (TERTULLIAN). Human beings are children of God through grace, not by nature; consequently, they were disinherited because of their rebellion. Because the Pharisees rebelled against God they are no longer children but strangers (ATHANASIUS).

The unclean Gentiles received the Lord, as should we (ORIGEN). We should love our Father just as wild beasts and infants naturally love their parent (BASIL). We should know God, our owner and master (GREGORY OF NAZIANZUS). We are nourished at the Lord's crib (AMBROSE). The righteous person does not shun the crib of Christ (AMBROSE). The whole world flocked to Christ's crib after the cross (CHRYSOSTOM). Mary laid the baby Christ in a crib to fulfill Isaiah's prophecy (JEROME). The ox and the donkey represent the Gentiles and the Jews who recognized Christ and came to him. We too may come to Christ, eat of his food and serve him (AUGUSTINE). Rational human beings are obligated to obey their Creator but often refuse to do so, revealing that they do not know God (VALERIAN). The beasts received Christ to their manger; we should not do less. Christ was in the manger and not the temple because he was rejected by the Jews (PETER CHRYSOLOGUS). Because all the earth belongs to the Lord, we should acknowledge him as the owner (CAESARIUS OF ARLES). The ox represents the Jews, who were under the yoke of the law; the donkey represents the Gentiles, who were unclean (BEDE).

Disharmony and judgment result from our failure to obey our master (BASIL). Isaiah foresaw the grace of Christ despite Israel's rejection of him (AUGUSTINE). Those who have denied the Son of God cannot be called the people of God (SALVIAN). Israel did not recognize the Messiah (JEROME). Those who do not live virtuous lives are evil (THEODORET). Despite having the prophets, the Jews did not recognize the Messiah when he came but instead rejected him (JUSTIN MARTYR). The people sinned, not acknowledging that God would judge them (PSEUDO-CLEMENT). Because our faith is weak we need correction for our iniquity (CLEMENT OF ALEXANDRIA). Those who reject warnings suffer serious consequences (CHRYSOSTOM). The Jewish people were led astray by their leaders (THEODORET). Sins wound and stain the soul and need the Word for cleansing (ORIGEN). One can bandage the wounds of the soul with gentle speech. The church tends to wounds with the oil that it has received (AMBROSE). Those who are penitent have their wounds bandaged, but not those who are unrepentant (JEROME).

Isaiah foretold the destruction of Jerusalem (JUSTIN MARTYR, HIPPOLYTUS, CHRYSOSTOM, CYRIL OF JERUSALEM). Because the Jews had forsaken God, his salvation was transferred from them to the Gentiles (ORIGEN). Although we are naturally the offspring of God, we are separated from him because of our sins (JEROME). Although the Jews had the prophets' message concerning Christ, only a remnant of them recognized him when he came (JUSTIN MARTYR). Salvation is not attained by human efforts, which produce pride, but by grace through faith (CHRYSOSTOM, AUGUSTINE). The remnant refers to those Jews who believed in Jesus Christ and were saved (JEROME).

1:1 The Vision of Isaiah

THE SPIRITUAL SENSE. CYRIL OF ALEXANDRIA: The word of the holy prophets is always difficult to surmise. It is filled with hidden meanings and is pregnant with announcements of divine mysteries. The end of the law and prophets is Christ, as Scripture says.[1] Those who want to expound these subtle matters must be diligent, I believe, to work in a logical way to thoroughly examine all of the symbols in the text to gain spiritual insight. First, the interpreter must determine the historical meaning and then interpret the spiritual meaning, in order for readers to derive benefit from every part of the text. The exposition must be clearly seen to be complete in every way. COMMENTARY ON ISAIAH, INTRODUCTION.[2]

---

[1]Rom 10:4. [2]PG 70:9.

MEANING OF VISION. BASIL THE GREAT: It is our task to pay diligent attention to the mind, so that it becomes clear-sighted, becoming perfect through appropriate exercises, while it is God's gift that the Spirit should illuminate us for the comprehension of his mysteries. The prophet puts "vision" first in his account and then introduces his report of the words, in order to show that he did not receive it through the faculty of hearing but is proclaiming the meaning of the word that has been impressed on his mind. For we need voice to indicate our thoughts, but God, affecting directly the very ruling aspect of the soul in those who are worthy, impresses on them the knowledge of his own will. COMMENTARY ON ISAIAH 1.8.[3]

VISION OF THE FUTURE. EUSEBIUS OF CAESAREA: A "vision," he says, not ordinary or perceptible with physical eyes, but a prophetic vision of things to come in far distant times; for just as one sees in a great tablet the invasion of enemies, ravagings of countryside, sieges of cities and enslavements of people, represented with the brilliance of color, the same way he seems to see a dream, but not a vision in sleep, when the divine spirit enlightens the soul. COMMENTARY ON ISAIAH 3.18-23.[4]

HISTORICAL CONTEXT OF THE VISION. EUSEBIUS OF CAESAREA: [The heading] indicated the ages of the kings, since there was a different state of affairs among the Jews, and events were to transpire in the distant future which never entered the mind or suspicion of the people of that time. Furthermore, it needs to be noted that the whole book, which only seems to be a single composition, was actually spoken over long periods of time, since there was need of extensive and precise understanding to discern the future, to determine the meaning of the events of the time and to suit the prophecy for the events that occurred in each reign. For the age of these kings covered fifty years in all, during which the things contained in this whole book were spoken. COMMENTARY ON ISAIAH 4.15-23.[5]

ISAIAH AN EVANGELIST. JEROME: [Isaiah] should be called an evangelist rather than a prophet, because he describes all the mysteries of Christ and the church so clearly that one would think he is composing a history of what has already happened rather than prophesying what is to come. PREFACE TO ISAIAH.[6]

JERUSALEM IS THE CHURCH. JEROME: It is also said in the old text that the people saw the voice of God.[7] The nonsense of Montanus remains silent about this, who thinks that it said the prophets would be coming in ecstasy and insanity of heart, for they could not see what they did not know. I know some from the heavens who interpret Judah and Jerusalem and Isaiah as figures of the person of the Lord our Savior, because it predicts the captivity of this province in our land and his subsequent return and ascension of the holy mountain in the last days. Adjudging all of this to be opposed to the faith of Christians, we despise it, and thus we interpret the truth of history spiritually, so that whatever they dream about the heavenly Jerusalem, we refer to the church of Christ and to those who either left her on account of sin or returned to their first position out of repentance. COMMENTARY ON ISAIAH 1.1.1.[8]

1:2 Rebellious Children

WITNESSES AGAINST JUDAH. CHRYSOSTOM: When Moses was going to bring Israel to the Promised Land, he had in full view all that they would do, that they were going to disregard those things he transmitted to them. "Listen, O heaven," he says, "and attend, O earth, to the words out of my mouth."[9] I give you as witnesses to heaven and earth, says Moses, that when you enter the Promised Land and you abandon the Lord God, you will be scattered abroad to all nations. Isaiah came, and the threat was going to be realized. You could not invite the deceased

---

[3]TASHT 7:10. [4]ECCI 156. [5]ECCI 154-55. [6]*Comm.* 24 4:850; PL 28:825-26. [7]Ex 20:18. [8]CCL 73:6. [9]Deut 32:1.

Moses and all those who had formerly heard and had died; so Isaiah calls to mind instead the elements that Moses brought forth as witnesses. HOMILY ON REPENTANCE AND ALMSGIVING 8.3.[10]

HUMANITY CREATED BY GOD. ORIGEN: All that exists was created by God, and there is nothing uncreated except the nature of the Father, Son and Holy Spirit. God, who is good by nature, wishing to have those whom he might benefit and who might enjoy the benefits received from him, made creatures worthy of himself, that is, who could receive him worthily. ON FIRST PRINCIPLES 44.8.[11]

KNOWING THE FATHER. TERTULLIAN: Our Lord frequently proclaimed God as a Father to us. He even gave us an instruction "that we call no one on earth father, but the Father whom we have in the heavens." So, in praying ["Our Father"] we are likewise obeying the precept. Those who recognize their Father are blessed! This is the reproach that is brought against Israel, to which the Spirit attests heaven and earth, saying, "I have begotten children, and they have not recognized me." ON PRAYER 2.[12]

NOT CHILDREN BY NATURE. ATHANASIUS: The one who is [begotten] from another by nature is a true child, just as Isaac was to Abraham, and Joseph was to Jacob, and as the radiance is to the sun. But those who are called children only from virtue and grace are called so not by nature but because of what they have received by grace. They still are not of the same nature as the one who gave them [the gift]. They are the ones who received the Spirit by participation, about whom it is said, "I produced and exalted children, but they rebelled against me." Of course, they were never really children *by nature*, and because of this and the fact that they reverted [to their former ways], the Spirit was taken away and they were disinherited. But when they again repent, God will receive them again and give them light. He will again call them children who at the

beginning had been given grace. FOUR DISCOURSES AGAINST THE ARIANS 1.11.37.[13]

NO LONGER CHILDREN. ATHANASIUS: And if they had examined with their understanding the things which were written, they would not have carefully fulfilled the prophecies which were against themselves, so as not to make their city now desolate, grace taken from them, and they themselves without the law, being no longer called children but strangers. FESTAL LETTER 10.[14]

1:3 The Ox and the Donkey

RECOGNIZE THE LORD. ORIGEN: That manger was the one the prophet meant when he said, "The ox knows his owner and the donkey his master's manger." The ox is a clean animal, and the donkey an unclean one. . . . The people of Israel did not know the manger of their Lord, but the unclean Gentiles did. . . . We should strive to recognize the Lord and to be worthy of knowing him. We should strive to appropriate not only his birth and fleshly resurrection but also his anticipated second coming in majesty. HOMILIES ON THE GOSPEL OF LUKE 13.7.[15]

LOVE FOR PARENTS. BASIL THE GREAT: If the love of children for their parents is a natural endowment and if this love is noticeable in the behavior even of brute beasts, as well as in the affection of human beings in early infancy for their mothers, let us not appear to be less rational than infants or more savage than wild beasts by alienating ourselves from him who made us by being unloving toward him. . . . This gratitude is characteristic not only of humans, but it is also felt by almost all animals, so that they attach themselves to those who have conferred some good upon them. THE LONG RULES 2.[16]

---

[10]FC 96:119*. [11]OSW 213**. [12]ANF 3:682*. [13]NPNF 2 4:328**. [14]NPNF 2 4:529*. [15]FC 94:55. [16]FC 9:236*.

Know Your Owner. Gregory of Nazianzus: Isaiah calls to you to know your owner, like the ox, and to know the manger of your Lord, like the donkey. On the Birth of Christ, Oration 38.17.[17]

Know the Lord's Crib. Ambrose: What is more evident than that it is said of the passion of the Lord: "The ox knows his owner and the donkey his master's crib." Let us, then, know the Lord's crib where we are nourished, fed and refreshed. Letter 36 (13.6).[18]

Crib of Christ. Ambrose: [The righteous person] does not say, "My portion consists of herds of oxen, donkeys or sheep," except, perhaps, he counts himself among those herds which know their owner and wishes to consort with that donkey which does not shun the crib of Christ . . . [For this person] that sheep is his portion which was led to the slaughter and the "Lamb which was dumb before his shearer and did not open his mouth."[19] In [Christ's] humiliation, judgment has been exalted. Letter 59 (14.93).[20]

The World Flocked to Him. Chrysostom: Before the cross not even the Jews knew him . . . while after the cross the whole world flocked to him. Homilies on the Gospel of John 80.[21]

Why a Manger? Jerome: His mother laid him in a manger. Joseph did not dare to touch him, for he knew he had not been begotten of him. In awe, he rejoiced at a son, but he did not dare to touch the Son. . . . Why in a manger? That the prophecy of Isaiah the prophet might be fulfilled. Homily 88 (On the Nativity).[22]

The Master's Manger. Augustine: Therefore "Jesus found a donkey and sat upon it."[23] . . . The donkey's colt upon which no one had sat (for this fact is found in the other Evangelists) we understand as the people of the nations which had not received the Lord's law. However, the donkey (because both beasts were led to the

Lord) is his community which came from the people of Israel, clearly not unbroken, but which recognized the Master's manger. Tractates on the Gospel of John 51.5.2.[24]

The Beast of Burden. Augustine: He who fills the world found no room in an inn. Placed in a manger, he became our food. Let the two animals, symbolic of two races, approach the manger, for "the ox knows his owner, and the donkey his master's crib." Do not be ashamed to be God's beast of burden. Carrying Christ, you will not go astray; with him burdening you, you make your way through devious paths. May the Lord rest upon us; may he direct us where he wishes; may we be his beast of burden and thus may we come to Jerusalem. Though he presses upon us, we are not crushed but lifted up; when he leads us, we shall not go astray. Through the Lord may we come to the child so that we may rejoice forever with the child who was born today. Sermon 189.4.[25]

Draw Near to the Manger. Augustine: The Leader and Shepherd of shepherds is announced to shepherds, and the food of the faithful lies in the manger of dumb beasts. . . . For that reason he sat upon the colt of a donkey when he entered Jerusalem amid the praises of the multitude surging around him.[26] Let us understand; let us draw near to the manger; let us eat of this food; let us bear the Lord, our Guide and Leader, so that under his direction we may come to the heavenly Jerusalem. Sermon 190.3.[27]

Shepherds and Magi. Augustine: In the persons of the shepherds and the magi, the ox began to recognize his owner and the donkey his Master's crib. From the Jews came the horned ox, since among them the horns of the cross were prepared for Christ; from the Gentiles came the

[17]NPNF 2 7:351. [18]FC 26:192. [19]Is 53:7. [20]FC 26:356*. [21]FC 41:368. [22]FC 57:221*. [23]Jn 12:14. [24]FC 88:274. [25]FC 38:22-23*; WSA 3 6:36**. [26]Mt 21:1-9. [27]FC 38:25; WSA 3 6:39-40.

long-eared donkey, since it was concerning them that the prophecy had been made: "A people, which I knew not, has served me: at the hearing of the ear they have obeyed me."[28] For the Owner of the ox and the Master of the donkey lay in a manger, yet he was furnishing common sustenance to both creatures. SERMON 204.2.[29]

ONE MANGER. AUGUSTINE: The ox from the Jews, the donkey from the Gentiles; both came to the one manger and found the fodder of the Word. SERMON 375.1.[30]

MAGNIFY THE LORD. AUGUSTINE: Therefore those oxen magnified the Lord, not themselves. See the ox magnifying his Lord because the ox has acknowledged his owner; observe the ox fearing that the ox's owner may be deserted and confidence be placed in the ox. How he is terrified of those who want to put hope in him! TRACTATES ON THE GOSPEL OF JOHN 10.7.3.[31]

KNOWING GOD. VALERIAN: I am often astonished at human conduct. Humans are endowed with wisdom and prudence, yet at whim they lightly reject the precepts of discipline. How different is the conduct which we see in the beasts! They avoid vices, carry out commands, submit to control and mold their spirits to perfect obedience. As a result, when need arises, they run against armed legions and charge head downward against the javelins of the foe. . . .

The person who is not aware of the obligation flowing from his condition of being a creature simply does not know God. HOMILY 1.[32]

ACKNOWLEDGE THE LORD. PETER CHRYSOLOGUS: If you did not recognize him soon along with the angels, do acknowledge him now, even though very late, in company with the beasts. Otherwise, while you loiter, you may be deemed less than those very animals with whom you were previously compared. . . . Yet you argue and quibble with the Jews who turned away from their inns their Master whom the beasts welcomed in

their cribs. SERMON 141.[33]

YOU HAVE NOT SOUGHT THE MASTER. PETER CHRYSOLOGUS: Why does the king of the Jews lie in a manger and not repose in the temple? Why is he not resplendent in purple rather than poorly clad rags? Why does he lie hidden in a cave and not on display in the sanctuary? The beasts have received in a manger him whom you have disdained to receive in his house. As it has been written. . . . But you, O Israel, have not sought out your Master. SERMON 156.[34]

RECOGNIZE THE OWNER. CAESARIUS OF ARLES: If the earth is the Lord's and the fullness thereof, we are his servants and farmers, and I do not know how we can fail to recognize him as the owner. SERMON 33.1.[35]

TURNED TO GRACE. BEDE: By the ox he designates the people of the Jews, who were accustomed to carry the yoke of the law and to ruminate upon its words; by the donkey he represents the people of the nations, who remained always unclean with the stains of idolatry. From both peoples a great many turned to the grace of the gospel and recognized the owner by whom they were created. [They] were seeking by means of his heavenly nourishing fare to grow toward perpetual salvation. HOMILIES ON THE GOSPELS 1.6.[36]

JUDGMENT. BASIL THE GREAT: If even among the barbarians harmony is maintained through subjection to a single leader, what should we think of the disharmony among us and our failure to be subject to the Lord's commands? We should realize that our good God gives us examples to teach us and lead us to conversion. On the great and awesome day of judgment he will use them as a demonstration of the shame and condemnation of

---

[28]Ps 18:44. [29]FC 38:79; WSA 3 6:99. [30]WSA 3 10:328. [31]FC 78:219. [32]17:305*. [33]FC 17:231-32. [34]FC 17:269. [35]FC 31:163. [36]CS 110:58-59*.

those who have not heeded his instruction. He has already said, and he continues to say, "The ox knows his owner and the donkey his master's manger; but Israel has not known me, and my people have not understood." PREFACE ON THE JUDGMENT OF GOD 7.[37]

FORESEEING CHRIST. AUGUSTINE: But, in fact, there were even in that people those that understood, having the faith which was afterwards revealed, not pertaining to the letter of the law but the grace of the Spirit. For they cannot have been without the same faith, who were able to foresee and foretell the revelation that would be in Christ, inasmuch as even those old sacraments were signs of those that should be. EXPLANATIONS OF THE PSALMS 78 (77).2.[38]

NOT THE PEOPLE OF GOD. SALVIAN THE PRESBYTER: They who have long since put aside the worship of God cannot be called the people of God. Neither can that people be said to see God who have denied the Son of God. THE GOVERNANCE OF GOD 4.[39]

ISRAEL MISSED CHRIST. JEROME: Like other Hebrews, Israel does not know its owner, nor does this people understand the cradle of its Lord. Here is the clear meaning: I adopted them as sons and made them a people peculiar to myself, the portion of my inheritance, and I called them my firstborn, but they did not cooperate, because they became dumb beasts to be conquered by favors and to recognize their shepherd and guardian. It does not compare them to dogs because a dog is the most clever kind of animal, which defends the dwelling of its owner for a little food. But the mind of the ox or ass is slower, animals that turn hard clumps of soil while pulling a plow behind some carriages and alleviate the workload of men by bearing heavy loads behind other carriages. Hence they are called beasts of burden, because they assist men. Although this verse can be understood as referring to God the Father, it seems instead to refer to the Son inasmuch as the people of Israel did not recognize him, nor did

they receive him whose day Abraham rejoiced to see and on whose advent all the hopes of the prophets hung. COMMENTARY ON ISAIAH 1.1.3.[40]

1:4 A Sinful, Estranged Nation

REJECTED VIRTUES. THEODORET OF CYR: When Isaiah calls them "evil seed," he does not mean to insult the ancestors of those to whom he was speaking. Rather he was denouncing their own wickedness, just as John the Baptist called the Jewish leaders "a brood of vipers"[41] and the Lord called them "an evil and adulterous generation."[42] They were called these things because they did not preserve the virtuous life of those who went before them. COMMENTARY ON ISAIAH 1.4.[43]

ISRAEL DID NOT RECOGNIZE CHRIST. JUSTIN MARTYR: The Jews who have the writings of the prophets did not understand this, and neither did they recognize Christ when he came. They even despise us who say that he has come, and, as it was prophesied, show that they crucified him. But in order that this may become clear to you, the following words were spoken through the aforementioned prophet Isaiah in the name of the Father: "The ox knows his owner and the donkey his master's crib; but Israel has not known me, and my people have not understood. Woe, sinful nation, people full of sins, evil seed, lawless children, you have forsaken the Lord." FIRST APOLOGY 36-37.[44]

SIN AND IGNORANCE. PSEUDO-CLEMENT OF ROME: When Isaiah, in the person of God, said, "Israel has not known me, and the people have not understood me," he did not mean there is another God who is known but that the known God was also unknown because when the people sinned they believed the good God would not chastise them, because they were ignorant of the righteousness of the known God. HOMILY 18.18.[45]

[37]PG 31:657. [38]NPNF 1 8:366*. [39]FC 3:91. [40]CCL 73:9. [41]Mt 3:7. [42]Mt 12:29. [43]SC 276:154. [44]ANF 1:175**. [45]ANF 8:329.

CORRECTION. CLEMENT OF ALEXANDRIA: Correction is a public rebuke of sin. [God] uses it in a manner that is particularly necessary for our instruction because of the weak faith of so many. For example, he says through Isaiah, "You have forsaken the Lord, you have provoked the holy one of Israel." CHRIST THE EDUCATOR 1.9.78.[46]

EXCORIATION. CLEMENT OF ALEXANDRIA: Excoriation is the most vigorous expression of disapproval. God employed excoriation as a remedy when he said through Isaiah, "Ah, sinful nation, a people full of sins, an evil seed, lawless children." CHRIST THE EDUCATOR 1.9.80.[47]

1:5 Sick and Faint

INCURABLE SICKNESS. CHRYSOSTOM: It shows utter contempt when, even with retributions, [the Israelites] do not become better. But even this is a kind of benefit—to be chastised. For they would have to admit that God not only condemned and rewarded but was also forgiving sinners. And certainly he was coaxing them with rewards and also chastising them with fear of punishments. COMMENTARY ON ISAIAH 1.3.[48]

HEAD AND HEART. THEODORET OF CYR: Isaiah calls the kings and the leaders the heads and the priests and teachers the heart. For what the heart is to the body, the priests and teachers are for the people, and what the head is for the body, the kings and leaders are for their subjects. COMMENTARY ON ISAIAH 1.5.[49]

1:6 Bleeding Wounds Not Bound

WOUNDS OF THE SOUL. ORIGEN: And just as there are some wounds that are cured by emollients, others that are cured by oil and others that need a bandage, there are still other wounds about which it is said, "It is not emollients or oil or bandages; but your land is desolate, your cities burned with fire." So there are some sins that pollute the soul, and for those sins one needs the lye of the Word, the soap of the Word. Yet some sins are not cured this way, because they do not pollute the soul. HOMILIES ON JEREMIAH 2.2.[50]

WOUNDS OF THE SOUL. ORIGEN: Isaiah teaches that there are certain wounds of the soul. . . . Without doubt, he is speaking about the transgressions of the people, because there are some to whom the medicine of the poultice must still be applied. Others may be sinners in such a degree that no cure can be found for them. HOMILIES ON LEVITICUS 8.5.5.[51]

WISE SPEECH MAY HEAL. AMBROSE: Let your exhortations be full of meaning. . . . Speech is a bandage that ties up the wounds of souls, and if anyone rejects this, he shows his despair of his own salvation. Likewise, with those who are vexed by a serious sore, use the oil of speech that you may soften their hardness of heart; apply a poultice; put on a bandage of salutary advice, so that you may never allow those who are astray or who are wavering regarding the faith or the observance of discipline to perish through the loss of courage and a breakdown of activity. LETTER 15 (7.36.7).[52]

THE CHURCH'S OIL. AMBROSE: They had nothing to pour. If they had had any oil, they would have poured it on their own wounds. Isaiah cries, "They cannot apply ointment or oil or bandage." But the church has oil, with which it tends the wounds of its children, that the wound may not harden and spread deep. [The church] has oil which it has received secretly. LETTER 41 (EX 1).19-20.[53]

UNREPENTANT SINNER. JEROME: You see now how the rebuilding of Jerusalem takes place: the broken heart is mended. . . . You wound your heart, and the Lord binds your wounds. . . . It refers to those who are penitent, but of the unre-

---

[46]FC 23:70* [47]FC 23:71**. [48]SC 304:56. [49]SC 276:154. [50]FC 97:24-25**. [51]FC 83:162*. [52]FC 26:79. [53]LCC 5:246.

pentant, Scripture says, their wounds "are not drained or bandaged or eased with salve." HOMILIES ON THE PSALMS 56 (PSALM 146).[54]

1:7-8 The Land Is Desolate

FULFILLED PROPHECY. JUSTIN MARTYR: You know very well that Jerusalem was laid waste just as it was prophesied. That it would be destroyed, and no one allowed to live there, was promised through the prophet Isaiah in this way: "Your land is desolate." . . . Indeed you are aware that it is guarded and no one is in it.[55] FIRST APOLOGY 47.4-6.[56]

FULFILLED PROPHECY. HIPPOLYTUS: What therefore? Have these things not come to be? Have the things announced by you not come to fruition? Is not their land, Judah, desolate? Is the holy place not burned? Are their ways not thrown down? Are their cities not laid waste? Do strangers not devour their lands? Do the Romans not rule over their land? ON THE ANTICHRIST 30.[57]

FUTURE CALAMITY. CHRYSOSTOM: Isaiah is not recalling events that have happened but is announcing events in the future. The prophets customarily use fear to demonstrate the truth of what they are saying. COMMENTARY ON ISAIAH 1.3.[58]

FULFILLED PROPHECY. CYRIL OF JERUSALEM: Isaiah lived almost [two] thousand years ago and saw Zion in a hut. The city was still standing, beautiful with public squares and clothed in honor; yet he says, "Zion shall be plowed like a field,"[59] foretelling what has been fulfilled in our day. Observe the exactness of the prophecy; for he said, "Daughter Zion will be left like a hut in a vineyard, like a shed in a melon patch." Now the place is full of melon patches. CATECHETICAL LECTURES 16.18.[60]

DESERTED. ORIGEN: Christ ceased to be in them. The Word deserted them. . . . The Jews

were left behind, and salvation passed to the Gentiles. God meant to spur on the Jews with envy. We contemplate God's mysterious plan, how for our salvation he rejected Israel. We ought to be careful. The Jews were rejected for our sake; on our account they were abandoned. We would deserve even greater punishment if we did nothing worthy of our adoption by God and of his mercy. In his mercy God adopted us and made us his sons [children] in Christ Jesus, to whom is glory and power for ages of ages. HOMILIES ON THE GOSPEL OF LUKE 5.4.[61]

SEPARATED FROM GOD. JEROME: But since the fruits were removed in this manner, only the drying arbors of the bushes and the cottages remain, the custodian having departed because there is nothing left for him to preserve. Therefore God omnipotent also abandons the temple and causes the city to be deserted. There is no need to prove this with words, especially to us who see Zion deserted and Jerusalem overthrown and the temple leveled to the ground. But the fact that he calls Zion a daughter displays the most clement affection of a parent. Neither is it any wonder that Zion is called a daughter, since Babylon also is frequently referred to as a daughter. For we are all children of God by nature, though we have been alienated from him by our own sins. Analogically, our souls can be called God's vineyard and a paradise of fruits, having God as its custodian provided that the mind, that is, the *nous*, presides. But if it is plundered by sin as though by wild beasts, then we are forsaken by God the custodian and rendered utterly alone. COMMENTARY ON ISAIAH 1.1.8.[62]

1:9 Without a Remnant, Destruction

DECEPTIVE TEACHERS. JUSTIN MARTYR: Moreover, those teachers who believe that the descen-

---

[54]FC 48:401. [55]In Justin's time, Jews were forbidden from gathering in Jerusalem in order to prevent any rebellious assembly from forming. [56]ANF 1:178**. [57]ANF 5:210. [58]SC 304:58. [59]This quotation is actually from Mic 3:12. [60]FC 64:87**. [61]FC 94:21-22. [62]CCL 73:14.

dants of Abraham according to the flesh will indeed share in the eternal kingdom, even if they are sinners without faith and disobedient to God, are deceiving themselves and you. These are speculations that the Scriptures demonstrate have absolutely no basis. If they did, Isaiah would not have said, "And except the Lord of hosts had left us seed, we had become as Sodom and Gomorrah." DIALOGUE WITH TRYPHO 140.3.2.[63]

REMNANT. JUSTIN MARTYR: The Gentiles were utterly ignorant of the one true God and worshiped things they themselves made. The Jews and Samaritans, though, had been given the Word of God by the prophets and have always waited for the coming of Christ. However, they did not recognize him when he came, except for a few who were to be saved. FIRST APOLOGY 53.6.[64]

SAVED BY FAITH. CHRYSOSTOM: He here shows that even the few that were saved were not saved through their own resources. Even they would have perished and suffered like Sodom. That is, they would have been completely destroyed—for Sodom was destroyed root and branch, and not even the smallest seed remained. He means to say that they too would have been like those, except that God demonstrated his goodness to them and saved them by faith. This happened as well in their visible captivity in which most of them were taken captive and perished, in which only a few were saved. HOMILIES ON ROMANS 16.10.[65]

GRACE. AUGUSTINE: Beware, O Christian, beware of pride. For though you are a follower of the saints, ascribe it always wholly to grace. That there should be any "remnant" in you, the grace of God has brought it to pass, not your own merits. SERMON 50 (100).4.[66]

LORD OF THE SABBATH. JEROME: It was shown above what the prophetic word threatened against Jerusalem and Judah, not pertaining to the time of the Babylonian captivity but to the end of the Romans, when the remnant of the Jewish people were saved in the apostles, and three thousand believed in one day and five thousand on another, and the gospel was spread throughout the entire world. "The Lord of hosts" is our Latin translation, following Aquila, of the Hebrew "Lord of the Sabbath," to which the Septuagint translators gave a double sense: either the Lord of powers or the Lord omnipotent. We also need to ask whether it was said about the Father or about the Son. But there is no doubt what we read in the twenty-third psalm: "Lift up your heads, gates, and be lifted up, eternal doors, and the king of glory will enter! Who is the king of glory? Lord of the sabbath."[67] The Lord of powers, he is the king of glory, referring to Christ, who ascended to heaven as victor after the triumph of the passion. And in another place it says about the Lord, the king of glory: "If they had known him, they never would have crucified the Lord of glory."[68] Not only according to the Apocalypse of John and the apostle Paul, therefore, but also in the Old Testament Christ is named as Lord of the sabbath, that is, Lord omnipotent. For if all things of the Father belong to the Son and, as he himself says in the Gospel, "All power in heaven and on the earth has been given to me"[69] and "All that is mine is yours, and I am glorified in them,"[70] why then does the title of omnipotence not also belong to Christ, so that just as he is God of God and Lord of Lord, he would also be the omnipotent Son of the omnipotent One? COMMENTARY ON ISAIAH 1.1.9.[71]

---

[63]ANF 1:269**. [64]ANF 1:180-81**. [65]PG 60:562-63. [66]NPNF 1 6:421*. [67]Ps 24:7-8 (23:7-8 LXX). [68]1 Cor 2:8. [69]Mt 28:18. [70]Jn 17:10. [71]CCL 73:14-15.

1:10-20 REJECTION OF FALSE RELIGION

¹⁰Hear the word of the Lord,
  you rulers of Sodom!
Give ear to the teaching of our God,
  you people of Gomorrah!
¹¹"What to me is the multitude of your
    sacrifices?
  says the Lord;
I have had enough of burnt offerings of rams
  and the fat of fed beasts;
I do not delight in the blood of bulls,
  or of lambs, or of he-goats.

¹²"When you come to appear before me,
  who requires of you
  this trampling of my courts?
¹³Bring no more vain offerings;*
  incense is an abomination to me.
New moon and sabbath and the calling of
    assemblies—
  I cannot endure iniquity and solemn
    assembly.
¹⁴Your new moons and your appointed feasts
  my soul hates;
they have become a burden to me,
  I am weary of bearing them.
¹⁵When you spread forth your hands,

I will hide my eyes from you;
even though you make many prayers,
  I will not listen;
  your hands are full of blood.
¹⁶Wash yourselves; make yourselves
    clean;
  remove the evil of your doings
  from before my eyes;
cease to do evil,
  ¹⁷learn to do good;
seek justice,
  correct oppression;
defend the fatherless,
  plead for the widow.

¹⁸ "Come now, let us reason together,
  says the Lord:
though your sins are like scarlet,
  they shall be as white as snow;
though they are red like crimson,
  they shall become like wool.
¹⁹If you are willing and obedient,
  you shall eat the good of the land;
²⁰but if you refuse and rebel,
  you shall be devoured by the sword;
  for the mouth of the Lord has spoken."

*LXX though you bring fine flour

Overview: God's pleasure is in his own sacrifice, not that of human beings (Ambrose). God honors repentance and a contrite heart. The old sacrifices were replaced by the sacrifice of Christ (Basil). God rejected the sacrifices of the people because of the people's laziness (Chrysostom). The sacrificial system of the Jews was instituted by God to prevent his people from succumbing to the constant threat of offering sacrifices to idols. Prayer is the spiritual sacrifice God desires (Tertullian). The Christian's sacrifice is kindness to the poor (Augustine). The sabbath that is acceptable to God is the eighth day, the day on which Jesus rose from the dead (Epistle of Barnabas). Every day of the week is the Lord's Day and is therefore a festal day (Origen). Sacrifices and other religious rituals done hypocritically are of no spiritual value (ATHANASIUS). The test of an offering's value is the intention of the one making the offering (CHRYSOSTOM, CYRIL OF ALEXANDRIA, LEO THE GREAT). The old sacrificial system has been annulled by Christ and replaced by spiritual offerings (EPISTLE OF BARNABAS). The temporal sabbath is profaned, but the eternal sabbath is divine (TERTULLIAN).

God does not hear the prayers of the arrogant (BASIL). The tongue is the hand of the one praying and should therefore be kept clean (CHRYSOSTOM). Christians multiply their sins when they lift to God sin-stained hands (AUGUSTINE). God does not respond to the prayers of the lazy person until that person learns that negligence was the cause of his or her dismay (ISAAC OF NINEVEH). Baptism washes the Christian clean (HIPPOLYTUS). Washing is not purification by water but is repentance (CHRYSOSTOM). When Christians fast, they should wash their faces (AUGUSTINE). As the bride of Christ the Christian should be clean and pure. Being cleansed of sin means ceasing to sin, not merely weeping over sin (GREGORY THE GREAT). Those who do not forgive others will not be forgiven (BEDE). God is pleased by those who believe in the gospel, not by those who offer sacrifices (JEROME).

The widow and the one who takes care of her are honored by God (TERTULLIAN). Christians should seek to defend those who have been wronged or are in need, and not only those who are reputable (CHRYSOSTOM). Those who repent will have their sins forgiven (JUSTIN MARTYR). Scarlet and crimson represent the blood of the prophets and of Christ, respectively (TERTULLIAN). God is able to heal all those suffering from sin (BASIL). God forgives his people, making them innocent (CYRIL OF JERUSALEM, AMBROSE). God's promise of forgiveness should not make one lax in living but should keep one from despair. It is even more important to ensure that one's soul is clean than one's body (CHRYSOSTOM).

The church is symbolized by white garments because it is pure through the grace of God (AUGUSTINE). Sins are buried in the water of baptism, and the one baptized is made clean (JOHN OF DAMASCUS). There are blessings for the flesh in the kingdom of God after the resurrection (TERTULLIAN). Those who are faithful to God will receive good things from him (AMBROSE). It is not free will but good will that is necessary for one to be a Christian. If one truly has the will to live properly, that person will do it (CHRYSOSTOM). The grace of God and the free will of humankind are to be affirmed (JOHN CASSIAN). It is wrong to believe God's grace is the result of his response to one's free will (CASSIODORUS). The sword of God does not destroy evildoers but devours them (JUSTIN MARTYR). God purges the dross from believers in the present so that they will need no penal cleansing in eternity (JOHN CASSIAN). There is a righteous judgment for those who remain in sin (FULGENTIUS).

1:11 No Delight in Sacrifices

REJECTION. AMBROSE: By saying that he does not delight in the sacrifices of the people, God is saying this: I abound in my own [sacrifice], I do not seek yours, I do not desire whole burnt offerings of rams and the fat of lambs and the blood of bulls and of goats. And do not come so into my sight. THE PRAYER OF JOB AND DAVID 4.9.33.[1]

REPENTANCE IS NECESSARY. BASIL THE GREAT: How do you hope to find any redemption for your souls through sacrifices that are offered in quantity but with no repentance worth mentioning? For God is merciful not through the blood of animals or through slaughter on the altar but upon the contrite heart. For "the sacrifice to God is a contrite heart."[2]

It is fitting for the same to be said to those who are lavish in their expiations but do not repent through their deeds. . . . Scripture says, "What is the multitude of your sacrifices to me?" So it dismisses the multitude and seeks after the

---

[1]FC 65:417**. [2]Ps 51:17.

single sacrifice.[3] COMMENTARY ON ISAIAH 1.24.[4]

NEW SACRIFICE. BASIL THE GREAT: Observe that God does not say that he does not wish for any blood, but for this particular blood from these particular animals. For he would not say that he does not wish for the blood that was poured out "in the last times for the annulment of sins,"[5] "which speaks more effectively than that of Abel,"[6] but he changes the sacrifices to the spiritual plane, since "the change of priesthood"[7] is about to happen. For if he rejects the physical sacrifices, he manifestly rejects the high priest according to the law.... They of the stock of Aaron are cast out, therefore, so that he [Christ] according to the order of Melchizedek might enter instead.[8] The "continuous sacrifices"[9] are no more, no more the sacrifices of the Day of Atonement,[10] no more "the ashes of the heifer which purify those that partake."[11] For the sacrifice is one, the Christ,[12] and the mortification of the saints according to him;[13] the sprinkling is one, the bath of regeneration;[14] the absolution of sins is one—the blood poured out for the salvation of the world.[15] Because of this God renounces the former things, so that he may establish the latter. COMMENTARY ON ISAIAH 1.26.[16]

1:12 Who Requires This?

SACRIFICES AS INSTRUCTION. CHRYSOSTOM: It is obvious that sacrifices were established as an instruction to inspire right living in the people and were not given as an end in themselves. When the people refused to do those works that were necessary in order to busy themselves with only sacrifices, God said that he would no longer accept the sacrifices.

The entire book of Leviticus offers laws that are very strict regarding sacrifices. Moreover, there are numerous laws concerning sacrifices scattered throughout the book of Deuteronomy, as well as other books. How then can God ask, "Who has required these things from your hands?" This is to teach us that God's will was not to make laws in this way but that the people

suffered from slothfulness in not abiding by this command. COMMENTARY ON ISAIAH 1.4.[17]

AWAY FROM IDOLATRY. TERTULLIAN: As for the burdensome sacrifices and the troublesome scrupulousness of their ceremonies and oblations, no one should blame the Jews, as if God specially required them for himself. . . . But he should see in those sacrifices a careful provision on God's part, which showed his wish to bind to his own religion a people who were prone to idolatry and transgression by that kind of services wherein consisted the superstition of that period. He did this in order to call them away from idolatry, while requesting sacrifices to be performed to himself, as if he desired that no sin should be committed in making idols. AGAINST MARCION 18.[18]

NEW SACRIFICE. TERTULLIAN: Now this is the spiritual victim which has set aside the earlier sacrifice. . . . The gospel teaches what God demands. "The hour is coming," he says, "when the true worshipers will worship the Father in spirit and in truth."[19] . . . We are the true worshipers and true priests who, offering our prayer in the spirit, offer sacrifice in the spirit—that is, prayer—as a victim that is appropriate and acceptable to God; this is what he has demanded and what he has foreordained for himself. ON PRAYER 28.[20]

GOD SEEKS US. AUGUSTINE: God seeks us, not what's ours. Anyway, the Christian's sacrifice is alms, or kindness to the poor. That is what makes God lenient toward sins. SERMON 42.1.[21]

1:13 Unacceptable Offerings

EIGHTH DAY. EPISTLE OF BARNABAS: You see

---

[3]See Rom 12:1. [4]TASHT 7:33-34. [5]Heb 9:26. [6]Heb 12:24. [7]Heb 7:12. [8]See Heb 5:6. [9]Ex 29:42. [10]Lev 25:9. [11]Heb 9:13; Num 19:9-10. [12]Eph 5:2. [13]2 Cor 4:10. [14]Tit 3:5. [15]Heb 9:12-14. [16]TASHT 7:36-37. [17]SC 304:64. [18]ANF 3:311-12**. [19]Jn 4:23. [20]FC 40:185. [21]WSA 3 2:234.

what he means: It is not the present sabbaths that I find acceptable but the one which I have made. After I have given rest to all things, I will make the beginning of the eighth day, which is the beginning of another world. It is for this reason that we celebrate on the eighth day, the day on which Jesus also rose from the dead, appeared and ascended into heaven. Epistle of Barnabas 15.8-9.[22]

Every Day Is Festal. Origen: Tell me, you who come to church only on festal days, are the other days not festal days? Are they not the Lord's days? It belongs to the Jews to observe religious ceremonies on fixed and infrequent days. . . . God hates, therefore, those who think that the festal day of the Lord is on one day. Homilies on Genesis 10.3.[23]

Hypocrisy. Athanasius: For actions not done lawfully and piously are not of advantage, though they may be reputed to be so, but they rather argue hypocrisy in those who venture upon them. Therefore, although such persons feign to offer sacrifices, yet they hear from the Father, "Your whole burnt offerings are not acceptable, and your sacrifices do not please me";[24] and although you bring fine flour, it is vanity; incense also is an abomination to me." Festal Letter 19.2.[25]

The Importance of Intention. Chrysostom: Listen to the words of the inspired writer: "Incense is an abomination to me"—as if to suggest the bad intention of the one offering the sacrifice. You see, just as in the present case the good person's virtue transformed the smoke and stench into an odor of fragrance, so in their case the malice of the one making the offering caused the fragrant incense to smell like an abomination. Consequently, let us earnestly take every opportunity, I beseech you, to demonstrate a sound attitude. This, after all, proves responsible for all our good things. You see, the good Lord is accustomed to heed not so much what is done from our own resources as the intention within, on

which we depend for our first move in doing these things, and he looks to that in either approving what is done by us or disapproving it. So whether we pray, or fast, or practice almsgiving (these, after all, being our spiritual sacrifices) or perform any other spiritual work, let us begin with a pure intention in performing it so that we may procure a reward worthy of our efforts. Homilies on Genesis 27.8.[26]

From Shadow to Truth. Cyril of Alexandria: How, tell me, can festivals that God hates be intended for continual and uninterrupted observance? Are we to say that God changed his mind, and that ordinances God originally said to be good, when he established them through Moses, are ridiculed by the prophets, so that we must conclude he who enjoined them made a mistake, and that he is subject to the same infirmities that afflict us? . . . He was in favor of the good for the ancients, but he wished, rather, that by passing from symbols and shadows into the beauty of the truth, they should commend the worship most well pleasing to him, and it is clear that such worship is intellectual and in spirit. Against Julian 9.[27]

The Proper Use of Self-Restraint. Leo the Great: When, from the teaching of ancient doctrine, dearly beloved, we undertake the fast of September to purify our souls and bodies, we are not subjecting ourselves to legal burdens. We are embracing the good use of self-restraint that serves the gospel of Christ. In this too, Christian virtue can "exceed that of the scribes and Pharisees,"[28] not by making void the law but by rejecting worldly wisdom. Sermon 92.2.[29]

1:14 New Moons and Festivals

New Law of Christ. Epistle of Barnabas: The aids of our faith are fear and patience. Allies to us

[22]ANF 1:147**. [23]FC 71:162-63. [24]Jer 6:20. [25]NPNF 2 4:545. [26]FC 82:168*. [27]MFC 9:29. [28]Mt 5:20. [29]FC 93:386.

are endurance and self-control. Where these things remain in purity in matters relating to the Lord, there wisdom, understanding, insight and knowledge are rejoicing with them. He has made it obvious to us through all the prophets that he does not require sacrifices, burnt offerings or oblations. . . . Therefore he has annulled these things, in order that the new law of our Lord Jesus Christ, which is free from the yoke of compulsion, might have an offering not made by humans. EPISTLE OF BARNABAS 2.2-6.[30]

Two Sabbaths. TERTULLIAN: Through this arises the question for us, what sabbath God willed us to keep? For the Scriptures point to an eternal sabbath and a temporal sabbath. For Isaiah the prophet says, "My soul hates your sabbaths," and in another place he says, "My sabbath you have profaned."[31] From which we discern that the temporal sabbath is human and the eternal sabbath is accounted divine. AN ANSWER TO THE JEWS 4.[32]

Humanity's Sabbaths. TERTULLIAN: God has here expressed an aversion to certain sabbaths. By calling them "your sabbaths" he means that the sabbaths he rejects are humanity's, and not his. He rejects them because they were celebrated without the fear of God by a people full of sins who love God "with the lip, not the heart."[33] AGAINST MARCION 12.[34]

1:15 I Will Not Listen

Sin of Arrogance. BASIL THE GREAT: Let those who do nothing right in life and think they are justified by the length of their prayer listen to these words. For the words of the prayer are not useful by themselves but only when they are offered up with earnest intent. Now the Pharisee also seemed to multiply his supplication. But what does the Scripture say? "The Pharisee stood and prayed thus to himself,"[35] not to God, for he turned back toward himself, since at all events he was in the sin of arrogance. COMMENTARY ON ISAIAH 1.36.[36]

The Tongue as the Hand Who Prays. CHRYSOSTOM: One asks, "What if I have been overcome?" Then cleanse yourself. "How, in what manner?" Weep, groan, give alms, apologize to the one who is offended, reconcile him to yourself in so doing, wash clean your tongue so that you will not offend God more grievously. If someone were to fill his or her hands with dung and embrace your feet asking something of you, you would push that person away with your foot rather than listen. Then why do you draw near to God in such a manner, because in reality the tongue is the hand of the one who prays, and by it we embrace the legs of God. HOMILIES ON THE GOSPEL OF MATTHEW 51.5.[37]

Holy Hands. AUGUSTINE: O foolish and wretched person, what are you doing? Why do you burden yourself with the weight of greater sins? Why do you inflict injury on God in addition to your contempt? Why, in order to provoke his wrath more quickly in manifestation of your punishment, do you extend to God your crime-stained hands when he who has commanded that only holy and unspotted hands be lifted up to him refuses to look at yours? Why do you beseech God with that mouth by which not long ago you spoke evil? Its prayers, however they be multiplied, are an abomination to him. ON THE CHRISTIAN LIFE 11.[38]

The Lazy and Negligent. ISAAC OF NINEVEH: Whenever [those who are lazy] pray to him, he does not quickly listen to them but waits until they grow weary and have learned in no uncertain manner that these things befell them because of their laziness and negligence. . . . Even if this was said of others, nonetheless it is written especially about those who have abandoned the way of the Lord. ASCETICAL HOMILIES 5.[39]

[30]ANF 1:137**. [31]Ezek 22:8 [32]ANF 3:155*. [33]Is 29:13. [34]ANF 3:363**. [35]Lk 18:11. [36]TASHT 7:50. [37]PG 58:516. [38]FC 16:32*. [39]AHSIS 46.

1:16 *Make Yourselves Clean*

BEAMS OF RIGHTEOUSNESS. HIPPOLYTUS: Beloved, see how the prophet predicted the washing of baptism. For the person who comes to the washing of regeneration with faith, renounces the devil, joins himself to Christ, denies the enemy, confesses that Christ is God, puts off the bondage and puts on the adoption is the one who emerges from the baptism "as bright as the sun," shining with beams of righteousness and, most importantly, returns a child of God and a joint heir with Christ. ON THE THEOPHANY 10.[40]

THE POWER OF REPENTANCE. CHRYSOSTOM: Let us become as clean as is possible. Let us wash away our sins. And the prophet teaches us how to wash them away, saying, "Wash yourselves, make yourselves clean, put away from my eyes the evil of your souls." . . . See that we must first cleanse ourselves, and then God cleanses us. He first said, "Wash yourselves, make yourselves clean," and then said, "I will make you white." . . . The power of repentance is then tremendous as it makes us white as snow and wool, even though sin had stained our souls. ON THE EPISTLE TO THE HEBREWS 12.4.[41]

PURIFY THE CONSCIENCE. CHRYSOSTOM: I say this, for in the prophet's words he does not mean bathing by water—the Jewish method of purification—but the purifying of the conscience. Let us also, then, be clean. HOMILIES ON THE GOSPEL OF JOHN 70.[42]

REPENTANCE WITHOUT PRETENSE. CHRYSOSTOM: Let us accept the medicine that obliterates our failures. Repentance is not what is spoken in words but what is confirmed by deeds, the repentance that obliterates the filth of impiety from the heart. . . . Why "before my eyes"? Because the eyes of people see differently, and the eye of God sees differently. . . . "Do not adulterate repentance with pretense," he says, "but, before my eyes, which examine what is secret, reveal the fruits of repentance." HOMILIES ON REPENTANCE AND ALMSGIVING 7.3.10.[43]

THE FACE AND THE HEART. AUGUSTINE: He [the one who is fasting] will wash his face,[44] that is, cleanse his heart, with which he will see God, no veil being interposed on account of the infirmity contracted from squalor; but being firm and steadfast, inasmuch as he is pure and guileless. . . . From the squalor, therefore, by which the eye of God is offended, our face is to be washed. SERMON ON THE MOUNT 2.42.[45]

STRETCHED ON THE CROSS. AUGUSTINE: So present yourself to such a head as a body worthy of him, to such a bridegroom as a worthy bride. . . . This is the bride of Christ, without stain or wrinkle. Do you wish to have no stain? Do what is written. . . . Do you wish to have no wrinkle? Stretch yourself on the cross. You see, you do not only need to be washed but also to be stretched, in order to be without stain or wrinkle; because by the washing sins are removed, while by the stretching a desire is created for the future life, which is what Christ was crucified for. SERMON 341.13.[46]

KEEPING CLEAN. GREGORY THE GREAT: He who does not keep innocence of life after weeping, neglects to be clean after washing; and those are not clean after washing who, though not ceasing to weep for their sins, yet commit again what has to be wept for. PASTORAL CARE 3.30.[47]

ANSWERED PRAYER. BEDE: Now they ask wrongly who persevere in sins and ill-advisedly entreat the Lord to forgive them the sins they do not at all forgive [others]. He condemns such as these through [the mouth of] Isaiah. . . . Still, having regard for such as these, Isaiah shows in what way they can obtain what they plead for when he goes on. HOMILIES ON THE GOSPELS 2.14.[48]

---

[40]ANF 5:237*. [41]PG 63:101-2. [42]FC 41:258. [43]FC 96:94-95. [44]Mt 6:17. [45]NPNF 1 6:47-48. [46]*WSA* 3 10:27. [47]ACW 11:204. [48]CS 111:127*.

THE WASHING OF REGENERATION. JEROME: "You are being washed; be clean." Instead of the sacrifices named above and holocausts and the abundance of fat and the blood of bulls and goats, instead of incense and new moons, the sabbath feast day and fastings, festivals and other solemnities, the religion of the gospel is what pleases me, that you would be baptized in my blood through the washing of regeneration, which alone is able to remove sins.[49] For no one will enter the kingdom of heaven who has not been reborn from water and the spirit. And the Lord himself, ascending to the Father, said, "Go and teach all the nations, baptizing them in the name of the Father, and the Son, and the Holy Spirit."[50] COMMENTARY ON ISAIAH 1.1.16.[51]

1:17 Care for Widows and Orphans

THE HONOR OF WIDOWHOOD. TERTULLIAN: God offers a brief summary through the prophet Isaiah of the honor that widows enjoy in the sight of God. . . . The Father defends these two types of people [widows and orphans] through divine mercy in proportion to their being destitute of human aid. Look how the widow's benefactor is put on a level with the widow herself, whose champion shall "reason with the Lord." TO HIS WIFE 8.[52]

GOD'S MERCY. CHRYSOSTOM: Do you see the great importance God places on mercy and of standing up for those who have been treated unjustly? We should pursue these good works, and by the grace of God will we receive the blessings to come. ON THE EPISTLE TO THE HEBREWS 12.4.[53]

THOSE IN NEED. CHRYSOSTOM: If you must visit someone, prefer to pay honor to orphans, widows and those in want rather than those who enjoy reputation and fame. BAPTISMAL INSTRUCTIONS 6.12.[54]

PITY THE WIDOW. CHRYSOSTOM: If you have

pity on the widow, your sins are washed away. HOMILIES ON 1 CORINTHIANS 23.6.[55]

1:18 Sins Washed White as Snow

REMISSION OF SIN. JUSTIN MARTYR: It was said through the prophet Isaiah how those who have sinned but repent will be freed from their sins. FIRST APOLOGY 61.[56]

THE LORD'S BLOOD. TERTULLIAN: In the scarlet color he indicates the blood of the prophets; in the crimson, that of the Lord, as the brighter. AGAINST MARCION 4.10.[57]

THE GREAT PHYSICIAN. BASIL THE GREAT: The great physician of souls is ready to cure your suffering; he is the ready liberator, not of you alone, but of all those enslaved by sin. LETTER 46.[58]

WOOL AS THE EMBLEM OF FORGIVENESS. CYRIL OF JERUSALEM: The Father will be seated, having "his garment white as snow, and the hair of his head like the pure wool."[59] This is spoken anthropomorphically. And the spiritual sense? That he is the King of such as are not defiled with sins. For God says, "Your sins shall be as white as snow, and shall be as wool." Wool is the emblem of forgiveness of sins, as also of innocence. CATECHETICAL LECTURES 15.19-21.[60]

A DOUBLE PURIFICATION. AMBROSE: [One] who is baptized is seen to be purified both according to the law and according to the gospel. According to the law, because Moses sprinkled the blood of the lamb with a bunch of hyssop;[61] according to the gospel, because Christ's garments were white as snow, when in the gospel he manifested the glory of his resurrection, [one] then whose guilt is remitted is made whiter than

[49]Cf. Jn 3:5; Tit 3:5. [50]Mt 28:19. [51]CCL 73:18. [52]ANF 4:43**. [53]PG 63:102. [54]ACW 31:98. [55]NPNF 1 12:136*. [56]ANF 1:183**. [57]ANF 3:358. [58]FC 13:127. [59]Dan 7:9. [60]LCC 4:162-63*. [61]Ex 12:22.

snow. ON THE MYSTERIES 7.34.[62]

CARE FOR THE WIDOW AND MINOR. AMBROSE: What shall I say of human judgments, since in the judgments of God the Jews are set forth as having offended the Lord in nothing more than violating what was due to widows and the rights of minors? This is proclaimed by the voices of the prophets as the cause that brought upon the Jews the penalty of rejection. This is mentioned as the only cause that will mitigate the wrath of God against their sin, if they honor the widow and execute true judgment for minors. Here also the likeness of the church is foreshadowed. You see, then, holy widows, that that office which is honored by the assistance of divine grace must not be degraded by impure desire. CONCERNING WIDOWS 2.13.[63]

ALLOW YOUR WOUND TO BE HEALED. CHRYSOSTOM: Should you have gone all lengths in wickedness, yet say to yourself, God is loving to humanity and desires our salvation. . . . Let us not therefore give up in despair; for to fall is not so grievous as to lie where we have fallen; nor to be wounded so dreadful as after wounds to refuse healing. . . . These things I say not to make you more negligent but to prevent your despairing. HOMILIES ON 1 CORINTHIANS 8.8 (4).[64]

A PURE SOUL. CHRYSOSTOM: Why do you deck out your body while you neglect your soul, enslaved as it is by impurity? Why do you not give as much thought to your soul as to your body? You ought, rather, to give it more care. Beloved, you ought at least to give it an equal amount of thought. Tell me, please, if someone should ask you which you would prefer: for your body to be glowing in health and to excel in beauty but to be clad in mean clothing, or for your body to be crippled and full of disease but adorned with gold and lavishly decked out— would you not choose by far to possess beauty as part of the very nature of your body rather than merely in the outward covering of your clothes? If

so, will you make this choice with regard to your body but just the opposite one in the case of your soul? If it is foul and noxious and black, what fruit do you think you will enjoy from your golden ornaments? But what insanity is this?

Apply this adornment within yourself and place these necklaces around your soul. For the ornaments placed about the body do not contribute either to its health or its beauty, since they do not make what is white, black—or what is discreditable, beautiful or good-looking. If you place ornaments about your soul, on the contrary, they quickly make it white instead of black, beautiful and comely instead of foul and deformed. HOMILIES ON THE GOSPEL OF JOHN 69.[65]

THE PURE CHURCH. AUGUSTINE: What is surprising about white garments symbolizing the church? SERMON 78.2.[66]

THE CONSTANT NEED FOR GRACE. AUGUSTINE: Humankind has need of God's grace not only to be made just when they are wicked, when they are changed, that is, from wicked to just, and when they are given good in return for evil, but grace must accompany them, and they must lean on it in order not to fall. This is why it is written of the church in the Song of Songs: "Who is this that comes up clad in white, leaning upon her kinsman?"[67] For she who could not do this of herself has been made white. And who has made her white but him who says by the prophet, "If your sins be as scarlet, they shall be made white as snow"? She was not gaining any good merit then at the time she was made white. But now that she has been made white, she walks aright, provided only that she continues to lean upon him who made her white. Accordingly, Jesus himself, upon whom the church leans, now that she has been made white, said to his disciples, "Without me you can do nothing."[68] ON GRACE AND FREE WILL 6.[69]

---

[62]NPNF 2 10:321*. [63]NPNF 2 10:393. [64]NPNF 1 12:47*. [65]FC 41:248-49*. [66]WSA 3 3:341. [67]Song 8:5 LXX. [68]Jn 15:5. [69]FC 59:265-66*.

DRAW NEAR TO CHRIST. JOHN OF DAMASCUS: Such therefore being the promises made by God to them that turn to him, don't delay . . . but draw near to Christ, our loving God, and be enlightened, and your face shall not be ashamed. For as soon as you go down into the bath of holy baptism, all the defilement of the old nature and all the burden of your many sins are buried in the water and pass into nothingness. And you come up from there a new person, pure from all pollution, with no spot or wrinkle of sin upon you. BARLAAM AND JOSEPH 32.[70]

1:19 Willing and Obedient

RENEWAL IN THE KINGDOM. TERTULLIAN: This passage means the blessings that await the flesh when in the kingdom of God it shall be renewed, and made like the angels, and waiting to obtain the things "which neither eye has seen nor ear heard, and which have not entered into the heart of man."[71] ON THE RESURRECTION OF THE FLESH 26.[72]

A PROLIFIC MOTHER. AMBROSE: Scripture promised these good things to the faithful when it said, "You shall eat the good things of the land." That we may obtain the good things, let us be like that good, the good that is without iniquity and without deceit and without severity but is with grace and holiness and purity and benevolence and love and justice. Thus goodness, like a prolific mother, embraces all the virtues. FLIGHT FROM THE WORLD 6.36.[73]

A GOOD WILL IS NEEDED. CHRYSOSTOM: Do you perceive that there is need only of the will? Of the will—not merely that faculty which is the common possession of all people—but good will. To be sure, I know that all people even now wish to fly up to heaven, but it is necessary to bring that desire to fruition by one's works. HOMILIES ON THE GOSPEL OF JOHN 1.[74]

DO THE GOOD DEEDS OF A GOOD WILL.

CHRYSOSTOM: Perhaps one will say, "I am willing (and no one is so void of understanding as not to be willing) but to will is not sufficient for me." No, it is sufficient, if you be duly willing and do the deeds of one that is willing. But as it is, you are not greatly willing. . . .

[One] that wills a thing as he ought puts also his hand to the means which lead to the object of his desire. HOMILIES ON 1 CORINTHIANS 14.5 (3).[75]

FREE WILL AND GRACE BELONG TOGETHER. JOHN CASSIAN: Who understands clearly how the sum of salvation is attributed to our will? . . .

What does this all mean except that in each of these cases both the grace of God and our freedom of will are affirmed, since even by his own activity a person can occasionally be brought to a desire for virtue, but he always needs to be helped by the Lord. CONFERENCE 13.9.2, 4.[76]

THE PELAGIAN ERROR. CASSIODORUS: There is also the Pelagians' second wickedness, for they so attribute free will to their human powers that they believe that they can devise or enact some good of their own accord without God's grace. . . . You interpret these and similar passages most perversely, believing that people take the first step of their good intentions of their own accord and subsequently obtain the help of the Godhead, so that (to express the matter sacrilegiously) we are the cause of his kindness and he is not the cause of his own. EXPOSITION OF THE PSALMS 50.7.[77]

1:20 Devoured by the Sword

GOD'S SWORD IN THE FIRE. JUSTIN MARTYR: The phrase "the sword shall devour you" does not mean that sinners will be killed by swords but that God's sword is the fire which is fueled by those who by their own volition do evil. . . . For were he to be speaking of a sword that cuts and

---

[70]LCL 34:503**. [71]1 Cor 2:9. [72]ANF 3:564. [73]FC 65:309. [74]FC 33:9. [75]NPNF 1 12:79-80*. [76]ACW 57:474-75. [77]ACW 51:499.

immediately kills, he would not have said, "will devour." First Apology 44.[78]

Fire-Tried Gold and Silver. John Cassian: Moreover, we know that even holy people have been given over bodily to Satan or to great sufferings on account of some slight sins. For the divine clemency does not permit the least blemish or stain to be found in them on the day of judgment. According to the words of the prophet, which are in fact God's, he purges away all the dross of their uncleanness in the present so that he may bring them to eternity like fire-tried gold or silver, in need of no penal cleansing. Conference 7.25.2.[79]

A Warning to the Recalcitrant. Fulgentius of Ruspe: He who forgives sins is proclaimed to be just and merciful; we know with the greatest of ease that the forgiveness of sins is granted only to the converted, and the punish-

ment of eternal damnation is inflicted only on those who remain in sin. . . .

In Isaiah is found a similar declaration from the divine Word against the recalcitrant who scorn the divine clemency. In this declaration it is made known that one obeys the divine commands not without reason and that one does not remain in evil without punishment. . . .

Who, I ask, is so hard and altogether inert that, in these words of the highest admonition, if he is not called to conversion out of the pleasure of what is promised, he is not at least compelled by the fear of punishment? Salvation will not accept the one who scorns the divine words, but the sword will devour him. On the Forgiveness of Sins 1.11.2-3.[80]

---

[78]ANF 1:177**. [79]ACW 57:264. [80]FC 95:122-23.

1:21-31 DESTRUCTION OF ISRAEL FOR FALSE RELIGION

[21]How the faithful city
  has become a harlot,
  she that was full of justice!
Righteousness lodged in her,
  but now murderers.
[22]Your silver has become dross,
  your wine mixed with water.*
[23]Your princes are rebels
  and companions of thieves.
Every one loves a bribe
  and runs after gifts.

They do not defend the fatherless,
  and the widow's cause does not come
  to them.

[24]Therefore the Lord says,
  the Lord of hosts,
  the Mighty One of Israel:
"Ah, I will vent my wrath on my enemies,
  and avenge myself on my foes.
[25]I will turn my hand against you
  and will smelt away your dross as with lye

and remove all your alloy.
[26] And I will restore your judges as at the
first,
and your counselors as at the beginning.
Afterward you shall be called the city of
righteousness,
the faithful city."

[27] Zion shall be redeemed by justice,
and those in her who repent, by
righteousness.
[28] But rebels and sinners shall be destroyed
together,

and those who forsake the LORD shall
be consumed.
[29] For you shall be ashamed of the oaks
in which you delighted;
and you shall blush for the gardens
which you have chosen.
[30] For you shall be like an oak
whose leaf withers,
and like a garden without water.
[31] And the strong shall become tow,
and his work a spark,
and both of them shall burn together,
with none to quench them.

*LXX your wine merchants mix the wine with water

OVERVIEW: To deny either the humanity or the divinity of Christ is to mix water and wine together (ATHANASIUS). One corrupts true doctrine when it is mixed with base speech (GREGORY OF NAZIANZUS, CHRYSOSTOM). God causes believers to endure trials in order to purge them of their small sins (JOHN CASSIAN). The faithful city is the church, which replaced Israel. Those who have abandoned the right way will be consumed if they do not repent (JEROME). Judgment against Judah ends with a remnant remaining (EUSEBIUS).

1:22 Wine Mixed with Water

CHRIST DIVINE AND HUMAN. ATHANASIUS: Someone who looks at what is done divinely by the Word and denies the body, or looks at what is proper to the body and denies the Word's presence in the flesh or from what is human, entertains low thoughts concerning the Word . . . as a Jewish vintner, mixing water with the wine, shall account the cross an offense, or as a Gentile, will deem the preaching folly. FOUR DISCOURSES AGAINST THE ARIANS 3.26.[1]

WORD OF TRUTH. GREGORY OF NAZIANZUS: And who is sufficient for these things? For we are

not as the many, able to corrupt the word of truth and mix the wine, which makes glad the heart of man,[2] with water. [We do not] mix, that is, our doctrine with what is common and cheap, and debased, and stale, and tasteless, in order to turn the adulteration to our profit and accommodate ourselves to those who meet us, and curry favor with everyone. [We do not] become ventriloquists[3] and chatterers, who serve their own pleasures by words uttered from the earth, and sink into the earth, and, to gain the special good will of the multitude, injure in the highest degree, no, ruin ourselves, and shed the innocent blood of simpler souls, which will be required at our hands.[4] IN DEFENSE OF HIS FLIGHT, ORATION 2.46.[5]

1:25-26 Refining Metal

THE UNDILUTED WORD. CHRYSOSTOM: For we will not mimic the false prophets who say that most things have been done by them. This is the meaning of "to corrupt," when someone dilutes the wine, or when someone sells something

---

[1] NPNF 2 4:413. [2] Ps 106:15. [3] "Wizards" in Is 8:19. [4] Ezek 3:20; 33:8. [5] NPNF 2 7:214*.

which ought to be given away freely. He seems to me to be both taunting them regarding money and hinting at the fact that they have mingled the things of God with their own things, as I have said. This is the accusation of Isaiah, who says, "Your wine merchants mingle wine with water." Even if this statement were about wine, one would not sin to say it of doctrine as well. He says, "We do not do this, but we offer to you what we have been given, pouring out the undiluted word." Homilies on 2 Corinthians 5.3.[6]

The Cleansing Fire. John Cassian: This occurs for the sake of cleansing, however, when he humbles his righteous ones for their small and as it were insignificant sins or because of their proud purity, giving them over to various trials in order to purge away now all the unclean thoughts . . . which he sees have collected in their inmost being, and in order to submit them like pure gold to the judgment to come, permitting nothing to remain in them that the searching fire of judgment might afterwards find to purge with penal torment. Conference 6.11.2.[7]

The City of Righteousness. Jerome: [This concerns] the faithful city of Zion, which later became a harlot. In place of the righteous, or righteousness, murderers dwelled within her. The Lord, therefore, turned his hand and purged her of impurities and removed all her alloy and restored her judges as at the beginning, and her counselors as of old. The prior judges were Moses and Joshua the son of Nun, and others from whom a book of sacred Scripture received its name. Later, David and other righteous kings were added. He will restore, therefore, a judge like them, or after the Babylonian captivity, as the Jews desire, Zerubbabel, Ezra, Nehemiah and other leaders who presided over the people until Hyrcanus, whom Herod succeeded as king. In any event, the apostles and those who believed through the apostles were established as more trustworthy and upright leaders of the church, in keeping with what we said at the beginning of

this vision, namely, that both the threat and the promise pertain to the time of the Lord's passion and to the faith that formed the church after his passion. "Afterward you will be called the city of the righteous, a faithful city." This prophetic word clearly embraces the church, composed of both the Jews and the Gentiles who would come to believe in the Lord. It is also the city of the righteous, that is, of the Lord our Savior, for she herself is called righteous about whom it was said, "A city set on a hill cannot be hidden."[8] Thus, calling her faithful, or *metropolim* according to the Septuagint, it shows that those who will believe in the Lord must also be known by these titles. Commentary on Isaiah 1.1.26.[9]

1:28 Those Who Forsake God

Will God Not Show Leniency? Jerome: Moreover, who can agree with the thesis that you [the Pelagians] set down as your next heading: "In the day of judgment, no leniency shall be shown to the ungodly and to sinners, but they shall be consumed in eternal fires," for you prevent God from showing mercy, and you pass judgment on the sentence of the judge before judgment day, so that if he wanted to spare the unjust and the sinner, he could not, in view of your prescription? For, you say, it is written in Psalm 103, "Let sinners be consumed out of the earth, and the unjust, so that they be no more."[10] And in Isaiah: "The unjust and the sinners shall burn together, and they who abandon God shall be consumed." And do you not know that a threat on the part of God at times hints at clemency? For he does not say that they shall be consumed in everlasting fires, but rather that they shall be consumed out of the earth and shall cease to be unjust. For it is one thing for them to avoid sin and injustice and quite another matter for them to perish forever and be consumed in eternal fires. Moreover, Isaiah, from whom you quote

---

[6]PG 61:431. [7]CSEL 13:168. [8]Mt 5:14. [9]CCL 73:24-25. [10]Ps 104:35 (103:35 LXX).

your testimony, says, "The unjust and the sinners shall burn together" (without adding the phrase "forever"), "and those who abandon God shall be consumed." This judgment refers, specifically, to heretics who have abandoned the right way of faith and will be consumed, if they are unwilling to return to God whom they have abandoned. AGAINST THE PELAGIANS 1.28.[11]

1:30 *Like an Oak with Fading Leaves*

THE PROPHET WARNS. EUSEBIUS OF CAE-

SAREA: In the beginning of his whole book, the prophet saw the "vision against Judah and against Jerusalem."[12] After listing all the many transgressions of the Jewish people and warning them about the complete destruction of Jerusalem, he brought to an end the spiritual sayings concerning them.[13] PROOF OF THE GOSPEL 2.3.[14]

---

[11]FC 53:272. [12]Is 1:1. [13]Eusebius means that because of their sins the Jewish people fade, so the church becomes the focus. [14]POG 1:80*.

2:1-6 THE COMING AGE OF PEACE

[1]The word which Isaiah the son of Amoz saw concerning Judah and Jerusalem.
[2]It shall come to pass in the latter days
    that the mountain of the house of the
        LORD
shall be established as the highest of the
        mountains,
    and shall be raised above the hills;
and all the nations shall flow to it,
    [3]and many peoples shall come, and say:
"Come, let us go up to the mountain of the
        LORD,
    to the house of the God of Jacob;
that he may teach us his ways
    and that we may walk in his paths."
For out of Zion shall go forth the law,
    and the word of the LORD from
        Jerusalem.

[4]He shall judge between the nations,
    and shall decide for many peoples;
and they shall beat their swords into
        plowshares,
    and their spears into pruning hooks;
nation shall not lift up sword against
        nation,
    neither shall they learn war any more.

[5]O house of Jacob,
    come, let us walk
    in the light of the LORD.

[6]For thou hast rejected thy people,
    the house of Jacob,*
because they are full of diviners[a] from the east
    and of soothsayers like the Philistines,
    and they strike hands with foreigners.

a Cn: Heb lacks *of diviners*   *LXX Israel

Overview: Christ's coming demonstrated the stark contrast between idolatry and true religion (Theodoret). The church is the indestructible mountain (Cyril of Jerusalem, Augustine). Christ is the mountain (Augustine, Gregory the Great). With the coming of Christ came the call of the Gentiles (Eusebius). The mountain is the church, built on the foundation of the apostles and prophets (Jerome). Nations and peoples are moving toward Christ and his church (Leander of Seville). Christians are encouraged to sing praise to God (Athanasius). Isaiah predicted the gospel of the New Testament (Theodoret, Basil). The apostles and their followers preached the gospel beginning in Jerusalem (Justin Martyr, Eusebius, Augustine, Bede). Jews and Gentiles are subject to the new law of God in Christ. Christ did not come as powerful in war but in peace (Tertullian). Peace comes only through Christ and his church (Athanasius, Chrysostom). One house of Jacob is born of flesh and blood, the other of faith and the spirit (Justin Martyr, Augustine). Jesus Christ is the light of the world, and we should come to him for forgiveness (Jerome).

2:2 The Lord's House Established

ANNOUNCEMENT OF THE INCARNATION. Theodoret of Cyr: [Isaiah] announces the wonderful and widespread demonstration of piety everywhere: idolatry will be destroyed, while the house of God will receive its due sign of universal respect.... After our Savior's appearing, idolatry will be shown and the beauty of truth will be unveiled. In this we will see the fulfillment of this announcement. Furthermore, by "last days" he means that time following incarnation. COMMENTARY ON ISAIAH 2.2.[1]

THE MOUNTAIN AS THE CHURCH. Cyril of Jerusalem: He calls the church a mountain when he says, "In the last days the mountain of the Lord's house shall be established." CATECHETICAL LECTURES 21.7.[2]

CHRIST THE MOUNTAIN. Augustine: The central place they are all coming to is Christ; he is at the center, because he is equally related to all; anything placed in the center is common to all....

Approach the mountain, climb up the mountain, and you that climb it, do not go down it. There you will be safe, there you will be protected; Christ is your mountain of refuge. And where is Christ? At the right hand of the Father, since he has ascended into heaven. SERMON 62A.3.[3]

THE VISION OF DANIEL. Augustine: It talks of a mountain, and the mountain is veiled to the party of Donatus.[4] ...

The holy Daniel saw a vision and wrote down what he saw, and he said that he had seen a stone hewn out of a mountain without hands. It is Christ, coming from the nation of the Jews, which was also a mountain, you see, because it has the kingdom....

What is the mountain over which the heretics stumbled? Listen to Daniel again: "And that stone grew and became a great mountain, such that it filled all the face of the earth."[5] How right the psalm is to say to Christ the Lord as he rises again, "Be exalted over the heavens, O God, and let your glory be over the whole earth."[6] What is your glory over the whole earth? Over the whole earth your church, over the whole earth your bride. SERMON 147A.4.[7]

OUR REDEEMER. Gregory the Great: Who is meant by "mountain of strength" but our Redeemer? FORTY GOSPEL HOMILIES 33.[8]

CHRIST IS THE SAVIOR OF ALL PEOPLES. Eusebius of Caesarea: One can take the time to learn in what manner the prophecies of the call

---

[1]SC 276:188-90. [2]NPNF 2 7:150. [3]WSA 3 3:171. [4]Donatus led a party out of the church over the question of clergy who had handed the Scriptures to authorities under the threat of persecution. Donatus and his followers believed the church had been corrupted by allowing these clergy to remain. [5]Dan 2:35. [6]Ps 57:11 (56:12 LXX); 108:5 (107:6 LXX). [7]WSA 3 4:454**. [8]CS 123:276.

of the Gentiles should be understood and that they were fulfilled only after the coming of our Savior. The beginning of the prophecy is consistent with the reality that the Lord descended not only for the salvation of the Jewish race but also for that of all people, in announcing to all peoples and all the inhabitants of the earth, "Hear, all peoples, and let the earth and all in it listen." Proof of the Gospel 6.13.[9]

Christ and His Church. Leander of Seville: The mountain is Christ, and the house of the God of Jacob is his one church, toward which the concourse of nations and assembly of peoples is moving by this pronouncement. Homily on the Triumph of the Church.[10]

The House of the Lord. Jerome: This mountain is in the house of the Lord, for which the prophet sighed when he said, "One thing I asked from the Lord, this I seek, that I might dwell in the house of the Lord all the days of my life,"[11] and about which Paul wrote to Timothy, "If I am late, you should know how to behave in the house of God, which is the church of the living God, the pillar and foundation of the truth."[12] This house was built on the foundation of the apostles and the prophets,[13] who are mountains themselves as imitators of Christ. About this house of Jerusalem the psalmist cried out: "Those who trust in the Lord are like Mount Zion, which dwells in Jerusalem; it will not be moved forever. The mountains surround her and the Lord surrounds his people."[14] Hence Christ also founds his church on one of the mountains and says to him, "You are Peter, and on this rock I will build my church, and the gates of the netherworld will not prevail against her."[15] Commentary on Isaiah 1.2.2.[16]

2:3 The Mountain of the Lord

The Saints of Old Encourage Us to Celebrate. Athanasius: Let us sing a victorious song of praise to the Lord!

Who will lead us to such a company of angels?

Who, longing for the heavenly feast and the angels' holiday, will say like the prophet, "I will lead them to the house of God: a multitude joyfully praising God and keeping festival"?[17] The saints of old encourage us to be like that, saying, "Come, let us go up to the mountain of the Lord, and to the house of the God of Jacob." Festal Letter 6.10-11.[18]

Gospel from Zion. Theodoret of Cyr: I am amazed at the persistence of some to interpret this passage in such a way as to conclude that this is a prediction of the return from Babylonian captivity. Which nations rushed to the temple after its rebuilding? What law was given from there? God gave the ancient law on Sinai, not Zion. Clearly Isaiah is referring to the New Testament, where the law was first given to the apostles and then delivered to all peoples by them. He announces that in addition to the law, the word would come from Zion. The term *word* is a title given to the message of the gospel. The blessed Luke says, "Those who were from the beginning eyewitnesses and ministers of the word delivered them to us."[19] He is not talking about God the Word but the message of the divine word. Zion is not where God the Word was from but where he taught the truth. Commentary on Isaiah 2.4.[20]

Gospel from Zion. Basil the Great: Ask a man of circumcision, a Jew after the flesh, which law and which word the prophet is talking about. About the law given through Moses? Let them show how this law comes "out of Zion." For Moses did not enter the land of possession, whereas Zion is in Judea.[21] The Scripture was mistaken then, according to them, using one name instead of another, for it said Zion instead of Sinai or Horeb. But it refers to the holy law. Which one? When was it given? Where was it

[9]POG 2:16-17. [10]FC 62:233. [11]Ps 27:4 (26:4 LXX). [12]1 Tim 3:15. [13]Cf. Eph 2:20. [14]Ps 125:1 (124:1 LXX). [15]Mt 16:18. [16]CCL 73:27-28. [17]Ps 42:4 (41:5 LXX). [18]NPNF 2 4:522*. [19]Lk 1:2. [20]SC 276:192-94. [21]Basil's point is that because Moses never entered Zion he could not have given the law to which Isaiah refers.

written? And "the word out of Jerusalem" as well? The Jew after the flesh says that Isaiah means preaching of the prophets. Yet the preaching of the prophets took place everywhere across Judea, not only in Jerusalem and throughout Israel but also in captivity, in Nineveh and throughout the earth. Let them restrain themselves then before the truth and receive the law giving of the Lord that comes from the watchtower, the God-bearing flesh from which he watched over human actions. "And the word of the Lord out of Jerusalem." Having started from there, the preaching of the gospel has been sown around the whole world. COMMENTARY ON ISAIAH 2.72.[22]

TWELVE WENT OUT. JUSTIN MARTYR: We can show you that this actually happened. For a group of twelve men went out from Jerusalem, and they were ignorant men, not trained in oratory. But through the power of God they witnessed to every race of humanity that they were sent out by Christ to teach the Word of God to all people. Now we who once killed one another no longer war against each other, but moreso we gladly die for the confession of Christ in order not to lie to or deceive our interrogators.[23] FIRST APOLOGY 39.[24]

A NEW LAW. EUSEBIUS OF CAESAREA: What can this law proceeding from Zion, which is different from what was made law by Moses in the desert at Mount Sinai, be but the word of the gospel through our Savior Jesus Christ which proceeds from Zion through all the nations? For clearly it was in Jerusalem and Mount Zion, where our Savior and Lord lived and taught, that the law of the new covenant originated and from which it proceeded to all people. PROOF OF THE GOSPEL 1.4.[25]

REPENTANCE BEGINS IN JERUSALEM. AUGUSTINE: The first law, the Old Testament, had come out of Mount Sinai by the lips of Moses; but it was foretold of the law Christ came to give: "The law shall come forth from Zion, and the word of the Lord from Jerusalem." This explains why

Christ ordered repentance to be preached in his name among all peoples but beginning in Jerusalem. CITY OF GOD 18.54.[26]

FORGIVENESS BEGINS IN JERUSALEM. BEDE: It was opportune that the preaching of repentance and the forgiveness of sins through confession of Christ's name should have started from Jerusalem. Where the splendor of his teaching and virtues, where the triumph of his passion, where the joy of his resurrection and ascension were accomplished, there the first root of faith in him would be brought forth; [there] the first shoot of the burgeoning church, like that of some kind of great vine, would be planted. Just so, by an increase in the spreading of the word, [the church] would extend the branches of her teaching into the whole wide world. . . . It was opportune that the preaching of repentance and the forgiveness of sins, good news to be proclaimed to idolatrous nations and those defiled by various evil deeds, should take its start from Jerusalem, lest any of those defiled, thoroughly terrified by the magnitude of their offenses, should doubt the possibility of obtaining pardon if they performed fruits worthy of repentance, when it was a fact that pardon had been granted to those at Jerusalem who had blasphemed and crucified the Son of God. HOMILIES ON THE GOSPELS 2.15.[27]

2:4 Judging the Nations

TRANSFORMED MINDS. TERTULLIAN: Long ago did Isaiah declare that "out of Zion should go forth the law, and the word of the Lord from Jerusalem," some other law, that is, and another word. In short, he says, "He shall judge among the nations and shall rebuke many people," meaning not those of the Jewish people only, but also of the nations which are judged by the new law of

---

[22]TASHT 7:85-86. [23]Justin is referring to persecuted Christians who could avoid death by denying Christ. To do so, however, would be to deceive. He means to say that Christians would rather die than deny Christ. [24]ANF 1:175*. [25]POG 1:24. [26]FC 24:180*. [27]CS 111:137-38*.

the gospel and the new word of the apostles, and are among themselves rebuked of their old error as soon as they have believed. And as the result of this, "They beat their swords into plowshares, and their spears (which are a kind of hunting instrument) into pruning hooks." That is to say, minds that once were fierce and cruel are changed by the gospel and the word of the apostles into good dispositions productive of good fruit. AGAINST MARCION 4.1.[28]

CHRIST, NOT MOSES. TERTULLIAN: The gospel will be this "way" of the new law and the new word in Christ, no longer in Moses. "And he shall judge among the nations," even concerning their error. "And these shall rebuke a large nation," that of the Jews themselves and their proselytes. "And they shall beat their swords into plowshares"; in other words, they shall change into pursuits of moderation and peace the dispositions of injurious minds, hostile tongues and all kinds of evil and blasphemy. . . . You learn here that Christ is promised not as powerful in war but pursuing peace. AGAINST MARCION 3.21.[29]

PEACE THROUGH CHRIST. ATHANASIUS: Who is the one who has done this, or who is the one who has joined together in peace people who once hated one another, except for the beloved Son of the Father, the Savior of all, even Jesus Christ, who because of his own love suffered all things for our salvation? For from ages past the peace he would initiate was promised. ON THE INCARNATION 52.1.[30]

PEACE THROUGH THE CHURCH. CHRYSOSTOM: Not only would the church be firm, steadfast and indestructible, but it would also gain great peace for the world. Governments and monarchies will be destroyed; there will be but one kingdom put together for all people, and, unlike in times past, its greater part will be at peace. For, in the past, all craftsmen and men in public life were trained in warfare and took their place among the ranks.

After the coming of Christ, all that was done away with, and wars were confined to widely separated areas. DEMONSTRATION AGAINST THE PAGANS 6.6.[31]

2:5-6 House of Jacob

TWO HOUSES OF JACOB. JUSTIN MARTYR: Our conclusion is that there were two seeds of Judah and two races, just as there are two houses of Jacob, one born of flesh and blood and the other born of faith and the Spirit. DIALOGUE WITH TRYPHO 135.6.5-8.[32]

JACOB IS NOT ISRAEL. AUGUSTINE: What did the prophet Isaiah mean when he announced that a mountain would be prepared on the summits of the mountains, to which all peoples were going to come? The law and the Word of God was going to proceed from Zion and Jerusalem to all nations, not from Mount Sinai to one nation. This we see most evidently fulfilled in Christ and the Christians. A little later the prophet says, "O house of Jacob, come and let us walk in the light of the Lord." Here, you [the Jews] will surely say your usual piece: "We are the house of Jacob," but listen a moment to what follows, and when you have said what you want to say, hear what you do not want to hear. The prophet continues, "For he has cast off his people, the house of Israel." Here say, "We are the house of Israel"; here acknowledge yourselves and forgive us for reminding you of these facts. IN ANSWER TO THE JEWS 8.[33]

NO PLACE FOR A PROUD ATTITUDE. AUGUSTINE: Dearly beloved, whether the Jews receive these divine testimonies with joy or with indignation, nevertheless, when we can, let us proclaim them with great love for the Jews. Let us not proudly glory against the broken branches; let us rather reflect by whose grace it is, and by much mercy, and on what root, we have been grafted

---

[28]ANF 3:346**. [29]ANF 3:339-40*. [30]NPNF 2 4:64*. [31]FC 73:213. [32]ANF 1:267. [33]FC 27:407*.

into. In Answer to the Jews 10.[34]

Walk in the Light. Jerome: For all who do evil hate the light and fail to come to the light lest their works be proven.[35] But you, the house of Jacob, the house of my people, come with me and let us walk together in the light of the Lord. Let us accept the gospel of Christ and be illuminated by him who said, "I am the light of the world."[36] And when this had been spoken to the people of the Jews, discerning that their hearts were impenitent and their hardened souls unbelieving, Isaiah made a note to the Lord, saying, "I exhort them, therefore, to come to you today and to be filled with me by your light, for you have abandoned your people, formerly the house of Jacob, on account of their sins." Commentary on Isaiah 1.2.5-6.[37]

[34]FC 27:414*. [35]Cf. Jn 3:20. [36]Jn 8:12. [37]CCL 73:31.

2:7-22 JUDGMENT FOR IDOLATRY

[7]Their land is filled with silver and gold,
  and there is no end to their treasures;
their land is filled with horses,
  and there is no end to their chariots.
[8]Their land is filled with idols;
  they bow down to the work of their hands,
  to what their own fingers have made.
[9]So man is humbled,
  and men are brought low—
  forgive them not!
[10]Enter into the rock,
  and hide in the dust
from before the terror of the Lord,
  and from the glory of his majesty.
[11]The haughty looks of man shall be brought low,
and the pride of men shall be humbled;
and the Lord alone will be exalted in that day.

[12]For the Lord of hosts has a day
  against all that is proud and lofty,
  against all that is lifted up and high;[b]

[13]against all the cedars of Lebanon,
  lofty and lifted up;
  and against all the oaks of Bashan;
[14]against all the high mountains,
  and against all the lofty hills;
[15]against every high tower,
  and against every fortified wall;
[16]against all the ships of Tarshish,
  and against all the beautiful craft.
[17]And the haughtiness of man shall be humbled,
  and the pride of men shall be brought low;
  and the Lord alone will be exalted in that day.
[18]And the idols shall utterly pass away.
[19]And men shall enter the caves of the rocks
  and the holes of the ground,
from before the terror of the Lord,
  and from the glory of his majesty,
  when he rises to terrify the earth.

[20]In that day men will cast forth
  their idols of silver and their idols of gold,

which they made for themselves to worship,
to the moles and to the bats,
²¹*to enter the caverns of the rocks*
and the clefts of the cliffs,
from before the terror of the LORD,

and from the glory of his majesty,
when he rises to terrify the earth.
²²*Turn away from man*
in whose nostrils is breath,
for of what account is he?

b Cn Compare Gk: Heb *low*

OVERVIEW: Isaiah denounced the misuse of possessions (CHRYSOSTOM). Idols can be statues, philosophy or heresies (ORIGEN). The highest idolatry is vanity (CASSIODORUS). Because of God's great works, no one should be ignorant of God's existence (TERTULLIAN).

2:7-8 A Land Filled with Idols

ABUSE OF POSSESSIONS. CHRYSOSTOM: Someone might ask, what is wrong with having silver or horses, particularly when what the people believed was not rigorous? How should we respond? The prophet was not criticizing the use of these possessions but the misuse of them. When he said, "Woe to the mighty,"[1] he was not condemning them for having possessions but for hoarding so much more than they needed. COMMENTARY ON ISAIAH 2.7.[2]

MENTAL IDOLS. ORIGEN: Not only do human beings "make gods for themselves"[3] from statues, but you will also find them "making gods for themselves" from their imaginations. For such people can imagine another god and creator of the world in a system different from the divine plan of the world recorded by the Spirit, other than the true world. These all have "made gods for themselves," and they have "worshiped the works of their hands." So, too, I believe is the case either among the Greeks who generate opinions, so to speak, of this philosophy or that, or among the heretics, the first who generate opinions. These have "made idols for themselves" and figments of the soul, and by turning to them "they worship the works of

their hands," since they accept as truth their own fabrications. HOMILIES ON JEREMIAH 16.9.1.[4]

THE VANITY THAT PERISHES. CASSIODORUS: Vanity is the general term for vices, but vain in the particular sense means that which is found alien to God. Just as trusting in the Godhead is fruitful constancy, so deviating from him is the vanity that perishes. . . . So those who burned with the most base love of idols are convicted, and the phrase is to be pronounced as a rebuke, as if the words were, "Why do you love the vanity by which you perish?" We ought to love things that are beneficial, not harmful, for it is better to curse the things that cause the punishment of lasting damnation to afflict us. EXPOSITION OF THE PSALMS 4.3.[5]

2:19 The Lord Rises to Terrify the Earth

THE CREATOR CAN BE KNOWN. TERTULLIAN: The Creator ought to be known even by the light of nature, for he may be understood from his works and may thereby become the object of a more widely spread knowledge. To him, therefore, does it appertain to punish such as do not know God, for none ought to be ignorant of him. In the apostle's phrase, "From the presence of the Lord, and from the glory of his power,"[6] he uses the words of Isaiah, who for that same reason attests the very same Lord as arising "to shake terribly the earth."[7] AGAINST MARCION 5.16.[8]

---

[1]Is 1:24. [2]SC 304:132. [3]Jer 16:20. [4]FC 97:177. [5]ACW 51:75**.
[6]2 Thess 1:9. [7]Tertullian means that Paul uses Isaiah in order to demonstrate that God is known by his works. [8]ANF 3:463*.

3:1-12 ISRAEL'S SIN AGAINST GOD

¹*For, behold, the Lord, the* LORD *of hosts,*
  is taking away from Jerusalem and
    from Judah
stay and staff,
  the whole stay of bread,
  and the whole stay of water;
²*the mighty man and the soldier,*
  the judge and the prophet,
  the diviner and the elder,
³*the captain of fifty*
  and the man of rank,
the counselor and the skilful magician
  and the expert in charms.
⁴*And I will make boys their princes,*
  and babes shall rule over them.
⁵*And the people will oppress one another,*
  every man his fellow
  and every man his neighbor;
the youth will be insolent to the elder,
  and the base fellow to the honorable.

⁶*When a man takes hold of his brother*
  in the house of his father, saying:
"You have a mantle;
  you shall be our leader,
and this heap of ruins
  shall be under your rule";
⁷*in that day he will speak out, saying:*

"I will not be a healer;
  in my house there is neither bread nor
    mantle;
you shall not make me
  leader of the people."
⁸*For Jerusalem has stumbled,*
  and Judah has fallen;
because their speech and their deeds are
  against the LORD,
  defying his glorious presence.

⁹*Their partiality witnesses against*
  them;
  they proclaim their sin like Sodom,
  they do not hide it.
Woe to them!
  For they have brought evil upon
  themselves.
¹⁰*Tell the righteous that it shall be well with*
  *them,**
  for they shall eat the fruit of their deeds.
¹¹*Woe to the wicked! It shall be ill with him,*
  for what his hands have done shall be
    done to him.
¹²*My people—children are their oppressors,*
  and women rule over them.
O my people, your leaders† mislead you,
  and confuse the course of your paths.

*LXX *Saying against themselves, "Let us bind the just, for he is burdensome to us"*   †LXX *they that call you blessed*

OVERVIEW: Grace was withdrawn from Israel because it rejected Christ (TERTULLIAN). The greatest sin of Israel was not idolatry but rejecting Christ (JUSTIN MARTYR). Isaiah foretold that the Jews would willfully reject the Messiah and plot against him (AMBROSE, EUSEBIUS, CYRIL OF JERU-SALEM, RUFINUS). Israel brought its scattering onto itself (ATHANASIUS). Those who have no shame about their sin often become immersed in it even more (GREGORY THE GREAT). Flattering a sinner contributes to even greater sin. Christians should put on Christ and not be concerned with gold and fine apparel (CYPRIAN). The one who does not follow the will of God misleads his people. Sinners should first be corrected in private, and only if they refuse to repent should it be taken to the whole church (JEROME). Those who serve God ought not to seek praise for their work (THEODORET).

3:1-3 Support Taken from Jerusalem and Judah

ISRAEL'S REJECTION OF CHRIST. TERTULLIAN: Consider whether what follows in the prophet has not received its fulfillment: "The Lord of hosts has taken away from Judah and from Jerusalem, among other things, both the prophet and the wise craftsman"; that is, his Holy Spirit, who builds the church, which is indeed the temple, and household and city of God. . . . And so in this manner the law and the prophets were until John, but the dews of divine grace were withdrawn from the nation. AGAINST MARCION 3.23.[1]

3:9-10 Bringing Evil on Themselves

THE CLIMAX OF ISRAEL'S SIN. JUSTIN MARTYR: The climax of your sin is that you hate the righteous one whom you killed, as well as those who by his grace are godly, righteous and loving. It is for this reason that the Lord said, "Woe to their soul, because they have taken evil counsel against themselves, saying, 'Let us take away the just one, for he is distasteful to us.'" Although you did not offer a sacrifice to Baal, like your ancestors, and did not offer cakes in groves and on hills to the heavenly army, you did not accept the Lord's Christ. Whoever does not know Christ does not know the will of God. Whoever rejects and hates him obviously rejects and hates the one who sent him.[2] Whoever does not have faith in him does not believe the words of the prophets who preached his good news and proclaimed him to all people. DIALOGUE WITH TRYPHO 136.[3]

A LINK TO CHRIST'S PASSION. AMBROSE: It is

the tribes, then, that are meant by the names of the patriarchs. From the tribe of Simeon come the scribes, from that of Levi the chief priests, who brought their wickedness to completion and filled up the entire measure of their fathers' ungodliness[4] in the passion of the Lord. They took counsel against the Lord Jesus, to kill him, even as Isaiah says, "Alas for their souls! Because they have devised an evil counsel against themselves, saying. 'Let us bind the just one, for he is profitless to us.'" They killed the prophets and apostles who announced the coming of the Lord of salvation and preached his glorious passion and resurrection. Thereafter, in their greed and out of their desire for earthly wickedness, they fled from sharing in the divine, from chastity of body and moderation of spirit, contempt for money and profit in grace. ON THE PATRIARCHS 3.13.[5]

GUILTY ACTIONS. EUSEBIUS OF CAESAREA: Immediately following, the prophet himself explains why he called them rulers of Sodom and people of Gomorrah: "Your hands are full of blood." Again a little later he says, "They have proclaimed their sin as Sodom and made it manifest. Woe to their souls, because they have taken evil counsel with themselves, saying, 'We will bind the just one, for he is a burden to us.'" Since he overtly speaks of blood and a plot against a just man, there is nothing else this could be than the plot against our Savior Jesus Christ. PROOF OF THE GOSPEL 2.3.[6]

PROPHECY FULFILLED. CYRIL OF JERUSALEM: They bound Jesus and led him to the meeting place of the high priest. Can you recognize that this was already written? Isaiah says, "Woe to their souls because they have taken evil counsel against themselves, saying, 'Let us bind the just one, for he is troublesome to us.'" Woe to their souls indeed! Let us see why. Isaiah was sawn in

---

[1]ANF 3:341*. [2]See Jn 15:23. [3]ANF 1:268. [4]See Mt 23:32. [5]FC 65:248-49*. [6]POG 1:79.

two, but afterwards the people were restored. Jeremiah was thrown into the dungeon, but the Jews had their wound healed. In these instances the sin was against a man, and therefore less. However, when they sinned not against a man but against God become human, then woe to their souls! Catechetical Lectures 13.12.[7]

Despite Many Good Works. Rufinus of Aquileia: For he [Jesus] had done so many good works among them. He had given sight to the blind, feet to the lame, the power of walking to the palsied, life also to the dead; for all these good works they paid him death as his price, appraised at thirty pieces of silver. It is related also in the Gospels that he was bound. This also the word of prophecy had foretold by Isaiah, saying, "Woe to their soul, who have devised a most evil device against themselves, saying, 'Let us bind the just one, seeing that he is unprofitable to us.'" Commentary on the Apostles' Creed 20.[8]

Scattered. Athanasius: Those who look upon their dispersion and the desolation of their city may not aptly say, "Woe to them, for they have imagined an evil imagination, saying against their own soul, let us bind the righteous man, because he is not pleasing to us." It is so true, for when they erred concerning the Scriptures, they did not know that "the one who digs a pit for his neighbor falls in it; and a serpent will bite the one who destroys a hedge."[9] Festal Letter 115.[10]

Deliberate Sin. Gregory the Great: Again, they are to be admonished that if they are not afraid of being wicked; they should at least be ashamed of being seen for what they are. Often a sin that is concealed is avoided, because a mind that is ashamed to be taken for what it does not fear to be in fact is sometimes ashamed to be in fact what it avoids appearing to be. On the other hand, when a person is shamelessly and notoriously wicked, then, the more freely he commits every kind of evil, the more he thinks it lawful, and in imagining it lawful, he is thereby without

doubt immersed in it all the more. Therefore, it is written, "They have proclaimed abroad their sin as Sodom, and they have not hid it." For if Sodom had concealed its sin, it would still have sinned, but in fear. But it had completely lost the curb of fear, in that it did not seek even darkness in its sinning. Therefore, it is said again, "The cry of Sodom and Gomorrah is multiplied."[11] For sin in words is sin in act, but sin that is cried out is sin committed with deliberation. Pastoral Care 3.31.[12]

3:12 Being Led Astray

Flattery Nourishes Sin. Cyprian: But now, what wounds can the conquered show, what injuries to gaping vitals, what tortures of the limbs, when faith did not fail in combat but perfidy arrived before the combat? Nor does the necessity of the crime excuse the one who was caught, where the crime is of the will. I do not say this to burden the cases of the brothers but rather to stimulate the brothers to prayers of satisfaction. For since it is written, "They that call you blessed send you into error and destroy the way of your steps," one who consoles the sinner with flattering blandishments furnishes the means for sinning and does not check transgressions but nourishes them. But one who rebukes at the same time that he instructs with firmer counsels urges a brother on to salvation.[13] The Lapsed 14.[14]

Put on Christ. Cyprian: Isaiah also, filled with the Holy Spirit, cries out and chides the daughters of Zion who have been defiled by gold and raiment, and he reproves those who have an abundance of harmful riches and withdraw from God for the sake of the pleasures of time....

---

[7]NPNF 2 7:85. [8]NPNF 2 3:551. [9]Eccles 10:8. [10]NPNF 2 4:534-35**. [11]Gen 18:20. [12]ACW 11:208-9*. [13]Following the third-century persecution of Christians by Emperor Decius, the church was faced with the question of dealing with those who had denied Christ under persecution. Cyprian, as bishop of Carthage, wrote *The Lapsed* to explain that the fallen (or lapsed) could be forgiven and allowed back into the church. [14]FC 36:69*.

This, God blames; this, he brands with reproach. By this he declares that they have been defiled; by this they have departed from the true adornment and have merited disgrace and shame. Having put on silk and purple, they cannot put on Christ; adorned with gold and pearls and necklaces, they have lost the adornments of the heart and soul. Who would not detest and shun what has caused another's ruin? Who would seek and take what has served as a sword and weapon for the death of another? If, on draining the cup, he who had taken the potion should die, you would know that what he drank was poison; if, after taking food, he who had taken it should perish, you would know that what could kill, when taken, was deadly. Seeing this you would not eat nor would you drink from that which had been used by those who died. Now what ignorance of the truth it is, what madness of mind to wish for what has always been and still is harmful, and to think that you yourself will not perish from the same causes from which you know that others have perished! THE DRESS OF VIRGINS 13.[15]

MISLEADING GOD'S PEOPLE. JEROME: Let us hearken to God, as he proclaims through Isaiah: "O my people, they that call you blessed lead you astray, throw you down headlong." Who is more guilty of throwing the people of God down headlong? He who relies on the power of the free will and scorns the help of the Creator and is secure in his own will, or he who fears the judgment of God at every thought of his precepts?[16] AGAINST THE PELAGIANS 2.24.[17]

PRIVATE REBUKE PREFERRED. JEROME: The Lord speaks by the mouth of Isaiah, saying, "O my people, they who call you happy cause you to err and destroy the way of your paths." How do you help me by telling my misdeeds to others? You may, without my knowing of it, hurt someone else by telling of my sins (or rather of those sins you slanderously attribute to me). While you are eager to spread the news everywhere, you may pretend to confide in individual people, giving them the impression that you have not talked to anyone else. This behavior is not intended to correct me but to indulge your own failings. The Lord commands that those who sin against us are to be approached privately or in the presence of a witness. If the one who is confronted continues in sin, then he or she is to be regarded as a heathen and a publican.[18] LETTER 125.19.[19]

THE DANGERS OF PRAISE. THEODORET OF CYR: Those who are zealous in the service of God, however, do not get a reward of praise, nor indeed do those who are concerned about the laws of God look for this return. For praise is often known to injure many, since it makes them less attuned and slows their pace. If a person thinks he has reached the goal of his endeavor—and praise gives him to understand that he has—he stops his race and victory eludes him. This was revealed by the God of the universe, speaking through the prophet: "My people, they that call you blessed, the same deceive you and destroy the way of your steps." For praise slackens the intensity of their zeal and prevents them from reaching the goal. ON DIVINE PROVIDENCE 9.9.[20]

---

[15]FC 36:42-43*. [16]Augustine contends that Pelagian's free will elevates the human role in salvation and diminishes God's role. [17]FC 53:336*. [18]Mt 18:15-17. [19]NPNF 2 6:251**. [20]ACW 49:122.

3:13—4:1 GOD'S JUDGMENT OF ISRAEL

[13]The LORD has taken his place to contend,
  he stands to judge his people.[d]
[14]The LORD enters into judgment
  with the elders and princes of his people:
"It is you who have devoured the vineyard,
  the spoil of the poor is in your houses.
[15]What do you mean by crushing my people,
  by grinding the face of the poor?" says the
    Lord GOD of hosts.

[16]The LORD said:
Because the daughters of Zion are haughty
  and walk with outstretched necks,
  glancing wantonly with their eyes,
mincing along as they go,
  tinkling with their feet;
[17]the Lord will smite with a scab
  the heads of the daughters of Zion,
  and the LORD will lay bare their secret
    parts.

[18]In that day the Lord will take away the
finery of the anklets, the headbands, and the
crescents; [19]the pendants, the bracelets, and the
scarfs; [20]the headdresses, the armlets, the
sashes, the perfume boxes, and the amulets;
[21]the signet rings and nose rings; [22]the festal
robes, the mantles, the cloaks, and the hand-
bags; [23]the garments of gauze, the linen garments, the turbans, and the veils.
  [24]Instead of perfume there will be
    rottenness;
  and instead of a girdle, a rope;
  and instead of well-set hair, baldness;
    and instead of a rich robe, a girding of
      sackcloth;
    instead of beauty, shame.[e]
[25]Your men shall fall by the sword
  and your mighty men in battle.
[26]And her gates shall lament and mourn;
  ravaged, she shall sit upon the ground.

[4:1]And seven women shall take hold of one
man in that day, saying, "We will eat our
own bread and wear our own clothes, only let
us be called by your name; take away our
reproach."

d Gk Syr: Heb judge peoples   e One ancient Ms: Heb lacks shame

---

OVERVIEW: Isaiah prophesies that the Lord will
suffer judgment at the hands of the elders (RUFI-
NUS). Christ will return with the angels and the
saints to judge (AUGUSTINE). The seven churches
are all the elect in Christ (VICTORINUS OF PE-
TOVIUM).

3:14 The Lord Judges

THE LORD SUFFERS. RUFINUS OF AQUILEIA: But,
says someone, "Are these things to be understood of the Lord? Could the Lord be held pris-
oner by men and dragged to judgment?" Of this
also the same prophet shall convince you. For he
says, "The Lord himself shall come into judgment with the elders and princes of the people."
The Lord is judged then according to the
prophet's testimony, and not only judged but
scourged and slapped on the face with the palms
[of men's hands], and spit on, and suffers every
insult and indignity for our sake. And because all
who should hear these things preached by the

apostles would be perfectly amazed, therefore also the prophet speaking in their person exclaims, "Lord, who has believed our report?"[1] For it is incredible that God, the Son of God, should be spoken of and preached as having suffered these things. For this reason they are foretold by the prophets, lest any doubt should spring up in those who are about to believe. COMMENTARY ON THE APOSTLES' CREED 21.[2]

COMING WITH HIS SAINTS. AUGUSTINE: Therefore, coming with all angels, together with him he shall have the saints also. For plainly says Isaiah also, "He shall come to judgment with the elders of the people." Those "elders of the people," then, those called "angels" in this passage, those thousands of many people made perfect coming from the whole world, are called "heaven." EXPLANATIONS OF THE PSALMS 50 (49).11.[3]

HE WILL NOT COME ALONE. AUGUSTINE: For not alone he shall come to judgment but with the elders of his people, to whom he has promised that they shall sit upon thrones to judge,[4] who even shall judge angels. These are the clouds Isaiah is speaking of. EXPLANATIONS OF THE PSALMS 68 (67).39.[5]

4:1 *Take Away Our Reproach*

SEVEN CHURCHES. VICTORINUS OF PETOVIUM: We read that the Holy Spirit announces in the mouth of Isaiah the number seven: "Seven women took hold of one man." The one man is Christ, though he was not born through a man's agency. The seven women are the seven churches, who receive his bread and are clothed with his apparel. They ask that their reproach be taken away and that they are called only by his name. The bread is the Holy Spirit who nourishes eternal life in those who have faith. The garments that they long to wear are the glory of immortality, of which the apostle Paul says, "This corruptible must put on incorruption, and this mortal must put on immortality."[6] COMMENTARY ON THE APOCALYPSE 1.16.[7]

---

[1]Is 53:1 LXX. [2]NPNF 2 3:551*. [3]NPNF 1 8:182**. [4]Mt 19:28. [5]NPNF 1 8:299**. [6]1 Cor 15:53. [7]ANF 7:345-46**.

4:2-6 RESTORATION OF JERUSALEM

[2]*In that day the branch of the LORD shall be beautiful and glorious, and the fruit of the land shall be the pride and glory of the survivors of Israel. *[3]And he who is left in Zion and remains in Jerusalem will be called holy, every one who has been recorded for life in Jerusalem, *[4]when the Lord shall have washed away the filth of the daughters of Zion and cleansed the bloodstains of Jerusalem* from its midst by a spirit of judgment and by a spirit of burning. *[5]Then the LORD will create over the whole site of Mount Zion and over her assemblies a cloud by day, and smoke and the shining of a flaming fire by night; for over all the glory there will be a canopy and a pavilion. *[6]It will be for a shade by day from the heat, and for a refuge and a shelter from the storm and rain.*

*LXX lacks *of Jerusalem*

Overview: God showed his magnificent generosity to humankind through his incarnation, resurrection and ascension. God calls humanity to be a part of his holy church (Bede). God removes the filth of the soul caused by sin (Clement of Alexandria, Origen). The Holy Spirit purged Israel because of her sins, just as the Spirit cleanses us from sin (Jerome). Human beings are stained because of the flesh. Those stains need to be cleansed (Origen).

4:2-4 Beautiful and Glorious, Called Holy

Christ's Generosity. Bede: The Lord indeed gave of his generosity in that he arranged to liberate the human race from the crime of its transgression through his only-begotten Son. He gave of his generosity because with the grace of the Holy Spirit he consecrated for his entry the temple of a virginal womb. And our earth gave its fruit because the same virgin who had her body from the earth bore a son who was coequal to God the Father in his divinity but by the reality of [his] flesh consubstantial with her. Concerning this, Isaiah also, looking toward the time of human redemption, said, "On that day the branch of the Lord will be in magnificence and in glory, and the fruit of the earth will be sublime." The branch of the Lord was in magnificence and glory when the undying Son of God, appearing temporally in the flesh as a bright light, poured out upon the world the greatness of his heavenly virtues. The fruit of the earth became sublime when the mortal flesh that God received from our nature, already rendered immortal in virtue of the resurrection, was raised up to heaven. Homilies on the Gospels 1.4.[1]

Unity of the Faith. Bede: But this enrollment of the whole world that is recalled as having been done by an earthly king also clearly designates the works of the heavenly king. Undoubtedly the reason he appeared in the world was so that from all the countries throughout the world he might gather the elect into the unity of his faith, just as he himself promised that he would write down their names forever in heaven. Also, the fact that all were going, in response to the edict of Augustus,[2] each to report to his own city, signifies what we must do spiritually as a service to our king. Indeed, our city is the holy church, which in part already reigns with the Lord in heaven. And after the end of this age the whole church will reign in a perfected state with him forever. We must all, then, go into this city, and there must be no excuse from such a salutary journey. We must pay the census [tax] which is due to the king who has been born—that is, we must comply with divine commands in the unity of the church now present and hasten by the tireless course of good works to our entry into the heavenly fatherland. Homilies on the Gospels 1.6.[3]

Spiritual Cleansing. Clement of Alexandria: The greatest cleansing is the spiritual washing that washes away the filth of the soul. The inspired word speaks of such a washing: "The Lord shall wash away the filth of the sons and daughters of Israel and shall wash away the blood from their midst." This refers to the blood of immortality as well as the killing of the prophets. He means by this purification, seen from the added phrase, "by the spirit of judgment and by the spirit of burning." The washing of the body, however, is physical and is accomplished only by water. In fact, it can even be done in fields far away from the baths. Christ the Educator 3.9.48.[4]

Stains Cleansed. Origen: Then the gospel says, "When the days of their purification were fulfilled, according to the law of Moses, they brought him into Jerusalem."[5] The passage says, on account of "their" purification. Who are "they"? If Scripture had said, "on account of 'her' purification"—that is, Mary's, who had given birth—then no question would arise. We would say confidently that Mary, who was a human being, needed purification after childbirth. But the passage reads, "the

---

[1]CS 110:33. [2]Lk 2:1-3. [3]CS 110:54. [4]ANF 2:283. [5]Lk 2:22.

days of their purification." Apparently it does not signify one but two or more. Did Jesus therefore need purification? Was he unclean or polluted with some stain? Perhaps I seem to speak rashly; but the authority of Scripture prompts me to ask. See what is written in the book of Job: "No man is clean of stain, not even if his life had lasted but a single day." The passage does not say, "No man is clean of sin," but "No man is clean of stain." "Stain" and "sins" do not mean the same thing. "Stain" is one thing, "sin" another. Isaiah teaches this clearly when he says, "The Lord will wash away the stains of the sons and daughters of Zion, and he will cleanse the blood from their midst. By the spirit of judgment he will purge the stain, and by the spirit of burning the blood."

Every soul that has been clothed with a human body has its own "stain." But Jesus was stained through his own will, because he had taken on a human body for our salvation. HOMILIES ON THE GOSPEL OF LUKE 14.3-4.[6]

THE SPIRIT OF BURNING. ORIGEN: When one has recognized the differences in sins, one can see how the Lord says in Isaiah, "The Lord will wash away the filth of the sons and daughters of Zion and will cleanse the blood from their midst by a spirit of judgment and a spirit of burning." Filth is washed away by a spirit of judgment. Blood is washed away by a spirit of burning. Even if you have not committed a sin that leads to death,[7] you have still sinned and have thereby become filthy. The Lord will wash away the filth of the sons and daughters of Zion, and he will cleanse the blood from among them. A spirit of judgment will be the recompense for filth, and a spirit of burning will be a recompense for the blood. Whenever we commit heinous sins, we do not need lye or washing with soap; rather we need the spirit of burning. HOMILIES ON JEREMIAH 2.2.[8]

WASHING AWAY THE FILTH. JEROME: When the daughters of Zion will have destroyed every adornment on account of pride, her gates will also be mourning and weeping, she herself will die alone,

and so many of her soldiers will be killed in war that a number of women will hardly be able to find one man. At that time the branch that bears the Christian name will arise, and the earth will give its fruit, and there will be exultation for those from Israel who will be saved, concerning whom it was also said above: "If the Lord of Hosts had not left us a seed, we would have become like Sodom and Gomorrah."[9] Observe also that not all of Israel will be saved, but only the remaining people in Zion and a remnant in Jerusalem, everyone who was written for life in Jerusalem, to whom the Lord said: "Rejoice because your names are written in heaven."[10] This signifies the apostles and those who would believe through the apostles.

"When the Lord will have washed away the filth of the daughters of Zion and cleansed the blood of Jerusalem from its midst by a spirit of judgment and a spirit of burning," then the remnant from Jerusalem will be saved—when their sins will be forgiven in the baptism of the Savior, and they will be cleansed by the blood of him whom the people invoked: "May his blood be upon us and upon our children."[11] Hence we read above: "When you raise your hands, I will not hear you, for your hands are covered with blood."[12] And later he attempts to move them to repentance, saying, "Wash, be clean."[13] Observe also that he will cleanse the filth of the daughters of Zion by a spirit of judgment, but the blood of Jerusalem by a spirit of burning, for what is light will be washed, but what is more heavily soiled will be scalded. John the Baptist spoke about this spirit of judgment and spirit of burning in the Gospel, when he said, "I baptize you with water, but the one who comes after me will baptize you with the Holy Spirit and with fire."[14] From this we learn that man provides only water, but God provides the Holy Spirit by whom both the filth is cleansed and the sins are purged in blood. COMMENTARY ON ISAIAH 2.4.2-4.[15]

[6]FC 94:57. [7]1 Jn 5:16. [8]FC 97: 25-26*. [9]Is 1:9. [10]Lk 10:20. [11]Mt 27:25. [12]Is 1:15. [13]Is 1:16. [14]Mt 3:11. [15]CCL 73:60-61.

5:1-7 A SONG FOR GOD'S BELOVED VINEYARD

¹Let me sing for my beloved
　a love song concerning his vineyard:
My beloved had a vineyard
　on a very fertile hill.*
²He digged it† and cleared it of stones,
　and planted it with choice vines;
he built a watchtower in the midst of it,
　and hewed out a wine vat in it;
and he looked for it to yield grapes,
　but it yielded wild grapes.

³And now, O inhabitants of Jerusalem
　and men of Judah,
judge, I pray you, between me
　and my vineyard.
⁴What more was there to do for my
　vineyard,
　that I have not done in it?
When I looked for it to yield grapes,
　why did it yield wild grapes?

⁵And now I will tell you
　what I will do to my vineyard.
I will remove its hedge,
　and it shall be devoured;
I will break down its wall,
　and it shall be trampled down.
⁶I will make it a waste;
　it shall not be pruned or hoed,
　and briers and thorns shall grow up;
I will also command the clouds
　that they rain no rain upon it.

⁷For the vineyard of the LORD of hosts
　is the house of Israel,
and the men of Judah
　are his pleasant planting;
and he looked for justice,
　but behold, bloodshed;
for righteousness,
　but behold, a cry!

*VG adds *called the son of oil*　†LXX *I made a hedge around it*

OVERVIEW: God laments that Israel has forsaken her Christ (JEROME). Let the vine give thanks to the vinedresser (EPHREM). The one who is beloved is the Son of God (ATHANASIUS). The church is a tower protected by God (AMBROSE). The Christian's soul should put aside the cares of the world and be free from earthly concerns (BASIL). Christians should bring forth good fruit (AUGUSTINE). God will send judgment on sin (ORIGEN). The apostles were to go to the Gentiles. The prophets were the clouds that were instructed not to rain upon rebellious Israel (JEROME). Preachers are clouds that pour rain throughout the world (CASSIODORUS).

5:1-2 A Song for the Vineyard

GOD'S LAMENT FOR ISRAEL. JEROME: The prophet sings a sorrowful song to the people of Israel, a song that he composed about the one of whom it is written in the Gospel: "When he saw her," referring beyond doubt to Jerusalem, "he wept over her and said, 'Would that you knew what will bring you peace, because the days are coming when your enemies will surround you and prevail over you and flatten both you and your children.'"[1] And again: "How often have I

---

[1]Lk 19:41-44.

desired to gather your children like a hen gathers her chicks under her wings, and you would not? Behold, your deserted house is abandoned,"[2] which is similar to what was said in the current song: "I will abandon the vineyard." But that Christ is called beloved and most dear, which Aquila understood to mean *patradelphon*, kindred through a father, the forty-fourth psalm teaches us in its inscription, "A song for the beloved,"[3] as does the voice of God the Father in the Gospel: "This is my beloved Son, with whom I am pleased."[4] We also read in the sixty-seventh psalm: "The Lord will send the word with great power to preachers, the King of hosts to the beloved."[5] This beloved, therefore, composed a mournful song for his vineyard, one that I will sing to my beloved and pathetic people. Or at least it can be understood to mean "I will sing to almighty God the Father the song of Christ who is my kindred," that is, begotten of my race. COMMENTARY ON ISAIAH 2.5.1.[6]

THE VINE GIVES THANKS. EPHREM THE SYRIAN: Let the vine give thanks to our Lord, the true vineyard.

> Souls were like young plants;
> He cultivated [his] vineyard, but he destroyed
>   the vineyard
> That gave sour grapes.
> Blessed be the one who uproots! . . .
> Let the vine eaten by the boar of the forest give
>   thanks
> To the true vinedresser, who himself worked
>   and guarded
> His fruit and offers fruit to the Lord of the
>   vineyard.
> Blessed be its vinedresser.

HYMNS ON THE NATIVITY 18.21-22.[7]

THE ONLY BEGOTTEN. ATHANASIUS: And in Isaiah it says, "I will sing to my beloved a song of my beloved touching my vineyard. My beloved has a vineyard." Who is the "Beloved" other than the only-begotten Son? FOUR DISCOURSES AGAINST THE ARIANS 4.24.[8]

FENCED WITH A RAMPART. AMBROSE: He fenced it [the church] in with a rampart, as it were of heavenly precepts and with the angels standing guard, for "the angel of the lord shall encamp round about them that fear him."[9] He placed in the church a tower, so to speak, of apostles, prophets and teachers, ready to defend the peace of the church. He dug around it, when he had freed it from the burden of earthly anxieties. For nothing burdens the mind more than exaggerated solicitude for the world and desire either for wealth or for power. SIX DAYS OF CREATION 3.12.50.[10]

THE HUMAN SOUL. BASIL THE GREAT: [God] calls us to produce much fruit so that we will not be cast into the fire because we do not. He constantly compares human souls with vines. He says, "My beloved has a vineyard on a hill in a fruitful place." And, "I planted a vineyard and put a hedge around it." Obviously he called human souls the vineyard, around which he puts the security of his commandments and his angels as a hedge.... He desires that we also hold fast to our neighbors with love like vines, and to rest on them, with the highest desires, in order that we may reach the greatest heights of lofty teachings, like climbing vines.... Our soul is "dug around" when we lay aside the cares of the world that burden our hearts. Therefore, the one who has laid aside carnal love and the desire of possessions and has deemed desire for small glory of greatest contempt has been dug around and liberated from the vain burden of the spirit of the world. HOMILIES ON THE HEXAEMERON 5.6.[11]

PRODUCE FRUIT. AUGUSTINE: So let me warn you, holy seedlings, let me warn you, fresh plants in the field of the Lord, not to have it said of you what was said of the vineyard of the house of Israel: "I expected it to produce grapes, but it pro-

---

[2]Mt 23:37-38. [3]Ps 45:1 (44:1 LXX). [4]Mt 3:17. [5]Cf. Ps 68:12-13 (67:13-14 LXX). [6]CCL 73:62-63. [7]ESH 162-63. [8]NPNF 2 4:442. [9]Ps 34:7 (33:8 LXX). [10]FC 42:104-5*. [11]NPNF 2 8:79*.

duced thorns." Let the Lord find good bunches of grapes on you, seeing that he was himself a bunch of grapes trodden in the winepress for you. Produce grapes, live good lives. Sermon 376a.2.[12]

5:4-6 The Vineyard Will Be Devoured

God Does Not Forsake Without Cause. Origen: See then how very bad sinning is, that they may be delivered to Satan, who holds captive the souls of those forsaken by God—though God does not forsake without cause or judgment those whom he has abandoned. For when he sends the rain for the vineyard and the vineyard bears thorns instead of grapes, what else will God do except order the clouds not to sprinkle rain on the vineyard? Homilies on Jeremiah 1.4.[13]

Apostles and Saints. Jerome: It is obvious enough that the prophet is referring to the apostles and to the saints; that they are not to rain his rain upon the Jews but upon the Gentiles. Homilies on the Psalms 34 (Psalm 107).[14]

Rain Will Not Fall. Jerome: The clouds are the prophets; the Lord commanded them to rain no rain upon Israel. The word of prophecy has turned to us. Homilies on the Psalms 56 (Psalm 146).[15]

Clouds Signify Preachers. Cassiodorus: The noise of the waters is great when sweet psalmody is offered, when guilt is removed by groans and tears, when thanks are rendered for a gift received. The different prayers of people resound in sacred churches like the crashing of the sea. He beautifully appends why the noise of the waters is great: it was because the clouds sent forth a sound. We have often said that clouds signify preachers, of whom Scripture says, "I will command my clouds not to pour rain on that land." They uttered that great sound when they made known the precepts of the Lord throughout the whole world. Exposition of the Psalms 76.18.[16]

Signs of Truth. Cassiodorus: Just as clouds when they rumble and clash (so the physicists tell us) send forth darts of lightning, so the words of the prophets shone out as signs of truth. In fact you often find the prophets in the divine Scriptures compared with clouds; for example, "And I will command the clouds not to rain upon it." Exposition of the Psalms 96.4.[17]

---

[12]WSA 3 10:349. [13]FC 97:5. [14]FC 48:247. [15]FC 48:403. [16]ACW 52:248*. [17]ACW 52:426.

5:8-24 SINS AGAINST GOD AND HIS PEOPLE

[8]Woe to those who join house to house,
   who add field to field,
until there is no more room,*
   and you are made to dwell alone
   in the midst of the land.†
[9]The Lord of hosts has sworn in my

hearing:
"Surely many houses shall be desolate,
   large and beautiful houses, without
   inhabitant.
[10]For ten acres of vineyard shall yield but
   one bath,

and a homer of seed shall yield but an
  ephah."

[11]Woe to those who rise early in the
  morning,
  that they may run after strong drink,
who tarry late into the evening
  till wine inflames them!
[12]They have lyre and harp,
  timbrel and flute and wine at their feasts;
but they do not regard the deeds of the Lord,
  or see the work of his hands.

[13]Therefore my people go into exile
  for want of knowledge;
their honored men are dying of hunger,
  and their multitude is parched with
  thirst.
[14]Therefore Sheol has enlarged its appetite
  and opened its mouth beyond measure,
and the nobility of Jerusalem[f] and her
  multitude go down,
  her throng and he who exults in her.
[15]Man is bowed down, and men are brought
  low,
  and the eyes of the haughty are humbled.
[16]But the Lord of hosts is exalted in justice,
  and the Holy God shows himself holy in
  righteousness.
[17]Then shall the lambs graze as in their
  pasture,
  fatlings and kids[g] shall feed among the
  ruins.

[18]Woe to those who draw iniquity with cords
  of falsehood,
  who draw sin as with cart ropes,
[19]who say: "Let him make haste,
  let him speed his work
  that we may see it;
let the purpose of the Holy One of Israel
  draw near,
  and let it come, that we may know it!"
[20]Woe to those who call evil good
  and good evil,
who put darkness for light
  and light for darkness,
who put bitter for sweet
  and sweet for bitter!
[21]Woe to those who are wise in their own
  eyes,
  and shrewd in their own sight!
[22]Woe to those who are heroes at drinking
  wine,
  and valiant men in mixing strong drink,
[23]who acquit the guilty for a bribe,
  and deprive the innocent of his right!

[24]Therefore, as the tongue of fire devours the
  stubble,
  and as dry grass sinks down in the flame,
so their root will be as rottenness,
  and their blossom go up like dust;
for they have rejected the law of the Lord
  of hosts,
  and have despised the word of the Holy
  One of Israel.

f Heb her nobility   g Cn Compare Gk: Heb aliens   *LXX so as to steal from their neighbor   †LXX shall you alone dwell in the midst of the earth?

Overview: The universe that God has created is far greater than material possessions (Ambrose). Christians should not concern themselves with worldly goods and desires, hoarding material possessions. The land suffers because of the sins of the people (Chrysostom). God is to be found in the sacred writings; those ignorant of the writings put themselves in danger (Caesarius of Arles).

Sins become an even greater danger when they are combined with other sins (AUGUSTINE). A person who adds sins upon one another lengthens the rope that will bind and scourge that person (BEDE). Those who prefer this life to the life to come have exchanged what is sweet for what is bitter (TERTULLIAN). Christians should take care not to call evil things good (AUGUSTINE). It is wrong to refuse a person justice in order to attain some reward in exchange (CAESARIUS OF ARLES). We should not tell people what they want to hear but what is most fitting (SALVIAN). There are those who rejoice in evil and reject what is good (JEROME). We should seek what is the common good, not what we desire (EPISTLE OF BARNABAS). Desiring only to follow one's own will, rather than God's, is representative of the sin of pride (JEROME, GREGORY THE GREAT).

5:8 Living Alone in the Land

THE HOUSE OF GOD. AMBROSE: Because your soul is a priceless thing, poor man, be on your guard. The soul is everlasting, although the flesh is mortal. Although you may lack money, you are not therefore devoid of grace. Although your house is not commodious, your possessions are not scattered. The sky is open, and the expanse of the world is free. The elements have been granted to all for their common use. Rich and poor alike enjoy the splendid ornaments of the universe.

Are the paneled ceilings decked with gold in the homes of the very wealthy more beautiful than the face of the heavens decorated with glistening stars? Are the estates of the rich more extensive than the surface of the world? Hence it was said of those who join house to house and estate to estate: "Shall you alone dwell in the midst of the earth?" You have actually a larger house, you man of low estate—a house wherein your call is heard and heeded. . . . The house of God is common to rich and poor. SIX DAYS OF CREATION 6.8.52.[1]

THE VALUES OF THIS LIFE. CHRYSOSTOM: You see, even if many people do not admit this in so many words but claim to believe in the doctrine of the resurrection and future retribution, nevertheless I take notice not of their words but of what they do day to day. That is to say, if you are looking forward to resurrection and retribution, why go chasing the values of this life to such an extent? Why, tell me, do you put yourself to such trouble day in and day out amassing more possessions than there is sand on the seashore, not to mention property and dwellings, as well as buying baths, often acquiring these things through robbery and greed and thus fulfilling that saying from the inspired author "Woe to those who add house to house, and join field to field so as to steal from their neighbor"? Cannot this sort of thing be seen happening day after day? One person says, "That house casts a terrible shadow on mine," and he invents countless pretexts to get hold of it, while another lays hold of a poor person's property and makes it his own. And what in fact is worse, remarkable and unheard of and quite beyond excuse, is for a person comfortably situated in one locality being able to move elsewhere without any good reason for wanting to, either on account of a change of circumstances or because constrained by physical disability; all over the place, in city after city, he is bent on procuring monuments to his own avarice and having timeless effigies of his own evil for all to see. He heaps all sins of this kind on his own head without feeling his heavy and troublesome burden, whereas enjoyment of them he leaves for others, not only after his departure from this life but even here before his demise. You see, no matter what he wishes, he is stripped of his possessions, they are all squandered, so to say, by his friends and left in tatters without the smallest part of them falling to him to enjoy. Yet why do I say enjoy? Even if he wanted, how could he with one stomach manage to dispose of such an abundance of good things? HOMILIES ON GENESIS 22.20 (6).[2]

---

[1]FC 42:265-66. [2]FC 82:83-84*.

5:10 *Little from Much*

EFFECTS OF SIN. CHRYSOSTOM: There are many instances in which the land suffers because of people's sins. Why are you surprised if the people's sin makes the land infertile and unfruitful when we caused it to be corrupt in the first place (and will again make it incorruptible)? . . . See Noah, for example. When humanity had become utterly perverse, turmoil ensued everywhere. Everything—the seed, the plants, all types of animals, the land, the sea, the air, the mountains, the valleys, the hills, the cities, the ramparts, the houses and the towers—everything was covered by the flood. When the time came for humanity to be replenished, the land was restored to the order and beauty it had before. It is clear that the land was restored in part as an honor to humanity. COMMENTARY ON ISAIAH 5.4.[3]

5:13 *For Lack of Knowledge*

KNOWLEDGE OF THE SACRED WRITINGS. CAESARIUS OF ARLES: What do servants think of themselves when they dare to despise the Lord's precepts, not even condescending to reread the letters of invitation whereby he asks them to the blessedness of his kingdom? If any one of us sends a letter to his administrator and he in turn not only fails to do what is commanded but even refuses to read over the orders, that person deserves to receive punishment, not pardon; imprisonment, not freedom. Similarly, one who refuses to read the sacred writings that have been transmitted from the eternal country should fear that he perhaps will not receive eternal rewards and even not escape endless punishment. So dangerous is it for us not to read the divine precepts that the prophet mournfully exclaims, "Therefore is my people led away captive, because they had not knowledge." . . . Doubtless, if a person fails to seek God in this world through the sacred lessons, God will refuse to recognize him in eternal bliss. SERMON 7.[4]

5:18 *Drawing Sins to Themselves*

ADDING SINS TO SINS. AUGUSTINE: For each and every person braids a rope for himself in his sins. . . . Who makes the rope long? Who adds sin to sin? How are sins added to sins? When the sins that have been committed are combined with other sins. He committed a theft; that no one may find out that he committed it, he seeks out an astrologer. It would be enough to have committed the theft; why do you want to join a sin to a sin? Look, two sins. When you are prevented from approaching the astrologer, you blaspheme the bishop. Look, three sins. When you hear, "Send him outside the church," you say, "I'm taking myself to Donatus's group."[5] Look, you add a fourth sin. TRACTATES ON THE GOSPEL OF JOHN 10.5.[6]

SCOURGED BY CORDS OF SIN. BEDE: Our Lord shows what reward awaits hypocritical workers when he made a scourge of cords and drove them all out of the temple.[7] They are cast out as sharers of the inheritance of the saints[8] if, after they are chosen to be among the saints, they either perform good acts deceitfully or evil acts openly. He also drives out the sheep and oxen when he shows the life and teaching of such persons deserve condemnation. The cords with which he expelled the wicked persons from the temple by scourging them are the progressive development of [their] evil actions, which provide material to the strict Judge for condemning those who are to be rejected. . . . The person who heaps sins upon sins, for which he will be condemned more severely, is like one lengthening the cords with which he can be bound and scourged, adding to them little by little. HOMILIES ON THE GOSPELS 2.1.[9]

---

[3]SC 304:228-30*. [4]FC 31:47. [5]Donatus had been the leader of a schismatic group that left the church over bishops who had handed over the Scripture to authority during a prior persecution. In the fifth century the Donatists were still a strong group. Augustine is saying that those who leave the church to join the Donatists have sinned. [6]FC 78:215-16. [7]Jn 2:14-15. [8]Col 1:12. [9]CS 111:5*.

5:20 *Evil for Good*

BITTER FOR SWEET. TERTULLIAN: For, in like manner, they also who oppose martyrdoms, representing salvation to be destruction, transmute sweet into bitter, as well as light into darkness. Thus, by preferring this very wretched life to that most blessed one, they put bitter for sweet, as well as darkness for light. SCORPIACE I.[10]

CALLING EVIL GOOD. AUGUSTINE: "Woe unto them that call evil good." For this text is to be understood to refer not to humans but to those things that make humans evil, and the prophet's accusation is rightly applied to one who calls adultery good. But if someone should call another good whom he believes chaste, not knowing that he is an adulterer, he is deceived not in his understanding of good and evil but through the secrets of human conduct. He is calling a person good whom he believes to possess that which indubitably is good. The adulterer he would call evil, the chaste person good, and he calls the person in question good simply through not knowing that he is an adulterer and not chaste. ENCHIRIDION 6.19.[11]

JUSTICE, NOT GREED. CAESARIUS OF ARLES: Some accept little gifts and presents and endeavor to corrupt just cases, as the prophet says: "Putting darkness for light, and light for darkness: saying what is sweet is bitter, and what is bitter, sweet." Therefore, they hear cases and decide them unjustly. They accept earthly gifts and lose eternal rewards; gaining money, they lose eternity. O miserable fellow, if you have done this or do it or attempt it, you pay attention to what you are acquiring but do not notice what you lose. By acquiring gold, you offend God, for while your money coffer is filled your conscience is weakened. In a few days or years your soul will leave your body; then the gold will remain in the coffer, but your unfortunate soul will descend into hell. However, if you had judged justly, refusing happily to serve avarice or dissipation, your soul would be lifted up to the kingdom full of

God and your moneybox would stay in the world without gold. Therefore I beseech you, brothers, and I adjure you by him who redeemed you with his precious blood, observe justice in every case with all your strength, and think more carefully of the salvation of your soul. SERMON 55.3.[12]

FALSE PRAISE. SALVIAN THE PRESBYTER: Must we be servile to the whim of those who are wicked? If they wish valueless praise conferred upon them, is it becoming that we, too, heap valueless and laughable praise on them? And this especially since they who wish to be ridiculous should not be laughed at by those who are honorable, just as they who desire to be decorated even with the label of false praise should not be praised in a lying manner. Our prime consideration should be not so much what they wish to hear as what it is fitting for us to say, especially since the prophet says, "Woe to them who speak sweet for bitter things and bitter for sweet things." THE GOVERNANCE OF GOD 8.[13]

GOOD AND EVIL. JEROME: It is of the same crime to call goodness, light and sweetness by contrary names as it is to apply the names of the virtues to evil, darkness and bitterness. This is directed against those who do not think it a sin to curse the good, nor consider it an offense to praise evil. The Jews called good evil, and light darkness, and sweetness bitterness, when they received Barabbas, thief and traitor,[14] while crucifying Jesus, who came only for the lost sheep of the house of Israel, to save those who were dying.[15] In Barabbas we can understand the devil, who though he was night and darkness, changed to appear as an angel of light.[16] Hence the apostle said, "What participation does righteousness have with iniquity? What does light have in common with darkness? What agreement does Christ have with Belial?"[17] For a lamp must not be taken and placed

---

[10]ANF 3:634. *Scorpiace* is the antidote for a scorpion's sting. [11]FC 2:385*. [12]FC 31:272*. [13]FC 3:224**. [14]Mt 27:16-26. [15]Mt 15:24. [16]Cf. 2 Cor 11:14. [17]2 Cor 6:14-15.

under a basket or a bed but should be set on a stand that it might illuminate everyone.[18] Nor should a tree that bears evil fruit be called a good tree. Hence it is told with mystical language in Genesis that God separated the light from the darkness, both of which were born above the waters in the beginning.[19] But the Savior himself testifies in the Gospel that he shall be called good: "The good shepherd lays down his life for his sheep."[20] He also calls himself light: "I am the light of the world."[21] And we say that he is the daily heavenly bread with which we are filled: "Taste and see how sweet is the Lord."[22] Commentary on Isaiah 2.5.20.[23]

5:21 Wise in Your Own Eyes

Seek the Common Good. Epistle of Barnabas: We should flee all vanity. We should utterly despise the works of the evil way. Do not live separately from one another, as though you have already become perfect, but come together and seek what is the common good. Epistle of Barnabas 4.10.[24]

Following One's Own Will. Jerome: Who is the greatest subverter of the people of God—he who, relying on the power of free choice, despises the help of the Creator and is satisfied with following his own will, or he who dreads to be judged by the details of the Lord's commandments? Against the Pelagians 2.7.[25]

We All Have Our Weaknesses. Gregory the Great: Those of you who are over others, pay special attention to your neighbors, particularly to those who have not been entrusted to your care. You do not know what good may lie hidden even in those you see doing something wrong. Let each of you, then, strive to be great in virtue, but nonetheless let him know that he is not so in some degree. Otherwise he may proudly attribute his greatness to himself and lose whatever good he has; he might even be rejected because of his sin of pride. Forty Gospel Homilies 4.[26]

---

[18]Mt 5:15. [19]Gen 1:4. [20]Jn 10:11. [21]Jn 8:12. [22]Ps 34:8 (33:9 LXX). [23]CCL 73:77. [24]ANF 1:139*. [25]NPNF 2 6:470. [26]CS 123:26.

5:25-30 GOD'S JUDGMENT ON HIS PEOPLE

[25]Therefore the anger of the Lord was
kindled against his people,
and he stretched out his hand against
them and smote them,
and the mountains quaked;
and their corpses were as refuse
in the midst of the streets.
For all this his anger is not turned away
and his hand is stretched out still.

[26]He will raise a signal for a nation afar off,
and whistle for it from the ends of the
earth;
and lo, swiftly, speedily it comes!
[27]None is weary, none stumbles,
none slumbers or sleeps,
not a waistcloth is loose,
not a sandal-thong broken;
[28]their arrows are sharp,

all their bows bent,
  their horses' hoofs seem like flint,
    and their wheels like the whirlwind.
²⁹Their roaring is like a lion,
  like young lions they roar;
they growl and seize their prey,

they carry it off, and none can rescue.
³⁰They will growl over it on that day,
  like the roaring of the sea.
And if one look to the land,
  behold, darkness and distress;
and the light is darkened by its clouds.

Overview: Christ was lifted up on the cross as a standard (Ignatius). Isaiah prophesies about the call of the Gentiles (Tertullian). At times, God punishes his people through their enemies (Eusebius).

5:25 The Hand of the Lord

Destruction Is a Punishment for Apostasy. Eusebius of Caesarea: "Therefore the anger of the Lord was kindled against his people." He wanted them to be a people of his own and to be called as such, but this is not what they wanted. Because of this he gives a sign of approaching war and of a multitude of the slain that would fill the mountains with dead corpses. The whole country would become full of their dead. All this would happen to them at the hands of the enemy invaders. The enemies did not do this on their own; rather, God himself brought them about, drawing and leading their enemies to the siege of the accused Israelites. Commentary on Isaiah 5.25.[1]

5:26a He Will Lift Up a Standard

The Cross. Ignatius: I give glory to Jesus Christ, the God who has imbued you with such wisdom. I am well aware that you have been made perfect in unwavering faith, like men nailed in body and spirit to the cross of our Lord Jesus Christ, and confirmed in love by the blood of Christ. In regard to our Lord, you are thoroughly convinced that he was of the race of David according to the flesh, and the Son of God by his will and power; that he was truly born of the Virgin and baptized by John in order that all due observance might be fulfilled by him;[2] that in his body he was truly nailed to the cross for our sake under Pontius Pilate and Herod the tetrarch (we are the most blessed fruit of his passion) so that, through his resurrection, he might raise for all ages in the one body of his church a standard for the saints and the faithful, whether among Jews or Gentiles. To the Smyrnaeans 6.1.[3]

5:26b They Shall Come with Speed

Call of the Nations. Tertullian: He [God] says the following about the Gentiles, those he was about to call together from the ends of the earth: "Behold, they shall come swiftly with speed." He says "swiftly" because of the hastening toward end times. He says "with speed" because they will not be weighed down by the weights of the ancient law. He says "they shall be filled" because it is a promise made only to those who hunger and thirst.[4] Against Marcion 4.15.[5]

---

[1]PG 24:121. [2]Cf. Mt 3:15. [3]FC 1:118. [4]Cf. Mt 5:6. [5]ANF 3:366.

6:1-8 ISAIAH BEFORE THE THRONE OF GOD

¹*In the year that King Uzziah died I saw the Lord sitting upon a throne, high and lifted up; and his train filled the temple. ²Above him stood the seraphim; each had six wings: with two he covered his face, and with two he covered his feet, and with two he flew. ³And one called to another and said:*

"Holy, holy, holy is the LORD of hosts;
the whole earth is full of his glory."

⁴*And the foundations of the thresholds shook at the voice of him who called, and the house was filled with smoke. ⁵And I said: "Woe is me! For I am lost;* for I am a man of unclean lips, and I dwell in the midst of a people of unclean lips; for my eyes have seen the King, the LORD of hosts!"*

⁶*Then flew one of the seraphim to me, having in his hand a burning coal which he had taken with tongs from the altar. ⁷And he touched my mouth, and said: "Behold, this has touched your lips; your guilt is taken away, and your sin forgiven. ⁸And I heard the voice of the Lord saying, "Whom shall I send, and who will go for us?" Then I said, "Here am I! Send me."*

*Vg I have kept silent; LXX I am pricked to the heart

OVERVIEW: Christ is the Lord of hosts (EUSE-BIUS). God is portrayed as a sovereign king (JE-ROME). The posture of sitting is a picture of God's condescension to humanity (CHRYSOSTOM). Uzziah's sin of pride caused a pause in prophetic activity, which resumed when he died (THEO-DORET). God appears to be sitting as an accommodation to humanity (CHRYSOSTOM).

God revealed his existence to Isaiah through a vision (THEODORET). Isaiah saw Christ in his vision (CYRIL OF ALEXANDRIA, CHRYSOSTOM). The seraphim around the throne may have been numerous (EUSEBIUS). They cover the face of God the Father (ORIGEN). God is seen to be a Trinity in the thrice-holy confession (AMBROSE, CAE-SARIUS OF ARLES, FULGENTIUS).

Christians should worship God in awe and wonder (CYRIL OF JERUSALEM, CHRYSOSTOM). Heaven will be spent in endless praise of God (AUGUSTINE). Christians should emulate the seraphim, who spoke to one another concerning the things of God (PSEUDO-DIONYSIUS). The angels' song reveals the Trinity (THEODORET, CYRIL OF ALEXANDRIA). The song of the Angels reveals the mystery of the Trinity (JEROME). The angels announce the incarnation (CYRIL OF ALEXAN-DRIA). God calls sinners to come before him for cleansing (SAHDONA).

Isaiah's sin was silence: he had to this point refused to preach (JEROME). After receiving the forgiveness of sin, the Christian's mouth offers praise to God (CASSIODORUS). Christians should not join in worldly discussion, as it defiles the lips (GREGORY THE GREAT). Faith in Christ removes the filth of sin (CYRIL OF ALEXANDRIA). The coal signifies that Christ is fully human and fully divine (JOHN OF DAMASCUS). God purifies believers in proportion to their sin (ORIGEN). Christ is the coal who has burned up our sins (AMBROSE). Christians should have remorse for their sin in order to receive forgiveness (PETER CHRYSOLO-GUS). A person with unrepentant lips cannot be in the service of God. Purity is required instead (JEROME).

6:1 The Lord on a Throne

The Glory of Christ. Eusebius of Caesarea: The prophet had seen Christ and the glory of Christ in the vision in which he said, "I saw the Lord of hosts sitting upon a throne, high and lifted up," and what follows. Proof of the Gospel 9.16.[1]

God as King. Jerome: We have talked about standing; we have talked about walking; let us talk about sitting. Whenever God is represented as seated, the portrayal takes one of two forms: either he appears as the ruler or as the judge. If he is like a king, one sees him as Isaiah does: "I saw the Lord seated on a high and lofty throne." There he is presented as the sovereign king. Homilies on the Psalms 14 (Psalm 81).[2]

God's Condescension. Chrysostom: It is obvious from the very words of Isaiah that he saw God because of God's condescension. He said, "I saw the Lord sitting on a high and lofty throne." But God is not sitting down. Beings with bodies sit. Isaiah also said, "on a throne." But God is not encompassed by a throne, because divinity cannot be contained within boundaries. That said, the seraphim could not endure the condescension of God although they were nearby.... He said, "And the seraphim stood around him," because he wanted to make it clear that although the seraphim are closer to the essence of God than human beings are, they cannot look upon his essence simply because they are closer to it. He is not referring to place in a localized sense. When he speaks of nearness, he is demonstrating that the seraphim are closer to God than we human beings are. Against the Anomoeans 3.16.[3]

Uzziah's Death Brings Return of Prophecy. Theodoret of Cyr: By speaking of Uzziah's death, the prophet informs us that it was Uzziah's sin that had brought an end to prophetic activity. At the beginning of his reign Uzziah had God's favor and was victorious over the Allophyles [foreigners] and other neighboring enemies. But he became blinded by pride because of

his victory. His pride caused him to usurp the honor of the priesthood. He took it on himself to trespass into the sanctuary of the temple and offer incense, though even the priests were not allowed to do this, as only the high priest had the right to enter the Holy of Holies. Azarias and other priests tried to stop him from doing this, but he ignored their warning.... It was not until after the death of the king that God granted this vision to the prophet, who had angered God by not identifying the culpability of the king. Commentary on Isaiah 6.1.[4]

Accommodation. Chrysostom: Why does God appear to be sitting on a throne with seraphim, when God does not sit?[5] He is accommodating himself to the ways of human beings. Commentary on Isaiah 6.1.78-81.[6]

Isaiah Recognizes God's Existence. Theodoret of Cyr: Isaiah has revealed the Father's existence but not his essence (which cannot be seen). In other places God reveals himself in ways that also demonstrate that no one has seen his essence. Abraham saw him in one way, Moses in another, Micah saw him in yet another way, which was different from the way Daniel saw him. Ezekiel saw God in yet another way. God's essence, however, does not have many different forms, because God is incorporeal, indivisible, simple, invisible and inaccessible. Commentary on Isaiah 6.1.[7]

Son of God in Glory. Cyril of Alexandria: No one can deny that the prophet saw the Son in the glory of God the Father, as John said: "Isaiah said this because he saw his glory and spoke of him [Christ]."[8] Look and see the great honor that is due to God, and see the authority he has over all creation. God is high and lifted up on a throne,

---

[1]POG 2:184. [2]FC 48:102-3*. [3]FC 72:102*. [4]SC 276:254-56. [5]Prior to this Chrysostom had argued that sitting was a bodily act and that because God does not have a body he could not, literally, be seen sitting. [6]SC 304:125*. [7]SC 276:258. [8]Jn 12:41.

crowned with the splendor of his reign. . . . In my view we should not think of the throne of God as lifted up in a physical way. That would be foolish and absurd. Rather, that the throne is said to be lifted up means that the reign of God transcends all things. That God is sitting refers to his immovability and that his blessings are everlasting and unchanging. COMMENTARY ON ISAIAH 1.4.[9]

6:2 Seraphs in Attendance

GOD'S ACCOMMODATION TO US. CHRYSOSTOM: Let us bring our discourse back to our earlier proposition and let us show that God, even by the accommodation of condescension, cannot be seen by the powers above. Tell me this. Why do the seraphim stretch forth their wings? There is no other reason than the statement made by the apostle: "Who dwells in unapproachable light."[10] And these heavenly virtues, who are showing this by their very actions, are not the only ones. There are powers higher than the seraphim, namely, the cherubim. The seraphim stood near; the cherubim are the throne of God. They are not called this because God has need of a throne but so that you may learn how great is the dignity of these very powers. AGAINST THE ANOMOEANS 3.24.[11]

THE ANGELIC GUARDS. EUSEBIUS OF CAE-SAREA: Some think there are two seraphim, but I, based on the idea expounded by the sacred Scripture, which says, "the seraphim stood round about him," think there are many, and they are bodyguards, as it were, like a crown from all sides, surrounding his throne with light and enlivened by him. COMMENTARY ON ISAIAH 6.2.[12]

6:3 Holy, Holy, Holy

SON AND SPIRIT. ORIGEN: My Hebrew master used to say that the two seraphim, which are described in Isaiah as having six wings each and as crying one to another and saying, "Holy, holy, holy is the Lord of hosts," were to be understood

to mean the only-begotten Son of God and the Holy Spirit. ON FIRST PRINCIPLES 1.3.[13]

TWO SERAPHIM ONLY. ORIGEN: My Hebrew teacher also used to teach as follows, that since the beginning or the end of all things could not be comprehended by any except our Lord Jesus Christ and the Holy Spirit, this was the reason why Isaiah spoke of there being in the vision that appeared to him two seraphim only, who with two wings cover the face of God, with two cover his feet and with two fly, crying one to another and saying, "Holy, holy, holy is the Lord of hosts; the whole earth is full of your glory." For because the two seraphim alone have their wings over the face of God and over his feet, we may venture to declare that neither the armies of the holy angels, nor the holy thrones, nor the dominions, nor principalities nor powers can wholly know the beginnings of all things and the ends of the universe. ON FIRST PRINCIPLES 4.3.[14]

UNDERSTAND THE DISTINCTIONS. AMBROSE: Cherubim and seraphim with unwearied voices praise him and say, "Holy, holy, holy is the Lord God of hosts." They say it not once, lest you should believe that there is but one; not twice, lest you should exclude the Spirit; they say not holies [in the plural], lest you should imagine that there is plurality, but they repeat three times and say the same word, that even in a hymn you may understand the distinction of persons in the Trinity and the oneness of the Godhead, and while they say this they proclaim God. ON THE HOLY SPIRIT 3.16.110.[15]

THAT WE MAY PRAISE WITH ANGELS. CYRIL OF JERUSALEM: We make mention also of the seraphim, whom Isaiah in the Holy Spirit saw standing around the throne of God, and with two of their wings veiling their face, and with two their feet, while with two they flew, crying,

---

[9]PG 70:172. [10]1 Tim 6:16. [11]FC 72:106. [12]PG 24:125; ECCI 52. [13]OFP 32. [14]OFP 311. [15]NPNF 2 10:151*.

"Holy, holy, holy is the Lord of hosts." For the reason of our reciting this confession of God, delivered down to us from the seraphim, is this, that so we may be partakers with the hosts of the world above in their hymn of praise. CATECHETICAL LECTURES 23.6.[16]

AWE AND WONDER. CHRYSOSTOM: Do you desire to learn how the powers above pronounce that name; with what awe, with what terror, with what wonder? "I saw the Lord," says the prophet, "sitting upon a throne, high, and lifted up; around him stood the seraphim; and one cried to another and said, "Holy, holy, holy, Lord God of hosts; the whole earth is full of his glory!" Do you perceive with what dread, with what awe, they pronounce that name while glorifying and praising him? But you, in your prayers and supplications, call upon him with much listlessness; when it would become you to be full of awe and to be watchful and sober! HOMILY CONCERNING THE STATUES 7.9.[17]

AWE AND WORSHIP. CHRYSOSTOM: What, then, do you think? Do you think that the angels in heaven talk over and ask each other questions about the divine essence? By no means! What are the angels doing? They give glory to God, they adore him, they chant without ceasing their triumphal and mystical hymns with a deep feeling of religious awe. Some sing, "Glory to God in the highest";[18] the seraphim chant, "Holy, holy, holy," and they turn away their eyes because they cannot endure God's presence as he comes down to adapt himself to them in condescension. AGAINST THE ANOMOEANS 1.35.[19]

LOOKING ON GOD. PSEUDO-DIONYSIUS: The scriptural declaration "they cried out to one another" means, I think, that they ungrudgingly impart to each other the conceptions resulting from their looking on God. And we should piously remember that in Hebrew the Scripture gives the designation of seraphim to the holiest of beings in order to convey that these are fiery hot

and bubbling over forever because of the divine life which does not cease to bestir them. ECCLESIASTICAL HIERARCHY 4.3.9.[20]

HEAVEN. AUGUSTINE: What are we going to do there? Tell me. Sleep? Yes, here people who have nothing to do just sleep. But there is no sleep there, because there is no weariness. So we aren't going to perform works of necessity, aren't going to sleep—what are we going to do? None of us must be afraid of boredom; none of us must imagine it's going to be so boring there. Do you find it boring now to be well? You can get tired of anything and everything in this age; can you get tired of being well? If you don't get tired of good health, will you get tired of immortality? So what activity are we going to engage in? "Amen" and "Alleluia." Here, you see, we do one thing and another, there one thing, I don't say day and night but day without end; what the powers of heaven, the seraphim, say now without ever getting bored: "Holy, holy, holy, Lord God of hosts." SERMON 211A.2.[21]

ONE HOLY SPIRIT. CAESARIUS OF ARLES: Isaiah, too, includes one Holy Spirit in the glory of the Trinity when he says, "I saw the Lord seated on a high throne; seraphim were stationed above and cried one to the other, "Holy, holy, holy is the Lord of hosts!" And in a following passage he says, "I heard the voice of the Lord saying, 'Go and say to this people: Listen carefully, but you shall not understand! Look intently, but you shall see nothing!'" SERMON 212.3.[22]

TRINITARIAN RELATIONSHIPS. FULGENTIUS OF RUSPE: The prophet Isaiah did not keep silent about this Trinity of persons and unity of nature revealed to him, when he says he saw the seraphim crying out, "Holy, holy, holy, Lord God of hosts." Therefore, where the triple "holy" is repeated, there is the Trinity of persons; where "God Lord of hosts" is said but once, we recog-

---

[16]NPNF 2 7:154*. [17]NPNF 1 9:394*. [18]Lk 2:14. [19]FC 72:66. [20]PDCW 230. [21]WSA 3 6:134. [22]FC 66:104*.

nize the unity of the divine nature. Therefore, in that Holy Trinity—and I keep on saying it so that it may be fixed in your heart the more firmly—the Father is one, who alone by his nature has generated the one Son from himself; and the Son is one, who alone has been born from the nature of the one Father; and the Holy Spirit is one, who alone proceeds from the essence of the Father and the Son. All of this is not possible for one person, that is, to generate oneself and to be born of oneself and to proceed from oneself. Therefore, because generating is different from being born and proceeding is something different again from generating and being born, it is obvious that the Father is different, the Son is different, and the Holy Spirit is different. The Trinity, therefore, refers to the persons of the Father and the Son and the Holy Spirit; unity, to the nature. TO PETER ON THE FAITH 6.[23]

THRICE HOLY. THEODORET OF CYR: Because the seraphim use the title *Lord* singularly in this song, but repeat "holy" three times (in reference to the Trinity), we know they are referring to the one essence of Deity. The praise "holy, holy, holy" properly indicates the Trinity, and the appellation "Lord of Hosts" indicates the oneness of the divine essence. Furthermore, the seraphim, in their song, praise the eternal essence for having filled both heaven and the entire earth with his glory. This happened through the incarnation of our God and Savior; because after the appearing of the Master, the nations received the illuminating ray of divine knowledge. COMMENTARY ON ISAIAH 6.3.[24]

ONE GOD. CYRIL OF ALEXANDRIA: The mouths of the seraphim are filled with blessings. They offer a doxology in turn, not in my opinion because they are tired but because they show respect to one another, both receiving and giving the doxology. They say "holy" three times and then conclude with "Lord of hosts." This demonstrates that the Holy Trinity exists in one divine essence. All hold and confess that the Father

exists, along with the Son and the Spirit. Nothing divides those who are named nor separates them into different natures. Just the opposite is true. We recognize one Godhead in three persons. COMMENTARY ON ISAIAH 1.4.[25]

TRINITY. JEROME: Because they cry out one to another or, according to the Hebrew, this one to that one, that is, mutually, they are exhorting each other to the praise of the Lord. And they say "Holy, holy, holy, Lord of hosts," that the mystery of the Trinity in one divine nature might be displayed. They also declare that no longer is it true only of the temple of the Jews, as before, but the whole earth is filled with the glory of him who deigned to assume a human body for our salvation and descend to earth. Moreover, when Moses had prayed to ask the Lord to spare this sinful people who had worshiped a calf, the Lord responded, "I will forgive them. Yet I live, and my name lives, for all the earth will be filled with my glory."[26] And the seventy-first psalm sings, "All the earth will be filled with his glory."[27] For this reason also did angels call to the shepherds, saying, "Glory to God in the highest and peace on earth to men of good will."[28] It is impious, therefore, to understand the two seraphim to be the Son and the Holy Spirit.[29] Let us teach instead, according to John the evangelist and the apostle Paul, that the Son of God and the Holy Spirit are said to be seen reigning in majesty. Some of the Latin [commentators] understand the two seraphim to be the Old and New Testaments, which speak only of the present age.[30] Thus they are said to have six wings and to cover the face and feet of God, and earnestly to provide a witness of the truth. Everything that they cry reveals the mystery of the Trinity. They also express wonderment to each other that the Lord of the sabbath who was in the form of God the Father accepted the form of a servant and humbled himself unto

---

[23]FC 95:64*. [24]SC 276:260-62. [25]PG 70:173. [26]Num 14:20-21. [27]Ps 72:19 (71:19 LXX). [28]Lk 2:14. [29]Cf. Origen *Commentary on Isaiah* 1.2 (Baehrens, p. 244 ll. 27-28). [30]Cf. Jerome *Epistulae* 84.3.

death, even death on a cross,[31] that no longer only those in heaven would know him, as before, but also those on earth. COMMENTARY ON ISAIAH 3.4.2-3.[32]

THE INCARNATION. CYRIL OF ALEXANDRIA: In announcing that the whole earth is full of his glory, the seraphim are predicting the mystery of the economy that will be brought to pass through Christ. Prior to the Word's becoming flesh the world was ruled by the devil, the evil one, the serpent, the apostate. The creature, rather than the Creator, was worshiped. But when the only-begotten Word of God became human, the entire earth was filled with his glory. COMMENTARY ON ISAIAH 1.4.[33]

6:5 A Man of Unclean Lips

SINNERS BEFORE GOD. SAHDONA: Let us, therefore, show awe when we sinners stand in the presence of this Majesty and speak. Even though we are so impure in our deeds he draws us close to the sight of himself in the Spirit; let us therefore repeat with trembling the words of the blessed prophet Isaiah: "Woe is me, for I am dazed: I am a man of unclean lips, yet my eyes have beheld the King, the Lord Almighty."

He can be seen by us in the Spirit even now, if we wish—not that he is contained on the throne in any form external to his nature, just "filling the temple with the extremity of his train," as the prophet beheld. No, he is hidden in the loftiness of his hiddenness in the inaccessible light of his nature where he lives and reigns over all the extremities of the universe in the majesty of his dominion. . . .

His creation is full of the splendor of his glory: "the seraphim" of fire "stand" there to honor him, the ranks of the many-eyed "cherubim"[34] escort his majestic Being, the bands of spiritual powers dash around ministering to him, the throngs of angels fly hither and thither with their wings, and all the orders of spiritual beings serve his Being in awe, crying "holy" in trembling and love, "as they cover their faces" with their wings at the splendor of his great and fearful radiance, ceaselessly crying out to one another the threefold sanctification of his exalted glory, "saying, holy, holy, holy, Lord Almighty, with whose glories both heaven and earth are full."

Let us therefore tremble at the magnitude of the sight of the ineffable one and at the sound that ceaselessly utters the praise of the hidden Being. And let us be filled with awe and trembling, falling on our faces in fear before him. Let us recognize our earthborn nature. Let us be aware of the base character of the dust we are made from. Let us join the prophet in saying, with feeling and with a penitent heart, "Woe is our state of confusion." Let us lay bare the foulness of our sins quite openly, accusing ourselves forcefully—just as it is said: "The just man condemns himself at the very beginning of his words."[35]

This is what we too should do at the commencement of our prayer, stating before God that we are not worthy to stand in his presence in our wretched state; and that, because our blind hearts have lost their sight through concentrating on what is below, dwelling in the darkness of the earth, we are unable to gaze on the great sight of him whose glory blinds the vision of the angels of light. Again, how are we able to speak with unclean lips about his great holiness? BOOK OF PERFECTION 5-9.[36]

WOE IS ME. JEROME: According to the Hebrew, Isaiah cries out in anguish and says, "Woe is me because I have held my peace,[37] because I am a man of unclean lips and I dwell in the midst of a people that has unclean lips, and I have seen with my eyes the Lord of hosts!" Because of his virtues, he deserved to enjoy the sight of God, and, because of his awareness of his sins, he confessed that his lips were unclean. Not because he had said anything that was contrary to the will of

---

[31]Phil 2:7-8. [32]CCL 73:86-87. [33]PG 70:176. [34]Ezek 10:12. [35]Prov 18:17. [36]CS 101:204-6*. [37]I.e., "kept silent."

God, but because he had held his peace, deterred either by fear or modesty, and because he had not exercised the prerogative of a prophet, of condemning a sinful nation. When we, who flatter the rich and accept sinful persons, rebuke sinners, is it for the sake of base gain? Unless, perhaps, we speak with complete frankness to those whose wealth we stand in need of. We may act otherwise; we may refrain from every type of sin, but, if we keep silent about the truth, we are certainly committing a sin. AGAINST THE PELAGIANS 2.24.[38]

THE HIDDEN REGION OF THE HEART. CASSIODORUS: By "mouth" [or lips] is meant the hidden region of the heart, from which God's praise is efficaciously sung. So he rightly proclaims after the forgiveness of his sin that his lips will be opened and that his mouth can announce the praise of the Lord. EXPOSITION OF THE PSALMS 5.17.[39]

CLEANSE OUR MOUTHS. CASSIODORUS: We must especially follow the commandments, and signing our lips with the seal of the cross we must pray to the Lord that he may cleanse our mouths, which are disfigured with human foulness. EXPOSITION OF THE PSALMS 141.8.[40]

WORLDLY CONVERSATION. GREGORY THE GREAT: Purity of heart and simplicity are most precious in the sight of Almighty God, who is fully pure and simple in nature. Set apart from the ways of the world, the servants of God are strangers to its vain talk and thus avoid disturbing and soiling their minds in idle conversation. . . . We are drawn downward by mingling in continual conversation with people of the world. It is with good reason that Isaiah, after seeing the Lord, the King of hosts, accuses himself of this very fault. In a spirit of repentance he says, "Woe is me, because I have held my peace; because I am a man of unclean lips." And why are his lips unclean? Because, as he explains immediately, "I dwell in the midst of a people that has unclean lips." Grieving that his own lips are unclean, he shows us that he contracted this defilement by living among a people that had unclean lips.

To take part in the talk of worldly people without defiling our own heart is all but impossible. If we permit ourselves to discuss their affairs with them, we grow accustomed to a manner of speech unbecoming to us, and we end clinging to it with pleasure and are no longer entirely willing to leave it. We enter upon the conversation reluctantly, as a kind of condescension, but we find ourselves carried along from idle words to harmful ones, from trivial faults to serious guilt, with the result that our lips are more defiled with foolish words, and our prayers further and further removed from God's hearing. . . . Why should we be surprised, then, if God is slow to hear our petitions when we on our part are slow to hear God's command or pay no attention whatever to it? DIALOGUES 3.15.[41]

6:6 A Burning Coal

APOSTOLIC TEACHING. CYRIL OF ALEXANDRIA: Let our lips be touched by the divine coal, which burns away out sins and consumes the filth of our transgressions. Moreover, it makes us zealous by the Spirit. By saying "taken from the altar with tongs," Isaiah means that we receive faith in and knowledge of Christ from the teachings or announcements in the law and the prophets, in which the word of the holy apostles confirms the truth. By quoting from the law and the prophets, the apostles convince their hearers and "touch their lips with the burning coal" in order to lead them to confess faith in Christ. COMMENTARY ON ISAIAH 1.4.[42]

TWO NATURES. JOHN OF DAMASCUS: With eyes, lips and faces turned toward it, let us receive the divine burning coal, so that the fire of the coal may be added to the desire within us to consume

[38]FC 53:336-37*. [39]ACW 51:508. [40]ACW 53:404. [41]FC 39:139-40*. [42]PG 70:181-84.

our sins and enlighten our hearts, and so that by this communion with the divine fire we may be set afire and deified. Isaiah saw a live coal, and this coal was not plain wood but wood joined with fire. Thus also, the bread of communion is not plain bread but bread joined with the God-head. And the body joined with the Godhead is not one nature. On the contrary, that of the body is one, whereas that of the Godhead joined with it is another—so that both together are not one nature but two. ORTHODOX FAITH 4.13.[43]

6:7 Sin Blotted Out

PURIFIED WITH FIRE. ORIGEN: We read also in Isaiah that the prophet is purified with fire by "one of the seraphim which was sent to him, when he took with a pair of tongs one coal from those which were upon the altar; and he touched the lips of the prophet and said, Behold, I have taken away your iniquities." These appear to me to be mystical and to indicate that the coals are put on the members of each in proportion to his sins, if he is worthy to be purified. For since the prophet says here, "I have unclean lips; also I dwell in the midst of a people who have unclean lips." For this reason, "a coal taken up with a pair of tongs" by the seraphim cleanses his lips. . . . The cleansing of his lips indicates that Isaiah's sin continually would be found only in words, but he would not have sinned in any act or deed. Otherwise, he would have said since I have an unclean body or I have unclean eyes, if he had sinned in desiring what belongs to something other than his lips. He would have said I have unclean hands, if he had polluted these with unjust deeds. But now since possibly he was aware of his transgression in word alone, about which the Lord says, "Likewise, you will give an account for every useless word on the day of judgment";[44] because it is difficult even for the perfect to escape the fault of the word, the prophet was likewise in need only of a purification of his lips. HOMILIES ON LEVITICUS 9.7.2.[45]

FORGIVENESS OF SIN. AMBROSE: Tell me, then, whoever you are who deny the divinity of the Holy Spirit. The Spirit could not be liable to sin, who rather forgives sin. Does an angel forgive? Does an archangel? Certainly not, but the Father alone, the Son alone and the Holy Spirit alone [can forgive sins]. Now one is obviously able to avoid that which he has power to forgive.

But perhaps someone will say that the seraph said to Isaiah, "Behold, this has touched your lips and shall take away your iniquities and purge away your sins." Shall take away, he says, and shall purge, not I will take away, but that fire from the altar of God, that is, the grace of the Spirit. For what else can we piously understand to be on the altar of God but the grace of the Spirit? Certainly not the wood of the forests or the soot and coals. Or what is so in accordance with piety as to understand according to the mystery that it was revealed by the mouth of Isaiah that everyone should be cleansed by the passion of Christ, who as a coal according to the flesh burnt up our sins, as you read in Zechariah: "Is not this a brand snatched from the fire? Now Joshua was clothed in filthy garments."[46] ON THE HOLY SPIRIT 1.10.112.[47]

REMORSE FOR SIN. PETER CHRYSOLOGUS: But let us at this time feel remorse with all the affection of our hearts. Let us admit that we are wretched in this misery of the flesh.[48] Let us weep with holy groans because we, too, have unclean lips. Let us do all this to make that one of the seraphim bring down to us, by means of the tongs of the law of grace, a flaming sacrament of faith taken for us from the heavenly altar. Let us do this to make him touch the tip of our lips with such delicate touch as to take away our iniquities, purge away our sins and so enkindle our mouths to the full flame of complete praise that the burning will be one that results in salvation, not pain.

---

[43]FC 37:359*. [44]Mt 12:36. [45]FC 83:189-90**. [46]Zech 3:2-3. [47]NPNF 2 10:108**. [48]By "flesh" Peter means humanity's sinful nature.

Let us beg, too, that the heat of that coal may penetrate all the way to our hearts. Thus we may draw not only relish for our lips from the great sweetness of this mystery but also complete satisfaction for our senses and minds. SERMON 57.[49]

6:8 *Whom Shall I Send?*

OBEDIENT SERVICE TO GOD. JEROME: When Isaiah had seen the Lord seated high upon a lofty throne, what does he say? "Woe is me, because I am in sorrow; because I am a man of unclean lips, and I dwell in the midst of a people that has unclean lips." Pay attention to his exact words: Woe is me because of my unclean lips. After that, what does he tell us? Because his lips are soiled, one of the seraphim is sent to him, and the seraph taking a burning coal from the altar touches with it Isaiah's lips and tongue and purifies his mouth. Then what does the seraph say? "See," he said, "now that this has touched your lips, your tongue is cleansed." Then immediately, what does the Lord say? "Whom shall I send? Who will go for us?" O divine secrets of Scripture! As long as Isaiah's tongue was treacherous and his lips unclean, the Lord does not say to him, Whom shall I send, and who shall go? His lips are cleansed, and immediately he is appointed the Lord's spokesman; hence it is true that the person with unclean lips cannot prophesy, nor can he be sent in obedient service to God. "With fiery coals of the desert." Would to heaven this solitude were granted us, that it would clear away all wickedness from our tongue, so that where there are thorns, where there are brambles, where there are nettles, the fire of the Lord may come and burn all of it and make it a desert place, the solitude of Christ. HOMILIES ON THE PSALMS 41 (PSALM 119).[50]

PURITY AND SERVICE. JEROME: It was not with temerity and arrogance that the prophet promised his own conscience that he would go, but with fidelity, for his lips were cleansed and the iniquity of his sins washed away and purified. When the Lord had said to Moses, therefore, "Come, I will send you to Pharaoh, the king of Egypt,"[51] he too responded with humility, not contempt, saying, "I beg you, Lord, to send another because I am not worthy," or as we read in Hebrew, "Send him whom you were about to send,"[52] for he who had been educated with all the wisdom of the Egyptians had heard nothing about the cleansing of his lips. Isaiah also offered himself for ministry by the grace of the Lord with which he was cleansed, not by his own merit. But others think that Isaiah offered himself because he thought that the message to be announced to the people was favorable, because he heard, "Go and say to this people: 'You will hear with your ears and not understand, you will see and not recognize.'"[53] Subsequently, therefore, when the voice of the Lord had said to him "Cry," he did not cry immediately but inquired, "What shall I cry?"[54] Jeremiah also, to whom it had been said, "Take this cup and make all the nations to whom I will send you drink from it,"[55] willingly accepting the cup of punishments to give to the enemy nations that they would drink and vomit and fall, later heard, "Go and first make Jerusalem drink from it,"[56] to which he replied, "You deceived me, Lord, and I was deceived."[57] This observation pertains to the Hebrews, but we acknowledge that others were obedient, not impetuous, in offering themselves to be sent by the Lord.[58] COMMENTARY ON ISAIAH 3.6.8.[59]

---

[49]FC 17:104-5*. [50]FC 48:309-10*. [51]Ex 3:10. [52]Ex 4:10-13. [53]Is 6:9. [54]Is 40:6. [55]Jer 25:15. [56]Jer 25:17-18. [57]Jer 20:7. [58]Cf. Origen *Commentary on Isaiah* 6.1 (Baehrens, p. 268). [59]CCL 73:90.

6:9-13 GOD'S JUDGMENT OF JUDAH

⁹And he said, "Go, and say to this people:
　'Hear and hear, but do not understand;
　see and see, but do not perceive.'
¹⁰Make the heart of this people fat,
　and their ears heavy,
　and shut their eyes;
　lest they see with their eyes,
　and hear with their ears,
　and understand with their hearts,
　and turn and be healed."
¹¹Then I said, "How long, O Lord?"
And he said:
　"Until cities lie waste

　without inhabitant,
　and houses without men,
　　and the land is utterly desolate,
¹²and the LORD removes men far
　away,
　and the forsaken places are many in
　　the midst of the land.
¹³And though a tenth remain in it,
　it will be burned again,
like a terebinth or an oak,
　whose stump remains standing
　when it is felled."
The holy seed is its stump.

OVERVIEW: Some see Christ with human eyes but do not recognize that he is also divine (MAXIMUS OF TURIN). Election is through the grace of God, not the merits of human beings (AUGUSTINE). The apostles preached in the midst of a people who had rejected Christ and were therefore desolate (EUSEBIUS).

6:9-10 Dullness of Mind

SPIRITUAL EYES. MAXIMUS OF TURIN: But he appeared not so much for the eyes of human beings as for their salvation, for even though he was first seen by fleshly eyes when he was born of the virgin, still he did not appear because the eye of faith did not as yet recognize his power. Hence it is said to the Jews by the prophet: "Seeing you will see and will not see"; that is, the Savior whom they discerned with their fleshly eyes they did not see in a spiritual light. SERMON 101.2.[1]

MERCY AND JUDGMENT. AUGUSTINE: Behold mercy and judgment: mercy upon the elect, who have obtained the justice of God, but judgment upon the others who have been blinded. And yet the former have believed, because they have willed, while the latter have not believed, because they have not willed. Hence mercy and judgment were brought about in their own wills. Clearly this election is through grace, not at all through merits. PREDESTINATION OF THE SAINTS 6.[2]

6:11 The Land Desolate

DESOLATION. EUSEBIUS OF CAESAREA: See here that the rest of the earth is desolate, and those who remain on the earth alone are said to multiply. These must be the disciples of the Savior, going forth from the Hebrews to all people. Like a seed left behind they have brought forth much fruit, which are the churches of the Gentiles in every dwelling place. In addition, when he says that only those who remain from the falling away of the Jews will multiply, he also says that the Jews themselves are desolate. For he says of them, "Their land shall be left desolate." And this was

---

[1]ACW 50:228. [2]FC 86:231.

said to them before by the same prophet, saying, "Your land is completely desolate, your cities burned with fire, before you strangers will devour your country."[3]

When was this fulfilled other than in the time of our Savior? Before they dared to do evil things to him, their land was not desolate, their cities not burned with fire, and strangers did not devour their country. Our Savior and Lord predicted what was to happen to them through that prophetic announcement, saying, "Your house is left to you desolate." It was not long from the prediction of that moment that the Romans laid siege to them and brought them to desolation.

The prophetic word gives the reason for the desolation by showing the cause of their fall, making the understanding of it clear. When they heard our Savior teaching among them but would not listen with the ear of the mind and did not understand who he was, seeing him with their eyes and not with the eyes of their spirit, "they hardened their heart, closed the eyes of their mind, and made their ears heavy."[4] As the prophecy says, their cities would become desolate such that no one would live in them because of this. In addition, their land would become desolate, and only a few would remain, being kept like fruitful seed who would proceed to all people and multiply on the earth. PROOF OF THE GOSPEL 2.3.[5]

---

[3]Is 1:7. [4]Mt 13:15. [5]POG 1:83-84.

7:1-25 THE PROMISE OF EMMANUEL

[1]In the days of Ahaz the son of Jotham, son of Uzziah, king of Judah, Rezin the king of Syria and Pekah the son of Remaliah the king of Israel came up to Jerusalem to wage war against it, but they could not conquer it. [2]When the house of David was told, "Syria is in league with Ephraim," his heart and the heart of his people shook as the trees of the forest shake before the wind.

[3]And the LORD said to Isaiah, "Go forth to meet Ahaz, you and Shear-jashub[b] your son, at the end of the conduit of the upper pool on the highway to the Fuller's Field, [4]and say to him, 'Take heed, be quiet, do not fear, and do not let your heart be faint because of these two smoldering stumps of firebrands, at the fierce anger of Rezin and Syria and the son of Remaliah. [5]Because Syria, with Ephraim and the son of Remaliah, has devised evil against you, saying, [6]"Let us go up against Judah and terrify it, and let us conquer it for ourselves, and set up the son of Tabe-el as king in the midst of it," [7]thus says the Lord GOD:

It shall not stand,
    and it shall not come to pass.
[8]For the head of Syria is Damascus,
    and the head of Damascus is Rezin.
(Within sixty-five years Ephraim will be broken to pieces so that it will no longer be a people.)

⁹*And the head of Ephraim is Samaria,*

and the head of Samaria is the son of Remaliah.

If you will not believe,

*surely you shall not be established.'"**

¹⁰*Again the* LORD *spoke to Ahaz,* ¹¹*"Ask a sign of the* LORD *your God; let it be deep as Sheol or high as heaven."* ¹²*But Ahaz said, "I will not ask, and I will not put the* LORD *to the test."* ¹³*And he said, "Hear then, O house of David! Is it too little for you to weary men, that you weary my God also?* ¹⁴*Therefore the Lord himself will give you a sign. Behold, a young woman*ⁱ *shall conceive and bear*ʲ *a son, and shall call his name Immanu-el.*ᵏ ¹⁵*He shall eat curds and honey when he knows how to refuse the evil and choose the good.* ¹⁶*For before the child knows how to refuse the evil and choose the good,*† *the land before whose two kings you are in dread will be deserted.* ¹⁷*The* LORD *will bring upon you and upon your people and upon your father's house such days as have not come since the day that Ephraim departed from Judah—the king of Assyria."*

¹⁸*In that day the* LORD *will whistle for the fly which is at the sources of the streams of Egypt, and for the bee which is in the land of Assyria.* ¹⁹*And they will all come and settle in the steep ravines, and in the clefts of the rocks, and on all the thornbushes, and on all the pastures.*

²⁰*In that day the Lord will shave with a razor which is hired beyond the River—with the king of Assyria—the head and the hair of the feet, and it will sweep away the beard also.*

²¹*In that day a man will keep alive a young cow and two sheep;* ²²*and because of the abundance of milk which they give, he will eat curds; for every one that is left in the land will eat curds and honey.*

²³*In that day every place where there used to be a thousand vines, worth a thousand shekels of silver, will become briers and thorns.* ²⁴*With bow and arrows men will come there, for all the land will be briers and thorns;* ²⁵*and as for all the hills which used to be hoed with a hoe, you will not come there for fear of briers and thorns; but they will become a place where cattle are let loose and where sheep tread.*

h *That is A remnant shall return*   i *Or virgin*   j *Or is with child and shall bear*   k *That is God is with us*   * *LXX understand*   † *LXX adds he will reject the evil by choosing the good*

OVERVIEW: Unbelievers do not comprehend the prophecies concerning Christ because they do not have faith (EUSEBIUS). One must first believe in order to have understanding (RUFINUS, AUGUSTINE). One must first believe the Scriptures and then seek the meaning of them (BASIL). Ahaz did not ask for a sign because God would have exalted himself by giving one. The virgin birth was a sign of something marvelous and extraordinary (JEROME). Isaiah announced that the Messiah would be born of a virgin (JUSTIN MARTYR, JEROME, THEOPHYLACT, CHRYSOSTOM, AUGUSTINE).

Christ was divine and human; he was God who experienced a human birth (TERTULLIAN, LACTANTIUS, MAXIMUS OF TURIN, ATHANASIUS, GREGORY OF NAZIANZUS, BEDE). The Son of the Virgin is God. Christ's birth was to demonstrate his true humanity (CHRYSOSTOM). "Emmanuel" signifies both divine and human natures of Jesus (BEDE). Christ was unique in that he rejected evil and accepted the good from the beginning of his human life (ORIGEN). Isaiah announced the virgin birth as a sign of the Messiah's birth (CHRYSOSTOM, EUSEBIUS). Because Christ was God, he recognized the difference between right and wrong even when he was a child (JOHN OF DAMASCUS). Christ was truly a human being (JEROME).

7:9 No Understanding Without Belief

IGNORANCE CAUSED BY UNBELIEF. EUSEBIUS OF CAESAREA: It is essential to notice that the statement means that those who read it do not only need understanding but also faith; and not only faith but also understanding. Those of the circumcision who do not believe in the Christ of God, though even now they hear these words, do not have understanding of the subject of this prophecy because they do not hear with the mind. The only reason for their lack of understanding is their lack of faith, as the prophecy clearly reveals both about them and to them. PROOF OF THE GOSPEL 7.1.[1]

FIRST BELIEVE. RUFINUS OF AQUILEIA: That the way to understand, therefore, may be open to you, you do rightly first of all, in professing that you believe; for no one embarks upon the sea and trusts himself to the deep and liquid element unless he first believes it possible that he will have a safe voyage. Neither does the husbandman commit his seed to the furrows and scatter his grain on the earth, but in the belief that the showers will come, together with the sun's warmth, through whose fostering influence, aided by favoring winds, the earth will produce and multiply and ripen its fruits. Nothing in life can be transacted if there be not first a readiness to believe. What wonder then, if, coming to God, we first of all profess that we believe, seeing that, without this, not even common life can be lived. COMMENTARY OF THE APOSTLES' CREED 3.[2]

SIMPLE FAITH. AUGUSTINE: According to the teaching of the Catholic church, the Christian mind must first be nourished in simple faith, in order that it may become capable of understanding things heavenly and eternal. Thus it is said by the prophet: "Unless you believe, you shall not

understand." Simple faith is that by which, before we attain to the height of the knowledge of the love of Christ so that we may be filled with all the fullness of God, we believe that the dispensation of Christ's humiliation was not without reason, in which he was born and suffered as man, foretold so long before by the prophets through a prophetic race, a prophetic people, a prophetic kingdom. REPLY TO FAUSTUS THE MANICHAEAN 12.46.[3]

UNDERSTANDING BY WISDOM. AUGUSTINE: "Unless you believe, you shall not understand," showing that as righteousness is by faith, understanding comes by wisdom. Accordingly, in the case of those who eagerly demand evident truth, we must not condemn the desire but regulate it, so that beginning with faith it may proceed to the desired end through good works. REPLY TO FAUSTUS THE MANICHAEAN 22.53.[4]

UNDERSTANDING FOLLOWS FAITH. AUGUSTINE: If you are not able to understand, believe, that you may understand. Faith goes before; understanding follows after; since the prophet says, "Unless you believe, you shall not understand. SERMON 68 (118).1.[5]

FAITH, THEN UNDERSTANDING. AUGUSTINE: The mysteries and secrets of the kingdom of God first seek for believing people, that they may make them understanding. For faith is understanding's step, and understanding faith's attainment. This the prophet expressly says to all who prematurely and in undue order look for understanding and neglect faith. SERMON 76.1.[6]

LET FAITH PRECEDE REASON. AUGUSTINE: So, then, in some points that bear on the doctrine of salvation, which we are not yet able to grasp by reason—but we shall be able to sometime—let faith precede reason, and let the heart be cleansed

[1]POG 2:54. [2]NPNF 2 3:543. [3]NPNF 1 4:198**. [4]NPNF 1 4:292*. [5]NPNF 1 6:465*. [6]NPNF 1 6:481.

by faith so as to receive and bear the great light of reason; this is indeed reasonable. Therefore the prophet said with reason: "If you will not believe, you will not understand"; thereby he undoubtedly made a distinction between these two things and advised us to believe first so as to be able to understand whatever we believe. It is, then, a reasonable requirement that faith precede reason, for, if this requirement is not reasonable, then it is contrary to reason, which God forbid. But, if it is reasonable that faith precede a certain great reason that cannot yet be grasped, there is no doubt that, however slight the reason which proves this, it does precede faith. LETTER 120.[7]

BELIEVE THE SCRIPTURES. BASIL THE GREAT: Certainly one must have faith in the Scriptures as containing the divine mind, and thus one must proceed to the understanding of what is written in them. For one must go beyond the types and thus apprehend the truth of what has been shown to us. First one must believe in the Scriptures with the simple faith that they are "inspired by God and useful"[8] and then go on to examine subtly and enquiringly the meaning contained in them. COMMENTARY ON ISAIAH 7.197.[9]

GOD'S EXALTATION. JEROME: "And Ahaz said, 'I will not ask and I will not tempt the Lord.'" It is not from humility but from pride that he does not wish to ask for a sign from the Lord. For although it is written in Deuteronomy, "You shall not tempt the Lord your God,"[10] and the Savior would use this as testimony against the devil,[11] when Ahaz was told to ask for a sign he should have fulfilled the commandment in obedience, especially since both Gideon and Manoah sought and received signs.[12] Although it was according to the ambiguity of the Hebrew expression *ulo enasse adonai* that everyone translated this as "I will not tempt the Lord," it can also be read as "I will not exalt the Lord." For the impious king knew that if he had asked for a sign, he would have received one, and the Lord would have been glorified. Like a worshiper of idols, therefore, who sets up altars

on all the street corners[13] and on mountains and in forests,[14] he also was a fanatic for capriciousness. He did not want to ask for a sign because he was commanded to do so. COMMENTARY ON ISAIAH 3.7.12.[15]

7:14 A Virgin Shall Conceive

VIRGIN BIRTH A SIGN. JEROME: By no means will God speak in many and various ways, according to the apostle Paul,[16] nor according to another prophet will he be represented through the hands of the prophets,[17] but he who previously spoke through others will himself say "Here I am."[18] The bride in the Song of Songs also asked in this regard: "O that you would kiss me with the kisses of your mouth!"[19] For "the Lord of hosts is himself the King of glory."[20] He will descend to a virginal womb and will enter and exit through the eastern gate that always remains closed,[21] concerning which Gabriel said to the virgin: "The Holy Spirit will come upon you, and the power of the Most High will overshadow you; therefore the one who will be born to you is holy and will be called the Son of God."[22] And Proverbs writes, "Wisdom built itself a home."[23] Thus when it is said, "The Lord himself will give you a sign," this should refer to something new and marvelous. COMMENTARY ON ISAIAH 3.7.14.[24]

VIRGIN CONCEPTION. JUSTIN MARTYR: And again hear what was prophesied through Isaiah the prophet, that he would be born of a virgin. He said, "Behold, the virgin shall conceive and bear a son, and they will call his name, God with us." Through the prophetic spirit God announced beforehand that things which are unimaginable and believed to be impossible for human beings would take place, in order that when it occurred it would be believed and received by faith because

---

[7]FC 18:302. [8]2 Tim 3:16. [9]TASHT 7:237. [10]Deut 6:16. [11]Mt 4:7. [12]Judg 6:36-40; 13:8-11. [13]Cf. Mt 6:5. [14]Cf. Ezek 6:13. [15]CCL 73:101-2. [16]Heb 1:1. [17]Cf. Hos 12:10. [18]Is 58:9. [19]Song 1:1. [20]Ps 24:10 (23:10 LXX). [21]Ezek 44:1-2. [22]Lk 1:35. [23]Prov 9:1. [24]CCL 73:102-3.

it had been promised. In order to ensure that someone does not accuse us of saying the same things as the poets, who say that Zeus came to women for sexual pleasure, we will explain the words of this prophecy clearly.[25] The phrase "behold, the virgin shall conceive" means that the virgin would conceive without intercourse. If she had in fact had intercourse with someone, she would not have been a virgin. God's power came on the virgin, overshadowed her and caused her to conceive while she remained a virgin. FIRST APOLOGY 33.[26]

WHAT DOES *ALMAH* MEAN? JEROME: Isaiah tells of the mystery of our faith and hope: "Behold, a virgin shall conceive, and bear a son, and shall call his name Emmanuel." I know that the Jews are accustomed to meet us with the objection that in Hebrew the word *almah* does not mean a virgin but "a young woman." And, to speak truth, a virgin is properly called *bethulah*, but a young woman, or a girl, is not *almah* but *naarah*! What then is the meaning of *almah*? A hidden virgin, that is, not merely virgin, but a virgin and something more, because not every virgin is hidden, shut off from the occasional sight of men.[27] AGAINST JOVINIANUS 1.32.[28]

VIRGIN AND SIGN. THEOPHYLACT: The Jews say that it is not written in the prophecy "virgin" but "young woman." To which it may be answered that "young woman" and "virgin" mean the same thing in Scripture, for in Scripture "young woman" refers to one who is still a virgin. Furthermore, if it was not a virgin that gave birth, how would it be a sign, something extraordinary? Listen to Isaiah, who says, "For this reason the Lord himself shall give you a sign," and immediately he adds, "Behold, the virgin." So if it were not a virgin that would give birth, it would not be a sign. The Jews, then, alter the text of Scripture in their malice, putting "young woman" instead of "virgin." But whether the text reads "young woman" or "virgin," it should be understood in either case that it is a virgin who will give birth so

that the event may be a miraculous sign. EXPLANATION OF MATTHEW 23.[29]

GOD'S BIRTH. TERTULLIAN: What is the sign? "Behold, a virgin shall conceive and bear a son." In fact, a virgin did conceive and gave birth to "Emmanuel,[30] God with us." This is the new birth: a man born from God. God was born in the man, taking the flesh of the old human race without the help of the old human seed. God took the flesh in order to reform the old human race with a new seed. In other words, he spiritually cleansed the old human race by removing its old stains. ON THE FLESH OF CHRIST 17.[31]

GOD AND HUMAN. LACTANTIUS: He [God] was with us on the earth, when he assumed flesh; and he was no less God in man, and man in God. That he was both God and man was declared before by the prophets. EPITOME OF THE DIVINE INSTITUTES 44.[32]

GOD'S FIRST DWELLING PLACE. MAXIMUS OF TURIN: The manner of his birth proves the truth about the Lord: a virgin conceived without knowing a man; her belly was filled, having been touched by no embrace; and her chaste womb received the Holy Spirit, whom her pure members preserved and her unsullied body carried. Behold the miracle of the mother of the Lord! She is a virgin when she conceives, a virgin when she brings forth, a virgin after birth. What glorious virginity! What splendid fruitfulness! The world's goodness is born, and there is no pain of childbirth. The womb is emptied, a child is brought forth, and still virginity is not violated. For it was fitting that when God was born, the value of chastity should increase, and that one who was untouched should not be violated by his

---

[25]Justin is seeking to explain that the conception of Mary did not involve sexual relations between her and God. [26]ANF 1:174**. [27]For Jerome, the argument is over the proper understanding of the Hebrew word *almah*. He contends it is used to speak of a virgin who is hidden to men. [28]NPNF 2 6:370. [29]EBT 21. [30]"Emmanuel" in Greek; "Immanuel" in Hebrew. [31]ANF 3:536. [32]ANF 7:239.

coming—he who came to heal what was injured—and that bodily purity should not be harmed by him who bestows virginity on those who have been baptized and had formerly been unchaste. The child who has been born, then, is placed in a crib. This is God's first dwelling place, and the ruler of heaven does not disdain these straitened circumstances—he whose home was the virginal womb. Clearly Mary was a fit habitation for Christ not because of the nature of her body but because of the grace of her virginity. SERMON 61B.2.[33]

GOD IN FLESH. ATHANASIUS: But what does this passage mean, if not that God has come in the flesh? LETTER 60.6.[34]

BORN OF A WOMAN. GREGORY OF NAZIANZUS: Humanity was blended with God, and he was one. The more powerful predominated in order that I might become god just as he became human. Although he was already begotten, he was born of a woman, who was a virgin. Because his birth was from a woman, it was human. Because she was a virgin, it was divine. He had neither a human father nor a divine mother. ON THE SON, THEOLOGICAL ORATION 3(29).19.[35]

GOD IS WITH US. CHRYSOSTOM: You have heard, therefore, that the Father is called Lord. Come now, and let me show you that the Son is called God. "Behold, the virgin shall be with child, and shall give birth to a son, and they shall call his name Immanuel, which means, 'God is with us.'" Did you see how both the name Lord is given to the Father and the name God is given to the Son? In the psalm, the sacred writer said, "Let them know that *Lord* is your name."[36] Here Isaiah says, "They shall call his name Immanuel." AGAINST THE ANOMOEANS 5.15.[37]

CHRIST A CHILD. CHRYSOSTOM: To prevent you from thinking that his coming to earth was an accommodation, as those others were, and to give you solid grounds for truly believing that his was

real flesh, he was conceived, born and nurtured.[38] That his birth might be made manifest and become common knowledge, he was laid in a manger,[39] not in some small room but in a lodging place before a throng of people. This was the reason for the swaddling clothes and also for the prophecies spoken long before. The prophecies showed not only that he was going to be a man but also that he would be conceived, born and nurtured as any child would be. Isaiah proclaimed this when he said, "Behold, the virgin will conceive and bear a son, and they will call his name Immanuel." He eats butter and honey. And again, the same prophet said, "A child is born to us, a son is given to us."[40] Do you see how these prophecies foretold his infancy? AGAINST THE ANOMOEANS 7.49.[41]

THE BIRTH IS A SIGN. CHRYSOSTOM: What precedes this passage also gives us its meaning. He does not simply say, "Behold, the virgin will conceive." First he said, "Behold, the Lord will give you a sign," and then he adds to it, "Behold, the virgin will conceive." If the one who was to give birth was not a virgin but the conception occurred in the natural manner, then what sort of sign would this be? A sign must be extraordinary and strange, or how else could it be a sign? HOMILIES ON THE GOSPEL OF MATTHEW 5.3.[42]

THE MESSAGE OF THE MIRACLES. AUGUSTINE: Christ was born a visible man of a human virgin mother, but he was a hidden God because God was his Father. So the prophet had foretold: "Behold, the virgin shall be with child and shall bring forth a son; and they shall call his name Emmanuel, which is interpreted, God with us."[43] To prove that he was God, Christ worked many miracles, some of which—as many as seemed

---

[33]ACW 50:251. [34]NPNF 2 4:577. [35]SC 250:218. [36]Ps 83:18 (82:19 LXX). [37]FC 72:143. [38]Chrysostom recognizes various "appearances" of God in the Old Testament and refers to them as God's accommodation to humanity. The incarnation, however, is a genuine coming of God and not a mere "appearance" of God's presence. [39]Lk 2:6-7. [40]Is 9:6. [41]FC 72:205-6. [42]PG 57:57. [43]Mt 1:23.

necessary to establish his claim—are recorded in the Gospels. Of these miracles the very first was the marvelous manner of his birth; the very last, his ascension into heaven in his body risen from the dead. CITY OF GOD 18.46.[44]

CHRISTIANS AND ABRAHAM. AUGUSTINE: But who shall say that Christ and Christians have no connection with Israel, seeing that Israel was the grandson of Abraham, to whom first, as afterwards to his son Isaac, and then to his grandson Israel himself, that promise was given, which I have already mentioned, namely: "In your seed shall all nations be blessed"?[45] That prediction we see now in its fulfillment in Christ. For it was of this line that the Virgin was born, concerning whom a prophet of the people of Israel and of the God of Israel sang in these terms: "Behold, a virgin shall conceive, and bear a son; and they shall call his name Emmanuel." For by interpretation, Emmanuel means "God with us."[46] This God of Israel . . . has forbidden the worship of other gods, . . . has forbidden the making of idols, . . . has commanded their destruction, . . . has by his prophet predicted that the Gentiles from the ends of the earth would say, "Surely our fathers have worshiped lying idols, in which there is no profit." This same God is he who, by the name of Christ and by the faith of Christians, has ordered, promised and exhibited the overthrow of all these superstitions. HARMONY OF THE GOSPELS 1.26.[47]

MANY LONGED TO SEE HIS DAY. AUGUSTINE: You must appreciate, brothers and sisters, what a tremendous desire possessed the saints of old to see the Christ. They knew he was going to come, and all those who were living devout and blameless lives would say, "Oh, if only that birth may find me still here! Oh, if only I may see with my own eyes what I believe from God's Scriptures!" The saints who knew from the holy Scripture that a virgin was going to give birth as you heard when Isaiah was read: "Behold, a virgin shall conceive in the womb and shall bear a son, and his

name shall be called Emmanuel." What Emmanuel means the Gospel declares to us, saying, "which is interpreted, God with us."[48] So do not let it surprise you, unbelieving soul, whoever you are, do not let it strike you as impossible that a virgin should give birth, and in giving birth remain a virgin. Realize that it was God who was born, and you will not be surprised at a virgin giving birth. So then, to prove to you how the saints and just men and women of old longed to see what was granted to this old man Simeon,[49] our Lord Jesus Christ said, when speaking to his disciples, "Many just men and prophets have wished to see what you see and have not seen it; and to hear what you hear and have not heard it."[50] SERMON 370.3.[51]

BORN FROM A VIRGIN. AUGUSTINE: Do you hesitate or refuse to believe his birth of a virgin, when you ought rather to believe that thus it was fitting for God to be born man? Learn that this, too, was foretold by the prophet: "Behold, a virgin shall conceive and bear a son, and his name shall be called Emmanuel, which is interpreted, God with us." You will not doubt, therefore, the motherhood of a virgin if you want to believe the nativity of a God who does not relinquish the government of the universe and comes in flesh among human beings; who bestows fecundity on his mother yet does not diminish her integrity. ON FAITH IN THINGS UNSEEN 3.5.[52]

TWO NATURES. BEDE: The Savior's name, because of which he is called "God with us" by the prophet, signifies both natures of his one person. For he who, born before time from the Father, is God himself in the fullness of time, became Emmanuel (that is, "God with us") in his mother's womb, because he deigned to take the weakness of our nature into the unity of his per-

[44]FC 24:163-64. [45]Gen 22:18. [46]Mt 1:23. [47]NPNF 1 6:94*. [48]Mt 1:23. [49]Simeon was a righteous man looking for the coming Messiah. He blessed Jesus in the temple when Jesus' parents took him there when he was eight days old (Lk 2:25-34). [50]Mt 13:17. [51]WSA 3 10:309. [52]FC 4:457*.

son when "the Word was made flesh and dwelt among us."[53] In a wonderful manner he began to be what we are, while not ceasing to be what he had been, assuming our nature in such a way that he himself would not lose what he had been. HOMILIES ON THE GOSPELS 1.5.[54]

VIRGIN BIRTH A SIGN. CHRYSOSTOM: Were she not to be a virgin, the birth would not have been a sign. A sign is something that differs from the normal way things happen, that is outside the natural manner. A sign is so unusual and unexpected that someone who sees it or hears of it sees that it is out of the ordinary. It is called a "sign" because it is significant. Were the birth to be like normal births, it would not have been significant. If the prophecy is about a woman giving birth in the normal manner, like what happens every day, then why call it a sign? COMMENTARY ON ISAIAH 7.5.[55]

VIRGIN, NOT YOUNG WOMAN. EUSEBIUS OF CAESAREA: House of David, from this time on when you encounter your enemies, call upon the one who is named Immanuel. The meaning of the title, which is "God with us," reveals the power of the Word. Believe this sign, be courageous, and do not call upon the gods of Damascus. Do not enlist those who have no assistance to offer. Rather, call upon Immanuel, the God who will "be with" people at the appropriate time. Take heart with confidence, trusting in the power of the title. . . . If the prophet had said, "They will call his name Immanuel," he would have been speaking only of a future time. This would have caused doubt for some, because when the Savior was born of the virgin his name was not Immanuel but Jesus, as the angel had instructed Joseph, saying, "Do not fear to take Mary as your wife, for that which is conceived in her is of the Holy Spirit. She will bear a son, and you shall call his name Jesus, for he will save his people from their sins."[56] If the prophecy was "they will call his name Immanuel," then how would the Savior had fulfilled it, when his name was Jesus and not

Immanuel? But this is not how it was written, because not everyone would call him by this title. The prophetic word says accurately, "You shall call." . . . Some scribes, because they did not understand this, wrote, "they will call" rather than "you shall call" in the Gospel of Matthew, even though the prophecy does not read this way. The Hebrew word translated in the passage is "you shall call," as is used by all the translations. Some translators translate the word for "virgin" as "young woman." There is no reason to think that the virgin was not also a young woman; in fact it is likely that the virgin who conceived the Savior was not fully grown but a young maiden. COMMENTARY ON ISAIAH 1.44.56-105.[57]

7:15-16 He Will Refuse Evil and Choose Good

CHOOSING GOOD IS NATURAL TO GOD. JOHN OF DAMASCUS: Now, since the Lord was not a mere man but was also God and knew all things, he stood in no need of reflection, inquiry, counsel or judgment. He also had a natural affinity for good and antipathy for evil. Thus it is in this sense that the prophet Isaiah, too, says, "Before the child shall know to refuse the evil, he will choose the good. For before the child knows to refuse the evil and to choose the good, he will reject the evil by choosing the good." The "before" shows that he made no inquiry or investigation in a human manner but that since he was God and divinely subsisted in the flesh—that is to say, was personally united to the flesh—by the fact of his very being and his knowing all things he naturally possessed the good. ORTHODOX FAITH 3.14.[58]

FED WITH CURDS AND HONEY. JEROME: This is said ["The child grew in wisdom and in age before God and men"][59] in order to establish the truth of his human body. Nevertheless, wrapped in swaddling clothes and fed with curds and

---

[53]Jn 1:14. [54]CS 110:47. [55]SC 304:314. [56]Mt 1:20-21. [57]PG 24:133-36. [58]FC 37:302-3*. [59]Lk 2:52.

honey, he will have the judgment to distinguish between good and evil, that rejecting evil he might choose the good. It does not say that he will in fact reject and choose but that he would learn to reject and to choose, so that we might know through such words that this pertains to the infant's human body, not to divine wisdom. Finally, it must be believed that the angels who announced to shepherds the news of the infant lying in a manger and the magi who came from the east to worship him were chosen. Herod, the scribes and the Pharisees, on the other hand, were condemned because they slaughtered thousands of children for the sake of one infant. COMMENTARY ON ISAIAH 3.7.15.[60]

---

[60]CCL 73:106.

8:1—9:1 JUDGMENT AGAINST ZION

[1]Then the LORD said to me, "Take a large tablet and write upon it in common characters, 'Belonging to Maher-shalal-hash-baz.'"[l] [2]And I got reliable witnesses, Uriah the priest and Zechariah the son of Jeberechiah, to attest for me. [3]And I went to the prophetess, and she conceived and bore a son. Then the LORD said to me, "Call his name Maher-shalal-hash-baz; [4]for before the child knows how to cry 'My father' or 'My mother,' the wealth of Damascus and the spoil of Samaria will be carried away before the king of Assyria."

[5]The LORD spoke to me again: [6]"Because this people have refused the waters of Shiloah* that flow gently, and melt in fear before[m] Rezin and the son of Remaliah; [7]therefore, behold, the Lord is bringing up against them the waters of the River, mighty and many, the king of Assyria and all his glory; and it will rise over all its channels and go over all its banks; [8]and it will sweep on into Judah, it will overflow and pass on, reaching even to the neck; and its outspread wings will fill the breadth of your land, O Immanu-el."

[9]Be broken, you peoples, and be dismayed;
   give ear, all you far countries;
gird yourselves and be dismayed;
   gird yourselves and be dismayed.
[10]Take counsel together, but it will come to nought;
   speak a word, but it will not stand,
   for God is with us.[x]
[11]For the LORD spoke thus to me with his strong hand upon me, and warned me not to walk in the way of this people, saying: [12]"Do not call conspiracy all that this people call conspiracy, and do

65

not fear what they fear, nor be in dread. [13]*But the LORD of hosts, him you shall regard as holy; let him be your fear, and let him be your dread.* [14]*And he will become a sanctuary, and a stone of offense, and a rock of stumbling to both houses of Israel, a trap and a snare to the inhabitants of Jerusalem.* [15]*And many shall stumble thereon; they shall fall and be broken; they shall be snared and taken."*

[16]*Bind up the testimony, seal the teaching among my disciples.* [17]*I will wait for the LORD, who is hiding his face from the house of Jacob, and I will hope in him.* [18]*Behold, I and the children whom the LORD has given me are signs and portents in Israel from the LORD of hosts, who dwells on Mount Zion.* [19]*And when they say to you, "Consult the mediums and the wizards who chirp and mutter," should not a people consult their God? Should they consult the dead on behalf of the living?* [20]*To the teaching and to the testimony! Surely for this word which they speak there is no dawn.* [21]*They will pass through the land,* [n] *greatly distressed and hungry; and when they are hungry, they will be enraged and will curse* [o] *their king and their God, and turn their faces upward;* [22]*and they will look to the earth, but behold, distress and darkness, the gloom of anguish; and they will be thrust into thick darkness.*

9 [p]*But there will be no gloom for her that was in anguish. In the former time he brought into contempt the land of Zebulun and the land of Naphtali, but in the latter time he will make glorious the way of the sea, the land beyond the Jordan, Galilee of the nations.*

l That is *The spoil speeds, the prey hastes*   **m** Cn: Heb *rejoices in*   **x** Heb *immanu el*   **n** Heb *it*   **o** Or *curse by*   **p** Ch 8.23 in Heb   *LXX Siloam

---

OVERVIEW: Christ was said to be Emmanuel because he was God among humanity (CHRYSOSTOM, THEOPHYLACT). Christ possessed all strength even as a child (JUSTIN MARTYR). Isaiah's prophecy concerning Christ having riches was fulfilled in the gifts of the magi (AUGUSTINE). The gospel is the Word of God sent into the world (EUSEBIUS). The king of Assyria stands for the Antichrist (HIPPOLYTUS). Christians are the spoils of victory from the nations (ORIGEN). Christ is the stone over whom unbelievers stumble (AUGUSTINE). Christians are not only brothers of Christ but also his children (CHRYSOSTOM). Isaiah's promise of Christ's self-revelation to Zebulun and Naphtali was fulfilled in Cana (JEROME).

8:3 Naming the Son

WHY THE NAME CHANGE. CHRYSOSTOM: How

was it, then, one may say, that his name was not called Emmanuel but Jesus Christ? Because he did not say "you shall call" but "they shall call," that is, the multitude and the issue of events. For here he uses an event (i.e., God being "with us") as a name; and this is customary in Scripture, to substitute the events that take place for names. Therefore, to say, "they shall call" him "Emmanuel" means nothing else than that they shall see God among humanity. For he has always been among them, but never so manifestly. HOMILIES ON THE GOSPEL OF MATTHEW 5.2.[1]

NAMED FOR THE EVENT. THEOPHYLACT: The Jews say, "How then is it that he was not called Emmanuel but Jesus Christ?" One may answer: The prophet did not say "you shall call" but "they shall call." That is, the events and deeds of his life

[1]PG 57:56-57.

will show that he is God and that he keeps company with us. For holy Scripture gives names that are derived from the events of one's life; for example, "Call his name Plunder Swiftly." Yet where does it record that anyone was ever called by such a name? But since error was despoiled and taken captive at the moment of the Lord's birth, Scripture gives this as his name, which he acquires from the event. EXPLANATION OF MATTHEW 1.[2]

8:4 Wealth of Damascus Carried Away

CHRIST'S POWER. JUSTIN MARTYR: And the words of Isaiah, "He shall take the power of Damascus and the spoils of Samaria," meant that the power of the wicked demon that dwelt in Damascus should be crushed by Christ at his birth. This is shown to have taken place. For the magi, held in servitude (as spoils) for the commission of every wicked deed through the power of that demon, by coming and worshiping Christ, openly revolted against the power that had held them as spoils, which power the Scripture indicated by parable to be located in Damascus. And in the parables that sinful and wicked power is fittingly called Samaria. Now, even among you none can deny that Damascus was and is a part of the land of Arabia, although it now belongs to Syro-Phoenicia. So it would be to your advantage, my friends, to learn what you do not understand from us Christians, who have received the grace of God, and not to exert every effort to defend your peculiar teachings and scorn those of God. DIALOGUE WITH TRYPHO 78.[3]

STRENGTH AND RICHES. AUGUSTINE: For, before the child knew how to call his father and mother, as Isaiah had prophesied of him, he took the strength of Damascus and the spoils of Samaria. That is, before he uttered human speech through his humanity, he took the strength of Damascus or that which gave confidence to Damascus. For, in the estimation of the world, that city had flourished for some time on account of her riches. But preeminence in riches is gained

by gold, and the magi as suppliants offered gold to Christ. SERMON 202.2.[4]

8:5-8 The Waters of Shiloah

FIGURATIVE EXPLANATION. EUSEBIUS OF CAESAREA: Obviously the only way to preserve the understanding of this passage is to explain its spiritual meaning. By the softly proceeding water of Siloam it means the gospel teaching of the word of salvation, because Siloam means "sent with a message." This would be God the Word, who was sent by the Father, of whom Moses says, "A ruler will not fail from Judah, nor a prince from his loins, until the one for whom it is stored up comes, and he is the expectation of the nations."[5] For rather than "for whom it is stored up" the Hebrew has "Siloam." The same word, Siloam, is used the same way in this passage for Isaiah, that is to say, "the one who is sent." PROOF OF THE GOSPEL 7.1.[6]

ANTICHRIST. HIPPOLYTUS: [Isaiah] uses the "king of Assyria" as a symbol for the Antichrist. ON THE ANTICHRIST 57.15-16.[7]

8:9 The Nations Conquered

CHRIST'S SPOILS OF VICTORY. ORIGEN: And what the same prophet said has been fulfilled. "God is with us. Know this, O nations, and be conquered." For we who are from the nations have been conquered and overcome. And we who bend our necks beneath his grace stand forth as a kind of spoils of his victory. ON FIRST PRINCIPLES 4.1.5.[8]

8:14-15 Many Shall Stumble

CHRIST THE STONE. AUGUSTINE: Christ rose again from the seed of David, as the son of David, because he had emptied himself. How did he empty himself? By taking what he was not, not by

---

[2]EBT 21*. [3]ANF 1:238**. [4]FC 38:72. [5]Gen 49:10. [6]POG 2:70. [7]ANF 5:216. [8]OSW 174-75.

losing what he was. He emptied himself; he humbled himself. Though he was God, he made himself known as a man. He was despised as he walked the earth, though he made the sky. He was despised as a mere man, as though he had no power. Not only despised, but on top of that also killed. He was a stone lying flat; the Jews stumbled over him and were shaken. But what does he say about that himself? "Whoever stumbles over this stone will be shaken; but as for anyone upon whom this stone comes, it will crush him." First he lay flat, and they stumbled; he will come from above and crush them, after they have been shaken. SERMON 92.2.[9]

8:18 The Children the Lord Has Given

CHRIST'S CHILDREN. CHRYSOSTOM: Not only do we become his brothers but even his children, for he says, "Behold, I and my children, whom God has given me." Not only do we become his children but also his members and his body.[10] As if the things already mentioned were not enough to prove the love and kindness that he shows toward us, he set down another thing, greater and more intimate than these, when he spoke of himself as our head.[11] BAPTISMAL INSTRUCTIONS 12.14 (2.2).[12]

CHRIST IN CANA. JEROME: First it must be noted that Matthew's Gospel uses the text of the Septuagint, not the Hebrew: "Jesus, hearing that John had been handed over, departed to Galilee. Leaving Nazareth, he came and lived in Capernaum, which is near the sea at the end of Zebulun and Naphtali. This was to fulfill what was said through the prophet Isaiah: 'In the land of Zebulun and Naphtali, by the way of the sea across the Jordan in Galilee of the Gentiles, the people who sat in darkness have seen a great light; upon those who sat in the region of the shadow of death a light has dawned.' From that moment, Jesus began to preach and to say, 'The kingdom of heaven approaches.'"[13] And the evangelist John reports that Jesus performed his first sign, changing water into wine, when he was invited to attend a wedding in Cana with his disciples: "Jesus performed the first of his signs in Cana of Galilee and revealed his glory, and his disciples believed in him."[14] Hence, the Septuagint reads, "Drink this first and do it quickly." For the land of Zebulun and the land of Naphtali were the first to see the miracles of Christ, that they who first saw the Lord perform a sign would be the first to drink the potion of faith. According to the Hebrew, it is also said to be the first time that the [lifting of the] burden of sins was revealed, because the Savior first preached the gospel in the region of these two tribes. . . .

But it calls this sea the lake of Gennesaret, which is formed from the influx of the Jordan.[15] On its shore are situated Capernaum, Tiberias, Bethsaida and Chorazin, in whose regions the Lord spent a great deal of time. He did so to enable the people who sat or walked in darkness to see the light—not a little light as from other prophets but a great light, as from him who said in the Gospel, "I am the light of the world."[16] And upon those who lived in the region of the shadow of death, a light has dawned. This region lies between death and the shadow of death, I believe, because death belongs to those who directed themselves straight to the underworld with their dead works: "For the soul that sins will die."[17] But the shadow of death pertains to those who do not depart from life when they sin, for they are still able to do penance if they wish. COMMENTARY ON ISAIAH 3.9.1-2.[18]

---

[9]WSA 3 3:467. [10]See 1 Cor 12:27. [11]See Eph 1:22-23. [12]ACW 31:177. [13]Mt 4:12-17. [14]Jn 2:11. [15]Cf. Lk 5:1. [16]Jn 8:12. [17]Ezek 18:20. [18]CCL 73:122-23.

9:2-7 THE MESSIANIC KING

^{2q}*The people who walked in darkness*
have seen a great light;
those who dwelt in a land of deep darkness,
on them has light shined.
^{3}*Thou hast multiplied the nation,*
thou hast increased its joy;
they rejoice before thee
as with joy at the harvest,
as men rejoice when they divide the spoil.
^{4}*For the yoke of his burden,*
and the staff for his shoulder,
the rod of his oppressor,
thou hast broken as on the day of
Midian.
^{5}*For every boot of the tramping warrior*
in battle tumult
and every garment rolled in blood

will be burned as fuel for the fire.
^{6}*For to us a child is born,*
to us a son is given;
and the government* will be upon his
shoulder,
and his name will be called
"Wonderful Counselor,† Mighty God,
Everlasting Father, Prince of Peace."
^{7}*Of the increase of his government and of*
peace
there will be no end,
upon the throne of David, and over his
kingdom,
to establish it, and to uphold it
with justice and with righteousness
from this time forth and for evermore.
The zeal of the LORD of hosts will do this.

q Ch 9.1 in Heb   *LXX *whose beginning*   †LXX *the messenger (or angel) of great counsel*

OVERVIEW: Isaiah looked toward Christ as the light that would shine in darkness (AMBROSE, LEO, ORIGEN). Christ, though only one person, is God and a human being (AMBROSE, AUGUSTINE). The Son being given does not imply subordination, because he gave himself as God (AMBROSE). Christ is called a child because of his purity and innocence (CASSIODORUS). Simplicity and innocence characterize children (MAXIMUS OF TURIN). The government on his shoulders was the power of the cross (JUSTIN MARTYR, AMBROSE). Christ is the beginning of all virtue (AMBROSE). Christ carried the cross on his shoulders so that he could reign as the king of the new age (TERTULLIAN). Isaac prefigured Christ when he carried wood for his sacrifice (CAESARIUS OF ARLES). The title "counselor" does not diminish Christ's divine status (CHRYSOSTOM).

We learn from Isaiah that Jesus Christ is God (APHRAHAT). Christ came to lead us back to God's peace by his act of reconciliation (BEDE). It is a wonder that God should show himself as a baby (EPHREM). Being born of the Virgin, Christ possessed the reality of his mother's flesh (LEO THE GREAT). The mother of Christ is the mother of God because the child born of her is called the mighty God (THEODORET).

Christ was called the Angel of Great Counsel because he brought the message of the kingdom of heaven and the will of the Father (AUGUSTINE, BEDE, CHRYSOSTOM, GREGORY OF NYSSA, NOVATIAN). Christ was the teacher of all truths (JUSTIN MARTYR). Christ appears as an angel on occasion (NOVATIAN). Christ, the light of life, was raised for those in the shadow of death (BEDE). Christ pronounced judgment on Israel and salvation for the Gentiles (JEROME). Human peace comes to an end, but the peace of Christ is never-ending (CHRYSOSTOM, JOHN CASSIAN, BEDE). Christ was God in the flesh, bringing peace to humanity (JOHN CASSIAN). Solomon was a type of Christ. The Roman peace at the birth of Christ showed Christ's mission of peace. Christ's peace is brought to fruition through the ministry of the church (BEDE).

9:2 The People in Darkness Will See Light

GOD'S GRACE. AMBROSE: Hence he was in the shadow of life, whereas sinners are in the shadow of death. According to Isaiah, the people who sinned sat in the shadow of death. For these a light arose, not by the merits of their virtues but by the grace of God. There is no distinction, therefore, between the breath of God and the food of the tree of life. No one can say that he can acquire more by his own efforts than what is granted him by the generosity of God. ON PARADISE 5.29.[1]

CHRIST THE LIGHT. LEO THE GREAT: Although he filled all things with his invisible majesty, [Christ] came, nevertheless, to those who had not known him, as if from a very remote and deep seclusion. At that time, he took away the blindness of ignorance, as it has been written: "For those sitting in darkness and in the shadow of death, a light has risen."[2] SERMON 25.3.[3]

SPIRITUAL MEANING OF DARKNESS. ORIGEN: Now the expression *darkness* will likewise be used to refer to two corresponding concepts. The statement "And God called the light day, and the darkness he called night"[4] is an example of the more common meaning. An example of the spiritual meaning occurs in the statement "The people who sat in darkness . . . and in the shadow of death, light has dawned on them." COMMENTARY ON THE GOSPEL OF JOHN 13.134.[5]

9:6 A Child Is Born, a Son Is Given

A CHILD IS BORN. AMBROSE: So we have in another place: "A child is born to us, and a son is given to us." In the term *child* there is an indication of age; in the term *son* a reference to the fullness of Godhead. He was made of his mother and born of the Father, but as the same person he was born and given. Do not think of two but of one. For the Son of God is one person, born of the Father and sprung from the virgin. The names differ in order but unite in one, just as the scriptural lesson just read teaches: "Man was made in her, and the Highest himself has founded her."[6] He was man indeed in body, but the Highest in power. And while he is God and man through diversity of nature, he is the same person, not two persons, though being God and man. He has, therefore, something peculiar to his own nature and something in common with us, but in both cases he is one and in both he is perfect. ON HIS BROTHER SATYRUS 1.12.[7]

BOTH GOD AND HUMAN. AUGUSTINE: We read, "A child is born to us," because we see him in the nature of a servant, which he had because the Virgin conceived and brought forth a son. However, because it was the Word of God who became flesh in order to dwell among us, and because he remains what he was (that is, really God hidden in the flesh), we use the words of the angel Gabriel and call "his name Emmanuel."[8] He is properly called God with us to avoid thinking of God as one person and the humanity [in Christ] as another. SERMON 187.4.[9]

GOD GAVE HIMSELF. AMBROSE: And not only did the Father send the Son but also gave him, as the Son himself gave himself. For we read, "Grace to you from God our Father and the Lord Jesus Christ, who gave himself for our sins."[10] If they think that the Son was subjected to God because he was sent, they cannot deny that it was of grace

---

[1]FC 42:307. [2]Mt 4:16. [3]FC 93:101. [4]Gen 1:5. [5]FC 89:96. [6]Ps 87:5 (86:5 LXX). [7]FC 22:166-67*. [8]Mt 1:23; Is 7:14. [9]FC 38:16**. [10]Gal 1:3-4.

that he was given. But he was given by the Father, as Isaiah said: "Unto us a child is born, unto us a son is given." But he was given by the Spirit and was sent by the Spirit. For since the prophet has not defined by whom he was given, he shows that he was given by the grace of the Trinity; and inasmuch as the Son himself gave himself, he could not be subject to himself according to his Godhead. Therefore that he was given could not be a sign of subjection in the Godhead. ON THE HOLY SPIRIT 3.2.9.[11]

CHRIST'S PURITY. CASSIODORUS: We often find the Lord Christ described as a child because of the purity of his innocence. The simplicity of youth bestows on a child the blessing of aversion from vices and from the malice of the world. As Christ himself attested, "Of such is the kingdom of heaven."[12] "Child" is used in the text: "Behold my child whom I have chosen, my beloved in which my soul delights,"[13] and in another passage: "A child is born to us, and a son bestowed on us." EXPOSITION OF THE PSALMS 68.18.[14]

CHRIST'S INNOCENCE. CASSIODORUS: In the holy Scripture Christ is often called a child because of his innocence of mind. As Isaiah says, "For a child has been born to us, and a son has been given to us." EXPOSITION OF THE PSALMS 85.16.[15]

INNOCENCE. MAXIMUS OF TURIN: For this reason the apostles are told, "unless you change and become like this child."[16] He does not say "like these children" but "like this child." He chooses one; he proposes one. Let us see, then, who he might be, who is proposed to the disciples to be imitated. I do not think that he is from the people, nor from the ordinary crowd, nor from the vast multitude—this one who was given, through the apostles, as an example of holiness to the entire world. I do not think, I say, that he is from the ordinary crowd but from heaven. For he is the child from heaven about whom the prophet Isaiah says, "A child is born to us, a son is given to us." Clearly he is the child who, like an innocent, did not curse when he was cursed, did not strike back when he was struck,[17] but rather in his very suffering prayed for his enemies, saying, "Father, forgive them, for they know not what they do."[18] Thus simplicity, which nature has given to infants, the Lord augmented with the virtue of mercy. SERMON 54.2.[19]

ON HIS SHOULDER. JUSTIN MARTYR: "A child is born to us, and a son is given to us, and the government is upon his shoulders." This signifies the power of the cross, which, at his crucifixion, he placed on his shoulders, as shall be demonstrated more clearly as we proceed in this discourse. FIRST APOLOGY 35.[20]

CHRIST'S DIVINE POWER. AMBROSE: Accordingly, to call the nations to the grace of his resurrection—which is the rich and fertile land that bears everlasting fruits, fruits a hundredfold and sixtyfold[21]—he bowed his shoulder to labor, bowed himself to the cross, to carry our sins. For that reason the prophet says, "whose government is on his shoulder." This means, above the passion of his body is the power of his divinity, or it refers to the cross that towers above his body. Therefore he bowed his shoulder, applying himself to the plow—patient in the endurance of all insults, and so subject to affliction that he was wounded on account of our iniquities and weakened on account of our sins.[22] ON THE PATRIARCHS 6.31.[23]

CHRIST IS THE BEGINNING OF VIRTUE. AMBROSE: Christ, then, is the beginning of our virtue. He is the beginning of purity, who taught maidens not to look for the embraces of humanity[24] but to yield the purity of their bodies and minds to the service of the Holy Spirit rather than to a husband. Christ is the beginning of fru-

---

[11]NPNF 2 10:136-37**. [12]Mk 10:14-15. [13]Is 42:1. [14]ACW 52:151-52*. [15]ACW 52:335*. [16]Mk 10:14-15. [17]See 1 Pet 2:23. [18]Lk 23:34. [19]ACW 50:132. [20]ANF 1:174**. [21]See Mt 13:8; Mk 4:8. [22]See Is 53:3-5. [23]FC 65:259. [24]See 1 Cor 7:29, 34.

gality, for he became poor, though he was rich. Christ is the beginning of patience, for when he was reviled, he reviled not again. When he was struck, he did not strike back. Christ is the beginning of humility, for he took the form of a servant, though in the majesty of his power he was equal with God the Father.[25] From him each various virtue has taken its origin.

For this cause, then, that we might learn these different virtues, "a son was given us, whose beginning was upon his shoulder." That "beginning" is the Lord's cross—the beginning of strong courage, wherewith a way has been opened for the holy martyrs to enter the sufferings of the holy war. On the Christian Faith 3.7.52-53.[26]

The One New King. Tertullian: Likewise Isaiah also says, "For unto us a child is born." But what is there unusual in this, unless he speaks of the Son of God? "To us is given he whose government is upon his shoulder." Now, what king is there who bears the ensign of his dominion upon his shoulder, and not rather upon his head as a diadem, or in his hand as a scepter, or else as a mark in some royal apparel? But the one new King of the new ages, Jesus Christ, carried on his shoulder both the power and the excellence of his new glory, even his cross; so that, according to our former prophecy, he might thenceforth reign from the tree as Lord. Against Marcion 3.19.[27]

The Mystery of Christ's Cross. Caesarius of Arles: When Isaac himself carried the wood for the sacrifice of himself, in this, too, he prefigured Christ our Lord, who carried his own cross to the place of his passion. Of this mystery much had already been foretold by the prophets: "And his government shall be upon his shoulders." Christ, then, had the government upon his shoulders when he carried his cross with wonderful humility. Not unfittingly does Christ's cross signify government: by it the devil is conquered and the whole world recalled to the knowledge and grace of Christ. Sermon 84.3.[28]

Equal Honor to the Son. Chrysostom: When Scripture wishes to show that God needs no one, it says that he has no counselor.[29] When it wishes to show the equal honor of the Only Begotten, it calls the Son of God his counselor. Against the Anomoeans 11.14.[30]

The Implication of Christ's Names. Aphrahat: Furthermore, we must prove that this Jesus was beforehand promised from ancient times in the prophets and was called the Son of God. David said, "You are my son; today I have begotten you."[31] Again he said, "In the glories of holiness, from the womb, from of old, I have begotten you, a child."[32] And Isaiah said, "Unto us a child is born, unto us a son is given, and his government was upon his shoulder, and his name shall be called Wonderful, and Counselor, and mighty God of the ages, and Prince of peace. And to the increase of his government and to his peace there is no end." Therefore tell me, O wise teacher of Israel, who is he that was born and whose name was called "child" and "son" and "Wonderful" and "Counselor," the "mighty God of the ages," and "Prince of peace," "to the increase of" whose government and to whose "peace [he said], there is no end?" For if we call Christ the Son of God, David taught us [this]; and that we call him God, this we learned from Isaiah. "And his government was laid upon his shoulder"; for he bore his cross and went out from Jerusalem. And that he "was born as a child," Isaiah again said, "Behold, the virgin shall conceive and bear; and his name shall be called Immanuel, which is, our God with us."[33] Demonstration 17.9.[34]

He Has Come to Reconcile the World. Bede: Surely the entire divinely arranged plan of our Redeemer's [coming] in the flesh is the reconciliation of the world—it was for this purpose that he became incarnate, for this he suffered, for

---

[25]Phil 2:6-8. [26]NPNF 2 10:250*. [27]ANF 3:337*. [28]FC 47:17*. [29]See Is 40:13. [30]FC 72:275. [31]Ps 2:7. [32]Ps 110:3 (Pesh.). [33]Is 7:14; Mt 1:23. [34]NPNF 2 13:390**.

this he was raised from the dead—that he might lead us, who had incurred God's anger by sinning, back to God's peace by his act of reconciliation. Hence he was rightly given the name "Father of the world to come" and "Prince of peace" by the prophet; and the apostle, writing about him to those from among the nations who had believed, said, "And coming, he brought the good news of peace to you who were from far off and peace to those who were near, since through him we both have access in one Spirit to the Father."[35] HOMILIES ON THE GOSPELS 2.9.[36]

THE WONDER OF HIS BIRTH. EPHREM THE SYRIAN: Today was born the child, and his name was called Wonderful! For a wonder it is that God should reveal himself as a baby. HYMNS ON THE NATIVITY 1.[37]

GENUINE FLESH. LEO THE GREAT: [Eutyches] might have read the words of the same prophet: "A child is born to us, and a son is given to us, and the government is upon his shoulders: and they shall call his name, angel of the Great Counsel, God the Mighty, the Prince of peace, Father of the world to come." And he would not speak nonsense, saying that the Word was made flesh in such a way that Christ, born from the Virgin's womb, had a man's form yet did not have the reality of his mother's body. LETTER 28.[38]

MOTHER OF GOD. THEODORET OF CYR: But the prophet who predicted the Emmanuel has written of him a little further on that "unto us a child is born, unto us a son is given; and the government shall be upon his shoulders; and his name is called angel of great counsel, wonderful, counselor, mighty God, powerful, Prince of peace, Father of the age to come." Now if the baby born of the virgin is styled "Mighty God," then it is only with reason that the mother is called "mother of God." For the mother shares the honor of her offspring, and the Virgin is both mother of the Lord Christ as man and again is his servant as Lord and Creator and God. LETTER 152.[39]

CHRIST COMES AS A MESSENGER. AUGUSTINE: The fact that the one who talked to Moses is called both the angel of the Lord and the Lord raises a big problem, which calls not for hasty assertion but for careful investigation. There are two opinions that can be put forward about it, of which either may be true, since they both fit the faith. When I say that either may be true, I mean whichever of them was intended by the writer. When we are searching the Scriptures, we may of course understand them in a way in which the writer perhaps did not; but what we should never do is understand them in a way which does not square with the rule of faith, with the rule of truth, with the rule of piety.[40] So I am offering you both opinions. There may be yet a third that escapes me. Anyway, of these two propositions, choose whichever you like. Some people say that the reason why he is called both the angel of the Lord and the Lord is that he was in fact Christ, of whom the prophet says plainly that he is "the angel of great counsel." "Angel" is a word signifying function, not nature. "Angel" is Greek for the Latin *nuntius*.[41] So "Messenger" is the name of an action: you are called a messenger for doing something, namely, for bringing some message. Now who would deny that Christ brought us a message about the kingdom of heaven? And then an angel, that is to say, a messenger, is sent by the one who wants to give a message by him. And who would deny that Christ was sent? So often did he say, "I did not come to do my own will but the will of him who sent me,"[42] that he of all people is the one who was sent. After all, that pool at Siloam "means Sent."[43] That is why he told the man whose eyes he anointed with mud to wash his face there. No one's eyes are opened except those of the person who is cleansed by Christ. So then, the angel and the Lord are one and the same. SERMON 7.3.[44]

---

[35]Eph 2:17-18. [36]CS 111:80. [37]NPNF 2 13:223**. [38]FC 34:94-95. [39]NPNF 2 3:332**. [40]Augustine warns the reader against interpreting Scripture contrary to the intention of the author, or contrary to Christian belief and/or practice. [41]English "messenger." [42]Jn 6:38. [43]Jn 9:7. [44]WSA 3 1:234*.

The Father's Herald. Bede: Clothed in flesh, [Christ] descended into the water as "an angel of great counsel,"[45] that is, as a herald of the Father's will to Jewish people. By his deeds and his teaching he moved sinners, so that he would be killed—he who, by his bodily death, was able not only to heal those who were ailing spiritually but also to bring the dead back to life. The movement of the water,[46] then, suggests the Lord's passion, which occurred by the Jewish nation being moved and stirred up. Homilies on the Gospels 1.23.[47]

The Son Reveals the Father. Chrysostom: The Son of God is said to be the angel of great counsel because of his many other teachings, but especially because he revealed his Father to humankind. Homilies on the Gospel of John 81.[48]

Christ's Names Point to His Divinity. Chrysostom: Come now, and let me show you that the Son is called God. "Behold, the virgin shall be with child and shall give birth to a son, and they shall call his name Immanuel, which means, 'God is with us.'"[49] Did you see how both the name Lord is given to the Father and the name God is given to the Son? In the psalm, the sacred writer said, "Let them know that *Lord* is your name."[50] Here Isaiah says, "They shall call his name Immanuel." And again, he says, "A child is born to us, and a son is given to us; and his name shall be called Angel of Great Counsel, God the Strong, the Mighty One." Against the Anomoeans 5.15.[51]

Christ Reveals the Father's Will. Gregory of Nyssa: For we too say plainly that the prophet, wishing to make manifest the mystery concerning Christ, called the self-existent "Angel," that the meaning of the words might not be referred to the Father, as it would have been if the title of "Existent" alone had been found throughout the discourse. But just as our word is the revealer and messenger (or "angel") of the move-

ments of the mind, even so we affirm that the true Word that was in the beginning, when he announces the will of his Father, is styled "angel" (or "messenger"), a title given to him on account of the operation of conveying the message. And as the sublime John, having previously called him "Word,"[52] so introduces the further truth that the Word was God, that our thoughts might not at once turn to the Father, as they would have done if the title of God had been put first. So too does the mighty Moses, after first calling him "Angel," teach us in the words that follow that he is none other than the self-existent himself, that the mystery concerning the Christ might be foreshown, by the Scripture assuring us by the name Angel that the Word is the interpreter of the Father's will, and, by the title of the "self-existent," of the closeness of relation subsisting between the Son and the Father. And if Eunomius should bring forward Isaiah also as calling him "the 'angel' of mighty counsel," not even so will he overthrow our argument. For there, in clear and incontrovertible terms, there is indicated by the prophecy the dispensation of his humanity; for "unto us," he says, "a child is born, unto us a son is given, and the government shall be upon his shoulder, and his name is called the angel of mighty counsel." . . . For as the "angel" (or "messenger") gives information from someone, even so the Word reveals the thought within, the seal shows by its own stamp the original mold, and the image by itself interprets the beauty of that whereof it is the image, so that in their signification all these terms are equivalent to one another. For this reason the title *angel* is placed before that of the "self-existent," the son being termed "angel" as the exponent of his Father's will, and the "existent" as having no name that could possibly give a knowledge of his essence, but transcending all the power of names to express. Against Eunomius 11.3.[53]

---

[45]LXX. [46]See Jn 5:2-9. [47]CS 110:223*. [48]FC 41:377. [49]Is 7:14; Mt 1:23. [50]Ps 83:18 (82:19 LXX). [51]FC 72:143. [52]Jn 1:1. [53]NPNF 2 5:235*.

HERALD OF THE FATHER'S WILL. NOVATIAN: Because he is of God, he is rightly called God, since he is the Son of God; and because he is subject to the Father and herald of the Father's will, he is proclaimed "Angel of Great Counsel." . . . The title [angel] does, however, suit the person of Christ, since he is not only God, inasmuch as he is the Son of God, but also a messenger, inasmuch as he is the herald of the Father's economy of salvation. Heretics must realize that they are acting contrary to the Scriptures when they say they believe that Christ was also an angel but do not want to admit that he is also the God who they read came frequently to visit the human race in the Old Testament. ON THE TRINITY 18.9-10.[54]

CHRIST THE TEACHER. JUSTIN MARTYR: [By] calling him "the Angel of great counsel," did not Isaiah predict that Christ would be a teacher of those truths that he expounded when he came upon this earth? For he alone openly taught the great counsels that the Father intended for those who either were or shall be pleasing to him, as well as for those people or angels who withdrew from his will. DIALOGUE WITH TRYPHO 76.[55]

BOTH GOD AND A MESSENGER. NOVATIAN: The title of angel is also appropriate to Christ because he was made "the Angel of Great Counsel." He is an angel because he lays bare the heart of the Father,[56] as John declares. For if John says that this Word, who lays bare the bosom of the Father, was also made flesh,[57] so that he could lay bare the heart of the Father, it follows that Christ is not only man but also an angel. And the Scriptures show not only that he is an angel but also that he is God. This is what we too believe. For, if we will not admit that it was Christ who then spoke to Hagar,[58] we must either make an angel God or reckon God the Almighty Father among the angels. ON THE TRINITY 18.22-23.[59]

A LIGHT FOR ALL PEOPLE. BEDE: "Which will be to all people," not to all the people of the Jews, nor to all the people of the nations, but to all the people who, either from the Jews or from the nations of the whole world, are brought together in one flock to one confession of Christ. From one and the same partaking of the mysteries of Christ they are called "Christian." . . .

The light of life rose for those of us dwelling in the region of the shadow of death. HOMILIES ON THE GOSPELS 1.6.[60]

HIS NAME SHALL BE CALLED WONDERFUL. JEROME: After two names, therefore [child and son], he will be called by another six names: wonderful, counselor, God, mighty, father of the coming age, prince of peace. For the names are not to be joined into couplets as many think, such that we would read "wonderful counselor" and "mighty God." Instead "wonderful," which is *pele* in Hebrew, is to be read separately, as is "counselor," or what is called *yôʿēṣ* in their language. The title "God" also, whom the Hebrews call *ēl*, stands on its own. Thus in subsequent passages where we read, "For you are God and we were unaware,"[61] and again, "I am God and there is no other beyond me,"[62] along with many similar statements, the Hebrew uses *ēl* where Latin uses Deus. And "mighty," which comes next, is called *gibbôr* in Hebrew. Hence when the same prophet remembers "They will lay their trust upon God, the Holy One of Israel in truth, and the remnant of Jacob upon the mighty God,"[63] the Hebrew text has *ēl gibbôr* for "mighty God." But anyone who reads that the Savior is our peace, according to the apostle Paul,[64] will have no doubt that the father of the coming age and of the resurrection, which is completed in our vocation, is also the prince of peace who said to the apostles, "My peace I give to you, my peace I bequeath to you."[65] The Septuagint in my opinion, terrified as it was by the majesty of these names, did not dare to say of a child that he must be called God and so forth but wrote in place of the six names, which it did

---

[54]FC 67:69**. [55]ANF 1:236**. [56]Jn 1:18. [57]Jn 1:14. [58]Gen 16:7. [59]FC 67:72. [60]CS 110:60-61. [61]Is 45:15. [62]Is 45:22. [63]Is 10:20-21. [64]Cf. Eph 2:14. [65]Jn 14:27.

not have in Hebrew, "angel of great counsel, and I will bring peace and his salvation upon the princes," which seems to me to have the following meaning: He who announced to us that Israel would be thrown down for a while and that the nations would be healed is the angel of great counsel who also gave peace to its princes, apostles and apostolic men, and bequeathed dogmatic healing to their believers. Commentary on Isaiah 3.9.16-17.[66]

9:7 No End of Peace

Christ's Peace Is Unending. Chrysostom: Listen to how Isaiah predicted this long beforehand when he said, "and his name shall be called Messenger of Great Counsel, Wonderful Counselor, God the Strong, the Mighty One, the Prince of peace, Father of the world to come."

No one could say this of a mere man, as is obvious even to those who are very eager to show how stubborn they can be. No man from the beginning of time has been called God the Mighty or Father of the world to come or the Prince of peace. For Isaiah said, "There is no end of his peace." And what did happen makes it clear that this peace has spread over the whole earth and sea, over the world where people dwell and where no one lives, over mountains, woodlands and hills, starting from that day on which he was going to leave his disciples and said to them, "My peace I give to you; not as the world gives do I give to you."[67]

Why did Christ speak in this way? Because the peace which comes from a human being is easily destroyed and subject to many changes. But Christ's peace is strong, unshaken, firm, fixed, steadfast, immune to death and unending. Demonstration Against the Pagans 2.8-10.[68]

His Kingdom Without End. John Cassian: Surely the coming of God in the flesh could not remain hidden from humanity, since the prophet had openly said about him, as though to the whole human race: "behold your God,"[69] and "this is your God,"[70] and again "the mighty God,

Father of the coming world, Prince of peace," and "of his kingdom there will be no end." Once God had come, however, did his coming remain hidden from those who openly confessed? Was Peter ignorant of the advent of God when he said, "You are Christ, the Son of the living God"?[71] Did Martha not know the one in whom she believed or the meaning of what she was saying when she declared, "Lord, I believe that you are Christ, the Son of the living God who has come into the world"?[72] Finally, was not everyone who asked him to heal diseases or to replace lost limbs or to raise the dead petitioning God's omnipotence rather than humanity's weakness? On the Incarnation of the Lord Against Nestorius 7.10.[73]

Christ's Peace. Bede: When Israel had been saved through the apostles, all the world flocked to the threshold of truth and of the peacemaker Solomon, of whom it was said, "His dominion will be increased and there will be no end of peace." For he [Christ] is "the stone broken off from the mountain,"[74] and in his earthly reign of faith, as he falls upon his enemy, he alone possesses a peaceful dominion throughout the earth. Commentary on the Acts of the Apostles 3.[75]

Peace to the World. Bede: And, indeed, just as in his divinity the Mediator between God and human beings[76] foresaw the mother of whom he willed to be born when he should so will, so also in his humanity he chose the time that he wished for his nativity. Moreover, he himself granted that that [time] should be such as he willed, namely, that in a calm among the storm of wars a singular tranquility of unusual peace should cover the whole world.

. . . He chose a time of utmost peace as the time when he would be born because this was the

---

[66]CCL 73:126-27. [67]Jn 14:27. [68]FC 73:195*. [69]Is 40:9. [70]Is 25:9. [71]Mt 16:16. [72]Jn 11:27. [73]CSEL 17:366. [74]Dan 2:45. [75]CS 117:45. [76]1 Tim 2:5.

reason for his being born in the world, that he might lead the human race back to the gifts of heavenly peace. . . . Our Lord was born in a time of peace, so that even by the circumstance of the time he might teach that he was the very one of whom the prophecy sent before [him] spoke: "His sovereignty will be multiplied, and there will be no end of peace." . . .

The very author of peace and the Maker of time sent before him a time of peace, and thus when he appeared in the flesh he opened an approach to light and proclaimed the joys of eternal peace first to the house of Jacob (that is, the Israelite people), and then to all the nations which came streaming to him. And we must not pass over the fact that the serenity of that earthly peace, at the time when the heavenly king was born, not only offered testimony to his grace but also provided a service, since it bestowed on the preachers of his word the capability of traveling over the world and spreading abroad the grace of the gospel wherever they wished. HOMILIES ON THE GOSPELS 1.6.[77]

SOLOMON, A TYPE OF CHRIST. BEDE: All these things, as the apostle teaches, "were done as an example for us"[78] and were written down for us, and so we must scrutinize them carefully for their spiritual meaning. King Solomon, whose name means "peaceful," typologically designates our Redeemer himself, of whom Isaiah says, "His sovereignty will be increased, and there will be no end of peace." The temple that he built is his catholic church, which he gathers into the one structure of his faith and charity from all the believers throughout the world, as it were from living stones.[79] HOMILIES ON THE GOSPELS 2.24.[80]

PRAYER FOR PEACE WITHOUT END. BEDE: This voice of repentance is that of the Jewish people and of all who found in Christ access to the salvation for which they were searching. I now know with certainty that you are the one concerning whom it was said "his government

will be increased and there will be no end to peace" and that you govern the kingdom in which the pure of heart will see God with unceasing happiness. I beg you, therefore, to strengthen and increase the faith that you imparted to me through the bestowal of your sacraments and heavenly gifts. Thus, having received the pledge of the Spirit, may I remain confident that you will forevermore preserve from destruction the generation of works which were begotten by my heart after the washing of my body and that you will never remove my name from the heavenly home which you deigned to grant to my fathers who, through the law, faithfully and devoutly awaited your coming. FOUR BOOKS ON 1 SAMUEL 4.24.[81]

HIS KINGDOM WILL INCREASE. BEDE: It is beyond doubt that Solomon, whose name means "peaceful," both by his name itself as well as by the most peaceful kingdom he established, signifies the one about whom Isaiah said, "His government will be increased, and there will be no end to peace." Hiram, on the other hand, whose name in Latin means "living gloriously," expresses figuratively the glorious believers from the Gentiles, along with their life and faith. Indeed, no one denies that Hiram, inasmuch as he was a king who assisted Solomon with his royal power in building the house of the Lord, prefigures those lords of earthly realities who would be converted to the faith. By [their] noble assistance the church would be supported, increased and strengthened against schismatic heretics and pagans, even more often than by its principal decrees.[82] Solomon, therefore, sought Hiram's help in the work of the temple because the Lord, when he came in the flesh and made plans to build the church as his own beloved home, clearly chose assistants in this work not only from the

---

[77]CS 110:52-53. [78]1 Cor 10:6. [79]1 Pet 2:5. [80]CS 111:249. [81]CCL 119:229. [82]Bede is arguing that just as Hiram aided Solomon in building the temple, so will human rulers aid the church in building its kingdom on earth.

Jews but also from the Gentiles.[83] He took ministers of the word from both peoples. TWO BOOKS ON THE TEMPLE 1.69-79.[84]

SOLOMON'S PEACE. BEDE: What does the spiritual house or temple that King Solomon made for the Lord in Jerusalem signify? Solomon himself, whose name means "peaceful," is a fitting symbol of the one about whom the prophet sang, "His government will be increased, and there will be no end to peace." [This is] the same one concerning whom the apostle also wrote to the church of the Gentiles, "and he came and preached peace to you who were far off and peace to those who were near, for through him we both have access in one Spirit to the Father."[85]

That it took Solomon seven years to build the temple,[86] which he completed and dedicated in the eighth year, was a sign that for seven years, or the entire span of the present age, the Lord would build the church as a heavenly dwelling for the gathered faithful. In the future life, however, when he appears in the glory of the resurrection, he will complete and perfect the church and raise it forevermore to the joy of life immortal in the vision of his beauty. Our resurrection, then, is rightly signified by the number eight, since the just will be raised from the dead on the eighth day, that is, after the seventh of the sabbath. THREE BOOKS ON EZRA AND NEHEMIAH 1.14-30.[87]

A REPOSE OF PEACE. BEDE: In this verse, Solomon signifies the everlasting light by "length of days," the survival of death by "years of life" and the state of happiness to be discovered by "growth in peace."[88] Isaiah refers to the same reality when he says, "His government will be increased, and there will be no end to peace." For when the people of God are obedient to God's law, both historically and at the present time, they are enabled to live for a long time in the repose of peace. THREE BOOKS ON THE

PROVERBS OF SOLOMON 1.3.[89]

THE SPIRITUAL KING OF ISRAEL. BEDE: Solomon gave the name "parables" or "metaphors" to this book [Proverbs] because he wanted us to understand it profoundly, not just according to the literal sense. He prefigures the Lord in this respect, who would speak to the crowds through parables. For just as Solomon's own name and peaceful reign foretold the enduring kingdom of Christ and of the church, concerning which it is written "his government will be increased, and there will be no end to peace upon the throne of David and his kingdom," so also did his construction and dedication of the temple artfully refer to the building of holy church, which will be dedicated for all eternity at the resurrection. The testimony of the crowds of people who greeted Christ with palm branches and praises at his entry into Jerusalem also declares him to be the son of David and the spiritual king of Israel. THREE BOOKS ON THE PROVERBS OF SOLOMON 1.1.[90]

THE THRONE OF DAVID. BEDE: Isaiah said, "His government will be increased, and there will be no end to peace upon the throne of David and his kingdom, to confirm and strengthen it in right judgment and justice."

He did not say "to acquire the glory of worldly riches" or "to have victory over many peoples and cities" or "to conquer the powerful," but "to confirm it in right judgment and justice."

For it is through this that the church is strengthened and the kingdom of Christ is extended both within each of the faithful and throughout the entire world. EXPOSITION OF THE GOSPEL OF LUKE 1.1.33.[91]

---

[83]1 Kings 5. [84]CCL 119A:148-49. [85]Eph 2:17-18. [86]1 Kings 6:38. [87]CCL 119A:241. [88]Prov 3:2. [89]CCL 119B:38. [90]CCL 119B:23. [91]CCL 120:32.

9:8-21 GOD'S JUDGMENT

⁸The Lord has sent a word against Jacob,
  and it will light upon Israel;
⁹and all the people will know,
  Ephraim and the inhabitants of Samaria,
  who say in pride and in arrogance of
    heart:
¹⁰"The bricks have fallen,
  but we will build with dressed stones;
the sycamores have been cut down,
  but we will put cedars in their place."*
¹¹So the LORD raises adversaries' against
    them,
  and stirs up their enemies.
¹²The Syrians on the east and the
    Philistines on the west
  devour Israel with open mouth.
For all this his anger is not turned away
  and his hand is stretched out still.
¹³The people did not turn to him who smote
    them,
  nor seek the LORD of hosts.
¹⁴So the LORD cut off from Israel head and
    tail,
  palm branch and reed in one day—
¹⁵the elder and honored man is the head,
  and the prophet who teaches lies is the
    tail;
¹⁶for those who lead this people lead them
    astray,

and those who are led by them are
    swallowed up.†
¹⁷Therefore the Lord does not rejoice over
    their young men,
  and has no compassion on their fatherless
    and widows;
for every one is godless and an evildoer,
  and every mouth speaks folly.
For all this his anger is not turned away
  and his hand is stretched out still.

¹⁸For wickedness burns like a fire,
  it consumes briers and thorns;
it kindles the thickets of the forest,
  and they roll upward in a column of smoke.
¹⁹Through the wrath of the LORD of hosts
  the land is burned,
and the people are like fuel for the fire;
  no man spares his brother.
²⁰They snatch on the right, but are still
    hungry,
  and they devour on the left, but are not
    satisfied;
each devours his neighbor's⁵ flesh,
²¹Manasseh Ephraim, and Ephraim
    Manasseh,
  and together they are against Judah.
For all this his anger is not turned away
  and his hand is stretched out still.

r Cn: Heb the adversaries of Rezin   s Tg Compare Gk: Heb the flesh of his arm   *LXX and cut down sycamores and cedars, and let us build for ourselves a tower   †Vg and they that call this people blessed, shall cause them to err: and they that are called blessed shall be thrown down, headlong

OVERVIEW: The message originally sent to the Jews was rejected by them and has now been believed by the Gentiles (GREGORY THE GREAT). Christians should offer to God their best works (PACHOMIUS). It is better to turn when we err than to be free from correction when we stumble (GREGORY OF NAZIANZUS). God's judgment is designed to produce repentance in those he loves

(GREGORY THE GREAT). Those who hold the right faith are the head of all people; heretics are the tail (APONIUS). Christians should avoid the pursuit of worldly glory and false teaching (PRIMASIUS). When church leaders fall, the entire church suffers (GREGORY THE GREAT). Leaders should desire heavenly and not earthly things (GREGORY OF NAZIANZUS). The Son of God purified the womb of Mary (EPHREM).

9:8 A Word Against Jacob

AGAINST JACOB. GREGORY THE GREAT: Jacob is called the destroyer, but Israel the one who sees God. Does not Jacob symbolize the Jews? And what does Israel represent, if not the people of the Gentiles? The latter, whom Jacob strove to destroy by bodily death, have surely come to see God with the eyes of faith. The word sent to Jacob fell on Israel, therefore, because the one whom the Jews rejected when he came to them has now been discovered and believed by the Gentiles. MORALS ON THE BOOK OF JOB 1.2.57.[1]

9:10 The Fallen Replaced

STONES HAVE FALLEN. GREGORY THE GREAT: Because the prophet recognized that the Jewish people would perish from the faith and because he foresaw that there would arise within the church holy apostles, through whom many of the Gentiles would be established in the strength of faith and life, he spoke with great encouragement, saying, "The stones have fallen, but we will build with square stones." Having foreseen the rise of the apostles, martyrs and doctors of the holy church, he was less troubled by the fall of the stones, which represents the judgment of the Jews, because he also saw the work of Almighty God, which is the holy church built from square stones.

Four tables were built from the square stones, therefore, inasmuch as faith, life, patience and kindness were given from the lives of the saints as an example for the people to follow, that they might already have a foretaste of the table. That is, the people might know the virtues through which they can offer a sacrifice of prayer to Almighty God on the altars of their hearts.

Whatever good the faithful people of the holy church have done or continue to do, then, they first received from the exemplary lives of their preachers. For how could they have acquired this foretaste of the table if they had not found the square stones?

Let's look briefly at each of them, dearest brothers. Do you want to see an instance of faith? "For me, to live is Christ and to die is gain."[2] Would you like to know what life is like? "The world is crucified to me and I to the world."[3] Do you want to hear what patience sounds like? "To the present hour we hunger, we are buffeted and homeless, and we labor, working with our hands. We are cursed and we bless, we are persecuted and we endure, we are slandered and we implore."[4] HOMILIES ON EZEKIEL 2.9.5.[5]

THE WORKS OF CAIN. PACHOMIUS: Whoever offers God his choicest goods is likened to Abel's works, while the one who brings cheap things is likened to the works of Cain[6] or to the one who laughed at his father and went to tell his two brothers,[7] or again to the one who decided to build a tower in the plain of Shinar,[8] forgetting the one who had piloted him on the boat and had saved him from the water of the flood and blessed his fathers. Now he said, fleeing, "Come, let us dress stones and cut sycamores and cedars, and let us build a tower for ourselves." LETTER 3.10.[9]

9:13 The Lord Who Smote Them

REPENTANCE IN JUDGMENT. GREGORY THE GREAT: Against them the prophet complains to the Lord, saying, "You have bruised them, and they have refused to receive correction."[10] . . .

[1]CCL 143:95; LF 18:107. [2]Phil 1:21. [3]Gal 6:14. [4]1 Cor. 4:11-13. [5]CCL 142:359-60. [6]Gen 4:3. [7]Gen 9:22. [8]Gen 11:2-9. [9]CS 47:57. [10]Jer 5:3.

Hence again the Lord says, "The people are not returned to him who has struck them." . . . Hence the Lord reproaches the people of Israel, captive yet not converted from their iniquity, saying, "The house of Israel is become dross to me; all these are brass, and tin, and iron and lead, in the midst of the furnace."[11] This is as though he said unmistakably, "I wished to purify them in the fire of tribulation, and I wanted them to become silver or gold. But they have turned from me in the furnace into brass, and tin, and iron and lead, because even in tribulation they have rushed forward not to virtue but to vices." When brass is struck, it gives off a greater sound than do other metals. He . . . who when chastised breaks forth into sounds of murmuring has turned to brass in the midst of the furnace. Tin, however, when skillfully treated, presents the deceptive appearance of silver. He therefore who is not free from the vice of pretence in the midst of tribulation has become tin in the furnace. But he uses iron who plots against the life of the neighbor, and he is iron in the furnace when he does not put away in his tribulations the wickedness of doing harm to neighbors. Lead, again, is heavier than the other metals. He then is found to be lead in the furnace who is so weighed down by the burden of his sin that even in tribulation he is not raised above earthly desires. Pastoral Care 3.13.[12]

A Fatherly Rebuke. Gregory of Nazianzus: It is better to turn again when we err than to be free from correction when we stumble. For whom the Lord loves he chastens,[13] and a rebuke is a fatherly action. Every soul that is not chastised is not healed. Is not then freedom from chastisement a hard thing? But to fail to be corrected by the chastisement is still harder. On His Father's Silence, Oration 16.15.[14]

9:14-15 Cut Off Head and Tail

Head and Tail. Aponius: He who may have been at the head of the flock of Christ is now made the tail of another flock, as God declared

through Isaiah: "The prophet who teaches lies is the tail." Everyone among the people who is of right faith, even though he may hold a lower position or office, is beyond doubt at the head of the people by virtue of his right faith. But if he were to depart from the head, great though he may seem among the heretics, he becomes the tail by teaching lies. No longer a lamb who hears the voice of the Lord, he is now made like a wandering goat by following in the footsteps of the evil flock. Exposition of Song of Songs 2.23.[15]

Those Who Bless the People. Primasius: Remember what is written in Isaiah: "The elder and honored man is the head, and the prophet who teaches lies is the tail, and there will be some who delight my people while deceiving them, and those who are delighted will be cast headlong." Thus it is clear that some desire to master those domains which all the saints and teachers of the truth are zealous to avoid, namely, worldly glory and the deception of harmful preaching. The power in their tails, therefore, extends back into this life for five months, where the lie is able to marshal the wicked or temporarily to torture the spiritual.[16] Commentary on the Apocalypse 3.9.[17]

Priests and Prophets. Gregory the Great: Where the head and the tail are said through the prophet to be destroyed, it is clear that priests are designated by the head and prophets by the tail. The crown, therefore, is removed from the head when those who are seen to preside over the body of the church abandon the rewards of heavenly compensation. Once its leaders fall, normally, the army that follows them also succumbs. Hence, soon after the condemnation of the leaders, Job comments on the manifold afflictions of the church: "He destroyed me on every side, and I perish; and he has removed my hope like uprooting a tree."[18] For the church is destroyed on every side and perishes in the persons of its sick mem-

[11]Ezek 22:18. [12]ACW 11:128-29*. [13]Prov 3:12. [14]NPNF 2 7:252*. [15]CCL 19:53. [16]See Rev 9:5-10. [17]CCL 92:151. [18]Job 19:10.

bers when those who seem to be its strength are corrupted, that is, when the crown is removed from the head because its leaders have abandoned their pursuit of eternal rewards. It is in reference to the sick who have fallen that Job then adds, fittingly: "and he removed my hope like uprooting a tree." A tree is felled by a gust of wind. And what is more similar to a person who falls into unrighteousness as a result of being terrorized with threats than a tree that loses its straightness because of the wind? MORALS ON THE BOOK OF JOB 3.14.43-44.[19]

9:16-17 Those Who Lead

UNWORTHY SERVANTS. GREGORY OF NAZIANZUS: He [Paul] lived not to himself but to Christ and his preaching. He crucified the world to himself,[20] and being crucified to the world and the things which are seen, he thought all things little[21] and too small to be desired. [He thought this] even though from Jerusalem and round about to Illyricum[22] he had fully preached the gospel, even though he had been prematurely caught up to the third heaven, and had had a vision of Paradise, and had heard unspeakable words.[23] Such was Paul, and everyone of similar spirit with him. But we fear that in comparison with them, we may be foolish princes of Zoan, or

extortionists who exact the fruits of the ground or falsely bless the people. IN DEFENSE OF HIS FLIGHT, ORATION 2.56.[24]

9:18 A Cleansing Fire

CHRIST SANCTIFIED MARY'S WOMB. EPHREM THE SYRIAN: Mary said to him, "How can this be, since no man has known me?" He said to her, "The Holy Spirit will come, and the power of the Most High will overshadow you."[25] Why did he not mention the Father's name but instead the name of his Power and the name of the Holy Spirit? Because it was fitting that the Architect of the works [of creation] should come and raise up the house that had fallen and that the hovering Spirit should sanctify the buildings that were unclean. Thus, if the Progenitor entrusted the judgment that is to come to his [Son], it is clear that he accomplished the creation of humanity and its restoration through him as well. He was the live coal that had come to kindle the briars and thorns. He dwelt in the womb and cleansed it and sanctified the place of the birth pangs and the curses. COMMENTARY ON TATIAN'S DIATESSARON 25.[26]

---

[19]CCL 143A:724-25; LF 21:145-46. [20]Gal 6:14. [21]Phil 3:8. [22]Rom 15:19. [23]2 Cor 12:2-4. [24]NPNF 2 7:217. [25]Lk 1:34-35. [26]ECTD 53.

10:1-19 DESTRUCTION OF JUDAH'S ENEMIES

[1]Woe to those who decree iniquitous decrees,
   and the writers who keep writing
     oppression,
[2]to turn aside the needy from justice
   and to rob the poor of my people of their
     right,

that widows may be their spoil,
   and that they may make the fatherless
     their prey!
[3]What will you do on the day of punishment,
   in the storm which will come from afar?
To whom will you flee for help,

and where will you leave your wealth?
⁴Nothing remains but to crouch among the
  prisoners
    or fall among the slain.
For all this his anger is not turned away
  and his hand is stretched out still.

⁵Ah, Assyria, the rod of my anger,
  the staff of my fury!ᵗ
⁶Against a godless nation I send him,
  and against the people of my wrath I
    command him,
to take spoil and seize plunder,
  and to tread them down like the mire
    of the streets.
⁷But he does not so intend,
  and his mind does not so think;
but it is in his mind to destroy,
  and to cut off nations not a few;
⁸for he says:
"Are not my commanders all kings?
⁹Is not Calno like Carchemish?
  Is not Hamath like Arpad?
  Is not Samaria like Damascus?
¹⁰As my hand has reached to the kingdoms
    of the idols
  whose graven images were greater than
    those of Jerusalem and Samaria,
¹¹shall I not do to Jerusalem and her idols
  as I have done to Samaria and her
    images?"

¹²When the Lord has finished all his work
on Mount Zion and on Jerusalem he ᵘwill punish the arrogant boasting of the king of Assyria
and his haughty pride. ¹³For he says:
  "By the strength of my hand I have done it,
    and by my wisdom, for I have

understanding;
I have removed the boundaries of peoples,
  and have plundered their treasures;
  like a bull I have brought down those
    who sat on thrones.
¹⁴My hand has found like a nest
  the wealth of the peoples;
and as men gather eggs that have been
    forsaken
  so I have gathered all the earth;
and there was none that moved a wing,
  or opened the mouth, or chirped."

¹⁵Shall the axe vaunt itself over him who
    hews with it,
  or the saw magnify itself against him
    who wields it?
As if a rod should wield him who lifts it,
  or as if a staff should lift him who is not
    wood!
¹⁶Therefore the Lord, the LORD of hosts,
  will send wasting sickness among his
    stout warriors,
and under his glory a burning will be
    kindled,
  like the burning of fire.
¹⁷The light of Israel will become a fire,
  and his Holy One a flame;
and it will burn and devour
  his thorns and briers in one day.
¹⁸The glory of his forest and of his fruitful
    land
  the LORD will destroy, both soul and body,
  and it will be as when a sick man wastes
    away.
¹⁹The remnant of the trees of his forest will
    be so few
  that a child can write them down.

t Heb a staff it is in their hand my fury   u Heb I

Overview: God will one day judge every thought and action (Gregory of Nazianzus). The promises of God serve to sustain his people during times of suffering (Horsiesi). The enemy of God boasts in his wickedness (Eusebius). Those who are proud are the enemies of God (Jerome). God's enemies seek to deceive the godly by their boasting (Athanasius). Death was the cause of the Fall and is the fountain of all evils (John Cassian). God has love for all of humankind (Theodoret). The Gentiles were filled with the knowledge of the truth when they received the Spirit of God (Verecundus). God used Sennacherib as an instrument of his judgment (Aphrahat). The church is led by the power of God (Pachomius). The Holy Spirit is light and fire, since he illuminates and consumes (Ambrose).

10:3 On the Day of Visitation

The Day of Visitation. Gregory of Nazianzus: "What shall we do in the day of visitation?" One of the prophets terrifies me [with this question], whether that of the righteous sentence of God against us or that upon the mountains and hills, of which we have heard. Whatever and whenever it may be, he will reason with us and oppose us and set before us[1] those bitter accusers, which are our sins, contrasting our wrongdoings with our benefits, striking thought with thought, scrutinizing action with action and calling us to account for the image[2] that has been blurred and spoiled by wickedness. He will finally lead us away self-convicted and self-condemned, no longer able to say that we are being unjustly treated—a thought that is able even here sometimes to console in their condemnation those who are suffering. On His Father's Silence, Oration 16.8.[3]

Look to the Promises. Horsiesi: [Christ] said to Peter, the prince of the apostles, "Simon, [son] of John, do you love me more than these?"[4] He answered, "Lord, you know I love you." He said to him, "Feed my lambs." He asked him a

second time, "Simon [son] of John, do you love me?" He answered, "Yes, Lord, you know I love you." He said to him, "Feed my sheep." And he ordered him to feed his sheep a third time, and in Peter he enjoined this office on all of us, diligently to feed the sheep of the Lord, that on the day of his visitation we may, for our toil and watchfulness, receive what he promised us in the gospel, saying, Father, I wish that where I am, there also shall be my minister. Let us look to the promises and rewards; then in an attitude of faith we will more easily stand all our pains, walking as the Lord himself walked, who is the one promising the rewards. The Testament of Horsiesi 18.[5]

10:13 By the Strength of His Hand

Boasting in Strength. Eusebius of Caesarea: These are the words of God's antagonist, boasting in the strength of his wickedness, as he threatens to steal and obliterate the divisions of the nations delivered by the Most High to the angels. And loudly [he] cries that he will spoil the earth, and shake the whole human race, and change them from their former good order. Proof of the Gospel 4.9.[6]

Prince of the Proud. Jerome: All sins must be avoided, to be sure, because all sins are contrary to God, but they vary in degree. The proud, for example, are God's enemies. "God resists the proud but gives grace to the humble."[7] The devil is the prince of the proud. "Lest he be puffed up with pride," says holy Scripture, "and incur the condemnation passed on the devil,"[8] for everyone who glorifies himself in his heart is partner to the devil, who used to say, "By my own power I have done it, and by my wisdom, for I am shrewd. I have moved the boundaries of peoples." . . . All other failings deserve the mercy of the Lord because, in humility, they are submitted to the

---

[1]Mt 25:8. [2]Gen 1:26. [3]NPNF 2 7:250**. [4]Jn 21:15-17. [5]CS 47:182-83. [6]POG 1:178*. [7]Jas 4:6. [8]1 Tim 3:6.

tribunal of God; pride alone, because it honors itself beyond its power, resists God. The adulterer or the fornicator does not dare to raise his eyes to heaven; in defection of soul, he looks for God's mercy; yet this one whom conscience bows down and humbles to the ground, it also elevates to heaven. When pride and inordinate desire for glory raise up a person, they at the same time abase him, for by his sin they make him an enemy of God. HOMILIES ON THE PSALMS, ALTERNATE SERIES, PSALM 93.[9]

FEAR NOT THE ADVERSARY. ATHANASIUS: And by the prophet, "the enemy said, I will pursue and overtake,"[10] and again by another, "I will grasp the whole world in my hand as a nest, and take it up as eggs that have been left." Such, in a word, are their boasts and professions that they may deceive the godly. But not even then ought we, the faithful, to fear his appearance or give heed to his words. For he is a liar and speaks of truth never a word. And though speaking words so many and so great in his boldness, without doubt, like a dragon he was drawn with a hook by the Savior,[11] and as a beast of burden he received the halter round his nostrils, and as a runaway his nostrils were bound with a ring, and his lips bored with an armlet.[12] And he was bound by the Lord as a sparrow, that we should mock him. LIFE OF ST. ANTHONY 24.[13]

10:14 Found Like a Nest

A DEATH FROM PRIDE. JOHN CASSIAN: And so God, the Creator and Healer of all, knowing that pride is the cause and fountain head of evils, has been careful to heal opposites with opposites, that those things which were ruined by pride might be restored by humility. For the one says, "I will ascend into heaven,"[14] and the other, "My soul was brought low even to the ground."[15] . . . The one says, "As eggs are gathered together which are left, so have I gathered all the earth"; the other says, "I am like a pelican of the wilderness . . . and am become as a sparrow dwelling

alone on a roof."[16] . . . If we look at the reason for our original fall and the foundations of our salvation, and [if we] consider by whom and in what way the latter were laid and the former originated, we may learn, either through the fall of the devil, or through the example of Christ, how to avoid so terrible a death from pride. INSTITUTES 12.8.[17]

GOD'S LOVING CARE FOR ALL HUMANITY. THEODORET OF CYR: Behold, then, how the Maker of the universe has always shown a loving care for humanity, not merely for the race of the descendants of Abraham but for all the descendants of Adam; through one tribe he has led all tribes to a knowledge of himself. He used them for this purpose both when they were religious and when they were paying the penalty for their sins. For instance, Nebuchadnezzar, the arrogant tyrant, who raised up the golden image and called on all to adore it, said, "I will gather in my hand the whole earth as a nest, as eggs that lie abandoned will I gather it." ON DIVINE PROVIDENCE 10.54.[18]

THE WEALTH OF THE PEOPLES. VERECUNDUS: "My hand found the strength of the people like a nest. And like abandoned eggs are collected, so I gathered all the earth. No one moved a wing, or opened a mouth, or chirped." "You sent your Spirit and the sea covered them; they descended to the depths like lead in the mighty water."[19] When the Spirit of the Lord was sent, the Egyptians were immersed in the waters of the sea. Although we desire to see ourselves there in the word of the Lord, which is also fulfilled in us, we would do better to apply this passage to the Gentiles, who were filled with the knowledge of the truth when they received the Spirit of God. To this the prophet bore witness: "All the earth is filled with the knowledge of the Lord, like the

[9]FC 57:100-101*. [10]Ex 15:9. [11]Job 41:1. [12]Job 41:2. [13]NPNF 2 4:202. [14]Is 14:13. [15]Ps 44:25 (43:26 LXX). [16]Ps 101:6-7 LXX. [17]CSEL 17:210-11. [18]ACW 49:151-52*. [19]Ex 15:10.

waters covering the sea."[20]

"They descended to the depths like lead in the mighty water." The "depths" are to be understood as carnal living, which tosses them to and fro on waves of sin. It drowns their self-absorbed souls and sends them to the bottom. Gossip, jealousy, depravity, cruelty and envy are the waves of worldly vice. COMMENTARY ON THE CANTICLE OF EXODUS 1.10-11.[21]

10:15 Shall the Ax Exalt Itself?

THE AX IN THE HANDS OF HIM THAT CUTS. APHRAHAT: For you, Sennacherib, are the ax in the hands of him that cuts, and you are the saw in the hands of him that saws, and the rod in the hand of him that wields you for chastisement, and you are the staff for smiting. You are sent against the fickle people, and again you are ordained against the stubborn people, that you may carry away the captivity and take the spoil; and you have made them as the mire of the streets for all people and for all the Gentiles. And when you have done all these things, why are you exalted against him who holds you, and why do you boast against him who saws with you, and why have you reviled the holy city? DEMONSTRATION 5.4.[22]

THE IMPORTANCE OF GOOD WORKS. PACHO-

MIUS: Let us consider therefore those to whom God has granted power, to see if we may deserve to serve them and to cling to their doctrine, putting aside all pride and resisting with great courage the sin, which fearlessly operates in bodies; for death has been swallowed up by victory. On the other hand, how weak we are in this age, knowing that the church is to stand and to be led toward what is good. . . . You know that the ax does not boast without the man who uses it to cut . . . but we must fight to be able to have peace with those who keep the commandments of God. LETTER 4.4.[23]

10:17 The Light of Israel

A CONSUMING FIRE. AMBROSE: And Isaiah shows that the Holy Spirit is not only light but also fire, saying, "And the light of Israel shall be for a fire." So the prophets called him a burning fire, because in those three points we see more intensely the majesty of the Godhead; since to sanctify is of the Godhead, to illuminate is the property of fire and light, and the Godhead is customarily pointed out or seen in the appearance of fire: "For our God is a consuming fire," as Moses said.[24] ON THE HOLY SPIRIT 1.14.[25]

---

[20]Is 11:9. [21]CCL 93:10-11. [22]NPNF 2 13:353*. [23]CS 47:60. [24]Deut 4:24. [25]NPNF 2 10:112*.

10:20-34 RETURN OF THE REMNANT

[20]*In that day the remnant of Israel and the survivors of the house of Jacob will no more lean upon him that smote them, but will lean upon the LORD, the Holy One of Israel, in truth.* [21]*A remnant will return, the remnant of Jacob, to the mighty God.* [22]*For though your people Israel be as the sand of the sea, only a remnant of them will return. Destruction is decreed, overflowing with right-*

eousness. [23]For the Lord, the LORD of hosts, will make a full end, as decreed, in the midst of all the earth.*

[24]Therefore thus says the Lord, the LORD of hosts: "O my people, who dwell in Zion, be not afraid of the Assyrians when they smite with the rod and lift up their staff against you as the Egyptians did. [25]For in a very little while my indignation will come to an end, and my anger will be directed to their destruction. [26]And the LORD of hosts will wield against them a scourge, as when he smote Midian at the rock of Oreb; and his rod will be over the sea, and he will lift it as he did in Egypt. [27]And in that day his burden will depart from your shoulder, and his yoke will be destroyed from your neck."[†]

> He has gone up from Rimmon,[v]
>   [28]he has come to Aiath;
> he has passed through Migron,
>   at Michmash he stores his baggage;
> [29]they have crossed over the pass,
>   at Geba they lodge for the night;
> Ramah trembles,
>   Gibeah of Saul has fled.
> [30]Cry aloud, O daughter of Gallim!
>   Hearken, O Laishah!
>   Answer her, O Anathoth!
> [31]Madmenah is in flight,
>   the inhabitants of Gebim flee for safety.
> [32]This very day he will halt at Nob,
>   he will shake his fist
>   at the mount of the daughter of Zion,
>   the hill of Jerusalem.

> [33]Behold, the Lord, the LORD of hosts
>   will lop the boughs with terrifying
>   power;
> the great in height will be hewn down,
>   and the lofty will be brought low.
> [34]He will cut down the thickets of the
>   forest with an axe,
>   and Lebanon with its majestic trees[w] will
>   fall.

v Cn: Heb *and his yoke from your neck, and a yoke will be destroyed because of fatness*   w Cn Compare Gk Vg: Heb *with a majestic one*   *LXX *He will finish the work (or word [logon]) and cut it short in righteousness: because the LORD will make a short work (or word) in all the world.*   †Vg *from before the oil*

Overview: The remnant that was promised salvation included the apostles and thousands of other Jews saved after the resurrection of Christ (Augustine). The remnant is those who have been freed by grace (Ambrose). Not all people will be saved, but only the few; and they will be saved by faith (Chrysostom). Isaiah prophesies that a remnant of the Jews will believe in Christ and be saved (Augustine, Gregory the Great). The Lord's Prayer is an example of the simplicity of faith (Cyprian). The Golden Rule was a summary of the law (Tertullian). God does not take pleasure in large numbers but in faithfulness (Gregory of Nazianzus). The messenger of God should preach the simple message of the apostles (Rufinus). Jesus' two commandments are a summary of all that Christians need to know (Augustine). The followers of Christ were anointed by the Spirit, breaking the tyranny of evil (Gregory the Great). The lofty are the rich, who have been elevated to a higher position because of their wealth (Tertullian).

Isaiah spoke of the initial judgment against the people's sins, but Christ later would cut the roots as well (Ephrem). Isaiah prophesied that Jerusalem, along with its important inhabitants, would fall. Jerusalem's destruction was connected with the birth of Christ (Eusebius). Lebanon refers to the temple of the Jews (Jerome).

10:21-22 A Remnant Will Return

A Remnant Has Been Saved. Augustine: May the remnant be saved, as Isaiah said, "and the remnant has" clearly "been saved." For out of them were the twelve apostles, out of them more than five hundred brothers, to whom the Lord showed himself after his resurrection.[1] Out of their number were so many thousands baptized,[2] who laid the price of their possessions at the apostles' feet. Thus then was fulfilled the prayer here made to God: "For your servant David's sake, turn not away the presence of your anointed."[3] Explanations of the Psalms 132 (131).10.[4]

Grace Is Free. Ambrose: This, then, is what the patriarch Isaac says, "You shall serve your brother. But the time will be when you shall shake off and loose his yoke from your neck."[5] He means that there will be two peoples, one the son of the slave girl, the other of the free woman[6]—for the letter is a slave, whereas grace is free.[7] The people that is attentive to the letter is going to be a slave as long as it needs to follow the expounder of learning in the spirit. Then that will also come to pass what the apostle says, "that the remnant may be saved by reason of the election made by grace."[8] "You shall serve your brother," but then you will perceive your advancement in servitude only when you begin to obey your brother voluntarily and not under compulsion. Jacob and the Happy Life 3.13.[9]

The Way of Faith. Chrysostom: Do you also see that he does not say that all will be saved but only those who are worthy will be saved? . . . He does not speak of the "sands of the sea" without cause, but he does so to remind them of the ancient promise they had made themselves unworthy of.[10] Why are you bothered, as though the promise has not been kept? The prophets demonstrate that not everyone will be saved. . . . It not only demonstrates that only a few will be saved, and not everyone, but also says how they will be saved. How are they to be saved, and by what manner will God consider them to be worthy? . . . Faith is such that it holds salvation in a few short words. Homilies on Romans 16.9.[11]

Jews Who Have Believed. Augustine: The remnant means the Jews who have believed in Christ. Many of them, we remember, did believe in the days of the apostles, and even today there are some converts, although very few. City of God 17.5.[12]

---

[1] 1 Cor 15:6. [2] Acts 2:41. [3] Ps 132:10 (131:10 LXX). [4] NPNF 1 8:618. [5] Gen 27:40. [6] See Gal 4:22-31. [7] See 2 Cor 3:6. [8] Rom 9:27. [9] FC 65:154. [10] See Gen 15:5. The stress is on Abraham's faith in God. [11] PG 60:562. [12] FC 24:38-39.

FORETOLD IN THE SCRIPTURES. AUGUSTINE: And it is their own Scriptures that bear witness that it is not we who are the inventors of the prophecies touching Christ. That is why many of them, who pondered these prophecies before his passion and more especially after his resurrection, have come to believe in him, as was foretold: "For if your people, O Israel, shall be as the sand of the sea, a remnant of them shall be converted." CITY OF GOD 18.46.[13]

THE HOLY VINEYARD. AUGUSTINE: Through this Son of man, Christ Jesus, and from his remnant, that is, the apostles and the many others who from among the Israelites have believed in Christ as God, and with the increasing plenitude of the Gentiles, the holy vineyard[14] is being completed. IN ANSWER TO THE JEWS 6.[15]

A REMNANT WILL BE SAVED. GREGORY THE GREAT: But grace from above sometimes looks upon these mighty men and afflicts them by the very employments caused by their abundant goods and intersperses with their prosperity adverse but profitable tribulation. [This is done] in order that, being sorrowful, they may turn to their heart and learn how vainly they are engaged in perishable pursuits. . . . This can be especially understood also of the Jews. . . . Because they are to be admitted to the faith at the end of the world . . . it is said by Isaiah, "if the number of the children of Israel shall be as the sand of the sea, a remnant shall be saved." For the light returns to them when they themselves return to confess the power of our Redeemer. MORALS ON THE BOOK OF JOB 5.27.25-26.[16]

10:23 A Full End

A SHORT WORD. CYPRIAN: What wonder, most beloved brothers, if such [the Lord's Prayer] is the prayer that God has taught, who by his instruction has abbreviated our every prayer in a saving word? This had already been foretold by Isaiah the prophet, when filled with the Holy Spirit, he spoke of the majesty and loving kindness of God. He said, "He will finish the word and cut it short in righteousness, because the Lord will make a short word in all the world." For when the Word of God, our Lord Jesus Christ, came to all, and gathering together the learned and unlearned alike, he gave forth the precepts of salvation to every sex and age, he made a concise compendium of his precepts. [This was] so that the memory of the learners might not be burdened in heavenly discipline but might learn quickly what was necessary to a simple faith. THE LORD'S PRAYER 28.[17]

SUMMARY OF THE DECALOGUE. TERTULLIAN: When God made statements such as "You shall not murder; you shall not commit adultery; you shall not steal; you shall not bear false witness,"[18] he was teaching me to refrain from doing to others what I would be unwilling to do to myself. Therefore the precept offered in the Gospel belongs only to the one who first drew it up in ancient times, arranging it according to his own teaching in a formula that could easily be understood. This was predicted in another passage in which the Lord, that is, Christ, was "to make a concise word on the earth."[19] AGAINST MARCION 4.16.[20]

NO PLEASURE IN NUMBERS. GREGORY OF NAZIANZUS: Three gathered together in the name of the Lord[21] count for more with God than tens of thousands of those who deny the Godhead. Would you prefer the whole of the Canaanites to Abraham alone?[22] or the men of Sodom to Lot?[23] or the Midianites to Moses,[24] when each of these was a pilgrim and a stranger? How do the three hundred men with Gideon, who bravely lapped,[25] compare with the thousands who were put to flight? Or the servants of Abraham, who

---

[13]FC 24:164*. [14]See Is 5:1. [15]FC 27:400. [16]LF 23:218. [17]FC 36:151**. [18]Ex 20:13-16. [19]Tertullian's point is that the Golden Rule is a concise summary of the Ten Commandments. [20]ANF 3:372*. [21]Mt 18:20. [22]Gen 12:6; 13:12. [23]Gen 19:1. [24]Ex 2:15. [25]Judg 7:5.

scarcely exceeded them in number, with the many kings and the army of tens of thousands whom, few as they were, they overtook and defeated?[26] Or how do you understand the passage that though the number of the children of Israel be as the sand of the sea, a remnant shall be saved?[27] And again, I have left me seven thousand men, who have not bowed the knee to Baal?[28] . . . God has not taken pleasure in numbers. THE LAST FAREWELL, ORATION 42.7.[29]

THE SIMPLE WORD. RUFINUS OF AQUILEIA: I find, indeed, that some eminent writers have published treatises on these matters piously and briefly written. Moreover, I know that the heretic Photinus has written on the same, with the object not of explaining the meaning of the text to his readers but of wresting things simply and truthfully said in support of his own dogma.[30] Yet the Holy Spirit has taken care that in these words nothing should be set down which is ambiguous or obscure or inconsistent with other truths; for therein is that prophecy verified, "Finishing and cutting short the word in equity: because a short word will the Lord make upon the earth."[31] It shall be our endeavor, then, first to restore and emphasize the words of the apostles in their native simplicity. COMMENTARY ON THE APOSTLES' CREED I.[32]

A SUMMARY WORD. AUGUSTINE: One might perhaps suppose that in regard to the knowledge of righteousness we have all we need; inasmuch as our Lord, summing and shortening his word upon the earth, has said that upon two commandments hang all the law and the prophets, and he put those commandments in the plainest words: "You shall love the Lord your God with all your heart and with all your soul and with all your mind,"[33] and "You shall love your neighbor as yourself."[34] ON THE SPIRIT AND THE LETTER 36.[35]

10:27 His Yoke Destroyed

A HOLY ANOINTING. GREGORY THE GREAT: It

was said by Moses, "They drew honey from the rock, and oil from the hardest rock."[36] . . . But because according to Paul, "the rock was Christ,"[37] they drew honey from the rock who saw the deeds and miracles of our Redeemer; and they drew oil from the hard rock because they were found worthy to be anointed with the outpouring of the Holy Spirit after his resurrection. . . . The gift of the holy anointing flowed out of him through the breathing forth of the Spirit. Of this oil the prophet said, "The yoke will be destroyed from before the oil." FORTY GOSPEL HOMILIES 26.[38]

THE OIL OF THE SPIRIT. GREGORY THE GREAT: It is possible that the Holy Spirit himself was denoted by the name of oil, concerning which it is said through the prophet: "and the yoke will rot at the presence of the oil." The yoke rotted at the presence of oil because when we are anointed with the grace of the Holy Spirit, we are liberated from the bondage of our slavery. Then, with the prideful tyranny of the evil spirit broken, the yoke with which the necks of our freedom was oppressed is destroyed. Again, it is written about the oil: "My beloved had a vineyard on a hill called the son of oil." The son of oil represents the faithful people, whose faith in God is generated by the interior anointing of the Holy Spirit.

Although it has been burdened in the past with many tribulations, therefore, let the holy church call to mind the gifts of the Spirit and the marvelous prophecies which it now possesses, and let it lament its silence, saying, "The rock poured out for me streams with oil."[39] MORALS ON THE BOOK OF JOB 4.19.24.[40]

10:33 The Lofty Brought Low

THE RICH HUMBLED. TERTULLIAN: And who

---

[26]Gen 14:14. [27]Rom 9:27. [28]1 Kings 19:18; Rom 11:4. [29]NPNF 2 7:388. [30]Photinus was a fourth-century heretic in Galatia who held Christ to be a mere human being. [31]Rom 9:28. [32]NPNF 2 3:542. [33]Mt 22:37. [34]Mt 22:39. [35]LCC 8:247. [36]Deut 32:13. [37]1 Cor 10:4. [38]CS 123:203. [39]Job 29:6. [40]LF 21:415-16**.

are these but the rich? Because they have indeed received their consolation, glory and honor, and a lofty position from their wealth. AGAINST MARCION 4.15.[41]

10:34 Thickets Cut with an Ax

BRANCHES, NOT THE ROOTS. EPHREM THE SYRIAN: [God spoke] of the branches (thickets), not the root. When the measure of the people's sins was complete, John came and took up the roots of their trees. "For the ax is laid to the roots of the trees,"[42] [the roots] which Isaiah had left [untouched]. When will this be, if not at the rising forth of the true One, who was designated by the [image of] the staff and the shoot, and upon whom rests the Spirit, who is referred to as being sevenfold.[43] COMMENTARY ON TATIAN'S DIATESSARON 3.15.[44]

LEBANON IS JERUSALEM. EUSEBIUS OF CAESAREA: In this instance Lebanon means Jerusalem . . . which the Word warns will fall with all of the men of greatness and glory. PROOF OF THE GOSPEL 2.3.[45]

THE DESTRUCTION OF LEBANON. EUSEBIUS OF CASESAREA: In this instance the birth of Christ from the seed of Jesse and David is joined with the destruction of Lebanon and the call of the Gentiles. PROOF OF THE GOSPEL 8.4.[46]

LEBANON WILL FALL. JEROME: What Scripture once said cryptically, however, it now expresses more clearly: "for the glorious trees are ruined."[47] I want to know what is meant by the cedars of Lebanon that burned, the firs that wailed and the pines that fell. "The glorious trees," it says, "are ruined." "Wail, oaks of Bashan,"[48] that is, of confusion and shame, for the thickest forest, which in Hebrew is called besor and is translated by the Septuagint as "densely wooded" [nemorosus], has been felled. In other words, wail because the temple, which had grown to unassailable strength, having been constructed by many different kings

and rulers and later by Herod, was demolished by the invading Romans.

Certain persons not familiar with this locale believe that Lebanon and the firs, pines and oaks, as well as Bashan and the dense or fortified forests, signify the competing powers of which Ezekiel had spoken under the names of Assyria and Pharaoh. "Behold, Assyria is a cedar in Lebanon, with strong branches and dense foliage, of great height, with its top reaching to the clouds; the waters nourished it and the abyss exalted it," etc.[49] They think that Assyria and the Pharaoh represent either competing powers or the proud or rulers, about which we read also in the psalms. "The voice of the Lord breaks the cedars, the Lord breaks the cedars of Lebanon,"[50] and in another place, "For the Lord of hosts has a day against all that is proud and lofty, against all that is lifted up and high," and shortly further "against all the cedars of Lebanon, lofty and lifted up."[51] They claim that it was to this, the nation of Lebanon, that it was prophesied: "Lebanon with its majestic trees will fall."

We, however, hold to the first interpretation, primarily because it corresponds with what follows: "The voice of the shepherds wails because their glory is ruined; the voice of the lions roars because the pride of Jordan is ruined."[52] According to the Septuagint's translation, "The voice of the shepherds mourns because their glory has been made wretched; the voice of the lions roars because Jordan's groaning is despondent." The whole of the chapter is contained in these short verses. What the text once called cedars, firs, pines and the oaks of Bashan, what it called trees, as in "for the glorious trees are ruined," it now, through the use of another metaphor, calls shepherds, that is, rulers and teachers. These, the leaders of the people, ought to weep and

---

[41]ANF 3:369; see also Clement of Rome's commentary on Is 13:11. [42]Mt 3:10; Lk 3:9. [43]Is 11:1-2. [44]ECTD 80. [45]POG 2:145*. [46]POG 2:145*. [47]Zech 11:2. [48]Zech 11:2. [49]Ezek 31:3-4. [50]Ps 29:5 (28:5 LXX). [51]Is 2:12-13. [52]Zech 11:3.

grieve because their glory and majesty and beauty are ruined and destroyed, clearly referring to the temple in which they gloried. Commentary on Zechariah 3.11.1-3.[53]

[53]CCL 76A:848-50.

11:1-9 THE MESSIANIC KING

[1]There shall come forth a shoot* from the
    stump† of Jesse,
and a branch‡ shall grow out of his roots.
[2]And the Spirit of the LORD shall rest upon
    him,
        the spirit of wisdom and understanding,
        the spirit of counsel and might,
        the spirit of knowledge§ and the fear of
        the LORD#
[3]And his delight shall be in the fear of the
    LORD.

He shall not judge by what his eyes see,
    or decide by what his ears hear;
[4]but with righteousness he shall judge the
    poor,
        and decide with equity for the meek of
        the earth;
and he shall smite the earth with the rod of
    his mouth,
        and with the breath of his lips he shall
        slay the wicked.

[5]Righteousness shall be the girdle of his
    waist,
        and faithfulness the girdle of his loins.

[6]The wolf shall dwell** with the lamb,
    and the leopard shall lie down with the
    kid,
and the calf and the lion and the fatling
    together,††
    and a little child shall lead them.
[7]The cow and the bear shall feed;
    their young shall lie down together;
    and the lion shall eat straw like the ox.
[8]The sucking child shall play over the hole
    of the asp,
        and the weaned child shall put his hand
        on the adder's den.
[9]They shall not hurt or destroy
    in all my holy mountain;
for the earth shall be full of the knowledge of
    the LORD
        as the waters cover the sea.

*LXX rod or scepter   †LXX root   ‡LXX flower   §LXX adds and piety   #LXX adds shall fill him   **LXX feed   ††LXX adds shall feed together

OVERVIEW: Christ would rise from Mary as a flower rises from a stem (JEROME). By the fruit of the root he will graft us onto his tree (EPHREM).

The call of the Gentiles came at the predicted birth of Christ (EUSEBIUS). Christians should not concern themselves with crowns of flowers, because theirs is the Flower of Jesse (Tertullian). Christ derives his human existence from Jesse and David through Mary the virgin (Tertullian, Novatian, Aphrahat, Gregory of Elvira, Ephrem, Ambrose, Chromatius, Bede). At his second coming Christ will possesses one staff from the Gentiles and another staff from the descendants of Jesse (Aphrahat). Jesus' only human lineage was from David, the son of Jesse, through the Virgin (Ephrem). Christ had to be born in Nazareth because he was the son of a branch, or scepter (Ephrem, Bede). Christ is the flower who pours out a fragrance in the world (Ambrose). From the root of Jesse has come pardon to the captives (Jerome). The gospel found in the New Testament was hidden in the root of the Old Testament (Augustine). Christ's birth was without the involvement of any seed (Quodvultdeus).

Prophetic predictions were no longer needed after Christ because the gifts of the Spirit came to fruition in him (Justin Martyr). After the resurrection, the Spirit was continually with the Lord's followers (Novatian). The spirit of fear leads to the spirit of wisdom (Ambrose, Augustine). The Holy Spirit is the river that waters the lands (Ambrose). The number seven denotes the sevenfold work of the one Spirit of God (Augustine, Cassiodorus, Orosius). The seven lamps are the seven gifts of the Holy Spirit distributed to believers (Gregory the Great, Bede). The Holy Spirit filled Jesus (Faustus of Riez).

As Christ is the angel of great counsel, so too is the Holy Spirit the spirit of counsel (Ambrose). The sevenfold operation of the Holy Spirit is similar to Jesus' beatitudes in the Sermon on the Mount. Faith comes from mercy, not by merit (Augustine). The fullness of the spirit, not known even by the saints (Bede), permanently possesses the soul whom it has seized (John Cassian). The Spirit is one, but his activities or "spirits" (Gregory of Nazianzus) are diverse (Cyril of Jerusalem). Christ is the fountainhead of the Spirit (Novatian). Christ judges the rich and poor equally (Cyril of Jerusalem,

Bede). The Spirit and the two-edged sword proceed from Christ's mouth (Fulgentius, Victorinus).

Christians are called to gird up their minds (Athanasius). The belt is spiritual, not physical (Chrysostom). Indeed, it represents the word of God (Eusebius). Different types of people become one in the church (Jerome). The wolf and the lamb represent present history and the future after the resurrection (Irenaeus). The gospel transforms even savage people into gentle followers of Christ (Eusebius). The lion learns to be docile from the ox and lamb (Jerome, Chrysostom). Jews and Gentiles were joined together by Christ in one covenant (Jerome). The church will be diverse, comprising the barbarian and the learned (Chrysostom, Gregory the Great). Kings, peasants and the poor all gather around the one table of Christ (Quodvultdeus).

God will recreate the world in the innocent condition it was in before the Fall (Gregory of Elvira). In the church, those who have had their sins cleansed are compared with the innocent (Ambrose). The enemy of the Christian is a carnal life represented by straw (Gregory the Great). Even little children can overcome the enemy by the power of God (Gregory the Great, Tertullian). The incarnation was Christ putting his hand into the snake's den (Ambrose). The gospel has spread throughout the whole world (Athanasius, Chrysostom). Scripture is the sea carrying believers to their eternal homeland (Gregory the Great).

11:1 A Shoot from Jesse

Mary Is from the Root of Jesse. Jerome: Until the beginning of the vision, or the burden of Babylon, which Isaiah the son of Amos saw, his entire prophecy was about Christ, a prophecy that we want to explain piecemeal lest the ideas and discussions thereof together confuse the reader's memory. The Jews interpreted the branch and the flower from the root of Jesse to be the Lord himself because the power of his governance is demonstrated in the branch and his beauty in the flower. But we understand the branch from the root of Jesse to be the holy Virgin Mary, who had no shoot connatural to herself. About her we read above: "Behold, a virgin will conceive and bear a son."[1] And the flower is the Lord our Savior, who said in the Song of Songs, "I am the flower of the field and the lily of the valleys."[2] In place of "root," which only the Septuagint translated, the Hebrew text has *geza,* which Aquila and Symmachus and Theodotus interpret as *kormon,* that is, "stem." And they translated "flower," which the Hebrew text calls *nēṣer,* as "bud" to show that after a long time in Babylonian captivity, no longer possessing any glory from the sprout of the old kingdom of David, Christ would rise from Mary as though from her stem. The educated of the Hebrews believe that what all the ecclesiastics sought in the Gospel of Matthew but could not find, where it was written "Because he will be called a Nazarene,"[3] was taken from this place. But it should be noted that *nēṣer* was written here with the [Hebrew] letter *ṣade* [צ], the peculiar sound of which—somewhere between *z* and *s*—the Latin language does not express. COMMENTARY ON ISAIAH 4.11.1-3.[4]

GRAFTING ONTO HIS TREE. EPHREM THE SYRIAN: By the fruit of the root he will graft us onto his tree. HYMNS ON THE NATIVITY 3.17.[5]

THE CALL OF THE GENTILES. EUSEBIUS OF CAESAREA: This shows in an obvious way that the birth of Christ would be from the root of Jesse, who was the father of David. This points toward the birth which the Gentiles would follow, having been prophetically announced by way of signs. PROOF OF THE GOSPEL 2.3.[6]

SEED OF JESSE. EUSEBIUS OF CAESAREA: It is prophesied that one will come forth of the seed of Jesse, that is to say, of David, many years after the death of both David and Solomon. PROOF OF THE GOSPEL 7.3.[7]

A FLOWER FOR THE SPIRIT'S GRACE. TERTULLIAN: In him dwelt the fullness of the Spirit; therefore I acknowledge him to be "the rod of the stem of Jesse." His blooming flower shall be my Christ, upon whom has rested, according to Isaiah, "the spirit of wisdom and understanding, the spirit of counsel and might, the spirit of knowledge and piety, and of the fear of the Lord." Now to no man, except Christ, would this diversity of spiritual proofs suitably apply. He is indeed like a flower for the Spirit's grace, reckoned indeed of the stem of Jesse but thence to derive his descent through Mary. AGAINST MARCION 3.17.[8]

A VIRGIN SHALL CONCEIVE. NOVATIAN: The same rule of truth[9] teaches us to believe, after the Father, also on the Son of God, Christ Jesus, the Lord our God, but the Son of God—of that God who is both one and alone, namely, the Founder of all things, as already has been expressed above. For this Jesus Christ, I will once more say, the Son of this God, we read of as having been promised in the Old Testament and we observe to be manifested in the New, fulfilling the shadows and figures of the Old Testament types, being the embodiment of truth. For as well the ancient prophecies as the Gospels testify him to be the son of Abraham and the son of David. Genesis itself anticipates him when it says, "To you will I give it, and to your seed."[10] He is spoken of when Scripture shows how a man wrestled with Jacob; he too, when it says, "There shall not fail a prince from Judah, nor a leader from between his thighs, until he shall come to whom it has been promised; and he shall be the expectation of the nations."[11] He is spoken of by Moses when he says, "Provide another whom you may send."[12] He is again spoken of by the same, when he [Moses] testifies, saying, "A prophet will God

---

[1]Is 7:14. [2]Song 2:1. [3]Mt 2:23. [4]CCL 73:147. [5]ESH 87. [6]POG 1:89*. [7]POG 2:90. [8]ANF 3:335. [9]A summary of Christian belief. [10]Gen 17:8. [11]Gen 49:10. [12]Ex 4:13.

raise up to you from your brothers; listen to him as if to me."[13] [Moses] bears witness of him, finally, when he says, "You shall see your life hanging in doubt night and day, and you shall not believe him."[14] Isaiah also refers to him: "There shall go forth a rod from the root of Jesse, and a flower shall grow up from his root." The same also when he says, "Behold, a virgin shall conceive and bear a son."[15] ON THE TRINITY 9.[16]

TWO CAMPS. APHRAHAT: Jacob also prayed when he returned back from Laban, and he was rescued from the hands of his brother, Esau. He prayed as follows, confessing and saying, "With my staff have I crossed this river Jordan, and now I have become two camps."[17] Wondrous symbol of our Savior! When our Lord first came, the staff left the stem of Jesse, just like Jacob's staff; and when he returns from his Father's house at his second coming, he goes back to him with two camps, one from the people [Israel], the other from the peoples [nations]—just like Jacob who returned to his father Isaac with two camps. DEMONSTRATION 4.6.[18]

FROM HIS ROOTS. GREGORY OF ELVIRA: Just as when a lion is born from a lion, the nature is not changed but is shown to have a common source, so also one who is born from God cannot be anything other than God. But he calls him a lion's cub for the purpose of signifying the Son. Indeed, he adds "from a sprout, my son, you have gone up,"[19] because he wants to show us that Christ came from the sprout of Judah, as it was also said through the prophet Isaiah: "there will come forth a rod [*virga*] out of the root of Jesse, and a flower will go up from his root." This Jesse was the father of David, from whose root, that is, source, the Virgin Mary [*maria virgo*] was born. That Isaiah refers to a "rod" [*virga*] and to a "flower" from the rod suggests that the flower which is Christ would be born from a virgin [*virgine*]. ORIGEN'S TRACTATE ON THE BOOKS OF HOLY SCRIPTURE 6.35-36.[20]

NOT FROM JOSEPH. EPHREM THE SYRIAN: He is the son of Mary, however, and not the son of Joseph. He did not appear in the body from any other lineage, except from David. COMMENTARY ON TATIAN'S DIATESSARON 26.[21]

LILY OF THE VALLEY. AMBROSE: The root of Jesse the patriarch is the family of the Jews, Mary is the rod, Christ the flower of Mary, who, about to spread the good odor of faith throughout the whole world, budded forth from a virgin womb, as he himself said: "I am the flower of the plain, a lily of the valley."[22] ON THE HOLY SPIRIT 2.5.[23]

A FLOWER WILL ARISE. AMBROSE: Scripture also expresses the Son's incarnation beautifully: "from a bud you have gone up,"[24] for like a plant of the earth he was to be conceived in the womb of a virgin. And like a fragrant flower sent forth from the maternal bosom in the splendor of the dawn, he was to go up for the redemption of the whole world, as Isaiah says: "There will come forth a rod out of the root of Jesse, and a flower will blossom from his root." The root is the family of the Jews, the rod is Mary, and the flower is her Christ. It is right, therefore, that the rod which is of royal lineage from the house of David, whose flower is Christ, who vanquished the foul odor of worldly filth, poured forth the fragrance of eternal life. ON THE PATRIARCHS 4.19-20.[25]

THE FLOWER OF MARY. AMBROSE: Also in Isaiah is it written: "There will come forth a rod out of the root of Jesse, and a flower will go up from his root." The root is the family of the Jews, the rod is Mary, and the flower is her Christ. When he blossoms in our land, makes fragrant the field of the soul, and flourishes in his church, we can no longer fear the cold or rain, but only anticipate

---

[13]Deut 18:15. [14]Deut 28:66. [15]Is 7:14. [16]ANF 5:618**. [17]Gen 32:10. [18]CS 101:10. [19]Gen 49:9. [20]CCL 64:50. [21]ECTD 54. [22]Song 2:1 LXX. [23]NPNF 2 10:119. [24]See Gen 49:9; whereas Jerome's translation reads *a praeda fili mi ascendisti*, Ambrose's text evidently has *ex germine mihi ascendisti*. [25]CSEL 32 2:135.

the day of judgment. APOLOGY ON DAVID 8.43.[26]

A VIRGIN BRANCH. CHROMATIUS OF AQUILEIA: Elsewhere, the Holy Spirit also speaks of the Virgin about to give birth when he says, "There will come forth a rod out of the root of Jesse, and a flower will arise from his root." The rod from the root of Jesse signifies the Virgin Mary, who found her origins in the stem of Jesse through David. For, as the Evangelist or apostle reveals, out of the tribe of David came the Virgin Mary, from whom the flower of human flesh arose in Christ.[27] This is the rod which, having been placed in the ark of testimony to be a sign for everlasting memory, has now by a new and wonderful mystery, without moisture from the earth, brought forth the fruit of the almond.[28] It is by this miracle that Aaron's priesthood was confirmed.[29] TRACTATE ON MATTHEW 2.5.[30]

PARDON FOR THE CAPTIVES. JEROME: The land that before brought forth thorns, hears in Isaiah the blessing: "A shoot shall sprout from the stump of Jesse, and from his roots a bud shall blossom." "You have turned away the captivity of Jacob."[31] The Lord has come, therefore, to proclaim pardon to captives. There is a parallel to this in another passage of Scripture: "He led captivity captive,"[32] that is, we, who in former times had been captured by the devil to perdition, now are led away by the Savior to salvation. HOMILIES ON THE PSALMS, ALTERNATE SERIES, PSALM 84.[33]

CHRIST HIDDEN IN THE ROOT. AUGUSTINE: David was the king of Israel and the son of Jesse at a certain time in the Old Testament, when the New Testament was still hidden there in the Old, like a fruit in its root. For if you seek the fruit in its root, you will not find it. But neither would you find the fruit in the branch, unless it had first come from the root.

At that time, then, the first people had come from the seed of Abraham carnally. The second people, those who belong to the New Testament, also belong to the seed of Abraham, but spiritually. Those first people who were still carnal, therefore, among whom very few prophets understood both what was to be desired from God and when to announce it publicly, foretold this future time and the advent of our Lord Jesus Christ.

Insofar as Christ himself was born according to the flesh, he was hidden in the root, in the seed of the patriarchs, and was to be revealed at a certain time, like fruit appearing on the branch, as it is written: "A rod will bloom from the root of Jesse." The same is true of the New Testament, which was hidden in Christ throughout those earlier times and was known only to the prophets and to a very small group of godly persons, not as the manifestation of present realities but as a revelation of future events. For what does it mean, brothers, if I can remind you of one specific event, that Abraham, sending his faithful servant to betroth a wife to his only son, makes him swear to him and in the oath says to him, "Put your hand under my thigh and swear"?[34] What was in the thigh of Abraham upon which the man put his hand and swore? What was there, except what was then promised to him: "in your seed, all the peoples will be blessed"?[35] The thigh signifies the flesh. From the flesh of Abraham, through Isaac and Jacob and, without naming everyone, through Mary, came our Lord Jesus Christ. EXPLANATIONS OF THE PSALMS 72.1.[36]

A BRANCH WILL BEAR FRUIT. QUODVULTDEUS: We believe, therefore, in the immortal and invisible God, not in him whom the infidels have fashioned to be God, who is both an adulterer and a thunderer, but in the true God, Creator and Ruler of all the world.

We also hold to Jesus Christ his Son, formerly promised through the prophets, and we know

---

[26]CSEL 32 2:388. [27]See Mt 1:1-17; Lk 3:23-38. [28]See Ezek 37:19-20. [29]Num 17:1-10; Heb 9:4. [30]CCL 9A:205. [31]Ps 85:1 LXX. [32]Eph 4:8. [33]FC 57:50-51*. [34]Gen 24:2. [35]Gen 22:18. [36]CCL 39:986-87.

that the promise has been fulfilled. Yet, because we were not present when it was fulfilled, we are also commanded to believe it. The Jews were present then, however, from whose race the Savior himself chose apostles through whom the faith has reached us. As a member of the very race in which and from which he deigned to be born, the prophet Isaiah predicted a long time ago: "Behold, a virgin will conceive in the womb and will bear a son, and you will call his name Emmanuel, which means 'God with us.' ";[37] And elsewhere [we read]: "There will come forth a rod out of the root of Jesse, and a flower will go up from his root." The branch signifies the Virgin Mary, and the flower of the rod represents the Son of the Virgin, the Lord Jesus Christ. Before these things took place, the Jews read about it and did not understand. . . . Christ was born from a virgin like a flower from a branch, without the involvement of any seed. He was born a small infant and a great king. ON THE CREED 2.3.14-2.4.6.[38]

CONCEPTION IN NAZARETH. BEDE: The prophet Isaiah bears witness that our Redeemer had to be conceived in Nazareth when he says, "A *nazareus* will ascend from his root." The term *nazareus* has the meaning of "flower" or "clean."[39] The Son of God made incarnate for us can properly be named by this term, both because he adopted the nature of a human being clean from all vices and because in him the font and origin of spiritual fruits came forth for all believers, since to them he both pointed out examples and granted the fruits of living properly and blessedly. HOMILIES ON THE GOSPELS 1.6.[40]

FROM THE STOCK OF JESSE. BEDE: Now [Mary] saw that she herself, who had arisen from the stock of Jesse, had conceived God's Son of the Holy Spirit. HOMILIES ON THE GOSPELS 1.7.[41]

HISTORY AND ALLEGORY. BEDE: For it is history when something is reported as having been done or said in plain discourse according to the letter; for example, the people of Israel, after they had been delivered from Egypt, are said to have made a tabernacle for the Lord in the wilderness. It is allegory when the presence of Christ and the sacraments of the church are designated by mystical words or things; by words, certainly, as when Isaiah says, "A shoot [*virga*] shall come forth from the root of Jesse, and a flower shall rise up from his root," which is to say openly, "The Virgin Mary will be born from the stock of David, and Christ will proceed from his lineage"; and by things, as when the people delivered from Egyptian slavery through the blood of the lamb signifies the church freed from the devil's domination by the passion of Christ. ON THE TABERNACLE 1.6.[42]

THE ROOT AND THE SPIRIT. BEDE: The seven lamps[43] are the seven gifts of the Holy Spirit, all of which remain in our Lord and Redeemer forever and are distributed in his members (that is, in all the elect) according to his will. Therefore the seven lamps are set upon the lampstand because upon our Redeemer, the firstborn "from the root of Jesse," rested "the Spirit of wisdom and of understanding, the Spirit of counsel and of fortitude, the Spirit of knowledge and of godliness," and he was filled "with the Spirit of the fear of the Lord." As he himself also says through the same prophet, "The Spirit of the Lord is upon me because the Lord has anointed me."[44] ON THE TABERNACLE 1.9.[45]

THE SOURCE OF ALL BLESSING. BEDE: The prophet Isaiah testified that it was necessary that our Redeemer be conceived in Nazareth when he said, "There will come forth a rod out of the root of Jesse, and a *nazareus* will go up from his root." *Nazareus* can be translated either as "flower" or as "pure." The Son of God who was made flesh for us can rightly be called by these names because he

---

[37]Is 7:14. [38]CCL 60:338-39. [39]Derived from Jerome's *Nom.* (CC 72:137, 24, 27). [40]CS 110:55*. [41]CS 110:69. [42]TTH 18:25-26. [43]Rev 1:12. [44]Is 61:1; Lk 4:18. [45]TTH 18:39.

assumed a human nature which was pure of every vice and because he is the font and source of spiritual fruit for all who believe in him, to whom he also both showed an example and granted the gift of righteous and blessed living. HOMILIES ON THE GOSPELS 1.6.[46]

11:2-3 The Spirit of the Lord Will Rest on Him

THE SPIRIT RESTED. JUSTIN MARTYR: The Scriptures state that these gifts of the Holy Spirit were bestowed upon him, not as though he were in need of them but as though they were about to rest upon him, that is, to come to an end with him, so that there would be no more prophets among [his] people as of old. DIALOGUE WITH TRYPHO 87.[47]

THE SPIRIT OF THE LORD. NOVATIAN: Moreover, the apostle Paul says, "Having the same Spirit; as it is written, 'I believed, and therefore have I spoken'; we also believe, and therefore speak."[48] He is therefore one and the same Spirit who was in the prophets and apostles, except that in the former he was occasional, in the latter always. But in the former not as being always in them, in the latter as abiding always in them; and in the former distributed with reserve, in the latter entirely poured out; in the former given sparingly, in the latter liberally bestowed; not yet manifested before the Lord's resurrection, but conferred after the resurrection. For, he said, "I will ask the Father, and he will give you another Advocate, that he may be with you for ever, even the Spirit of truth."[49] And, "When he, the Advocate, shall come, whom I shall send to you from my Father, the Spirit of truth who proceeds from my Father."[50] And, "If I do not go away, that Advocate shall not come to you; but if I go away, I will send him to you."[51] And, "When the Spirit of truth shall come, he will direct you into all the truth."[52] And because the Lord was about to depart to the heavens, he gave the Paraclete out of necessity to the disciples; so as not to leave them

in any degree orphans,[53] which was hardly desirable, and forsake them without an advocate and some kind of protector.

For this is he who strengthened their hearts and minds, who marked out the Gospel sacraments, who was in them the enlightener of divine things; and they being strengthened, feared, for the sake of the Lord's name, neither dungeons nor chains, nay, even trod under foot the very powers of the world and its tortures. For they were henceforth armed and strengthened by the same Spirit, having in themselves the gifts which this same Spirit distributes and appropriates to the church, the spouse of Christ, as her ornaments. This is he who places prophets in the church, instructs teachers, directs tongues, gives powers and healings, does wonderful works, often discrimination of spirits, affords powers of government, suggests counsels and orders and arranges whatever other gifts there are of charismata. . . . This is he who, after the manner of a dove, when our Lord was baptized, came and abode upon him, dwelling in Christ full and entire, and not maimed in any measure or portion; but with his whole overflow copiously distributed and sent forth, so that from him others might receive some enjoyment of his graces: the source of the wholeness of the Holy Spirit remaining in Christ, so that from him might be drawn streams of gifts and works, while the Holy Spirit dwelt richly in Christ. For truly Isaiah, prophesying this, said, "And the Spirit of wisdom and understanding shall rest upon him, the Spirit of counsel and might, the Spirit of knowledge and piety; and the Spirit of the fear of the Lord shall fill him." This selfsame thing also he said in the person of the Lord himself, in another place. "The Spirit of the Lord is upon me; because he has anointed me, he has sent me to preach the gospel to the poor."[54] ON THE TRINITY 29.[55]

[46]CCL 122:39. [47]ANF 1:243**. [48]2 Cor 4:13. [49]Jn 14:16-17. [50]Jn 15:20. [51]Jn 16:7. [52]Jn 16:13. [53]Jn 14:18. [54]Is 61:1. [55]ANF 5:640-41**.

THE FEAR OF THE LORD. AMBROSE: The fear of the righteous, therefore, is the complete, golden foundation of prudence. It is also a tribunal for the teaching of Christ and for the apostolic word. The word of the saints is a good likeness of the same: an image of truth, as it were. See how the fear of the saints is made to be their golden foundation.[56] Read Isaiah and see how he elevates fear to make it blameless and good: "the Spirit of wisdom and understanding, the Spirit of counsel and strength, the spirit of knowledge and piety, the Spirit of holy fear." He elevates fear that he might possess what can follow from it, for holy fear is shaped by wisdom, instructed by understanding, directed by counsel, empowered by strength, ruled by knowledge and adorned with piety. Take up the fear of the Lord. Irrational and foolish fear belongs to the "fighting without and fear within"[57] which would have afflicted Paul, had he not taken the Lord for his consolation. EXPOSITION OF PSALM 118 5.39.[58]

THE SEVEN GIFTS OF THE SPIRIT. AMBROSE: So, then, the Holy Spirit is the river, and the abundant river, which according to the Hebrews flowed from Jesus in the lands, as we have received it prophesied by the mouth of Isaiah.[59] This is the great river that flows always and never fails. And not only a river, but also one of copious stream and overflowing greatness, as also David said: "The stream of the river makes glad the city of God."[60]

For neither is that city, the heavenly Jerusalem, watered by the channel of any earthly river, but that Holy Spirit, proceeding from the fount of life, by a short draught of whom we are satiated, seems to flow more abundantly among those celestial thrones, dominions and powers, angels and archangels, rushing in the full course of the seven virtues of the Spirit. For if a river rising above its banks overflows, how much more does the Spirit, rising above every creature, when he touches the low-lying fields of our minds, as it were, make glad that heavenly nature of the creatures with the larger fertility of his sanctification.

And let it not trouble you that either here it is said "rivers"[61] or elsewhere "seven Spirits,"[62] for by the sanctification of these seven gifts of the Spirit, as Isaiah said, is signified the fullness of all virtue; the Spirit of wisdom and understanding, the Spirit of counsel and strength, the Spirit of knowledge and godliness, and the Spirit of the fear of God. One, then is the river, but many the channels of the gifts of the Spirit. This river, then, goes forth from the fount of life. ON THE HOLY SPIRIT 1.16.[63]

FAITH AND MERCY. AUGUSTINE: A person would not have wisdom, understanding, counsel, fortitude, knowledge, piety and fear of God unless, according to the prophet's words, he had received "the spirit of wisdom and of understanding, of counsel and of fortitude, of knowledge and of godliness, and of fear of God." . . . And a person would not have power and love and sobriety, except by receiving the Spirit of whom the apostle speaks: "We have not received the spirit of fear but of power and of love and of sobriety."[64] So also one would not have faith unless he received the spirit of faith of which the same apostle says: "But having the same spirit of faith, as it is written, 'I believed, therefore I have spoken,' we also believe therefore we speak also."[65] Thus he shows very plainly that faith is not received because of merit but by the mercy of him who has mercy on whom he will,[66] when he says of himself: "I have obtained mercy to be faithful."[67] LETTER 194.[68]

THE LADDER OF ASCENT AND DESCENT. AUGUSTINE: For if Paul had said only "Jesus Christ,"[69] he would have included Jesus Christ according to his divinity, according to his being the Word who was with God, Jesus Christ the Son of God. Yet children cannot receive what is said in this manner. How, therefore, do they who are fed milk receive it?[70] "Jesus Christ," he said,

---

[56]See Song 5:15. [57]2 Cor 7:5. [58]CSEL 62:103-4. [59]Is 66:12. [60]Ps 46:4 (45:5 LXX). [61]Jn 7:38. [62]Rev 5:6. [63]NPNF 2 10:113-14. [64]2 Tim 1:7. [65]2 Cor. 4:13. [66]Rom 9:18. [67]1 Cor 7:25. [68]FC 30:310-11*. [69]See 1 Cor 2:2. [70]See 1 Cor 3:2.

"and him crucified." Feed upon what he did for you, and you will grow to know him as he is.

Some ascend the ladder,[71] therefore, and some descend on it.[72] Who are those that ascend? They who make progress toward the knowledge of spiritual realities. Who are those that descend? They who, although enjoying as great a knowledge of spiritual realities as is possible for humans, nevertheless descend to the level of children to speak of such things that children can understand, so that those who had been nourished with milk might be made fit and strong enough to receive spiritual food. Isaiah, brothers, was himself among those who descended to us, for the steps upon which he descended are obvious. In reference to the Holy Spirit, he said "the Spirit of wisdom and understanding, of counsel and fortitude, of knowledge and piety, the Spirit of the fear of God rested upon him," he began from wisdom and descended toward fear. See how the teacher descended from wisdom toward fear; you who learn, if you are to make progress, must ascend from fear to wisdom. For it is written, "The fear of the Lord is the beginning of wisdom."[73] Listen, therefore, to the psalms. EXPLANATIONS OF THE PSALMS 119.2.[74]

SEVEN AND THE SPIRIT. AUGUSTINE: The Holy Spirit is denoted in Scripture principally by the number seven, whether in Isaiah or in the Apocalypse, where the seven spirits of God are referenced most clearly under the sevenfold operation of one and the same Spirit. The Spirit's sevenfold operation is also indicated through the prophet Isaiah: "the Spirit of wisdom and understanding, of counsel and fortitude, of knowledge and piety, the Spirit of the fear of God rested upon him." This fear of the Lord should be understood as pure, enduring forever.[75] EXPLANATIONS OF THE PSALMS 150.1.[76]

ADD SEVEN TO TEN. AUGUSTINE: "The love of God has been poured out in our hearts through the Holy Spirit who has been given to us."[77]

That the Holy Spirit is suggested by the number seven anybody knows who can read. But listen anyway, those of you who read carelessly, or perhaps cannot read. This is how God presents the Holy Spirit through the prophet Isaiah: "The Spirit," he says, "of wisdom and understanding, of counsel and fortitude, of knowledge and piety, the Spirit of the fear of God." This is the sevenfold Spirit who is also called down upon the newly baptized. The law is the Decalogue; the Ten Commandments, you see, were written on tablets, but stone ones still, because of the stubborn hardness of the Jews. After the Spirit came, what does the apostle say? "You yourselves are our letter, not written with ink but with the Spirit of the living God; not on tablets of stone, but on the fleshly tablets of the heart."[78] Take away the Spirit, the letter kills, because it finds the sinner guilty, doesn't set him free. That's why the apostle says, "For we are not sufficient of ourselves to think anything as coming from ourselves; but our sufficiency is from God, who has made us sufficient to be ministers of the new covenant, not in the letter, but in the Spirit. For the letter kills, but the Spirit brings to life."[79] So add seven to ten, if you wish to fulfill all justice. When you are commanded by the law to do something, ask the Spirit to help you. SERMON 229M.2.[80]

DISTINGUISH BETWEEN YOUR FEARS. AUGUSTINE: Now in respect of this passage of the apostle, we must be on our guard against supposing that we have not received the spirit of the fear of God, which is undoubtedly a great gift of God, and concerning which the prophet Isaiah says, "The Spirit of the Lord shall rest upon you, the spirit of wisdom and understanding, the spirit of counsel and might, the spirit of knowledge and piety, the spirit of the fear of the Lord." It is not the fear with which Peter denied Christ that we have received the spirit of, but that fear concerning which Christ himself says, "Fear him who has

[71]Gen 28:10-22. [72]Augustine wants the readers to see the importance of simple faith. [73]Ps 111:10 (110:10 LXX). [74]CCL 40:1779. [75]See Ps 19:9 (18:10 LXX). [76]CCL 40:2191. [77]Rom 5:5. [78]2 Cor 3:2-3. [79]2 Cor 3:6. [80]WSA 3 6:317.

power to destroy both soul and body in hell; yes, I say to you, 'Fear him.' "[81] This, indeed, he said, lest we should deny him from the same fear which shook Peter; for such cowardice he plainly wished to be removed from us when he, in the preceding passage, said, "Be not afraid of them that kill the body, and after that have no more that they can do."[82] It is not of this fear that we have received the spirit, but of power, and of love and of a sound mind. On Grace and Free Will 39.[83]

Seven Lamps, Seven Gifts. Bede: The seven lamps are the seven gifts of the Holy Spirit, all of which remain in our Lord and Redeemer forever and are distributed in his members (that is, in all the elect) according to his will. On the Tabernacle 1.9.[84]

Recognize the Spirit's Activities. Cassiodorus: As we said earlier, the seven-formed Spirit has been denoted here, as you easily infer by calculation and recognize by his activity. But we must regard this Holy Spirit as one and the same as him whose virtues are known by Isaiah's witness to be the same seven which we have mentioned: the Spirit of wisdom, of understanding, of counsel, of courage, of knowledge, of piety, of fear of the Lord; and he distributes these to each as he wills. It should not trouble you that everywhere Isaiah ascribes the words to the voice of the Holy Spirit, for clearly "voice" is associated with the whole Trinity. We read of the Father's voice when he says, "This is my beloved Son in whom I am well pleased,"[85] and again of the Son's voice in the words "Saul, Saul, why do you persecute me?"[86] Likewise in the Acts of the Apostles we read of the Holy Spirit: "Separate for me Paul and Barnabas, for the work to which I have called them."[87] Exposition of the Psalms 28.9.[88]

Apocalyptic Connections. Paulus Orosius: Scripture testifies that "a great and strong angel exclaimed in heaven: Who is worthy to open the book and to break its seal? No one was

able to open the book or to look at it, neither in heaven nor on earth nor under the earth."[89] John wept and lamented that none of all the rational creatures in the universe was found worthy to open the book to look at it. One of the elders consoled John as he wept and said, "Do not cry, John. Behold, the Lion from the tribe of Judah, the root of David, was victorious in opening the book and breaking its seal."[90] What, I ask, is this book which no one was ever able to receive from the hand of the living, except "he who walks without sin and does justice"?[91] It is not enough that he walk without sin or that he be a lamb, but he must be a slain lamb who crowned purity with the witness of the passion of life, having seven horns and seven eyes, which are the seven spirits of God. These undoubtedly are "the Spirit of wisdom and understanding, the Spirit of counsel and strength, the spirit of knowledge and piety, and the Spirit of the fear of the Lord." What, therefore, is this book? It is the book of judgment, I believe. For "the Father judges no one but has given all judgment to the Son."[92] Defense Against the Pelagians 15.5-10.[93]

Seven Children. Gregory the Great: Indeed, seven children are born to us when, through the conception of a good thought, seven virtues of the Holy Spirit arise within us. The prophet enumerates these interior offspring of the Spirit's impregnation of the mind when he says, "the Spirit of the Lord will rest upon him, the Spirit of wisdom and understanding, the Spirit of counsel and strength, the spirit of knowledge and piety, and the Spirit of the fear of the Lord will fill him." Morals on the Book of Job 1.1.27.[94]

Seven Steps. Gregory the Great: There are seven steps to the gate because the way to heav-

[81]Lk 12:5. [82]Lk 12:4. [83]NPNF 1 5:460*. [84]TTH 18:39. [85]Mt 3:17. [86]Acts 9:4. [87]Acts 13:2. [88]ACW 51:281-82*. [89]Rev 5:2-3. [90]Rev 5.5. [91]Ps 15:2 (14:2 LXX). [92]Jn 5:22. [93]CSEL 5:624-25. [94]CCL 143:45; LF 18:53.

enly life is opened to us through the sevenfold grace of the Holy Spirit.[95] Isaiah locates this sevenfold grace in our Head himself, or in his body which we are: "The Spirit of the Lord will rest upon him, the Spirit of wisdom and understanding, the Spirit of counsel and strength, the spirit of knowledge and piety, and the Spirit of the fear of the Lord will fill him." He is speaking here from the perspective of heaven, clearly numbering the steps in descending rather than ascending order: wisdom, understanding, counsel, strength, knowledge, piety and fear. Because it is written, "the fear of the Lord is the beginning of wisdom,"[96] the way consists beyond doubt in ascending from fear to wisdom, not in regressing from wisdom to fear, for wisdom surely has perfect charity. It is also written: "Perfect charity casts out fear."[97] The prophet, therefore, because he reasoned from heavenly realities to the lower things, began with wisdom and descended toward fear.

We, however, who strive from the earthly toward the heavenly, enumerate the same steps in the ascending order to enable us to make progress from fear to wisdom. In our minds, then, the first step on the way to heaven is the fear of the Lord, the second godliness, the third knowledge, the fourth strength, the fifth counsel, the sixth understanding, and the seventh wisdom. For the fear of the Lord is in the mind. But what kind of fear is it if it is not accompanied by godliness? HOMILIES ON EZEKIEL 2.7.7.[98]

TEN AND SEVEN. GREGORY THE GREAT: You know that in the Old Testament every work is prescribed by the Ten Commandments, but in the New Testament the power of the same work is given to the increased number of faithful through the sevenfold grace of the Holy Spirit. The prophet foretells this when he speaks of "the spirit of wisdom and understanding, the spirit of counsel and strength, the spirit of knowledge and devotion, and he will fill him with the spirit of the fear of the Lord." A person acquires the ability to work in this Spirit who acknowledges faith

in the Trinity, believing that Father and Son and the same Holy Spirit are one power and confessing that they are of one substance. Because there are seven commandments, given, as I have said, more widely by the New Testament, and ten given by the Old Testament, all of our power and work can be fully comprised by ten and seven. FORTY GOSPEL HOMILIES 24.[99]

THE SPIRIT OF THE LORD. BEDE: Only of the mediator between God and humanity, the man Jesus Christ, can it be said truthfully, "And the Spirit of the Lord will rest upon him, the Spirit of wisdom and understanding, the Spirit of counsel and strength, the Spirit of knowledge and piety, and the Spirit of the fear of the Lord will fill him." Each of the saints, on the other hand, receives not the fullness of his Spirit but receives from his fullness only as the Spirit grants it, for "to one is given through the Spirit a word of wisdom, and to another a word of knowledge according to the same Spirit, to another faith in the same Spirit, to another the grace of healing in the one Spirit, to another the working of miracles, to another prophecy, to another the discernment of spirits, to another different kinds of languages, to another the interpretation of words. One and the same Spirit operates all of these gifts, dividing to each person as he wills."[100] HOMILIES ON THE GOSPELS 1.2.[101]

UPON THE LORD JESUS. FAUSTUS OF RIEZ: We read in Isaiah that the Spirit of the Lord descended upon the Lord Jesus, "the Spirit of wisdom and understanding, the Spirit of counsel and strength, the Spirit of knowledge and piety." It is in reference to this same Spirit of the Lord who descended upon the Savior in a holy outpouring that the Son said through Isaiah, "The

---

[95]Gregory here makes the connection of Isaiah with Jacob's ladder (Gen 28:10-22) as seen in Augustine *Explanations of the Psalms* (see pp. 99-100). [96]Ps 111:10 (110:10 LXX). [97]1 Jn 4:18. [98]CCL 142:320-21. [99]CS 123:182-83; cf. Augustine *Sermon* 229 (see p. 100). [100]1 Cor 12:8-11. [101]CCL 122:8*.

Spirit of the Lord is upon me,"[102] and that Matthew the Evangelist said, "Behold, the heavens opened, and he saw the Spirit of God descending upon him like a dove."[103] Luke the Evangelist, moreover, clearly teaches that the Spirit of God whom the Savior received in baptism is the Holy Spirit: "Jesus, full of the Holy Spirit, returned from the Jordan."[104] TWO BOOKS ON THE HOLY SPIRIT 1.7.[105]

ONE IN COUNSEL. AMBROSE: As the Son is the Angel of great counsel, so, too, is the Holy Spirit the Spirit of Counsel, that you may know that the Counsel of the Father, the Son and the Holy Spirit is one. Counsel, not concerning any doubtful matters, but concerning those foreknown and determined. LETTER 50.[106]

THE SERMON ON THE MOUNT AND ISAIAH. AUGUSTINE: It seems to me, therefore, that the sevenfold operation of the Holy Spirit, of which Isaiah speaks, coincides with these stages and maxims.[107] However, the order is different. In Isaiah, the enumeration begins from the higher, while here it begins from the lower; in the former, it starts from wisdom and ends at the fear of God. But "the fear of the Lord is the beginning of wisdom."[108] Therefore, if we ascend step by step, as it were, while we enumerate, the first grade is the love of God; the second is piety; the third is knowledge; the fourth is fortitude; the fifth is counsel; the sixth is understanding; the seventh is wisdom. The fear of God coincides with the humble, of whom it is here said, "Blessed are the poor in spirit."[109] SERMON ON THE MOUNT 1.11.[110]

FAITH COMES FROM MERCY. AUGUSTINE: If we say that faith goes before and that the merit of grace is in it, what merit does a man have before faith so as to receive faith? For, what has he that he has not received? And if he has received it, why does he glory as if he had not received it?[111] Just as a man would not have wisdom, understanding, counsel, fortitude, knowledge, piety and fear of

God unless, according to the prophet's words, he had received "the spirit of wisdom and of understanding, of counsel and of power, of knowledge and of godliness, and of fear of God." In the same way, he would not have power and love and sobriety, except by receiving the Spirit of whom the apostle speaks: "We have not received the spirit of fear but of power and of love and of sobriety."[112] So also he would not have faith unless he received the spirit of faith of which the same apostle says, "But having the same spirit of faith, as it is written: 'I believed for which cause I have spoken,' we also believe for which cause we also speak."[113] Thus he shows very plainly that faith is not received because of merit but by the mercy of him who has mercy on whom he will, when he says of himself: "I have obtained mercy to be faithful."[114] LETTER 194.[115]

THE FULLNESS OF HIS SPIRIT. BEDE: In truth, not all the saints receive the fullness of his Spirit, but they receive from his fullness, insofar as he grants it. HOMILIES ON THE GOSPELS 1.2.[116]

THE SPIRIT SHALL FILL HIM. JOHN CASSIAN: About this text you should first take care to observe that Isaiah does not say that "the spirit of fear shall rest upon him" but "shall fill him." The power of it is so abundant that if once it possesses a person in its strength, it possesses his mind to the exclusion of all else. Linked with the charity that never fails, it fills and permanently possesses the soul whom it has seized, and it cannot be lessened by the temptations of any this-worldly happiness. CONFERENCE 11.13.[117]

ONE AND INDIVISIBLE. CYRIL OF JERUSALEM: Isaiah signifies that the Spirit was indeed one and indivisible, but his operations diverse. CATECHETICAL LECTURES 16.30.[118]

---

[102]Is 61:1. [103]Mt 3:16. [104]Lk 4:1. [105]CSEL 21:111. [106]FC 26:265. [107]See Mt 5:3-9. [108]Prov 1:7 LXX. [109]Mt 5:3. [110]FC 11:27. [111]1 Cor 4:7. [112]2 Tim 1:7. [113]2 Cor 4:13. [114]1 Cor 7:25. [115]FC 30:310-11*. [116]CS 110:10. [117]LCC 12:256**. [118]FC 64:93*.

ACTIVITIES OF THE SPIRIT. GREGORY OF NAZIANZUS: I think Isaiah loves to call the activities of the Spirit "spirits." ON PENTECOST, ORATION 41.3.[119]

THE FOUNTAINHEAD OF THE SPIRIT. NOVATIAN: In Christ alone he dwells fully and entirely, not lacking in any measure or part; but in all his overflowing abundance dispensed and sent forth, so that other men might receive from Christ a first outpouring, as it were, of his graces. For the fountainhead of the entire Holy Spirit abides in Christ, that from him might be drawn streams of grace and wondrous deeds because the Holy Spirit dwells richly in Christ. ON THE TRINITY 29.11.[120]

11:4 Judging the Poor in Righteousness

THE IMPARTIAL JUDGE. CYRIL OF JERUSALEM: He [Christ] does not esteem the learned above the simple, nor the rich above the poor. CATECHETICAL LECTURES 15.23.[121]

JUSTICE FOR THE POOR. BEDE: Hence, when Isaiah said "he will judge the poor with justice," he was without doubt speaking of those very persons to whom it was said, "Blessed are you poor, for yours is the kingdom of God."[122] FOUR BOOKS ON 1 SAMUEL 1.7.6.[123]

THE BREATH OF HIS MOUTH. FULGENTIUS OF RUSPE: That the Holy Spirit also proceeds from the Son, the prophetic and apostolic teaching shows us. So Isaiah says concerning the Son, "He shall strike the earth with the rod of his mouth, and with the breath of his lips he shall kill the wicked." Concerning him the apostle also says, "Whom the Lord Jesus will kill with the breath of his mouth."[124] The one Son of God himself, showing who the Spirit of his mouth is, after his resurrection, breathing on his disciples, says, "Receive the Holy Spirit."[125] "From the mouth," indeed, of the Lord Jesus himself, says John in the Apocalypse, "a sharp, two-edged word came

forth."[126] The very Spirit of his mouth is the sword itself that comes forth from his mouth. To PETER ON THE FAITH 54.[127]

THE TWO-EDGED SWORD. VICTORINUS OF PETOVIUM: And Paul, speaking of Antichrist to the Thessalonians, says, "Whom the Lord Jesus will slay by the breath of his mouth."[128] And Isaiah says, "By the breath of his lips he shall slay the wicked." This, therefore, is the two-edged sword issuing out of his mouth. COMMENTARY ON THE APOCALYPSE 1.14.[129]

11:5 Righteousness Will Be His Belt

THE BELT ABOUT HIS LOINS. ATHANASIUS: At all times let us stand firm, but especially now, although many afflictions overtake us and many heretics are furious against us. Let us then, my beloved brothers, celebrate with thanksgiving the holy feast that now draws near to us, "girding up the loins of our minds,"[130] like our Savior Jesus Christ, of whom it is written, "Righteousness shall be the girdle of his loins, and faithfulness the girdle of his reins." FESTAL LETTER 3.[131]

SPIRIT LANGUAGE. CHRYSOSTOM: He is not speaking of a literal, physical belt, for all the language in this passage he employs in a spiritual sense. HOMILIES ON EPHESIANS 23.[132]

TRUTH AND RIGHTEOUSNESS. EUSEBIUS OF CAESAREA: "Righteousness shall be the girdle of his waist, and truth the girdle of his loins." As a king has a belt made of gold and precious stones, so in a prophetic manner, he speaks about the belt made of righteousness and truth. By the belt we may also understand the divinity of the Word, because he is righteousness, according to the apostle: "He is the source of your life in

---

[119]NPNF 2 7:379. [120]FC 67:102. [121]FC 64:68. [122]Lk 6:20. [123]CCL 119:61. [124]2 Thess 2:8. [125]Jn 20:22. [126]Rev 1:16. [127]FC 95:94. [128]2 Thess 2:8. [129]ANF 7:345. [130]1 Pet 1:3. [131]NPNF 2 4:515*. [132]NPNF 1 13:163-64*.

Christ Jesus, whom God made our wisdom, our righteousness and sanctification and redemption."[133] He is also the truth, according to Evangelist: "I am the way, and the truth, and the life."[134] The Word being the righteousness and the truth that comes from the root of Jesse, his waist [belt] points out to his attribute as king and warrior as the Word who conquers the invisible powers and hosts. COMMENTARY ON ISAIAH 11.7.[135]

11:6 The Wolf and the Lamb

THE PEACE OF THE PEOPLE OF GOD. JEROME: The others are easy to understand according to the vivifying spirit. For Paul the wolf, who first persecuted and lacerated the church, about whom it was said, "Benjamin is a rapacious wolf,"[136] lived with a lamb—that is, either with Ananias, by whom he was baptized,[137] or with the apostle Peter, to whom it was said, "Feed my lambs."[138] And the leopard, which first did not change its spots, once it was washed in the fountain of the Lord lay down with the kid—not the goat on the left[139] but the one that is sacrificed at the pasch of the Lord. It is also to be noted that the lamb and the kid will not dwell and recline with the wolf and the leopard, but the wolf and the leopard will imitate the innocence of the lamb and the kid.

The lion, previously most ferocious, and the sheep and the calf lingered together. We also see in the church today that the rich and the poor, the powerful and the humble, kings and peasants, remain together and are ruled in the church by small children, whom we understand to be the apostles and apostolic men, men who are unskilled in rhetoric but not in knowledge. When they are federated among themselves by the discipline of the Lord, such that their families also are united, then the saying will be implemented: "Their young will lie down together." The lion, moreover, will not eat meat but hay, because it feeds on simple food. Observe also that the cow will not eat meat, but the lion will eat hay. I

believe that "hay" in sacred Scripture is understood to be simple words, as is "wheat," the inner marrow, the meaning which is found in the letter. And it frequently happens that secular men unacquainted with the mysteries are fed by a simple reading of the Scriptures.

The infant also, who is a child with respect to evil,[140] places his hand in the hole of the asp and demons flee from the besieged bodies of men. One who is weaned no longer takes nourishment from the milk of infants but now feeds on solid food.[141] He puts his hand in the den of the serpent, that is, the habitation of Satan himself, and extracts him from it. Hence the apostles were given power to tread on serpents and scorpions and every strength of the enemy.[142] And venomous beasts were previously unable to harm or to kill those who will have lived on God's holy mountain, which means the church, about which it is said in the Gospel, "A city set on a hill cannot be hidden."[143] COMMENTARY ON ISAIAH 4.11.6-9.[144]

THE WOLF AND THE LAMB. CHRYSOSTOM: The prophet also foretold the kinds of people from whom the church would be established. Not only the meek and the mild and the good would form the church. The wild, the inhuman and men whose ways were like those of wolves and lions and bulls would flock together with them and form one church. Hear how the prophet foretold the diversity of this flock when he said, "Then a wolf shall feed with a lamb." And by this he showed the simplicity of the way of life the church's rulers would live. DEMONSTRATION AGAINST THE PAGANS 6.8.[145]

WILD BEASTS. EUSEBIUS OF CAESAREA: [Isaiah] continues prophetically to show the transformation of all different races of humanity, barbarian and Greek . . . through the teaching of

---

[133]1 Cor 1:30. [134]Jn 14:6. [135]PG 24:172. [136]Gen 49:27. [137]Acts 9:17-18. [138]Jn 21:15. [139]Mt 25:33. [140]Cf. 1 Cor 14:20. [141]Cf. Heb 5:12-14. [142]Lk 10:19. [143]Mt 5:14. [144]CCL 73:151-52. [145]FC 73:214.

Christ. . . . The irrational animals and wild beasts in the passage represent the Gentiles, who are naturally like animals. One who comes from the seed of Jesse will rule over the Gentiles. This is the genealogy of our Savior and Lord, in whom the Gentiles now believe and hope. PROOF OF THE GOSPEL 3.2.[146]

FEEDING TOGETHER. CHRYSOSTOM: When he says, "Every valley shall be filled, and every mountain and hill shall be brought low, and the rough ways shall be made smooth,"[147] he is signifying the exaltation of the lowly, the humiliation of the self-willed, the hardness of the law changed into easiness of faith. For it is no longer toils and labors, says he, but grace and forgiveness of sins, affording great facility of salvation. Next he states the cause of these things, saying, "All flesh shall see the salvation of God,"[148] no longer Jews and proselytes only, but also all earth and sea and the entire human race. Because by "the crooked things" he signified our whole corrupt life, publicans, harlots, robbers, magicians, as many as having been perverted before afterwards walked in the right way: much as he himself likewise said, "Publicans and harlots go into the kingdom of God before you,"[149] because they believed. And in other words also again the prophet declared the selfsame thing, thus saying, "Then wolves and lambs shall feed together." For similarly here by the hills and valleys, he meant that incongruities of character are blended into one and the same evenness of self-restraint, so also there, by the characters of the brute animals indicating the different human dispositions, he again spoke of their being linked in one and the same harmony of godliness. HOMILIES ON THE GOSPEL OF MATTHEW 10.3.[150]

WOLVES AND SHEEP. IRENAEUS: I am aware that some try to refer these [prophecies] to fierce people of diverse nations and of different kinds of behavior, who have believed, and when they have believed have come to agree with the righteous. But although this is now true of various kinds of

people who have come from different nations to the one conviction of the faith, nevertheless [it will also be true] in the resurrection of the just with reference to these animals. AGAINST HERESIES 5.[151]

THE OX AND THE LION. JEROME: Not of course that the ox may learn ferocity from the lion but that the lion may learn docility from the ox. LETTER 130.8.[152]

THE LION AND THE LAMB. CHRYSOSTOM: I have heard many saying, "The threats of a king are like the wrath of a lion";[153] being full of dejection and lamentation. What then should we say to such? That he who said, "The wolves and the lambs shall feed together; and the leopard shall lie down with the kid, and the lion shall eat straw like the ox," will be able to convert the lion into a mild lamb. HOMILIES CONCERNING THE STATUES 3.5.[154]

A COVENANT WILL BE STRUCK. JEROME: "And I will strike for you a covenant on that day with the beasts of the field, the birds of the air and with what crawls on the ground; and I will destroy the bow, the sword and war from the earth; and I will make them sleep in safety."[155] According to the Septuagint, "And I will arrange for them a covenant on that day with the beasts of the field, the birds of the air and with what crawls on the ground; and I will destroy war from the earth; and I will make them live in hope."[156] When all talk of false religion is removed from the people who confess the Lord and, he said, when they call me "my husband,"[157] no longer daring to cry to "Baal" (which means "my idol"), then I will strike for them a covenant and an agreement with the beasts of the field and with the birds of the sky and with what crawls on the ground. Of this

---

[146]POG 1:111*. [147]Is 40:4. [148]Is 40:5. [149]Mt 21:31. [150]NPNF 1 10:64*. [151]LCC 1:395*. [152]NPNF 2 6:266. [153]Prov 19:12. [154]NPNF 1 9:356. [155]Hos 2:18. [156]Hos 2:18. [157]Hos 2:16.

moment Isaiah also speaks: "The wolf will dwell with the lamb, and the leopard will lie down with the kid, and the calf, the lion and the lamb will remain together, and a small child will lead them." The cow and the bear will feed together and relax with their young; and the lion will eat hay like the ox, no longer desiring to eat flesh and blood at all, but enjoying its food with the pure and simple. To enable him to receive Cornelius from the Gentiles, it was revealed and commanded to Peter that he could eat any animal and that he should consider nothing to be unclean when, after being seized with thanksgiving, he later heard: "What God has purified, you must not call common."[158] At the coming of the Lord our Savior, therefore, after the triumph of his resurrection and ascension to the Father, two walls will be joined at the cornerstone by him who "made both one."[159] He called her "pitied" who was once called "not pitied,"[160] and he called them his people who was once called "not my people."[161] And the bow, the sword and war will be destroyed, granting peace to all. For instruments of war are unnecessary when there is no one to wage war. Israel will be joined to the Gentiles, and what was said in Deuteronomy will be fulfilled: "Rejoice, Gentiles, with his people."[162] For "God is known in Judah, his name is great in Israel."[163] COMMENTARY ON HOSEA 1.2.18.[164]

A LOVE THAT REFORMS. GREGORY THE GREAT: For behold, we who appear clothed in a religious habit have come together from various states of life in the world for the sake of faith in the omnipotent Lord and for hearing his word. We were gathered from many kinds of iniquity into the concord of holy church to make it seen clearly that what was said through the prophet Isaiah about the promise of the church has been accomplished: "The wolf shall dwell with the lamb, and the leopard will lie down with the kid." For it is through the organs of holy charity that the wolf will dwell with the lamb, since those who were plunderers in the world now rest in peace with

the meek and the tame. And the leopard will lie down with the kid because the person who was stained with the multitude of his sins now agrees to be humbled with the person who despises himself and confesses himself to be a sinner. Isaiah also adds, "and the calf and the lion and the sheep will remain together." One who prepares himself as a daily sacrifice to God through a contrite heart, and another who once raged with cruelty like a lion, and yet another who remains in the simplicity of his innocence like a lamb have all come together in the folds of holy church. Behold the kind of charity that enkindles, consumes, melds and reforms such a diversity of minds as though into one species of gold. HOMILIES ON EZEKIEL 2.4.3.[165]

SHALL FEED. QUODVULTDEUS: The promise will be fulfilled when kings, peasants and the poor all gather equally around the one table of Christ (believed and seen by us); according to the prophet Isaiah: "Then the wolf will dine with the lamb, and the leopard will lie down with the kid, and the cow, the lion and the lamb will eat straw together, and a small child will feed them." THE BOOK OF PROMISES AND PREDICTIONS OF GOD 3.39.46.[166]

11:7 The Cow and the Bear

THE COW AND THE LION. GREGORY OF ELVIRA: Where and when, therefore, will this blessing[167] be accomplished except in the kingdom of God, where grain, wine and oil are in abundance? The earth will yield its fruit generously and every evil will be destroyed, as Isaiah said: "In those days, the lion will eat straw with the ox, the wolf and the lamb will feed together, and a small child will put his hand in the den of an asp without being harmed." In his kingdom, God will recreate the world as wonderfully as it was made at the begin-

---

[158]Acts 10:15; 11:9. [159]Eph 2:14. [160]Hos 1:6, 8. [161]Hos 1:9; cf. Rom 9:25. [162]Deut 32:43 LXX; Rom 15:10. [163]Ps 76:1 (75:1 LXX). [164]CCL 76:29-30. [165]CCL 142:259-60. [166]CCL 60:186-87. [167]See Gen 27:28.

ning, before the first man sinned. For after he violated the word of God, all things were corrupted, profaned and cursed when God said, "Cursed is the ground because of your works."[168] The passing form of this world,[169] therefore, will become the kingdom of the saints and the liberation of creation. ORIGEN'S TRACTATE ON THE BOOKS OF HOLY SCRIPTURE 5.36-37.[170]

THE GIFT OF WATER. AMBROSE: The gift of water is so great that it causes both oxen and lions to feed, in correspondence with that prophetic saying about the holiness of the church: "Then the wolf and the lamb will feed together, and the lion will eat straw with the ox." Nor is it any marvel that water operates the same way in the church, such that thieves whose sins were washed away may be compared with the innocent. SIX DAYS OF CREATION 5.2.6.[171]

THE LION SHALL EAT STRAW. GREGORY THE GREAT: For when Isaiah observed the life of sinners devoured by the ancient and insatiable enemy, he said, "The lion shall eat straw like the ox." But what is signified by the words *hay* and *straw* except the life of the carnal? Of which it is said by the prophet, "All flesh is hay."[172] He then who here is "Behemoth,"[173] is there a "lion"; they who are here called "hay," are there called "straw." But the mind strives to enquire why this lion in Isaiah, or Behemoth as he is called by the voice of the Lord, is in both passages compared not with a horse but an ox. But we ascertain this the sooner, if we consider what is the difference of foods in the two animals. For horses eat hay, however dirty, but drink clean water only. But oxen drink water, however filthy, but feed only on clean hay. What then is it, for which this Behemoth is compared with an ox, which feeds on clean food, except that which is said of this ancient enemy by another prophet; "His food is choice."[174] MORALS ON THE BOOK OF JOB 6.32.18.[175]

A SMALL CHILD. GREGORY THE GREAT: It is also added here: "and a small child will lead

them." Who is this small child, if not the one about whom it was written: "A child is born to us, a son is given to us"?[176] HOMILIES ON EZEKIEL 2.4.3.[177]

11:8 A Small Child Shall Put His Hand Near an Asp

THE CAVE OF AN ASP. TERTULLIAN: Happily the Creator has promised by Isaiah to give this power even to little children, of putting their hand in the cockatrice den and on the hole of the young asps without at all receiving hurt. And, indeed, we are aware . . . that under the figure of scorpions and serpents are portended evil spirits, whose very prince is described by the name of serpent, dragon and every other most conspicuous beast in the power of the Creator. This power the Creator conferred first of all upon his Christ, even as the ninetieth psalm says to him: "Upon the asp and the basilisk[178] shall you tread; the lion and the dragon shall you trample under foot."[179] So also Isaiah: "In that day the Lord God shall draw his sacred, great and strong sword" (even his Christ) "against that dragon, that great and tortuous serpent; and he shall slay him in that day."[180] AGAINST MARCION 4.24.[181]

HIS HAND. AMBROSE: Hear how the antidote was administered to the flesh: the Word of God became flesh, put his hand into the serpent's den, removed the venom and took away sin. In other words, "from sin, he condemned sin in the flesh."[182] EXPLANATION OF THE TWELVE PSALMS 37.4.[183]

11:9 The Earth Will Know the Lord

THE EARTH IS FULL. ATHANASIUS: But now, to

---

[168]Gen 3:17. [169]1 Cor 7:31. [170]CCL 69:42-43. [171]CSEL 32 1:145. [172]Is 40:6. [173]Job 40:15. [174]Hab 1:16. [175]LF 31:524-25. [176]Is 9:6. [177]CCL 142:260. [178]A monster lizard. [179]Ps 91:13 (90:13 LXX). [180]Is 27:1. [181]ANF 3:388. [182]Rom 8:3. [183]CSEL 64:139.

all the earth has gone forth their voice, and all the earth has been filled with the knowledge of God,[184] and the disciples have made disciples of all the nations,[185] and now is fulfilled what is written: "They shall be all taught of God."[186] And then what was revealed was but a type; but now the truth has been manifested. FOUR DISCOURSES AGAINST THE ARIANS 1.13.8.[187]

THE SPREAD OF THE GOSPEL. CHRYSOSTOM: The successful spread of the gospel message all over the world was also predicted. DEMONSTRATION AGAINST THE PAGANS 6.4.[188]

SCRIPTURE AND THE SEA. GREGORY THE GREAT: Paul testifies to our Redeemer when he says, "He was made a curse for us."[189] The wood of the cross is also announced through the prophet, who said, "The Lord reigned from a tree,"[190] and again, "Let us put wood in his bread."[191] But the wood of the cross is explicitly revealed through the gospel, where the prophesied passion of the Lord is described.

This very same cross is also maintained in words and works through the apostles, as when Paul writes, "The world is crucified to me and I to the world," and again, "May I glory in nothing except the cross of our Lord Jesus Christ."[192] For us who strive to reach the eternal homeland, therefore, sacred Scripture is the sea in its four aspects. It announces the cross because it bears us on a tree to the land of the living. Had the prophet not found a likeness between sacred Scripture and the sea, he never would have said,

"The earth is full of the knowledge of the Lord, like the waters covering the sea." It follows, then: "The four had one likeness and their appearance and work was like a wheel within a wheel."[193] The four had one likeness because what the law proclaimed, so also did the prophets; and what the prophets announced, the gospel set forth; and what the gospel set forth, the apostles proclaimed throughout the world. The likeness of the four is one, therefore, because even though the divine words are distinct with regard to time, they are nevertheless unified to those who hear them.

"And their appearance and work was like a wheel within a wheel."[194] The wheel within a wheel is the New Testament within the Old, as we have already said, for what the Old Testament signifies, this the New Testament displays. Let me speak succinctly of complex matters. What does it mean that Eve is produced from a sleeping Adam if not that the church is formed from the dying Christ? What does it mean that Isaac bore wood as he was led to be sacrificed and that he continued to live after he had been laid on the altar, if not that our Redeemer himself bore the wood of the cross as he was led along and that he died in sacrifice for us according to his humanity but nevertheless remained immortal in his divinity? HOMILIES ON EZEKIEL 1.6.13-15.[195]

---

[184]Ps 76:1 (75:1 LXX). [185]Mt 28:19. [186]Jn 6:45; Is 54:13. [187]NPNF 2 4:341*. [188]FC 73:213*. [189]Gal 3:13. [190]Ps 96:10 (95:10 LXX). [191]Jer 11:19 LXX. [192]Gal 6:14. [193]Ezek 1:16. [194]Ezek 1:16. [195]CCL 142:74-75.

11:10-16 THE MESSIANIC AGE

[10]*In that day the root of Jesse shall stand as an ensign to the peoples; him shall the nations seek, and his dwellings shall be glorious.**

[11]*In that day the Lord will extend his hand yet a second time to recover the remnant which is left of his people, from Assyria, from Egypt, from Pathros, from Ethiopia, from Elam, from Shinar, from Hamath, and from the coastlands of the sea.*

[12]*He will raise an ensign for the nations,*
    and will assemble the outcasts of Israel,
and gather the dispersed of Judah
    from the four corners of the earth.
[13]*The jealousy of Ephraim shall depart,*
    and those who harass Judah shall be cut
        off;
Ephraim shall not be jealous of Judah,
    and Judah shall not harass Ephraim.
[14]*But they shall swoop down upon the*
shoulder of the Philistines in the west,
    and together they shall plunder the
        people of the east.
They shall put forth their hand against
        Edom and Moab,
    and the Ammonites shall obey them.
[15]*And the* LORD *will utterly destroy*
        the tongue of the sea of Egypt;
and will wave his hand over the River
        with his scorching wind,
and smite it into seven channels
        that men may cross dryshod.
[16]*And there will be a highway from*
        Assyria
    for the remnant which is left of his
        people,
as there was for Israel
        when they came up from the land of
        Egypt.

*LXX *and his rest will be his honor;* Vg *and his sepulcher will be glorious*

OVERVIEW: Christ was not only God but also a human being (THEODORET). Christ's death led to his exaltation. The place of Christ's burial was a blessed place of honor. Eventually a remnant of Israel will receive Christ and be saved (JEROME). The Antichrist will be proclaimed king but will be destroyed (HIPPOLYTUS). The Lord silences false doctrine, philosophy and superstition (GREGORY THE GREAT).

11:10-11 The Nations Will Seek the Root of Jesse

THE ROD OF JESSE. THEODORET OF CYR: Now Jesse was the father of David, and the promise with an oath was made to David. The prophet would not have spoken of the Lord Christ as a rod growing out of Jesse if he had only known him as God. DIALOGUE 1.[1]

HIS SEPULCHER SHALL BE GLORIOUS.
JEROME: Here is the meaning: his death will be glorious so that what the Savior prayed in the Gospel might be fulfilled: "Father, glorify me with the glory that I had with you before the world came to be." This was said about his nativity and about other sacraments in the public view. He came to death who was not accustomed to bearing the name of the dead but because perpetual life was in Christ, it was called "rest." But we,

[1]NPNF 2 3:172.

in order to make the meaning clear to the reader, replaced "rest" and "dormancy" with another word of the same meaning: "sepulcher."[2] At that time therefore, when the gospel of Christ shines in all the world and the earth is filled with the knowledge of God, like waters of the sea covering the land, the root of Jesse and he who arises from his stem will be a sign to all the people, that they might see the sign of the Son of Man in heaven.[3] He will have a horn in his hands, in which are hidden his strength, that when he is exalted he might draw all things to himself.[4] COMMENTARY ON ISAIAH 4.11.10.[5]

HIS RESTING PLACE. JEROME: Long before this tomb [of Christ] was hewn out by Joseph,[6] its glory was foretold in Isaiah's prediction, "his rest shall be glorious," meaning that the place of the Lord's burial should be held in universal honor. LETTER 46.5.[7]

A REMNANT OF ISRAEL. JEROME: In that day, that is, at the time of which it was also spoken above, when the root of Jesse will arise as a sign for the peoples, or to rule the nations, the Lord will send forth his hand a second time that all of Israel may be saved at the end of the world when the fullness of the Gentiles will enter,[8] by no means according to our Judaizers. But we should understand all these things as pertaining to the first advent. For since only one day is indicated both here and above, we are unable to refer the former to the first advent and the latter to the second, such that the events that follow and those that preceded would not be referred to Christ, whom the Jews contended had not yet come, but would still come in the future. After the calling of the Gentiles, therefore, who were formerly thought to be the tail,[9] Israel will be known as the tail, that the Lord may put forth his hand a second time and take possession of the remnant of his people, about whom we also read above: not all of Israel but that portion of Israel to be saved, which will remain from Assyria and Egypt and diverse parts of the world. For first the

twelve apostles and the seventy[10] and the one hundred twenty souls[11] and the five hundred to whom the Lord appeared at once,[12] then the three thousand[13] and the five thousand[14] are Jews who will have believed in the Lord. COMMENTARY ON ISAIAH 4.11.11-14.[15]

11:14 Swooping and Plundering

THE FALSE KING. HIPPOLYTUS: He [the Antichrist] shall be proclaimed king by them, and shall be magnified by all, and shall prove himself an abomination of desolation to the world. FRAGMENTS FROM COMMENTARY ON DANIEL 2.40.[16]

11:15 The Tongue of the Sea of Egypt

THE TONGUE OF THE SEA. GREGORY THE GREAT: It is said, as Paul witnesses, "And from sin he condemned sin."[17] He bound his tongue with a cord, because by means of the likeness of sinful flesh he swept away all his deceitful arguments from the hearts of his elect. For behold, when the Lord appears in the flesh, the tongue of Leviathan is bound, because, when his truth had become known, those doctrines of falsehood were silenced.

For where is now the error of the academicians, who endeavor to establish on sure grounds that nothing is sure, who with shameless brow demand from their hearers belief in their assertions, when they declare that nothing is true? Where is the superstition of the mathematicians, who, looking up at the courses of the constellations, make the lives of men to depend on the motions of the stars? Though the birth of twins often scatters their doctrine to the winds; for though born at one and the same moment, they do not remain in the same kind of life. Where are those many false teachings, which we abstain

---

[2]Jerome is here comparing the Septuagint to the Latin translation. [3]Cf. Mt 24:30. [4]Cf. Hab 3:4; Jn 12:32. [5]CCL 73:153. [6]That is, Joseph of Arimathea. See Mt 27:59-60; Lk 23:50-53. [7]NPNF 2 6:62*. [8]Cf. Rom 11:25-26. [9]Cf. Deut 28:13, 44. [10]Lk 10:1. [11]Acts 1:15. [12]1 Cor 15:6. [13]Acts 2:41. [14]Acts 4:4. [15]CCL 73:154. [16]ANF 5:184. [17]Rom 8:3.

from enumerating, for fear of digressing far from the course of our commentary? But every false doctrine has now been silenced, because the Lord has bound the tongue of Leviathan by the cord of his incarnation. Whence it is also well said by the prophet: "And the Lord shall lay waste the tongue of the Egyptian sea." For the "tongue of the sea" is the knowledge of secular learning. But it is well called "the Egyptian sea," because it is darkened with the gloom of sin. The Lord, therefore, laid waste the tongue of the Egyptian sea, because by manifesting himself in the flesh, he destroyed the false wisdom of this world. The tongue of Leviathan is, therefore, bound with a cord, because the preaching of the old sinner was bound by the likeness of sinful flesh. MORALS ON THE BOOK OF JOB 6.33.18-19.[18]

---

[18]LF 31:574.

12:1-6 SONGS OF DELIVERANCE AND THANKSGIVING

[1]You will say in that day:
"I will give thanks to thee, O LORD,
for though thou wast angry with me,
thy anger turned away,
and thou didst comfort me.

[2]"Behold, God is my salvation;
I will trust, and will not be afraid;
for the LORD GOD is my strength and my song,
and he has become my salvation."

[3]With joy you will draw water from the wells of salvation. [4]And you will say in that day:
"Give thanks to the LORD,
call upon his name;
make known his deeds among the nations,
proclaim that his name is exalted.

[5]"Sing praises to the LORD, for he has done gloriously;
let this be known[x] in all the earth.
[6]Shout, and sing for joy, O inhabitant of Zion,
for great in your midst is the Holy One of Israel."

x Or this is made known

OVERVIEW: Jesus is the healing waters that will save his people (JEROME). A fountain of eternal life flowed from Christ's wounds (AMBROSE, JEROME, FACUNDUS OF HERMIANE, CASSIODORUS, GREGORY THE GREAT). The judged will desire the water of salvation (AMBROSE).

12:3 Water from the Wells of Salvation

DRINK FROM WELLS OF SALVATION. JEROME: The one whom he entitled "Emmanuel" above,[1] then "take the spoils," "hasten to plunder,"[2] and with other names, he now calls "Savior," lest there appear to be another beyond him whom Gabriel announced to the Virgin, saying, "And you will call his name Jesus, for he will save his people."[3] He also prophesies that waters are to be drawn from his fonts—not from the waters of the rivers of Egypt, which were stricken,[4] nor from the waters of the rivers of Rezin, but from the fonts of Jesus, for this is what "Savior" expresses in the Hebrew language. Hence Jesus himself cried out in the Gospel, "Let anyone who thirsts come to me and drink. Whoever believes in me, as the Scripture says, 'rivers of living water will flow from his heart.' This," adds the evangelist, "he said of the Holy Spirit, whom those who believed in him were about to receive."[5] Jesus also says elsewhere in the Gospel, "The one who drinks from the water that I shall give him will never thirst again, for the water that I will give him will become in him a font of water springing up to eternal life."[6] We understand the fonts of the Savior to be evangelical doctrine, about which we read in the sixty-seventh psalm, "Blessed be the Lord God in the congregations from the fonts of Israel."[7] COMMENTARY ON ISAIAH 4.12.3.[8]

THE WELLS OF SALVATION. AMBROSE: The foolishness of those who have eyes with which to see their wounds is superior to the wisdom of those who do not.[9] Admonished by the spiritual vision of his foolishness, then, the king showed himself so obviously to be afflicted with miseries that he was able to find the cure, which is repentance. Judas, on the other hand, who bought a field with the reward from his iniquity, could not find the cure. "I am afflicted with miseries," the king said, "and I am utterly bowed down; all day long I walk in sorrow."[10] Are we to understand the "utterly" of his "utterly bowed down" as referring to the fullness of the legal requirements for repentance? Or, better, shall we not understand it mystically as referring to Christ, who is himself

the fullness of the law, who allowed himself to be stoned, his body suffering the wounds of death? Christ's wounds, however, were redolent with the fragrance of grace, not the stench of repentance. Hence it was not death's decay that flowed from his wounds, as is the case with all other men, but it was the fountain of eternal life, as Scripture teaches us: "And water will spring up with delight from the fountains of salvation." His wounds gushed forth, therefore, that we might drink of salvation. All sinners of the world will drink to overthrow sin, but each person must be considered individually. Christ was afflicted with miseries to make blessed those who were ensconced in misery. No one will call a man miserable who may be righteous. He himself said, "No one will make you wretched." He was bowed down that we might be raised up; he bore sorrow to bring us joy, according to which it is written: "For if I make you sorrowful, who will bring me joy except those whom I brought sorrow?"[11] The very one who was made sorrowful by the Lord Jesus Christ will bring joy to Christ and will be made joyful by Christ. We recognize, therefore, that satisfaction does not need to be made by us. We are utterly bowed down, that is, not only in offering our faith in Christ but also our perseverance in suffering. And we should rejoice in our sufferings, as Christ also rejoiced in his sufferings. What he took up for his servants, we should undergo for the Lord. EXPLANATION OF THE TWELVE PSALMS 37.31-32.[12]

WATER WILL SPRING UP. AMBROSE: Although my mind would fail if you were to ask how Christ is rich in poverty, the well of divine Scripture does not fail, for the apostle said, "The Lord Jesus was made poor when he was rich, that by his poverty you might become rich."[13] But what is that poverty which makes rich? Let's consider the matter by focusing on the venerable sacrament

[1]Is 7:14. [2]Is 8:3. [3]Mt 1:21. [4]Ex 7:20. [5]Jn 7:37-39. [6]Jn 4:13-14. [7]Ps 68:26 (67:27 LXX). [8]CCL 73:158. [9]See Ps 38:5 (37:6 LXX). [10]Ps 38:6 (37:7 LXX). [11]2 Cor 2:2. [12]CSEL 64:160-61. [13]2 Cor 8:9.

itself. What can be purer or simpler than it? No one is soaked in the blood of a bull, as the sacred rites of the Gentiles are said to have, nor is any sinner washed with the blood of goats and rams, for these acts cleanse only the flesh but do not absolve sins. Rather, "water will spring up with delight from the fountains of salvation," and "a heavenly table will be prepared in your presence and a glorious, intoxicating cup."[14] These are the things of rich simplicity in which Christ's precious poverty consists. Because poverty is also good with respect to morals, the Lord said, "Blessed are the poor in spirit,"[15] and we find in the psalms, "For the Lord will save the humble of spirit."[16] I believe that poverty also abounds in gathering together, if faith abounds. For this reason, the apostle said, "Their great poverty abounds in the riches of their simplicity."[17] EXPLANATION OF THE TWELVE PSALMS 40.4-5.[18]

TOO LATE TO BE A TEACHER. AMBROSE: There will be a great chasm, therefore, between the wealthy and the poor, because merits cannot be altered after death. As the wealthy man is led down to the furnace, he desires to draw a cooling draft from the poor, since water is refreshment for the soul in pain, concerning which Isaiah said, "And water will spring up with delight from the fountains of salvation." But why is he tormented prior to judgment? Because the punishment for luxuriant living is to be lacking in pleasure. For the Lord also said, "There will be weeping and grinding of teeth when you see Abraham, Isaac and Jacob and all the prophets in the kingdom of heaven."[19] Very late does the wealthy man begin to be a teacher, when he still has time for learning but not for teaching. EXPOSITION OF THE GOSPEL OF LUKE 8.18-19.[20]

YOU WILL DRAW WATER. JEROME: "More majestic than the voices of many waters or the mighty waves of the sea."[21] These are the waters of Shiloah which run in silence,[22] about which Isaiah speaks: "You will draw water from the fountains of salvation"; and the psalmist: "Bless the Lord from the fountains of Israel."[23] Again, Isaiah says about the Lord our Savior: "He will live in a dwelling on high, made of the strongest rock; bread will be given him, and his water supply will be sure."[24] COMMENTARY ON EZEKIEL 14.47.1.[25]

THE HOLY FONT. FACUNDUS OF HERMIANE: But after discussing this sermon of the venerable Bishop Paul, Saint Cyril addressed the people and said, "The blessed prophet Isaiah, preaching tenderly about future teachers in Christ, said, 'Draw water from the fountains of salvation with joy.'" Behold, therefore, we drew water from the holy font. But I say that our prophesying teacher, having been enlightened through feasts of the Holy Spirit, was drawing our attention to the great and sacred mystery of the Savior, through which we who believe in him were saved. To JUSTINIAN 1.5.39-40.[26]

HE FILLS THE THIRSTY. CASSIODORUS: We say that God is . . . a fountain because he fills the thirsty and empty. EXPOSITION OF THE PSALMS 35.10.[27]

STREAMS OF TRUTH. GREGORY THE GREAT: And who is this strong man, except him of whom the Lord says in the Gospel, "No man can enter into a strong man's house and spoil his goods, unless he first bind the strong man."[28] The Lord, therefore, bound the fountains and the torrents when he spread in the hearts of his apostles the streams of truth. Of whom it is said again by another prophet; "With joy shall you draw water from the fountains of the Savior." MORALS ON THE BOOK OF JOB 6.33.20.[29]

[14]Ps 23:5 (22:5 LXX). [15]Mt 5:3. [16]Ps 33:19 (32:19 LXX). [17]2 Cor 8:2. [18]CSEL 64:231-33. [19]Lk 13:28. [20]CCL 14:304-5. [21]Ps 93:4 (92:4 LXX). [22]See Is 8:6. [23]Ps. 68:26 (67:27 LXX). [24]Is 33:16. [25]CCL 75:707. [26]CCL 90A:36. [27]CCL 97:322. [28]Mk 3:27. [29]LF 31:575*.

13:1-22 ORACLE AGAINST BABYLON

¹The oracle concerning Babylon which Isaiah
the son of Amoz saw.
    ²On a bare* hill raise a signal,
        cry aloud to them;
    wave the hand for them to enter
        the gates of the nobles.
    ³I myself have commanded my consecrated
        ones,
        have summoned my mighty men to
        execute my anger,
        my proudly exulting ones.

    ⁴Hark, a tumult on the mountains
        as of a great multitude!
Hark, an uproar of kingdoms,
        of nations gathering together!
The LORD of hosts is mustering
        a host for battle.
    ⁵They come from a distant land,
        from the end of the heavens,
the LORD and the weapons of his
        indignation,
        to destroy the whole earth.

    ⁶Wail, for the day of the LORD is near;
        as destruction from the Almighty it will
        come!
    ⁷Therefore all hands will be feeble,
        and every man's heart will melt,
        ⁸and they will be dismayed.
Pangs and agony will seize them;
        they will be in anguish like a woman in
        travail.
They will look aghast at one another;
        their faces will be aflame.

    ⁹Behold, the day of the LORD comes,
        cruel, with wrath and fierce anger,
to make the earth a desolation
        and to destroy its sinners from it.
    ¹⁰For the stars of the heavens and their
        constellations
        will not give their light;
the sun will be dark at its rising
        and the moon will not shed its light.
    ¹¹I will punish the world for its evil,
        and the wicked for their iniquity;
I will put an end to the pride of the
        arrogant,
        and lay low the haughtiness of the
        ruthless.
    ¹²I will make men more rare than fine gold,
        and mankind than the gold of Ophir.
    ¹³Therefore I will make the heavens
        tremble,
        and the earth will be shaken out of its
        place,
at the wrath of the LORD of hosts
        in the day of his fierce anger.
    ¹⁴And like a hunted gazelle,
        or like sheep with none to gather
        them,
every man will turn to his own people,
        and every man will flee to his own land.
    ¹⁵Whoever is found will be thrust through,
        and whoever is caught will fall by the
        sword.
    ¹⁶Their infants will be dashed in pieces
        before their eyes;
their houses will be plundered
        and their wives ravished.

*¹⁷Behold, I am stirring up the Medes
  against them,
  who have no regard for silver
  and do not delight in gold.
¹⁸Their bows will slaughter the young
  men;
  they will have no mercy on the fruit of
  the womb;
  their eyes will not pity children.
¹⁹And Babylon, the glory of kingdoms,
  the splendor and pride of the Chaldeans,
will be like Sodom and Gomorrah
  when God overthrew them.
²⁰It will never be inhabited*

*or dwelt in for all generations;
no Arab will pitch his tent there,
  no shepherds will make their flocks lie
  down there.
²¹But wild beasts will lie down there,
  and its houses will be full of howling
  creatures;
there ostriches will dwell,
  and there satyrs will dance.
²²Hyenas will cry in its towers,
  and jackals in the pleasant palaces;
its time is close at hand
  and its days will not be prolonged.*

*Old Latin *dark*

OVERVIEW: On a bare hill raise a signal giving glory to God (JEROME). Christians lift up a banner to God when they exalt the virtue of the cross (GREGORY THE GREAT). The day of the Lord will come unexpectedly (AMBROSE). There will be no rescue from eternal judgment (CHRYSOSTOM). God humbles the proud (CLEMENT OF ROME). Because only a few will be saved, one cannot suppose that all of the Jews will be saved (EUSEBIUS). God will destroy Babylon (JEROME). Fathers who raise wild animals are to blame (CHRYSOSTOM).

13:2 Lift a Banner

ON A BARE HILL RAISE A SIGNAL. JEROME: Hence it is often said to sinners: give glory to God! But Babylon and the entire region of the Chaldeans are called dark or gloomy mountains, as in the beginning of Isaiah, where we find written against Babylon: "Raise the signal on a dark mountain," which in Hebrew is called *nishpeh*. SIX BOOKS ON JEREMIAH 3.17.2-3.[1]

A HIGH MOUNTAIN. GREGORY THE GREAT: And this covenant is well said to be a shady and thick mountain, because it is darkened by the thick obscurities of allegories. Again, by a mountain is designated the apostate angel, as is said to preachers concerning the ancient enemy under the character of the king of Babylon, "Lift you up a banner upon the gloomy mountain." Holy preachers lift up a banner above the gloomy mountain when they exalt the virtue of the cross. MORALS ON THE BOOK OF JOB 6.33.2.[2]

13:8 Pangs and Agony

LIKE PAINS OF CHILDBIRTH. AMBROSE: The day of the Lord comes suddenly, it says, and in an unexpected way like the pains of childbirth, which forestall all one's efforts to hide them. LETTER 32 (8.56.12).[3]

13:9 Destroying Sinners from the Earth

TO DESTROY ITS SINNERS. CHRYSOSTOM: For there will be none to stand by, none to rescue, nowhere the face of Christ, so mild and calm. But as those who work in the mines are delivered over to certain cruel people and see none of their

---

[1]CCL 64:130-31. [2]LF 31:555*. [3]FC 26:159.

friends but those only that are set over them, so will it be then also: or rather not so, but even far more grievous. HOMILIES ON THE GOSPEL OF MATTHEW 43.5.[4]

13:11 Ending the Pride of the Arrogant

PRIDE OF THE ARROGANT. CLEMENT OF ROME: You have opened "the eyes of our hearts"[5] so that we realize you alone are "highest among the highest, and ever remain holy among the holy."[6] "You humble the pride of the arrogant, overrule the plans of the nations, raise up the humble and humble the haughty. You make rich and make poor; you slay and bring to life; you alone are the guardian of spirits and the God of all flesh." You see into the depths:[7] you look upon humankind's deeds; you aid those in danger and "save those in despair."[8] You are the Creator of every spirit and watch over them. You multiply the nations on the earth, and from out of them all you have chosen those who love you through Jesus Christ, your beloved Son. Through him you have trained us, made us saints and honored us. 1 CLEMENT 59.3.[9]

13:14 Like a Hunted Gazelle

HUNTED GAZELLE. EUSEBIUS OF CAESAREA: In this way the word [Scripture] clearly shows the few who will be saved in the day of the ruin of those who are evil. Therefore, one cannot expect that all those who are uncircumcised and all of the Jewish nation, without exception, will receive the promises of God. PROOF OF THE GOSPEL 2.3.[10]

13:17 Raising the Medes

THE MEDES. JEROME: Hence he was ordered by the prophet to speak to the sons of Ammon and to reproach them, for they would have to be captured, and he directed a word also to the sword. . . . But even more is said through Isaiah in his vision against Babylon: "Behold, I will raise the Medes up against them;" and shortly later: "This Babylon, glorious among the kingdoms, the proud possession of the Chaldeans, will be destroyed by God like Sodom and Gomorrah. It will remain uninhabited forever." COMMENTARY ON EZEKIEL 7.21.28-32.[11]

13:21 Houses Full of Howling Creatures

HOWLING CREATURES. CHRYSOSTOM: There are people who are even worse than wild donkeys, living in the wilderness and kicking. In fact, most of the young people among us are like this. They have wild desires and jump around, kicking and going around unbridled. They spend all their energy on unbecoming behavior. The fathers are to blame. While they hire horse breakers to discipline their horses and do not let the young colt stay untamed for long, they overlook their own young people. The youth are unbridled and have no self-control. They disgrace themselves through their sexual sins, through gambling and through going to the wicked theater. HOMILIES ON THE GOSPEL OF MATTHEW 59.7.[12]

---

[4]NPNF 1 10:276*. [5]Eph 1:18. [6]Is 57:15. [7]Sir 16:18-19. [8]Jdt 9:11. [9]LCC 1:70-71. [10]POG 1:92*. [11]CCL 75:292-93. [12]NPNF 1 10:370**.

14:1-11 RETURN FROM EXILE

[1]The LORD will have compassion on Jacob and will again choose Israel, and will set them in their own land, and aliens will join them and will cleave to the house of Jacob. [2]And the peoples will take them and bring them to their place, and the house of Israel will possess them in the LORD's land as male and female slaves; they will take captive those who were their captors, and rule over those who oppressed them.

[3]When the LORD has given you rest from your pain and turmoil and the hard service with which you were made to serve, [4]you will take up this taunt against the king of Babylon:

"How the oppressor has ceased,
    the insolent fury[y] ceased!
[5]The LORD has broken the staff of the
    wicked,
    the scepter of rulers,
[6]that smote the peoples in wrath
    with unceasing blows,
    that ruled the nations in anger

with unrelenting persecution.
[7]The whole earth is at rest and quiet;
    they break forth into singing.
[8]The cypresses rejoice at you,
    the cedars of Lebanon, saying,
'Since you were laid low,
    no hewer comes up against us.'
[9]Sheol beneath is stirred up
    to meet you when you come,
it rouses the shades to greet you,
    all who were leaders of the earth;
it raises from their thrones
    all who were kings of the nations.
[10]All of them will speak
    and say to you:
'You too have become as weak as we!
    You have become like us!'
[11]Your pomp is brought down to
    Sheol,
    the sound of your harps;
maggots are the bed beneath you,
    and worms are your covering."

y One ancient Ms Compare Gk Syr Vg: The meaning of the Hebrew word is uncertain

---

OVERVIEW: God's will is fulfilled suddenly (CLEMENT OF ROME). The Jews will possess the nations (JUSTIN MARTYR). The king of Babylon represents the one who was responsible for the beginning of evil; the enemy of Christ (ORIGEN, HIPPOLYTUS). It befits Christians to be on guard against former temptations (VERECUNDUS).

14:1 He Will Come Quickly

COME QUICKLY. CLEMENT OF ROME: Truly his will shall be fulfilled swiftly and suddenly, as the Scripture testifies. 1 CLEMENT 23.[1]

THE STRANGER. JUSTIN MARTYR: [Jewish] proselytes have no need of a new covenant, since, as one and the same law binds all who are circumcised, Scripture speaks of them as follows: "And the stranger also shall be joined to them and shall adhere to the house of Jacob." DIALOGUE WITH TRYPHO 123.[2]

14:4 A Taunt Song Against the King of Babylon

---

[1]FC 1:29. [2]ANF 1:261**.

THE KING OF BABYLON. ORIGEN: According to Isaiah, in which lament is offered on behalf of the king of Babylon, much can be learned about the origin and beginning of evil. Evil derived its existence from some who had lost their wings by following the one who was first to lose his own wings. AGAINST CELSUS 6.43.[3]

THE SHAMEFUL TYRANT. HIPPOLYTUS: We will show in what follows that these things are not said of someone else but of that tyrant, the one without shame, the enemy of God, as Isaiah says. ON THE ANTICHRIST 15.[4]

THE OPPRESSOR. VERECUNDUS: Because the

Lord Jesus would destroy their staff, that is, their power to oppress, Isaiah said, "How has the oppressor ceased and the tax ended? Was his oppressor's staff destroyed?" It befits Christians to be cautious, therefore, and it is right for the people of the Lord to be observant, lest oppressors who had once been repelled by divine grace should rouse themselves again to demand the kind of taxes which are paid with spiritual delinquency. COMMENTARY ON THE CANTICLE OF DEUTERONOMY 2.10.[5]

---

[3]ANF 4:593*. [4]ANF 5:207*. [5]CCL 93:26-27.

14:12-32 THE FALL FROM HEAVEN

[12]"How you are fallen from heaven,
  O Day Star, son of Dawn!
How you are cut down to the ground,
  you who laid the nations low!*
[13]You said in your heart,
  'I will ascend to heaven;
above the stars of God
  I will set my throne on high;
I will sit on the mount of assembly
  in the far north;[†]
[14]I will ascend above the heights of the
    clouds,
  I will make myself like the Most High.'
[15]But you are brought down to Sheol,
  to the depths of the Pit.
[16]Those who see you will stare at you,
  and ponder over you:

'Is this the man who made the earth
    tremble,
  who shook kingdoms,
[17]who made the world like a desert
    and overthrew its cities,
  who did not let his prisoners go home?'
[18]All the kings of the nations lie in glory,
  each in his own tomb;
[19]but you are cast out, away from your
    sepulchre,
  like a loathed untimely birth,[z]
clothed with the slain, those pierced by the
    sword,
  who go down to the stones of the Pit,
  like a dead body trodden under foot.
[20]You will not be joined with them in burial,
  because you have destroyed your land,

you have slain your people.

"May the descendants of evildoers
    nevermore be named!
[21]Prepare slaughter for his sons
    because of the guilt of their fathers,
lest they rise and possess the earth,
    and fill the face of the world with cities."

[22]"I will rise up against them," says the LORD of hosts, "and will cut off from Babylon name and remnant, offspring and posterity, says the LORD. [23]And I will make it a possession of the hedgehog, and pools of water, and I will sweep it with the broom of destruction, says the LORD of hosts."

[24]The LORD of hosts has sworn:
"As I have planned,
    so shall it be,
and as I have purposed,
    so shall it stand,
[25]that I will break the Assyrian in my land,
    and upon my mountains trample him
        under foot;
and his yoke shall depart from them,
    and his burden from their shoulder."
[26]This is the purpose that is purposed
    concerning the whole earth;

and this is the hand that is stretched out
    over all the nations.
[27]For the LORD of hosts has purposed,
    and who will annul it?
His hand is stretched out,
    and who will turn it back?

[28]In the year that King Ahaz died came this oracle:
[29]"Rejoice not, O Philistia, all of you,
    that the rod which smote you is
        broken,
for from the serpent's root will come forth
    an adder,
    and its fruit will be a flying serpent.
[30]And the first-born of the poor will feed,
    and the needy lie down in safety;
but I will kill your root with famine,
    and your remnant I[a] will slay.
[31]Wail, O gate; cry, O city;
    melt in fear, O Philistia, all of you!
For smoke comes out of the north,
    and there is no straggler in his ranks."

[32]What will one answer the messengers of
    the nation?
"The LORD has founded Zion,
    and in her the afflicted of his people find
        refuge."

z Cn Compare Tg Symmachus: Heb *a loathed branch*   a One ancient Ms Vg: Heb *he*   *LXX How has Lucifer, that rose in the morning, fallen from heaven! He that sends orders to all the nations is crushed to the earth.   †LXX I will sit on a lofty mount, on the lofty mountains toward the north.

OVERVIEW: Lucifer fell from heaven because of his pride (JEROME). The enemy is a fallen being of light. The one fallen from heaven cannot be Nebuchadnezzar or any other human being (ORIGEN). Lucifer descended from better to worse in his fall from heaven (EUSEBIUS). Lucifer fell from heaven because he wanted to be like God (JEROME). Pride was the reason for Lucifer's fall (AUGUSTINE). Nebuchadnezzar was destroyed because of his pride (APHRAHAT). Lucifer fell not because of any sinful actions but because of his prideful tongue (JEROME, AMBROSE, JOHN CASSIAN). Death comes to all, showing the limitation of human pride (CHRYSOSTOM). The devil, a robber and accuser, can find no fault in Christ (AUGUSTINE), nor can he take the exalted place of

God (CASSIODORUS). God's wrath on obstinate sinners is unbearable (VERECUNDUS). God uses even bad circumstances for good, and his will prevails (CHRYSOSTOM). The flying serpent, or basilisk, can destroy even from a distance (GREGORY THE GREAT). Christians must guard against the sin of pride (AMBROSE).

14:12 Fallen from Heaven

LUCIFER'S FALL. JEROME: For greater ease of understanding we translated this phrase as follows: "How you have fallen from heaven, Lucifer, who arose in the morning." But if we were to render a literal translation from the Hebrew, it would read, "How you have fallen from heaven, howling son of the dawn." Lucifer is also signified with other words. And he who was formerly so glorious that he was compared to a bearer of lightning is now told that he must weep and mourn. Just as Lucifer scatters the darkness, it says, glowing and shining with a golden hue, so also your stepping forth to the peoples and the public seemed like a shining star. But you who spoke with arrogance, who wounded the nations, fell to the earth. I have obtained so great a power that heaven should stand still for me, and the stars above deserve to be thrown under my feet. Nevertheless, the Jews wanted to be understood as the heaven and stars of God, inasmuch as it continues, "I will sit in the mount of the covenant," that is, in the temple where the laws of God are hidden, "and on the sides of the north," that is, in Jerusalem. For it is written, "Mount Zion, the sides of the north."[1] Nor was his pride satisfied with desire for the heavens, but it would break forth with such madness that he would claim for himself likeness to God. COMMENTARY ON ISAIAH 5.14.12-14.[2]

THE LIGHTBEARER. ORIGEN: It is most clearly proved by these words that he who formerly was Lucifer and who "arose in the morning" has fallen from heaven. For if, as some suppose, he was a being of darkness, why is he said to have formerly been Lucifer or lightbearer? Or how could he "rise in the morning" who had in him no light at all? . . . So he was light once . . . when "his glory was turned into dust." ON FIRST PRINCIPLES 1.5.[3]

FALLEN FROM HEAVEN. ORIGEN: How can we possibly suppose that what is said in many places by Scripture, especially in Isaiah, about Nebuchadnezzar is said about a human being? For no human being is said to have "fallen from heaven" or to have been "Lucifer" or the one who "arose every morning." ON FIRST PRINCIPLES 4.3.9.[4]

THE GREAT TEMPTER. EUSEBIUS OF CAESAREA: The Word clearly demonstrates many things in this passage: the lunacy of that spirit, his fall from what was good to what was bad, and the result of his fall. Having pronounced many terrible threats against humanity he realized that they had the possibility of falling into evil by virtue of their own free will. Therefore he turned them from a good state to a bad one, leading the many souls by the lure of desire to every fashion of evil. There was no device he did not attempt. With the myths of the gods and impure stories he tempted his victims with the things they loved and the things that gave them pleasure. . . . Soon, according to the blessed apostle, they no longer pondered the works of God that still illumined the heavens. PROOF OF THE GOSPEL 4.9.[5]

SON OF THE DAWN. JEROME: Lucifer fell, Lucifer who used to rise at dawn; and he who was raised in a paradise of delight had the well-earned sentence passed upon him: "Though you exalt yourself as the eagle, and though you set your nest among the stars, thence will I bring you down, says the Lord."[6] For he had said in his heart, "I will exalt my throne above the stars of God," and

[1]Ps 48:2 LXX. [2]CCL 73:168-69. [3]OFP 50. [4]OSW 196. [5]POG 1:179*. [6]Obad 4.

"I will be like the Most High." Letter 22.4.[7]

You Are Cut Down. Augustine: It was by a kind of strength that man offended, so as to require to be corrected by weakness: for it was by a certain "pride" that he offended; so as to require to be chastened by humility. All proud persons call themselves strong people. Therefore have many [others] "come from the East and the West" and have attained "to sit down with Abraham, and Isaac and Jacob, in the kingdom of heaven."[8] Therefore, how was it that they so attained? Because they would not be strong. What is meant by "would not be strong"? They were afraid to presume of their own merits. They did not "go about to establish their own righteousness," that they might "submit themselves to the righteousness of God."[9] . . . Behold! you are mortal; and you bear about you a body of flesh that is corrupting away: "And you shall fall like one of the princes. You shall die like human beings"[10] and shall fall like the devil. What good does the remedial discipline of mortality do you? The devil is proud, as not having a mortal body, as being an angel. But as for you, who have received a mortal body, and to whom even this does no good, so as to humble you by so great weakness, you shall "fall like one of the princes." This then is the first grace of God's gift, to bring us to the confession of our infirmity, that whatever good we can do, whatever ability we have, we may be that in him; that "he that glories, may glory in the Lord."[11] "When I am weak," he says, "then am I strong."[12] Explanations of the Psalms 39 (38).18.[13]

The Text Refers to Lucifer. Augustine: For example, what is said in Isaiah, "How he is fallen from heaven, Lucifer, son of the morning!" and the other statements in that context that speak of the king of Babylon are of course to be understood of the devil. However, the statement that is made in the same place, "He that sent orders to all nations is crushed on the earth," does not altogether fitly apply to the head himself. Christian Instruction 3.37.[14]

14:13-14 I Will Ascend to Heaven

I Will Ascend. Aphrahat: Now Nebuchadnezzar said, "I will ascend to heaven and exalt my throne above the stars of God and sit in the lofty mountains that are in the borders of the north." Isaiah said concerning him: "Because your heart has thus exalted you, therefore you shall be brought down to Sheol, and all that look upon you shall be astonished at you." Demonstration 5.4.[15]

The Power of the Tongue. Jerome: Read in the letter of James how much evil the tongue can cause. The tongue knows no middle way; either it is a great evil or a great good; a great good when it acknowledges that Christ is God, a great evil when it denies that Christ is God. Let no one, therefore, harbor the illusion and claim: I have not committed sin in act; if I sinned, I sinned with my tongue. What more monstrous sin is there than blasphemy against God? Yet it is the tongue that is sinning. Why did the devil fall? Because he committed theft? Because he committed murder? Because he committed adultery? These are certainly evils, but the devil did not fall because of any of these; he fell because of his tongue. What was it that he said? "I will scale the heavens; above the stars I will set up my throne; I will be like the Most High!" Monks surely, then, have no right to think they are safe and say: We are in the monastery, and so we do not commit serious offenses; I do not commit adultery; I do not steal; I am not a murderer; I am not guilty of parricide; and so of all the rest of the big vices. But the devilish sins are those of the tongue. It is outrageous to detract from my brother; I am killing my brother with my tongue, for, "Everyone who hates his brother is a murderer."[16]

Listen to what Solomon says: "Death and life are in the power of the tongue."[17] "In the power of

[7]NPNF 2 6:23*. [8]Mt 8:11. [9]Rom 10:3. [10]Ps 82:7. [11]1 Cor 1:31. [12]2 Cor 12:10. [13]NPNF 1 8:117*. [14]NPNF 1 2:573**. [15]NPNF 2 13:353*. [16]1 Jn 3:15. [17]Prov 18:21.

the tongue," do you see how much evil there is in the tongue? It has power, for what does he say? "In the power of the tongue." HOMILIES ON THE PSALMS 41 (PSALM 119).[18]

I WILL ASCEND. AMBROSE: How injurious to the servants of God can be the proud one who exalts himself against God and says, "I will ascend into heaven and seat my throne above the stars of heaven; I will sit on the highest mountain above the tall mountains of the north; I will ascend above the clouds; and I will be like the Most High." It is no wonder, then, that the stubborn of spirit who will not yield to God is also able to oppress humanity. How will he preserve the confidence and faith of others who, through arrogant sacrilege and fantasy, promotes himself to equality with the omnipotent Lord? How does one who fails to liberate prisoners slander him who alone made void all the earth, caused kings to tremble, destroyed cities and laid waste the entire earth? We must be careful, therefore, that he not destroy the walls guarding our souls, or compromise our mind's defenses or seat his throne above the stars. He seats his throne above the stars when he deceives the elect and when he oppresses the just, whose works shine like the stars in heaven. EXPOSITION OF PSALM 118.16.15-16.[19]

LIKE THE MOST HIGH. AMBROSE: When the Lord Jesus redeemed the human race through his obedience, he reformed justice. The serpent, however, introduced sin through his disobedience, a sin which we are now able to identify as pride, the author of which is the devil, whom the prophet portrayed as saying, "I will seat my throne above the clouds and I will be like the Most High." Yet he who was so wicked that he would not honor the Lord our God taught his disciples to be even worse. Thus, whereas the devil exalted himself to the degree that he desired to be similar and equal to the Most High, his disciple is signified by the apostle who would become so indignant as to judge himself already similar and equal to God. For it is written, "The

man of iniquity and the son of perdition will be revealed, who opposes and extols himself above everything which is called god."[20] He presumes that he is equal to the teacher, or, in this case, even superior. The Lord said to his disciples, "You will do greater things than these,"[21] to indicate that whereas the serpent acquired more for himself than he gave to others, Christ would give his disciples more to accomplish than even he had done on earth, for he wanted to triumph in his disciples and to deceive the prince of the world. EXPOSITION OF PSALM 118.3.34.[22]

IMPORTANT CONTRASTS. JOHN CASSIAN: The one says, "I will exalt my throne above the stars of God"; the other, "Learn of me, for I am meek and lowly of heart."[23] The one says, "I know not the Lord and will not let Israel go";[24] the other, "If I say that I know him not, I shall be a liar like unto you: but I know him and keep his commandments."[25] The one says, "My rivers are mine, and I made them";[26] the other, "I can do nothing of myself, but my Father who abides in me, he does the works."[27] The one says, "All the kingdoms of the world and the glory of them are mine, and to whomsoever I will, I give them";[28] the other, "Though he were rich, yet he became poor, that we through his poverty might be made rich."[29] The one says, "As eggs are gathered together which are left, so have I gathered all the earth, and there was none that moved the wing or opened the mouth, or made the least noise";[30] the other, "I am become like a solitary pelican; I watched and became as a sparrow alone upon the roof."[31] The one says, "I have dried up with the sole of my foot all the rivers shut up in banks";[32] the other, "Cannot I ask my Father, and he shall presently give me more than twelve legions of angels?"[33] If we look at the reason of our original fall and the foundations of our salvation, and [if

---

[18]FC 48:306-7. [19]CSEL 62:360-61. [20]2 Thess 2:3-4. [21]See Jn 14:12. [22]CSEL 62:60-61. [23]Mt 11:29. [24]Ex 5:2. [25]Jn 8:55. [26]Ezek 24:3. [27]Jn 5:30; 14:10. [28]Lk 4:6. [29]2 Cor 8:9. [30]Is 10:14. [31]Ps 102:7-8 (101:7-8 LXX). [32]Is 37:25. [33]Mt 26:53.

we] consider by whom and in what way the latter were laid and the former originated, we may learn, either through the fall of the devil or through the example of Christ, how to avoid so terrible a death from pride. ON THE INSTITUTES 12.4.[34]

THE JUST SHALL LAUGH. JOHN CASSIAN: And because he "loved the words of ruin,"[35] with which he had said, "I will ascend into heaven," and the "deceitful tongue," with which he had said of himself, "I will be like the Most High," and of Adam and Eve, "You shall be as gods," therefore "shall God destroy him forever and pluck him out and remove him from his dwelling place and his root out of the land of the living." Then "the just," when they see his ruin, "shall fear, and shall laugh at him and say" (what may also be most justly aimed at those who trust that they can obtain the highest good without the protection and assistance of God): "Behold the man that did not make God his helper but trusted in the abundance of his riches and prevailed in his vanity."[36] ON THE INSTITUTES 12.4.[37]

DEATH COMES TO ALL. CHRYSOSTOM: There were some who dared in the opinion of the multitude to immortalize themselves and, notwithstanding that the very sense of sight bore witness to their mortality, were ambitious to be called gods and were honored as such; to what a length of impiety would not many people have proceeded, if death had not gone on teaching all humanity the morality and corruptibility of our nature? Hear, for instance, what the prophet says of a barbarian king, when seized with this frenzy: "I will exalt," he says, "my throne above the stars of heaven; and I will be like unto the Most High." HOMILIES CONCERNING THE STATUES 11.4.[38]

WHO WAS THE ROBBER? AUGUSTINE: "He deemed it no robbery to be God's equal, yet he emptied himself and took on the form of a slave."[39] This was by no means robbery! Who was the robber, then? Adam. And the primordial rob-

ber? The being who seduced Adam. How, then, did the devil seize what did not belong to him? "I will set my throne in the north; I shall be like the Most High," he said. He grabbed for himself something not given to him; that was robbery. The devil tried to usurp what had not been granted to him and thereby lost what he had been given. Then from the cup of his own pride he offered a drink to the humans he was trying to seduce, saying, "Taste it, and you will be like gods."[40] They too wanted to make a grab at divinity, and they lost their happiness. The devil robbed and paid for it; but Christ declares, "I was discharging a debt, though I had committed no robbery."[41]

As the Lord approached his passion, he testified, "Now the prince of this world (that is, the devil) is coming, and he will find nothing in me (that means, he will find no justification for killing me). But so that the world may know that I am doing my Father's will, rise, let us leave here."[42] And he went out to his passion, to pay back where he had committed no robbery. What else does his statement mean—"he will find nothing in me"? He will find no fault. Had the devil found anything missing from his house? Let the devil pursue any robbers he may find; "he will find nothing in me." EXPLANATIONS OF THE PSALMS 68.[43]

GOD'S NATURE DOES NOT CHANGE. CASSIODORUS: The devil regarded himself as great when he said, "I will set my throne at the north, and I will be like the Most High." Even today proud people count themselves greater than all others. But no one can be truly called great except God alone, for nothing can be remotely compared with his power; he is subject to no change but continues always in the glory of his nature. EXPOSITION OF THE PSALMS 85.10.[44]

---

[34]CSEL 17:209*. [35]Ps 51:6. [36]Ps 52:6-9 (51:6-9 LXX). [37]CSEL 17:209. [38]NPNF 1 9:414*. [39]Phil 2:6-7. [40]Gen 3:5. [41]Ps 69:4 (LXX 68:4). [42]Jn 14:30-31. The parenthetical comments are Augustine's. [43]WSA 3 17:375. [44]ACW 52:332.

THE GREAT ACCUSER. CASSIODORUS: And again: "I shall set my seat to the north, and I will be like the Most High." So he is rightly termed a calumniator, for while performing cruel deeds he always lays accusations against the devoted. Scripture elsewhere says of him, "He shall humble the oppressor, and he shall continue with the sun."[45] So they most justly ask that the humble be not betrayed to the proud, the ingenuous to the liar, the pious to the ungrateful, for the persons whom those persecutors cannot seduce they treat with more savage violence. EXPOSITION OF THE PSALMS 118.122.[46]

14:21 Lest They Neither Fail to Rise or Fill the Earth with Wars

THE JUDGMENT OF BOTH EXCESSIVE SUBMISSIVENESS OR OBSTINACY. VERECUNDUS: God's warning is twofold, one directed toward the submissive and the other toward obstinate minds. As was said about the submissive: "I will punish their crimes with a rod and their sins with a whip, but I will not remove my mercy from them or deceive them in my truth."[47] But the wrath of God's rebuke upon obstinate sinners is unbearable, as Isaiah testifies: "The descendants of the evil will never be named. Prepare their sons to be killed for the iniquity of their fathers. They will not rise, or inherit the earth or fill the face of the world with children. 'And I will rise against them,' says the Lord of hosts, 'and I will destroy the name of Babylon and its seed and offspring,'" said the Lord." COMMENTARY ON THE CANTICLE OF MANASSES 7.6.[48]

14:27 Who Will Frustrate What the Lord Has Purposed

THE STORY WILL END WELL. CHRYSOSTOM: For their part they plotted to hand him [Joseph] over to death, distress, slavery and the worst of evil fates; but God who is skillful in devising good used the wickedness of the plotters for the credit of him whom they had plotted to sell. Lest anyone think that these things happened through some coincidence or reversal of circumstances, by the very men who opposed and hindered them God brings about the events that they tried to prevent, using Joseph's enemies as servants for his credit. From this you may learn that what God has planned no one will scatter, and no one will turn aside his lofty hand, so that when people plot against you, you may not fall or be annoyed but may keep in mind that the plot leads to good at the end, if only you endure nobly whatever happens to you. HOMILIES ON LAZARUS AND THE RICH MAN 4.[49]

GOD'S WILL STANDS. CHRYSOSTOM: What God has reared up and wishes to remain, no one can tear down. In the same way, what he has destroyed and wishes to stay destroyed, no one can rebuild. DISCOURSES AGAINST JUDAIZING CHRISTIANS 5.11.6.[50]

14:29 From the Roots of a Serpent

ROOTS OF A SERPENT. GREGORY THE GREAT: But because this Leviathan is called in another place not merely a serpent but also a flying serpent, because he rules over unclean spirits or reprobate people, as Isaiah says, "Out of the serpent's root shall come forth a flying serpent," we must attentively observe how a basilisk destroys, that by the doings of the basilisk, his malice may be more plainly made known to us. For a basilisk does not destroy with its bite but consumes with its breath. It often also infects the air with its breath and withers with the mere blast of its nostrils whatever it has touched, even when placed at a distance. MORALS ON THE BOOK OF JOB 6.33.62.[51]

---

[45]Ps 72:4-5. [46]ACW 53:232. [47]Ps 89:32-33 (LXX 88:32-33). [48]CCL 93:151. [49]OWP 92. [50]FC 68:138. [51]LF 31:613**.

15:1-9 ORACLE AGAINST MOAB

[1]An oracle concerning Moab.
  Because Ar is laid waste in a night
  Moab is undone;
because Kir is laid waste in a night
  Moab is undone.
[2]The daughter of Dibon[b] has gone up
  to the high places to weep;
over Nebo and over Medeba
  Moab wails.
On every head is baldness,
  every beard is shorn;
[3]in the streets they gird on sackcloth;
  on the housetops and in the squares
  every one wails and melts in tears.
[4]Heshbon and Ele-aleh cry out,
  their voice is heard as far as Jahaz;
therefore the armed men of Moab cry
    aloud;
  his soul trembles.
[5]My heart cries out for Moab;
  his fugitives flee to Zoar,

to Eglath-shelishiyah.
For at the ascent of Luhith
  they go up weeping;
on the road to Horonaim
  they raise a cry of destruction;
[6]the waters of Nimrim
  are a desolation;
the grass is withered, the new growth fails,
  the verdure is no more.
[7]Therefore the abundance they have gained
  and what they have laid up
they carry away
  over the Brook of the Willows.
[8]For a cry has gone
  round the land of Moab;
the wailing reaches to Eglaim,
  the wailing reaches to Beer-elim.
[9]For the waters of Dibon[c] are full of blood;
  yet I will bring upon Dibon[c] even more,
a lion for those of Moab who escape,
  for the remnant of the land.

b Cn: Heb the house and Dibon c One ancient Ms Vg Compare Syr: Heb Dimon

---

OVERVIEW: Moab is to be understood spiritually (JEROME). There is coming judgment and destruction (VERECUNDUS).

15:1 An Oracle Concerning Moab

THE SPIRITUAL INTERPRETATION OF MOAB. JEROME: In a certain way, there is a circumcision that is both carnal and spiritual. Concerning the spiritual circumcision, it is said by the apostle Paul, "For we are of the true circumcision, who worship God in spirit, and glory in Christ Jesus, and do not put confidence in the flesh."[1] And further, for the sake of distinguishing the spiritual

Israel, it is said of the carnal, "You see Israel according to the flesh,"[2] and "You are Gentiles according to the flesh."[3] Thus Moab is to be taken here in a spiritual sense, which is interpreted as "from the father,"[4] that is, "the paternal waters," conceived by incest and drunkenness, because he was brought forth when the father was in a certain sense absent, that is, unawares. In many places of Scripture we read concerning Moab, especially in the book of Numbers, where Balak, the king of the Moabites, invited Balaam the

---

[1]Phil 3:3. [2]1 Cor 10:18. [3]Eph 2:11. [4]Literal Hebrew translation of "Moab."

soothsayer for the purpose of cursing. Balaam prophesied mystically, among other things, against Moab: "A star will arise from Jacob, and a man will rise up out of Israel, and he will strike the leaders of Moab."[5] COMMENTARY ON ISAIAH 6.15.[6]

15:3 In the Streets Everyone Wails

IN THE STREETS. VERECUNDUS: Indeed, it is not inappropriate that the author of the abyss, the devil, should be identified with the abyss, as he is also called death, being the head of death: "Where, O death, is your sting?"[7] And the voice of death or the abyss groans with pain, since he sees that the power to prey upon the people he possessed from the beginning is being taken away. But if, perchance, you have little faith in my own words, we can produce the testimony of Isaiah: "Shall the prey be taken from the strong, or will the captive be rescued from the mighty? But thus says the Lord: 'The captives will indeed be taken away from the strong, and what was stolen by the mighty will be rescued.'"[8] For no one denies that the mighty cry in protest and suffer as a result of losing their spoils, except those who think that the devil is of lesser malice or that he is altogether uninvolved. But persons with such opinions are inept and deceived. Turn instead to the teachers of truth, whose knowledge I can only introduce to you, that it might be yours, reader, to explore within more attentively. Jeremiah uses Moab as a figure for the prince of the world in describing his devastation and groaning: "There is lamentation in all the dwellings of Moab and in its streets, for I have shattered Moab like a useless vessel, said the Lord."[9] Isaiah also bears witness to the coming destruction: "Moreover, Moab's army wails; its soul groans for itself," and again: "Everyone wails upon its roofs and in its streets." In this way, they suffer that they were despoiled of the people. Daily they groan over their plundering. Consequently, they do not cease to attack us also, in the hopes that they can recapture something of what was taken from them. COMMENTARY ON THE CANTICLE OF HABAKKUK 6.12.[10]

---

[5]Num 24:17. [6]PL 24:238. [7]1 Cor 15:55. [8]Is 49:24-25. [9]Jer 48:38. [10]CCL 93:137.

16:1-14 DESTRUCTION OF THE VINEYARDS

[1]They have sent lambs
    to the ruler of the land,
from Sela, by way of the desert,
    to the mount of the daughter of Zion.*
[2]Like fluttering birds,
    like scattered nestlings,
so are the daughters of Moab
    at the fords of the Arnon.
[3]"Give counsel,

    grant justice;
make your shade like night
    at the height of noon;
hide the outcasts,
    betray not the fugitive;
[4]let the outcasts of Moab
    sojourn among you;
be a refuge to them
    from the destroyer.

When the oppressor is no more,
  and destruction has ceased,
and he who tramples under foot
  has vanished from the land,
⁵then a throne will be established in
    steadfast love
  and on it will sit in faithfulness
  in the tent of David
one who judges and seeks justice
  and is swift to do righteousness."

⁶We have heard of the pride of Moab,
  how proud he was;
of his arrogance, his pride, and his
    insolence—
his boasts are false.
⁷Therefore let Moab wail,
  let every one wail for Moab.
Mourn, utterly stricken,
  for the raisin-cakes of Kir-hareseth.

⁸For the fields of Heshbon languish,
  and the vine of Sibmah;
the lords of the nations
  have struck down its branches,
which reached to Jazer
  and strayed to the desert;

its shoots spread abroad
  and passed over the sea.
⁹Therefore I weep with the weeping of Jazer
  for the vine of Sibmah;
I drench you with my tears,
  O Heshbon and Ele-aleh;
for upon your fruit and your harvest
  the battle shout has fallen.
¹⁰And joy and gladness are taken away
  from the fruitful field;
and in the vineyards no songs are sung,
  no shouts are raised;
no treader treads out wine in the presses;
  the vintage shout is hushed.ᵈ
¹¹Therefore my soul moans like a lyre for
    Moab,
  and my heart for Kir-heres.
¹²And when Moab presents himself, when
he wearies himself upon the high place, when
he comes to his sanctuary to pray, he will not
prevail.
¹³This is the word which the LORD spoke
concerning Moab in the past. ¹⁴But now the
LORD says, "In three years, like the years of a
hireling, the glory of Moab will be brought into
contempt, in spite of all his great multitude, and
those who survive will be very few and feeble."

d Gk: Heb I have hushed   *Vg send you a lamb as ruler of the land from the rock of the wilderness to the mount of the daughter of Zion

---

OVERVIEW: Isaiah prophesies the church. Ruth is the fulfillment of the prophecy concerning Moab (JEROME). The tent of David is the church, and the throne is Christ's (EUSEBIUS). The victories of the churches of Moab testify to the dominion of Christ (JEROME).

16:2 The Daughters of Moab Are Like Scattered Nestlings

LAMBS SENT BY WAY OF THE DESERT. JEROME:

Send forth the lamb, the ruler of the earth, from the rock of the desert to the mount of the daughter of Zion." The interpretation that we provide is not history but prophecy. For every prophecy is enveloped in enigmas and precise statements; while it is speaking of one thing, it moves to another, for if it were to preserve the written order it would be a narrative, not a prophecy. This then is the meaning: O Moab, in whom the lion is about to rage and from whom no one who remains can be saved, take consolation in this: the immaculate Lamb who will take away the sins of the world, he who shall rule the world, will come forth from you. From the rock of the desert—that is, from Ruth, who was widowed when her husband died—Obed was begotten from Boaz and Jesse from Obed and David from Jesse and Christ from David. We will interpret the mount of the daughter of Zion to be either the city of Jerusalem herself or, according to a holy understanding, the church which should be established at the summit of the virtues. COMMENTARY ON ISAIAH 5.16.1.[1]

ATTEND TO THE SPIRITUAL SENSE. JEROME: Then, as for Job, that pattern of patience, what mysteries are there not contained in his discourses? Commencing in prose the book soon glides into verse and at the end once more reverts to prose. By the way in which it lays down propositions, assumes postulates, adduces proofs and draws inferences, it illustrates all the laws of logic. Single words occurring in the book are full of meaning. To say nothing of other topics, it prophesies the resurrection of humankind's bodies at once with more clearness and with more caution than anyone has yet shown. "I know," Job says, "that my redeemer lives, and that at the last day I shall rise again from the earth; and I shall be clothed again with my skin, and in my flesh shall I see God. Whom I shall see for myself, and mine eyes shall behold, and not another. This my hope is stored up in my own bosom."[2] I will pass on to Joshua, son of Nun[3]—a type of the Lord in name as well as in deed—who crossed over Jordan, subdued hostile kingdoms, divided the land among the conquering people and who, in every city, village, mountain, river, hill-torrent and boundary which he dealt with, marked out the spiritual realms of the heavenly Jerusalem, that is, of the church.[4] In the book of Judges every one of the popular leaders is a type. Ruth the Moabite fulfills the prophecy of Isaiah: "Send you a lamb, O Lord, as ruler of the land from the rock of the wilderness to the mount of the daughter of Zion." Under the figures of Eli's death and the slaying of Saul, Samuel shows the abolition of the old law.

Again in Zadok and in David he bears witness to the mysteries of the new priesthood and of the new royalty. The third and fourth books of Kings called in Hebrew *Malachim* give the history of the kingdom of Judah from Solomon to Jeconiah, and of that of Israel from Jeroboam the son of Nebat to Hosea, who was carried away into Assyria. If you merely regard the narrative, the words are simple enough, but if you look beneath the surface at the hidden meaning of it, you find a description of the small numbers of the church and of the wars that the heretics wage against it. The twelve prophets whose writings are compressed within the narrow limits of a single volume have typical meanings far different from their literal ones. Hosea speaks many times of Ephraim, of Samaria, of Joseph, of Jezreel, of a wife of whoredoms and of children of whoredoms,[5] of an adulteress shut up within the chamber of her husband, sitting for a long time in widowhood and in the garb of mourning, awaiting the time when her husband will return to her.[6] Joel the son of Pethuel describes the land of the twelve tribes as spoiled and devastated by the palmerworm, the cankerworm, the locust and the blight.[7] He predicts that after the overthrow of the former people the Holy Spirit shall be poured out upon God's servants and handmaids;[8] the same spirit, that is, which was to be poured out in the upper chamber at Zion upon the 120 believers.[9] These believers rising by gradual and regular gradations from one to fifteen form the steps to which there is a mystical allusion in the "psalms of degrees."[10] Amos, although he is only "a herdsman" from the country, "a gatherer of sycamore fruit,"[11] cannot be explained in a few words. LETTER 53.8.[12]

16:5 A Throne Established

THE THRONE IS CHRIST'S. EUSEBIUS OF CAE-

[1]CCL 73:179. [2]Job 19:25-27. [3]Num 27:18. [4]See Gal 4:6. [5]Hos 1:2. [6]Hos 3:1, 3-4. [7]Joel 1:4. [8]Joel 2:29. [9]Acts 1:13, 15. [10]Pss 120—134. [11]Amos 7:14. [12]NPNF 2 6:99-100*.

SAREA: According to Aquila, "his throne will be established in mercy," or according to Theodotion, "the throne will be established with mercy." Who will establish the throne? Or how is Christ born from the posterity of David? The throne will be established by the Moabites, according to the text; and Christ who is born from the tent (tabernacle) of David will sit upon the throne. By "the tent of David" the prophet means the church of God. David himself is called christ because from his posterity Christ is born according to flesh.[13] Therefore, the tent (tabernacle) of David is the church, and the throne belongs to the head of the church. It refers to the humanity of Christ. Therefore, one should contemplate on the mystery of Christ revealed in the prophecy only in the Holy Spirit; and in such a cautious contemplation curiosity and speculation must be tamed.[14] COMMENTARY ON ISAIAH 16.1-5.[15]

THE DOMINION OF MERCY. JEROME: "And a throne will be prepared in mercy, and on it will sit in truth, in the tabernacle of David, one who judges and seeks judgment and quickly renders

what is just." The Hebrews interpret this to mean that Hezekiah, a just man, after having expelled the Assyrians, will retain the throne of David and rule Judah, adjudging the people of God to be subject to himself in truth. Others understand that it is about Christ. With the antichrist reduced to dust and with the oppressor who had trampled all the earth removed, Christ the King will come and sit in the tabernacle of David and render to each person according to his works on the day of judgment.[16] Neither is there any doubt that this chapter prophesies of Christ. But we are also able to understand the same thing in the first advent and to demonstrate in the tabernacle of the church that the surging victories of the churches of Moab in all the earth testify to the dominion of Christ. COMMENTARY ON ISAIAH 5.16.5.[17]

---

[13]Christ, the anointed one, was born of a Moabite (Ruth). [14]Cyril's call is to avoid speculations on the mystery of Christ, perhaps especially on the mode of unity of human and divine in Christ, which was a subject of heated debates in his lifetime. [15]PG 24:201. [16]Cf. Mt 16:27; Rom 2:6. [17]CCL 73:180-81.

17:1-14 JUDGMENT AGAINST IDOLATRY

[1]An oracle concerning Damascus.
Behold, Damascus will cease to be a city,
and will become a heap of ruins.
[2]Her cities will be deserted for ever;[e]
they will be for flocks,
which will lie down, and none will make them afraid.
[3]The fortress will disappear from Ephraim,

and the kingdom from Damascus;
and the remnant of Syria will be
like the glory of the children of Israel,
says the LORD of hosts.

[4]And in that day
the glory of Jacob will be brought low,
and the fat of his flesh will grow lean.

⁵*And it shall be as when the reaper gathers*
    standing grain
  and his arm harvests the ears,
  and as when one gleans the ears of grain
    in the Valley of Rephaim.
⁶*Gleanings will be left in it,*
  as when an olive tree is beaten—
two or three berries
  in the top of the highest bough,
four or five
  on the branches of a fruit tree,
       says the LORD *God of Israel.*

⁷*In that day men will regard their Maker,*
and their eyes will look to the Holy One of
Israel; ⁸*they will not have regard for the altars,*
the work of their hands, and they will not look
to what their own fingers have made, either
the Asherim or the altars of incense.
⁹*In that day their strong cities will be like*
the deserted places of the Hivites and the
Amorites,ᶠ which they deserted because of the
children of Israel, and there will be desolation.

¹⁰*For you have forgotten the God of your*
  salvation,
  and have not remembered the Rock of
    your refuge;
therefore, though you plant pleasant plants
  and set out slips of an alien god,
¹¹*though you make them grow on the day*
  that you plant them,
  and make them blossom in the morning
    that you sow;
yet the harvest will flee away
  in a day of grief and incurable pain.

¹²*Ah, the thunder of many peoples,*
  they thunder like the thundering of
    the sea!
Ah, the roar of nations,
  they roar like the roaring of mighty
    waters!
¹³*The nations roar like the roaring of many*
    waters,
  but he will rebuke them, and they will
    flee far away,
chased like chaff on the mountains before
  the wind
  and whirling dust before the storm.
¹⁴*At evening time, behold, terror!*
  Before morning, they are no more!
This is the portion of those who despoil us,
  and the lot of those who plunder us.

e Cn Compare Gk: Heb *the cities of Aroer are deserted* f Cn Compare Gk: Heb *the wood and the highest bough* *Vg *in the day of your planting, the wild vine*

OVERVIEW: The remnant is those who believe in the Lord (EUSEBIUS). Idolatry is senseless (JOHN OF DAMASCUS). The "waves of the sea" represent invading armies, for example, Sennacherib, which are turned away from Jerusalem and scattered like dust in a storm (JEROME).

17:4-8 The Glory of Jacob

BERRIES ON AN OLIVE BRANCH. EUSEBIUS OF CAESAREA: By this it is clearly promised that the glory of Israel and all her riches will be taken away, and only a few, who like the few berries on an olive branch can be counted easily, will be left. These are the ones who believe in the Lord. Just after this there is a prophecy of the entire human race turning away from the error of idolatry and recognizing the God of Israel. PROOF OF THE GOSPEL 2.3.[1]

¹POG 1:92*.

They Will Not Look. John of Damascus:
Those who trust in idols are foolish. Idols are their
own creations, things they made with their own
hands, but they turn around and say, "These idols
are our creators." How can these people say that
something they made is their creator? Moreover,
they guard their idols, so that they will not be stolen by thieves. What foolishness! If idols cannot
guard and protect themselves, how can they guard
and save others? Barlaam and Joseph 10.[2]

17:12-14 They Will Flee

The Assyrians Are Scattered Like Dust.
Jerome: Those who believe that the captivity of
Damascus discussed above was inflicted by the
Romans also refer what is written here to the
time of Christ and the apostles: "People will bow
to their Creator, and their eyes will look to the
holy one of Israel." They further think that what
follows, namely, "You will plant faithful plants,
and you will sow strange seeds; in the day of your
planting, the wild grape" applies to the infidelity
of the Jews. And this little passage that we just set
forth they interpret as concerning the peoples

who persecute the church. The next line, "he will
rebuke him, and he will flee far away," they
receive as concerning the devil, demonstrating
the destruction of persecutors and demons
through a tropological interpretation. We, however, follow the original order and complete the
historical foundation with a historical culmina-
tion. Woe, it says, to all the nations who wage
war against my people, whose attack was strong
enough to be compared to the waves of the sea.
But when raging warriors come and inundate my
land, then their prince Sennacherib will flee from
them, rebuked, and they will be scattered like
dust in a plundering storm. As the top of a whirlwind revolves, so will he be struck by an angel
when he approaches Jerusalem to besiege her. He
will come in the morning and witness his powerful army destroyed. And "this is the portion of
those who despoil us." This prophet speaks either
in the person of the people or as though uniting
himself to his nation. Commentary on Isaiah
5.17.12-14.[3]

---

[2]LCL 34:139**. [3]CCL 73:187-88.

18:1-7 THE LAND OF ETHIOPIA

[1]Ah, land of whirring wings*
　　which is beyond the rivers of Ethiopia;
[2]which sends ambassadors by the Nile,
　　in vessels of papyrus upon the waters!
Go, you swift messengers,
　　to a nation, tall and smooth,
to a people feared near and far,
　　a nation mighty and conquering,
　　whose land the rivers divide.

[3]All you inhabitants of the world,
　　you who dwell on the earth,
when a signal is raised on the mountains,
　　look!
　　When a trumpet is blown, hear!
[4]For thus the Lord said to me:
"I will quietly look from my dwelling
　　like clear heat in sunshine,
　　like a cloud of dew in the heat of

harvest."

*⁵For before the harvest, when the blossom
  is over,
  and the flower becomes a ripening grape,
he will cut off the shoots with pruning
  hooks,
  and the spreading branches he will hew
  away.
⁶They shall all of them be left
  to the birds of prey of the mountains
  and to the beasts of the earth.
And the birds of prey will summer*

*upon them,
  and all the beasts of the earth will
  winter upon them,*

*⁷At that time gifts will be brought to the
Lord of hosts
  from a people tall and smooth,
    from a people feared near and far,
  a nation mighty and conquering,
    whose land the rivers divide,
to Mount Zion, the place of the name of
the Lord of hosts.*

*LXX woe to the wings of the vessels of the land

Overview: Reference to areas beyond Ethiopia emphasizes Israel's idolatry (Cyril of Alexandria). The "wings of the vessels" are the churches, and the sea is the world, in which the church is set like a ship tossed in the deep but not destroyed (Hippolytus).

18:1-2 Beyond the Rivers of Ethiopia

The Israelites Follow Other Gods.

Cyril of Alexandria: Someone might wonder and say to himself, "Why does the prophetic oracle addressed to Damascus now mention the land that is beyond the rivers of Ethiopia?" At certain times the Israelites foolishly abandoned God the Savior of all and fell into the error of worshiping many gods. Paying no heed whatsoever to the law given by Moses, they were chastised by God, at times through foes who rose up against them and at times by other catastrophes. Although they should have repented and been healed, ceased their wicked way, walked in the commandments and sought help from God, they made alliances with their neighbors, first with the kings in Damascus, then with those in Egypt. Not only this. They also embraced the gods of the nations that had come to their aid and wasted no time in emulating their ways. Hence the prophet now turns

his attention to the Egyptians.

The Israelites, in particular those living in Jerusalem, had approached the Egyptians and pleaded with them to become allies. They needed their support because they were being invaded by the Babylonians. As God says in the words of the prophet, "Woe to those who go down to Egypt for help, who trust in horses and chariots."[1] The Egyptians were zealous in their devotion to idols. Therefore he calls them a people desperate and beaten down. Desperate because they did not know the one who is by nature truly God, beaten down because they had allowed their minds to become subject to the deceptions of demons, trodden down under their feet. Commentary on Isaiah 2.3.18.[2]

The Wings of the Vessels Are the Churches. Hippolytus: The word of Isaiah: "Woe to the wings of the vessels of the land, beyond the rivers of Ethiopia: (woe to him) who sends sureties by the sea, and letters of papyrus [on the water; for nimble messengers will go] to a nation anxious and expectant, and a people strange and bitter against them; a nation hopeless and trodden down."

---

[1]Is 31:1. [2]*Comm.* 24 4:855; PG 70:436-37.

But we who hope for the Son of God are persecuted and trodden down by those unbelievers. For the "wings of the vessels" are the churches; and the sea is the world, in which the church is set like a ship tossed in the deep but not destroyed. For she has with her the skilled pilot, Christ. And she bears in her midst also the trophy over death, for she carries with her the cross of the Lord. For her prow is the east, and her stern is the west, and her hold is the south, and her tillers are the two Testaments. And the ropes that stretch around her are the love of Christ, which binds the church. And the net which she bears with her is the layer of the regeneration which renews the believing from which also come these glories. As the wind, the Spirit from heaven is present by whom those who believe are sealed. She has also anchors of iron accompanying her, that is, the holy commandments of Christ himself, which are strong as iron. She also has mariners on the right and on the left, assessors like the holy angels by whom the church is always governed and defended. The ladder in her leading up to the sail-yard is an emblem of the passion of Christ, which brings the faithful to the ascent of heaven. And the topsails aloft on the yard are the company of prophets, martyrs and apostles, who have entered into their rest in the kingdom of Christ. ON THE ANTICHRIST 58-59.[3]

---

[3]ANF 5:216-17.

19:1-15 GOD'S JUDGMENT AGAINST EGYPT

[1]An oracle concerning Egypt.
Behold, the LORD is riding on a swift* cloud
    and comes to Egypt;
and the idols of Egypt will tremble at his
    presence,
    and the heart of the Egyptians will melt
    within them.
[2]And I will stir up Egyptians against
    Egyptians,
    and they will fight, every man against his
    brother
and every man against his neighbor,
city against city, kingdom against
    kingdom;
[3]and the spirit of the Egyptians within them
    will be emptied out,
    and I will confound their plans;
and they will consult the idols and the
    sorcerers,
    and the mediums and the wizards;
[4]and I will give over the Egyptians
    into the hand of a hard master;
and a fierce king will rule over them,
    says the Lord, the LORD of hosts.

[5]And the waters of the Nile will be dried up,
    and the river will be parched and dry;
[6]and its canals will become foul,
    and the branches of Egypt's Nile will
    diminish and dry up,

reeds and rushes will rot away.
⁷There will be bare places by the Nile,
    on the brink of the Nile,
and all that is sown by the Nile will dry up,
    be driven away, and be no more.
⁸The fishermen will mourn and lament,
    all who cast hook in the Nile;
and they will languish
    who spread nets upon the water.
⁹The workers in combed flax will be in
        despair,
    and the weavers of white cotton.
¹⁰Those who are the pillars of the land will
        be crushed,
    and all who work for hire will be grieved.

¹¹The princes of Zoan are utterly foolish;
    the wise counselors of Pharoah give
        stupid counsel.

How can you say to Pharaoh,
    "I am a son of the wise,
    a son of ancient kings"?
¹²Where then are your wise men?
    Let them tell you and make known
    what the LORD of hosts has purposed
        against Egypt.
¹³The princes of Zoan have become fools,
    and the princes of Memphis are deluded;
those who are the cornerstones of her tribes
    have led Egypt astray.
¹⁴The LORD has mingled within her a spirit
        of confusion;
and they have made Egypt stagger in all her
        doings
    as a drunken man staggers in his vomit.
¹⁵And there will be nothing for Egypt
    which head or tail, palm branch or reed,
        may do.

* Vg will ascend upon a light

OVERVIEW: The swift cloud is either a symbol of heaven or of Christ's body, not weighted down by sin, or the Virgin Mary (CHRYSOSTOM, JEROME, BEDE). Those who rejoiced at the coming of the Lord were moved by his birth (AUGUSTINE). The Lord took on a body not stained by sin and ascended to the right hand of the Father (CHROMATIUS OF AQUILEIA, BEDE).

Egypt means the whole sinful world (TERTULLIAN). Jesus went to Egypt to destroy their idols (CYRIL OF JERUSALEM). Christ was the Word of God, who visited Egypt in visible fashion (EUSEBIUS). The prophecy of the incarnation has been fulfilled, in that many throughout Egypt worship the God of the Bible (EUSEBIUS). Isaiah prophesies that Christ will come to Egypt because the Egyptians were the first to practice polytheism (EUSEBIUS). As a human being Christ flees Herod to Egypt, but as God he shakes the idols of the Egyptians (THEODORET). The Lord's coming to

Egypt refers to the struggle between believers and nonbelievers (BEDE). The oracle against Egypt refers to the entire world, kingdom fighting against kingdom (ISIDORE OF SEVILLE). By raising Christ from the dead, he made the counsel of those who spoke evil empty (AMBROSE). Secular teaching is a shallow well that will dry up, but the gospel is living water (BEDE).

19:1 The Lord Rides on a Swift Cloud

ENTER INTO EGYPT. JEROME: Appreciate what that means: The Lord comes, the Lord and Savior, into the Egypt in which we live; the Lord comes into the land of darkness where Pharaoh is. But he does not come save riding on a swift cloud. Now what is this swift cloud? I think it is holy Mary with child of no human seed. This swift cloud has come into the world and brought with it the Creator of the world. What does Isaiah say? "The

Lord will enter into Egypt upon a swift cloud; and the idols of Egypt shall be shattered." The Lord has come, and the false gods of Egypt tremble violently, crash together and are destroyed. Homilies on the Psalms 24 (Psalm 96).[1]

The Cloud as the Virgin. Jerome: We must think of that swift cloud as befitting either the body of the Savior, because his body was light, not weighted down by any sin; or certainly holy Mary, who was heavy with child by no human seed. Behold the Lord has entered the Egypt of this world on a swift cloud, the Virgin. Homilies on the Psalms 11 (Psalm 77).[2]

Egypt as the Whole World. Tertullian: Egypt is sometimes understood to mean the whole world in [Isaiah], because of superstition and malediction. An Answer to the Jews 9.[3]

A Prophecy Concerning Egypt. Augustine: It is relevant to recall that holy Isaiah uttered a particular prophecy concerning Egypt: "And the idols of Egypt shall be moved at his presence, and the heart of Egypt shall melt within them" and the rest.

In the same class with these prophets were those who rejoiced because they knew he had come whom they had been expecting. Such were Simeon and Anna, who recognized Jesus when he was born, and Elizabeth, who, in the Spirit, realized that he had been conceived, and Peter, who, by revelation of the Father, affirmed, "You are the Christ, the son of the living God."[4] City of God 8.23.[5]

The Lord Ascended. Bede: The psalmist spoke of this solemnity [when he said], "God has ascended with a shout of jubilation, and the Lord with the sound of the trumpet."[6] He ascended with a shout of jubilation, since he sought heaven as the disciples rejoiced in the glory of his being lifted up. He ascended with the sound of the trumpet, since he went up to the throne of his heavenly kingdom as the angels heralded his return to judge the living and the dead.

How God, who is present always and everywhere and does not change from place to place, ascended, the same [inspired writer] declares elsewhere, saying, "He who makes a cloud his stairway and walks upon the wings of the winds."[7] He calls the substance of human weakness with which "the sun of righteousness"[8] clothed himself, that [the sight of him] might be borne by human beings, a cloud. Hence Isaiah says, "Behold, the Lord will ascend upon a swift cloud and will enter Egypt, and the idols of Egypt will be shaken before his face." The Lord ascended upon a swift cloud so that when he entered Egypt he might overturn its idols when "the Word was made flesh and dwelt among us."[9] He took upon himself a body immune from all stains of iniquity and entered the world in it, so that he might destroy the cult of idolatry and make clear the true light of divinity to the shadowy and dark hearts of the Gentiles. He who is not enclosed in a place willed to go from place to place by means of this cloud, his human nature; in it he who always remains invisible in his divinity willed to suffer mockery, scourging and death; by means of it he who fills the heavens in the power of his divinity ascended into heaven, crowned with the power of his resurrection. Homilies on the Gospels 2.15.[10]

The Importance of the Cloud. Chrysostom: [At the Mount of Transfiguration] the Father uttered a voice out of the cloud. Why out of the cloud? Because this is how God appears. For a "cloud and darkness are around him."[11] "He sits on a light cloud," and "He makes clouds his chariot."[12] "A cloud received him out of their sight."[13] "As the Son of Man coming in the clouds."[14]

His voice comes from a cloud so that they might believe that the voice proceeds from God. Homilies on the Gospel of Matthew 56.5.[15]

---

[1]FC 48:193*. [2]FC 48:88. [3]ANF 3:162**. [4]Mt 16:16. [5]FC 14:64**. [6]Ps 47:5 (LXX 46:6). [7]Ps 104:3 (LXX 103:3). [8]Mal 4:2. [9]Jn 1:14. [10]CS 111:142-43. [11]Ps 97:2. [12]Ps 104:3. [13]Acts 1:9. [14]Dan 7:13. [15]NPNF 1 10:348**.

The Cloud Is a Symbol. Chrysostom: That it was Jesus himself [at the ascension] they knew from the fact that he had been conversing with them (for had they seen only from a distance, they could not have recognized him by sight), but that he is taken up into heaven the angels themselves inform them. Observe how it is ordered, that not all is done by the Spirit, but the eyes also do their part. But why did "a cloud receive him"?[16] This too was a sure sign that he went up to heaven. Not fire, as in the case of Elijah, nor fiery chariot,[17] but "a cloud received him"; which was a symbol of heaven, as the prophet says, "Who makes the clouds his chariot";[18] it is of the Father himself that this is said. Therefore he says, "on a cloud"; in the symbol, he would say, of the divine power, for no other power is seen to appear on a cloud. For hear again what another prophet says: "The Lord sits upon a light cloud." Homilies on the Acts of the Apostles 2.[19]

Christ Will Come into Egypt. Eusebius of Caesarea: This prophecy says that the one who is begotten after the God and Lord of all things, meaning the Word of God, will come into Egypt, and not undercover or invisibly or without a body but riding on a light cloud, or better "on thick light." This is the meaning of the Hebrew word. Let the Hebrew children tell us when after the time of Isaiah the Lord visited Egypt, and which Lord it was. The God over all is one. Let them tell us how he is said to ride on "thick light" and to come to any particular place on the earth. Let them interpret "thick light" and explain why the Lord is not said to visit Egypt without it. Let them also say when the prophecy that the Egyptian idols made with hands would be shaken and Egyptians would fight Egyptians by the coming of the Lord is to have been fulfilled. Proof of the Gospel 6.20.[20]

The Idols Will Tremble. Eusebius of Caesarea: Now one can consider that the prophecy has not been fulfilled if the following are true: if the Egyptians in our own time cannot be seen to

have abandoned the gods of their fathers and calling on the God of the prophets; throughout every town and city in the country of Egypt there are not altars built to the God that previously only the Hebrews acknowledged; the idols have not been shaken. . . . How can we deny that the prophecies of ages past have been fulfilled? They promised beforehand that the Lord would not come to Egypt in an incorporeal manner but on a light cloud, or better "on a thick light," which is the meaning of the Hebrew word. This figuratively speaks of his incarnation. The prophecy continues by calling him a human being who is the Savior, saying, "And he shall send to them a man who is a savior."[21] The Hebrew here is, "And he shall send to them a savior who will save them." This clear demonstration leads me to conclude that there is no doubt of the time of the promise of the appearing of the Lord. Proof of the Gospel 8.5.[22]

The Idols of Egypt. Eusebius of Caesarea: I suppose that the reason why it is foretold that the Lord would come to Egypt is this: The Egyptians are said to have been the first to practice the errors of polytheism. . . . And Holy Scripture witnesses that they were the enemies of God's people from the very beginning, for it is written that their ancient king confessed that he did not know the Lord, when he said, "I do not know the Lord, and I will not let Israel go."[23] So, then, it is because Scripture wishes to show the great marvel of the divine power of Christ that it foretells his going to Egypt, in predicting that the Egyptians will undergo an extraordinary conversion, when it goes on to say, "And the Egyptians shall know the Lord, who before knew him not, and shall pray to the Lord,"[24] and so on. . . . Here it is predicted of Egypt and its people that they will not acknowledge idols any more but will acknowledge the Lord revealed by the Jewish prophets. Now if we cannot see this actually ful-

---

[16]Acts 1:9. [17]See 2 Kings 2:11. [18]Ps 104:3. [19]NPNF 1 11:13. [20]POG 2:37*. [21]Is 19:20. [22]POG 2:147-48*. [23]Ex 5:2. [24]Is 19:20.

filled before our eyes, we must not say that the Lord's coming to Egypt has taken place. But if beyond all need of argument the truth is shown by facts and reveals clearly to the most unobservant the Egyptians rescued from hereditary superstition, and followers of the God of the prophets who foretold that this would take place, serving him only and greeting every form of death for their duty to him, to what else can we attribute it but to the Lord coming to Egypt, as the prophecy before us predicted? PROOF OF THE GOSPEL 9.2.[25]

HE SHAKES THE IDOLS OF EGYPT. THEODORET OF CYR: Therefore all the human qualities of the Lord Christ, hunger, I mean, and thirst and weariness, sleep, fear, sweat, prayer, and ignorance, and the like, we affirm to belong to our nature which God the Word assumed and united to himself in effecting our salvation. But the restitution of motion to the maimed, the resurrection of the dead, the supply of loaves and all the other miracles we believe to be works of the divine power. In this sense I say that the same Lord Christ both suffers and destroys suffering; suffers, that is, as touching the visible, and destroys suffering as touching the ineffably indwelling Godhead. This is proved beyond question by the narrative of the holy Evangelists, from whom we learn that when lying in a manger and wrapped in swaddling clothes, he was announced by a star, worshiped by magi and hymned by angels. Thus we reverently discern that the swaddling bands and the lack of a bed and all the poverty belonged to the manhood; while the journey of the magi and the guiding of the star and the company of the angels proclaim the Godhead of the unseen. In like manner he makes his escape into Egypt and avoids the fury of Herod by flight, for he was man; but as the prophet says, "He shakes the idols of Egypt," for he was by nature God. LETTER 151.[26]

THE SHADOW OF HIS BODY. AMBROSE. Hear that the flesh of the Lord was a shadow: "Behold, the Lord is seated on a light cloud and will come

to Egypt." David also said, "Protect me under the shadow of your wings."[27] The shadow was emptied, therefore, for us whom the sun of iniquity had consumed. For we saw Christ in a shadow when the faith was first arising. Now that he illuminates the entire world, we nevertheless still see him through the shadow of his body, which is the church, not yet face to face, for our bodily eyes are incapable of beholding the brilliance of his divinity. And this shadow daily protects all the earth. An imprisonment, therefore, was advantageous: "God imprisoned all things in unbelief, that he might have mercy on all."[28] EXPOSITION OF PSALM 118 19.6.[29]

A HOLY BODY. CHROMATIUS OF AQUILEIA: But Isaiah announced the Lord's future trip to Egypt[30] some time ago when he said, "Behold, the Lord will be seated upon a light cloud and will come to Egypt." By this saying, the mystery of the Lord's incarnation is clearly shown. For because the Lord himself, "dawning from on high,"[31] is called "the sun of justice,"[32] it is not without merit that he was foretold to be coming "upon a light cloud," that is, in a holy body which no sin was able to weigh down. It was under the veil of this corporeal cloud that he concealed the light of his majesty. TRACTATE ON MATTHEW 6.1.[33]

HE COVERED HIS RADIANCE. CHROMATIUS OF AQUILEIA: To make himself visible, the "sun of justice"[34] assumed a human body like a cloud, according to which it was said, "Behold, the Lord will come upon a light cloud." What is the cloud upon which the Lord, the sun of justice, was predicted to arrive if not the cloud of the human body, through which the appearance of his divine radiance was shielded? But just as the sun is less visible to us when covered by a cloud, even though its nature remains unchanged, so also the Son of God did not cease to retain the glory of his

---

[25]POG 2:154-55**. [26]NPNF 2 3:328*. [27]Ps 17:8 (16:8 LXX). [28]Rom 11:32. [29]CSEL 62:425*. [30]See Mt 2:13-15. [31]Lk 1:78. [32]Mal 4:2. [33]CCL 9A:220. [34]Mal 4:2.

divinity when he covered his radiance with the cloud of a human body. The Gospel said that "his face shone like the sun and his clothing was made as white as snow"[35] to show the power of his divine radiance, through which even his clothing was made white like snow. "And behold, Moses and Elijah appeared and spoke with them," it continues.[36] The Lord had already promised the glory of this vision long ago to the same Moses, saying, "You will see my back [*posteriora mea*]."[37] He used "posterior" here to indicate that he would reveal himself to Moses at a posterior time, after his assumption of the body. "But Peter responded and said to him, 'Lord, it is good for us to be here. If you like, let's pitch three tents here, one for you, one for Moses, and one for Elijah.'"[38] TRACTATE ON MATTHEW 54A.3.[39]

NEVER IN DARKNESS. JEROME: Behold, the Lord has entered the Egypt of this world on a soft cloud, the Virgin. "He led them with a cloud by day."[40] Beautifully said, by day, for the cloud was never in darkness but always in light. "And all night with a glow of fire."[41] "For you darkness itself is not dark, and night shines as the day."[42] "And all night with a glow of fire." "The Lord our God is a consuming fire."[43] A consuming fire. The psalmist did not say what the fire is consuming; he left that to our intelligence. HOMILIES ON THE PSALMS 11 (PSALM 77).[44]

THE CREATOR COMES. JEROME: "The Lord is riding on a swift cloud on his way to Egypt." Appreciate what that means: the Lord comes, the Lord and Savior, into the Egypt in which we live; the Lord comes into the land of darkness where Pharaoh is. But he does not come save riding on a swift cloud. Now what is this swift cloud? I think it is holy Mary with child of no human seed. This swift cloud has come into the world and brought with it the Creator of the world. What does Isaiah say? "The Lord will enter into Egypt upon a swift cloud; and the idols of Egypt shall be shattered." The Lord has come, and the false gods of Egypt tremble violently, crash together and are

destroyed. This is the cloud that in Alexandria destroyed Sarapis;[45] no general did it, no mortal man, but this cloud that came into Alexandria. HOMILIES ON THE PSALMS 24 (PSALM 96).[46]

SAVING STREAMS OF WISDOM. BEDE: Such brief downpours are rightly compared with the shallow, inflated boasting of secular teaching which often seems to pour forth an endless, deep river of eloquence and broad learning but soon dries up entirely, as though it had never existed at all, where the sun of justice and the summer of evangelical radiance shine. The Lord himself laments this state of affairs through the prophet: "They abandoned me, the fountain of living water, and dug for themselves broken cisterns which cannot hold water."[47] Isaiah also says, "Behold, the Lord will ascend upon a light cloud and will come to Egypt," and again, "The water of the sea will dry up and the river will be desolate and arid." "A well of living waters," he said, "which flows from Lebanon,"[48] that is, from the church, whose life is both clear and deep. For Lebanon, which means "clarity," fills its camps with saving streams of wisdom for its subjects, as though they were an audience, like the Lord promises in the Gospel: "Whoever believes in me, as Scripture teaches, 'rivers of living water will flow from his heart.'"[49] Explaining this, the Gospel adds, "He said this about the Spirit, whom those who believed in him would receive."[50] SIX BOOKS ON THE SONG OF SONGS 3.4.15.[51]

BORN HOLY. BEDE: The blessed Virgin, being purely human, was unable to receive bodily all the plenitude of divinity.[52] But the power of the Most High overshadowed her,[53] that is, her body received the incorporeal light of divinity. The prophet comments on this beautifully: "Behold,

---

[35]Mt 17:2 [36]Mt 17:3. [37]Ex 33:23. [38]Mt 17:4. [39]CCL 9A Suppl:629-30. [40]Ps 78:14. [41]Ps 78:14. [42]Ps 139:12. [43]See Deut 4:24; Heb 12:29. [44]FC 48:88. [45]Sarapis was an Alexandrian pagan deity that Jerome claims was destroyed by the Lord. [46]FC 48:193*. [47]Jer 2:13. [48]Song 4:15. [49]Jn 7:38; cf. Is 44:3; 58:11. [50]Jn 7:39. [51]CCL 119B:268-69*. [52]See Col 2:9. [53]Lk 1:35.

the Lord will ascend upon on a light cloud and will come to Egypt," which is to say, Behold, the coeternal Word of God the Father, the light from light who was born before the ages, will receive at the end of the age a flesh and soul not burdened with any sin, and he will enter the world from a virginal womb, like a bridegroom from his chamber.[54] Therefore, what will be born will be called holy, the Son of God.[55] In distinction from our holiness, Jesus alone is said to be born holy. EXPOSITION OF THE GOSPEL OF LUKE 1.1.35.[56]

SPIRITUAL WARFARE AMID AN EVIL PEACE. BEDE: But if the entire world is divided against itself with respect to faith in Christ, each home contains both infidels and believers. A good war is waged, therefore, to disrupt an evil peace. Isaiah also announced prophetically under the figure of Egypt: "Behold, the Lord will ascend upon a light cloud and will come to Egypt, and the idols of Egypt will tremble at his presence and the hearts of the Egyptians will melt within them, and I will cause Egyptians to attack Egyptians." Clearly this refers to a struggle between proponents of the faith and its enemies. EXPOSITION OF THE GOSPEL OF LUKE 4.12.51.[57]

19:2 Provoking Egypt Against Egypt

APPLYING TO SCRIPTURE THE RULES OF TIME. ISIDORE OF SEVILLE: Daughters of Tyre, daughters of the nations, from species to genus. Through Tyre, neighbor to the land of prophecy, the psalmist signifies all the people who would come to believe in Christ. Rightly, therefore, does he continue: "The wealthy of the earth will all seek your face."[58] The Lord also threatens Assyria through the prophet Isaiah, saying, "I will destroy the Assyrian in my land, and I will crush him on my mountains";[59] "and the Lord will destroy Babylon, glorious and famous among the kingdoms, as he destroyed Sodom and Gomorrah."[60] It is possible that the Lord began to admonish only the city of Babylon at the beginning of Isaiah, but as he spoke against it, he crossed from species to

genus and turned to address his word generally toward all the earth. Surely, if he were not speaking against the entire world, he would not have added later: "I will destroy the whole earth, and I will visit evil upon the world,"[61] and other such statements that pertain to the eradication of the corrupted world. Consequently, he also adds, "This is the decision that I have made concerning the whole earth and this is its hand extended over all the peoples."[62] . . . He was addressing the entire world under the figure of Babylon, saying, "I will destroy the whole earth, and I will visit evil upon the world," along with similar declarations pertaining to the world's extermination. [But] he also turned his attention back toward Babylon, as though from genus to species, and made remarks that relate specifically to that city: "Behold, I am raising Media up against them."[63] For during Balthasar's reign, Babylon was taken by Media. So also, the "oracle of Egypt" intends for Egypt to be understood as a personification of the entire world when it says, "And I will cause Egyptians to fight against Egyptians, kingdom against kingdom," since it is written that Egypt possessed only one kingdom, not many.

The fifth rule of time is that the greater part can be implied through the lesser or the lesser through the greater. With regard to the three days of the Lord's burial, for instance, the whole is taken from the part, since he lay in the tomb neither for three full days nor for three full nights. And the part can be taken from the whole, for after the Lord had established that "the length of a man's life will be one hundred and twenty years,"[64] only one hundred years passed before the great flood. Also, whereas God predicted that the children of Israel would be slaves in Egypt for four hundred years and would then depart,[65] they were not enslaved for four hundred years, since they had escaped slavery under Joseph's rule. Yet again, the whole is also here

---

[54]Ps 18:6. [55]Lk 1:35. [56]CCL 120:33-34. [57]CCL 120:262. [58]Ps 45:12. [59]Is 14:25. [60]Is 13:19. [61]Is 13:5, 11. [62]Is 14:26. [63]Is 13:17. [64]Gen 6:3. [65]See Gen 15:13.

subjoined from the part, since they did not depart Egypt immediately after the four hundred years, as promised, but did so after four hundred and thirty years had transpired. Events that are still in the future but are narrated as though they have already occurred also belong to this rule of time. For example, "They pierced my hands and feet and counted all of my bones,"[66] and "they divided my clothing among themselves,"[67] and similar passages in which what has yet to occur is related as a historical event. Anything predicated of the future, however, is spoken from our perspective. But when the future is said to have happened, it must be understood from the perspective of God's eternity, since what is still in the future for us has already been accomplished according to God's predestination, for whom everything in the future has been accomplished.

The sixth rule of time is that of recapitulation, which consists in Scripture returning to what it had already narrated. For instance, when it discussed the sons of the sons of Noah, Scripture said that they had their own language among their own people. Afterwards, however, as though subsequent in time, we read, "And all the earth was of one language, and everyone spoke with one voice."[68] How, therefore, could the sons of Noah have had their own language if there were only one language for everyone, unless the narrative regressed in order to recapitulate what had already transpired? THREE BOOKS OF THOUGHTS 1.19.7-16.[69]

19:11 Wise Counselors Turned to Folly

VAIN IS THE COUNSEL. AMBROSE: For this reason the Father says to him, "Return to me," calling forth from earth to heaven the one whom he had sent for our salvation. And so, raising up his only-begotten Son, he made empty the counsel of those who spoke evil—on this account Isaiah also says, "Vain is the counsel of your spirit"— and he abolished all the reproaches which they directed as if they were shooting arrows. He destroyed the power of those who were trusting in their own strength and not in God. ON THE PATRIARCHS 11.49.[70]

---

[66]Ps 22:16-17 (21:17-18 LXX). [67]Ps 22:18 (21:19 LXX). [68]See Gen 11:1, 6. [69]PL 83:582-85. [70]FC 65:267-68.

19:16-25 CONVERSION OF EGYPT AND ASSYRIA

[16]In that day the Egyptians will be like women, and tremble with fear before the hand which the LORD of hosts shakes over them. [17]And the land of Judah will become a terror to the Egyptians; every one to whom it is mentioned will fear because of the purpose which the LORD of hosts has purposed against them.

[18]In that day there will be five cities in the land of Egypt which speak the language of Canaan and swear allegiance to the LORD of hosts. One of these will be called the City of the Sun.

[19]In that day there will be an altar to the LORD in the midst of the land of Egypt, and a pillar to the LORD at its border. [20]It will be a sign and a witness* to the LORD of hosts in the land of Egypt;

when they cry to the Lord because of oppressors he will send them a savior,†and will defend and deliver them. ²¹*And the Lord will make himself known to the Egyptians; and the Egyptians will know the Lord in that day and worship with sacrifice and burnt offering, and they will make vows to the Lord and perform them.* ²²*And the Lord will smite Egypt, smiting and healing, and they will return to the Lord, and he will heed their supplications and heal them.*

²³*In that day there will be a highway from Egypt to Assyria, and the Assyrian will come into Egypt, and the Egyptian into Assyria, and the Egyptians will worship with the Assyrians.*

²⁴*In that day Israel will be the third with Egypt and Assyria, a blessing in the midst of the earth,* ²⁵*whom the Lord of hosts has blessed, saying, "Blessed be Egypt my people, and Assyria the work of my hands, and Israel my heritage."*

*LXX lacks *witness*   †LXX *man

Overview: The five cities of Egypt are the five languages of the world (Aponius). The five cities of Egypt are the five senses (Bede). A replica temple was erected in Egypt by Onias the high priest (Jerome). The Donatists interpreted the temple in Egypt to refer to their church, but it prophetically referred to the church spread throughout the entire world (Augustine). The Virgin gave birth to a human being (Ambrose). Christ was both God and a human being (Lactantius).

19:18 *Five Cities in Egypt*

Hebrew, Greek, Coptic, Latin and Syriac: Five Cities. Aponius: Like one body has five senses and five movements by which all of its works are performed, so also are five different personas typified in this Canticle, each through the image of a spouse, not counting the "sixty queens" and "eighty concubines" and "adolescents without number," or "daughters," and "the only child of her mother," who calls herself a "wall," and she who "has no breasts."[1]

These five personas, I believe, denote five languages. Hebrew, the first of all languages, was the language of those from among whom the church was first assembled at the coming of Christ and to whom the first Gospel was addressed in Hebrew through the apostle Matthew. Greek is the language of those collaborators of the apostles, the Evangelists Mark and Luke, who are

shown to be the first after the Hebrews to have gone on their missions. Egyptian, with which Mark the disciple of the apostles was not unfamiliar, is the tongue of those to whom he was sent as a teacher; the example he left them flowers still today with holy piety. Latin, which the ancients called Auxonian after King Auxonius, is the language of the one who has Peter, prince of the apostles, as its teacher and patron; decorated with the jewels of his doctrine,[2] it is united by participation in Christ. It is to it, we believe, that it was said, "How beautiful are your feet in sandals, daughter of the prince!"[3] Fifthly, Assyrian, also called Syriac, is the tongue of the country to which the nation of ten tribes, the kingdom of Ephraim, was led away captive.[4] By proclaiming the merit of its religion through this tongue, the people were made one body. Assyrian, then, represents the nation which was led by the Word of God "out of the wilderness"[5] where Christ was not honored and out of the thorny conduct of humanity, to be settled in the delightful garden of sanctity.[6]

After or apart from these languages, all the others under heaven, once converted to Christ, will be grafted into them like a limb onto a body. For everyone who believes in one omnipotent God and confesses one Redeemer, Christ, the

---

[1]Song 6:7-8; 8:8-10. [2]See Is 61:10. [3]Song 7:1. [4]See 2 Kings 17:1-6. [5]Song 8:5. [6]See Song 8:13.

Son of God, and receives the one Holy Spirit who proceeds from both, together constitutes the one body of the church, which is unified, as we have said, as though by the five senses. And it was prophesied quite clearly in mystery through the prophet Isaiah, I believe, that these five languages would become one language rejoicing in the praises of its one Creator by holding firm to the one faith. The coming of such a time was predicted when he said, "There will be in that day," the day when the Lord will break the chains of his people, "five cities in the land of Egypt speaking the language of Canaan, one of which will be called the city of the sun."

We know that "Egypt" means "obscurity" or "darkness," which characterized the entire world before the incarnation of Christ, as blessed John the Evangelist taught when he said, "The light shone in the darkness, and the darkness has not overtaken it."[7] Zechariah also taught that Christ came "to illuminate those who were sitting in darkness and the shadow of death."[8] And the Savior himself declared, "I am the light of the world."[9] "Canaan," on the other hand, means "glowing chalice." Who else are we able to understand as a glowing chalice except the Holy Spirit, who, after the ascension of the Lord, was first sent by the Father and the Son to the apostles while their faith was still cold? Of him it is said in the Acts of the Apostles that "he rested upon each one like a flame."[10] He filled those who spoke the one praise of the one God in the tongue of every nation, such that they appeared intoxicated to the unaware.[11] Having received from this chalice, the five prophesied cities now speak the marvels of the omnipotent God with one mouth or one tongue, "that our Lord Jesus Christ," as Paul, teacher of the Gentiles, shows, "is to the glory of God the Father,"[12] and that "no one can say that Jesus Christ is Lord except in the Holy Spirit."[13]

The name "city of the sun" designates the one Hebrew language itself, whose kingdom is seated in Jerusalem. There is the throne, there is the temple, the holy place of worship, and there is the kingdom of Judah, whence came Christ, the Sun of Justice.[14] It is from Jerusalem, which was previously called Heliopolis, meaning "city of the sun," that light is shed throughout the entire, darkened body of the world. From it, a healing balm is applied to every member of the church. And it was of this sun that the prophet predicted, "For you who fear the Lord, the sun of justice will rise, and healing is in its rays; and you will leap like young bulls in the middle of the herd, and you will trample your enemies until they become like the dust under your feet."[15] EXPOSITION OF SONG OF SONGS, EPILOGUE 89-93.[16]

CITIES IN EGYPT. BEDE: The servant is "faithful in very little"[17] who does not defile the word of God but speaks as though he were speaking from God and with God in Christ. For whatever gifts we receive at present are very little and very poor in comparison with those of the future, since "now we know only partially and prophesy only partially, but when the perfect comes, the partial will pass away."[18] The ten cities[19] are souls coming to the grace of the gospel through the word of the law. And because he must be glorified, the one who will invest the money of the word worthily for God is placed over them. Hence one successful investor addressed the cities over whom he presided, that is, the souls whose governance he had accepted, asking, "What is our hope or joy or crown of glory? Is it not you before the Lord Jesus?"[20]

"And another came, saying, 'Lord, your mina has made five minas.'"[21] This servant is representative of those who were sent to evangelize the uncircumcised. The Lord had given him one mina for preaching, which means one and the same faith which is also believed by the circumcised.[22] He made five minas because people who had previously been enslaved to their bodily senses he converted to the grace of evangelical

---

[7]Jn 1:5. [8]Lk 1:79. [9]Jn 8:12. [10]Acts 2:3. [11]See Acts 2:13. [12]See Phil 2:11. [13]1 Cor 12:3. [14]See Mal 4:2. [15]Mal 4:2-3. [16]CCL 19:308-10. [17]Lk 19:17. [18]1 Cor 13:9-10. [19]See Lk 19:17. [20]1 Thess 2:19. [21]Lk 19:18. [22]See Gal 2:7.

faith. "And he said to him, 'You will be over five cities,'"[23] that is, you will shine greatly and on high with the faith and conversion of those souls whom you imbued. Isaiah also spoke mystically about this: "In that day there will be five cities in the land of Egypt who speak the language of Canaan." The five cities in the land of Egypt are the five senses of the body we use in this world, namely, vision, hearing, taste, smell and touch. He who looks at a woman with concupiscence, he who shuts his ears not to hear the poor, he who gets drunk with wine, which is dissipation, he who delights in crowning himself with fresh roses, whose hands are covered with blood and whose right hand is filled with bribes, represents the five cities that speak the language of Egypt, that is, that perform the works of darkness with all of their senses, for Egypt sings of the darkness. But he who blocks his ears not to hear of blood and closes his eyes not to see evil, he who tastes and sees how sweet is the Lord, who castigates his body and makes it his slave, who is able to say with the apostle "we are the fragrance of Christ to God,"[24] represents the cities of those who speak the altered language of Canaan. And the one who delivered them from darkness by his teaching is rightly rewarded with the leadership of five cities because he is being honored not only for his own progress but also for that of those whom he called to the light. EXPOSITION OF THE GOSPEL OF LUKE 5.19.17-19.[25]

19:19 An Altar to the Lord

IN THE MIDST OF EGYPT. JEROME: During the conflict between Antiochus the Great and the generals of Ptolemy, Judea, which lay between them, was rent into contrary factions, the one group favoring Antiochus and the other favoring Ptolemy. Finally the high priest, Onias, fled to Egypt, taking a large number of Jews along with him, and he was given by Ptolemy an honorable reception. He then received the region known as Heliopolis, and by a grant of the king, he erected a temple in Egypt like the temple of the

Jews, and it remained standing up until the reign of Vespasian, over a period of 250 years. But then the city itself, which was known as the City of Onias, was destroyed to the very ground because of the war which the Jews had subsequently waged against the Romans. There is consequently no trace of either city or temple now remaining. But as we were saying, countless multitudes of Jews fled to Egypt on the occasion of Onias's pontificate, and the land was filled with a large number from Cyrene as well. For Onias affirmed that he was fulfilling the prophecy written by Isaiah: "There shall be an altar of the Lord in Egypt, and the name [inscription] of the Lord shall be found in their territories." And so this is the matter referred to in this passage: "The sons of the transgressors of your people,"[26] who forsook the law of the Lord and wished to offer blood sacrifices to God in another place than what he had commanded. They would be lifted up in pride and would boast that they were fulfilling the vision, that is, the thing that the Lord had enjoined. But they shall fall to ruin, for both temple and city shall be afterwards destroyed. COMMENTARY ON DANIEL 3.11.146.[27]

A SIGN IN EGYPT. AUGUSTINE: The prophet Isaiah says this about Egypt: "In that day there will be an altar of the Lord in the land of the Egyptians and an inscription to the Lord at its border. It will be a sign forever to the Lord in the land of the Egyptians, for they will cry to the Lord against their assailants, and the Lord will send them a savior who will be determined to save them. And the Lord will be known to the Egyptians, and they will fear the Lord in that day and make sacrifices to him and promise vows to him and fulfill them. And the Lord will strike the Egyptians with plagues and heal them by his mercy, and they will turn to the Lord, and he will listen to them and heal them." What do they [i.e.,

---

[23]Lk 19:19. [24]2 Cor 2:15. [25]CCL 120:338-39. [26]Dan 11:14. [27]CCL 75A:908-9; JCD 125-26.

members of the Donatist sect][28] say to this? Why do they not share with the church what was foretold of the Egyptians? Or, if Egypt signifies the world by prophetic prefiguration, why are they not in communion with the church of the world? Consequently, they search the Scriptures and, against so many sure and clear witnesses through which the church of Christ is shown to be diffused throughout the entire world, they offer just one witness in an attempt to demonstrate that the church of Christ perished from all other peoples and remained only in Africa, as though from another beginning, not from Jerusalem but from Carthage, where they first elevated one bishop against another. LETTER TO THE CATHOLICS ON THE SECT OF DONATISTS 16.41-42.[29]

19:20 A Savior Who Will Defend and Deliver

A SAVIOR. AMBROSE: If the waters bore a man, could not a virgin give birth to a man? What man? Him of whom we read: "The Lord will send them a man, who will save them, and the Lord will be known in Egypt." LETTER 44 (15.7).[30]

HE WAS A MAN. LACTANTIUS: He was called "Christ" from the anointing. Then, that the same one was a human being Jeremiah shows, saying, "And he is man, and who has known him?"[31] And Isaiah, "And the Lord shall send them a man, who shall save them, and judging them he will heal them." THE DIVINE INSTITUTES 4.13.[32]

HE WAS GOD AND MAN. LACTANTIUS: That he was both God and man was declared before by the prophets. That he was God, Isaiah thus declares, "They shall fall down before you, they shall make supplication to you, since God is in you, and we knew it not, even the God of Israel. They shall be ashamed and confounded, all of them who oppose themselves to you, and shall go unto confusion."[33] . . . Likewise that he was man . . . Isaiah also thus speaks, "and the Lord shall send them a man who shall save them, and with judgment shall he heal them." EPITOME OF THE DIVINE INSTITUTES 44.[34]

---

[28]The Donatists split from the Catholic church over the question of impurity, as epitomized by the handing over of the Scriptures to authorities. [29]CSEL 52:286-87. [30]FC 26:228. [31]Jer 17:9. [32]FC 49:274. [33]Is 45:14-16. [34]ANF 7:239*.

20:1-6 ORACLE AGAINST EGYPT

[1]In the year that the commander in chief, who was sent by Sargon the king of Assyria, came to Ashdod and fought against it and took it,—[2]at that time the LORD had spoken by Isaiah the son of Amoz, saying, "Go, and loose the sackcloth from your loins and take off your shoes from your feet," and he had done so, walking naked and barefoot—[3]the LORD said, "As my servant Isaiah has walked naked and barefoot for three years as a sign and a portent against Egypt and Ethiopia, [4]so shall the king of Assyria lead away the Egyptians captives and the Ethiopians exiles, both the

young and the old, naked and barefoot, with buttocks uncovered, to the shame of Egypt. [5]*Then they shall be dismayed and confounded because of Ethiopia their hope and of Egypt their boast.* [6]*And the inhabitants of this coastland will say in that day, 'Behold, this is what has happened to those in whom we hoped and to whom we fled for help to be delivered from the king of Assyria! And we, how shall we escape?'"*

Overview: The beauty of character should not be covered in vanity (Clement of Alexandria). Isaiah's nakedness symbolized the captivity to come (Jerome, Ambrose). Christians should look to things above, not things below, and not be ashamed of their Lord (Ambrose). The islands are churches in the midst of the world (Jerome).

20:1-2 Isaiah's Nakedness a Sign

Naked and Barefoot. Clement of Alexandria: Just as the bare framework of the body is revealed once the accumulated tissue is stripped away, so magnificent beauty of character will become manifest if only it is not shrouded in the nonsense of vanity. But to trail around garments that reach down even to the feet is nothing more than ostentatiousness. Christ the Educator 2.10.113.[1]

A Sign of the Future. Jerome: "And the Spirit entered me and set me upon my feet and spoke to me, saying, 'Go and enclose yourself within your house.'"[2] Unable to bear the glory of the Lord standing before him, he fell on his face, only to be raised up by the indwelling Spirit. When the Spirit set him upon his feet and spoke, saying, "Go and enclose yourself within your house," this is what he meant: "Because you were strengthened by the appearance of the Lord's majesty, you should neither fear nor be terrified of anything, but return to your house (either to tend to the needs of the body, as some think, or to signify the future siege) and, as a barefoot, naked Isaiah announced for three years the coming captivity and nakedness of the people, so also your own enclosure in the house will itself be a prophet announcing the siege of the city of Jeru-

salem." Commentary on Ezekiel 1.3.23b-24.[3]

Without Blushing. Jerome: Isaiah goes naked without blushing as a type of captivity to come. Letter 40.[4]

Naked. Ambrose: Someone perhaps will say, "Was it not disgraceful for a man to walk naked among the people since he must meet both men and women? Must not his appearance have shocked the gaze of all, but especially that of women? Do we not ourselves generally abhor the sight of naked men? And are not men's private parts covered with clothing that they may not offend the gaze of onlookers by their unsightliness?"

I agree, but you must consider what this act represented and what was the reason for this outward show; it was that the young Jewish youths and maidens would be led away into exile and walk naked, "as my servant Isaiah walked," he says, "naked and barefoot." This might have been expressed in words, but God chose to enforce it by an example that the very sight might strike more terror, and what they shrank from in the body of the prophet they might utterly dread for themselves. Wherein lay the greater abhorrence: in the body of the prophet or in the sins of the disbelievers? Letter 28 (6.27.13).[5]

And He Had Done So. Ambrose: That it may be more fully clear that prophets look not to themselves or what lies at their feet but to heavenly things, Stephen, when he was being stoned,[6] saw the heavens open and Jesus standing at the

---

[1]FC 23:186-87. [2]Ezek 3:24. [3]CCL 75:40-41. [4]NPNF 2 6:54. [5]FC 26:146-47*. [6]Acts 7.

right hand of God. Then he did not feel the blows of the stones, he did not heed the wounds of his body, but, fastening his eyes on Christ, he clung to him. So, too, Isaiah did not notice his nakedness but made himself the instrument of God's voice, that he might proclaim what God spoke within him. LETTER 28 (6.27.10).[7]

Do Not Be Ashamed. AMBROSE: Truly I grieve that while falsehood is so respected, there should be such negligence as regards the truth, that many are ashamed of seeming too devoted to our holy religion, not considering his words who says, "Whosoever shall be ashamed of me before men, of him will I also be ashamed before my Father which is in heaven."[8] But Moses was not thus ashamed, for though invited into the royal palace he "esteemed the reproach of Christ greater riches than the treasures of Egypt."[9] David was not thus ashamed when he danced before the ark of the testimony in the sight of all the people.[10] Isaiah was not thus ashamed when he walked naked and barefoot through the people, proclaiming the heavenly oracles. . . .

But the things that viewed corporeally are unseemly, when viewed in regard to holy religion become venerable, so that they who blame such things will involve their own souls in the net of blame. Thus Michal reproves David for his dancing and says to him, "How glorious was the king of Israel today, who uncovered himself today in the eyes of his handmaids!" And David answered her, "It was before the Lord, who chose me before your father and before all his house to appoint me ruler over the people of the Lord, over Israel."[11] LETTER 27 (6.27.3).[12]

20:6 Coastlands and Islands

Christ as the Foundation. JEROME: Even as islands have been set in the midst of the sea, churches have been established in the midst of this world, and they are beaten and buffeted by different waves of persecution. Truly these islands are lashed by waves every day, but they are not submerged. They are in the midst of the sea, to be sure, but they have Christ as their foundation, Christ who cannot be moved. HOMILIES ON THE PSALMS 24 (PSALM 96).[13]

---

[7]FC 26:148*. [8]Mk 8:38. [9]Heb 11:26. [10]2 Sam 6:14. [11]2 Sam 6:20-22. [12]LF 45:346-47*. [13]FC 48:192.

21:1-17 CONCERNING BABYLON, EDOM AND ARABIA

[1]The oracle concerning the wilderness of the sea.
  As whirlwinds in the Negeb sweep on,
    it comes from the desert,
    from a terrible land.
[2]A stern vision is told to me;

the plunderer plunders,
    and the destroyer destroys.
  Go up, O Elam,
    lay siege, O Media;
  all the sighing she has caused
    I bring to an end.

³*Therefore my loins are filled with anguish;*
pangs have seized me,
like the pangs of a woman in travail;
I am bowed down so that I cannot hear,
I am dismayed so that I cannot see.
⁴*My mind reels, horror has appalled me;*
the twilight I longed for
has been turned for me into trembling.
⁵*They prepare the table,*
they spread the rugs,
they eat, they drink.
Arise, O princes,
oil the shield!*
⁶*For thus the Lord said to me:*
"Go, set a watchman,
let him announce what he sees.
⁷*When he sees riders, horsemen in pairs,*
riders on asses, riders on camels,
let him listen diligently,
very diligently."
⁸*Then he who saw^g cried:*
"Upon a watchtower I stand, O Lord,
continually by day,
and at my post I am stationed
whole nights.
⁹*And behold, here come riders,*
horsemen in pairs!"†
And he answered,
"Fallen, fallen is Babylon;
and all the images of her gods

he has shattered to the ground."
¹⁰*O my threshed and winnowed one,*
what I have heard from the LORD of hosts,
the God of Israel, I announce to you.

¹¹*The oracle concerning Dumah.*
One is calling to me from Seir,
"Watchman, what of the night?
Watchman, what of the night?"
¹²*The watchman says:*
"Morning comes, and also the night.
If you will inquire, inquire;
come back again."

¹³*The oracle concerning Arabia.*
In the thickets in Arabia you will lodge,
O caravans of Dedanites.
¹⁴*To the thirsty bring water,*
meet the fugitive with bread,
O inhabitants of the land of Tema.‡
¹⁵*For they have fled from the swords,*
from the drawn sword,
from the bent bow,
and from the press of battle.
¹⁶*For thus the Lord said to me, "Within a*
year, according to the years of a hireling, all the
glory of Kedar will come to an end; ¹⁷and the
remainder of the archers of the mighty men of
the sons of Kedar will be few; for the LORD,
the God of Israel, has spoken."

g One ancient Ms: Heb a lion   *Vg Babylon, my beloved, has become a strange spectacle to me: set the table and behold in the mirrors those who eat and drink; rise up, you princes, and snatch up your shields!   †LXX he comes riding in a chariot and pair   ‡Vg south

OVERVIEW: Despite treacherous opposition, we must proclaim the faith (GREGORY OF NAZIANZUS). The table is an exhortation to battle (JEROME). Christ's disciples strengthen one another in ministry (PETER CHRYSOLOGUS). Only a remnant of the Jews believed the gospel (EUSEBIUS).

Failure to believe in Christ is refusal to see the light and emerge from the darkness. Bread is a symbol of proper Christian doctrine (GREGORY THE GREAT).

21:2 Dealing Treacherously

**LET THE TREACHEROUS DEAL TREACHER-
OUSLY.** GREGORY OF NAZIANZUS: We receive the
Son's light from the Father's light in the light of the
Spirit: that is what we ourselves have seen and
what we now proclaim—it is the plain and simple
explanation of the Trinity. Let the treacherous deal
treacherously, let the transgressor transgress—we
shall preach what we know. We shall climb a lofty
mountain and shout it out, if we are not given a
hearing below. We shall extol the Spirit; we shall
not be afraid. If we do have fear, it will be of
silence, not of preaching. ON THE HOLY SPIRIT,
THEOLOGICAL ORATION 5 (31).3.[1]

21:5 Prepare the Table

THE TABLE. JEROME: And in testimony of the
fact that Babylon was captured during a banquet,
Isaiah clearly exhorts it to battle when he writes,
"Babylon, my beloved, has become a strange spectacle to me: set the table and behold in the mirrors those who eat and drink; rise up, you
princes, and snatch up your shields!" COMMEN-
TARY ON DANIEL 2.5.31.[2]

21:7-9 Horsemen in Pairs

TWO BY TWO. PETER CHRYSOLOGUS: [In the
Gospels it is said,] "And he began to send them
forth two by two."[3] He sent them two by two that
no one of them, being abandoned and alone,
might fall into a denial, like Peter,[4] or flee, like
John.[5] Human frailty quickly falls if it proudly relies on itself, despises companions and is unwilling to have a colleague. As Scripture says, "Woe
to him that is alone, for when he falls, he has
none to lift him up."[6] The same Scripture testifies
how much one is strengthened by another's aid,
when it states, "A brother that is helped by his
brother is like a strong city."[7]

. . . This was done also to fulfill the prophecy
of Isaiah, who testified that he had seen a rider of
a two-horse chariot, when he heard it said to him,
"What do you see?" And he replied, "I see a rider
of a two-horse chariot." Because of this he cried

out right away that Babylon had fallen, and all its
graven gods.

Who doubts, brothers, that by this two-horse
chariot Christ was riding upon his saving journeys, since he sees that through the apostles'
preaching temples have fallen, idols have perished, the bleating of herds has ceased and the
victims, along with even the very altars with their
perfume of incense, have already disappeared
through all the centuries. SERMON 170.[8]

21:10 Threshed and Winnowed

FORSAKEN AND TORTURED. EUSEBIUS OF CAE-
SAREA: Notice how in this passage he does not
call those of the circumcision to hear the unspeakable words, but only those whom he calls
"forsaken and tortured." These were those of the
time of the apostles who regretted and lamented
the evil of humanity. PROOF OF THE GOSPEL 2.3.[9]

21:11 Watchman, What of the Night?

WATCHMAN. GREGORY THE GREAT: Again he
says, "Watchman, what of the night? Watchman,
what of the night? The watchman said, 'The
morning comes, and also the night.'" For "the
watchman came by night," in that the guardian of
the human race even showed himself manifest in
the flesh, and yet Judea, being close pressed by
the darkness of its faithlessness, never knew him.
Where it is well added in the voice of the watchman, "The morning comes, and also the night."
For by his presence has a new light shone out
upon the world, and yet the former darkness
remained in the hearts of unbelievers. And it is
well said, "They shall grope in the noonday as in
the night," for we search out by groping that
which we do not see with our eyes. Now the Jews
had seen his undisguised miracles, and yet they
still went on seeking him, as it were groping for

---

[1]NPNF 2 7:318. [2]JCD 62; CCL 75A:828. [3]Mk 6:7. [4]Mt 26:69-75.
[5]See Mk 14:50-52. Presumed to be John. [6]Eccl 4:10. [7]Prov 18:19.
[8]FC 17:280-81*. [9]POG 1:92-93*.

him, when they said, "How long do you make us to doubt? If you be the Christ, tell us plainly."[10] See, the light of miracles was before their eyes, yet stumbling in the darkness of their own hearts, they continued to grope in seeking for him." MORALS ON THE BOOK OF JOB 2.6.34.[11]

21:14 Meeting the One Who Flees

WITH HIS BREAD. GREGORY THE GREAT: Again, by bread is set forth the instruction of heavenly doctrine, as is said by the prophet, "You who dwell in the land of the south, meet with

bread him that is flying away." For they dwell in the land of the south who, placed within [the] holy church, are breathed upon by the love of the Spirit from on high. But he is flying who is wishing to escape from the evils of this world. He then who dwells in the land of the south should meet with bread him that is flying; that is, he who is already full of the Holy Spirit within the church should console with words of instruction the one who is endeavoring to escape from his evil ways. MORALS ON THE BOOK OF JOB 5.23.49.[12]

---

[10]Jn 10:24. [11]LF 18:338. [12]LF 23:42-43.

22:1-25 WARNING OF APPROACHING DESTRUCTION

[1]The oracle concerning the valley of vision.*
  What do you mean that you have gone up,
    all of you, to the housetops,†
  [2]you who are full of shoutings,
    tumultuous city, exultant town?
  Your slain are not slain with the sword
    or dead in battle.
  [3]All your rulers have fled together,
    without the bow they were captured.
  All of you who were found were captured,
    though they had fled far away.ᵇ
  [4]Therefore I said:
  "Look away from me,
    let me weep bitter tears;
  do not labor to comfort me
    for the destruction of the daughter of my people."

⁵*For the Lord GOD of hosts has a day*
    of tumult and trampling and confusion
    in the valley of vision,
a battering down of walls
    and a shouting to the mountains.
⁶*And Elam bore the quiver*
    with chariots and horsemen,ⁱ
    and Kir uncovered the shield.
⁷*Your choicest valleys were full of chariots,*
    and the horsemen took their stand at the gates.
⁸*He has taken away the covering of Judah.*

In that day you looked to the weapons of the House of the Forest, ⁹and you saw that the breaches of the city of David were many, and you collected the waters of the lower pool, ¹⁰and you counted the houses of Jerusalem, and you broke down the houses to fortify the wall. ¹¹You made a reservoir between the two walls for the water of the old pool. But you did not look to him who did it, or have regard for him who planned it long ago.

¹²*In that day the Lord GOD of hosts*
    called to weeping and mourning,
    to baldness and girding with sackcloth;
¹³*and behold, joy and gladness,*
    slaying oxen and killing sheep,
    eating flesh and drinking wine.
"Let us eat and drink,
    for tomorrow we die."
¹⁴*The LORD of hosts has revealed himself in my ears:*
"Surely this iniquity will not be forgiven you
    till you die,"
    says the Lord GOD of hosts.

¹⁵Thus says the Lord GOD of hosts, "Come, go to this steward, to Shebna, who is over the household, and say to him: ¹⁶What have you to do here and whom have you here, that you have hewn here a tomb for yourself, you who hew a tomb on the height, and carve a habitation for yourself in the rock? ¹⁷Behold, the LORD will hurl you away violently, O you strong man. He will seize firm hold on you, ¹⁸and whirl you round and round, and throw you like a ball into a wide land; there you shall die, and there shall be your splendid chariots, you shame of your master's house. ¹⁹I will thrust you from your office, and you will be cast down from your station. ²⁰In that day I will call my servant Eliakim the son of Hilkiah, ²¹and I will clothe him with your robe, and will bind your

girdle on him, and will commit your authority to his hand; and he shall be a father to the inhabitants of Jerusalem and to the house of Judah. ²²And I will place on his shoulder the key of the house of David; he shall open, and none shall shut; and he shall shut, and none shall open. ²³And I will fasten him like a peg in a sure place, and he will become a throne of honor to his father's house. ²⁴And they will hang on him[‡] the whole weight of his father's house, the offspring and issue, every small vessel, from the cups to all the flagons. ²⁵In that day, says the LORD of hosts, the peg that was fastened in a sure place will give way; and it will be cut down and fall, and the burden that was upon it will be cut off, for the LORD has spoken."

h Gk Syr Vg: Heb *from far away*   i The Hebrew of this line is obscure   *LXX *valley of Zion*   †Vg *the empty roof*   ‡LXX *everyone that is glorious in the house of his father shall trust in him*

OVERVIEW: The sinner is a valley of Zion, but the church is the mountain of Zion. The roof is symbolic of the heretical leader (JEROME). If we grieve over the death of the body, we should all the more grieve over the death of the soul (BASIL, CHRYSOSTOM). Like God, we should lament the destruction of the sinner and not find pleasure in it (BASIL). We should grieve not only for ourselves but also for all humanity (CHRYSOSTOM). Sinners bury their souls in sin (ATHANASIUS). We should long for spiritual food, not for physical food (CYPRIAN). The excesses of Shebna will be compensated when God establishes Eliakim (EUSEBIUS, CYRIL OF ALEXANDRIA).

22:1 Oracle Concerning the Valley of Zion

VALLEY OF ZION. JEROME: If, as I was saying, we are in the church, if we possess the faith of the church, of the apostles, of Christ, the truths of Christian teaching, we are the mountains of Zion. We do not want to be among the valleys of Zion; we want to be mountains of Zion. Zion, indeed, has its valleys; it has plains, too. The sinner is a valley of Zion, not a mountain. Someone may interpose, "You are giving us your own opinion." Let us call upon the testimony of Isaiah when Zion had fallen into sin, in which after many visions, the prophet mentions one against Idumea, one against Moab, one against Edom and the sons of Ammon, and lastly, "a vision of the valley of Zion." Because Zion had descended

from sublime faith, it fell recklessly from the mountain into the valley.

Before all else, then, let us flee from the valleys of Zion and come to the plains; from the plains, let us go to the hills, from the hills up the mountains. HOMILIES ON THE PSALMS 45 (PSALM 132).[1]

PRIDE AND FALSE KNOWLEDGE. JEROME: "Gog" is a Greek word translated in Latin by "roof" (*tectum*) and "magog" by "from the roof" (*de tecto*). All pride and false knowledge, therefore, that raises itself against the acknowledgment of the truth is indicated by these words. And this is the roof about which Isaiah spoke in his vision against the valley of Zion: "What has happened to you now, that you have all gone up to the empty roof?"[2] We shall understand "roof" to refer to the leaders of heretics and "from the roof" to those who accept their teaching. How beautiful it is, after so many mystical prophecies contained in this volume, to find at last a prophecy against Gog and Magog. COMMENTARY ON EZEKIEL 11.38.1-23.[3]

22:2 Not Dead in Battle

NOT SLAIN BY THE SWORD. BASIL THE GREAT: Now is the time to utter aloud those words of the prophet who said, "Who will give water to my head and a fountain of tears to my eyes, and I will

---

[1]FC 48:339*. [2]"Empty" (*vana*) is not included in modern editions of the Vulgate. [3]CCL 75:526-27.

weep for the slain of the daughters of my people?"[4] For, even if deep silence enfolds them and they lie dispossessed once and for all of their senses by the horrible deed (for by the deadly blow they have been deprived already of the very awareness of their condition), still we must not tearlessly disregard so great a fall. For, if Jeremiah judged those whose bodies were smitten in war worthy of innumerable laments, what should be said regarding so terrible a disaster to souls? "Your slain," it is said, "are not slain by the sword, and your dead are not dead in battle." But I bewail the sharp sting that causes real death, that is, grievous sin, and the fiery darts of the evil one, barbarously burning soul and body alike. LETTER 46.[5]

22:4 Weeping Bitter Tears

LET ME WEEP. CHRYSOSTOM: Grief is often capable of refreshing distressed souls and of rendering a burdened conscience light: consider how often women, when they have lost their most beloved children, break their hearts and perish if they are forbidden to mourn and to shed tears. But if they do all which those who are sad are apt to do, they are relieved and receive consolation. And what wonder that this should be the case with women, when you may even see a prophet affected in a similar manner? Therefore he was continually saying, "Leave me alone. I will weep bitterly. Do not try to comfort me over the destruction of the daughter of my people." So oftentimes sadness is the bearer of consolation; and if it is so with regard to this world, much more with regard to spiritual things. HOMILIES CONCERNING THE STATUES 18.8.[6]

BITTER TEARS. BASIL THE GREAT: Remember the compassion of God, how he heals with olive oil and wine. Do not despair of salvation. Recall the memory of what has been written, how he that falls rises again, and he that is turned away turns again,[7] he that has been smitten is healed, he that is caught by wild beasts escapes, and he

that confesses is not rejected. The Lord does not wish the death of the sinner, but that he return and live.[8] Be not contemptuous[9] as one who has fallen into the depths of sins.

There is still time for patience, time for forbearance, time for healing, time for amendment. Have you slipped? Rise up. Have you sinned? Cease. Do not stand in the way of sinners,[10] but turn aside; for then you will be saved when turning back you bewail your sins. In fact, from labors there is health; for sweat, salvation. So take heed, lest, in wishing to keep your contracts with others, you transgress your covenants with God that you confessed before many witnesses.[11] Do not, therefore, because of certain human considerations, hesitate to come to me. For, receiving my dead, I shall lament; I shall care for him, "I shall weep bitterly for the devastation of the daughter of my people." All welcome you, all will aid you in your sufferings. Do not lose heart; be mindful of the days of old. There is salvation; there is amendment. Have courage; do not despair. There is no law that passes sentence of death without pity, but grace, exceeding the chastisement, awaits the amendment. Not yet have the doors been closed; the Bridegroom listens;[12] sin is not the master. Again take up the struggle; do not draw back, but pity yourself and all of us in Jesus Christ, our Lord, to whom be glory and might, now and forever, for ages of ages. Amen. LETTER 44.[13]

GRIEF IS NECESSARY. CHRYSOSTOM: It is, after all, the practice of the prophets and the just to grieve not only for themselves but also for the rest of humankind. HOMILIES ON GENESIS 29.7.[14]

22:13 Let Us Eat and Drink

EAT AND DRINK. ATHANASIUS: Now we say that the wicked are dead, but not in an ascetic life opposed to sin; nor do they, like the saints, bear

---

[4]Jer 9:1. [5]FC 13:118-19*. [6]NPNF 1 9:461**. [7]Jer 8:4. [8]Ezek 18:32. [9]Prov 18:3. [10]Ps 1:1. [11]1 Tim 6:12. [12]Cf. Mt 25:10. [13]FC 13:114-15*. [14]FC 82:203.

about dying in their bodies. But it is the soul which they bury in sins and follies, drawing near to the dead and satisfying it with dead nourishment. [They are] like young eagles which, from high places, fly upon the carcasses of the dead, and which the law prohibited, commanding figuratively, "You are not to eat the eagle or any other bird that feeds on a dead carcass."[15] And it pronounced unclean any other animal that eats the dead, for these kill the soul with lusts and say nothing but "let us eat and drink, for tomorrow we die." FESTAL LETTER 7.2.[16]

TOMORROW WE DIE. CYPRIAN: That too great lust of food is not to be desired. In Isaiah: "Let us eat and drink, for tomorrow we shall die. This sin shall not be atoned for to you, even until you die." Also in Exodus: "And the people sat down to eat and drink, and rose up to play."[17] Paul, in the first [letter] to the Corinthians: "Food does not commend us to God; neither if we eat shall we abound, nor if we do not eat shall we lack."[18] And again: "When you come together to eat, wait one for another. If any is hungry, let him eat at home, that you may not come together for judgment."[19] Also to the Romans: "The kingdom of God is not food and drink but righteousness and peace, and joy in the Holy Spirit."[20] In the Gospel according to John: "I have food of which you don't know. My food is that I should do his will who sent me and should finish his work."[21] To QUIRINUS 3.60.[22]

22:15-24 Eliakim to Assume Shebna's Robe

THE GLORIOUS ROBE OF MINISTRY. EUSEBIUS OF CAESAREA: For all these things[23] will work for your destruction [i.e., Shebna's], since you have been deposed and rejected from the high priesthood, of which you showed yourself unworthy, God being a just judge who gives to each according to his worth. On you, then, he will bring these things; but on the other, Eliakim, whom he has assessed as his good servant and slave, he will invest with your robe and will honor by placing on him the crown of the high priesthood, whose ministry you had hitherto been entrusted with. For he is a man worthy of it. And since he has been promoted by God, unlike you he will not be proud and boastful. He will hold the place of a father toward all those who are going to be governed by him. Therefore, as to one who is soothing and gentle, [God] will give the glory of David, the most just and gentle king, in order to rule the people with great authority, so that none will gainsay his deeds. He will be rooted, established and placed securely at his ministry, so that no glorious member of the people shall contend or contrive envy, nor shall jealousy ever come into being on his account, but they shall "trust in him as in a father." COMMENTARY ON ISAIAH 148.6-20.[24]

THE MEASURE OF SPIRITUAL MATURITY. CYRIL OF ALEXANDRIA: When he says, "I will call my servant Eliakim" (the name Eliakim means resurrection of God), then everyone who is glorious in the house of his father will trust in him [Eliakim]. Yet what is the house of Christ's Father if not the church? And who are glorious there? Those who put their trust in Christ, and they are not just those who are glorious according to the judgment of this world. On the opposite they may be very small people according to that judgment. But God is just and unprejudiced. He repays everyone according to the measure of their spiritual age [maturity], as in that respect some are fathers yet others are still toddlers, babies and teenagers. COMMENTARY ON ISAIAH 22.10-14.[25]

---

[15]Lev 11:13. [16]NPNF 2 4:524**. [17]Ex 22:6. [18]1 Cor 8:8. [19]1 Cor 11:33. [20]Rom 14:17. [21]Jn 4:32, 34. [22]CCL 3:150-51. [23]Shebna's excesses; see Is 22:16. [24]ECCI 183. [25]PG 70:517-18.

23:1-18 ORACLE CONCERNING SIDON

¹The oracle concerning Tyre.
Wail, O ships of Tarshish,
    for Tyre is laid waste, without house or
      haven!
From the land of Cyprus
    it is revealed to them.
²Be still, O inhabitants of the coast,
    O merchants of Sidon;
your messengers passed over the sea^j
   ³and were on many waters;
your revenue was the grain of Shihor,
    the harvest of the Nile;
    you were the merchant of the nations.
⁴Be ashamed, O Sidon, for the sea has
     spoken,
    the stronghold of the sea, saying:
"I have neither travailed nor given birth,
    I have neither reared young men
    nor brought up virgins."
⁵When the report comes to Egypt,
    they will be in anguish over the report
     about Tyre.
⁶Pass over to Tarshish,
    wail, O inhabitants of the coast!
⁷Is this your exultant city
    whose origin is from days of old,
whose feet carried her
    to settle afar?
⁸Who has purposed this
    against Tyre, the bestower of crowns,
whose merchants were princes,
    whose traders were the honored of the
     earth?
⁹The Lord of hosts has purposed it,
    to defile the pride of all glory,

    to dishonor all the honored of the earth.
¹⁰Overflow your land like the Nile,
    O daughter of Tarshish;
    there is no restraint any more.
¹¹He has stretched out his hand over the
     sea,
    he has shaken the kingdoms;
the Lord has given command concerning
     Canaan
    to destroy its strongholds.
¹²And he said:
"You will no more exult,
    O oppressed virgin daughter of Sidon;
arise, pass over to Cyprus,
    even there you will have no rest."

¹³Behold the land of the Chaldeans! This is the people; it was not Assyria. They destined Tyre for wild beasts. They erected their siege towers, they razed her palaces, they made her a ruin.^k
¹⁴Wail, O ships of Tarshish,*
    for your stronghold is laid waste.
¹⁵In that day Tyre will be forgotten for seventy years, like the days of one king. At the end of seventy years, it will happen to Tyre as in the song of the harlot:
¹⁶"Take a harp,
    go about the city,
    O forgotten harlot!
Make sweet melody,
    sing many songs,
    that you may be remembered."
¹⁷At the end of seventy years, the Lord will visit Tyre, and she will return to her hire, and

will play the harlot with all the kingdoms of the world upon the face of the earth. [18]*Her merchandise and her hire will be dedicated to the LORD; it will not be stored or hoarded, but her merchandise will supply abundant food and fine clothing for those who dwell before the LORD.*

j One ancient Ms: Heb *who passed over the sea, they replenished you*   k The Hebrew of this verse is obscure   *LXX *Carthage*

OVERVIEW: God warned his people against foolishness even before the incarnation (ATHANASIUS). The prophet warns Sidon of danger, just as the sea warns sailors of danger (AMBROSE, THEODORET). Insolence and worldly living bring shame (GREGORY THE GREAT, AMBROSE). Israel has no excuse; the life of those under the law (Sidon) is convicted by the life of Gentiles (the sea) (GREGORY THE GREAT). Even when we are not ashamed of sin, we are ashamed of the names of particular sins (AMBROSE). The Savior left his rightful home to come to the sea of the world (JEROME). Tyre lay in waste for seventy years because of its harlotry (APHRAHAT). The commerce of Tyre is like the resources given to the church for support of its leaders (EUSEBIUS).

23:2 Like Merchants of Phoenicia

THE CARELESSNESS OF THE PEOPLE. ATHANASIUS: Still, it was when humanity was in this state that the Word—the Son—came to seek and to find that which was lost. Even before he came, he tried to restrain us from such foolishness, crying out, "Don't be like the horse and the mule which have no understanding and whose mouth must be held in with bit and bridle."[1] And because his own people were careless and acted as the wicked did, Isaiah, praying in the Spirit said, "You are to me like merchants of Phoenicia." FESTAL LETTER 2.3.[2]

23:4 Be Ashamed, Sidon

THE SEA HAS SPOKEN. AMBROSE: If all our acts and deeds depend on the fates acquired at our birth and not on principles of morality, why are laws established and statutes promulgated by which punishment is meted out to the wicked and security bestowed on the innocent? . . . Why does the farmer toil and not rather wait until it is time to convey into his storehouses the produce for which he has not labored, relying on the prerogatives of his birth? If he was destined by birth to be endowed with wealth without the expenditure of labor, he should undoubtedly wait until the earth brings forth fruit spontaneously without seed. If such were the case, he should not sink his ploughshare into the earth or put his hands on the curved scythe or undergo the expense of harvesting the grapes. Rather, the wine would without effort flow plenteously into his stock of jars. Without effort, too, he would let the wild olive berry exude its oil without the labor of grafting upon the trunk of the olive tree. In the same way a merchant who travels over the wide seas would not be in dread of the perils that threaten his own life, for it is within his power, because of a certain destiny allotted to him at birth, to come without labor into a wealth of treasure.

But this is far from the accepted opinion. As a matter of fact, the farmer cleaves the earth "with deep-driven plough"; "stripped he ploughs, stripped he sows"; stripped in the glowing "heat he thrashes on the floor the parched ears." The merchant, impatient when the east winds are blowing, ploughs the sea often when the course is unsafe. Insolent and rash men such as these are condemned by the prophet, who says, "Be ashamed, O Sidon, the sea speaks." That is to say, if dangers do not move you, then shame can check and modesty confound you. "Be ashamed, O Sidon," in which there is no place for virtue, no care for safety, no young men exercised in arms

[1]Ps 32:9. [2]NPNF 2 4:510**.

and ready to fight in defense of their country. They are anxiously and entirely preoccupied with gain and the benefits derived from commerce. Six Days of Creation 4.4.19.[3]

A Proof of Divine Providence. Theodoret of Cyr: To convince you of this, return again to the sea, and observe its depths, its extent, its division into bays, its shores, its port, the islands in its midst, the kinds of fishes in it and their species, shapes, variety and fondness for the shore. . . .

Since journeying by land is fraught with difficulty and the satisfaction of all our needs on such journeys is not only difficult but impossible, the surface of the sea is there to take vessels, small and large, and to provide much necessary cargo for those in short supply. A single frigate can be seen taking as much as many thousand beasts. To ease the burden for seafarers the Creator made islands as ports in which they could call, rest, buy their needs and then set sail again for their destination. "Be ashamed" then "at this multitude of blessings, said the sea."

For the words of the prophet apply more to you than to Sidon. For Sidon, ignoring the Creator, divided the divinity into many gods, mutilated the monotheistic form of worship and extended it to nonexistent deities, not indeed denying providence but ascribing it also to these false gods. For it would not offer sacrifice to these false gods unless it had fully persuaded itself that they provide assistance and avert disaster. But you who have been delivered from the error of polytheism and agree that all visible things are created; you, who adore their Creator, banish him from his creatures, set him completely outside his creation, assert that such an ordered universe is without a pilot and is borne about aimlessly like a ship without ballast. Be ashamed, then, at the blessings received from the sea, from the earth, from the air, from the sun and the sky that affords a roof over our heads. Respect the tribute you receive from creation. On Divine Providence 2.18, 20.[4]

Be Ashamed. Gregory the Great: Sidon is brought to shame, as it were, by the voice of the sea, when the life of one who is fortified and supposedly steadfast is reprobated in comparison with the lives of those who are worldly and are being tossed about in this world. For often there are those who, returning to the Lord after their sins of the flesh, evince themselves the more zealous in doing good works, as they realize they were worthy of condemnation for their deeds. And often certain people who persevere in preserving the integrity of the flesh, on perceiving that they have less to deplore, think to themselves that the innocence of their lives is sufficient and do not arouse themselves by zealously striving to be fervent in spirit. Pastoral Care 3.28.[5]

Be Ashamed, Sidon. Ambrose: Therefore, after being so often ploughed by returning merchants, "Be ashamed, O Sidon, has said the sea." This is the voice of the fatigued element, as it were, saying, "Be ashamed, Sidon"; that is: Merchant, you accuse my waves although you yourself are more restless than they. Blush indeed for shame since you are not disturbed by peril. More modest are the winds than your desires. They have their rests; never do your cravings for gain take holiday. Even when the weather is quiet, never are your ships quiet. The water is churned under the oar when it is at rest from the blast. "I have not been in labor," it says, "nor have I reared, nor have I nourished up young men." Why do they disquiet me whom I do not know, whom I do not acknowledge? On Helia and Fast 19.71.[6]

Israel Has No Excuse. Gregory the Great: Divine Providence has compassed us about and cut off all excuse. All openings to people's equivocating arts are in every way closed. A Gentile, one without the law, is brought forward to confound the iniquity of those that are under the law; which is well and summarily shown by

---

[3]FC 42:142-44*. [4]ACW 49:30-31. [5]ACW 11:197*. [6]CSEL 32 2:454.

the prophet, when he says, "Be ashamed, O Sidon, says the sea." For in Sidon we have a figure of the steadfastness of those settled upon the foundation of the law, and in the sea of the life of the Gentiles. Accordingly, "Be ashamed, O Sidon, says the sea," because the life of those under the law is convicted by the life of Gentiles, and the conduct of people in a state of religion is put to confusion by the conduct of those living in the world, so long as the first do not, even under vows, observe what they hear enjoined in precepts. The latter by their manner of life keep those ways so that they are not in any wise bound by legal enactments. Morals on the Book of Job, Preface to Book 1.5.[7]

23:14 Wail, Ships of Tarshish

Unseemly Words. Ambrose: "Howl," he says—he repeats it—"O you ships of Carthage, for your strength is laid waste. And it shall come to pass in that day, Tyre shall be abandoned;" and below, "but after seventy years, Tyre shall be as the song of a harlot." Behold what words the prophet employs, and how he does not avoid the baseness of words of this kind. We ourselves sometimes avoid them, not because our tongue is more chaste than theirs, but our authority inferior. For very great is the force of words in the vivid exposition of such things, so that they who do not blush at their sins blush at least at the names of their sins. "Tyre shall be," he says, "as the song of a harlot." Beware, lest, when someone sees those dances being performed, and unseemly words being sung, he says, "Behold, Tyre has become the song of a harlot." On Helia and Fast 20.73-74.[8]

He Left His Native Homeland. Jerome: Furthermore, the Hebrews claim that Tarshish generally represents the sea, as in the psalms: "With a violent wind, you will destroy the ships of Tarshish,"[9] that is, the sea, and in Isaiah: "Wail, ships of Tarshish." I recall speaking about this several years ago in a letter to Marcella. The prophet, therefore, was not seeking to flee to a

specific place,[10] but he was hastening to continue toward wherever it was the sea would take him. Indeed, a terrified fugitive is rightly more interested in seizing the first opportunity to sail than he is in selecting a place of refuge. This also we are able to say: he who thought that "God is known in Judea" only and that "his name is great in Israel" only,[11] once he felt him in the waves of the sea, confessed and said, "I am a Hebrew, and I fear the Lord of heaven who made the sea and the dry land."[12] But if he made the sea and the dry land, how can you who abandoned the dry land think it possible to avoid the Creator of the sea in the midst of the sea? At the same time, the salvation and conversion of the sailors taught him that the great multitude at Nineveh could also be saved by confessing like he did.

We are able to say of our Lord and Savior that he left his native homeland, assumed flesh and, in a manner of speaking, fled from heaven and came to Tarshish. That is, [he came] to the sea of this world, about which it is said elsewhere: "This is the sea, great and vast, where there are creatures without number and animals both small and large. Ships navigate there with the dragon whom you formed to play in it."[13] Commentary on Jonah 1.3.[14]

23:15 Tyre Will Be Forgotten

Seventy Years. Aphrahat: This Tyre also lay waste seventy years like Jerusalem, which sat in desolation seventy years. Demonstration 5.9.[15]

23:17 At the End of Seventy Years

At the End. Aphrahat: Now we see that Tyre was inhabited and was opulent after it had "wandered seventy years," and after it had received the reward of its prostitutions. Demonstration 21.6.[16]

---

[7]LF 18:17-18**. [8]CSEL 32 2:456. [9]Ps 47:7. [10]See Jon 1:3. [11]Ps 75:2. [12]Jon 1:9. [13]Ps 104:25-26. [14]CCL 76:381-82. [15]NPNF 2 13:356. [16]NPNF 2 13:395*.

23:18 *The Merchandise of Sidon*

The Consecrated Commerce. Eusebius of Caesarea: To seek out the exact form of the reading, I gave my attention to the translation of Aquila, which says, "And it will happen that its commerce and wages are consecrated to the Lord." Thus the Hebrew has, precisely, "commerce and wages" without the articles, not, according to the Septuagint, "*the* commerce and *the* wages," by which it appears to mean all the commerce and all the wages. According to Aquila, "Its commerce and wages are consecrated to the Lord." Not its whole commerce or its whole wages, but a part of the commerce and a part of the wages are consecrated to the Lord. And this is what has been fulfilled in our day. For the church of God is established in the city of Tyre, as indeed in the rest of the nations, and many of the wages in it and what is stored up for business are offered to the church and consecrated to the Lord. The things that people bring, they offer in piety, not for themselves in order to enjoy the gifts offered to God but "for those who dwell before the Lord." (Namely, [these gifts are] for those who serve at the altar, "for the Lord had enjoined that those who preach the gospel should live by the gospel" and "those who serve at the altar share in the sacrificial offerings."[17]) Commentary on Isaiah 152.23-153.2.[18]

---

[17]1 Cor 9:13. [18]ECCI 79-80.

24:1-23 JUDGMENT AND DELIVERANCE

[1]Behold, the Lord will lay waste the earth
    and make it desolate,
    and he will twist its surface and scatter
    its inhabitants.
[2]And it shall be, as with the people, so with
    the priest;
    as with the slave, so with his master;
    as with the maid, so with her mistress;
as with the buyer, so with the seller;
    as with the lender, so with the borrower;
    as with the creditor, so with the
    debtor.
[3]The earth shall be utterly laid waste and
    utterly despoiled;
    for the Lord has spoken this word.

[4]The earth mourns and withers,
    the world languishes and withers;
    the heavens languish together with the
    earth.
[5]The earth lies polluted
    under its inhabitants;
for they have transgressed the laws,
    violated the statutes,
    broken the everlasting covenant.
[6]Therefore a curse devours the earth,
    and its inhabitants suffer for their guilt;
therefore the inhabitants of the earth are
    scorched,
    and few men are left.
[7]The wine mourns,

the vine languishes,
all the merry-hearted sigh.
⁸The mirth of the timbrels is stilled,
the noise of the jubilant has ceased,
the mirth of the lyre is stilled.
⁹No more do they drink wine with singing;
strong drink is bitter to those who drink
it.
¹⁰The city of chaos is broken down,
every house is shut up so that none can
enter.
¹¹There is an outcry in the streets for lack of
wine;
all joy has reached its eventide;
the gladness of the earth is banished.
¹²Desolation is left in the city,
the gates are battered into ruins.
¹³For thus it shall be in the midst of the
earth
among the nations,
as when an olive tree is beaten,
as at the gleaning when the vintage is
done.

¹⁴They lift up their voices, they sing for joy;
over the majesty of the LORD they shout
from the west.
¹⁵Therefore in the east give glory to the
LORD;*
in the coastlands of the sea,† to the name
of the LORD, the God of Israel.
¹⁶From the ends of the earth we hear songs
of praise,
of glory to the Righteous One.
But I say, "I pine away,

I pine away. Woe is me!
For the treacherous deal treacherously,
the treacherous deal very treacherously."

¹⁷Terror, and the pit, and the snare
are upon you, O inhabitant of the earth!
¹⁸He who flees at the sound of the terror
shall fall into the pit;
and he who climbs out of the pit
shall be caught in the snare.
For the windows of heaven are opened,
and the foundations of the earth
tremble.
¹⁹The earth is utterly broken,
the earth is rent asunder,
the earth is violently shaken.
²⁰The earth staggers like a drunken man,
it sways like a hut;
its transgression lies heavy upon it,
and it falls, and will not rise again.

²¹On that day the LORD will punish
the host of heaven, in heaven,
and the kings of the earth, on the earth.
²²They will be gathered together
as prisoners in a pit;
they will be shut up in a prison,
and after many days they will be
punished.
²³Then the moon will be confounded,
and the sun ashamed;
for the LORD of hosts will reign
on Mount Zion and in Jerusalem
and before his elders he will manifest his
glory.

*Aramaic (or Peshitta) *Glorify the Lord in doctrine*   †LXX *Therefore shall the glory of the Lord be in the isles of the sea*

OVERVIEW: The people should let their piety persuade their priests to live properly (GREGORY OF NAZIANZUS). Ungodly priests will lead their people astray (GREGORY THE GREAT). Only the remnant remains (Eusebius). The islands represent the church (Primasius, Eusebius), and the sea represents the nations (Cyril of Alexandria). The church announces the glory of Christ (Primasius). The moon will be ashamed on the day of judgment (Jerome, Bede).

24:2 As with the People, So with the Priests

So with the Priests. Gregory of Nazianzus: Nor indeed is there any distinction between the state of the people and that of the priesthood: but it seems to me to be a simple fulfillment of the ancient curse, "As with the people, so with the priest."[1] Nor again are the great and eminent men affected otherwise than the majority; no, they are openly at war with the priest, and the piety of the people is an aid to their powers of persuasion. And indeed, provided that it is on behalf of the faith and of the highest and most important questions, let the people be thus disposed, and I do not blame them. To say the truth, I go so far as to praise and congratulate the people. In Defense of His Flight, Oration 2.82.[2]

The Shepherd Has Become a Wolf. Gregory the Great: We are put as guards in the vineyards, but we do not cultivate our own. When we are involved with external affairs, we neglect to watch over our own activities. I think that God suffers greater outrage from no one, dearly beloved, than from priests. Those he has placed to reprove others he sees giving an example of wickedness in their own lives. We who ought to have restrained sin, ourselves commit it. More seriously, priests who ought to give of their own possessions frequently plunder the goods of others. If they see others living humbly and chastely, they often make fun of them. Consider what will become of the flocks when wolves become shepherds! They undertake to guard the flock and are not afraid to waylay the Lord's flock.

We do not seek to gain souls; we devote ourselves daily to our own pursuits, we attend to earthly matters, we strive for human praise with all our will. From being set over others we have greater freedom to do anything we like, and so we turn the ministry we have received into an occasion for display. We abandon God's cause, and we devote ourselves to earthly business; we accept a place of holiness and involve ourselves in earthly deeds. What is written in Hosea is truly fulfilled in us: "And so it will be, like people, like priest."[3] Forty Gospel Homilies 19.[4]

Priests. Gregory the Great: And this indeed is what the Lord, in the wrath of just retribution, menaced through the prophet, saying, "And there shall be like people, like priest."[5] For the priest is as the people, when one who bears a spiritual office acts as do others who are still under judgment with regard to their carnal pursuits. Pastoral Care 2.7.[6]

24:6 Inhabitants of the Earth Are Scorched

Few Are Left. Eusebius of Caesarea: After he rebukes those of the circumcision who have trespassed the law of the covenant of God and warns them with what he has written, he prophesies that only a small number of them will be saved. These few are those whom the apostle calls "the remnant according to the election of grace."[7] Proof of the Gospel 2.3.[8]

24:15 Glorify the Lord

Glorify the Lord! Primasius: "And God remembered Babylon the great, who came into his sight."[9] This designates the confused multitude of all the lost. "That he might give it to drink from the wine of his wrath."[10] The retribution of due punishment to be returned to the wicked is here recorded. "And all the islands fled, and no mountains could be found."[11] I believe that these islands

---

[1]Hos 4:9. [2]NPNF 2 7:221*. [3]Hos 4:9. [4]CS 123:145. [5]Hos 4:9. [6]NPNF 2 12:17. [7]Rom 11:5. [8]POG 1:93*. [9]Rev 16:19. [10]Rev 16:19. [11]Rev 16:20.

and mountains are literary figures for the church on account of the prominence of its stability, concerning which it is also said through Isaiah: "Glorify the Lord in doctrine, the name of the Lord God of Israel in the islands of the sea." COMMENTARY ON THE APOCALYPSE 4.16.[12]

THE CHURCH AS THE ISLAND IN THE SEA.
EUSEBIUS OF CAESAREA: "Therefore, the glory of the Lord is in the islands of the sea." That pertains obviously to the church, which is located in the midst of the godless nations as if an island in the sea. It is in that island that the glory of the Lord shines. COMMENTARY ON ISAIAH 7.19.[13]

THE SEA REPRESENTS THE NATIONS. CYRIL OF ALEXANDRIA: By "sea" he means the multitude of nations, and by "coastlands," perhaps, he means cities. All their inhabitants will "raise their voices" when the divine wrath comes upon them. But the majesty of Christ will somehow be in the sea, that is, in all those nations, and they will realize that it is through divine Providence that they are destroyed and annihilated. They are destroyed because their impiety provoked the Almighty God; hence they will reject their gods who are unable to help them. That is how the majesty of the Lord is celebrated. It is clear that the purpose of the prophecy is to point to the mystery of Christ and to remind about the coming salvation in him. . . . Now, when the preaching of the holy apostles, which leads the nations from the idolatry to the grace of Christ, is spread to the ends of the earth, then, he says, "they shall cry aloud from the sea," that is, all the nations of the world. COMMENTARY ON ISAIAH 2.5.24.[14]

24:16 Praise from the Ends of the Earth

THE GLORY OF THE RIGHTEOUS. PRIMASIUS: "The Spirit of the Lord filled the world."[15] But that will be done with the broken horns of sinners. The horns of the righteous one are said to be exalted,[16] concerning which Isaiah prophesied: "From the ends of the earth we heard praises

announcing the glory of the righteous one." The church is understood to have seven horns, as does every world in which the sevenfold grace of the Spirit rules on account of his remarkable sevenfold operation. And eyes are mentioned here[17] because of illumination. It is in relation to this, I believe, that Zechariah said, "These seven are the eyes of the Lord, which run through all the earth."[18] COMMENTARY ON THE APOCALYPSE 2.5.[19]

24:23 The Moon Will Be Ashamed

THE MOON. JEROME: He [Isaiah] was pricked by the thorn of sin;[20] you are decked with the flowers of virtue. "The moon shall be ashamed, and the sun confounded, when the Lord shall punish the host of heaven on high." This is explained by another passage. "Even the stars are unclean in his sight";[21] and again, "He charges his angels with folly."[22] The moon is ashamed, the sun is confounded, and the sky covered with sackcloth. Shall we fearlessly and joyously, as though we were free from all sin, face the majesty of the Judge? After all, the mountains shall melt away, that is, all who are lifted up by pride, and all the host of the heavens, whether they are stars or angelic powers, shall fade away like heavens when the heavens shall be rolled together as a scroll. AGAINST THE PELAGIANS 2.24.[23]

OVERSHADOWING BRILLIANCE. BEDE: The stars on the day of judgment will be seen obscurely, not because of a gradual waning of their own light but due to the overwhelming brilliance of the true light, who is the supreme Judge coming in majesty, and the light of the Father and the holy angels.[24] Nevertheless, nothing should prevent us from understanding that the sun, the moon and other stars will be deprived temporarily of their own light, as happened to the sun

---

[12]CCL 92:235. [13]PG 24:261. [14]PG 70:545-48. [15]Wis 1:7. [16]See Rev 5:6; Ps 75:10 (74:11 LXX). [17]Rev 5:6. [18]Zech 4:10. [19]CCL 92:85-86. [20]Is 6:5 LXX. [21]Job 25:5. [22]Job 4:18. [23]NPNF 2 6:470**. [24]See Mt 24:29.

at the Lord's passion.[25] But because the moon, which should have been full at that time, lay hidden behind the earth, Joel's prophesy remains unfulfilled still today, for after he had said "the sun will be turned to darkness," he added, "and the moon to blood before the great and magnificent day of the Lord comes."[26] Isaiah also spoke about the day of judgment, saying, "The moon will be ashamed and the sun confounded when the Lord of hosts reigns on Mount Zion and in Jerusalem and is glorified in the presence of Jerusalem's elders." Exposition of the Gospel of Mark 4.13.24.[27]

---

[25]See Mt 24:29; Lk 23:45.   [26]Joel 2:31; Acts 2:20.   [27]CCL 120:600.

25:1-12 SONG OF THANKSGIVING

[1]O Lord, thou art my God;
I will exalt thee, I will praise thy name;
for thou hast done wonderful things,
    plans formed of old, faithful and sure.
[2]For thou hast made the city a heap,
    the fortified city a ruin;
the palace of aliens is a city no more,
    it will never be rebuilt.
[3]Therefore strong peoples will glorify thee;
    cities of ruthless nations will fear thee.*
[4]For thou hast been a stronghold to the poor,
    a stronghold to the needy in his distress,
    a shelter from the storm and a shade from the heat;
for the blast of the ruthless is like a storm against a wall,
    [5]like heat in a dry place.
Thou dost subdue the noise of the aliens;
    as heat by the shade of a cloud,
    so the song of the ruthless is stilled.

[6]On this mountain the Lord of hosts will make for all peoples a feast of fat things, a feast of wine on the lees, of fat things full of marrow, of wine on the lees well refined.† [7]And he will destroy on this mountain the covering that is cast over all peoples,‡ the veil that is spread over all nations. [8]He will swallow up death for ever,§ and the Lord God will wipe away tears from all faces, and

the reproach of his people he will take away from all the earth; for the LORD has spoken.

⁹It will be said on that day, "Lo, this is our God; we have waited for him, that he might save us.# This is the LORD; we have waited for him; let us be glad and rejoice in his salvation."**

¹⁰For the hand of the LORD will rest on this mountain, and Moab shall be trodden down in his place, as straw is trodden down in a dung-pit. ¹¹And he will spread out his hands in the midst of it as a swimmer spreads his hands out to swim; but the LORD will lay low his pride together with the skillˡ of his hands. ¹²And the high fortifications of his walls he will bring down, lay low, and cast to the ground, even to the dust.

l The meaning of the Hebrew word is uncertain   *LXX *Therefore shall the poor people bless thee, and cities of injured men shall bless thee*   †LXX *on this mount they shall drink gladness, they shall drink wine*   ‡LXX *they shall anoint themselves with ointment in this mountain*   §LXX *Death has prevailed and swallowed men up*   #LXX *Behold our God in whom we have trusted*   **LXX *we have exulted and will rejoice in our salvation*

OVERVIEW: The "wonderful things" are the anointing of Christians and the Eucharist (EUSEBIUS). Israel's neighbors, at first impoverished, are brought to glorify God. Simeon is an example of one in Israel anticipating the coming of Christ (CYRIL OF ALEXANDRIA). The anointing is the Christian practice of anointing the newly baptized with oil (CYRIL OF JERUSALEM). The good news was transferred from the Jews to the nations (RUFINUS). The church can know that the sacraments are pure because they are the Lord's (PRIMASIUS), and it will rejoice in Christ's blood (wine) (CYRIL OF ALEXANDRIA). Before the resurrection, death was bitter. We must avoid pride, so that death will not overcome us (AMBROSE). There is coming a time when the flesh will be overcome (AUGUSTINE). Christ is the victor over death (EUSEBIUS, JEROME, CYRIL OF ALEXANDRIA). In the future rest there will be no sorrow (BASIL). When Isaiah says, "Behold our God," we can see that this refers to Christ (CYRIL OF ALEXANDRIA).

25:1 I Will Exalt the Lord

GOD'S COUNSEL. EUSEBIUS OF CAESAREA: The "wonders" of Isaiah were the promises to the Gentiles, and not to Israel, of anointing with sweet-smelling oil and myrrh. They naturally received the name of Christian from this anointing. In addition he promises the "wine of joy" to the Gentiles, using a shadow to allude to the sac-

rament of the new covenant of Christ, which is now openly celebrated among the Gentiles. PROOF OF THE GOSPEL 1.10.[1]

25:3 People Will Glorify God

THE NATIONS GLORIFY GOD. CYRIL OF ALEXANDRIA: Israel was called to the knowledge of God through the tutoring of the law and was richly endowed with the things of God. It was delivered [from Egypt] and inherited the Promised Land. Although there were many other peoples living in other parts of the world, all were alien to spiritual matters and heavenly things. They had not tasted the gifts that come from God. They were, as it were, naked and unclothed, enjoying neither divine protection nor shelter from on high, nor the spiritual wealth that comes from virtue nor other things worthy of praise or admiration.

When Christ appeared, destroying the arrogance of the devil, he led the nations to God the Father, and they basked in the splendor of the true light and shared in his glory. Enjoying the splendor of the way of life according to the gospel, they offered hymns of thanksgiving to the God and Father for these gifts. Thus the text says, you have carried out a "faithful plan formed of old," O Lord, recapitulating all things in Christ and

---

[1]POG 1:61*.

enlightening those in darkness, destroying the mighty powers of this age. That is, like "fortified cities the impoverished people will bless you" and whole cities will "glorify you." Having become a "help to all" and "protection" to those whose ancestral traditions were impoverished, you have saved them from wicked people. Commentary on Isaiah 3.1.25.[2]

25:5 The Fainthearted Thirst for Zion

Simeon Thirsts for the Coming of Christ. Cyril of Alexandria: Perhaps this is what the prophet is referring to, that is, those in Israel who were thirsting for the coming of the Savior. They desired to see the Savior and Redeemer of all. One such person was the righteous Simeon. When he took the infant Jesus in his arms, he said, "Lord, now let your servant depart in peace, according to your word; for mine eyes have seen your salvation which you have prepared in the presence of all peoples, a light for revelation to the Gentiles, and for glory to your people Israel."[3] Commentary on Isaiah 3.1.25.[4]

25:6 Anointed with Ointment

Anoint Themselves. Cyril of Jerusalem: Having been counted worthy of this holy chrism,[5] you are called Christians, verifying the name also by your new birth. For before you were deemed worthy of this grace, you had properly no right to this title but were advancing on your way toward being Christians.

Moreover, you shall know that in the old Scripture there lies the symbol of this chrism. For at the time Moses imparted to his brother the command of God and made him high priest, he anointed him after bathing him in water. And Aaron was called Christ or anointed, evidently from the typical anointing. So also the high priest, in advancing Solomon to the kingdom, anointed him after he had bathed in Gihon.[6] To them, however, these things happened in a figure, but to you not in a figure but in truth; because

you were truly anointed by the Holy Spirit. Christ is the beginning of your salvation. He is truly the first fruit, and you are what follow. If the first fruit is holy, obviously its holiness will pass to the remainder also.

Keep this teaching unspotted, for it shall teach you all things, if it abide in you. . . . For this holy thing is a spiritual safeguard of the body and salvation of the soul. Of this the blessed Isaiah prophesying of old time said, "On this mountain shall the Lord make for all nations a feast; they shall drink wine, they shall drink gladness, they shall anoint themselves with ointment." Catechetical Lectures 11.5-7.[7]

For All Nations. Rufinus of Aquileia: Moreover, this same Isaiah foretells that while those who were engaged in the study of the law from childhood to old age did not believe, to the Gentiles every mystery should be transferred. His words are, "And the Lord of hosts shall make a feast on this mountain for all nations." . . . This was the counsel of the Almighty respecting all the nations. Commentary on the Apostles' Creed 19.[8]

A Shelter from the Heat. Primasius: They will not hunger[9] because they will feed upon living bread, for he said, "I am the living bread which came down from heaven."[10] Neither will they thirst, because they will drink from a cup so splendid as to enact in them the truth he spoke: "Whoever believes in me will never thirst";[11] and again: "Whoever drinks from the water I give him will receive in himself a fountain of water springing up to eternal life."[12] Neither will the sun strike them, nor will they be burned by the deadly fire of its heat. God made a similar promise to his church through Isaiah, saying that he would be "a shelter from the storm, a shade from

[2]*Comm. 24* 4:857*; PG 70:557-60. [3]Lk 2:29-32. [4]*Comm. 24* 4:857-58*; PG 70:560. [5]In the fourth century, Christians in the Jerusalem church were anointed with oil before and after their baptism. This anointing, or chrism, was a part of the baptismal service. [6]1 Kings 1:39. [7]NPNF 2 7:150**. [8]NPNF 2 3:551. [9]Rev 7:16; cf. Is 49:10. [10]Jn 6:51. [11]Jn 6:35. [12]Jn 4:13-14.

the heat." Here he declares the purity of his sacraments to thrive in his own and that none of them will be oppressed by the heat of temptation. "For the Lamb in the midst of the throne governs them."[13] Previously it had said that the Lamb seated on the throne received the scroll,[14] but now it says that the Lamb in the midst of the throne governs them. It does so to teach that there is one throne for the Father and for the Son, since the Father is in the Son and the Son is in the Father, that is, in the midst of the church, which the one, whole, triune God inhabits through faith. COMMENTARY ON THE APOCALYPSE 2.7.[15]

THE WINE OF FEASTING AND JOY. CYRIL OF ALEXANDRIA: Having said that the Lord will reign in Zion and Jerusalem, Isaiah leads us to the mystical meaning of the passage. Thus Zion is interpreted as a high place that is good for surveillance, and Jerusalem is the vision of the world. In fact, the church of Christ combines both: it is high and visible from everywhere, and is, so to speak, located on the mountain. The church may be understood as high also in another way: there is nothing low in it, it is far removed from all the mundane things, as it is written, "I will be exalted among the nations, I will be exalted in the earth!"[16] Equally elevated are its orthodox and divine doctrines; thus the doctrine about God or about the holy and consubstantial Trinity is true, pure and without guile. "The Lord of hosts will make for all people," not just for the Israelites elected for the sake of their patriarchs but for all the people of the world. What will he make? "A feast of wines on the lees; they will drink joy, they will drink wine. They will be anointed with myrrh on the mountain." This joy, of course, means the joy of hope, of the hope rooted in Christ, because we will reign with him, and with him we will enjoy every spiritual joy and pleasure that surpasses mind and understanding. By "wine" he points to the mystical sacrament, that of the bloodless sacrifice, which we celebrate in the holy churches. COMMENTARY ON ISAIAH 25.6-7.[17]

25:8 God Will Wipe Away Tears from Every Eye

DEATH IS SWALLOWED UP. AMBROSE: In the Old Testament the jaw of death is bitter, since it is said, "Strong death is all devouring." In the New Testament the jaw of death is sweet, for it has swallowed death, as the apostle says: "Death is swallowed up in victory! O death, where is your victory? O death, where is your sting?"[18] LETTER 50 (6.31.9).[19]

PRIDE MUST BE SWALLOWED. AMBROSE: Stricken by the indecency of this act [the golden calf], Moses broke the tablets and shattered the head of the calf and beat it to powder in order to destroy all traces of impiety.[20] The first tablets were broken so that the second ones might be repaired whereon, through the teaching of the gospel, faithlessness, now utterly destroyed, vanished. Thus Moses shattered that Egyptian pride and by the authority of the eternal law checked that loftiness overreaching itself. Therefore David says, "And the Lord will break the cedars of Lebanon, and shatter them like the calf of Lebanon.[21] Thus the people swallowed all faithlessness and pride, so that impiety and haughtiness might not swallow them. For it is better that each person be master of his flesh and its vices, that it may not be said of him that all-powerful death has devoured him, but rather, "death is swallowed up in victory!"[22] LETTER 87 (7.78.5).[23]

LUST WILL BE OVERCOME. AUGUSTINE: The apostle said, "With the mind I serve the law of God, but with the flesh the law of sin,"[24] not by giving my members over to committing iniquities but only by feeling lust, without however giving a hand to unlawful lust. So when he said, "With the mind I serve the law of God, but with the flesh the law of sin," he went on to add, "There is

---

[13]Rev 7:17. [14]See Rev 5:1-10. [15]CCL 92:131. [16]Ps 47:7-8 (46:8-9 LXX). [17]PG 70:561. [18]1 Cor 15:54-55. [19]FC 26:268. [20]Ex 32:19-20. [21]Ps 28:5-6. [22]1 Cor 15:54. [23]FC 26:486*. [24]Rom 7:25.

therefore no condemnation now for those who are in Christ Jesus."[25] For those who are in the flesh there is condemnation; for those who are in Christ Jesus no condemnation. In case you should assume this is going to be the case after becoming a Christian, that is why he added "now."

What you must look forward to afterward is not even to have any lust in you which you have to contend with, which you have to combat, which you must not consent to, which you have to curb and tame; look forward to its simply not being there afterward. I mean to say, if what is now contending with us from its base in this mortal body is going to be there afterward, the taunt "Where, death, is your striving?" will be untrue. So let us be quite clear about what it is going to be like afterward. Then, you see, will come about the word that is written: "Death has been swallowed up in victory. Where, death, is your striving? Where, death, is your sting? For the sting of death is sin; but the power of sin, the law."[26] Because desire was increased, not extinguished, by being forbidden. The law gave sin power by simply commanding through the letter without assisting through the spirit. SERMON 155.2.[27]

LOVE OVERCOMES DEATH. EUSEBIUS OF CAESAREA: Now the laws of love summoned him even as far as death and the dead themselves, so that he might summon the souls of those who were long time dead. And so because he cared for the salvation of all for ages past and that "he might bring to nothing him that has the power of death,"[28] as Scripture teaches, here again he underwent the dispensation in his mingled natures: as man, he left his body to the usual burial, while as God he departed from it. For he cried with a loud cry, and said to the Father, "I commend my spirit,"[29] and departed from the body free, in no way waiting for death, who was lagging as it were in fear to come to him. No, rather, he pursued him from behind and drove him on, trodden under his feet and fleeing, and he burst the eternal gates of his dark realms and

made a road of return back again to life for the dead there bound with the bonds of death. Thus too, his own body was raised up, and many bodies of the sleeping saints arose and came together with him into the holy and real city of heaven, as rightly is said by the holy words: "Death has prevailed and swallowed people up; but again the Lord God has taken away every tear from every face." And the Savior of the universe, our Lord, the Christ of God, called Victor, is represented in the prophetic predictions as reviling death and releasing the souls that are bound there, by whom he raises the hymn of victory. PROOF OF THE GOSPEL 4.12.[30]

HELL AND THE DEVIL ARE OVERCOME. JEROME: "Where, O death, is your strife? Where, O death, is your sting?" Commenting upon the power of this testimony, Paul infers "the sting of death is sin, and the power of sin is the law. Yet thanks be to God, who gave us victory through our Lord Jesus Christ."[31] Because he interpreted the resurrection of the Lord in this way, we dare not nor are we able to interpret it differently. Death can be understood as hell and as the devil, who was strangled by the death of Christ. In this connection, Isaiah also said, "Growing stronger, he devoured death," and again, "the Lord has wiped every tear from every face." The two brothers who divided from one another at death,[32] according to the history of that time, are understood to be Israel and Judah, that what was then partially prefigured might now be known fully[33] and that Israel and Judah might be liberated and redeemed along with every human family. COMMENTARY ON HOSEA 3.13.14-15.[34]

CHRIST CONQUERS DEATH. CYRIL OF ALEXANDRIA: It is appropriate and necessary that at the time the "mystery" is handed over,[35] the "resur-

---

[25]Rom 8:1. [26]1 Cor 15:54-55. [27]WSA 3 5:84-85**. [28]Heb 2:14. [29]Lk 23:46. [30]POG 1:186*. [31]1 Cor 15:55-57. [32]See Hos 13:15. [33]See 1 Cor 13:12. [34]CCL 76:149-50. [35]Teaching the Apostles' Creed to catechumens.

rection of the dead" is included. For at the time we make the confession of faith at holy baptism, we say that we expect the resurrection of the flesh. And so we believe. Death overcame our forefather Adam on account of his transgression and like a fierce wild animal it pounced on him and carried him off amid lamentation and loud wailing. Men wept and grieved because death ruled over all the earth. But all this came to an end with Christ. Striking down death, he rose up on the third day and became the way by which human nature would rid itself of corruption. He became the first born of the dead, and the first fruits of those who have fallen asleep.[36]

We who come afterward will certainly follow the first fruits. He turned suffering into joy, and we cast off our sackcloth. We put on the joy given by God so that we can rejoice and say, "Where is your victory O death?"[37] Therefore every tear is taken away. For believing that Christ will surely raise the dead, we do not weep over them, nor are we overwhelmed by inconsolable grief like those who have no hope. Death itself is a "reproach of the people" for it had its beginning among us through sin. Corruption entered in on account of sin, and death's power ruled on earth. Commentary on Isaiah 3.1.25.[38]

The Curse Is Overcome. Cyril of Alexandria: And since the holy Virgin brought forth as man God united personally to flesh, we say that she is the mother of God. [This is] not because the nature of the Word had a beginning of existence from the flesh, for "in the beginning was the Word, and the Word was with God, and the Word was God";[39] he is the Creator of the ages, coeternal with the Father and Creator of all things. As we have stated before, having united humanity to himself personally he even endured birth in the flesh from the womb. He did not require because of his own nature as God a birth in time and in the last stages of the world. He was born in order that he might bless the very beginning of our existence and in order that, because a woman bore him when he was united to the flesh,

the curse against the whole race might be stopped. The curse was sending our bodies from the earth to death, and by him abolishing the saying, "in pain shall you bring forth children,"[40] the words of the prophet might be shown to be true, "strong death has swallowed them up," and again "God has taken away every tear from every face." Third Letter to Nestorius 17.18.[41]

Every Tear Wiped Away. Basil the Great: For eternal rest lies before those who have struggled through the present life observant of the laws, a rest not given in payment for a debt owed for their works but provided as a grace of the munificent God for those who have hoped in him. Then, before he describes the good things there, telling in detail the escape from the troubles of the world, he gives thanks for them to the liberator of souls, who has delivered him from the varied and inexorable slavery of the passions. But what are these good things?

"For he has delivered my soul from death, my eyes from tears, my feet from falling."[42] God describes the future rest by a comparison with things here. Here, he says, the sorrows of death have compassed me, but there he has delivered my soul from death. Here the eyes pour forth tears because of trouble, but there, no longer is there a tear to darken the eyes of those who are rejoicing in the contemplation of the beauty of the glory of God. "For God has wiped away every tear from every face." Homilies on the Psalms 114.[43]

25:9 Behold Our God

"God" Refers to Christ. Cyril of Alexandria: You recognize the one who gives you joy to drink and wine in addition, anointing those in spiritual Zion with myrrh. You recognize that he is true God and Son of God by nature, and although he appeared in the form of a servant,[44] by

---

[36]1 Cor 15:20. [37]1 Cor 15:55-56. [38]*Comm.* 24 4:859; PG 70:564. [39]See Jn 1:1. [40]Gen 3:16. [41]FC 76:89-90**. [42]Ps 114:8. [43]FC 46:357*. [44]See Phil 2:7.

becoming man he became the source of salvation and life for all, being in all things like those on earth though without sin. The prophet indicates that they are all but pointing [to Christ] with their finger when they say, "Behold our God in whom we have hoped, and we will rejoice in our salvation." I think that this text applies especially to the Israelites who were nurtured in the words of Moses and were not ignorant of the predictions of the holy prophets. They waited for the time of the coming of the Savior and Redeemer, the Lord Jesus Christ. Therefore, as I have already said, Zechariah the father of John [the Baptizer] when he prophesied in the Spirit said of Christ, "He has raised up a horn of salvation."[45] And Simeon when he took the holy child in his arms said, "Behold, my eyes have seen the salvation which you have prepared before the face of all people."[46] Recognize then what had been announced of old, the one who is the hope of all, the Savior and Redeemer, they said, according to Isaiah, "Behold our God."

They confess that God will give rest on this mountain. And it seems to me that mountain here refers to the church, for it is there that one finds rest. For we heard the words of Christ: "Come to me, all who labor and are heavy laden, and I will give you rest."[47] COMMENTARY ON ISAIAH 3.1.25.[48]

---

[45]Lk 1:69. [46]Lk 2:30-31. [47]Mt 28:11. [48]*Comm.* 24 4:860; PG 70:564-65.

26:1-10 SONG OF VICTORY

[1]*In that day this song will be sung in the land of Judah:*
"*We have a strong city;*
    he sets up salvation
    as walls and bulwarks.
[2]*Open the gates,*
    that the righteous nation which keeps faith
    may enter in.
[3]*Thou dost keep him in perfect peace,*
    whose mind is stayed on thee,
    because he trusts in thee.
[4]*Trust in the* LORD *for ever,*
    for the LORD GOD
    is an everlasting rock.
[5]*For he has brought low*
    the inhabitants of the height,
    the lofty city.
He lays it low, lays it low to the ground,
    casts it to the dust.
[6]*The foot tramples it,*
    the feet of the poor,
    the steps of the needy."

[7]*The way of the righteous is level;*
    thou[m] *dost make smooth the path of the righteous.*
[8]*In the path of thy judgments,*
    O LORD, *we wait for thee;*
thy memorial name
    is the desire of our soul.
[9]*My soul yearns for thee in the night,*

> my spirit within me earnestly seeks
> thee.*
> For when thy judgments are in the
> earth,
> the inhabitants of the world learn
> righteousness.

> [10]If favor is shown to the wicked,
> he does not learn righteousness;
> in the land of uprightness he deals
> perversely
> and does not see the majesty of the
> LORD.

m Cn Compare Gk: Heb *thou (that art) upright*   *LXX *my spirit seeks you very early in the morning*

OVERVIEW: Christ possessed a body and a soul, and those who believe in him find safety. Christ is the city (VERECUNDUS, APONIUS). God's mercy is in his law (AMBROSE). Vigils are useful in the life of the believer (NICETAS OF REMESIANA, CAESARIUS OF ARLES, CHRYSOSTOM). We should long for God in this present life, symbolized by the night. Anyone who seeks the truth is enflamed with love (GREGORY THE GREAT). The wicked are deprived of the Lord's blessings (ATHANASIUS). The wicked will not see the glory of God (AUGUSTINE, CHRYSOSTOM, GREGORY THE GREAT).

26:1 A Strong City for Us

THE SAVIOR IS A STRONG CITY. APONIUS: Hence, if they find anyone outside, they beat, wound and rob him[1] by not believing in the true flesh of Christ that was nailed to the cross, from whom true blood flowed when pierced by a lance, and by not believing in the true God who bore a true soul and laid it down freely and raised it up freely. Isaiah prophesied about this city and, indeed, demonstrated with his finger, when he said, "Behold, our Savior is a strong city, fortified with walls and bulwarks." EXPOSITION OF SONG OF SONGS 8.24-25.[2]

CHRIST IS THE PROPHESIED CITY. APONIUS: For this reason, it seems to me that the wall[3] represents the people who are acquainted with the one omnipotent God, having been brought near to the Word of the Father, about whom Isaiah prophesied, saying, "The Savior is our strong city. A wall and a bulwark is established in him."

This indicates that Christ was shown to be equipped with a true soul and true flesh for the redemption of the world. But those who have already attained greater perfection, who are prepared to have their blood shed for the sake of his name, who by their own example offer unbelievers access to salvation, are compared with gates. For although the Word of God clothed himself with the nature of every human person for the liberation of the human race, it is nevertheless true that anyone becomes the wall or the gate of the prophesied city, that is of Christ, who, bearing God's image and holding fast to the true faith, merits with his holy works to contain the Word himself, as he promised through the prophet: "I will dwell within them, and I will be their God."[4] EXPOSITION OF SONG OF SONGS 12.32.[5]

TURN YOUR VISION TO THE SAVIOR. VERECUNDUS: When Hezekiah, the king of Judah and son of Ahaz, was gravely ill and had learned of his coming death by the prophecy of Isaiah, he turned his face to the wall and wept bitterly.[6] Immediately the Lord in his mercy not only averted the destruction of imminent death but also added fifteen years to the man's life. Then, at last, Hezekiah sang this song.[7] Hezekiah, a holy man who reigned at that time over all of Israel, displayed the Lord's form: clearly he had every movement of body, soul and mind in subjection to himself, and he accepted the consequences of his infirmity and weakness. He knew without

---

[1]See Song 5:7. [2]CCL 19:191. [3]See Song 8:9-10. [4]Ex 29:45; 2 Cor 6:16. [5]CCL 19:282. [6]See 2 Kings 20:1-3. [7]See Is 38:10-20.

doubt through the prophetic message that the end of his life was approaching. For the longer we seem to live, the more indubitably is our future death foreknown to us. And if we turn our face to the wall when struck by the fear of death, that is, if we direct the vision of our hearts to the Savior, who is here represented by the wall because he is elsewhere called "a wall," we will be saved, inasmuch as he saves the faithful who dwell within him from a great many attacks. "In the city of our strength," says Isaiah, "is the Savior established as a wall and a fortress." Behold, the Savior is said to be a wall. COMMENTARY ON THE CANTICLE OF EZEKIEL 5.1-2.[8]

26:9 My Soul Yearns for You

SEEK GOD IN THE NIGHT. NICETAS OF REMESIANA: And now, beloved, I ought to say a word about the antiquity of the tradition and the utility of vigils. It is easier to begin a work if we keep before our eyes how useful it is. The devotion to vigils is very old. It has been a household tradition among the saints. It was the prophet Isaiah who cried out to the Lord: "My soul has yearned for you in the night. Indeed, my spirit within me seeks you early in the morning." VIGILS OF THE SAINTS 4.[9]

CONTINUALLY REFLECT ON THE WORD. CAESARIUS OF ARLES: For this reason, as I have already said, you ought to read and listen to the sacred lessons with such eagerness that you may be able to speak about them and teach them to others in your own homes and elsewhere, wherever you are. As you, like clean animals, ruminate the Word of God by continuous reflection, you may be able to procure useful favor for yourselves, that is, their spiritual meaning, and with God's help give it to others. Then will be fulfilled in you what is written: "Your cup overflows!"[10] Moreover, you will fulfill what the blessed apostle encourages and advises when he says, "The fact is that whether you eat or drink—whatever you do—you should do all for the glory of God."[11] If

infirmity does not prevent it, fast daily. Hasten to the vigils with cheerful and fervent devotion because of what is written: "O God, my soul yearns for you in the night"; and again: "To you I pray, O Lord; at dawn you hear my voice";[12] and still further: "At midnight I rise to give thanks to your name, O Lord."[13] To this our Lord and Savior also exhorts and encourages us when he says in the Gospel: "Be on guard, and pray that you may not undergo the test."[14] May he himself deign to grant this, to whom are honor and might together with the Father and the Holy Spirit, world without end. SERMON 198.5.[15]

I WILL SEEK YOU IN THE NIGHT. CHRYSOSTOM: [In monasteries] at the crowing of the rooster their leader comes, and gently touching the sleeper with his foot, rouses them all. For there are none sleeping naked. Then as soon as they have arisen they stand up and sing the prophetic hymns with much harmony and well-composed tunes. And neither harp nor pipe nor other musical instrument utters such sweet melodies as you hear from the singing of these saints in their deep and quiet solitudes. And the songs themselves too are suitable and full of the love of God. "In the night," they say, "lift up your hands to God. With my soul have I desired you in the night; truly with my spirit within me will I seek you early." HOMILIES ON 1 TIMOTHY 14.[16]

THE PRESENT LIFE IS THE NIGHT. GREGORY THE GREAT: For "night" is this present life,[17] and as long as we are in it, we are covered with a mist of uncertain imaginations as far as the sight of inward objects is concerned. For the prophet was sensible that he was held by a certain mist in his sight of the Lord, when he says, "My soul longed for you in the night." As if he were to say, I long to behold you in the obscurity of this present life,

---

[8]CCL 93:117. [9]FC 7:58*. [10]Ps 22:5 LXX. [11]1 Cor 10:31. [12]Ps 5:3 (5:4 LXX). [13]Ps 119:62. [14]Mt 26:41. [15]FC 66:52*. [16]NPNF 1 13:456*. [17]See Job 33:15.

but I am still surrounded by the mist of infirmity. MORALS ON THE BOOK OF JOB 5.23.39.[18]

SEEKING GOD IN THE MORNING. GREGORY THE GREAT: Anyone who has been able to reach out for the truth has been on fire with this love. For this reason David said, "My soul has thirsted for the living God; when shall I come and appear before the face of God?"[19] And he counseled us, saying, "Seek his face continually."[20] And for this reason the prophet said, "My soul has desired you in the night, and with my spirit within my breast I will watch for you in the morning." And again the church says to the Lord in the Song of Songs, "I have been wounded with love."[21]

It is right that the soul, after bearing in its heart a wound of love brought on by its burning desire, should reach out for healing at the sight of the doctor. And so, again, it says, "My soul melted when he spoke."[22] The heart of a person who does not seek the face of his Creator is hardened by his wickedness, because in itself it remains cold. But if it now begins to burn with the desire of following him whom it loves, it runs since the fire of love has melted it. Its desire makes it anxious. Everything that used to please it in the world seems worthless; it finds nothing agreeable outside of its Creator; things that once delighted the heart afterwards become grievously oppressive. Nothing brings it consolation in its sadness as long as the one it desires is not beheld. The heart sorrows. Light itself is loathsome. Scorching fire burns away the rust of sin in the heart. The soul is inflamed as if it were gold, for gold loses its beauty through use, but fire restores its brightness. FORTY GOSPEL HOMILIES 25.[23]

26:10 Let the Ungodly Be Taken Away

THE WICKED RECEIVE JUDGMENT. ATHANASIUS: When, by such faith and knowledge, the Lord's people have embraced this true life, they surely receive the joy of heaven. The wicked, on the other hand, since they don't care about the Lord's life, are rightly deprived of its blessings. For, "let the wicked be taken away so that he shall not see the glory of the Lord." In the end they, like everyone else, shall hear the universal proclamation of the promise, "Awake, sleeper, and rise up from the dead."[24] They shall rise and knock on the doors of heaven, saying, "Open to us."[25] The Lord, however, will rebuke them for rejecting knowledge of him and will tell them, "I do not know you."[26] FESTAL LETTER 7.2.[27]

NOT ALL WILL SEE GOD. AUGUSTINE: In the resurrection itself it is not easy to see God, except for those who are clean of heart; hence, "Blessed are the clean of heart, for they shall see God."[28] From here on he begins to speak of that world where all who rise again will not see God, but only those who rise to eternal life. The unworthy will not see him, for of them it is said, "Let the wicked be taken away lest he behold the brightness of the Lord." But the worthy will see him, and of such the Lord spoke when, though present, he was not seen, saying, "He that loves me keeps my commandments, and he that loves me shall be loved of my Father, and I will love him and will manifest myself to him."[29] LETTER 27 (177.11).[30]

ONLY THE PURE IN HEART WILL SEE GOD. AUGUSTINE: In this human form the good will see him in whom they have believed; the wicked, him whom they have despised. But the wicked will not see him in the form of God in which he is equal to the Father, for as the prophet says, "The wicked shall be taken off that he may not see the glory of the Lord," and, on the other hand, "Blessed are the clean of heart, for they shall see God."[31] SERMON 214.9.[32]

THE WICKED WILL NOT SEE THE GLORY OF GOD. AUGUSTINE: Then, therefore, we shall

---

[18]LF 23:33-34*. [19]Ps 42:2 (41:3 Vg). [20]Ps 105:4 (104:4 Vg). [21]Song 2:5. [22]Song 5:6. [23]CS 123:190*. [24]Eph 5:14. [25]Mt 25:11. [26]Lk 13:25. [27]NPNF 2 4:523-24**. [28]Mt 5:8. [29]Jn 14:21, 23. [30]FC 20:195*. [31]Mt 5:8. [32]FC 38:140*.

come and we shall enjoy the one thing; but the one thing will be all things to us. For what was it I said, my brothers, when I began to speak? What is that sufficiency which we shall possess when we shall have no need? What is the sufficiency which we shall possess? I had intended to say, "What will God give to us which he will not give to them?" "Let the wicked be taken away that he may not see the glory of God." Hence God will give his glory to us so that we may enjoy it; and the wicked will be taken away that he may not see the glory of God. God himself will be the entire sufficiency which we shall possess as our own. Greedy one, what did you seek to gain? What does anyone, for whom God is not enough, seek from God? SERMON 255.6.[33]

THE WONDER OF GOD'S GLORY. CHRYSOSTOM: Our Lord Jesus Christ came on this account, too, that we might see not only his glory here but also the glory to come. Therefore he said, "I will that where I am they also may be, in order that they may behold my glory."[34] Now, if this glory here has been so bright and splendid, what could one say of that other? It will not appear on this corrupt earth or while we are in our perishable bodies but in that immortal and everlasting creation, and with so much brightness that it is impossible to put it into words. Oh, blessed, and thrice-blessed, and blessed many times over, they who are deemed worthy to become beholders of that glory! With reference to it the prophet says, "Away with the impious, that he may not behold the glory of the Lord." HOMILIES ON THE GOSPEL OF JOHN 13 (12.3).[35]

THE VISION OF GOD'S GLORY. GREGORY THE GREAT: His coming means his return from the judgment to his kingdom. The Lord comes to us after the judgment, because he lifts us up from his human appearance in the contemplation of his divinity; his coming means that he leads us to the vision of his glory. We see in his divinity after the judgment the one we beheld in his humanity at the judgment. At the judgment he comes in the form of a servant and appears to everyone, since it is written, "They will look on him whom they pierced."[36] When the condemned fall down to their punishment, the righteous are led to the brightness of his glory, as is written: "The wicked is taken away, so that he will [not] see the glory of the Lord." FORTY GOSPEL HOMILIES 20.[37]

---

[33]FC 38:355*. [34]Jn 17:24. [35]FC 33:118*. [36]Jn 19:37. [37]CS 123:152.

26:11-21 GOD'S HELP AND VICTORY

[11]O LORD, thy hand is lifted up,
 but they see it not.
Let them see thy zeal for thy people, and
 be ashamed.
 Let the fire for thy adversaries consume

 them.*
[12]O LORD, thou wilt ordain peace for us,†
 thou hast wrought for us all our works.
[13]O LORD our God,
 other lords besides thee have ruled over

us,

but thy name alone we acknowledge.
¹⁴They are dead, they will not live;
they are shades, they will not arise;‡
to that end thou hast visited them with
destruction
and wiped out all remembrance of them.
¹⁵But thou hast increased the nation, O
LORD,
thou hast increased the nation; thou art
glorified;
thou hast enlarged all the borders of the
land.

¹⁶O LORD, in distress they sought thee,
they poured out a prayerⁿ
when thy chastening was upon them.
¹⁷Like a woman with child,
who writhes and cries out in her pangs,
when she is near her time,
so were we because of thee, O LORD;
¹⁸we were with child, we writhed,§
we have as it were brought forth wind.#

We have wrought no deliverance in the
earth,
and the inhabitants of the world have not
fallen.**
¹⁹Thy dead shall live, their bodiesº shall
rise.††
O dwellers in the dust, awake and sing
for joy!
For thy dew is a dew of light,‡‡
and on the land of the shades thou wilt
let it fall.

²⁰Come, my people, enter your chambers,
and shut your doors behind you;
hide yourselves for a little while
until the wrath§§ is past.
²¹For behold, the LORD is coming forth out
of his place
to punish the inhabitants of the earth for
their iniquity,
and the earth will disclose the blood shed
upon her,
and will no more cover her slain.

n Heb uncertain   o Cn Compare Syr Tg: Heb my body   *LXX jealousy shall seize upon an untaught nation, and now fire shall devour the adversaries   †LXX give us peace   ‡Vg
giants shall not rise up again   §LXX because of your fear (reverence)   #LXX the spirit of your salvation   **LXX we shall not fall, but all that dwell upon the land shall fall   ††LXX and
they that are in tombs shall be raised   ‡‡LXX healing   §§LXX adds of the Lord

OVERVIEW: Zeal that is full of hatred will destroy (AUGUSTINE). The fire is the indignation the enemies of the church felt for believers (CASSIODORUS). God will devour his enemies (GREGORY OF NAZIANZUS). The truly wise entrust themselves to the power of the Godhead (CASSIODORUS). God will give us peace through Christ (AUGUSTINE, CHRYSOSTOM, CYRIL OF ALEXANDRIA). Only fear offending God (CHRYSOSTOM). Any good that people do is a result of God working in them (CASSIODORUS, BEDE). We should give thanks to God for his good works in us (GREGORY THE GREAT).

Though Christ reigns over all, those who

believe in him are said to be possessed by him (AUGUSTINE, ATHANASIUS). The dead are sinners, and the giants are those consumed by pride (GREGORY THE GREAT). The soul is ready to receive the gospel (AMBROSE). Souls are pregnant that receive the faith (JEROME, FULGENTIUS). The righteous glory in reverence for the Lord. Believers produced the spirit of salvation because of their fear of the Lord. The spirit of salvation is spiritual rebirth and the promised resurrection (AMBROSE), which brings the richest joy (AUGUSTINE). The church is pregnant with the spirit of salvation (BEDE).

The judgment of God is balanced by his mercy

(GREGORY OF NAZIANZUS). All those who are dead will be raised from the dead, but the righteous will be raised to eternal joy and sinners to eternal punishment (AUGUSTINE, CHRYSOSTOM, CYRIL OF JERUSALEM, IRENAEUS). Bodies will be raised from the dead, and not just souls (JOHN OF DAMASCUS). Dew is the light of wisdom and the healing of souls (APONIUS). Christ is dew to those who need his mercy (JEROME). Everyone will be raised from the dead (TERTULLIAN). Once the body has been raised from the dead, it is immortal (NICETAS OF REMESIANA, QUODVULTDEUS, JEROME). Death is rest until the resurrection (AUGUSTINE, JEROME, TERTULLIAN). All those who died before Christ are awaiting the time of the resurrection of the saints (CLEMENT OF ROME). Those who have gone into the chambers of the church are saved from judgment (ORIGEN, JEROME).

26:11 Adversaries Consumed by Fire

TWO KINDS OF ZEAL. AUGUSTINE: Note that there are two kinds of zeal, one full of love, the other full of hatred. The former is indicated in the words, "The zeal of your house has devoured me";[1] the latter, in the words, "Zeal has taken hold of the senseless people, and now fire shall devour your opponents." CITY OF GOD 20.12.[2]

SURROUNDED BY ENEMIES. CASSIODORUS: A fire went before the Lord's coming when the hearts of the unfaithful seethed at the preaching of the prophets so that they were fired with the heat of anger, and they debated the murder of those preachers. So this is the fire that shall go before him, but it devoured instead those who stirred it. As the prophet Isaiah said, "And now fire will devour your enemies." Next comes, "And shall burn his enemies round about." "Shall burn," as we have stated, refers to the indignation and sudden mental heat that the enemies of the holy church experienced at that time. "Round about" we must interpret as "on all sides," for as the preachers were few, a countless crowd of ene-

mies hemmed them in. EXPOSITION OF THE PSALMS 96.3.[3]

THE PUNISHMENTS OF THE UNGODLY. GREGORY OF NAZIANZUS: I know the glittering sword,[4] and the blade made drunk in heaven, bidden to slay, to bring to nothing, to make childless and to spare neither flesh nor marrow nor bones. I know him who, though free from passion, meets us like a bear robbed of her cubs, like a leopard in the way of the Assyrians,[5] not only those of that day, but if anyone now is an Assyrian in wickedness. Nor is it possible to escape the might and speed of his wrath when he watches over our impieties, and his jealousy, which knows to devour his adversaries, pursues his enemies to the death.[6] I know the emptying, the making void, the making waste, the melting of the heart and knocking of the knees together;[7] such are the punishments of the ungodly. ON HIS FATHER'S SILENCE, ORATION 16.7.[8]

26:12a Peace Ordained for Us

ENTRUST YOURSELVES TO GOD. CASSIODORUS: So they are truly wise who entrust themselves to the power and dispensation of the Godhead; him alone they seek, and the outcome is all that is good for them. This is the message of the prophet Isaiah: "Lord our God, give us your peace; for you have bestowed all things on us." Next comes: "And he gave ear to me." Note that this utterance to the Lord, so short but magnificent in its devotion, sought that he should deign to give ear; what is there that he has failed to give us when out of pity he has granted such a request? For his gaze on us spells deliverance and a bestowal of gifts so great that even the greedy suppliant ceases to beg for them. EXPOSITION OF THE PSALMS 76.2.[9]

WHAT SORT OF PEACE? AUGUSTINE: The time

[1]Ps 68:10. [2]FC 24:283*. [3]ACW 52:426*. [4]Ezek 21:9. [5]Hos 13:7-8. [6]Hos 8:3. [7]Nahum 2:10. [8]NPNF 2 7:249*. [9]ACW 52:239-40*.

when our external enemy the devil will be under our feet is when the internal enemy, covetousness, has been healed, and we shall be living in peace. What sort of peace? The sort that "eye has not seen nor ear heard."[10] What sort of peace? The sort that no imagination can conceive and no quarreling intrude on. What sort of peace? The sort about which the apostle said, "And the peace of God, which surpasses all understanding, will guard your hearts."[11] About this peace the prophet Isaiah says, "O Lord our God, give us peace, for you have given us everything you promised." You promised Christ; you have given him to us. You promised his cross and the shedding of his blood for the forgiveness of sins; you have given them to us. You promised his ascension and the sending of the Holy Spirit from heaven; you have given them to us. You promised us a church spread throughout the world; you have given it. You promised there would be heretics to try us and put us through our paces, and the church would triumph over their errors; you have given this. You promised the abolition of the idols of the heathen; you have given it. SERMON 77A.2.[12]

DEATH'S STING IS SIN. AUGUSTINE: What's the meaning of "Where, death, is your sting?" It means, "Where is sin?" You ask, and it is nowhere. "For the sting of death is sin."[13] They are the apostle's words, not mine. That is when we will be able to say, "Where, death, is your sting?" Sin will be nowhere, neither to take you captive, nor to assault you nor to tickle your consciousness. That is when we will not say, "Forgive us our debts."[14] But what will we say? "Lord our God, give us peace, for you have given us everything." SERMON 131.7.[15]

PUNISHMENT LEADS US TO GOD. CHRYSOSTOM: When you see a person living in wickedness and enjoying great prosperity without suffering any misfortune, you should mourn particularly for this reason, because although he is afflicted with a very serious disease and ulcer, he aggravates his illness, making himself worse by his lux-

ury and self-indulgence. For punishment is not evil, but sin is evil. The latter separates us from God, but the former leads us toward God and dissolves his anger. How do we know this? Hear what the prophet says, "Comfort, comfort my people, O priests, speak tenderly to Jerusalem . . . that she has received from the Lord's hand double for all her sins."[16] And elsewhere he says, "O Lord our God, give us peace; for you have given us all our due." HOMILIES ON LAZARUS AND THE RICH MAN 3.[17]

GOD'S PEACE PROVIDES ALL WE NEED. CYRIL OF ALEXANDRIA: And we have learned also to say in our prayers, "O Lord our God, grant us your peace, for you have given us everything," so that if anyone becomes partaker of the peace furnished by God, he will not be lacking any good thing. LETTER 39.2.[18]

ONLY FEAR OFFENDING GOD. CHRYSOSTOM: But I say all this now, and select all the histories that contain trials and tribulations and the wrath of kings and their evil designs, in order that we may fear nothing except offending God. For then also was there a furnace burning;[19] yet they derided it but feared sin. For they knew that if they were consumed in the fire, they should suffer nothing that was to be dreaded; but that if they were guilty of impiety, they should undergo the extremes of misery. It is the greatest punishment to commit sin, though we may remain unpunished; as on the other hand, it is the greatest honor and repose to live virtuously, though we may be punished. For sins separate us from God; as he himself speaks: "Have your sins separated between you and me?"[20] But punishments lead us back to God. As one says, "Give peace; for you have recompensed us for all things." Suppose anyone has a wound; which should we most deservedly fear, gangrene or the

[10]1 Cor 2:9. [11]Phil 4:7. [12]WSA 3 3:328. [13]1 Cor 15:54-56. [14]Mt 6:12. [15]WSA 3 4:320. [16]Is 40:1-2. [17]OWP 65. [18]FC 76:148. [19]Dan 3:19-30. [20]Is 59:2.

surgeon's knife? The steel or the devouring progress of the ulcer? Sin is a gangrene; punishment is the surgeon's knife. If someone has gangrene and does not have surgery, he does not merely remain ill, he gets worse. In the same way the sinner, though he is not punished, is the most wretched of people; and he is then especially wretched when he has no punishment and is suffering no distress. HOMILIES CONCERNING THE STATUES 6.14.[21]

26:12b All Our Works You Have Done for Us

GOD ACCOMPLISHES ALL. CASSIODORUS: "All have fallen."[22] Anyone who refuses to seek out a strong foundation necessarily falls. "Together they became useless," namely, with regard to the work for which they were created. "There is none who does good."[23] There was no one who would do good, because the Jews broke the commandments and the Gentiles spurned the law of nature. When anyone from either party did good, therefore, he knew that he was indebted to grace, not to nature, as the prophet said in reference to the Lord: "in the presence of whom no one is innocent."[24] Isaiah also says in his canticle: "O Lord our God, you will give us peace, for you have accomplished all of our works in us." EXPOSITION OF ROMANS 3.[25]

ALL FROM GOD'S GRACE. BEDE: "A man's steps are directed by the Lord."[26] Whoever walks a straight path composed of human steps does so not by the freedom of human judgment but by the governance of him to whom Isaiah said, "All of our works were accomplished by you." "What man can understand his way?"[27] In this it becomes clear that whatever goodness anyone possesses from himself he does not have except through the grace of God, because no one is able to understand through the freedom of his own judgment either what kind of future he will have or the quality and duration of conquests to come. THREE BOOKS ON THE PROVERBS OF SOLOMON 2.20.[28]

ALL OUR WORKS. GREGORY THE GREAT: Let us offer thanks to our Creator for the blessings we have received and humbly say with the prophet Isaiah, "For you have wrought all our works for us." HOMILIES ON EZEKIEL 1.4.16.[29]

26:13 O Lord, Take Possession of Us

POSSESS US. AUGUSTINE: Therefore Christ will hand the kingdom over to God and the Father when through him the Father will be known by sight, for his kingdom consists of those in whom he now reigns through faith. In fact, in one sense Christ's kingdom means his divine power according to which every created thing is subject to him; and in another sense his kingdom means the church in respect to the faith that it has in him. In accord with this meaning is the prayer of him who says, "Possess us," for it is not the case that [Christ] himself does not possess all things. This is also the meaning of the following statement: "When you were the slaves of sin, you were free from righteousness."[30] Therefore he will destroy every dominion and every authority and power, so that he who sees the Father through the Son will neither require nor be pleased with repose in his own or the power of any created thing. QUESTION 69.4.[31]

LORD OF ALL. ATHANASIUS: For the Son of God indeed, being himself the Word, is Lord of all. But we once were subject from the first to the slavery of corruption and the curse of the law. Then by degrees fashioning for ourselves things that were not, we served, as says the blessed apostle, "them which by nature are no gods."[32] Ignorant of the true God, we preferred things that were not to the truth. But afterwards, as the ancient people when oppressed in Egypt groaned, so when we too had the law "engrafted"[33] in us, according to the unut-

---

[21]NPNF 1 9: 387**. [22]Rom 3:12; Ps 14:3 (13:3 LXX). [23]Rom 3:12. [24]Ex 34:7. [25]PL 68:429. [26]Prov 20:24. [27]Prov 20:24. [28]CCL 119B:106-7. [29]CCL 142:66. [30]Rom 6:20. [31]FC 70:170-71. [32]Gal 4:8. [33]Jas 1:21.

terable sighings[34] of the Spirit made our interces-sion, "O Lord our God, take possession of us"; then, as "he became a house of refuge" and a "God and defense," so also he became our Lord. Nor did he then begin to be, but we began to have him for our Lord. Four Discourses Against the Arians 2.15.14.[35]

26:14 Those Who Are Dying Will Not Live

The Sinner Shall Not Live. Gregory the Great: For hence it is said by the prophet, "The dead shall not live; the giants shall not rise up again." For whom does he call "the dead" except sinners, and whom does he designate "giants" except those who over and above take pride in sin. Now the former do "not live," because by sin-ning they have forfeited the life of righteousness; these latter too "cannot rise up again" after death because after their transgression they are swollen with pride and do not have recourse to the reme-dies of penitence. Morals on the Book of Job 4.17.30.[36]

26:18 Bringing Forth the Spirit of Salvation

The Womb of the Soul. Ambrose: Nature provides woman with a womb in which a living person is brought to birth in the course of time. Such too is that characteristic of the soul which is ready to receive in its womblike recesses the seeds of our thoughts, to cherish them and to bring them forth as a woman gives birth to a child. This and no other is the meaning of the words of Isaiah: "We have conceived and brought forth the spirit of salvation."[37] Cain and Abel 1.10.47.[38]

We Conceived. Jerome: We, however, who heard the Lord our Savior say that those in Judea should flee to the mountains[39] also lift our own eyes to the mountains, concerning which it was written: "I raise my eyes to the mountains, whence comes my assistance."[40] And in another place [it is written], "Its foundation is in the holy

mountains,"[41] and "The Lord surrounds his peo-ple as the mountains surround them,"[42] and "The city set upon a mountain cannot be hidden."[43] We must shed the skin of the letter and, ascending Mount Zion barefoot with Moses, say, "I will cross over and see this great vision."[44] [This is] so that we can understand those souls to be preg-nant who conceived the beginning of faith from the seed of doctrine and from talking with God, who say with Isaiah, "Out of reverence for you, Lord, we have conceived and given birth, bringing the spirit of your salvation upon the earth." Let-ter 121.4.[45]

Pregnant with Faith. Jerome: The souls of those believers are pregnant who are able to say at the beginning of faith: "From reverence for you, Lord, we have conceived and given birth." Com-mentary on Amos 1.1.4-5.[46]

Faith Must Be Nourished. Fulgentius of Ruspe: Therefore faith can neither be conceived nor augmented in the human heart unless it is infused and nourished by the Holy Spirit. For we are reborn from the same Spirit from which Christ was born. The Spirit by which Christ is formed according to faith in the heart of each believer, therefore, is also the Spirit by which he was formed bodily in the womb of the Virgin. For this reason, it is in the person of the believer that the prophet cries out to the Lord: "Out of rever-ence for you, Lord, we conceived in the womb and brought forth; we have brought the spirit of your salvation upon the earth." Letter 17.40.[47]

The Righteous Glory in the Lord. Ambrose: Their cows did not miscarry, there-

---

[34]Rom 8:26. [35]NPNF 2 4:355. [36]CCL 143A:868; LF 21:298. [37]The LXX connects the two words *spirit* (wind) and *salvation* to form the phrase "the spirit of salvation." In the traditional Hebrew text, the Masoretic Text, these two words are separated by a disjunctive accent. Hence it reads, "we have given birth to wind (or spirit). Salvation has not been accomplished in the land." [38]CSEL 32 1:377. [39]See Mt 24:16. [40]Ps 121:1 (120:1 LXX). [41]Ps 87:1 (86:1 LXX). [42]Ps 125:2 (124:2 LXX). [43]Mt 5:14. [44]Ex 3:3. [45]CSEL 56:16. [46]CCL 76:219. [47]CCL 91A:594.

fore, but gave birth, so that their labor would be increased and that they would beget everything they conceived without reverence for God.[48] The righteous, however, take delight in an altogether different way. They glory not in the abundance of their wealth or the fruitfulness of their livestock but in the Lord, saying, "We were impregnated with reverence for you, and we brought forth the spirit of salvation." THE PRAYER OF JOB AND DAVID 2.4.15.[49]

YOUR DEAD SHALL LIVE. AMBROSE: Isaiah also, proclaiming the resurrection to the people, says that he is the announcer of the Lord's message, for we read thus: "For the mouth of the Lord has spoken, and they shall speak in that day."[50] And what the mouth of the Lord declared that the people should say is set forth later on, where it is written: "Because of your fear, O Lord, we have been with child and have brought forth the Spirit of your salvation, which you have poured forth upon the earth. They that inhabit the earth shall fall; they shall rise that are in the graves. For the dew which is from you is health for them, but the land of the wicked shall perish. Go, O my people, and enter into your chambers; hide yourselves for a little until the Lord's wrath pass by." ON HIS BROTHER SATYRUS 2.67.[51]

THE RICHEST JOY. AUGUSTINE: Even now let us rejoice somehow or other in this hope derived from the promises of one most faithful, until that richest of all possible joys arises, when "we shall be like him, because we shall see him as he is,"[52] and our joy nobody shall take from us. Of this hope, you see, we have also received already the acceptable and freely given pledge that is the Holy Spirit, who produces in our hearts the unutterable groanings of holy desire. "For we have conceived," as Isaiah says, "and have brought forth the spirit of salvation." And, "when a woman is in labor," the Lord says, "she has sorrow, because her day has come; but when she has brought forth, there is great joy, because a human being has been born into the world."[53] This will

be the joy that nobody will take away from us; on the day when we are brought forth into the eternal light from this conception of faith. So meanwhile let us fast and pray, while it is still the day of bringing forth. SERMON 210.7.[54]

THE CHURCH GIVES BIRTH. BEDE: "When a woman gives birth, she is sorrowful because her hour has come."[55] He refers to holy church as a woman on account of her fruitfulness in good works and because she never ceases to beget spiritual children for God. He says also in another place about this, "The kingdom of heaven is like yeast which a woman took and hid in three measures of flour until the whole [mass] was leavened."[56] A woman took some yeast when the church, by the Lord's generosity, secured the energy of love and faith from on high. She hid this "in three measures of flour until the whole [mass] was leavened" when she performed her ministry of imparting the word of life to parts of Asia [Minor], Europe and Africa, until all the bounds of the world were on fire with love for the heavenly kingdom. The one who said sadly to those who were departing from the purity of the faith, "My little children, for whom I am again in travail, until Christ be formed in you,"[57] was indicating that he was among this woman's members. They testified that they were among her members who were enkindled with heavenly desires, who cried out in praise of their Maker, "It is out of fear of you, Lord, that we have conceived and been in travail and given birth to the Spirit." HOMILIES ON THE GOSPELS 2.13.[58]

THE SPIRIT OF SALVATION. GREGORY OF NAZIANZUS: Let us talk about how "mercy is put in the balance"[59] as holy Isaiah declares, for goodness is not without discernment, as the first laborers in the vineyard fancied, because they

---

[48]See Job 21:10. [49]CSEL 32 2:241. [50]Is 25:8-9. [51]NPNF 2 10:184-85*. [52]1 Jn 3:2. [53]Jn 16:21. [54]WSA 3 6:122. [55]Is 65:13-14. [56]Lk 13:21. [57]Gal 4:19. [58]CS 111:120. [59]Is 28:17 LXX.

could not perceive any distinction between those who were paid alike.[60] And [let us talk about] how anger, which is called "the cup in the hand of the Lord"[61] and "the cup of falling which is drained,"[62] is in proportion to transgressions, even though he abates to all somewhat of what is their due and dilutes with compassion the unmixed draught of his wrath. For he inclines from severity to indulgence toward those who accept chastisement with fear and who after a slight affliction conceived and are in pain with conversion and bring forth the perfect spirit of salvation. But nevertheless he reserves the dregs, the last drop of his anger, that he may pour it out entire upon those who, instead of being healed by his kindness, grow obdurate, like the hard-hearted Pharaoh, that bitter taskmaster, who is set forth as an example of the power of God over the ungodly. ON HIS FATHER'S SILENCE, ORATION 16.4.[63]

26:19a The Dead Shall Rise

THE DEAD SHALL RISE. AUGUSTINE: The first part [of the verse] concerns the resurrection of the just, but the last few words may be taken to mean "the bodies of the wicked will fall into the ruin of damnation." In regard to the resurrection of the just, the attentive reader will notice some distinction. "The dead shall rise" refers to the first resurrection; "those in the graves" refers to the second; and in the following words we may not improperly find a reference to the saints whom the Lord will find alive on earth. As for the word "your dew is their health," we are not wrong in taking "health" to mean "immortality," that most perfect health which needs no daily medicine of ordinary food. CITY OF GOD 20.21.[64]

ALL WILL BE RAISED. CHRYSOSTOM: Isaiah made it clear that Christ will raise up all people when he said, "The dead shall be raised up again; even those in the tombs shall be raised up. For the dew from you is healing for them." That was not all. After his cross, after his slaughter, his glory will shine forth more brightly; after his resurrection, he will advance the message of his gospel still more. DEMONSTRATION AGAINST THE PAGANS 8.8.[65]

THE GRAVES WILL BE OPENED. CYRIL OF JERUSALEM: Isaiah the prophet says, "The dead men shall rise again, and those who are in the tombs shall awake." And the prophet Ezekiel, now before us, says most plainly, "Behold, I will open your graves and bring you up out of your graves."[66] And Daniel says, "Many of those who sleep in the dust of the earth shall arise, some to everlasting life and some to everlasting shame."[67]

And there are many Scriptures that testify of the resurrection of the dead. For there are many other sayings on this matter. But now, by way of remembrance only, we will make a passing mention of the raising of Lazarus on the fourth day[68] and just allude, because of the shortness of the time, to the widow's son also who was raised.[69] And merely for the sake of reminding you, let me mention the ruler of the synagogue's daughter,[70] and the rending of the rocks,[71] and how "there arose many bodies of the saints which slept,"[72] their graves having been opened. But especially be it remembered that "Christ has been raised from the dead."[73] CATECHETICAL LECTURES 18.15-16.[74]

THE MANNER OF RISING WILL BE DIFFICULT. CYRIL OF JERUSALEM: Do not listen to those who say that this body is not raised up; for raised it is, as Isaiah witnesses, saying, "The dead shall arise, and they in the tombs shall be raised." Or, as Daniel says, "Many of them that sleep in the dust of the earth shall arise, some to everlasting life and some to everlasting shame."[75] But while rising again is the common lot of all people, the manner of rising again is not alike for all. For while we all

---

[60]Mt 20:12. [61]Ps 75:9. [62]Is 51:17 LXX. [63]NPNF 2 7:248. [64]FC 24:305. [65]FC 73:221-22*. [66]Ezek 37:12. [67]Dan 12:2. [68]Jn 11. [69]Lk 7:12-14. [70]Mk 5:22-23. [71]Mt 27:51. [72]Mt 27:52. [73]1 Cor 15:20. [74]NPNF 2 7:138*. [75]Dan 12:2.

receive everlasting bodies, those bodies are not alike for all. That is to say, the righteous receive such bodies as may enable them to join with the band of angels throughout eternity, while sinners received bodies in which to undergo through the ages the torture of their sins. CATECHETICAL LECTURES 4.31.[76]

JOY AT THE RESURRECTION. IRENAEUS: Then too, Isaiah himself has plainly declared that there shall be joy of this nature at the resurrection of the just, when he says, "The dead shall rise again; those too who are in the tombs shall arise, and those who are in the earth shall rejoice. For the dew from you is health to them." AGAINST HERESIES 5.34.1.[77]

THE RESURRECTION OF THE BODY. JOHN OF DAMASCUS: Sacred Scripture . . . testifies to the fact that there will be a resurrection of the body. . . . Isaiah also [testifies that] "the dead shall rise and those in their graves be awakened." And it is obvious that it is not the souls that are put in the tombs but the bodies. ORTHODOX FAITH 4.27.[78]

26:19b *Dew from You Is Healing to Them*

THE DEW. APONIUS: About this dew[79] the prophet Isaiah proclaimed: "Your dew is their salvation," or, according to the Hebrew text, "For your dew is the dew of light." Here is clearly taught that the dew of which he speaks is the light of wisdom and the healing of souls, which is the doctrine of wisdom and truth, without which the soul is sickly and blind. EXPOSITION OF SONG OF SONGS 8.7.[80]

DEW BRINGS HEALTH. JEROME: We should love the dew about which Moses said, "May my words descend as the dew,"[81] and about which Isaiah also said, "The dead shall rise again, and all who were in the graves shall rise again, for the dew which is from you is their health." COMMENTARY ON HOSEA 2.6.5.[82]

HEALING DEW. JEROME: In the same way that the Lord becomes the light,[83] the way, the truth,[84] the bread,[85] the vine,[86] the fire,[87] the shepherd,[88] the lamb,[89] the door, and many other things to believers, so also does he become the dew to us who are in need of his mercy and know ourselves to be feverish with sin, about whom Isaiah said, "The dew which is from you is their health." COMMENTARY ON HOSEA 3.14.5-9.[90]

MEDICINE FOR THEIR BONES. TERTULLIAN: Unquestionably, if the people were indulging in figurative murmurs that their bones were become dry[91] and that their hope had perished—plaintive at the consequences of their dispersion—then God might fairly enough seem to have consoled their figurative despair with a figurative promise. Since, however, no injury had as yet alighted on the people from their dispersion, although the hope of the resurrection had very frequently failed among them, it is manifest that it was owing to the perishing condition of their bodies that their faith in the resurrection was shaken. God, therefore, was rebuilding the faith that the people were pulling down. But even if it were true that Israel was depressed at some shock in their existing circumstances, we must not on that account suppose that the purpose of revelation could have rested in a parable. Its aim must have been to testify a resurrection, in order to raise the nation's hope to even an eternal salvation and an indispensable restoration and thereby turn off their minds from brooding over their present affairs. This indeed is the aim of other prophets likewise. "You shall go forth," [says Malachi], "from your tombs, as young calves let loose from their bonds, and you shall tread down your enemies." And again [Isaiah says], "Your heart shall rejoice, and your bones shall spring up like the grass,"[92] because the grass also is renewed by the

---

[76]FC 61:134**. [77]ANF 1:563. [78]FC 37:402. [79]See Song 5:2. [80]CCL 19:183. [81]Deut 32:2. [82]CCL 76:66. [83]Jn 1:4. [84]Jn 14:6. [85]Jn 6:35. [86]Jn 15:5. [87]Jn 10:11. [88]Jn 1:29. [89]Jn 10:7. [90]CCL 76:156. [91]Ezek 37:1-2. [92]Is 66:14.

dissolution and corruption of the seed. In a word, if it is contended that the figure of the rising bones refers properly to the state of Israel,[93] why is the same hope announced to all nations, instead of being limited to Israel only, of reinvesting those bony remains with bodily substance and vital breath and of raising up their dead out of the grave? For the language is universal: "The dead shall arise and come forth from their graves; for the dew which comes from you is medicine to their bones." In another passage it is written: "All flesh shall come to worship before me, says the Lord."[94] When? When the fashion of this world shall begin to pass away. For he said before, "As the new heaven and the new earth, which I make, remain before me, says the Lord, so shall your seed remain."[95] Then also shall be fulfilled what is written afterwards: "And they shall go forth" [namely, from their graves] "and shall see the carcasses of those who have transgressed: for their worm shall never die, nor shall their fire be quenched; and they shall be a spectacle to all flesh,"[96] even to that which, being raised again from the dead and brought out from the grave, shall adore the Lord for his great grace. ON THE RESURRECTION OF THE FLESH 31.[97]

TRUE AND LASTING HEALTH. NICETAS OF REMESIANA: To remove all doubt about the resurrection of the body, take a single illustration from the course of nature. The apostle reminds us, "What you yourself sow is not brought to life, unless it dies."[98] Here you have a grain of wheat, dead and dry and sown in the earth. It is softened by the rain from heaven. Only when it decays does it spring to life and begin to grow. I take it that he who raises to life the grain of wheat for the sake of humankind will be able to raise to life the person himself who has been sown in the earth. He both can and wills to do this. What the rains do for the seed, the dew of the Spirit does for the body that is to be raised to life. Thus Isaiah cries to Christ, "Your dew is health for them," true health, since, once the bodies of the saints have been raised to life, they feel no pain, they

fear no death. They will live with Christ in heaven, who lived on earth according to the words and ways of Christ. This is the eternal and blessed life in which you believe. This is the fruit of all our faith and holy works. This is the hope on account of which we are born, believe and are reborn. It was on account of this that the prophets, apostles and martyrs sustained such endless toil and accepted death with joy. EXPLANATION OF THE CREED 12.[99]

THE SAINTS WERE RAISED. QUODVULTDEUS: Of the fulfilled promise (both believed and seen) wherein the bodies of the saints rose again at the death of the Lord, the prophet Isaiah said, "The dead will rise again, and all who were in the graves will be raised up, and all who are on the earth shall rejoice, for the dew which is from you is their medicine." Matthew the Evangelist confirms this, saying, "The earth shook and rocks were split and graves were opened and many bodies of the sleeping saints were raised. And going forth from their graves after his resurrection, they came to the holy city and appeared to many."[100] THE BOOK OF PROMISES AND PREDICTIONS OF GOD 3.29.[101]

26:20 Hide Until the Wrath Is Past

UNTIL THE WRATH IS PAST. AUGUSTINE: Certainly there are two things that make us hope for the bliss of the just and the end of all suffering: death and the resurrection from the dead. In death is rest, as the prophet says, "My people, enter into your chambers, hide yourself a little until the indignation of the Lord pass away." But in the resurrection there is perfect happiness in the whole person, that is, in flesh and spirit. Consequently we are not to think that both of these are to be marked by the labor of fasting but rather by the rejoicing of refreshment. LETTER 36.[102]

---

[93]Ezek 37:7-8. [94]Is 66:23. [95]Is 66:22. [96]Is 66:24. [97]ANF 3:567*. [98]1 Cor 15:36. [99]FC 7:52*. [100]Mt 27:51-53. [101]CCL 60:173. [102]FC 12:166*.

FOR A LITTLE WHILE. JEROME: "The hour will come in which all who are in the tombs shall hear the voice of the Son of God and shall come forth."[103] They shall hear with ears and come forth with feet. This Lazarus had already done. They shall, moreover, come forth from the tombs; that is, they who had been laid in the tombs, the dead, shall come and shall rise again from their graves. For the dew that God gives is healing to their bones. Then shall be fulfilled what God says by the prophet, "Go, my people, into your closets for a little while, until mine anger pass." The closets signify the graves, out of which is brought forth which had been laid therein. And they shall come out of the graves like young mules free from the halter. Their heart shall rejoice, and their bones shall rise like the sun; all flesh shall come into the presence of the Lord, and he shall command the fishes of the sea; and they shall give up the bones which they had eaten; and he shall bring joint to joint, and bone to bone;[104] and they who slept in the dust of the earth shall arise,[105] some to life eternal, others to shame and everlasting confusion. AGAINST JOHN OF JERUSALEM 33.[106]

THE GREAT PROCESS OF RESURRECTION. TERTULLIAN: When we read, "Go, my people, enter into your closets for a little while, until my anger passes away," we have in the closets graves, in which they will have to rest for a little while, who shall have at the end of the world departed this life in the last furious onset of the power of Antichrist. Why else did he use the expression *closets* in preference to some other receptacle, if it were not that the flesh is kept in these closets or cellars salted and reserved for use, to be drawn out thence on a suitable occasion? It is on a similar principle that embalmed corpses are set aside for burial in mausoleums and sepulchers, in order that they may be removed from there when the Master shall order it. Since, therefore, there is consistency in thus understanding the passage (for what refuge of little closets could possibly shelter us from the wrath of God?), it appears

that by the very phrase which he uses, "until his anger passes away," which shall extinguish Antichrist, he in fact shows that after that indignation the flesh will come forth from the sepulcher, in which it had been deposited previous to the bursting out of the anger. Now out of the closets nothing else is brought than that which had been put into them, and after the extirpation of Antichrist shall be busily transacted the great process of the resurrection. ON THE RESURRECTION OF THE FLESH 27.[107]

THE CLOSETS SIGNIFY THE GRAVE. CLEMENT OF ROME: All the generations from Adam to this day have passed away; but those who were made perfect in charity by the grace of God live among the saints; and they shall be made manifest at the judgment of the kingdom of Christ. For it is written, "Enter into your chamber a little while, until my wrath and anger pass, and I remember the good day and will raise you up out of your graves."[108] 1 CLEMENT 50.[109]

INTO YOUR CHAMBERS. ORIGEN: Therefore [Noah] constructs the ark and makes nests in it, that is, certain chambers in which animals of various kinds are received. The prophet also speaks of these chambers: "Go, my people, into your chambers, hide yourself a while until the fury of my anger pass away." This people, therefore, which is saved in the church is compared with all those, whether men or animals, which are saved in the ark. HOMILIES ON GENESIS 2.3.[110]

LIKE MULES FREE FROM THE HALTER. JEROME: "The hairs of your head are numbered."[111] If the hairs, I suppose the teeth would be more easily numbered. But there is no object in numbering them if they are some day to perish. "The hour will come in which all who are in the tombs shall hear the voice of the Son of God and

---

[103]Jn 5:25. [104]Ezek 37. [105]Dan 12:11. [106]NPNF 2 6:441*. [107]ANF 3:565*. [108]Ezek 37:12, "I will raise you up out of your graves," is attached to Is 26:20. [109]FC 1:48*. [110]FC 71:78. [111]Lk 12:7.

shall come forth."[112] . . . Then shall be fulfilled what God says by the prophet, "Go, my people, into your closets for a little while, until my anger pass." The closets signify the graves, out of which is brought forth which had been laid therein. And

they shall come out of the graves like young mules free from the halter. Against John of Jerusalem 33.[113]

---

[112]Jn 5:25. [113]NPNF 2 6:441*.

27:1-13 DOOM AND DELIVERANCE

[1]In that day the LORD with his hard and great and strong sword will punish Leviathan the fleeing serpent, Leviathan the twisting serpent, and he will slay the dragon that is in the sea.

[2]In that day:
"A pleasant vineyard, sing of it!
   [3]I, the LORD, am its keeper;*
every moment I water it.
Lest any one harm it,
   I guard it night and day;
   [4]I have no wrath.
Would that I had thorns and briers to
   battle!
   I would set out against them,
   I would burn them up together.
[5]Or let them lay hold of my protection,
   let them make peace with me,
   let them make peace with me."

[6]In days to come[q] Jacob shall take root,
   Israel shall blossom and put forth shoots,
   and fill the whole world with
      fruit.

[7]Has he smitten them as he smote those who
      smote them?
   Or have they been slain as their slayers
      were slain?
[8]Measure by measure,[r] by exile thou didst
      contend with them;
   he removed them with his fierce blast in
      the day of the east wind.
[9]Therefore by this the guilt of Jacob will be
      expiated,
   and this will be the full fruit of the
      removal of his sin:
when he makes all the stones of the altars
      like chalkstones crushed to pieces,
   no Asherim or incense altars will remain
      standing.
[10]For the fortified city is solitary,
   a habitation deserted and forsaken, like
      the wilderness;
there the calf grazes,
   there he lies down, and strips its
      branches.
[11]When its boughs are dry, they are broken;
   women come and make a fire of them.[t]
For this is a people without discernment;

therefore he who made them will not
    have compassion on them,
he that formed them will show them no
    favor.

[12]In that day from the river Euphrates to the Brook of Egypt the LORD will thresh out the grain, and you will be gathered one by one, O people of Israel. [13]And in that day a great trumpet will be blown, and those who were lost in the land of Assyria and those who were driven out to the land of Egypt will come and worship the LORD on the holy mountain at Jerusalem.

q Heb *Those to come*   r Compare Syr Vg Tg: *The meaning of the Hebrew word is unknown*   *LXX *I am a strong city, a city in a siege*   †LXX *Come you women that come from a sight*

OVERVIEW: Those who follow the serpent walk a crooked path (BASIL). The serpent promised the impossible and stole from humans what they already possessed. The serpent, as a slippery creature, slipped into the heart of humanity (GREGORY THE GREAT). The soul of the believer is a strong, walled city. The church is the strong city (AMBROSE). The women were the first witnesses to Jesus' resurrection to demonstrate that he was the Christ of the prophets (RUFINUS, TERTULLIAN).

27:1 The Lord Will Punish Leviathan

THE TWISTING SERPENT. BASIL THE GREAT: Let us earnestly endeavor, therefore, to flee every crooked and tortuous act, and let us keep our mind and the judgment of our soul as straight as a rule, in order that the praise of the Lord may be permitted to us since we are upright. In the same way the serpent, which is the author of sin, is called crooked, and the sword of God is drawn against the dragon, the crooked serpent, which makes many twists and turns in its progress. . . . Therefore one who follows the serpent shows that his life is crooked, uneven and filled with contrarieties; but one who follows after the Lord makes his paths straight and his footprints right. HOMILIES ON THE PSALMS 32.1.[1]

THE DECEITFUL SERPENT. GREGORY THE GREAT: For "Leviathan" is interpreted to be "their addition."[2] Whose "addition," then, but the

"addition" of people? And it is properly styled "their addition," for since by his evil suggestion he brought into the world the first sin, he never ceases to add to it day by day by prompting to worse things.

Or indeed it is in reproach that he is called Leviathan, that is, styled "the addition of men." For he found them immortal in Paradise, but by promising the divine nature to immortal beings, he as it were pledged himself to add somewhat to them beyond what they were. But while with flattering lips he declared that he would give what they did not have, he robbed them cunningly even of what they had. And hence the prophet describes this same Leviathan in these words, "Leviathan, the serpent: even Leviathan that crooked serpent." For this Leviathan crept near to people with tortuous windings through the false promise of what he would give them; for while he falsely promised things impossible, he really stole away even those which were possible. MORALS ON THE BOOK OF JOB 1.4.15.[3]

THE TWISTING SERPENT. GREGORY THE GREAT: For who is described by the designation of the "serpent" but our old enemy, at once slippery and crooked, who for the deceiving of humankind spoke with the mouth of a serpent? Of whom it is said by the prophet, "Leviathan

---

[1]FC 46:228-29. [2]See Job 3:8. Gregory contends that the title Leviathan is derived from the serpent's empty promise of the divine nature to humanity. [3]LF 18:194**.

the serpent, the crooked one"; who was for this reason allowed to speak with the mouth of a serpent, that by Leviathan's vessel humanity might learn what he was that dwelt within. For a serpent is not only crooked but slippery as well; and so because he stood not in the uprightness of truth, he entered into a crooked animal. . . . He spoke to man by means of a slippery animal because if one does not resist him, he secretly slips into the interior of the heart. Now "the dens" of this serpent were the hearts of wicked people. MORALS ON THE BOOK OF JOB 4.17.51.[4]

27:3 A City Besieged

A CITY BESIEGED. AMBROSE: It is the soul, too, that says, "I am a strong city, a city besieged." The city is besieged through Christ, the city is that heavenly Jerusalem,[5] in which there are interpreters of God's law and men skilled in doctrine in great abundance; through them one seeks the Word of God. ISAAC, OR THE SOUL 5.39.[6]

THE SOUL IS A WALL. AMBROSE: Therefore let us flee these evils and elevate our soul to the image and likeness of God. The flight from evils is the likeness of God, and the image of God is gained through the virtues. And so, like a painter, he has painted us with the colors of the virtues. "See, I have painted your walls, Jerusalem."[7] Let us not wipe away with the brush of neglect the props of the painted walls of our soul. And so "I have painted the walls,"[8] with which we can turn away the enemy. The soul has its walls; from them it stands forth and concerning them it says, "I am a strong city, a city besieged." By these walls it is guarded, and by them it is protected under siege. And truly the soul is a wall, which stretches forth over the camp. And therefore the bride says in the Song of Solomon, "I am a wall, and my breasts are like towers."[9] The wall that the Lord painted is good, even as he says: "On my hands I have painted your walls, and you are always in my

sight."[10] DEATH AS A GOOD 5.17-18.[11]

BESIEGED BY THE WORLD AND THE DEVIL. AMBROSE: You have in Isaiah the speech made by the soul of a just man or of the church: "I am a strong city, I am a city besieged," defended by Christ and besieged by the devil. But one whom Christ aids ought not to be fearful of a siege. [Such a person] is defended by spiritual grace and is besieged by the perils of this world. Hence also it is said in the Song of Songs, "I am a wall, and my breasts are as a tower."[12] The wall is the church, and the towers are her priests, who have full power to teach the natural and the moral sciences. SIX DAYS OF CREATION 6.8.49.[13]

27:11 A People of No Understanding

WITNESSES OF THE RESURRECTION. RUFINUS OF AQUILEIA: That the women were to see his resurrection, while the scribes and Pharisees and the people disbelieved, this also Isaiah foretold in these words, "You women, who come from beholding, come: for it is a people that has no understanding." COMMENTARY ON THE APOSTLES' CREED 30.[14]

A VISION OF ANGELS. TERTULLIAN: The women, returning from the sepulcher and from this vision of the angels, were foreseen by Isaiah, when he says, "Come, you women, who return from the vision," that is, "come" to report the resurrection of the Lord. It was well, however, that the unbelief of the disciples was so persistent, in order that to the last we might consistently maintain that Jesus revealed himself to the disciples as none other than the Christ of the prophets. AGAINST MARCION 4.43.[15]

---

[4]LF 21:313*. [5]See Heb 12:22. [6]FC 65:32-33. [7]Is 49:16. [8]Is 49:16. [9]Song 8:10. [10]Is 49:16. [11]FC 65:83-84*. [12]Song 8:10. [13]FC 42:262-63**. [14]NPNF 2 3:555*. [15]ANF 3:422*.

28:1-13 ORACLE AGAINST RELIGIOUS LEADERS

¹Woe to the proud crown of the drunkards of
  Ephraim,
  and to the fading flower of its glorious
  beauty,
  which is on the head of the rich valley of
  those overcome with wine!
²Behold, the Lord has one who is mighty
  and strong;
  like a storm of hail, a destroying tempest,
like a storm of mighty, overflowing waters,
  he will cast down to the earth with
  violence.
³The proud crown of the drunkards of
  Ephraim
  will be trodden under foot;
⁴and the fading flower of its glorious beauty,
  which is on the head of the rich valley,
will be like a first-ripe fig before the
  summer:
  when a man sees it, he eats it up
  as soon as it is in his hand.

⁵In that day the LORD of hosts will be a
  crown of glory,
  and a diadem of beauty, to the remnant of
  his people;
⁶and a spirit of justice to him who sits in
  judgment,
  and strength to those who turn back the
  battle at the gate.

⁷These also reel with wine
  and stagger with strong drink;
  the priest and the prophet reel with strong
  drink,
  they are confused with wine,
  they stagger with strong drink;
they err in vision,
  they stumble in giving judgment.
⁸For all tables are full of vomit,
  no place is without filthiness.

⁹"Whom will he teach knowledge,
  and to whom will he explain the
  message?
Those who are weaned from the milk,
  those taken from the breast?
¹⁰For it is precept upon precept, precept
  upon precept,
  line upon line, line upon line,
  here a little, there a little."*

¹¹Nay, but by men of strange lips
  and with an alien tongue
the LORD will speak to this people,†
  ¹²to whom he has said,
"This is rest;
  give rest to the weary;
and this is repose";
  yet they would not hear.
¹³Therefore the word of the LORD will be to
  them
precept upon precept, precept upon
  precept,
  line upon line, line upon line,
  here a little, there a little;
that they may go, and fall backward,
  and be broken, and snared, and taken.

*LXX Except affliction on affliction, hope upon hope; yet a little, and yet a little   †LXX by reason of the contemptuous words of the lips, by means of another language: for they shall speak to this people

Overview: The Lord will crown the remnant with hope and glory (Cyril of Alexandria). All disciples of Jesus should abstain from wine and drunkenness (Pachomius). Mature believers must endure tribulation in order to receive hope. Suffering is only temporary (Jerome). Speaking in other tongues is not necessary (Constitutions of the Holy Apostles). All of the Scriptures are designated together as the law (Augustine). The Holy Spirit gifted the apostles to speak in languages other than their own (Chrysostom, Gregory of Nazianzus).

28:5 A Crown of Glory to the Remnant

The Remnant of Israel. Cyril of Alexandria: The prophet expounds on the destiny of those in Israel who believed in Christ, because Israel did not perish completely, as the remnant of Israel was saved, according to the prophecy. Quite a number of people believed in Christ, and his apostles were, so to speak, the first fruit. Therefore at that time the Lord of hosts will be as a crown of hope and a diadem of glory to the remnant of his people. The Lord of hosts will crown the believers with hope and glory, that is, with hope of future blessings and with glory because they will reign with him. They will become the recipients of the highest honor and will be worthy of adoration and glory. What glory can be compared with that received in the kingdom of Christ? In another passage Isaiah also says, "You shall also be a crown of glory in the hand of the Lord and a royal diadem in the hand of your God,"[1] since Christ will crown those who believe in him with unending glory and bless them with the most joyous hope. And the remnant of Israel will participate in all of this after the others, the Gentiles, are received in Christ. Realizing their glory in Christ, they cry to their heavenly God and Father, "O Lord, crown us with the shield of your favor."[2] For when it pleased their God and Father, he revealed himself as an unbroken shield and became the Christ who defends us from the arrows of the evil one and keeps his people. Com-mentary on Isaiah 3.1.28.[3]

28:7 Reeling with Wine

Deranged by Wine. Pachomius: In fact, our fathers passed their lives in hunger, thirst and great mortification, by which they acquired purity. Above all they fled the wine habit, which is full of every evil. Troubles, tumults and disorders are caused in our members through the abuse of wine; this is a passion full of sin, it is sterility and the withering of fruit. For sensuality in unquenchable thirst stupefies the understanding, makes conscience overbold and snaps the rein on the tongue. Total joy is when we do not grieve the Holy Spirit, or become deranged by sensuality. As it is said, "The priest and the prophet were deranged by wine.". . . Therefore, all who have prepared to become disciples of Jesus should abstain from wine and drunkenness. Instructions 45.[4]

28:10 For a Little While These Things Must Be

A Little While. Jerome: "My conscience is at rest, and I know that it is not from any fault of mine that I am suffering; moreover affliction in this world is a ground for expecting a reward hereafter."[5] When the enemy was more than usually forward and ventured to reproach her to her face, she used to chant the words of the Psalter. . . .When she felt herself tempted, she dwelt upon the words of Deuteronomy. . . . In tribulations and afflictions she turned to the splendid language of Isaiah: "You that are weaned from the milk and drawn from the breasts, look for tribulation upon tribulation, for hope also upon hope. Yet a little while must these things be by reason of the malice of the lips and by reason of a spiteful

---

[1]Is 62:3. [2]Ps 5:12 (5:13 LXX). [3]PG 70:617. [4]CS 47:34-35. [5]Jerome quotes and comments on Paula (347-404), a devout woman who followed him from Rome to Palestine and founded a convent in Bethlehem.

tongue." This passage of Scripture she explained for her own consolation as meaning that the weaned, that is, those who have come to full age, must endure tribulation upon tribulation that they may be accounted worthy to receive hope upon hope. LETTER 108.18.[6]

AFFLICTION ON AFFLICTION. JEROME: We read in the book of Job how, while the first messenger of evil was yet speaking, there came also another;[7] and in the same book it is written, "Is there not a temptation"—or as the Hebrew better gives it—"a warfare to man upon earth?"[8] It is for this end that we labor, it is for this end that we risk our lives in the warfare of this world, that we may be crowned in the world to come. That we should believe this to be true of people is nothing wonderful, for even the Lord was tempted,[9] and of Abraham the Scripture bears witness that God tested him.[10] It is for this reason also that the apostle says, "We glory in tribulations . . . knowing that tribulation works perseverance; and perseverance, character; and character, hope. Now hope does not disappoint."[11] And in another passage [we read], "Who shall separate us from the love of Christ? Shall tribulation or distress or persecution or family or nakedness or peril or sword? As it is written, 'for your sake we are killed all the day long; we are accounted as sheep for the slaughter.'"[12] The prophet Isaiah comforts those in a similar case in these words: "You who are weaned from the milk, you who are drawn from the breasts, look for tribulation upon tribulation, but also for hope upon hope." For, as the apostle puts it, "The sufferings of this present time are not worthy to be compared with the glory which shall be revealed in us."[13] LETTER 130.7.[14]

28:11 The Lord Speaks to His People

WITH OTHER TONGUES. CONSTITUTIONS OF THE HOLY APOSTLES: It is not therefore necessary that every one of the faithful should cast out demons or raise the dead or speak with tongues, but such a one only who is graciously given this gift. For [it may contribute] to the salvation of the unbelievers, who are often put to shame not with the demonstration of the world but by the power of the signs, that is, such as are worthy of salvation. For all the ungodly are not affected by wonders, and hereof God is a witness, as when he says in the law: "With other tongues will I speak to this people, and with other lips, and yet will they by no means believe." For neither did the Egyptians believe in God, when Moses had done so many signs and wonders;[15] nor did the multitude of the Jews believe in Christ, as they believed Moses, who yet had healed every sickness and every disease among them.[16] CONSTITUTIONS OF THE HOLY APOSTLES 8.[17]

I WILL SPEAK. AUGUSTINE: Thus at times all the sayings of the ancient covenant of the sacred Scriptures are designated together by the name of law. For the apostle cites the testimony from the prophet Isaiah, where he says, "In other tongues and with other lips I will speak to this people," and yet he had prefaced this by saying, "In the law it is written."[18] ON THE TRINITY 15.17.30.[19]

THE GIFT OF FOREIGN LANGUAGES. CHRYSOSTOM: Someone might well ask how the apostles drew to themselves all these people. How did men who spoke only the language of the Jews win over the Scythian, the Indian, the Sarmatian and the Thracian? Because they received the gift of tongues through the Holy Spirit.[20] Not only did the apostles say this but also the prophets when they made both these facts clear, namely, that the apostles received the gift of tongues and that they failed to win over the Jews. Hear how the prophet showed this when he said, " 'In foreign tongues and with other lips I shall speak to this people, and in this way they shall not hear me,' says the Lord." DEMONSTRATION AGAINST THE PAGANS 7.2.[21]

---

[6]NPNF 2 6:204*. [7]Job 1:16. [8]Job 7:1. [9]Mt 4:1-11. [10]Gen 22:1. [11]Rom 5:3-5. [12]Rom 8:35-36. [13]Rom 8:18. [14]NPNF 2 6:264*. [15]Ex 7:3-4. [16]Deut 18:15. [17]ANF 7:479. [18]1 Cor 14:21. [19]FC 45:494. [20]Acts 2:4. [21]FC 73:215-16.

STRANGE SPEECH. GREGORY OF NAZIANZUS: They spoke with strange tongues and not those of their native land; and the wonder was great, a language spoken by those who had not learned it. And the sign is to them that do not believe, not to them that believe, that it may be an accusation of the unbelievers, as it is written, "With other tongues and other lips will I speak to this people, and not even so will they listen to me, says the Lord." But they heard. Here stop a little and raise a question. How are you to divide the words? For the expression has an ambiguity, which is to be determined by the punctuation. Did they each hear in their own dialect so that if I may so say, one sound was uttered but many were heard; the air being thus beaten and, so to speak, sounds being produced more clear than the original sound? Or are we to put the stop after "they heard" and then to add "them speaking in their own languages" to what follows, so that it would be speaking in the hearers' own languages, which would be foreign to the speakers? I prefer to put it this latter way; for on the other plan the miracle would be rather of the hearers than of the speakers; whereas in this it would be on the speakers' side. And it was they who were reproached for drunkenness, evidently because they by the Spirit wrought a miracle in the matter of the tongues. ON PENTECOST, ORATION 41.15.[22]

---

[22]NPNF 2 7:384.

28:14-22 ORACLE AGAINST CIVIL LEADERS

[14]Therefore hear the word of the LORD, you
  scoffers,
    who rule this people in Jerusalem!
[15]Because you have said, "We have made a
    covenant with death,*
    and with Sheol we have an agreement;
  when the overwhelming scourge passes
    through
    it will not come to us;
  for we have made lies our refuge,
    and in falsehood we have taken shelter";
[16]therefore thus says the Lord GOD,
  "Behold, I am laying in Zion for a
    foundation
    a stone, a tested stone,†
  a precious cornerstone, of a sure foundation:

  'He who believes will not be in haste.'‡
[17]And I will make justice the line,
    and righteousness the plummet;§
  and hail will sweep away the refuge of lies,
    and waters will overwhelm the shelter."
[18]Then your covenant with death will be
    annulled,
    and your agreement with Sheol will not
    stand;
  when the overwhelming scourge passes
    through
    you will be beaten down by it.
[19]As often as it passes through it will take
    you;
  for morning by morning it will pass
    through,

by day and by night;*
and it will be sheer terror to understand the
message.**
²⁰*For the bed is too short to stretch oneself*
on it,
and the covering too narrow to wrap
oneself in it.
²¹*For the LORD will rise up as on Mount*
Perazim,

he will be wroth as in the valley of
Gibeon;
to do his deed—strange is his deed!
and to work his work—alien is his work!
²²*Now therefore do not scoff,*
lest your bonds be made strong;
for I have heard a decree of destruction
from the Lord GOD of hosts upon the
whole land.

*LXX Hades   †LXX a costly and choice stone   ‡LXX shall by no means be ashamed   §LXX and my compassion shall be for just measures   #LXX and in the night there shall be an evil hope   **Vg and only the vexing alone shall supply understanding to the hearing

OVERVIEW: The strong in Jerusalem were those leaders who were teaching the doctrines of men, thereby placing burdens on the people (TERTULLIAN). By renouncing Satan, the believer annuls the covenant with death (CYRIL OF JERUSALEM). Some protect themselves by lying (VERECUNDUS). Christ is the foundation of the church (AMBROSE). The millstone symbolizes the help offered to the weak by Christ (PETER CHRYSOLOGUS). The stone is a symbol of Christ (GREGORY OF NYSSA). People cannot be built into the dwelling place of God until they have first laid the cornerstone, which symbolizes being born again. Jesus is seen to be the cornerstone (AUGUSTINE).

Salvation is in Christ, the precious cornerstone (CYRIL OF JERUSALEM). Christ is the cornerstone because he supports the Mosaic law and the gospel (EUSEBIUS). Christ gives to believers everlasting immortality as the cornerstone (FIRMICUS MATERNUS). Christ is the anointed stone (AUGUSTINE). Christ is symbolized as a stone in several places throughout Scripture (QUODVULTDEUS). Christ joins together different peoples into a unity (JEROME). Christians should not be ashamed of confessing Christ (AUGUSTINE). Those who believe in Christ find salvation, but those who reject him are destroyed as if a stone were to fall on them (JEROME, EPISTLE OF BARNABAS).

If we believe what the Scriptures say, we will discover much more hidden in them (ORIGEN). God gives mercy to the repentant but judgment to

the unrepentant (BASIL). There is mercy for those who accepted the chastisement of God with the proper attitude. Christ is the light of hope dispelling the darkness of evil (GREGORY OF NAZIANZUS). Some people begin to understand the precepts of God only when they are being judged for disobedience (GREGORY THE GREAT). The narrow bed teaches that there is no room for both Christ and Belial (JEROME). God's provision of salvation through his passion is unusual, as the attributes of suffering are not proper to God (GREGORY THE GREAT). The whole teaching of Scripture is contained in an abbreviated form in the Lord's Prayer and the creed (ISIDORE OF SEVILLE).

28:14-15 Hear the Word of the Lord!

WHO RULE IN JERUSALEM. TERTULLIAN: What, then, are the burdens that he censures? None but those which they were accumulating of their own accord, when they taught for commandments the doctrines of men; for the sake of private advantage joining house to house, so as to deprive their neighbor of his own; cajoling the people, loving gifts, pursuing rewards, robbing the poor of the right of judgment, that they might have the widow for a prey and the fatherless for a spoil. Of these Isaiah also says, "woe[1] to them that are

---

[1]Neither the Hebrew, Greek nor Latin text has the word *woe*, though it is implied by the context.

strong in Jerusalem!" AGAINST MARCION 4.27.[2]

A COVENANT WITH HELL. CYRIL OF JERUSALEM: When you renounce Satan, trampling underfoot every covenant with him, then you annul that ancient "league with hell," and God's paradise opens before you, that Eden, planted in the east, from which for his transgression our first father was banished. CATECHETICAL LECTURES 1.9.[3]

FALSEHOOD AS PROTECTION. VERECUNDUS: "He has become my help and my protector unto salvation."[4] They are said to be helpers who grant us their cooperation through specific acts. Protectors, however, are those who defend us with their power. Protection can take a variety of forms. For some, God is a protection, but deception becomes a protection for others, who lie about themselves, as Isaiah said: "We have established deception as our hope, and we are protected by lies." COMMENTARY ON THE CANTICLE OF EXODUS 1.3.[5]

28:16 A Stone for a Foundation

FAITH THE FOUNDATION OF JUSTICE. AMBROSE: The foundation of justice therefore is faith, for the hearts of the just dwell on faith. And the just man that accuses himself builds justice on faith, for his justice becomes plain when he confesses the truth. So the Lord says through Isaiah: "Behold, I lay a stone for a foundation in Zion." This means Christ as the foundation of the church. For Christ is the object of faith to all; but the church is as it were the outward form of justice; it is the common right of all. DUTIES OF THE CLERGY 1.29.[6]

WHY A MILLSTONE? PETER CHRYSOLOGUS: Therefore, brothers, we should be careful neither to give scandal to others nor to take it ourselves when another gives it. It is scandal that troubles the senses, perturbs the mind, confuses our judgment otherwise sharp. It is a scandal that changed an angel into the devil, an apostle into a traitor;

that brought sin into the world and allured humankind to death. . . . Scandal tempts the saints, fatigues the cautious, throws down the incautious, disturbs all things, confuses all people. . . . He uttered a warning to keep anyone else from coming to this, by saying, "It is impossible that scandals should not come; but woe to him through whom they come! It would be better for him if a millstone were hung about his neck and he were thrown into the sea, rather than that he should cause one of these little ones to sin."[7]

Why a millstone and not an ordinary stone? Because, while a millstone is grinding the grain, and pouring out the flour and separating the bran from the meal, it is simultaneously furnishing bread to those who are dutifully toiling. Rightly, therefore, is a millstone tied to the neck of the person who chooses to be a minister of scandal rather than of peace; the very same thing that should have drawn him to life may drag him down to death. For [such a person] has changed those senses given to aid him toward life into a stumbling block bringing death. Then they persuaded him to see something else, and hear, feel and relish something else than was in Christ and in his saving knowledge. In this way he has encompassed the cornerstone, the stone symbolizing help, the stone cut out without hands, that is, Christ, and he has turned it into a stumbling for the weak. SERMON 27.[8]

CHRIST IS THE STONE. GREGORY OF NYSSA: Jacob, hastening to seek a bride, met Rachel unexpectedly at the well. And a great stone lay upon the well, which a multitude of shepherds were [accustomed] to roll away when they came together and then gave water to themselves and to their flocks. But Jacob alone rolls away the stone and waters the flocks of his spouse.[9] The thing is, I think, a dark saying, a shadow of what should come. For what is the stone that is laid but Christ? For of him Isaiah says, "And I will lay in

[2]ANF 3:395. [3]FC 64:158. [4]See Ex 15:2. [5]CCL 93:5. [6]NPNF 2 10:24*. [7]Lk 17:1-2. [8]FC 17:74-75*. [9]Gen 29.

ISAIAH 28:14-22

the foundations of Zion a costly stone, precious, elect"; and Daniel likewise, "A stone was cut out but not by hand,"[10] that is, Christ was born without a man. ON THE BAPTISM OF CHRIST.[11]

THE UNIQUE CORNERSTONE. AUGUSTINE: Therefore, with the exception of this cornerstone,[12] I do not see how people are to be built into a house of God, to contain God dwelling in them,[13] without being born again, which cannot happen before they are born. LETTER 187.31.[14]

THE CORNERSTONE UNITES. AUGUSTINE: To the one group,[15] the infant at birth is shown as the chief cornerstone announced by the prophet; to the other group he is manifested at the very outset of his career. He has already begun to weld together in himself the two walls originally set in different directions, bringing shepherds from Judea and magi from the East. SERMON 199.1.[16]

THE CORNERSTONE AND THE TOMB. CYRIL OF JERUSALEM: Was his tomb made with hands? Does it rise above the ground, like the tombs of kings? Was the sepulcher made of stones joined together? And what is laid upon it? Tell us exactly, O prophets, about his tomb also, where it lies, and where we shall look for it. But they answer, "Look upon the solid rock which you have hewn,"[17] look and see. . . . I, who am "the chief corner stone, chosen, precious,"[18] lie for a while within a stone, I, who am "a stone of stumbling"[19] to the Jews but of salvation to them that believe. CATECHETICAL LECTURES 13.35.[20]

WHO IS THE CORNERSTONE? EUSEBIUS OF CAESAREA: Who can the cornerstone be other than the one who is the living and precious stone supporting two structures with his teaching making them one? He established the building of Moses, which was to remain until his day, and then he joined on to one side our building of the gospel. This is why he is called the cornerstone. PROOF OF THE GOSPEL 1.7.[21]

A STONE THAT STRENGTHENS. FIRMICUS MATERNUS: Your stone is one that ruin follows and the disastrous collapse of tumbling towers; but our stone, laid by the hand of God, builds up, strengthens, lifts, fortifies and adorns the grace of the restored work with the splendor of everlasting immortality.

For Isaiah says of this at the behest of the Holy Spirit: "Thus says the Lord: Behold, I lay a stone for the foundations of Zion, a precious stone, elect, a chief cornerstone, honored, and he that shall believe in it shall not be confounded." ERROR OF THE PAGAN RELIGIONS 20.[22]

WHY ANOINTED? AUGUSTINE: A stone anointed; why a stone? "Behold, I lay in Zion a stone, elect, precious; and he that believes on him shall not be confounded." Why anointed? Because Christ comes from "anointing" (chrisma). TRACTATES ON THE GOSPEL OF JOHN 7.23.[23]

CHRIST AS CORNERSTONE. QUODVULTDEUS: Isaiah wrote, "Behold, I lay a cornerstone in Zion as its foundation, elect and precious; he who believes in it will not be ashamed." The cornerstone is Christ, who, when Nathaniel came to him, explained what Jacob had seen in his dream: "You will see the heavens opened and the angels of God ascending and descending upon the Son of man."[24] For the Christ who descended "is the same one who ascends above all the heavens that he might fill everything."[25] But he lays a narrow path that leads to life.[26] THE BOOK OF PROMISES AND PREDICTIONS OF GOD 1.33-34.[27]

A RESTORATION OF UNITY. JEROME: This cornerstone[28] joins together both walls and restores two peoples to unity, concerning which

[10]Dan 2:5. [11]NPNF 2 5:521*. [12]1 Pet 2:6; Eph 2:20. [13]2 Cor 6:16. [14]FC 30:246. [15]The first group of people to which Augustine refers is the Jews, who had the prophetic announcements of Christ. The second group is the Gentiles. [16]FC 38:59*. [17]Is 51:1 LXX. [18]1 Pet 2:6. [19]1 Pet 2:8. [20]FC 64:28. [21]POG 1:46*. [22]ACW 37:87. [23]CCL 36:80. [24]Jn 1:51; cf. Gen 28:12. [25]See Eph 4:10. [26]See Mt 7:14. [27]CCL 60:41. [28]See Zech 14:10.

God said through Isaiah: "Behold, I will lay a cornerstone in Zion as its foundation, elect and precious; the one who believes in it will not be ashamed." It was his will to build further upon this cornerstone and other cornerstones, so that the apostle Paul would be able to say boldly, "built upon the foundation of the apostles and the prophets, with Jesus Christ himself being the chief cornerstone."[29] Commentary on Zechariah 3.14.10-11.[30]

By No Means Ashamed. Augustine: Here is what one believes with the heart unto justice and makes confession of with the mouth unto salvation. But you're afraid to confess it, in case people taunt you with it; and not ones who have not come to believe, because they too believe it inwardly. But in case those who are ashamed to confess it should taunt you with it, listen to what comes next. For Scripture says, "Nobody who believes in him shall be put to shame." Reflect on all this; stick to it all. This is prey, food not for the belly but for the intelligence. Sermon 279.9.[31]

He Who Believes. Jerome: Peter also spoke confidently about this stone of assistance:[32] "This is the stone rejected by you builders, which was made the cornerstone."[33] And Isaiah said, "Behold, I will lay a cornerstone in Zion as its foundation, elect and precious; the one who believes in it will not be ashamed."

"Therefore I say to you that the kingdom of God will be taken from you and given to the people who produce its fruit."[34] As I have said, the kingdom of God is often to be understood as sacred Scripture, which the Lord removed from the Jews and gave to us that we might produce its fruits. This is the vineyard that was given to the tenant farmers and vinedressers who did no work in it; possessing the Scriptures in name only, they will lose the fruits of the vineyard.

"Whoever falls on this stone will be broken, but the one upon whom it falls will be destroyed."[35] It is one thing to offend Christ through evil deeds

but another thing to deny him. The sinner who nevertheless still believes in him is the one who falls on the stone and is broken but not altogether destroyed, for he is preserved for salvation through patience. But the one upon whom it falls, that is, the one upon whom the stone itself rushes, is the one who denies Christ inwardly. He is destroyed so completely that not even a shard with which to draw a little water will remain. Commentary on Matthew 3 (21.42-44).[36]

A Hard Rock. Epistle of Barnabas: And again the prophet says, seeing that as a hard stone he was ordained for crushing, "Behold, I will put into the foundations of Zion a stone very precious, elect, a chief cornerstone, honorable." Then again [read] what he says: "And whosoever shall set his hope on him shall live forever."[37] Is our hope then set upon a stone? Far from it. But it is because the Lord has set his flesh in strength. For he says, "And he set me as a hard rock."[38] Epistle of Barnabas 6.[39]

Discern the Meaning of the Text. Origen: And if in reading the Scripture you stumble on a good thought that is a "stumbling stone and a rock of offense,"[40] blame yourself. For do not despair that this "stumbling stone and rock of offense" have meanings so as to fulfill the saying, "And the one who believes will not be put to shame."[41] Believe first, and you will discover much holy aid beneath the supposed offense. For if we ourselves receive the commandment not to speak a "careless word as we will render an account of it on the day of judgment,"[42] and if we earnestly aspire, as far as possible, to make it so that every word coming out of our mouth works both on us who speak it and on those who hear it, what else is there need to understand about the prophets than that every word spoken through their mouth was

[29]Eph 2:20. [30]CCL 76A:887-88. [31]WSA 3 8:65. [32]See Mt 21:42. [33]Acts 4:11. [34]Mt 21:43. [35]Mt 21:44. [36]CCL 77:198-99. [37]"To live forever" is a reading unique to the Epistle of Barnabas and appears to be drawn from the LXX of Genesis 3:22. [38]Is 50:7 LXX. [39]AF 141-42*. [40]Rom 9:32-33; 1 Pet 2:7; Is 8:14; Mt 18:7. [41]Rom 9:33. [42]Mt 12:36.

one which works? And do not be amazed if every word spoken by the prophets works a work which is fitting for a word. For I think that every extraordinary letter written in the words of God works, and there is not "an iota or one dot"[43] written in the Scripture which does not work in those who know to use the power of the Scriptures. FRAGMENTS FROM THE PHILOCALIA 10.1.[44]

28:17 For Just Measures

MERCY IN MEASURE. BASIL THE GREAT: The Judge wishes to have mercy on you and to share his own compassion, but on condition that he finds you humble after sin, contrite, lamenting much for your evil deeds, announcing publicly without shame sins committed secretly, begging the brothers to labor with you in reparation. In short, if he sees that you are worthy of pity, he provides his mercy for you ungrudgingly. But if he sees your heart unrepentant, your mind proud, your disbelief of the future life and your fearlessness of the judgment, then he desires the judgment for you. [This is like] a reasonable and kind doctor [who] tries at first with hot applications and soft poultices to reduce a tumor. But, when he sees that the mass is rigidly and obstinately resisting, casting away the olive oil and the gentle method of treatment, he prefers henceforth the use of the knife. Therefore [God] loves mercy in the case of those repenting, but he also loves judgment in the case of the unyielding. Isaiah says some such thing, too, to God: "Your mercy in measure." For he compares the mercy with the judgment of him who gives compensation by scale and number and weight according to the deserts of each. HOMILIES ON THE PSALMS 32.3.[45]

MERCY IN BALANCE. GREGORY OF NAZIANZUS: Discourse awhile on our present heavy blow,[46] about the just judgments of God, whether we grasp their meaning or are ignorant of their great depth.[47] How again "mercy is put in the balance," as holy Isaiah declares. For goodness is not without discernment, as the first laborers in the

vineyard[48] fancied, because they could not perceive any distinction between those who were paid alike. [Perceive] how anger, which is called "the cup in the hand of the Lord"[49] and "the cup of falling which is drained,"[50] is in proportion to transgressions, even though he shows mercy to every one according to what they are due and dilutes with compassion the unmixed draught of his wrath. For he inclines from severity to indulgence toward those who accept chastisement with fear, and who after a slight affliction conceive and are in pain with conversion, and bring forth the perfect spirit of salvation. But nevertheless he reserves the dregs,[51] the last drop of his anger, that he may pour it out entire upon those who, instead of being healed by his kindness, grow obdurate, like the hard-hearted Pharaoh,[52] that bitter taskmaster, who is set forth as an example of the power[53] of God over the ungodly. ON HIS FATHER'S SILENCE, ORATION 16.4.[54]

28:19 An Evil Hope in the Night

AN EVIL HOPE. GREGORY OF NAZIANZUS: Every time is suitable for your ablution, since any time may be your death.[55] With Paul I shout to you with that loud voice, "Behold now is the accepted time; behold now is the day of salvation";[56] and that now does not point to any one time but is every present moment. And again "Awake, you that sleep, and Christ shall give you light,"[57] dispelling the darkness of sin. For as Isaiah says, "In the night hope is evil," and it is more profitable to be received in the morning. ON HOLY BAPTISM, ORATION 40.13.[58]

PAIN LEADS TO UNDERSTANDING. GREGORY THE GREAT: Now righteous people conceive a dread of God before his indignation is stirred up against them; they fear him at rest, lest they

---

[43]Mt 5:18. [44]FC 97:278*. [45]FC 46:233*. [46]The death of his father. [47]Ps 36:6. [48]Mt 20:12. [49]Ps 75:9. [50]Is 51:17 LXX. [51]Ps 75:10. [52]Ex 5:6; 7:22. [53]Rom 9:17. [54]NPNF 2 7:248*. [55]The occasion is the funeral of Gregory's father. [56]2 Cor 6:2. [57]Eph 5:14. [58]NPNF 2 7:364*.

should feel him as moved. But, on the other hand, the wicked then for the first time fear to be smitten when they are under the rod, and terror then rouses them from the sleep of their insensibility when vengeance is troubling them. And hence it is said by the prophet, "And only the vexing alone shall supply understanding to the hearing." For when they have begun to be stricken in vengeance for the contempt and neglect of God's precepts, then they understand the thing that they heard. MORALS ON THE BOOK OF JOB 3.11.41.[59]

28:20 The Bed Too Narrow

A NARROW BED. JEROME: "The glory of the God of Israel was there"[60] not to delight the neighborhood but to annihilate the "idol of jealousy" and the temple by his very presence. Hence the destruction of the city and the temple followed shortly thereafter. It is also written in Isaiah that "a narrow bed cannot hold two persons, nor can a short blanket cover both," prefiguring that saying of the apostle: "What does Christ have in common with Belial, or the temple of God with an idol?"[61] COMMENTARY ON EZEKIEL 3.8.[62]

28:21 His Deed Is Strange

GOD'S STRANGE WORK. GREGORY THE GREAT: Hence Isaiah, contemplating our salvation and [Christ's] passion, well said: "That he may do his work, his strange work; that he may perform his work, his work is strange to him." For the work of God is to gather the souls that he created and call them back to the joys of the eternal light. But it is not the work [of] God in his essence to be flogged, to be smeared with spittle, to be crucified, to die and to be buried, but this is the work of a sinful person who deserved all these things for his sins. But [Jesus] himself bore our sins in his own body on the tree. And he who in his own nature always remains incomprehensible deigned to be comprehended in our nature and to be flogged, because if he had not assumed the attributes of our weakness he could never have raised us to the power of his

fortitude. . . . And he does his strange work that he might do his proper work, because insofar as he bore our sins in infirmity he led us who are his creatures to the glory of his fortitude in which he lives and reigns with God the Father in the unity of the Holy Spirit, God, through ages of ages. Amen. HOMILIES ON EZEKIEL 2.4.20.[63]

28:22 Works Cut Short by the Lord of Hosts

CUT SHORT. ISIDORE OF SEVILLE: They do not understand that God grants to each period of time what is appropriate. As he commanded marriage in the law, so in the gospel does he recommend virginity. In the law, an eye is to be offered for an eye, but in the gospel, the other side of the cheek is to be offered to one's assailant.[64] The former arrangement was for a weak people, whereas the latter is for the perfect. Nevertheless each order was adapted to its proper time. Yet it is not to be believed on the basis of this change that God is mutable. Instead, it should be proclaimed a miracle that while remaining immutable himself, God gave to each era its own distinctly appropriate order.

Sins were of lesser guilt under the Old Testament because only a shadow of the truth, not truth itself, was present therein. For the higher precepts of the New Testament reveal that we are to forsake some of those things to which the people of the shadow of truth were bound. Previously, for instance, fornication and the taking of retribution for injuries were permitted without punishment. In the New Testament, however, they are condemned with severe punishments.

The creed and the Lord's Prayer replace the whole law in sufficing to obtain the kingdom of heaven for the little ones of the church. For the entire breadth of Scripture is contained briefly in the Lord's Prayer and the creed. Thus does the prophet Isaiah say, "I heard from the Lord God of hosts about an abbreviation upon all the earth." THREE BOOKS OF THOUGHTS 1.20.1-21.1.[65]

---

[59]LF 21:26. [60]Ezek 8:4. [61]See 2 Cor 6:15-16. [62]CCL 75:94. [63]HGE 204*. [64]Mt 5:38-39. [65]PL 83:586-87.

28:23-29 THE PARABLE OF THE FARMER

²³*Give ear, and hear my voice;*
hearken, and hear my speech.
²⁴*Does he who plows for sowing plow*
continually?
does he continually open and harrow his
ground?
²⁵*When he has leveled its surface,*
does he not scatter dill, sow cummin,
and put in wheat in rows
and barley in its proper place,
and spelt as the border?
²⁶*For he is instructed aright;*
his God teaches him.

²⁷*Dill is not threshed with a threshing*
sledge,
nor is a cart wheel rolled over
cummin;
but dill is beaten out with a stick,
and cummin with a rod.
²⁸*Does one crush bread grain?*
No, he does not thresh it for ever;
when he drives his cart wheel over it
with his horses, he does not crush it.
²⁹*This also comes from the* LORD *of hosts;*
he is wonderful in counsel,
and excellent in wisdom.

OVERVIEW: Those who are married should labor to produce children who will remain virgins, being married to Christ (JEROME).

28:24 Plowing All Day?

PLOW ALL DAY. JEROME: I praise wedlock, I praise marriage, but it is because they give me virgins. I gather the rose from the thorns, the gold from the earth, the pearl from the shell. "Does the plowman plow all day to sow?" Shall he not also enjoy the fruit of his labor?[1] Wedlock is the more honored, the more what is born of it is loved. Why, mother, do you grudge your daughter her virginity? She has been reared on your milk, she has come from your womb, she has grown up in your bosom. Your watchful affection has kept her a virgin. Are you angry with her because she chooses to be a king's wife and not a soldier's? She has conferred on you a high privilege; you are now the mother-in-law of God. LETTER 22.20.[2]

---

[1] Jerome's argument is that marriage alone is not the full meaning of marriage. One has to look at the fruits of marriage, namely, the youth, in this case, virgins, who are born from it and go into the church. [2] NPNF 2 6:30*.

29:1-12 EVENTUAL RESTORATION

¹Ho Ariel, Ariel,
   the city where David encamped!
Add year to year;
   let the feasts run their round.
²Yet I will distress Ariel,
   and there shall be moaning and
      lamentation,
   and she shall be to me like an Ariel.
³And I will encamp against you round
      about,
   and will besiege you with towers
   and I will raise siegeworks against you.
⁴Then deep from the earth you shall speak,
   from low in the dust your words shall
      come;
your voice shall come from the ground like
      the voice of a ghost,
   and your speech shall whisper out of the
      dust.

⁵But the multitude of your foesˢ shall be like
      small dust,
   and the multitude of the ruthless like
      passing chaff.
And in an instant, suddenly,
   ⁶you will be visited by the LORD of hosts
with thunder and with earthquake and
      great noise,
   with whirlwind and tempest, and the
      flame of a devouring fire.

⁷And the multitude of all the nations that
      fight against Ariel,
   all that fight against her and her
      stronghold and distress her,
   shall be like a dream, a vision of the
      night.
⁸As when a hungry man dreams he is eating
   and awakes with his hunger not satisfied,
or as when a thirsty man dreams he is
      drinking
   and awakes faint, with his thirst not
      quenched,*
so shall the multitude of all the nations be
   that fight against Mount Zion.

⁹Stupefy yourselves and be in a stupor,
   blind yourselves and be blind!
Be drunk, but not with wine;
   stagger, but not with strong drink!
¹⁰For the Lord has poured out upon you†
   a spirit of deep sleep,
and has closed your eyes,† the prophets,
   and covered your heads, the seers.
¹¹And the vision of all this has become to
you like the words of a book that is sealed.
When men give it to one who can read, saying,
"Read this," he says, "I cannot, for it is sealed."
¹²And when they give the book to one who cannot read, saying, "Read this," he says, "I cannot read."

s Cn: Heb *strangers*   *LXX adds *and his soul has desired in vain*   †LXX *them*   ‡LXX *their*

OVERVIEW: Ariel refers to the strength of Zion (JEROME). The pleasures and riches of the world are like the food in a sleeping person's dreams (AM-BROSE, JEROME). The sleepy dreamer is like those who fail to recognize what is true (ORIGEN). Drunkenness is the straying of reason and the loss of our understanding; it can be caused by anger, evil desire, greed, and other passions (CHRYSOSTOM). Those who are judged by God are rendered drunk from the blows administered by God (GREGORY OF NAZIANZUS). Sinners are blinded to the truth because they are unwilling to receive it (AUGUSTINE). The deep sleep is the inability to recognize sin due to the wrath of God (CYPRIAN). Christ came to open the vision and the prophet, not to close them (EUSEBIUS). Before the coming of Christ, the true meaning of the Law, the Prophets and the Writings was sealed, but Christ unsealed the meaning (JEROME, HIPPOLYTUS, ORIGEN). Those who do not believe cannot understand the Scripture (PRIMASIUS, CYPRIAN). To understand Scripture we need a guide (JEROME).

29:1 Woe to Ariel

THE STORMING OF ZION. JEROME: [Zion] formed the city that David formerly stormed and afterwards rebuilt.[1] Of its storming it is written, "Woe to Ariel, to Ariel"—that is, God's lion[2] (and indeed in those days it was extremely strong). LETTER 108.9.[3]

29:8 Awaking with Hunger and Thirst Not Satisfied

A HUNGRY MAN DREAMS. AMBROSE: Let us speak of him who thought he was happy since he was chief butler and believed that this was the summit and crown of all power, that he would give the cup to the king.[4] This was his glory, this was his grandeur in this world; when he was deprived of this he felt sorrow, and when he was restored to it he rejoiced. But this is a dream, and all worldly power is a dream, not a reality. To be sure, he saw by way of a dream that his preeminent position was restored to him. Isaiah also says that people of this kind are such as take delight in prosperity in this world. One who eats and drinks in his sleep thinks he is filled with food and drink, but when he awakens, he begins to be more hungry; then he understands how

insubstantial were that dreamer's food and drink. Just so, one who is asleep in this world and does not open his eyes to the mysteries of God, as long as he is in a deep corporeal sleep, supposes that such worldly power is of some importance, seeing it, as it were, in his dreams. But when he has awakened, he discovers how insubstantial the pleasure of this world is. ON JOSEPH 6.38.[5]

THE DREAM OF RICHES. JEROME: Truly, this life is a dream, a dream of riches; for when we seem to have them within our grasp, immediately they slip away. Isaiah expresses this same thought: "As when a thirsty man dreams he is drinking and awakens faint and dry," so indeed are the riches of this world; while we are reaching out for them they are gone. HOMILIES ON THE PSALMS 9 (PSALM 75).[6]

A LACK OF ATTENTION. ORIGEN: And those who sleep are those who, when they ought to be taking heed and watching with the soul, are not doing this. But by reason of great want of attention they are nodding in resolution and are drowsy in their reflections, such as "in their dreaming defile the flesh, and set at nothing that which is highest in authority, and rail at dignities."[7] And these, because they are asleep, live in an atmosphere of vain and dreamlike fancies concerning realities. [They do not admit] the things that are actually true, but [they are] deceived by what appears in their vain imaginations. In regard to [them] it is said in Isaiah, "Like as when a thirsty man dreams that he is drinking, but when he has risen up is still thirsty, and his soul has cherished a vain hope, so shall be the wealth of all the nations, as many as have warred in Jerusalem." COMMENTARY ON MATTHEW 10.[8]

29:9 Drunk, but Not with Wine

---

[1]2 Sam 5:7, 9. [2]Hebrew *ariel* translated literally is "God's lion." [3]NPNF 2 6:199. [4]Gen 40:9-11. [5]FC 65:209-10. [6]FC 48:64. [7]Jude 8. [8]ANF 9:430*.

A More Dangerous Drunkenness. Chrysostom: Since you are reasonable, I know that after my exhortation you will not permit yourselves to go beyond the bounds of what you need. But now it is appropriate for me to urge you not only to turn aside from drinking to excess but also to avoid the drunkenness that comes without drinking wine. For this kind is more dangerous. Don't be astonished at what I say, for it is possible to be drunk without wine. That you may know that this is possible, listen to the prophet, who said, "Woe to those who are drunk not from wine." But what is this drunkenness that does not come from wine? It takes many and varied forms. For anger makes us drunk; so too, vainglory, haughty madness, and all the deadly passions that spring up in us produce a kind of drunkenness and satiety that darkens our reason. For drunkenness is nothing more than the distraction of our minds from their natural ways, the straying of reason and the loss of our understanding. Baptismal Instructions 5.4.[9]

Not with Wine. Chrysostom: Yes, it is possible to be drunk without wine; it is possible for a sober person to act as if he is drunk and to revel like a prodigal. If one could not get drunk without wine, the prophet would never have said, "Woe to those who are drunk not from wine"; if one could not get drunk without wine, Paul would never have said, "Do not be drunk with wine."[10] For he said this as if there were a possibility of getting drunk some other way. And it is possible. A person can be drunk with anger, with unseemly desire, with greed, with vainglory, with ten thousand other passions. For drunkenness is nothing other than a loss of right reason, a derangement and depriving the soul of its health. Discourses Against Judaizing Christians 8.1.1.[11]

We Have Refused to Be Healed. Gregory of Nazianzus: What are we to do now, my brothers, when crushed, cast down and drunk but not with strong drink or with wine, which excites and obfuscates but for a while, but with

the blow which the Lord has inflicted upon us? He says, "And you, O heart, be stirred and shaken,[12] and gives to the despisers the spirit of sorrow and deep sleep to drink."[13] To [them] he also says, "See, you despisers, behold, and wonder and perish."[14] How shall we bear his convictions; or what reply shall we make, when he reproaches us not only with the multitude of the benefits for which we have continued ungrateful, but also with his chastisements, and reckons up the remedies with which we have refused to be healed? On His Father's Silence, Oration 16.10.[15]

29:10 A Spirit of Deep Sleep

God's Just Judgments. Augustine: If they could not believe, what is the sin of a person not doing what he cannot do? But if they sinned by not believing, then they could believe and did not. . . . Then what will we answer about another testimony of the prophet that the apostle Paul cites, saying, "Israel did not obtain what he was seeking, but the election did obtain it. The rest indeed have been blinded, as it has been written, 'God gave them a spirit of insensibility, eyes that they should not see, and ears that they should not hear until this present day.' "[16]

You have heard, brothers, the question proposed; you see, of course, how profound it is. But we answer as best we can. "They could not believe," because Isaiah the prophet foretold this. But the prophet foretold it because God foreknew that it would be. Why they could not, however, if it should be asked of me, I quickly answer, because they were not willing. For God foresaw their evil will and he, from whom the future cannot be hidden, foretold it through the prophet.

But, you say, the prophet states another cause, not of their will. What cause does the prophet state? That "God gave them a spirit of insensibility, eyes that they should not see and ears that

[9]ACW 31:81-82. [10]Eph 5:18. [11]FC 68:205-6. [12]Hab 2:16. [13]Ps 60:2-3. [14]Hab 1:5; Acts 13:41. [15]NPNF 2 7:250. [16]Rom 11:7-8.

they should not hear, and he blinded their eyes and hardened their heart."[17] I answer that their will earned even this. For thus God blinds, thus God hardens by abandoning and not helping; and he can do this by a hidden judgment, but he cannot do it by an evil one. The piety of the religious ought altogether keep this unshaken and inviolate; as the apostle says when he was discussing this very same, most difficult question: "What shall we say, then? Is there injustice with God? Not at all!"[18] Therefore, if it is not at all the case that there is injustice with God, either when he helps, he acts mercifully, or when he does not help, he acts justly, because he does all things not with rashness but in judgment. Accordingly, if the judgments of the saints are just, how much more so those of the sanctifying and justifying God![19] Therefore they are just but hidden. TRACTATES ON THE GOSPEL OF JOHN 53.5.2-6.2.[20]

A DEEP SLEEP. CYPRIAN: Not to recognize sins lest penance follow is the wrath of God, as it is written: "And the Lord gave to them the spirit of a deep sleep," lest they actually return and be cured and be healed by their lamentations and just satisfactions after their sins. . . .

The first degree of felicity is not to sin; the second, to recognize the sins committed. In the former, innocence runs upright and unimpaired to save; in the latter, there follows the remedy to cure. They have lost both of these by offending God. . . . Or do you think, brother, that crimes against God are light matters, small and of little moment, because through them the majesty of an offended God is not sought, because the wrath and fire and day of the Lord are not feared, because, with Antichrist at hand, the faith of a militant people is disarmed while vigor and the fear of Christ are taken away? LETTER 59.13.[21]

29:11 Like a Book That Is Sealed

PROPHECY BROUGHT TO LIGHT. EUSEBIUS OF CAESAREA: For our Lord Jesus Christ did not come as it were to seal up the visions of the prophets. He rather opened and explained those that were of old obscure and sealed, tearing away so to say the seals impressed on them, and taught his disciples the meaning of the Holy Scriptures. Hence he says, "Behold, the lion of the tribe of Judah has prevailed, and he has opened the seals that were set on the book,"[22] in John's Apocalypse. What are these seals but the obscurities of the prophets? Isaiah knew them well and definitely says too: "And these words shall be as the words of the sealed book." The Christ of God did not come then to shut up the vision and the prophet but rather to open them and bring them to the light. PROOF OF THE GOSPEL 8.2.[23]

A SEALED BOOK. JEROME: What is the gate that is always closed, through which only the Lord God of Israel enters?[24] Surely it is that about which the Savior spoke in the Gospel: "Woe to you scribes and Pharisees, woe to you teachers of the law, woe to you who hold the key of knowledge. You do not enter yourselves, and you prevent those who would from entering."[25] Isaiah wrote about the same thing, using the metaphor of a book: "The words of this book are like sealed words; when you give them to a man who cannot read and tell him to read, he will respond: 'I don't know how to read.' And they will give it to a man who is able to read and tell him to read and he will say: 'I cannot read because it is sealed.'" This is the same book whose seal no one can break and open either in heaven or on earth or under the earth, except the one about whom John said in the Apocalypse: "Behold, the Lion of the tribe of Judah, the root and race of David, has conquered so that he can open the book and break its seal."[26] Before the Savior assumed a human body and humbled himself, taking the form of a servant,[27] the law was closed, the prophets were closed, all knowledge of the Scriptures was closed, and paradise was closed. After he had hung on the cross,

---

[17]Rom 11:8. [18]Rom 9:14. [19]1 Cor 1:30. [20]FC 88:293-94*. [21]FC 51:184-85. [22]Rev 5:5. [23]POG 2:121-22. [24]See Ezek 44:2. [25]See Lk 11:52. [26]Rev 5:5. [27]See Phil 2:7.

however, and said to the thief, "Today you will be with me in paradise,"[28] immediately the veil of the temple was cut and everything was opened. And once the veil has been removed, we will say, "But we all contemplate the glory of the Lord with unveiled face and are being transformed into his very image from glory to glory."[29] COMMENTARY ON EZEKIEL 13.44.1-3.[30]

A GREAT OBSCURITY. JEROME: He who had revealed manifold truth to Daniel now signifies that the things he has said are matters of secrecy. And he orders him to roll up the scroll containing his words and set a seal upon the book, with the result that many shall read it and inquire as to its fulfillment in history, differing in their opinions because of its great obscurity. And as for the statement, "Many shall pass over" or "go through,"[31] this indicates that it will be read by many people. For it is a familiar expression to say, "I have gone through a book," or "I have passed through an historical account." Indeed this is the idea that Isaiah also expressed in regard to the obscurity of his own book: "And the sayings of that book shall be like the words of a book that is sealed." COMMENTARY ON DANIEL 4.12.[32]

THE SEAL IS NOW BROKEN. HIPPOLYTUS: And that the things spoken of old by the law and the prophets were all sealed, and that they were unknown to people, Isaiah declares when he says, "And they will deliver the book that is sealed to one that is learned, and will say to him, 'Read this;' and he will say, 'I cannot read it, for it is sealed.' " It was right and necessary that the things spoken of old by the prophets should be sealed to the unbelieving Pharisees, who thought that they understood the letter of the law, and be opened to the believing. The things, therefore, which of old were sealed, are now by the grace of God the Lord all open to the saints. FRAGMENTS FROM COMMENTARY ON DANIEL 2.19.[33]

COVERED WITH A GREAT VEIL. ORIGEN: And clearly, if we hear negligently, if we bring no zeal

to learning and understanding, not only are the Scriptures of the law and prophets but also of the apostles and Gospels covered for us with a great veil. I fear, however, lest by too much negligence and dullness of heart the divine volumes are not only veiled to us but also sealed, so that "if a book should be put into the hand of a man who cannot read to be read, he would say, 'I cannot read'; if it should be put into the hands of a man who can read, he would say, 'It is sealed.' " Whence it is shown that we must not only employ zeal to learn the sacred literature, but we must also pray to the Lord and entreat "day and night"[34] that the Lamb "of the tribe of Judah" may come and himself taking "the sealed book" may deign to open it.[35] For it is he who "opening the Scriptures" kindles the hearts of the disciples so that they say, "Was not our heart burning within us when he opened to us the Scriptures?"[36] HOMILIES ON EXODUS 12.4.[37]

DEPRIVED OF FRUIT. PRIMASIUS: This is also why Isaiah would say to the Jews: "Behold, all of these words will be to you like the words of a sealed book." The skilled reader and the illiterate are equally said to be deprived of fruit, since one is prevented by the seal from penetrating what lies hidden within and the other is shackled by ignorance. COMMENTARY ON THE APOCALYPSE 2.5.[38]

UNDERSTANDING WILL COME. CYPRIAN: Isaiah [prophesied] that the Jews would not understand the holy Scriptures, but that they would become intelligible in the last times, after Christ had come: "And all these words shall be to you as the words of a book that is sealed, which, if you shall give to a man that knows letters to read, he shall say, I cannot read, for it is sealed. . . . But in that day the deaf shall hear the words of the book, and they who are in darkness and in a

---

[28]Lk 23:43. [29]2 Cor 3:18. [30]CCL 75:643-44. [31]Dan 12:4. [32]JCD 147. [33]ANF 5:181*. [34]See Ps 1:2; Josh 1:8. [35]See Rev 5:5. [36]Lk 24:32. [37]FC 71:372. [38]CCL 92:87-88.

cloud; the eyes of the blind shall see."[39] To Quirinus 1.4.[40]

A LEARNED GUIDE. JEROME: In the Apocalypse a book is shown sealed with seven seals,[41] which if you deliver to one that is learned saying, "Read this," he will answer you, "I cannot, for it is sealed." How many there are today who fancy themselves learned, yet the Scriptures are a sealed book to them, and one which they cannot open save through him who has the key of David, "he that opens and no man shuts; and shuts and no man opens."[42] In the Acts of the Apostles the holy eunuch[43] when reading Isaiah is asked by Philip, "Do you understand what you are reading?" The man answered, "How can I, except some man should guide me?"[44] To digress for a moment to myself, I am neither holier nor more diligent than this eunuch, who came from Ethiopia . . . and was so great a lover of the law and of divine knowledge that he read the holy Scriptures even in his chariot. Yet although he had the book in his hand and took into his mind the words of

the Lord, no, even had them on his tongue and uttered them with his lips, he still did not know him, who—not knowing—he worshiped in the book. Then Philip came and showed him Jesus, who was concealed beneath the letter. Wondrous excellence of the teacher! In the same hour the eunuch believed and was baptized; he became one of the faithful and a saint. He was no longer a pupil but a master; and he found more in the church's font there in the wilderness than he had ever done in the gilded temple of the synagogue. These instances have been just touched upon by me (the limits of a letter forbid a more discursive treatment of them) to convince you that in the Holy Scriptures you can make no progress unless you have a guide to show you the way. LETTER 53.5-6.[45]

---

[39]Is 29:11, 18. [40]CCL 3:9. [41]Rev 5:1. [42]Rev 3:7. [43]Or rather "man," for so the Scripture calls him in Acts 8:27. [44]Acts 8:30-31. [45]NPNF 2 6:98*.

29:13-24 A NEW RELATIONSHIP WITH GOD

[13]And the Lord said:
"Because this people draw near with their mouth
and honor me with their lips,
while their hearts are far from me,
and their fear of me is a commandment of men learned by rote;*
[14]therefore, behold, I will again
do marvelous things with this people,
wonderful and marvelous;

and the wisdom of their wise men shall perish,[†]
and the discernment of their discerning men shall be hid."[‡]

[15]Woe to those who hide deep from the LORD their counsel,
whose deeds are in the dark,
and who say, "Who sees us? Who knows us?"

¹⁶*You turn things upside down!*
    Shall the potter be regarded as the clay;
that the thing made should say of its maker,
    "He did not make me";
or the thing formed say of him who formed
    it,
    "He has no understanding"?

¹⁷*Is it not yet a very little while*
    until Lebanon shall be turned into a
    fruitful field,
    and the fruitful field shall be regarded as
    a forest?
¹⁸*In that day the deaf shall hear*
    the words of a book,
and out of their gloom and darkness
    the eyes of the blind shall see.
¹⁹*The meek shall obtain fresh joy in the*
    LORD,
    and the poor among men shall exult in
    the Holy One of Israel.
²⁰*For the ruthless shall come to nought and*
    the scoffer cease,

and all who watch to do evil shall be cut
    off,
²¹*who by a word make a man out to be an*
    offender,
    and lay a snare for him who reproves in
    the gate,
    and with an empty plea turn aside him
    who is in the right.

²²*Therefore thus says the* LORD, *who*
redeemed Abraham, concerning the house of
Jacob:
    "Jacob shall no more be ashamed,
    no more shall his face grow pale.
²³*For when he sees his children,*
    the work of my hands, in his midst,
    they will sanctify my name;
they will sanctify the Holy One of Jacob
    and will stand in awe of the God of Israel.
²⁴*And those who err in spirit will come to*
    understanding,
    and those who murmur will accept
    instruction."

*LXX but in vain do they worship me, teaching the commandments and doctrines of men   †*LXX I will destroy*   ‡*LXX I will hide*

OVERVIEW: Some people preach the gospel with their lips but not their heart (AUGUSTINE). One cannot praise God and live a wicked life (CAESARIUS OF ARLES). Sinners give thanks to God when they receive what they want, but their hearts do not praise God. God knows the state of the heart, even if the lips confess sins to him. God is everywhere, but we are far from him when we sin (CASSIODORUS). God does not desire repetition of praises but a heart free of worldly concerns (CHRYSOSTOM). We confess Christ not with our lips alone, but by obeying him and honoring him with our hearts (PSEUDO-CLEMENT, MAXIMUS OF TURIN, AMBROSE).

God is offended when human tradition subverts divine precepts (CYPRIAN). A right attitude of the soul is more precious than simply offering phrases to God (GREGORY OF NYSSA). The hearts of the people were far from God because they lacked faith (ARNOBIUS THE YOUNGER). We are distant from God when we sin or are ashamed of him. While we sing with our lips, we should draw near to God with our hearts (AUGUSTINE, FULGENTIUS). Although heretics may frequently repeat the name of Christ, God does not inhabit them. Isaiah is writing about those who claim to know God but deny him with their works (JEROME). We should ensure that our lives are consistent with the profession of our lips (EUSEBIUS OF GAUL).

The wisdom of the world cannot replace the gospel (AUGUSTINE). God will bring to nothing those who practice idle discourse concerning the Scriptures (CLEMENT OF ALEXANDRIA). There is no other wisdom than God's wisdom (CYPRIAN). We should prefer the plain words of the apostles to the discussions of the philosophers (JEROME). Scripture warns us from thinking our sin is hidden from God (CLEMENT OF ALEXANDRIA). As the potter God rightly judges sinners and offers grace to some of his choosing (AUGUSTINE). While we are clay, the craftsman has made us more worthy than clay (CHRYSOSTOM). Though we are dirt before God, he has condescended to us (SAHDONA). Isaiah prophesied about Gentiles coming into the city of God and Jews who would be faithless. By "day" Isaiah means numerous moments of divine grace, not one specific day (BEDE).

29:13 Hearts Far from God

HEARTS FAR FROM ME. AUGUSTINE: Leah, too, received children by her handmaid, from the desire of having a numerous family. Zilpah, her handmaid, is, interpreted, an open mouth.[1] So Leah's handmaid represents those who are spoken of in Scripture as engaging in the preaching of the gospel with open mouth but not with open heart. Thus it is written of some, "This people honor me with their lips, but their heart is far from me." To such the apostle says, "You that preach that a man should not steal, do you steal? You that say a man should not commit adultery, do you commit adultery?"[2] REPLY TO FAUSTUS THE MANICHAEAN 22.55.[3]

THIS PEOPLE DRAW NEAR. CAESARIUS OF ARLES: According to what the prophet says, "This people honors me with their lips, though their hearts are far from me." To them the Holy Spirit exclaims, "But to the wicked person God says, 'Why do you recite my statutes and profess my covenant with your mouth?'"[4] It is as if he were saying it does you no good to praise God. It is profitable for those who live well to praise him, but if you praise him and do not abandon your sins, it avails nothing. Why do you praise me?

Listen to the Scriptures say, "Unseemly is praise on a sinner's lips."[5] If you live a wicked life and say good things, you do not yet praise God. Again, if when you have begun to live well you attribute it to your own merits, you do not yet praise God. I do not want you to be a robber deriding the cross of our Lord, but neither do I want you as his temple to throw away his merits in you and conceal his wounds. SERMON 133.4.[6]

HYPOCRITICAL SPEECH. CASSIODORUS: The habit of sinners is . . . after they have achieved the aspiration of their most wicked plans, they then give thanks to the Godhead since they have attained their wish. But they in their utter wretchedness do not realize that he originates only successful aspirations that are holy. "They shall bless" not with their hearts but their mouths, the source of hypocritical utterances for the most part. As Isaiah says, "This people glorify me with their lips, but their heart is far from me." EXPOSITION OF THE PSALMS 48.14.[7]

THEIR HEART IS FAR FROM ME. CASSIODORUS: If the fear of God is not mingled with love, he is not sought in the heart's entirety. It is certain that it is the keenest of sins for a person to say that he confesses to him with his tongue, while his heart deep down is at odds with him; does God not know all that goes on within us? . . . He does not hear merely what the tongue proclaims, as a human person does. It is the person who faithfully believes his testimonies who truly loves him. *Fides* (faith) gets its name from words uttered (*quod fiant dicta*). The Lord himself offers a testimony like this verse when he says, "This people glorifies me with their lips, but their heart is far from me." EXPOSITION OF THE PSALMS 77.37.[8]

OUR DEEDS DISTANCE US FROM GOD. CASSIODORUS: Though we never withdraw ourselves

---

[1]Gen 29—30. [2]Rom 2:21-22. [3]NPNF 1 4:293*. [4]Ps 50:16 (49:16 LXX). [5]Sir 15:9. [6]FC 47:248*. [7]ACW 51:475-76*. [8]ACW 52:264**.

from the Lord since he is wholly everywhere, we nonetheless become distant when we are displaced through the nature of our deeds. EXPOSITION OF THE PSALMS 94.1.[9]

GOD DESIRES TO WRITE ON THE HEART. CHRYSOSTOM: If we do not see our children deriving any benefit from the teachers we send them to, then we blame the teachers and take our children to other teachers. What excuse will we have for putting so much emphasis on earthly things but not putting emphasis on virtue? Our teachers here [at church] are far more numerous. No less than the prophets and apostles and patriarchs and all righteous people are set over you as teachers in every church. And there is no profit in merely chanting out two or three psalms, making the accustomed prayers at random and then being dismissed. Do you think this is enough for your salvation? Have you not heard the prophet (or rather God through the prophet) say, "These people honor me with their lips, but their heart is far from me"?

To keep this from being the case with us as well, then wipe out the letters and impressions the devil has engraved on your souls, and bring me a heart that has been set free from worldly tumults so I can write on it what I want to. HOMILIES ON THE GOSPEL OF MATTHEW 11.9.[10]

CONFESS GOD THROUGH YOUR DEEDS. PSEUDO-CLEMENT OF ROME: Since, then, [Christ] has bestowed such mercy on us, first that we the living do not sacrifice to gods who are dead or worship them but through him know the Father of truth—what is true knowledge concerning him except not to deny him through whom we knew the Father? He himself says, "He who confessed me before men, I will confess him before my father."[11] This, then, is our reward, if we confess him through whom we were saved. But how do we confess him? By doing what he says, and not disobeying his commandments, and honoring him not only with our lips but "with all our heart and all our mind."[12] And he says also in

Isaiah: "This people honor me with their lips, but their heart is far from me." 2 CLEMENT 3.[13]

BELIEVE WITH THE HEART. MAXIMUS OF TURIN: Suppose someone says, "We are Christians too; we believe in the Lord, the Savior." But it is necessary to believe in deed and not in word, not with the tongue but with the heart, lest it also be said to us, "This people honors me with their lips, but their heart is far from me." SERMON 102.3.[14]

THE FORM OF RIGHTEOUSNESS. AMBROSE: Again the form of righteousness is described and magnified when Scripture says, "The law of his God is in his heart, and his stride will not be broken."[15] The law of God is in the heart of the righteous. Which law? It is not the written law but the natural law, because "the law was not laid down for the righteous but for the unrighteous."[16] The law is in his heart, not superficially, as it is on the lips of the Jews, for "he who believes with his heart is justified."[17] The one who believes also speaks, but the one who speaks does not necessarily believe. For instance, the people did not believe about whom it is written: "This people honors me with their lips, but their hearts are far from me." EXPLANATION OF THE TWELVE PSALMS 36.69.[18]

THE COMMANDMENTS OF MEN. CYPRIAN: What is this obstinacy or what is this presumption to place human tradition before the divine plan and not to notice that God is offended and angered as often as human tradition subverts and disregards the divine precepts? He cries and says through Isaiah, the prophet, "This people honors me with their lips, but their heart is far separated from me. In vain, moreover, they honor me, teaching the commandments and doctrines of men." LETTER 74.3.[19]

---

[9]ACW 52:409. [10]NPNF 1 10:73-74**. [11]Mt 10:32. [12]Mk 12:30. [13]FC 1:66-67*. [14]ACW 50:230-31. [15]Ps 37:31 (36:31 LXX). [16]1 Tim 1:9. [17]Rom 10:10. [18]CSEL 64:128. [19]FC 51:287-88*.

THE HEART SUPPLIES THE MOTIVE. GREGORY OF NYSSA: For speaking in this way or in that is not the cause of the thought within us, but the hidden conception of the heart supplies the motive for such and such words, "for from the abundance of the heart the mouth speaks." We make the words interpret the thought; we do not by a reverse process gather the thought from the words. Should both be at hand, a person may certainly be ready in both, in clever thinking and clever expression; but if the one should be wanting, the loss to the illiterate is slight, if the knowledge in his soul is perfect in the direction of moral goodness. "This people honors me with their lips, but their heart is far from me." What is the meaning of that? That the right attitude of the soul toward the truth is more precious than the propriety of phrases in the sight of God, who hears the "groanings that cannot be uttered."[20] Phrases can be used in opposite senses; the tongue readily serving, at his will, the intention of the speaker; but the disposition of the soul, as it is, so is it seen by him who sees all secrets. AGAINST EUNOMIUS 1.37.[21]

WE MUST HAVE FAITH. ARNOBIUS THE YOUNGER: For God is necessary to all things, but nothing is necessary to him. Because, however, he loved everything he created, by the great grace of his kindness he deemed it worthy to invite the soul to come to him through the law, through trials of virtue, through sorrows of the heart, and through the greatness of human works. He gave not only the bread of angels, therefore, but also the flesh of innumerable birds to the concupiscent, even to the ungrateful.[22] And lest their descendants fail to fear the unpunished crime of the ungrateful, "the wrath of God came upon them when their food was still in their mouths" because they did not believe in his wonders.[23] "Their days vanished in emptiness and their years in partying."[24] Truly, as I have said, you will not desire to do good unless you are compelled by the fear of suffering evil: "When he killed them," it says, "they sought him, repented, and came to him immediately."[25] It was then that "they remembered that God is their helper and their defense."[26] But only those who said, "You are our God" are the ones who "lied to him with their tongues, for their hearts were not right within them."[27] Consequently the Lord said, "This people loves me with its lips, but its heart is far from me." Why these people in particular? Because "they did not have faith in his covenant."[28] For "without faith," said the apostle, "it is impossible to please God."[29] COMMENTARY ON THE PSALMS 77.[30]

A DISTANT HEART. AUGUSTINE: This is why he can say, "My friends and neighbors drew near and stood against me; and my neighbors stood far off."[31] Do you understand what I mean? I have called those who approached him "neighbors," yet they stood far off; for though they drew near in body, they stood far away in their hearts. Who was so near physically as those who hoisted him onto the cross? Yet who so far away in heart as those who uttered blasphemies? Far distance of this latter kind was mentioned by Isaiah; listen to what he said about being near while really being far away: "This people honors me with its lips (that means, they are physically near), but its heart is far from me." The same people are said to be near and yet far: near with their lips, far away in their hearts.

However, the fearful apostles certainly ran far away, so we can more simply and obviously refer the saying to them, understanding it to mean that some of them drew near and others stood far off. Even Peter, who had been bold enough to follow our Lord, was so far off that when questioned and frightened, he three times denied the Lord with whom he had earlier promised to die.[32] EXPLANATIONS OF THE PSALMS 37.17.[33]

---

[20]Rom 8:22. [21]NPNF 2 5:85*. [22]See Ps 78:25-27 (77:25-27 LXX). [23]Ps 78:30-31 (77:30-31 LXX). [24]Ps 78:33 (77:33 LXX). [25]Ps 78:34 (77:34 LXX). [26]Ps 78:35 (77:35 LXX). [27]Ps 78:36-37 (77:36-37 LXX). [28]Ps 78:37 (77:37 LXX). [29]Heb 11:6. [30]CCL 25:113-14. [31]Ps 38:11 (37:11 LXX). [32]See Mt 26:69-75; Mk 14:66-72; Lk 22:56-62. [33]WSA 3 16:160.

God Perceives the Heart. Augustine: "See, Lord, I will not keep my lips sealed, you know it."[34] My lips speak, and I will not restrain them. My lips speak to the ears of men and women, but you know my heart. "Lord, I will not keep my lips sealed, you know it." A human being hears one thing, but God perceives something else. This is emphasized because our proclamation must not be with our lips only, so that it could be said of us, "Do what they tell you, but do not imitate what they do."[35] Nor must it be said of us, as it was said of that people who praised God with their mouths but not their hearts, "This people honors me with its lips, but its heart is far from me." Sing with your lips, but draw near to him with your heart, for "the faith that issues in righteousness is in the heart, and the confession that leads to salvation is made with the lips."[36] This was true of the thief who hung on the cross with the Lord and from the cross acknowledged the Lord. Others failed to recognize the Lord even as he performed miracles, but this man recognized him as he hung upon the cross. The thief was nailed securely in all his limbs: his hands were immobilized by nails, his feet were transfixed, and his whole body fastened to the wood. That body had no use of its other members, but his heart had the use of his tongue. With his heart he believed, and with his lips he made confession. "Lord, remember me when you come into your kingdom," he said.[37] He hoped for salvation as a distant prospect and would have been content to receive it after a long delay; his hope stretched toward a far-off future, but the day was not delayed. He prayed, "Remember me when you come into your kingdom," but Christ replied, "Truly I tell you, today you will be with me in paradise."[38] Explanations of the Psalms 39.15.[39]

A Distant Heart. Fulgentius of Ruspe: God cannot be separated from his creatures by time or space but only by their iniquities. Of the iniquitous, therefore, he said, "This people honors me with their lips, but their heart is far from

me." He also said, "I am a God who draws near, not a God who remains far away. If a man tries to hide, will I not see him? Do I not fill heaven and earth?"[40] Nevertheless, blessed David himself said, "Those who distance themselves from you will perish."[41] Book to Victor Against the Sermon of Fastidios the Arian 5.1.[42]

God Does Not Inhabit Them. Jerome: This oration is directed against all who act with iniquity.[43] It is summarized neatly in one sentence by the seventy-second Psalm, wherein the prophet says, "How good is the God of Israel to those who are upright in heart! But my feet had almost been moved and my step had nearly slipped, for I was jealous of sinners when I saw the ease of their lives."[44] This is said particularly against heretics, who, because they are impious, prosper in their ways and generate children of their own, whom they deceive with heresy. They conspire and act with iniquity, all of this for the purpose of plundering the church and of portraying themselves as having been planted by God and having sunk roots and produced children and bore fruit, even while continuing in the wickedness of their intentions. Although they frequently repeat the name of Christ, God does not inhabit them, as Isaiah said: "This people honors me with their lips, but their heart is far from me."

"And you know me, Lord, you see me and you prove my heart to be with you. Gather them as sheep for the slaughter and sanctify them on the killing day."[45] There is no scandal, he says, because all the impious or heretics flourish only for a while, but "you know me, Lord, and you prove my heart to be with you." Commentary on Jeremiah 3.2.2-3.3.1.[46]

Their Works Deny Him. Jerome: But if we are impure and unfaithful, all things are profane

---

[34]Ps 40:10 (LXX 39:10). [35]Mt 23:3. [36]Rom 10:10. [37]Lk 23:42. [38]Lk 23:43. [39]WSA 3 16:210-11. [40]Jer 23:23-24. [41]Ps 73:27 (LXX 72:27). [42]CCL 91:289. [43]See Jer 12:1-2. [44]Ps 73:1-2 (LXX 72:1-2). [45]Jer 12:3. [46]CCL 74:120-21.

to us, either due to heresy inhabiting our hearts or to a sinful conscience.[47] Moreover, if our conscience does not accuse us and if we have pious trust in the Lord, "we will pray with the spirit and we will pray with the mind; we will sing with the spirit and sing with the mind,"[48] and we will be far removed from those about whom it is here written: "their minds and consciences are polluted."[49]

"They claim to know God, but they deny him with their deeds. They are accursed, disobedient and repelled by every good deed."[50] It is about these persons whose minds and consciences are polluted, who claim to know God but deny him with their deeds, that it is said in Isaiah: "This people honors me with their lips, but their heart is far from me." See how they honor God with their lips while fleeing from him in their heart; professing belief in God with words, their works deny him. COMMENTARY ON TITUS 1.15-16.[51]

WORD AND LIFE MUST FIT TOGETHER. EUSEBIUS OF GAUL: We heard in the Gospel the voice of the Lord saying, "Not everyone who says to me 'Lord, Lord' will enter the kingdom of heaven."[52] To whom does this word pertain? It is doubtlessly to those to whom he had said in another place: "This people honors me with their lips, but their heart is far from me." We should be vigilant, therefore, that our lives remain consonant and harmonious with the profession of our lips, for if our works cry out to God with sincerity of conscience and probity of life, the mercy of the Lord will turn toward us whom he has heard. HOMILY 7.1.[53]

29:14 The Wisdom of Their Wise Men Will Perish

SHADOWS IN THE HUMAN SOUL. AUGUSTINE: But perhaps Pelagius thinks that the name of Christ is necessary so that we may learn by his gospel how we ought to live, but not so that by his grace we may also be helped to lead good lives. At least, this consideration should lead him to

admit that there are wretched shadows in the human soul, which knows how to tame a lion but not how to live. But are a free will and the natural law sufficient for us to know this? This is the "wisdom of speech" by which "the cross of Christ is made void."[54] But he said, "I will destroy the wisdom of the wise," because that cross cannot be made void. And immediately is overthrown that "wisdom" through the "foolishness of preaching," by which those who believe are healed. For if the natural power through free will is sufficient for us not only to know how we ought to live but actually to live well, "then Christ died in vain,"[55] "then is the scandal of the cross made void."[56] . . . Ignorant of the justice of God, you are seeking to establish your own justice, and you have not submitted to the justice of God. For even as Christ is the end of the law, so also is he the savior of corrupted human nature, to justice for all who believe. ON NATURE AND GRACE 40.47.[57]

IDLE DISCOURSE. CLEMENT OF ALEXANDRIA: It is of . . . those . . . who practice idle discourse that God's Scriptures say superbly: "I will destroy the wisdom of the wise and bring to nothing the cleverness of the clever."[58] STROMATEIS 1.3.[59]

A FALSE PATIENCE. CYPRIAN: Philosophers also declare that they pursue this virtue, but their patience is as false as is their wisdom, for how can anyone be either wise or patient unless he knows the wisdom and patience of God? For he himself warns and states concerning those who think that they are wise in this world: "I will destroy the wisdom of the wise, and the prudence of the prudent I will reject."[60] . . . Therefore, if their wisdom is not true, their patience cannot be true either. For if that man who is humble and meek is patient, and yet we see that the philosophers are not humble or meek but very pleasing to themselves, and displeasing to God by the very fact

[47]See Tit 1:15. [48]See 1 Cor 14:15. [49]Tit 1:15. [50]Tit 1:16. [51]PL 26:576. [52]Mt 7:21. [53]CCL 101:77. [54]1 Cor 1:17. [55]Gal 2:21. [56]Gal 5:11. [57]FC 86:57-58*. [58]1 Cor 1:19. [59]FC 85:39. [60]1 Cor 1:19.

that they are pleasing to themselves, it is evident that patience is not found where there is the arrogant boldness of an affected freedom and the shameless boasting of the proud and half-naked breast. THE GOOD OF PATIENCE 2.[61]

BRING TO NOTHING THE UNDERSTANDING OF THE WISE. JEROME: From my youth up until now I have spent many years in writing various works and have always tried to teach my hearers the doctrine that I have been taught publicly in church. I have not followed the philosophers in their discussions but have preferred to acquiesce in the plain words of the apostles. For I have known that it is written, "I will destroy the wisdom of the wise and will bring to nothing the understanding of the prudent," and "the foolishness of God is wiser than men."[62] This being the case, I challenge my opponents thoroughly to sift all my past writings and, if they can find anything that is faulty in them, to bring it to light. One of two things must happen. Either my works will be found edifying and I shall confute the false charges brought against me; or they will be found blameworthy and I shall confess my error.[63] LETTER 133.12.[64]

29:15 Woe to Those Who Hide Their Counsel

WHO SEES US? CLEMENT OF ALEXANDRIA: He forgets the words of the Educator: "Every man that passes beyond his own bed, who says in his soul: Who sees me? Darkness compasses me about, and the walls cover me, and no man sees my sins: whom do I fear? The Most High will not remember."[65] Such a person is most wretched, for he fears only the human observation and thinks to hide from God. "He does not know," Scripture continues, "that the eyes of the Most High Lord are far brighter than the sun, beholding all the ways of men and looking into the most hidden parts."[66] Another time, the Educator gives warning through Isaiah: "Woe to you who made your counsel in secret and say: Who sees us?"

A light that can be seen by the senses may pass unnoticed, but that which illumines the mind cannot be ignored. CHRIST THE EDUCATOR 2.10.99.[67]

29:16 The Creator and the Created

POWER OVER THE CLAY. AUGUSTINE: Scripture says to Pharaoh, "To this purpose have I raised you that I may show my power in you; and that my name may be declared throughout all the earth."[68] Then, making a conclusion to both passages, he says, "Therefore he has mercy on whom he will and whom he will he hardens."[69] Obviously he treats neither of these with injustice but both with mercy and truth; in spite of that there is an uprising of insolent weakness on the part of those who attempt to comprehend the unsearchable depth of the judgment of God[70] according to the interpretations of the human heart. The apostle refutes this view when he says, "You will say therefore to me: Why does he then find fault? For who resists his will?"[71] Let us imagine this as said to us. What other answer should we make than the one he made? If such ideas disturb us also because we, too, are human, we all have need to listen to the apostle saying, "O man, who are you that replies against God? Shall the thing formed say to him that formed it: Why have you made me thus? Or has not the potter power over the clay, of the same lump to make one vessel unto honor, another unto dishonor?"[72] If this lump of clay were of such indifferent value that it deserved nothing good any more than it deserved anything evil, there would be reason to see injustice in making of it a vessel unto dishonor. But when, through the free will of the first man alone, condemnation extended to the whole lump of clay, undoubtedly if vessels are made of it unto honor, it is not a question of justice not forestall-

---

[61]FC 36:263-64. [62]1 Cor 1:25. [63]Jerome posits that either he will prove his case or he will admit to error. Obviously this is a rhetorical device; Jerome has no intention of admitting any error. [64]NPNF 2 6:279. [65]Sir 23:18. [66]Sir 23:19. [67]FC 23:176*. [68]Ex 9:16. [69]Rom 9:16-18. [70]Rom 11:33. [71]Rom 9:19. [72]Rom 9:20-21.

ing grace, but of God's mercy. If, however, vessels are made of it unto dishonor, it is to be attributed to the judgment of God, not to his injustice—far be from us the thought that there could be any such with God! Whoever is wise in this matter with the Catholic church does not argue against grace in favor of merit, but he sings mercy and judgment to the Lord, that he may not ungratefully deny his mercy or unjustly upbraid his judgment. LETTER 186.[73]

REGARDED AS CLAY. CHRYSOSTOM: If a man seems more comely to look upon than clay, this difference was not produced by a change of nature but by the wisdom of the craftsman. Why? Because you are no different from the clay. If you refuse to believe this, let the coffins and the cinerary urn convince you. And you will know that this is the truth if you have gone to visit the tombs of your forebearers. Therefore there is no difference between the clay and the potter.[74] AGAINST THE ANOMOEANS 2.36.[75]

DUST CONVERSES WITH ITS MAKER. SAHDONA: God comes down to the level of sinful men and women; the good Lord speaks with his rebellious servants; the holy one calls those who are impure to forgiveness. Humanity created out of mud addresses its Fashioner with familiarity; dust converses with its Maker. Let us, therefore, show awe when we sinners stand in the presence of this Majesty and speak. Even though we are so impure in our deeds, he draws us close to the sight of himself in the spirit; let us therefore repeat with trembling the words of the blessed prophet Isaiah: "Woe is me, for I am dazed: I am a man of unclean lips, yet my eyes have beheld the King, the Lord Almighty."[76] BOOK OF PERFECTION 5.[77]

29:17 Lebanon Turned into a Fruitful Field

UNEXPECTED TRANSFORMATION. BEDE: Note that [Paul] taught Greeks in Jerusalem, and Jews in Damascus[78] which is a Gentile city, even though this should signify that Gentiles were to be included in the city of God and Jews were to fall into the faithlessness of the Gentiles, in accordance with what Isaiah said, "Lebanon shall be changed into Carmel,[79] and Carmel shall be regarded as a wasteland." COMMENTARY ON THE ACTS OF THE APOSTLES 9.[80]

29:18 In That Day the Deaf Will Hear

THE DEAF WILL HEAR. BEDE: Neither was heaven created in any six-day period and the stars illuminated and the dry land separated from the water and the trees and vegetation planted. Rather, Scripture customarily uses "day" to denote an unspecified period of time, as the apostle did when he said, "Behold, this is the day of salvation."[81] He was not referring to a particular day but to the entirety of the time of the present life in which we labor for eternal salvation. The prophet also spoke not of one specific day but of numerous moments of divine grace, saying, "In that day, the deaf will hear the words of this book." Moreover, it is difficult to understand how in one day God made heaven and earth and all the brush of the field and every plant of every region, unless we say that all creatures were created simultaneously in formless matter, according to which it is written: "He who lives forever created all things together."[82] ON GENESIS 1.2.4-5.[83]

---

[73]FC 30:204-5*. [74]Chrysostom means that human beings are made from clay as well. [75]FC 72:85. [76]Is 6:5. [77]CS 101:204. [78]Acts 9:22. [79]The Hebrew word Carmel can be translated "fruited field." [80]CS 117:90. [81]2 Cor 6:2. [82]Sir 18:1. [83]CCL 118A:40.

30:1-17 JUDAH'S ATTEMPT TO SOLICIT EGYPT'S HELP AGAINST ASSYRIA

[1]"Woe to the rebellious children," says the
LORD,
"who carry out a plan, but not mine;
and who make a league, but not of my
spirit,
that they may add sin to sin;
[2]who set out to go down to Egypt,
without asking for my counsel,
to take refuge in the protection of
Pharaoh,
and to seek shelter in the shadow of
Egypt!
[3]Therefore shall the protection of Pharaoh
turn to your shame,
and the shelter in the shadow of Egypt to
your humiliation.
[4]For though his officials are at Zoan
and his envoys reach Hanes,
[5]every one comes to shame
through a people that cannot profit them,
that brings neither help nor profit,
but shame and disgrace."

[6]An oracle on the beasts of the Negeb.
Through a land of trouble and anguish,
from where come the lioness and the lion,
the viper and the flying serpent,
they carry their riches on the backs of asses,
and their treasures on the humps of
camels,
to a people that cannot profit them.
[7]For Egypt's help is worthless and empty,
therefore I have called her
"Rahab who sits still."

[8]And now, go, write it before them on a
tablet,
and inscribe it in a book,
that it may be for the time to come
as a witness for ever.
[9]For they are a rebellious people,
lying sons,
sons who will not hear
the instruction of the LORD;
[10]who say to the seers, "See not";
and to the prophets, "Prophesy not to us
what is right;
speak to us smooth things,
prophesy illusions,
[11]leave the way, turn aside from the
path,
let us hear no more of the Holy One of
Israel."

[12]Therefore thus says the Holy One of
Israel,
"Because you despise this word,
and trust in oppression and perverseness,
and rely on them;
[13]therefore this iniquity shall be to you
like a break in a high wall, bulging out,
and about to collapse,
whose crash comes suddenly, in an
instant;
[14]and its breaking is like that of a potter's
vessel
which is smashed so ruthlessly
that among its fragments not a sherd is
found
with which to take fire from the hearth,

or to dip up water out of the cistern."

¹⁵*For thus said the Lord GOD, the Holy*
    One of Israel,
"In returning and rest you shall be saved;
  in quietness and in trust shall be your
    strength."*
And you would not, ¹⁶*but you said,*
"No! We will speed upon horses,"

therefore you shall speed away;
and, "We will ride upon swift steeds,"
  therefore your pursuers shall be swift.
¹⁷*A thousand shall flee at the threat of*
  one,
  at the threat of five you shall flee,
till you are left
  like a flagstaff on the top of a mountain,
  like a signal on a hill.

*LXX and you will know where you have been when you trusted in vanities

OVERVIEW: We should continually take refuge in God (CHRYSOSTOM). Reprimand is disapproval expressed in correction (CLEMENT OF ALEXANDRIA). Those who have abandoned the faith strive against God's ordinance (CYPRIAN). God's prophecies against the Jews were written down so they would be remembered when the events came to pass. It is an insult to hear someone speak without replying (CHRYSOSTOM). Isaiah prophesied that the chief priests would claim that Jesus' body was stolen rather than raised from the dead (CYRIL OF JERUSALEM). We are saved by God's goodness when we repent of our sins (CAESARIUS OF ARLES, CYRIL OF JERUSALEM). We should rest in God's forgiveness of our sins (FULGENTIUS). It is never too late to repent (JEROME). Even the greatest sinner will find forgiveness of sin by repentance (PACIAN OF BARCELONA). We will defeat our enemies through prayer (JEROME).

30:1 Woe to Rebellious Children

GOD DESIRES TO BE OUR REFUGE. CHRYSOSTOM: Let every man and woman among us, whether meeting together at church or remaining at home, call upon God with much earnestness, and he will doubtless accede to these petitions. Whence does this appear evident? Because he is exceedingly desirous that we should always take refuge in him and in everything make our requests to him; [he desires that we] do nothing and speak nothing without him. For men, when

we trouble them repeatedly concerning our affairs, become slothful and evasive and conduct themselves unpleasantly toward us; but with God it is quite the reverse. Not when we apply to him continually respecting our affairs, but when we fail to do so, then is he especially displeased. Hear at least what he reproves the Jews for, when he says, "You have taken counsel, but not of me, and made treaties but not by my Spirit." For this is the custom of those who love; they desire that all the concerns of their beloved should be accomplished by means of themselves; and that they should neither do anything, nor say anything, without them. . . . Let us not then be slow to take refuge in him continually; and whatever be the evil, it will in any case find its appropriate solution. HOMILIES CONCERNING THE STATUES 3.5.[1]

STRONGLY WORDED BLAME. CLEMENT OF ALEXANDRIA: Reprimand is disapproval expressed in correction or strongly worded blame. The Educator resorts to this method of training when he says through Isaiah, "Woe to you, apostate children, says the Lord, that you would take counsel and not of me, and make treaties and not of my Spirit." He flavors each pronouncement in turn with the tart spice of fear to whet the appetite of his people for salvation and make them more aware of it, just as wool to be dyed is usually steeped first in an astringent to

---

[1]NPNF 1 9:356.

prepare it to preserve the dye. CHRIST THE EDU-CATOR 1.9.78.[2]

THIEVES AND ROBBERS. PSEUDO-CYPRIAN: Moreover, in the same [Gospel] he also says, "All who have come before are thieves and robbers."[3] Who are such but the deserters of the faith and the transgressors of God's church, who strive against God's ordinance—whom the Holy Spirit rightly rebukes by the prophet, saying, "You have taken counsel, but not by me; and have made a confederacy, but not by my Spirit, to add sin to sin." TO NOVATIAN 2.3-4.[4]

30:8 Inscribed as a Witness Forever

IN A BOOK. CHRYSOSTOM: [Isaiah] set his prophecy down in writing in a new[5] book so that, after his prophecy was fulfilled, what he had written might bear witness against the Jews of what the inspired prophet predicted to them a long time before. This is why he did not simply write it in a book, but in a new book, a book capable of staying sturdy for a long time without easily falling apart, a book which could last until the events described in it would come to pass. DISCOURSES AGAINST JUDAIZING CHRISTIANS 5.4.6.[6]

30:10 Seers and Prophets

DO NOT SPEAK TO US. CHRYSOSTOM: What insults a person more: when he says something and receives no answer or when he is silent and receives no answer? Obviously a person is most insulted when he speaks and receives no answer. God is insulted when he speaks and you will not heed what he says. They said in ancient days to the prophets, "Do not speak to us." But you do worse. You say, "Speak to us, but we will not obey." They turned the prophets away in order to keep them from speaking, sensing that there was some sort of awe or obligation in the voice itself. But you, with excessive contempt, do not even do this. Believe me, if you stopped our mouths by

putting your hand over them, it would not be as great of an insult as it is for you to hear but not obey. HOMILIES ON THE ACTS OF THE APOSTLES 19.[7]

DO NOT TELL THE TRUTH. CYRIL OF JERUSALEM: The chief priests and the Pharisees, through the agency of Pilate, sealed the tomb; but the women saw him who was risen. . . . The chief priests lacked understanding, but the women beheld with their own eyes. When the soldiers came into the city and told the chief priests what had happened, they said to the soldiers, "Say, his disciples came by night and stole him while we were sleeping."[8] Well did Isaiah foretell this also, in their persons: "But tell us, and relate another error." Christ has risen and come back from the dead, and by a bribe they persuade the soldiers. CATECHETICAL LECTURES 14.14.[9]

30:15 In Returning and Rest You Will Be Saved

YOU SHALL BE SAVED. CAESARIUS OF ARLES: Let us, then, devoutly think over these truths, dearest brothers, while it is still within our power to do so with the help of God. As we shudder at the wounds of our sins as at deadly poisons, let us apply ourselves to almsgiving, prayer and fasting. Above all, by a charity that loves not only friends but even enemies, let us have recourse to the mercy of that heavenly Physician to recover the health of our souls as if by spiritual remedies. For he himself said, "I take no pleasure in the death of the sinner, but rather in the wicked man's conversion, that he may live";[10] and again: "When you groan and are converted, you shall be saved." In his goodness may he lead us to this salvation, who together with the Father and the Holy Spirit lives and reigns forever and ever. Amen. SERMON 150.5.[11]

---

[2]FC 23:70*. [3]Jn 10:8. [4]CCL 4:138. [5]The origin of the reading "new book" is uncertain. The Hebrew text and its versions all have simply "book" or "book of precept(s)." [6]FC 68:112-13. [7]NPNF 1 11:127**. [8]Mt 28:13. [9]FC 64:40-41. [10]Ezek 18:32. [11]FC 47:326-27*.

THE POWER OF REPENTANCE. CYRIL OF JERUSALEM: Would you know the power of repentance? Would you understand this strong weapon of salvation and the might of confession? By confession Hezekiah routed 185,000 of the enemy.[12] That was important, but it was little compared to what shall be told. The same king's repentance won the repeal of the sentence God had passed on him. For when he was sick, Isaiah said to him, "Give charge concerning your house, for you shall die, and not live."[13] What expectation was left? What hope of recovery was there when the prophet said, "For you shall die"? But Hezekiah did not cease from penitence, for he remembered what was written: "In the hour that you turn and lament, you shall be saved." He turned his face to the wall, and from his bed of pain his mind soared up to heaven—for no wall is so thick as to stifle reverent prayer—"Lord," he said, "remember me."[14] "For it is sufficient for my healing if you remember me. You are not subject to circumstances but are yourself the legislator of life. For not on birth and conjunction of stars, as some vainly say, does our life depend. No, you are the arbiter, according to your will, of life and the duration of life." He whom the prophet's sentence had forbidden to hope was granted fifteen further years of life, the sun turning back its course in witness thereof. Now while the sun retraced its course for Hezekiah, for Christ it was eclipsed, the distinction marking the difference between the two, I mean Hezekiah and Jesus. Now if even Hezekiah could revoke God's decree, shall not Jesus grant the remission of sins? Turn and lament, shut your door and beg for pardon, that God may remove from you the scorching flames. For confession has the power to quench even fire; it can tame even lions. CATECHETICAL LECTURES 2.15.[15]

DISCIPLINE PREVENTS CONDEMNATION. FULGENTIUS OF RUSPE: So useful are trials for Christians that through them, our spirit becomes a sacrifice to God. For it is written in the psalm: "The sacrifice acceptable to God is a broken spirit; a broken and contrite heart, O God, you will not despise."[16] Enlightened by this and innumerable other texts of this type, let us hasten as rapidly as possible to be converted to God absolutely.... Converted, let us never despair of the forgiveness of sins, holding on to the faithful promise of the Lord who says, "In returning and rest, you will be saved." Let us put up with the pressures and trials of the present time with patient courage, and let us never depart from the fear of the Lord. For the apostle commands us to "endure in affliction."[17] He bears witness that the correction of the present time is of great avail to us for avoiding the punishment of the future judgment, saying, "But since we are being judged by the Lord, we are being disciplined so that we may not be condemned along with the world."[18] LETTER 7.20-21.[19]

NEVER TOO LATE TO REPENT. JEROME: It is never too late to repent. You may have gone down from Jerusalem and may have been wounded on the way; yet the Samaritan will set you upon his beast and will bring you to the inn and will take care of you.[20] Even if you are lying in your grave, the Lord will raise you though your flesh may stink.[21] At least imitate those blind men for whose sake the Savior left his home and heritage and came to Jericho. They were sitting in darkness and in the shadow of death when the light shone upon them.[22] For when they learned that it was the Lord who was passing by, they began to cry out, saying, "You son of David, have mercy on us."[23] You too will have your sight restored, if you cry to him and cast away your filthy garments at his call.[24] "When you shall turn and repent then shall you be saved, and then shall you know where you have been." LETTER 147.9.[25]

HE WILL PARDON THE PENITENT. PACIAN OF

[12]2 Kings 19:35. [13]2 Kings 20:1. [14]2 Kings 20:2. [15]FC 61:104-5*. [16]Ps 51:17 (50:19 LXX). [17]Rom 12:12. [18]1 Cor 11:32. [19]FC 95:364-65. [20]Lk 10:30-34. [21]Jn 11:39-44. [22]Lk 1:79. [23]Mt 9:27. [24]Mk 10:50. [25]NPNF 2 6:293*.

BARCELONA: The Apocalypse also threatens the seven churches unless they should repent. Nor would he, indeed, threaten the impenitent unless he pardoned the penitent. God himself also says, "Remember then from where you have fallen, and repent."[26] And again, "When, having returned, you shall mourn, then shall you be saved and know where you have been." Let no one so despair of the vileness of a sinful soul that he believe that God has no need for him anymore. The Lord wishes that not one of us should perish. Even those of little worth and the humblest are sought after. If you do not believe it, consider this. Behold, in the Gospel the single piece of silver is sought after, and when [it is] found [it] is shown to the neighbors.[27] The little sheep, although it has to be carried back on his supporting shoulders, is not burdensome to the shepherd.[28] Over a single sinner who repents, the angels in heaven rejoice and the celestial choir exults. Come then, you sinner. Do not cease your entreaties. You see where there is rejoicing over your return! ON PENITENTS 12.3.[29]

30:17 A Thousand Fleeing at the Threat of One

A THOUSAND SHALL FLEE. JEROME: When Moses fought against Amalek, it was not with the sword but with prayer that he prevailed.[30] Therefore, if we wish to be lifted up, we must first prostrate ourselves. . . . We do not understand the prophet's words: "One thousand shall flee at the rebuke of one." We do not cut away the causes of the disease, as we must do to remove the disease itself. Else we should soon see the enemies' arrows give way to our javelins, their caps to our helmets, their saddle horses to our chargers. LETTER 60.17.[31]

---

[26]Rev 2:5. [27]See Lk 15:8-9. [28]See Lk 15:4-7. [29]FC 99:86*. [30]Ex 17:11. [31]NPNF 2 6:130*.

30:18-33 HOPE FOR THE AFFLICTED

[18]*Therefore the* LORD *waits to be gracious to you;*
   therefore he exalts himself to show mercy to you.
For the LORD *is a God of justice;*
   blessed are all those who wait for him.
[19]*Yea, O people in Zion who dwell at Jerusalem; you shall weep no more. He will surely be gracious to you at the sound of your cry; when he hears it, he will answer you.* [20]*And though the Lord give you the bread of adversity and the water of affliction, yet your Teacher will not hide himself any more, but your eyes shall see your Teacher.* [21]*And your ears shall hear a word behind you, saying, "This is the way, walk in it," when you turn to the right or when you turn to the left.* [22]*Then you will defile your silver-covered graven images and your gold-plated molten images. You will scatter them as unclean things; you will say to them, "Begone!"*

---

²³*And he will give rain for the seed with which you sow the ground, and grain, the produce of the ground, which will be rich and plenteous. In that day your cattle will graze in large pastures;* ²⁴*and the oxen and the asses that till the ground will eat salted provender, which has been winnowed with shovel and fork.* ²⁵*And upon every lofty mountain and every high hill there will be brooks running with water, in the day of the great slaughter, when the towers fall.* ²⁶*Moreover the light of the moon will be as the light of the sun, and the light of the sun will be sevenfold, as the light of seven days, in the day when the* LORD *binds up the hurt of his people, and heals the wounds inflicted by his blow.*

²⁷*Behold, the name of the* LORD *comes from far,*
   burning with his anger, and in thick rising smoke;
his lips are full of indignation,
   and his tongue is like a devouring fire;
²⁸*his breath is like an overflowing stream*
   that reaches up to the neck;
to sift the nations with the sieve of destruction,
   and to place on the jaws of the peoples a bridle that leads astray.

²⁹*You shall have a song as in the night when a holy feast is kept; and gladness of heart, as when one sets out to the sound of the flute to go to the mountain of the* LORD, *to the Rock of Israel.* ³⁰*And the* LORD *will cause his majestic voice to be heard and the descending blow of his arm to be seen, in furious anger and a flame of devouring fire, with a cloudburst and tempest and hailstones.* ³¹*The Assyrians will be terror-stricken at the voice of the* LORD, *when he smites with his rod.* ³²*And every stroke of the staff of punishment which the* LORD *lays upon them will be to the sound of timbrels and lyres; battling with brandished arm he will fight with them.* ³³*For a burning place*^t *has long been prepared; yea, for the king*^u *it is made ready, its pyre made deep and wide, with fire and wood in abundance; the breath of the* LORD, *like a stream of brimstone, kindles it.*

t Or *Topheth*   u Or *Molech*

OVERVIEW: God calls, invites and waits on us. God shows the way of salvation to those who are straying. The grace of God and free will are in harmony with one another. Those who know the divine law will be blessed (JOHN CASSIAN). Even when we reject his words, God still calls us and waits on us (GREGORY THE GREAT). Our way is guided by meditating on the Word of God (JOHN CASSIAN). God calls us back to himself and offers us forgiveness when we sin (GREGORY THE GREAT). The Holy Spirit will rain down and germinate the seed of the saving Word we have heard. Isaiah proclaims that God's creation is blessed (JOHN CASSIAN). Isaiah describes the glory of the future life (BEDE).

30:18 The Lord Waits to Have Grace on You

HE WAITS FOR US. JOHN CASSIAN: For he calls and invites us, when he says, "All the day long I stretched forth my hands to a disobedient and gainsaying people";[1] and he is invited by us when we say to him, "All the day long I have stretched forth my hands unto you."[2] He waits for us, when it is said by the prophet, "Therefore the Lord waits to have compassion upon us"; and he is waited for by us, when we say, "I waited patiently for the Lord, and he inclined to me," and "I have waited for your salvation, O Lord."[3] Conference 13.12.[4]

30:19 He Will Answer Your Cry

God's Providence Goes Before Us. John Cassian: The divine protection, then, is always inseparably present to us, and so great is the love of the Creator for his creature that his providence not only stands by it but even goes constantly before it. The prophet, who has experienced this, confesses it very clearly when he says, "My God will go before me with his mercy."[5] When he notices good will making an appearance in us, at once he enlightens and encourages it and spurs it on to salvation, giving increase to what he himself planted and saw arise from our own efforts. For, he says, "before they cry, I will hear them. I will hear them when they are still speaking."[6] And again: "As soon as he hears the voice of your cry, he will respond to you." Not only does he graciously inspire holy desires, but also he arranges favorable moments in one's life and the possibility of good results, and he shows the way of salvation to those who are straying. Conference 13.8.3-4.[7]

Grace and Free Will Are in Harmony. John Cassian: These two then, namely, the grace of God and free will, seem opposed to each other but really are in harmony. And we gather from the system of goodness that we ought to have both alike, lest if we withdraw one of them from man, we may seem to have broken the rule of the church's faith. For when God sees us inclined to will what is good, he meets, guides. and strengthens us. For "at the voice of your cry, as soon as he shall hear, he will answer you"; and

"Call upon me," he said, "in the day of tribulation, and I will deliver you, and you shall glorify me."[8] And again, if he finds that we are unwilling or have grown cold, he stirs our hearts with salutary exhortations, by which a good will is either renewed or formed in us. Conference 13.11.[9]

30:20 You Will See Your Teachers

Unceasing Meditation. John Cassian: "Let waters from your own fountain flow in abundance for you, but let your waters pass through into your streets."[10] And according to the prophet Isaiah, "You shall be like a watered garden and like a fountain of water whose waters shall not fail. And the places that have been desolate for ages shall be built in you; you shall raise up the foundations of generation and generation; and you shall be called the repairer of the fences, turning the paths into rest."[11] And that blessedness shall come upon you which the same prophet promises: "And the Lord will not cause your teacher to flee away from you any more, and your eyes shall see your teacher. And your ears shall hear the word of one admonishing you behind your back. This is the way, walk in it, and go not aside either to the right hand or to the left." And so it will come to pass that not only every purpose and thought of our heart but also all the wanderings and rovings of your imagination will become to you a holy and unceasing pondering of the divine law. Conference 14.13.[12]

He Waits for Us. Gregory the Great: He has seen us sinning and has borne with it. He who forbade us to sin before we did it does not stop waiting to pardon us even after we have sinned. The one we have rejected is calling us. We have turned away from him, but he has not turned away. Hence Isaiah said, "Your eyes shall

---

[1]Rom 10:21. [2]Ps 88:9 (87:10 LXX). [3]Ps 40:2 (39:2 LXX); 119:166 (118:166 LXX). [4]CSEL 13:382. [5]Ps 58:11 LXX. [6]Is 65:24. [7]ACW 57:474. [8]Ps 50:15 (49:15 LXX). [9]CSEL 13:77. [10]Prov 5:16. [11]Is 58:11-12. [12]CSEL 13:416.

see your teacher, and your ears shall hear the voice of a counselor behind you." A person is counseled to his face, so to speak, when he is created for righteousness and receives the precepts of rectitude. When he despises these precepts, it is as if he is turning his back to his Creator's face. But he still follows behind us and counsels us that we have despised him, but he still does not cease to call us. We turn our backs on his face, so to speak, when we reject his words, when we trample his commandments under foot; but he who sees that we reject him still calls out to us by his commandments and waits for us by his patience, stands behind us, and calls us back when we have turned away. FORTY GOSPEL HOMILIES 34.[13]

30:21 This Is the Way, Walk in It

A WORD BEHIND YOU. JOHN CASSIAN: If, then, such matters are carefully received, if they are hidden and consigned within the quiet places of the mind, if they are marked in silence, they will later be like a wine of sweet aroma bringing gladness to the human heart. Matured by long reflection and by patience, they will be poured out as a great fragrance from the vessel of your heart. Like some everlasting spring they will flow out from the channels of experience and from the flowing waters of virtue. They will come bounding forth, running, unceasing, from, as it were, the abyss of your heart. . . . And, as the prophet Isaiah declares, "You will be like a well-watered garden, like a flowing spring whose waters will never fail. And places emptied for ages will be built up in you. You will lift up the foundations laid by generation after generation. You will be called the builder of fences, the one who turns the pathways toward peace."[14] That blessing promised by the prophet will come to you: "And the Lord will not cause your teacher to fly far away from you, and your eyes will look upon your guide. And your ears shall hear the word of warning from behind, 'This is the path. Walk along it and turn neither to the right nor to the left.'" CONFERENCE 14.13.[15]

YOUR EARS SHALL HEAR. GREGORY THE GREAT: God opens the bosom of his loving kindness to us if we return to him after sinning, for he says by the prophet, "If a man puts away his wife, and she goes from him and marries another man, shall he return to her any more? Shall not that woman be polluted and defiled? But you have prostituted yourself to many lovers; nevertheless return to me, says the Lord."[16] Note how the plea of justice is proposed in regard to the wife who commits fornication and is deserted, and yet, for us who return after our fall, it is not justice but loving kindness that is shown. The inference is obvious, namely, that if our sins are spared with such great love, how great would be our wickedness if we sinned but failed to return after our sin, and what pardon can the wicked expect from him who does not cease to call them after they have sinned! This mercy of God in calling us after our sin is well expressed by the prophet, when it is said to him who turns away from him: "And your eyes shall see your teacher, and you ears shall hear the word of one admonishing you behind your back." PASTORAL CARE 3.28.[17]

THE VOICE OF A COUNSELOR. GREGORY THE GREAT: We are truly repentant if we weep bitterly over the actions we have committed. Let us consider the riches of our Creator's attitude toward us. He has seen us sinning, and has borne with it. He who forbade us to sin before we did it, does not stop waiting to pardon us even after we have sinned. The one we have rejected is calling us. We have turned away from him, but he has not turned away. Hence Isaiah said, "Your eyes shall see your Teacher, and your ears shall hear the voice of a Counselor behind you." A person is counseled to his face, so to speak, when he is created for righteousness and receives the precepts of rectitude. When he despises these precepts, it is as if he is turning his back to his Creator's face. But he still follows behind us, and counsels us that we have despised him but that he still does

---

[13]CS 123:296. [14]Is 58:11-12. [15]JCC 168*. [16]Jer 3:1. [17]ACW 11:194*.

not cease to call us. We turn our backs on his face, so to speak, when we reject his words, when we trample his commandments under foot; but he who sees that we reject him, and still calls out to us by his commandments, and waits for us by his patience, stands behind us, and calls us back when we have turned away. FORTY GOSPEL HOMILIES 34.17.[18]

30:23 He Will Give Rain

SEED. JOHN CASSIAN: For "in a good heart wisdom will rest," and "he that fears the Lord shall find knowledge with righteousness."[19] But that we must attain to spiritual knowledge in the order of which we have already spoken, we are taught also by the blessed apostle. For when he wanted not merely to draw up a list of all his own virtues but rather to describe their order, that he might explain which follows what, and which gives birth to what, after some others he proceeds as follows: "In watchings, in fastings, in chastity, in knowledge, in long suffering, in gentleness, in the Holy Spirit, in love unfeigned."[20] And by this enumeration of virtues he evidently meant to teach us that we must come from watchings and fastings to chastity, from chastity to knowledge, from knowledge to long suffering, from long suffering to gentleness, from gentleness to the Holy Spirit, from the Holy Spirit to the rewards of love unfeigned. When then by this system and in this order you too have come to spiritual knowledge, you will certainly have, as we said, not barren or idle learning but what is vigorous and fruitful. And the seed of the word of salvation that has been committed by you to the hearts of your hearers will be watered by the plentiful showers of the Holy Spirit that will follow. And according to this the prophet promised, "The rain will be given to your seed, wherever you shall sow in the land, and the bread of the corn of the land shall be most plentiful and fat." CONFERENCE 14.16.[21]

30:26 The Light of the Moon

AS THE LIGHT OF THE SUN. JOHN CASSIAN: Does not Scripture say universally of all the things that were created by God, "Behold, everything that God made was very good"?[22] . . . The things that belong to the present, then, are not declared good in a merely minimal sense but are emphatically "very good." For, in fact, they are useful for us while we are living in this world, whether to sustain life or as medicine for the body or on account of some benefit unknown to us. Or else they are very good in that they let us "see the invisible things of God, his eternal power and his divinity, from the creation of the world, through things that have been made graspable"[23]—that is, from the great and well-ordered construction and arrangement of the world—and let us contemplate them from the existence of everything that is in it. Yet all of these will be unable to maintain their title to goodness if they are compared with the future age, where no mutability in good things and no corruption of true blessedness is to be feared. The blessedness of this world is described as follows: "The light of the moon shall be as the light of the sun, and the light of the sun shall be sevenfold, as the light of seven days." The things that are great, then, and splendid and marvelous to behold will immediately seem empty if they are compared with the future promises in faith. CONFERENCE 23.3.2-4.[24]

THE GLORY OF THE FUTURE LIFE. BEDE: Moreover, when the day of judgment has been completed and the glory of the future life has become evident with the new heaven and the new earth, then will come to pass what the same prophet announced elsewhere: "The light of the moon will be as the light of the sun, and the light of the sun will be increased sevenfold, like the light of seven days." EXPOSITION OF THE GOSPEL OF MARK 4.13.24.[25]

---

[18]CS 123:296. [19]Prov 14:33; Eccl 32:20. [20]2 Cor 6:5-6. [21]CSEL 13:420-21. [22]Gen 1:31. [23]Rom 1:20. [24]ACW 57:792. [25]CCL 120:600.

IN REMEMBRANCE OF HEAVENLY LIFE. BEDE: Why should the lunar reckoning be calculated from the noontide hours, seeing that the moon had not yet been placed in the heavens or gone forth over the earth? On the contrary, none of the feast days of the law began and ended at noon or in the afternoon, but all did so in the evening. Or else perchance it is because sinful Adam was reproached by the Lord "in the cool of the afternoon"[26] and thrust out from the joys of Paradise. In remembrance of that heavenly life which we changed for the tribulation of this world, the change of the moon, which imitates our toil by its everlasting waxing and waning, ought specifically to be observed at the hour in which we began our exile. In this way every day we may be reminded by the hour of the moon's changing of that verse, "a fool changes as the moon"[27] while the wise man "shall live as long as the sun,"[28] and that we may sigh more ardently for that life, supremely blessed in eternal peace, when "the light of the moon shall be as the light of the sun, and the light of the sun shall be sevenfold, as the light of seven days." Indeed, because (as it is written) "from the moon is the sign of the feast day,"[29] and just as the first light of the moon was shed upon the world at eventide, so in the law it is compulsory that every feast day begin in the evening and end in the evening.[30] THE RECKONING OF TIME 3.43.[31]

A NEW HEAVEN AND A NEW EARTH. BEDE: But when there will be a new heaven and a new earth after the judgment—which is not one heaven and earth replacing another but these very same ones which will shine forth, having been renewed by fire and glorified by the power of the resurrection—then, as Isaiah predicts, "The light of the moon will be as the light of the sun, and the light of the sun will be sevenfold, as the light of seven days." THE RECKONING OF TIME 6.70.[32]

---

[26]Gen 3:8. [27]Sir 27:11. [28]Ps 72:5 (71:5 LXX). [29]Sir 43:7. [30]See Ex 12:18. [31]TTH 29:116*; CCL 123B:413-14. [32]TTH 29:244; CCL 123B:540.

31:1-9 WARNING TO GOD'S ENEMIES

¹Woe to those who go down to Egypt for help
and rely on horses,
who trust in chariots because they are many
and in horsemen because they are very
strong,
but do not look to the Holy One of Israel
or consult the LORD!
²And yet he is wise and brings disaster,
he does not call back his words,
but will arise against the house of the
evildoers,
and against the helpers of those who
work iniquity.
³The Egyptians are men, and not God;
and their horses are flesh, and not spirit.
When the LORD stretches out his
hand,
the helper will stumble, and he who is
helped will fall,
and they will all perish together.

⁴For thus the Lord said to me,
As a lion or a young lion growls over his
prey,
and when a band of shepherds is called
forth against him
is not terrified by their shouting
or daunted at their noise,
so the Lord of hosts will come down
to fight upon Mount Zion and upon its
hill.
⁵Like birds hovering, so the Lord of hosts
will protect Jerusalem;
he will protect and deliver it,
he will spare and rescue it.

⁶Turn to him from whom youᵛ have deeply

revolted, O people of Israel. ⁷For in that day
every one shall cast away his idols of silver and
his idols of gold, which your hands have sin-
fully made for you.
⁸"And the Assyrian shall fall by a sword,
not of man;
and a sword, not of man, shall devour
him;
and he shall flee from the sword,
and his young men shall be put to forced
labor.
⁹His rock shall pass away in terror,
and his officers desert the standard in
panic,"
says the Lord, whose fire is in Zion,
and whose furnace is in Jerusalem.*

v Heb the   *LXX Blessed is he who has seed in Zion, and kindred in Jerusalem

OVERVIEW: While it is not wrong to go to Egypt, it is wrong to change to the ways of the Egyptians (AMBROSE). If we repent and return to God, he will forgive us (JEROME). The furnaces symbolize hearts that were made to burn with love (BEDE, GREGORY THE GREAT). The seed of love that is planted in the heart brings forth salvation (JOHN OF DAMASCUS).

31:1 Woe to Those Who Go to Egypt for Help

DOWN TO EGYPT. AMBROSE: Let our course take us to regions above, because it is better to ascend. Finally, as was read today, "Woe to them that go down to Egypt." Surely it is not wrong to go to Egypt, but to change to the ways of the Egyptians, to change to the violence of their treachery and to the ugliness of their wantonness—this is wrong. He that changes in this way descends, and one who descends falls. Let us keep away, then, from the Egyptian who is a man, but [let us] not [keep away] from God. Even the king of Egypt himself fell under the dominion of his own vices

and in comparison with him Moses was accounted a god, ruling over kingdoms and sub-jecting powers to himself. So we read that it was said to Moses: "I shall make you a god to Pha-raoh."[1] LETTER 81 (1.6.7).[2]

31:6 Return to God

RETURN. JEROME: In place of the last clause ["But you have played the harlot with many lov-ers; yet return again to me, says the Lord."] the true Hebrew text (which is not preserved in the Greek and Latin versions) gives the following: "you have forsaken me, yet return, and I will receive you, says the Lord."[3] Isaiah also speaking in the same sense uses almost the same words: "Return," he cries, "O children of Israel, you who devise a deep and sinful counsel. Return to me, and I will redeem you. I am God, and there is no God else beside me; a just God and a Savior; there is nothing beside me. Look to me, and be saved, all the ends of the earth."[4] Remember this

¹Ex 7:1. ²FC 26:457-58*. ³Jer 3:1. ⁴Is 45:21-22.

and show yourselves men: bring it again to mind, O you transgressors. Return in heart and remember the former things of old: for I am God and there is none else."[5] LETTER 122.2.[6]

31:9 *His Furnace Is in Jerusalem*

GOD'S FURNACE. BEDE: If the breads of the furnace[7] that were baked in secret signify the interior devotion of the mind of the faithful confirmed by the fire of charity, breads which were also commanded by the law to be offered in the sacrifice of the Lord,[8] it is most fitting that the hearts which were made to burn constantly with the flame of intimate love and virtue and to beget words are symbolized through the furnaces in which the same breads were baked. The prophet spoke beautifully about these things when he referred to "the Lord whose fire is in Zion and whose furnace is in Jerusalem." It is also written: "Did our hearts not burn within us when he spoke along the way and opened the Scriptures to us?"[9] THREE BOOKS ON EZRA AND NEHEMIAH 3.[10]

FIERY LOVE FOR GOD. GREGORY THE GREAT: Of this love that is begun here to be perfected from the sight of the Lord in the eternal kingdom Isaiah rightly speaks, saying, "The Lord lives, whose fire is in Zion, and his furnace in Jerusalem." It is, however, greater to be a furnace than a fire because a fire can also be small, but a larger flame is kindled in a furnace. Zion truly is said to be speculation but Jerusalem the vision of peace. Truly we sometimes catch a glimpse of our peace here in order there later to see it fully. Therefore through the Lord's love the fire is in Zion and his furnace in Jerusalem because here we burn in some measure with the flames of his love when we glimpse him, but there we shall burn totally when we shall fully see him whom we love. HOMILIES ON EZEKIEL 2.9.10.[11]

A SEED IN ZION. JOHN OF DAMASCUS: The prescription of the law must be taken in the more spiritual sense. For there is a spiritual seed which through charity and the fear of God is conceived in the womb of the soul, which in turn travails and brings forth the spirit of salvation. It is in this sense that the passage is to be taken which reads, "Blessed is he who has seed in Zion and kindred in Jerusalem." What, indeed! Even though one is a fornicator, a drunkard or an idolater, will he be blessed, provided only that he has seed in Zion and kindred in Jerusalem? No one in his right mind would say that. ORTHODOX FAITH 4.24.[12]

---

[5]Is 46:8-9. [6]CSEL 56:62. [7]See Neh 12:37 (LXX 12:38). [8]See Lev 2:4. [9]Lk 24:32. [10]CCL 119A:382-83. [11]HGE 264-65. [12]FC 37:395-96*.

32:1-20 THE COMING AGE OF TRUE JOY

[1]*Behold, a king will reign in righteousness,*
    and princes will rule in justice.
[2]*Each will be like a hiding place from the wind,*
        a covert from the tempest,
    like streams of water in a dry place,
        like the shade of a great rock in a weary land.

³Then the eyes of those who see will not be
closed,
and the ears of those who hear will
hearken.
⁴The mind of the rash will have good
judgment,
and the tongue of the stammerers will
speak readily and distinctly.
⁵The fool will no more be called noble,
nor the knave said to be honorable.
⁶For the fool speaks folly,
and his mind plots iniquity:
to practice ungodliness,
to utter error concerning the LORD,
to leave the craving of the hungry
unsatisfied,
and to deprive the thirsty of drink.
⁷The knaveries of the knave are evil;
he devises wicked devices
to ruin the poor with lying words,
even when the plea of the needy is
right.
⁸But he who is noble devises noble
things,
and by noble things he stands.

⁹Rise up, you women who are at ease, hear
my voice;
you complacent daughters, give ear to my
speech.
¹⁰In little more than a year
you will shudder, you complacent
women;
for the vintage will fail,
the fruit harvest will not come.
¹¹Tremble, you women who are at ease,
shudder, you complacent ones;

strip, and make yourselves bare,
and gird sackcloth upon your loins.
¹²Beat upon your breasts for the pleasant
fields,
for the fruitful vine,
¹³for the soil of my people
growing up in thorns and briers;
yea, for all the joyous houses
in the joyful city.
¹⁴For the palace will be forsaken,
the populous city deserted;
the hill and the watchtower
will become dens for ever,
a joy of wild asses,
a pasture of flocks;
¹⁵until the Spirit is poured upon us from on
high,
and the wilderness becomes a fruitful
field,
and the fruitful field is deemed a
forest.
¹⁶Then justice will dwell in the wilderness,
and righteousness abide in the fruitful
field.
¹⁷And the effect of righteousness will be
peace,
and the result of righteousness, quietness
and trust for ever.
¹⁸My people will abide in a peaceful
habitation,
in secure dwellings, and in quiet resting
places.
¹⁹And the forest will utterly go down,ʷ
and the city will be utterly laid low.
²⁰Happy are you who sow beside all waters,
who let the feet of the ox and the ass
range free.

w Cn: Heb *And it will hail when the forest comes down*

224

OVERVIEW: Our opponents accuse us of confessing a novel idea (CYRIL OF ALEXANDRIA). We should apply wise counsel to our deliberations (CLEMENT OF ALEXANDRIA). The house of joy is the mind of the wicked, which does not consider the coming judgment. Silence is the sign of a righteous mind. Fools consider the reprimand of the wise to be nothing (GREGORY THE GREAT). The Christian is to accept the Old and the New Testaments (AMBROSE). Jews and Gentiles are gathered into one faith (CLEMENT OF ALEXANDRIA). Water represents the mind of the good person who follows the preaching of the faith (GREGORY THE GREAT). The person who preaches the gospel is blessed (GREGORY OF NAZIANZUS). Christians are content with the simple gospel (JEROME).

32:6 Speaking Folly, Plotting Iniquity

THE FOOL SPEAKS FOLLY. CYRIL OF ALEXANDRIA: And they [our opponents] even joined in censuring us, as if we thought the opposite to the things that we have already written. But I learn that they say this also, namely, that recently we have accepted a doctrinal statement, or a new creed, perhaps, I suppose, because we lightly esteem the ancient and august one. "The fool will say foolish things, and his heart will think nonsense." However, we say this, that no individuals have demanded an explanation from us, nor have we accepted one newly coined by others. For the divinely inspired Scripture and the vigilance of our holy Fathers and the creed formulated by those who are in every way orthodox are sufficient for us. LETTER 40.7.[1]

32:8 Godly Counsel Shall Stand

WISE DELIBERATION. CLEMENT OF ALEXANDRIA: Abraham is the more praiseworthy in that "he went as the Lord told him."[2]

It was from here that one of the wise men of Greece drew the simple saying "Follow God."[3] . . . Deliberation is an investigation of the right

means to pursue in present circumstances. Wise deliberation is the application of practical wisdom to deliberations. Well? Does God, after Cain's forgiveness, consequently introduce the repentance of Enoch in demonstration that forgiveness naturally breeds repentance?[4] Pardon is not constituted for remission of penalty but for cure. STROMATEIS 2.15.69-70.[5]

32:13 Thorns and Briers

ABANDONED TO SINFUL HABITS. GREGORY THE GREAT: If those very persons, who amid the darkness of the present life shine bright by virtuous attainments—if they also cannot be void of contagion, with what guilt of wickedness are those bound, who still live after the flesh? If those persons cannot be free from sin who are already walking in the way of heavenly desires, what about those who still lie under the loads of sinful habits, who, abandoned to the gratifications of their fleshly part, still bear the yoke of rottenness? So Peter says, "And if the righteous scarcely be saved, where shall the ungodly and the sinner appear?"[6] And it is said by Isaiah, "Upon the land of my people shall come up thorns and briars; how much more upon all the houses of joy in the joyous city." The "house of joy in the joyous city" is the mind of the wicked, which neglects to regard the punishments that are destined to come, in the gratification of the flesh, and going away from itself, it revels in empty mirth. MORALS ON THE BOOK OF JOB 4.17.23.[7]

32:17 Works of Righteousness Shall Be Peace

THE SERVICE OF JUSTICE. GREGORY THE GREAT: One addicted to much speaking fails entirely to keep on the straight path of righteousness, so the prophet testifies, saying . . .

---

[1]FC 76:157. [2]Gen 12:4. [3]Pythagoras. Clement assumes the Greek philosophers whom he admires had read the Scriptures and drawn their thoughts from them. [4]Gen 5:24. [5]FC 85:205*. [6]1 Pet 4:18. [7]LF 21:295**.

"The service of justice shall be quietness," that is, he indicates that the righteousness of the mind is lacking where there is not restraint on immoderate speaking. MORALS ON THE BOOK OF JOB 2.7.58.[8]

THE CALL TO SILENCE. GREGORY THE GREAT: It is the practice of the impertinent ever to answer by the opposite to what is said rightly, lest if they assent to the things asserted, they should seem inferior. . . . When wisdom reprimands sins by the mouth of the righteous, it sounds like superfluity of talkativeness to the ears of the foolish. For assertive people deem nothing right except what they themselves think, and they consider the words of the righteous to be idle to the degree that they find them to be different from their own notions. . . . As long as any one lets himself go in words, the gravity of silence being gone, he parts with the safekeeping of the soul. For this reason it is written, "And the work of righteousness, silence." So Solomon says, "He who has no rule over his own spirit in talking is like a city that is broken down and without walls."[9] And he says again, "In the multitude of words sin is not lacking."[10] . . . the value of a true sentence is lost when it is not delivered under the keeping of discretion. . . . A true sentence against the wicked, if it is aimed at the virtue of the good, loses its own virtue and bounds back with blunted point. . . . But the wicked cannot hear good words with patience, and, neglecting to amend their life, they brace themselves up with words of rejoinder. MORALS ON THE BOOK OF JOB 2.10.2.[11]

32:20 Where the Ox and Donkey Tread

THEY THAT SOW BY EVERY WATER. AMBROSE: Accordingly, like a perfect man learned in the law and made firm in the gospel, accept the faith of both Testaments, for, as we read today, "Blessed is he who sows upon every water, where the ox and the donkey tread," that is, who sows upon the people who follow the teaching of both Testaments. This is the ploughman's ox, wearing the yoke of the law, of which the law says, "You shall not muzzle the ox that treads out your corn,"[12] for this ox has the horns of holy Scripture. But in the Gospel the Lord, representing the people of the Gentiles, mounts the colt of a donkey.[13] LETTER 68 (9.64.9).[14]

OX AND DONKEY. CLEMENT OF ALEXANDRIA: The prophet says, "Blessed is he that sows into all waters, whose ox and donkey tread," [that is] the people, from the law and from the Gentiles, gathered into one faith. STROMATEIS 6.1.1.[15]

THE WATERS ARE PEOPLES. GREGORY THE GREAT: By water, peoples are denoted, as it is said by John, "Now the waters are peoples."[16] By water likewise, not only the tide of peoples drifting away, but also the minds of good men who follow the preachings of faith are denoted, as the prophet says, "Blessed are you who sow upon all waters." And it is said by the psalmist, "The voice of the Lord is upon the waters."[17] MORALS ON THE BOOK OF JOB 19.6.[18]

THE WORD OF PREACHING. GREGORY THE GREAT: What else is meant by "seed" but the word of preaching? It is as the truth says in the Gospel, "A sower went forth to sow";[19] and the prophet says, "Blessed are you who sow upon all waters." What else but the church ought to be understood by the threshing floor? Of this it is said by the voice of the forerunner: "And he will thoroughly purge his floor."[20] MORALS ON THE BOOK OF JOB 6.31.9.[21]

BLESSED ARE THEY. GREGORY OF NAZIANZUS: Only let us not be condemned for frivolity by asking for little, and for what is unworthy of the giver. Blessed is he from whom Jesus asks drink,

---

[8]CCL 143:378; LF 18:411**. [9]Prov 25:28 Vg. [10]Prov 10:19. [11]CCL 143:534-35; LF 18:575-76**. [12]Deut 25:4. [13]Lk 19:30-37. [14]FC 26:409*. [15]ANF 2:480*. [16]Rev 17:15. [17]Ps 29:3. [18]LF 21:400*. [19]Mt 13:3. [20]Mt 3:12. [21]LF 31:431*.

as he did from that Samaritan woman, and gives a well of water springing up unto eternal life.[22] Blessed is he that sows beside all waters, and upon every soul, tomorrow to be ploughed and watered, which today the ox and the donkey tread, while it is dry and without water, and oppressed with lack of rationality. And blessed is he who, though he be a "valley of rushes,"[23] is watered out of the house of the Lord; for he is made fruit-bearing instead of rush-bearing and produces that which is for the food of man, not that which is rough and unprofitable. And for the sake of this we must be very careful not to miss the grace. ON HOLY BAPTISM, ORATION 40.27.[24]

WHERE THE DONKEY TREADS. JEROME: Let them take as much pleasure as they please in their Gallican geldings;[25] we will be satisfied with the simple "donkey" of Zechariah, loosed from its halter and made ready for the Savior's service, which received the Lord on its back and so fulfilled Isaiah's prediction: "Blessed is he that sows beside all waters, where the ox and the donkey tread under foot." LETTER 27.3.[26]

---

[22]Jn 4:7. [23]Joel 3:18. [24]NPNF 2 7:370*. [25]Jerome has in mind the literary fashion of his detractors in elevating by any means the simple humility of the gospel which speaks of Christ riding not a handsome gelding but a humble donkey. [26]NPNF 2 6:44*.

33:1-24 GOD'S VICTORY AND THE RESTORATION OF ZION

[1]Woe to you, destroyer,
    who yourself have not been destroyed;
you treacherous one,
    with whom none has dealt treacherously!
When you have ceased to destroy,
    you will be destroyed;
and when you have made an end of dealing
    treacherously,
    you will be dealt with treacherously.

[2]O LORD, be gracious to us; we wait for
    thee.
    Be our arm every morning,
    our salvation in the time of trouble.
[3]At the thunderous noise peoples flee,
    at the lifting up of thyself nations are
    scattered;
[4]and spoil is gathered as the caterpillar
    gathers;
    as locusts leap, men leap upon it.

[5]The LORD is exalted, for he dwells on
    high;
    he will fill Zion with justice and
    righteousness;
[6]and he will be the stability of your times,
    abundance of salvation, wisdom, and
    knowledge;
    the fear of the LORD is his treasure.*

[7]Behold, the valiant ones[y] cry without;
    the envoys of peace weep bitterly.

⁸The highways lie waste,
   the wayfaring man ceases.
Covenants are broken,
   witnesses[z] are despised,
   there is no regard for man.
⁹The land mourns and languishes;
   Lebanon is confounded and withers
      away;
Sharon is like a desert;
   and Bashan and Carmel shake off their
      leaves.

¹⁰"Now I will arise," says the LORD,
   "now I will lift myself up;
   now I will be exalted.
¹¹You conceive chaff, you bring forth stubble;
   your breath is a fire that will consume
      you.
¹²And the peoples will be as if burned to lime,
   like thorns cut down, that are burned
      in the fire."

¹³Hear, you who are far off, what I have
      done;
   and you who are near, acknowledge my
      might.
¹⁴The sinners in Zion are afraid;
   trembling has seized the godless:
"Who among us can dwell with the
      devouring fire?
   Who among us can dwell with
      everlasting burnings?"[†]
¹⁵He who walks righteously and speaks
      uprightly,
   who despises the gain of oppressions,
who shakes his hands, lest they hold a bribe,
   who stops his ears from hearing of
      bloodshed
   and shuts his eyes from looking upon evil,

¹⁶he will dwell on the heights;
   his place of defense will be the fortresses
      of rocks;
   his bread will be given him, his water
      will be sure.

¹⁷Your eyes will see the king in his beauty;
   they will behold a land that stretches afar.
¹⁸Your mind will muse on the terror:
   "Where is he who counted, where is he
      who weighed the tribute?
   Where is he who counted the towers?"
¹⁹You will see no more the insolent people,
   the people of an obscure speech which you
      cannot comprehend,
   stammering in a tongue which you
      cannot understand.
²⁰Look upon Zion, the city of our appointed
      feasts!
   Your eyes will see Jerusalem,
   a quiet habitation, an immovable tent,
whose stakes will never be plucked up,
   nor will any of its cords be broken.
²¹But there the LORD in majesty will be for
      us
   a place of broad rivers and streams,
where no galley with oars can go,
   nor stately ship can pass.
²²For the LORD is our judge, the LORD is
      our ruler,
   the LORD is our king; he will save us.

²³Your tackle hangs loose;
   it cannot hold the mast firm in its place,
   or keep the sail spread out.

Then prey and spoil in abundance will be
      divided;
   even the lame will take the prey.

*²⁴And no inhabitant will say, "I am
  sick";*

*the people who dwell there will be
  forgiven their iniquity.*

y The meaning of the Hebrew word is uncertain   z One ancient Ms: Heb *cities*   *LXX *They shall be delivered up to the law; our salvation is our treasure; there is wisdom and knowledge and piety toward the Lord; these are treasures of righteousness.*   †LXX *Who can tell you of the eternal place?*

OVERVIEW: Christ is called by many names so that we can learn something about God (CHRYSOSTOM).

We should endure tribulation with the hope of salvation (THEODORE). The riches of our salvation cannot be preserved without the fear of the Lord (JOHN CASSIAN). God gives eternal treasures such as wisdom (LEO THE GREAT). True wealth is possessing the spiritual virtues God gives. The prophets were grieved that Israel would reject their Messiah (BEDE). God gives to us the ability to hear the word and believe (EPISTLE OF BARNABAS).

Abraham's bosom is a temporary place that offers some foresight into what the eternal heaven will be (TERTULLIAN). God is a living fire who purifies (VERECUNDUS). Christians should demand neither payment nor human favors for their good deeds (GREGORY THE GREAT). Christians should not take bribes (ISIDORE OF SEVILLE). Bread signifies perfection (GREGORY THE GREAT). Whoever cleanses his heart from lies will see God (APHRAHAT).

The pure eyes of the saints will see Christ in his beauty. While the disciples saw Christ coming in his kingdom, the resurrected saints will see him perfectly in his beauty (BEDE). At his second coming Christ will appear in power and glory rather than humility (HIPPOLYTUS). The cave was Christ's tomb, but when he was resurrected he was seen in his beauty (ADAMNAN).

If we meditate on the fear of the Lord, then evil thoughts will diminish (PACHOMIUS). The teachings of the church are plain and simple to understand (GREGORY THE GREAT). God's greatest and most noble act is saving humanity (CLEMENT OF ALEXANDRIA).

33:2 Our Salvation in the Time of Trouble

COUNTLESS NAMES. CHRYSOSTOM: The master of the church has many names: being called the Father, the way,[1] the life,[2] the light,[3] the arm, the propitiation,[4] the foundation,[5] the door,[6] the sinless one,[7] the treasure,[8] Lord, God, Son, the only begotten, the form of God,[9] the image[10] of God. So it is with the church itself. Does one name suffice to present the whole truth? By no means. But for this reason there are countless names, that we may learn something concerning God, though it is but a small part. HOMILY ON EUTROPIUS 2.6.[11]

IN TIME OF TRIBULATION. THEODORE: Then, O beloved, if we have been able to admire that man [Apa], let us not be discouraged by tribulation, for what we endure today is only a small part of what those men[12] endured. "Our salvation [comes] in time of tribulation." INSTRUCTIONS 3.3.[13]

33:6 The Fear of the Lord Is His Treasure

REVERENCE FOR THE LORD. JOHN CASSIAN: It must follow that any one solidly established in the perfection of this love will rise to that more excellent and more sublime stage that is the fear derived from love. This is not a terror in the face of punishment or a desire for reward. Rather it is something that comes from the very greatness of love. It is the mixture of respect and affection that a son has for a very indulgent father, a brother for a brother, a friend for a friend, a wife for a husband. This is the fear whose splendor has been elegantly described by one of the prophets. "Wis-

---

[1]Jn 14:6. [2]Jn 14:6. [3]Jn 1:8-9. [4]1 Jn 2:2. [5]1 Cor 3:11. [6]Jn 10:7. [7]1 Jn 3:5. [8]Cf. Mt 6:21. [9]Phil 2:6. [10]Col 1:15. [11]NPNF 1 9:256**. [12]Joseph, Job, David and others of their kind. [13]CS 47:94.

dom and knowledge are the riches of salvation, but its treasure is the fear of the Lord." He could not have more clearly described the dignity and the merit of this fear when he said that the riches of our salvation, namely, true wisdom and the knowledge of God, cannot be preserved except by the fear of the Lord. This is the fear to which saints, and not sinners, are invited by the prophetic oracles.... Someone holding to this fear of the Lord is certain to lack no perfection. Conference 11.13.[14]

Riches That Cannot Be Lost. Leo the Great: But, since there are many kinds of treasures and different grounds for joy, each one's treasure corresponds to the movement of their desire. If it is an appetite for earthly things, it makes those who share in it not happy but wretched. Those who "savor the things above, not what is on earth,"[15] and are not eager for what perishes but for what is eternal, have hidden, incorruptible resources, in that about which the prophet says, "In your treasure is our salvation. There wisdom and knowledge and holiness are from the Lord. These are the treasures of his justice."

Through them, with God's grace helping us, even earthly goods are transformed into heavenly, as long as many use their wealth, either left them by law or otherwise acquired, as instruments of goodness. When they distribute, from what they can count as overabundance, to the support of the poor, they collect for themselves riches that cannot be lost, so that what they have withdrawn for alms cannot be credited to expense, and they properly keep their heart where they have "their treasure."[16] It is most blessed to use wealth of this kind that it may grow, and not fear lest it be destroyed. Sermon 92.3.[17]

Genuine Wealth. Bede: But "true wealth"[18] signifies either the joy of eternal life itself, concerning which it is written, "the riches of his inheritance in the saints,"[19] or those spiritual virtues with which the fullness of life is attained,

about which Isaiah said, "the riches of salvation, wisdom, and knowledge; the fear of the Lord himself is its treasure."

"And if you are unfaithful with goods that are not yours, who will give you something of your own?"[20] The resources of this world are alien to us, that is, external to the nature of our habitat, "for we brought nothing into this world and we are without doubt unable to take anything from it."[21] Our possession is the kingdom of heaven, our life is Christ, and our wealth consists in the fruitfulness of spiritual works, about which Solomon said, "The redemption of a man's soul is his wealth."[22] Exposition of the Gospel of Luke 5.16.11-12.[23]

33:7 The Angels of Peace Will Weep Bitterly

Weep Bitterly. Bede: But if you want to see that the ancient prophets were terribly sad and aggrieved about the future blinding of their nation, which was the cause of our illumination, listen to Isaiah, for when he was sent to announce beforehand the grace of the Lord's coming, saying that "a light has arisen upon those who dwell in the region of the shadow of death," he responded immediately to the advent of the same light, saying "you have enlarged the nation; you have not increased its joy."[24] And elsewhere, while commemorating the despondency of this people, Isaiah said, among other things, "the messengers of peace will weep bitterly," referring to the prophetic heralds of the divine word. Four Books on 1 Samuel 3.16.1.[25]

33:13 Hearing What God Has Done

They Shall Hear. Epistle of Barnabas: And again he speaks concerning the ears, [meaning] how he circumcised our hearts, for the Lord says in the prophet, "in the hearing of the ear

[14]JCC 152*. [15]Col 3:2. [16]Mt 6:21. [17]FC 93:387-88. [18]Lk 16:11. [19]Eph 1:18. [20]Lk 16:12. [21]1 Tim 6:7. [22]Prov 13:8. [23]CCL 120:299. [24]Is 9:2. [25]CCL 119:138.

they obeyed."[26] And again he says, "They who are far away shall surely hear, they shall know what I have done," and "Be circumcised in your hearts, says the Lord."[27] . . . So, then, he circumcised our ears that we might hear the word and believe. EPISTLE OF BARNABAS 9.[28]

33:14 *The Devouring Fire*

THE ETERNAL PLACE. TERTULLIAN: The Scripture itself . . . expressly distinguishes between Abraham's bosom, where the poor man dwells, and the infernal place of torment. "Hell" (I take it) means one thing, and "Abraham's bosom" another. "A great gulf" is said to separate those regions and to hinder a passage from one to the other.[29] Besides, the rich man could not have "lifted up his eyes,"[30] and from a distance too, except to a superior height, and from the said distance all up through the vast immensity of height and depth. . . . There is some determinate place called Abraham's bosom, and it is designed for the reception of souls of Abraham's children, even from among the Gentiles (since he is "the father of many nations," which must be classed amongst his family), and of the same faith as that with which he himself believed God, without the yoke of the law and the sign of circumcision. This region, therefore, I call Abraham's bosom. Although it is not in heaven, it is yet higher than hell, and it is appointed to afford an interval of rest to the souls of the righteous, until the consummation of all things shall complete the resurrections of all people with the "full recompense of their reward."[31] This consummation will then be manifested in heavenly promises. . . . Amos, however, tells us of "those stories towards heaven"[32] which Christ "builds"—of course for his people. There also is that everlasting abode of which Isaiah asks, "Who shall declare to you the eternal place, but he (that is, of course, Christ) who walks in righteousness, speaks of the straight path, and hates injustice and iniquity?" Now, although this everlasting abode is promised, and the ascending stories (or steps) to heaven are

built by the Creator, who further promises that the seed of Abraham shall be even as the stars of heaven, by virtue certainly of the heavenly promise, why may it not be possible, without any injury to that promise, that by Abraham's bosom is meant some temporary receptacle of faithful souls, wherein is even now delineated an image of the future and where is given some foresight of the glory of both judgments? AGAINST MARCION 4.34.[33]

A FIRE THAT PURIFIES. VERECUNDUS: "He looked upon them, and the nations shook and the mountains quickly scattered."[34] The sight of the Lord shattered what was hardened and melted what was tightly compact, so that the truth expressed by Isaiah might be evident, for God is a living fire who advances to purify, not to kill: "Who among you can dwell with the devouring fire, or who among you can walk with eternal flames?" Whomever he looks upon, therefore, and touches with his warmth, he melts on the spot. Consequently, when he will later look upon the nations with mercy and judge them to be most worthy of redemption through his Christ, immediately their hardness will be shattered. COMMENTARY ON THE CANTICLE OF HABAKKUK 6.5.[35]

33:15 *One Who Walks Righteously*

FREE FROM EVERY GIFT. GREGORY THE GREAT: There are indeed some who do not receive a price in money from an ordination, and yet they bestow holy orders as a human favor and only seek the recompense of praise for it. Undoubtedly these are not granting freely what they have received freely, because they seek payment in esteem for the holy office they have conferred. Hence the prophet, when he was describing the righteous man rightly, said that "he is one who keeps his hands clean of every gift." He did not

[26]Ps 18:44. [27]Jer 4:4. [28]FC 1:204-5. [29]Lk 16:26. [30]Lk 16:23. [31]See Heb 2:2; 10:35; 11:26. [32]Amos 9:6. [33]ANF 3:406. [34]Hab 3:6. [35]CCL 93:129.

say that he is one who keeps his hands free of a gift but added "every," because a gift given from deference is one thing, a gift from the hand another, and a gift from the tongue still another. A gift from deference is submission conferred without being deserved, a gift from the hand is money, a gift from the tongue esteem. Therefore whoever grants holy orders "keeps his hands free from every gift" when he not only demands no money but not even human favors for the sacred gifts. FORTY GOSPEL HOMILIES 17.[36]

THE THREE WAYS OF DECEIT. GREGORY THE GREAT: We must bear in mind also, that there are three ways in which deceit itself is practiced. Its aim is either the secret interest of our fellow creatures' feelings; or the breath of applause; or some outward advantage. Contrary to this, it is rightly said of the righteous man by the prophet: "Blessed is he who shakes his hands clear of every favor." . . . Now every righteous man "shakes his hands clear of every favor" if in whatever he does right, he neither aims to win vainglory from the affections of his fellow creatures, nor applause from their lips, nor a gift from their hands. . . . Therefore, because our very good actions themselves cannot escape the word of ambushed sin unless they are guarded every day by anxious fear, it is rightly said in this place by the holy man, "I was afraid of all my works." MORALS ON THE BOOK OF JOB 2.9.53.[37]

TRUTH VIOLATED. ISIDORE OF SEVILLE: Taking bribes is a violation of the truth. Therefore, it is said of the just man: "He who cleanses his hands of every gift will live on the heights." THREE BOOKS OF THOUGHTS 3.54.3[38]

33:16 Bread Shall Be Given

BREAD FOR THE MATURE. GREGORY THE GREAT: "Bread" signifies perfection, as Paul attested while exhorting the weak to conversion: "I gave you milk to drink, not food, for you were then and still remain unable to eat."[39] If milk is for children, then bread is only for the perfect. Consequently, it was said about the strength of the perfect man: "He will live upon the heights, a fortress of rocks will be his dwelling, bread will be given to him." SIX BOOKS ON 1 KINGS 6.67 (16.1).[40]

33:17 Your Eyes Will See the King

THE KING IN HIS BEAUTY. APHRAHAT: Whosoever loves humility shall be heir in the land of life. Whosoever wishes to make peace shall be one of the sons of God.[41] Whosoever knows the will of his Lord, let him do that will, that he may not be beaten much.[42] Whosoever cleanses his heart from deceits, "his eyes shall behold the King in his beauty." Whosoever receives the Spirit of Christ, let him adorn his inner man. Whosoever is called the temple of God,[43] let him purify his body from all uncleanness. DEMONSTRATION 6.1.[44]

YOUR EYES WILL SEE. BEDE: Through the sacraments of his humanity with which we have been imbued, we may be able to attain the contemplation of the glory of his divinity, that contemplation which he himself in his faithful benevolence pledged to his faithful servants when he said, "One who has my commandments and keeps them, he it is who loves me. One who loves me will be loved by my Father, and I will love him and manifest myself to him."[45] He says, "I will manifest myself"—that is, "Not in such a way that everyone can look at me, or in such a way that even the unfaithful can see me and crucify me, but in such a way that only the pure eyes of the saints can see 'the King of ages in his beauty.' " In this way I will show myself to those who love me, so as to reward them for their love. Therefore let us hope, as we have said, that through the visible nature of his humanity we may be able to

---

[36]CS 123:123-24. [37]LF 18:534-35. [38]PL 83:726. [39]1 Cor 3:2. [40]CCL 144:589. [41]Mt 5:9. [42]Lk 12:47. [43]1 Cor 3:16-17. [44]NPNF 2 13:364. [45]Jn 14:21.

ascend to see the beauty of his divinity, if we keep these sacraments as we have received them, unblemished in the worthy honor of justice and holiness and truth, if we follow his example in his human way of life, and if we humbly follow the words of the teaching which he ministered to us through his humanity. Homilies on the Gospels 1.19.[46]

A Future Vision of Glory. Bede: The disciples indeed saw him coming in his kingdom, for on the mountain they saw him shining in that brightness with which he will be seen in his kingdom by all the saints when the judgment has been brought to completion. But since the eyes of the disciples were still mortal and corruptible, they were then unable to sustain what the whole church of the saints will have the power to look upon when she has become incorruptible through resurrection. Concerning this it is written, "Their eye will see the king in his beauty." Homilies on the Gospels 1.24.[47]

The Two Advents of the Lord. Hippolytus: Two advents of our Lord and Savior are indicated in the Scriptures. The one [is] his first advent in the flesh, which took place without honor by reason of his being set at nothing, as Isaiah spoke of him in the past, saying, "We saw him, and he had no form nor comeliness, but his form was despised (and) rejected above all men; a man smitten and familiar with bearing infirmity (for his face was turned away); he was despised, and esteemed not."[48] But his second advent is announced as glorious, when he shall come from heaven with the host of angels and the glory of his Father, as the prophet says, "You shall see the King in glory"; and, "I saw one like the Son of man coming with the clouds of heaven; and he came to the Ancient of Days, and he was brought to him. And there were given him dominion, and honor, and glory, and the kingdom; all tribes and languages shall serve him: his dominion is an everlasting dominion, which shall not pass away."[49] On the Antichrist 44.[50]

See the King. Adamnan: But it also must be noted that the Savior's tomb, above which a memorial canopy is often seen, can properly be called a cave or a den. Clearly, then, it was about the Lord Jesus Christ in the tomb that the prophet prophesied, "He lived in a high cave of fortified rocks," and shortly thereafter added, with regard to the apostles rejoicing at the resurrection of the Lord: "You will see the king in his glory." On the Holy Places 1.2.13.[51]

33:18 Your Heart Will Meditate on the Terror

The Call to Meditate. Pachomius: And if you want all these thoughts to diminish in you and not to have power over you, then recite in your heart without ceasing every fruit that is written in the Scriptures, having in yourself the resolution to walk in them, as it is written in Isaiah, "Your heart shall meditate on the fear" of the Lord, and all these things shall cease from you, little by little. Life of Pachomius (Sahidic) 4.[52]

33:21 A Place of Wide Rivers

A Wider Interpretation. Gregory the Great: For the plainly spoken words of these interpretations have made the views of the ancient fathers clear to us. If we view the words of the text according to the plain meaning of the words and not according to the obscured meaning of allegory, then we will see that Isaiah exclaimed (as interpreted by the holy church), "The place of rivers, the broadest and open streams." For the sayings of the Old Testament were as narrow and close streams, which brought together the various views in their culture. But the teachings of the holy church are broad and open streams, because its declarations are at once many in number to those who find them and are plain to those who

---

[46]CS 110:188**. [47]CS 110:236. [48]Is 53:2-5. [49]Dan 7:13-14. [50]ANF 5:213*. [51]CCL 175:188. [52]CS 45:453.

seek them. MORALS ON THE BOOK OF JOB 4.18.60.[53]

33:22 The Lord Is Our King

HE WILL SAVE US. CLEMENT OF ALEXANDRIA: This is the greatest and noblest of all God's acts: saving humanity.[54] But those who labor under some sickness are dissatisfied if the physician prescribes no remedy to restore their health. How, then, can we withhold our sincerest gratitude

from the divine Educator when he corrects the acts of disobedience that sweep us on to ruin and uproots the desires that drag us into sin, refusing to be silent and connive at them, and even offers counsels on the right way to live? Certainly we owe him the deepest gratitude. CHRIST THE EDUCATOR 1.12.100.[55]

---

[53]CCL 143A:926; LF 21:361**. [54]See Jer 30:11; Mt 18:11. [55]FC 23:88-89*.

34:1-17 THE DESTRUCTION OF GOD'S ENEMIES

[1]*Draw near, O nations, to hear,*
and hearken, O peoples!
Let the earth listen, and all that fills it;
the world, and all that comes from it.
[2]*For the LORD is enraged against all the*
nations,
and furious against all their host,
he has doomed them, has given them
over for slaughter.
[3]*Their slain shall be cast out,*
and the stench of their corpses shall rise;
the mountains shall flow with their
blood.
[4]*All the host of heaven shall rot away,*
and the skies roll up like a scroll.
All their host shall fall,
as leaves fall from the vine,
like leaves falling from the fig tree.

[5]*For my sword has drunk its fill in the*

heavens;
behold, it descends for judgment upon
Edom,
upon the people I have doomed.
[6]*The LORD has a sword; it is sated with*
blood,
it is gorged with fat,
with the blood of lambs and goats,
with the fat of the kidneys of rams.
For the LORD has a sacrifice in Bozrah,
a great slaughter in the land of Edom.
[7]*Wild oxen shall fall with them,*
and young steers with the mighty bulls.
Their land shall be soaked with blood,
and their soil made rich with fat.

[8]*For the LORD has a day of vengeance,*
a year of recompense for the cause of
Zion.
[9]*And the streams of Edom[a]* shall be turned*

into pitch,
and her soil into brimstone;
her land shall become burning pitch.
[10]Night and day it shall not be quenched;
its smoke shall go up for ever.
From generation to generation it shall lie
waste;
none shall pass through it for ever and
ever.
[11]But the hawk and the porcupine shall
possess it,
the owl and the raven shall dwell in it.
He shall stretch the line of confusion over it,
and the plummet of chaos over[b] its nobles.
[12]They shall name it No Kingdom There,
and all its princes shall be nothing.

[13]Thorns shall grow over its strongholds,
nettles and thistles in its fortresses.
It shall be the haunt of jackals,
an abode for ostriches.
[14]And wild beasts shall meet with hyenas,

the satyr shall cry to his fellow;
yea, there shall the night hag alight,
and find for herself a resting place.

[15]There shall the owl nest and lay[†]
and hatch and gather her young in her
shadow;
yea, there shall the kites be gathered,
each one with her mate.
[16]Seek and read from the book of the
LORD:
Not one of these shall be missing;
none shall be without her mate.
For the mouth of the LORD has
commanded,
and his Spirit has gathered them.
[17]He has cast the lot for them,
his hand has portioned it out to them
with the line;
they shall possess it for ever,
from generation to generation they shall
dwell in it.

a Heb *her streams*   **b** Heb lacks *over*   *LXX *her streams*   †LXX *there has the hedgehog made its nest*

OVERVIEW: The heavenly vaults will be opened (CHRYSOSTOM). This world and all its evils will fade away at the end (CYRIL OF JERUSALEM). From the beginning God spread out the heavens. There is contention and not peace in this world. Every sinner will die by the spiritual sword of God (JEROME). Hell is a dreadful place of judgment. Thoughts that exasperate and sinful deeds that wound arise in the reprobate mind (GREGORY THE GREAT). The hedgehog symbolizes the duplicity of the insincere mind (JEROME).

34:4 The Skies Roll Up Like a Scroll

ROLLED UP AS A SCROLL. CHRYSOSTOM: Daniel said, "I beheld in the night a vision, and saw one coming with the clouds of heaven as the Son of

man, and he came on to the Ancient of Days and was brought near to him. To him was given the dominion and the honor and the kingdom. And all people, tribes and tongues will serve him. His dominion is an eternal dominion, which shall not pass away. And his kingdom shall not be destroyed."[1] . . . Then all the gates of heaven will be opened, or rather the heaven itself is taken away. For we read, "The heaven shall be rolled up like a scroll," wrapped up to the middle like the skin and covering of some tent, so as to be made into a more useful shape. LETTER TO THE FALLEN THEODORE 1.12.[2]

A FAIRER WORLD WILL BE REVEALED. CYRIL

---

[1]Dan 7:13-14. [2]NPNF 1 9:101.

OF JERUSALEM: So, our Lord Jesus Christ comes from heaven, and he comes with glory at the last day to bring this world to its close. For this world will accomplish its course, and the world that once came into being is hereafter to be renewed. For seeing that corruption, theft, adultery and every form of sin has been poured out on the earth, and in the world fresh blood has been ever mingled with previous blood,[3] this astonishing habitation filled with iniquity is not to last. This world passes away that the fairer world may be revealed. Now would you have this proved by the express words of Scripture? Listen to these from Isaiah: "And the heavens shall be rolled together as a scroll; and all the stars shall fall down, as the leaf falls off from the vine, and as a falling fig from the fig tree." CATECHETICAL LECTURES 15.3.[4]

THE HEAVENS WILL BE ROLLED UP. JEROME: "You have spread out the heavens like a tent cloth." The prophet means to say that from the beginning God spread out the heavens, just as if he were unfolding a scroll and rolling it back again, as it is written in Holy Scripture: "And the heavens shall be rolled up like a scroll." You have constructed your palace upon the waters, as similarly in Genesis,[5] there were waters above the firmament and, likewise, below the firmament. "You travel on the wings of the wind." This typifies the presence of God everywhere. HOMILIES ON THE PSALMS 30 (PSALM 103).[6]

34:5 The Sword Descends for Judgment

STRIFE FOR THE PRESENT. JEROME: To us this life is a race course: we contend here, we are crowned elsewhere. No one can lay aside fear while serpents and scorpions beset his path. The Lord says, "My sword has drunk its fill in heaven," and do you expect to find peace on the earth? No, the earth yields only thorns and thistles, and its dust is food for the serpent.[7] "For our wrestling is not against flesh and blood but against the principalities, against the powers, against the world rulers of this darkness, against

the spiritual hosts of wickedness in the heavenly places."[8] We are hemmed in by hosts of foes; our enemies are upon every side. The weak flesh will soon be ashes: one against many, it fights against tremendous odds. Not till it has been dissolved, not till the prince of this world has come and found no sin therein,[9] not till then may you safely listen to the prophet's words: "You shall not be afraid for the terror by night nor the arrow that flies by day; nor for the trouble which haunts you in darkness."[10] . . . When the hosts of the enemy distress you, when your body is hot with fever and your passions roused, when you say in your heart, "What shall I do?" Then Elisha's words shall give you your answer, "Fear not, for they that be with us are more than they that be with them."[11] He shall pray, "Lord, open the eyes of your handmaid that she may see." And then when your eyes have been opened, you shall see a fiery chariot like Elijah's waiting to carry you to heaven,[12] and you shall joyfully sing, "Our soul has become free like a bird out of the snare of the fowlers: the snare is broken and we have been set free."[13] LETTER 22.3.[14]

A SPIRITUAL SWORD. JEROME: Because God did not spare the sinful angels who lost their heavenly home through their own fault, therefore does he say through Isaiah, "My sword in heaven is satiated." For every sinner among the people will die by the sword, yet not by a physical sword (there are many and varied ways to die other than by a sword) but by the spiritual sword with which all who fail to do penance must be stricken. COMMENTARY ON ZECHARIAH 1.5.1-4.[15]

34:8 The Day of the Lord's Vengeance

A DESCRIPTION OF HELL. GREGORY THE GREAT: It [sacred Scripture] has a dreadful

---

[3]Hos 4:2. [4]LCC 4:149. [5]See Gen 1:7. [6]FC 48:223*. [7]Gen 3:14, 18. [8]Eph 6:12. [9]Jn 14:30. [10]Ps 91:5-7. [11]2 Kings 6:16. [12]2 Kings 2:11; 6:17. [13]Ps 124:7. [14]NPNF 2 6:23. [15]CCL 76A:786-87.

appearance[16] when, describing hell, it says, "The day of the vengeance of the Lord, the year of recompense of the judgment of Zion. And the streams thereof shall be turned into pitch, and the ground thereof into brimstone: and the land thereof shall become burning pitch. Night and day it shall not be quenched . . . forever." HOMILIES ON EZEKIEL 1.6.18.[17]

34:13 Thorns Shall Spring Up

NETTLES AND THORNS. GREGORY THE GREAT: Which conduct the Lord by the prophet well reproves, under the character of Babylon, saying, "Thorns and nettles shall spring up in her houses, and the bramble in their fortresses." For what do we understand by "nettles" but the irritations of thoughts, and what by "thorns" but the piercing of sins? Nettles therefore and thorns spring up in the houses of Babylon, because in the disorder of a reprobate mind there arise longings of thoughts that exasperate and sinful deeds that wound. MORALS ON THE BOOK OF JOB 6.33.10.[18]

34:15 There the Hedgehog Had Its Hole

THE HEDGEHOG. GREGORY THE GREAT: It is rightly said by the prophet, under the similitude of Judea, against the soul that sins and excuses itself, "There has the hedgehog had its hole." Here the term hedgehog symbolizes the duplicity of the insincere mind that craftily defends itself. For when the hedgehog is discovered, its head is seen,

its feet are obvious, its whole body revealed; but the moment it is captured, it gathers itself up into a ball, draws in its feet, hides its head, and the thing disappears in the hands of him who holds it, whereas before all the parts were visible.

Such, indeed, is the case of insincere minds when detected in their transgressions. The head of the hedgehog is seen in that one perceives from what beginnings the sinner approaches his crime. The feet of the hedgehog are visible, because one sees by what steps the evil was done. Then by quickly giving excuses, the insincere mind gathers up its feet, inasmuch as it tries to hide every vestige of its sin. It withdraws its head, because it claims through strange pleas that no evil ever began. The thing [i.e., the sinner] remains, as it were, in the hand of him who holds it like a ball. The one who reproves the evil suddenly no longer sees the sins that he had known earlier and holds the sinner enfolded in his own mind. The one who had seen everything at the moment of capturing the sinner (like a hedgehog) loses all knowledge of the sinner, being deluded by the subterfuges of his wicked pleas. Therefore the hedgehog has its nest in the wicked, that is, the duplicity of a malicious mind that conceals itself in the obscurity of its self-defense by drawing itself into a ball. PASTORAL CARE 3.11.[19]

---

[16]See Ezek 1:18, in reference to which "dreadful appearance" is here quoted by Gregory. [17]HGE 62. [18]CCL 143B:1678; LF 31:563**. [19]ACW 11:118-19**.

35:1-10 RESTORATION OF ZION

¹The wilderness and the dry land shall be
  glad,
  the desert shall rejoice and blossom;
like the crocus ²it* shall blossom
  abundantly,
  and rejoice with joy and singing.
The glory of Lebanon shall be given to it,
  the majesty of Carmel and Sharon.
They shall see the glory of the LORD,
  the majesty of our God.

³Strengthen the weak hands,
  and make firm the feeble knees.
⁴Say to those who are of a fearful heart,
  "Be strong, fear not!
Behold, your God
  will come with vengeance,
with the recompense of God.
  He will come and save you."†

⁵Then the eyes of the blind shall be opened,
  and the ears of the deaf unstopped;
⁶then shall the lame man leap like a hart,
  and the tongue of the dumb sing for joy.

For waters shall break forth in the
  wilderness,
  and streams in the desert;
⁷the burning sand shall become a pool,
  and the thirsty ground springs of water;
the haunt of jackals shall become a swamp,ᶜ
  the grass shall become reeds and rushes.

⁸And a highway shall be there,
  and it shall be called the Holy Way;
the unclean shall not pass over it,ᵈ
  and fools shall not err therein.
⁹No lion shall be there,
  nor shall any ravenous beast come up on
  it;
they shall not be found there,
  but the redeemed shall walk there.
¹⁰And the ransomed of the LORD shall
  return,
  and come to Zion with singing;
everlasting joy shall be upon their heads;
  they shall obtain joy and gladness,
  and sorrow and sighing shall flee
  away.

c Cn: Heb *in the haunt of jackals is her resting place*   d Heb *it and he is for them a wayfarer*   *LXX *And the desert places of Jordan*   †LXX *us*

OVERVIEW: The desert is a symbol of the Gentiles, who did not possess the good things of God (EUSEBIUS). The desert is a symbol of the soul that is parched. Carmel is a symbol of the soul that has received grace through the Spirit. The great trees of Lebanon refer to God's regenerating humanity (GREGORY OF NYSSA). The honor of the Mosaic law was transferred to the Gentiles (EUSEBIUS). God turned the Judean desert into a place of honor: the church (BEDE).

Christ is called Lord because he is God incarnate (CYRIL OF ALEXANDRIA). The glory of the Lord was seen at his baptism (EUSEBIUS). Isaiah prophesied that the Gentiles would come to faith in God through Christ (BEDE). Weak hands and feeble knees refer to the palsy that is healed by God (TERTULLIAN). Faith in God is our strength (AMBROSE). Isaiah prophesies about those who repent upon hearing the preaching of John the Baptist (CHROMATIUS). Christians should flee the wicked world (AMBROSE).

The prophecy of Isaiah is fulfilled in part in the account of the men who brought the lame man to be healed by Christ (EUSEBIUS). Christ did not send an ambassador but himself came to save us (AUGUSTINE). The one who was sent to save us came by his own will (QUODVULTDEUS). Christ as God incarnate was announced beforehand by Isaiah. Christ is distinguished as God by his preaching and his acts of power (TERTULLIAN). Isaiah prophesies concerning Christ's work of healing (CHRYSOSTOM, NOVATIAN). Christ was God incarnate, seen by his great works (CHROMATIUS). The Creator put on the creature and performed miraculous acts (LEO THE GREAT). Christ's miracles were the literal fulfillment of prophecy (CHROMATIUS, ATHANASIUS, TERTULLIAN, JUSTIN MARTYR, NOVATIAN, ORIGEN).

Christ came to the destitute Gentiles and offered them living water (JUSTIN MARTYR). There is one doctrine of truth that nourishes many hearers (GREGORY THE GREAT). Hope enables us to endure until we are delivered (AUGUSTINE). The other life brings the absence of all pain and sorrow (CHRYSOSTOM, CAESARIUS OF ARLES, JOHN OF DAMASCUS). Eternal joy begins after the resurrection (TERTULLIAN). As good approaches, pain and sorrow flee (JOHN CASSIAN, AMBROSE). There is continual joy in the kingdom of God (JOHN CASSIAN). When death is swallowed up, there will be no corruption of body or soul (FULGENTIUS). For the faithful there is coming perfect health (PRIMASIUS).

35:1 The Desert Will Rejoice and Blossom

THE DESERT SHALL REJOICE. EUSEBIUS OF CAESAREA: This, too, was fulfilled, was clearly fulfilled, by our Savior's miraculous works after John's preaching. Notice therefore how he bears good tidings to the desert, not generally or to any desert but to one particular desert by the bank of the Jordan. This was because John lived there and baptized there, as Scripture says, "John was in the desert baptizing."[1] . . . I think the desert here is a symbol of that which of old was void of all God's good things, I mean the church of the Gentiles. And the river by the desert that cleanses all that are bathed therein is a figure of some cleansing spiritual power, of which the Scriptures speak, saying, "The movements of the river make glad the city of God."[2] And this means the ever-flowing stream of the Holy Spirit welling from above and watering the city of God, which is the name for life according to God. This river of God, then, has reached even to the desert, that is the Gentile church, and even now supplies it with the living water that it bears. PROOF OF THE GOSPEL 9.6.[3]

REJOICE AND BLOSSOM. EUSEBIUS OF CAESAREA: Here also the coming of God for salvation, bringing many blessings, is precisely foretold. The prophet says that there will be a cure for the deaf, sight for the blind, yes, even healing for the lame and tongue-tied, and this was fulfilled only at the coming of our Savior Jesus Christ, by whom the eyes of the blind were opened, and the deaf regained their hearing.[4] Why need I say, how many palsied and deaf and lame also received physical cure by the hands of his disciples? And how many others, afflicted with various diseases and maladies, received of him healing and salvation, according to the inspired prediction of prophecy and according to the unimpeachable testimony of the holy Gospels? And the prophecy here disguises under the name of "desert" the church of the Gentiles,[5] which for long years deserted of God is being evangelized by those of whom we are speaking, and it says that besides other blessings the glory of Lebanon will be given to the desert. Now it is customary to call Jerusalem Lebanon allegorically, as I will show, when I have time, by proofs from holy Scripture. This prophecy before us, therefore, teaches that by God's presence with men the glory of Lebanon will be given to that which is called "desert," that is to say, the church of the

---

[1]Mk 1:4. [2]Ps 46:4. [3]POG 2:164*. [4]Mt 11:5. [5]Eusebius means that the Gentiles did not possess the law and the prophets.

Gentiles. Proof of the Gospel 6.21.[6]

The Soul That Is Parched. Gregory of Nyssa: And where shall we place that oracle of Isaiah, which cries to the wilderness, "Be glad, O thirsty wilderness. Let the desert rejoice and blossom as a lily, and the desolate places of Jordan shall blossom and shall rejoice"? For it is clear that it is not to places without soul or sense that he proclaims the good tidings of joy, but he speaks, by the figure of the desert, of the soul that is parched and unadorned. On the Baptism of Christ.[7]

The Excellence of Carmel. Gregory of Nyssa: And "the excellence of Carmel" is given to the soul that bears the likeness to the desert, that is, the grace bestowed through the Spirit. For since Elijah dwelt in Carmel, and the mountain became famous and renowned by the virtue of him who dwelt there, and since moreover John the Baptist, illustrious in the spirit of Elijah, sanctified the Jordan, therefore the prophet foretold that "the excellence of Carmel" should be given to the river. On the Baptism of Christ.[8]

The Glory of Lebanon. Gregory of Nyssa: And "the glory of Lebanon," from the similitude of its lofty trees, he transfers to the river. For as great Lebanon presents a sufficient cause of wonder in the very trees that it brings forth and nourishes, so is the Jordan glorified by regenerating people and planting them in the paradise of God. And of them, as the words of the psalmist say, ever blooming and bearing the foliage of virtues, "the leaf shall not wither,"[9] and God shall be glad, receiving their fruit in due season, rejoicing, like a good planter, in his own works. On the Baptism of Christ.[10]

Holiness in the Desert. Eusebius of Caesarea: Moreover, it is said in this prophecy that the glory of Lebanon and the honor of Carmel shall be given to this wilderness. What is the glory of Lebanon but the worship performed

through the sacrifices of the Mosaic law, which God refused in the prophecy which says, "Why do you bring me Lebanon from Sheba? And of what service to me is the multitude of your sacrifices?"[11] He has transferred the glory of Jerusalem to the desert of Jordan, since, from the times of John, the ritual of holiness began to be performed not at Jerusalem but in the desert. In like manner, too, the honor of the law and of its more external ordinances was transferred to the wilderness of Jordan for the same reason, namely, that they who need the healing of their souls no longer hastened to Jerusalem but to that which was called the wilderness, because there the forgiveness of sins was preached. Proof of the Gospel 9.6.[12]

Judah Will Bear Fruit in the Desert. Bede: After John was killed, the Lord saw the time drawing near and withdrew to a deserted place called Bethsaida.[13] This teaches mystically that a deserted Judah, which had beheaded its prophets by not believing them, would later become fruitful in the desert of a church that possessed no man of the Word. Hence, the beautiful Bethsaida means "house of fruitfulness." For it was about it that Isaiah said, "The desert and the dry land will rejoice, and the wilderness will exult and bloom like the lily," and again, "they will see the glory of the Lord and the beauty of our God." Exposition of the Gospel of Luke 3.9.10.[14]

35:2 Seeing the Glory of the Lord

The Lord. Cyril of Alexandria: Observe how he names him Lord and calls him God, seeing that he speaks in the Spirit; note that he knew the Emmanuel[15] would not be simply a man bearing God nor, of a truth, as one assumed as an agent. But he knew that he was truly God and incarnate. . . . For our Lord Jesus Christ showed himself to us having divine strength, and his arm

---

[6]POG 2:42*. [7]NPNF 2 5:523. [8]NPNF 2 5:523. [9]Ps 1:4. [10]NPNF 2 5:523. [11]Jer 6:20; Is 1:11. [12]POG 2:164-65*. [13]See Lk 9:10. [14]CCL 120:198. [15]Is 7:14.

with authority, that is, with power and dominion. LETTER 1.31.[16]

GLORY AT CHRIST'S BAPTISM. EUSEBIUS OF CAESAREA: I believe the passage, "And my people shall see the glory of the Lord, and the majesty of God," refers to the presence of our Savior at the baptism, because it was there that the glory of the Savior was seen. PROOF OF THE GOSPEL 9.6.[17]

JUDAH AWESTRUCK. BEDE: Because a multitude of Gentiles followed it after Judah came to faith in the Lord's incarnation and an astonished partaker of the same grace hastened its own unexpected conversion, Judah exclaimed in surprise, "Who is this that ascends from the desert, flowing with delights, leaning upon my beloved?"[18] The church of the Gentiles ascends from the desert because the one who was deserted by its Creator for a very long time now arrives at his grace by the incremental steps of faith and good works, thus fulfilling what the prophet Isaiah said: "The desert and the dry land will rejoice, and the wilderness will exult and bloom like the lily." Indeed, she is truly flowing with those delights about which the spouse spoke above: "How beautiful you are, and how lovely, my dear, with delights,"[19] that is, with the delights of heavenly life. "Leaning upon my beloved" means leaning upon him without whose assistance she would be able neither to ascend above nor to rise again, for we are unable to possess either advancement in the virtues or the beginning of faith itself unless the Lord bestows them upon us.

Therefore, Judah was even more awestruck by this grace of the Gentiles' new conversion, a grace that it believed pertained only to itself and to those who were received in its rite through the mystery of circumcision, as the Acts of the Apostles made abundantly clear. SIX BOOKS ON THE SONG OF SONGS 5.8.4-5.[20]

35:3 Be Strong, You Relaxed Hands and Palsied Knees

RENEWED ENERGY. TERTULLIAN: The sick of the palsy is healed,[21] and that in public, in the sight of the people. For, says Isaiah, "they shall see the glory of the Lord and the excellence of our God." What glory, and what excellence? "Be strong, you weak hands and feeble knees" refers to the palsy. "Be strong; fear not." "Be strong" is not vainly repeated, nor is "fear not" vainly added; because with the renewal of the limbs there was to be, according to the promise, a restoration also of bodily energies: "Arise, and take up your couch";[22] and likewise moral courage not to be afraid of those who should say, "Who can forgive sins, but God alone?"[23] AGAINST MARCION 4.10.1.[24]

THE BALM OF UNSPOILED FAITH. AMBROSE: Therefore the traders came from Gilead,[25] that is, from their possessions of or dwelling in the law, and brought their wares to the church, so that that balm might heal the sins of the nations. Of them it is said, "Be strong, you hands that are feeble and you knees that are without strength." The balm is unspoiled faith. Such a faith Peter exhibited when he said to the lame man, "In the name of Jesus Christ of Nazareth, arise and walk."[26] And he arose and walked, as was right. Such a faith Peter had when he said to the paralytic, "Aeneas, the Lord Jesus heals you; get up and make your bed."[27] And he got up and made his bed. Such a faith he had when he said to the dead woman, "Arise in the name of our Lord Jesus Christ."[28] And the departed woman arose. With the mortar made from this cement those stones are fastened together from which God is able to raise up children to Abraham.[29] ON JOSEPH 3.17.[30]

THE TIME OF GRACE FORETOLD. CHROMATIUS OF AQUILEIA: The grace of this time in which John was exhorting sinners to repentance and

---

[16]FC 76:27*. [17]POG 2:165**. [18]Song 8:5. [19]Song 7:6. [20]CCL 119B:343. [21]Lk 5:16-26. [22]Mk 2:11. [23]Mk 2:7. [24]CCL 1:562. [25]Gen 37:25. [26]Acts 3:6. [27]Acts 9:34. [28]Acts 9:40. [29]See Mt 3:9. [30]FC 65:199.

baptizing those who confessed their sins in the desert, Isaiah previously witnessed when he said, "The desert will rejoice and blossom like the lily. The desert of the Jordan will bloom and exult. Strengthen the hands of the abandoned and bolster their weak knees. You who are lowly of soul, be encouraged and do not fear." Tractate on Matthew 10.1.[31]

The Footstep of the Spirit. Ambrose: Then let us flee the wickedness of this world, in which "the very days are evil,"[32] and flee it relentlessly. On that account Isaiah cries out, "Be strong, you hands which are feeble and you knees which are without strength." This means: Be strong, you knees, not of the body but of the soul, so that the footstep of the spirit can rise up straightway to the heights of heaven. Thus conduct will be more stable, life more mature, grace more abundant and discretion more guarded. Flight from the World 7.37.[33]

The Medicine of His Teaching. Eusebius of Caesarea: Now we have this prophecy fulfilled in the Gospels, partly, when they brought to our Lord and Savior a paralytic lying on a bed, who he made whole with a word;[34] and partly, when many that were blind and possessed with demons, yes, laboring under various diseases and weaknesses, were released from their sufferings by his saving power. Nor should we forget how even now throughout the whole world multitudes bound by all forms of evil, full of ignorance of Almighty God in their souls, are healed and cured miraculously and beyond all argument by the medicine of his teaching. Except that now we call him God as we should, as one who can work thus, as I have already shown in the evidence of his divinity. Yes, surely it is right now to acknowledge him to be God, since he has given proof of power divine and truly inspired.

For it was specifically God's work to give strength to the paralyzed, to give life to the dead, to supply health to the sick, to open the eyes of the blind, to restore the lame and to make the tongue-tied speak plainly, all of which things were done by our Savior Jesus Christ, because he was God. And they have been witnessed to by many throughout all the world that preach him—whose evidence unvarnished and truthful is confirmed by trial of torture, and by persistence even to death, which they have shown forth before kings and rulers and all nations, witnessing to the truth of what they preach. Proof of the Gospel 9.13.[35]

35:4 God Will Come and Save You

An Extreme Humility. Augustine: This is the divine arrangement, as far as any human being can investigate it, better minds in a better way, lesser minds less effectively; this divine arrangement is giving us hints of a great and significant mystery. Christ, you see, was going to come in the flesh, not anyone at all, not an angel, not an ambassador; but "he himself will come and save you." It wasn't anyone who was going to come; and yet how was he going to come? He was going to be born in mortal flesh, to be a tiny infant, to be laid in a manger, wrapped in cradle clothes, nourished on milk; going to grow up, and finally even to be done to death. So in all these indications of humility there is indeed a pattern of an extreme humility. Sermon 293.8.[36]

By His Own Will. Quodvultdeus: "This is the will of my Father," he said, "that all who see the Son and believe in him should have eternal life."[37] But notice that he who was sent also came by his own will, as the prophet Isaiah said: "Be encouraged, you who are lowly of soul, and do not fear. Behold, our God will bring judgment. God himself will come and save us." On the Approach to Grace 1.14.12-1.15.1.[38]

God Will Come. Quodvultdeus: Christ said, "I am in the Father, and the Father is in me," and

---

[31]CCL 9A:235. [32]Eph 5:16. [33]FC 65:310. [34]Mk 2:9-11. [35]POG 2:178*. [36]WSA 3 8:151-52*. [37]Jn 6:40. [38]CCL 60:453.

"Whoever sees me, sees the Father."[39] The inclusion of just one syllable, "and," distinguishes the Father from the Son. It also demonstrates that you possess neither the Father nor the Son.[40] Tell me, Arian, do you refer to the Father as God? And how! But what about the Son? Him too I profess to be God. You will do well to acknowledge this also, for when his coming in the flesh was announced beforehand, the prophet said about him, "Be encouraged, you who are lowly of soul, and do not fear. Behold, your God will bring the vengeance of retribution. God himself will come and save us." AGAINST FIVE HERESIES 6.38-39.[41]

PREACHING AND POWER. TERTULLIAN: The actions of Christ must be seen alongside the rule of the Scriptures.[42] Unless I am mistaken, we see that Christ's work consisted of two actions: preaching and power. Let us look at each of these in the order we have just listed them. First, Christ was announced as a preacher. Isaiah said, "Cry out loud, and do not hold back. Lift up your voice as a trumpet, and declare to my people their crimes and to the house of Jacob their sins. Then seek me day by day and desire to learn my ways, as a nation that has done righteousness and has not forsaken the judgment of God," and so forth.[43] Second, it was announced that Christ would do acts of power from the Father. Isaiah said, "Behold, our God will come with judgment; he will come and save us. Then the sick will be healed, the eyes of the blind will see, the ears of the deaf will hear, the mute will speak, and the lame will leap as a deer." AN ANSWER TO THE JEWS 9.[44]

35:5 The Eyes of the Blind Will Be Opened

THE MESSIAH PREDICTED. NOVATIAN: Isaiah also alludes to him: "There shall go forth a rod from the root of Jesse, and a flower shall grow up from his root."[45] The same also when he says, "Behold, a virgin shall conceive and bear a son."[46] He refers to him when he enumerates the heal-

ings that were to proceed from him, saying, "Then shall the eyes of the blind be opened, and the ears of the deaf shall hear. Then shall the lame man leap like a deer, and the tongue of the dumb shall be eloquent." Him also, when he sets forth the virtue of patience, saying, "His voice shall not be heard in the streets; a bruised reed shall he not destroy, and the smoking flax shall he not quench."[47] ON THE TRINITY 9.6.[48]

OTHER MARVELS. CHRYSOSTOM: And Isaiah went on to tell of other marvels and showed how Christ cured the lame, how he made the blind to see, and the mute to speak: "Then will the eyes of the blind be opened, then will the ears of the deaf hear." And thereafter he spoke of the other marvels: "Then will the lame man leap like a stag, and the tongue of those with impediments of speech will be clear and distinct." And this did not happen until his coming. DEMONSTRATION AGAINST THE PAGANS 3.9.[49]

SIGHT TO THE BLIND. CHROMATIUS OF AQUILEIA: Although these blind men[50] had no bodily eyes, they had the vision of faith and heart with which they were able to see the true and eternal Light, the Son of God, about whom it is written: "He was the true light which illumines everyone, coming into the world."[51] It was he who had predicted through the prophet Isaiah that he would come to give sight to the blind: "The Spirit of the Lord is upon me because he has anointed me. He has sent me to evangelize the poor and to restore sight to the blind."[52] Again Isaiah testified about the same one elsewhere: "Behold, our God will restore justice; he will come and save us. Then the eyes of the blind will be opened and the ears of the deaf will hear." David also bore witness to

---

[39]Jn 14:10. [40]Quodvultdeus is writing against the Arians, who rejected the deity of the Son. [41]CCL 60:286-87. [42]In this instance, by Scriptures Tertullian means the Old Testament. He is saying that Christ must be understood in the light of the Old Testament message about him. [43]Is 58:1-2. [44]ANF 3:164. [45]Is 11:1. [46]Is 7:13. [47]Is 42:2-3. [48]CCL 4:25. [49]FC 73:200. [50]See Mt 9:27-31. [51]Jn 1:9. [52]Is 61:1; Lk 4:18.

him, saying through the Holy Spirit: "The Lord raises up the downcast, the Lord frees the imprisoned, the Lord gives sight to the blind."[53] TRACTATE ON MATTHEW 48.1.[54]

MIRACULOUS WORKS. LEO THE GREAT: "God was in Christ reconciling the world to himself,"[55] and the Creator himself was wearing the creature which was to be restored to the image of its Creator. And after the divinely miraculous works had been performed, the performance of which the spirit of prophecy had once predicted, "then shall the eyes of the blind be opened and the ears of the deaf shall hear; then shall the lame man leap like a deer, and the tongue of the dumb shall speak plainly." SERMON 54.4.[56]

35:6a Then Shall the Lame Leap Like a Hart

THE STRIDES OF THE INTERIOR LIFE. CHROMATIUS OF AQUILEIA: But that these five thousand men are signs of divine power,[57] the Lord himself predicted through the prophet, saying, "Behold, I and the children whom God has given me will be signs in the house of Israel from the Lord of hosts on Mount Zion."[58] The same prophet later revealed the nature of these future signs when he said, "Then the eyes of the blind will be opened, and the ears of the deaf will hear, and the lame will leap like deer." We can recognize the fulfillment of this prophecy in the lame man who had been unable to walk since birth.[59]

If we look closely, we can also recognize the sacraments prefigured mystically in him, for the lame man received healing while looking toward Peter and John when he was at the Beautiful Gate of the temple. We too were lame prior to coming to the knowledge of Christ, in the sense that we were limping along the way of righteousness. Our halting strides were not those of the body, however, but those of the interior life. Whoever has gone astray from the way of righteousness or from the way of truth is altogether lame, even if his feet and legs are healthy, since he limps with

his mind and soul. For the journey of faith and truth is traveled not with bodily steps but with strides of the interior life. SERMON 1.3-4.[60]

THE LAME ONE LEAPS. ATHANASIUS: Now what can they [i.e., those who deny the incarnation] say to this, or how can they dare to face this at all?[61] For the prophecy not only indicated that God is to sojourn here but also announces the signs and the time of his coming. For they connect the blind recovering their sight, and the lame walking, and the deaf hearing, and the tongue of the one who stammers being made plain, with the divine coming which is to take place. Let them say, then, when such signs have come to pass in Israel, or where in Judah anything of the sort has occurred. Naaman, a leper, was cleansed,[62] but no deaf man heard nor lame walked. Elijah raised a dead man;[63] so did Elisha;[64] but none blind from birth regained his sight. For in good truth, to raise a dead man is a great thing, but it is not like the wonder wrought by the Savior. Only, if Scripture has not passed over the case of the leper and of the dead son of the widow, certainly had it come to pass that a lame man also had walked and a blind man recovered his sight, the narrative would not have omitted to mention this also.[65] Since, then, nothing is said in the [Old Testament] Scriptures, it is evident that these things had never taken place before. When, then, have they taken place, save when the Word of God himself came in the body? Or when did he come, if not when lame men walked,[66] and those who stammer were made to speak plainly,[67] and deaf men heard,[68] and men blind from birth regained their sight?[69] ON THE INCARNATION 38.[70]

---

[53]Ps 146:8 (LXX 145:8). [54]CCL 9A:436. [55]2 Cor 5:19. [56]CCL 138A:319-20. [57]See Acts 4:4. [58]Is 8:18; cf. Heb 2:13. [59]See Acts 3:1-10. [60]CCL 9A:4. [61]Athanasius is referring to the prophecy of Isaiah 35:3-6. [62]2 Kings 5:14. [63]1 Kings 17:22. [64]2 Kings 4:34-35. [65]Athanasius is arguing that since the Old Testament recorded the healing of Naaman and the raising of the widow's son from the dead, then certainly the healing of the lame and blind would have been recorded as well, had they occurred. [66]E.g., Mk 2:3-12. [67]E.g., Mt 9:33. [68]E.g., Mk 7:33. [69]Jn 9:1. [70]LCC 3:92.

35:6b *And the Tongue of the Mute Sings for Joy*

LITERAL PROPHECIES. TERTULLIAN: Let me dispel at once the . . . assertion that the prophets make all their announcements in figures of speech. Now, if this were the case, the figures themselves could not possibly have been distinguished, inasmuch as the verities would not have been declared, out of which the figurative language is stretched. And, indeed, if all are figures, where will be that of which they are the figures? How can you hold up a mirror for your face, if the face nowhere exists? But, in truth, all are not figures, but there are also literal statements; nor are all shadows, but there are bodies too. We have prophecies about the Lord himself even, which are clearer than the day. For it was not figuratively that the Virgin conceived in her womb. . . . Not even of his mighty works have [the prophets] used parabolic language. Or else, were not the eyes of the blind opened? Did not the tongue of the mute recover speech? Did not the relaxed hands and palsied knees become strong, and the lame leap like a deer? No doubt we are accustomed also to give a spiritual significance to these statements of prophecy, according to the analogy of the physical diseases that were healed by the Lord. But still they were all fulfilled literally, thus showing that the prophets foretold both senses, except that very many of their words can be taken only in a pure and simple signification and free from all allegorical obscurity. ON THE RESURRECTION OF THE FLESH 20.[71]

PREDICTIONS OF CHRIST. JUSTIN MARTYR: How it was prophesied that our Christ would heal all diseases and raise the dead, hear what was spoken, as follows: "At his coming the lame will leap like a deer, and the stammering tongue will be clear; the blind will see and lepers be cleansed, and the dead will arise and walk." That he did these things you can learn from the Acts of Pontius Pilate.[72] FIRST APOLOGY 48.[73]

WORKS OF HEALING. NOVATIAN: Isaiah bears witness to him when he sets before us the works of healing that were to be done by him. ON THE TRINITY 9.6.[74]

THE LAME AND THE BLIND. ORIGEN: That [Jesus] healed the lame and the blind, and that therefore we hold him to be the Christ and the Son of God, is manifest to us from what is contained in the prophecies: "Then the eyes of the blind shall be opened." AGAINST CELSUS 2.48.[75]

35:7 *Springs of Water*

CHRIST THE FOUNTAIN OF LIVING WATER. JUSTIN MARTYR: You can easily perceive how the Scriptures foretold that they who were destitute of the knowledge of God (I allude to the Gentiles who had eyes and saw not, hearts and understood not, but worshiped material idols) should abandon their idols and place their hope in Christ. . . . The fountain of living water that gushed forth from God upon a land devoid of the knowledge of God (that is, the land of the Gentiles) was our Christ, who made his appearance on earth in the midst of your people and healed those who from birth were blind and deaf and lame. He cured them by his word, causing them to walk, to hear and to see. By restoring the dead to life, he compelled the people of that day to recognize him. DIALOGUE WITH TRYPHO 69.[76]

TRUTH NOURISHES MANY. GREGORY THE GREAT: The Lord makes a promise about holy church through another prophet, saying, "The reed and the rushes will become green and luscious." I remember explaining elsewhere that reeds must be interpreted as scribes and rushes surely as hearers. But because both rushes and reeds are apt to grow beside the moisture of water and both benefit from the same water, and a reed

---

[71]ANF 3:559*. [72]Also called the Gospel of Nicodemus, a twenty-two-chapter Christian writing from the end of the third century A.D. [73]LCC 1:272-73*. [74]FC 67:43*. [75]ANF 4:449. [76]ANF 1:233**.

is indeed used for writing while it is impossible to write with a bulrush, what must we understand by the bulrush and the reed except that there is one doctrine of truth which nourishes many hearers? HOMILIES ON EZEKIEL 2.1.11.[77]

35:10 Toil and Groaning Have Passed Away

TOIL AND GROANING. AUGUSTINE: What about hope? Will that be there [i.e., in heaven]? Hope will not continue when the thing hoped for is there. Certainly hope is very necessary for us in our exile. It is what consoles us on the journey. When the traveler, after all, finds it wearisome walking along, he puts up with the fatigue precisely because he hopes to arrive. Rob him of any hope of arriving, and immediately his strength for walking is broken. So the hope also which we have here is part and parcel of the justice of our exile and our journey. Listen to the apostle himself. "Awaiting the adoption,"[78] he says, "we cannot yet say there is the bliss of which Scripture says, 'Toil and groaning have passed away.'" SERMON 158.8.[79]

THE WONDROUS LIFE TO COME. CHRYSOSTOM: I ask you to consider the condition of the other life, so far as it is possible to consider it; for no words will suffice for an adequate description. But from the things which are told us, as if by means of certain riddles, let us try and get some indistinct vision of it. "Pain and sorrow and sighing," we read, "have fled away." What then could be more blessed than this life? It is not possible there to fear poverty and disease. It is not possible to see any one injuring or being injured, provoking or being provoked, or angry, or envious, or burning with any outrageous lust, or anxious concerning the supply of the necessities of life, or bemoaning himself over the loss of some dignity and power. For all the tempest of passion in us is quelled and brought to nothing, and all will be in a condition of peace and gladness and joy, all things serene and tranquil, all will be daylight and brightness, and light, not

this present light but one excelling this in splendor as much as daylight is brighter than a lamp. For things are not concealed in that world by night or by a gathering of clouds. Bodies there are not set on fire and burned. For there is neither night nor evening there, nor cold nor heat, nor any other variation of seasons. But the condition is of a different kind, such as only they will know who have been deemed worthy of it. There is no old age there, nor any of the evils of old age, but all things relating to decay are utterly removed, and incorruptible glory reigns in every part. But greater than all these things is the perpetual enjoyment of relationship with Christ in the company of angels and archangels and the higher powers. LETTER TO THE FALLEN THEODORE 1.11.[80]

SORROWS SHALL PASS AWAY. CAESARIUS OF ARLES: The world is indeed harassed by the evil lives and statements of many people. This attack upon the good and the bad is just like when mud and an ointment are blown on the same wind; the one exhales a foul odor, while the other has a sweet fragrance. In order that everyone may understand this, I will reveal it more explicitly to you, my friend. Good and bad people are two urns, one of which contains rottenness, the other precious spices. When they are blown by the same fan, the urn that has spices gives forth a desirable fragrance, while the one that is a sewer returns an unbearable stench. Similarly, both good and bad people are troubled but are distinguished by the penetrating judgment of God. Whenever tribulation comes to the world, the good like a holy vessel thank God who has deigned to chastise them; those who are proud, dissolute or avaricious on the contrary blaspheme and murmur against God, saying, O God, what great evil have we done that we should suffer such calamities? Therefore, even if the good die in the midst of adversities, they will end a life full of labors and miseries but will receive eternal life

---

[77]HGE 165*. [78]Rom 8:23. [79]WSA 3 5:118*. [80]NPNF 1 9:99*.

from which "sorrow and mourning shall flee away." Unfaithful souls refuse to believe this, and while fettered with love for this life, they cannot keep it but lose it by their infidelity. Sermon 70.1.[81]

Fuel for Eternal Fire. John of Damascus: You are about to journey a long road, and you need many supplies. You shall arrive at the place eternal that has two regions, wherein are many mansions; one of which places God has prepared for them that love him and keep his commandments, full of all manner of good things. And they that attain to it shall live for ever in incorruption, enjoying immortality without death, where pain and sorrow and sighing are fled away. But the other place is full of darkness and tribulation and pain, prepared for the devil and his angels. In it also they shall be cast who by evil deeds have deserved it, who have bartered the incorruptible and eternal for the present world and have made themselves fuel for eternal fire. Barlaam and Joseph 14.124.[82]

Tears Shall Cease. Tertullian: "Everlasting joy," says Isaiah, "shall be upon their heads." Well, there is nothing eternal until after the resurrection. "And sorrow and sighing," he continues, "shall flee away." The angel echoes the same to John: "And God shall wipe away all tears from their eyes,"[83] from the same eyes indeed which had formerly wept and which might weep again if the loving kindness of God did not dry up every fountain of tears. And again: "God shall wipe away all tears from their eyes; and there shall be no more death," and therefore no more corruption, it being chased away by incorruption, even as death is by immortality. On the Resurrection of the Flesh 58.[84]

The Home of the Virtues. John Cassian: And in fact, if we look with the elevated gaze of our mind at the condition wherein the heavenly and supernal virtues that are truly in the kingdom of God make their home, what else should it be

thought to be than perpetual and continual joy? For what belongs so much to true blessedness and so befits it as continual tranquility and everlasting joy? . . . "They shall receive joy and gladness; sorrow and groaning shall flee away." Conference 1.13.3-4.[85]

The End Will Come. Ambrose: [God] is the same one who said to Jeremiah, "Behold, I place my words in your mouth as a fire."[86] David, therefore, also received this tongue of fire, so that he could speak of divine knowledge while enkindled with zeal: "Make known to me my end, O Lord."[87] He was not here asking about his own death or about the final resurrection. He was inquiring into that end of which the apostle spoke: "For the end will come when the Lord Jesus hands over the kingdom to God the Father and when he destroys every principality and power and when death is the last of all things to be destroyed,"[88] such that evil is defeated and eternal goodness is ignited. Therefore it was said, "Pain and wailing will flee." Explanation of the Twelve Psalms 38.16.[89]

Perpetual and Lasting Joy. John Cassian: For by these tokens the kingdom of God and the kingdom of the devil are distinguished: and in truth if lifting up our mental gaze on high we would consider that state in which the heavenly powers live on high, who are truly in the kingdom of God, what should we imagine it to be except perpetual and lasting joy? For what is so specially peculiar and appropriate to true blessedness as constant calm and eternal joy? And that you may be quite sure that this, which we say, is really so, not on my own authority but on that of the Lord, hear how very clearly he describes the character and condition of that world. "Behold," he says, "I create new heavens and a new earth; and the former things shall not be remembered nor come into mind. But

[81]FC 31:330*. [82]LCL 34:211*. [83]Rev 7:17. [84]ANF 3:590*. [85]ACW 57:51. [86]Jer 5:14; cf. Acts 2:3. [87]Ps 39:5 (38:5 LXX). [88]See 1 Cor 15:24, 26. [89]CSEL 64:196.

you shall be glad and rejoice forever in that which I create."[90] And again "joy and gladness shall be found therein: thanksgiving and the voice of praise, and there shall be month after month, and sabbath after sabbath."[91] And again: "They shall obtain joy and gladness; and sorrow and sighing shall flee away." And if you want to know more definitely about that life and the city of the saints, hear what the voice of the Lord proclaims to the heavenly Jerusalem: "I will make," he says, "your officers peace and your overseers righteousness. Violence shall no more be heard in your land, desolation nor destruction within your borders. And salvation shall take possession of your walls, and praise of your gates."[92] CONFERENCE 1.13.[93]

DEATH IS SWALLOWED UP IN VICTORY. FUL-GENTIUS OF RUSPE: When death is swallowed up in victory,[94] therefore, there will be no corruption of body or soul, for when all iniquity has been removed from us, no infirmity will remain. Indeed, it is about such matters that Isaiah said, "They will obtain joy and gladness; and pain and moaning will flee from them." THREE BOOKS TO TRASAMUNDUS 3.19.3.[95]

ENDURE TO THE END. PRIMASIUS: "The one who endures to the end will be saved."[96] By still

referring to this the text goes on reading: "On either side of the river is the tree of life with its twelve kinds of fruit, producing its fruit each month; and the leaves of the tree are for the healing of the nations. Nothing accursed will be found there anymore."[97] In the twelve months he suggests the idea of all times and designates eternity. Therefore where there is eternal greenness, no aridity will ever be allowed to exist. Where there is perfect and sound health, no infirmity is ever admitted, and also the prophet promises this by saying, "They shall obtain joy and gladness, and sorrow and sighing shall flee away." "The tree" is the one that we read to be "planted by streams of water," about which also Jeremiah says "that it sends out its roots by the stream,"[98] that is, places its hope and confidence in the Lord. In another sense the river of the water of life is recognized to signify rightly the fountain itself of life, that is, the Lord Jesus Christ, about whom we read, "For with you is the fountain of life; in your light we see light."[99] COMMENTARY ON THE APOCALYPSE 5.22.[100]

---

[90]Is 65:17-18. [91]Is 51:3; 66:23. [92]Is 60:17-18. [93]CSEL 13:19-20. [94]See 1 Cor 15:54. [95]CCL 91:163. [96]Mt 10:22. [97]Rev 22:2-3. [98]Jer 17:8. [99]Ps 36:9. [100]CCL 92:300.

36:1-22 THE ASSYRIAN ASSAULT ON JUDAH

[1]In the fourteenth year of King Hezekiah, Sennacherib king of Assyria came up against all the fortified cities of Judah and took them. [2]And the king of Assyria sent the Rabshakeh from Lachish to King Hezekiah at Jerusalem, with a great army. And he stood by the conduit of the upper pool on the highway to the Fuller's Field. [3]And there came out to him Eliakim the son of Hilkiah, who was over the household, and Shebna the secretary, and Joah the son of Asaph, the recorder.

⁴And the Rabshakeh said to them, "Say to Hezekiah, "Thus says the great king, the king of Assyria: On what do you rest this confidence of yours? ⁵Do you think that mere words are strategy and power for war? On whom do you now rely, that you have rebelled against me? ⁶Behold, you are relying on Egypt, that broken reed of a staff, which will pierce the hand of any man who leans on it. Such is Pharaoh king of Egypt to all who rely on him. ⁷But if you say to me, "We rely on the LORD our God," is it not he whose high places and altars Hezekiah has removed, saying to Judah and to Jerusalem, "You shall worship before this altar"? ⁸Come now, make a wager with my master the king of Assyria: I will give you two thousand horses, if you are able on your part to set riders upon them. ⁹How then can you repulse a single captain among the least of my master's servants, when you rely on Egypt for chariots and for horsemen? ¹⁰Moreover, is it without the LORD that I have come up against this land to destroy it? The LORD said to me, Go up against this land, and destroy it.'"

¹¹Then Eliakim, Shebna, and Joah said to the Rabshakeh, "Pray, speak to your servants in Aramaic, for we understand it; do not speak to us in the language of Judah within the hearing of the people who are on the wall." ¹²But the Rabshakeh said, "Has my master sent me to speak these words to your master and to you, and not to the men sitting on the wall, who are doomed with you to eat their own dung and drink their own urine?"

¹³Then the Rabshakeh stood and called out in a loud voice in the language of Judah: "Hear the words of the great king, the king of Assyria! ¹⁴Thus says the king: 'Do not let Hezekiah deceive you, for he will not be able to deliver you. ¹⁵Do not let Hezekiah make you rely on the LORD by saying, "The LORD will surely deliver us; this city will not be given into the hand of the king of Assyria." ¹⁶Do not listen to Hezekiah; for thus says the king of Assyria: Make your peace with me and come out to me; then every one of you will eat of his own vine, and every one of his own fig tree, and every one of you will drink the water of his own cistern; ¹⁷until I come and take you away to a land like your own land, a land of grain and wine, a land of bread and vineyards. ¹⁸Beware lest Hezekiah mislead you by saying, "The LORD will deliver us." Has any of the gods of the nations delivered his land out of the hand of the king of Assyria? ¹⁹Where are the gods of Hamath and Arpad? Where are the gods of Sepharvaim? Have they delivered Samaria out of my hand? ²⁰Who among all the gods of these countries have delivered their countries out of my hand, that the LORD should deliver Jerusalem out of my hand?'"

²¹But they were silent and answered him not a word, for the king's command was, "Do not answer him." ²²Then Eliakim the son of Hilkiah, who was over the household, and Shebna the secretary, and Joah the son of Asaph, the recorder, came to Hezekiah with their clothes rent, and told him the words of the Rabshakeh.

OVERVIEW: Isaiah included a passage from 2 Kings to demonstrate the truth of his own prophecies concerning Christ (THEODORET). The Sennacherib of this passage is not the same as the Sennacherib who captured Samaria. The identity of the Rabshakeh is uncertain, and his words should be considered false. The Eliakim of this passage, however, is the same Eliakim in Isaiah

22. Shebna the scribe is a different person from Shebna the leader of the temple. Hezekiah was confident that God would deliver Jerusalem from destruction at the hands of the Assyrians. The Rabshakeh refused to speak Aramaic for, they said, they had come to deliver a message to the people (JEROME). Christians should not attend the theater because of its filthy content (CHRYSOSTOM). The Rabshakeh strategized to win the Israelites' allegiance, but they remained loyal to King Hezekiah (JEROME).

36:1-2 Sennacherib Takes the Cities of Judah

THE TRUTH OF ISAIAH'S PROPHECY. THEODORET OF CYR: The book of 2 Kings also speaks of this event.[1] Isaiah has included it to his prophecy in order to show that his prophecy is true. Previously the prophet has made announcements concerning Babylon, Tyre, Egypt and other nations, but he is mostly concerned with the incarnation of our Savior, the unbelief and resultant judgment of Israel, and the call and salvation of the Gentiles. He has also announced Assyria's attack and their ultimate destruction. It follows that he would include this event here to demonstrate that his prophecies are true. By showing that the announcement related to Sennacherib is true, he can show that all his other prophecies will be fulfilled in the same way. COMMENTARY ON ISAIAH 36.1.[2]

THE IDENTITY OF SENNACHERIB. JEROME: I read in the commentary of a certain man that it was the same Sennacherib who also captured Samaria, which is altogether false. For sacred history reports that Pul, under Menahem the king of Israel, was the first king of the Assyrians to have plundered the ten tribes.[3] Second, Tiglath-pileser came to Samaria under Pekah the son of Remaliah.[4] Shalmaneser was then the third to have taken all of Samaria.[5] Fourth came Sargon, who fought against Ashdod,[6] and the fifth was Essarhadon, who held the Samaritans captive in the land of Judea. Sennacherib was the sixth who,

under Hezekiah king of Israel, laid siege to Jerusalem after he had captured Lachish and other cities of Judea.[7] But others think that these many names apply to one and the same person. COMMENTARY ON ISAIAH 11.36.1-10.[8]

THE IDENTITY OF THE RABSHAKEH AND HIS WORDS. JEROME: But the Jews claim that the Rabshakeh, who spoke the Hebrew language, was the son of the prophet Isaiah and was himself a betrayer, and that another remaining son of Isaiah was called Jashub, who also spoke our tongue. Others, moreover, believe that he was a Samaritan and that this is why he knew the Hebrew language and why he blasphemed the Lord with such audacity and impiety. We should therefore regard the words of the Rabshakeh to be false, first of all this: "You trust in that broken staff of a reed, in Egypt." For there is no history that sends Hezekiah to Egypt and makes Pharoah his assistant. But what he infers, "If you respond to me, 'We trust in the Lord our God,'" is true. Yet again he joins this truth to a lie, saying that Hezekiah removed God's high places and altars. For he did not do this against God but on behalf of God, so that with idolatry and the old error destroyed, he could command God to be worshiped in Jerusalem where his temple was located, although we observe the terrible custom of appointing people to sacrifice victims to God in the mountains and hills, where altars are already built. And wishing to demonstrate the paucity of hostages, the Rabshakeh promises two thousand horses, riders for whom Hezekiah is unable to produce. Thus it was not out of stupidity that he approached the Jewish people, who lacked a knowledge of horsemanship, but due to his observation of the commandments of God, who had enjoined through Moses on the king of Israel, "He will not multiply horses for himself, and he will not have many wives."[9] But, the Rabshakeh said, if you are

---

[1]2 Kings 18:13—20:18. [2]SC 295:346. [3]2 Kings 15:17-20. [4]2 Kings 15:29. [5]2 Kings 17:3-6. [6]Is 20:1. [7]2 Kings 18—19. [8]CCL 73:431-32. [9]Deut 17:16-17.

unable to withstand me, a servant of Sennacherib—even the least of his servants—how will you withstand such great power of the king? But to the possibility of Hezekiah responding "We trust in the Lord our God" the Rabshakeh replies cleverly and with prudence that he had not come on his own initiative, but at the request of the Lord. "The Lord said to me, 'Go up to that land and destroy it.'" This in short is his argument: Surely I would not have been able to come if it were not the will of the Lord. But since I came and captured many cities, with Jerusalem remaining intact, it is manifestly his will that I came. COMMENTARY ON ISAIAH 11.36.1-10.[10]

36:3 Eliakim and Shebna

THE IDENTITY OF HILKIAH. JEROME: Eliakim, the son of Hilkiah, who was leader of the house, went out to him, as well as Shebna the scribe and Joah the son of Asaph from the commentaries. This is the same Elakim, son of Hilkiah, about whom we read above in the vision of the valley of Zion: "I will call my servant Eliakim, son of Hilkiah, and I will clothe him in your tunic, and I will strengthen him with your girdle, and I will give your power into his hand, and he will be like a father to the inhabitants of Jerusalem and to the house of Judah."[11] COMMENTARY ON ISAIAH 11.36.1-10.[12]

THE IDENTITY OF SHEBNA. JEROME: But these things were said to Shebna, who was leader of the temple before Eliakim, about whom it is written, "Go, approach him who lives in the tabernacle, Shebna the leader of the temple."[13] Acting under the threat of the Rabshakeh, the Hebrews betrayed him to the Assyrians and handed over the lower part of Jerusalem to the enemies, and nothing remained of what the Assyrians had left behind except for the temple and the ark of Zion. Hence they err who think that the Shebna who now goes out with Eliakim and Joah to the Rabshakeh is the same as the one above. For that Shebna was made leader of the temple which, it is

said, was to be taken by the Assyrians. But this Shebna is a scribe, that is, a *grammateis* [Greek], which is called *sofer* in Hebrew, and is *homōnymos* [Greek] to the one above. COMMENTARY ON ISAIAH 11.36.1-10.[14]

36:4 Thus Says the King

THE PRESUMPTUOUS RABSHAKEH. JEROME: And the Rabshakeh told them: "Say to Hezekiah, 'Thus says the great king, the king of the Assyrians,'" and other things that are contained in the history. In this, the Rabshakeh is to be regarded as presumptuous because, like some sort of contrary power, he is imitating the habit of the prophets, inasmuch as they customarily use "Thus says the Lord" as a preface to display the authority and greatness of the speaker, whereas he now says, "Thus says the great king, the king of the Assyrians." COMMENTARY ON ISAIAH 11.36.1-10.[15]

HEZEKIAH'S CONFIDENCE. JEROME: The accusation of the Rabshakeh against Hezekiah is evidence that with all the cities of Judah taken captive he would still be confident in the Lord, as he said to the people: "Do not be afraid, nor quake at the king of the Assyrians and all the great multitude that he has with him. For we have a great deal more with us than he has with him. With him is the arm of flesh, but with us is the Lord our God, our help, who will fight for us." And the people were encouraged, it says, by these words of Hezekiah the king of Judah, which is why the Rabshakeh wanted to destroy what Hezekiah had created, so he said to the people, "Do not let Hezekiah seduce you," and "Do not let him cause you to rely upon the Lord God." COMMENTARY ON ISAIAH 11.36.11-21.[16]

36:11 The Request for Aramaic

---

[10]CCL 73:431. [11]Is 22:20-21. [12]CCL 73:430. [13]Is 22:15. [14]CCL 73:430-31. [15]CCL 73:430. [16]CCL 73:433.

THE RABSHAKEH REFUSES TO SPEAK ARAMAIC.
JEROME: But what Eliakim and Shebna and Joah
humbly requested, namely, "Speak to your servants in the Syrian language [Aramaic], for we
understand it, and do not speak to us in Hebrew
within the hearing of the people on the wall," has
this sense: Is it really necessary to fill the people
with unjustified terror and to spread panic?
Speak a language that these people do not understand, for we have knowledge of your tongue and
are familiar with the Syrian dialect, which is
common to us both. To this the Rabshakeh
replied arrogantly: "Did my master send me," he
said, "to your master rather than to the men who
sit on the wall?" Then he added, to supply the
threat of terror by showing that they would be
overtaken by hunger, poverty and thirst: "that
they would eat their own dung and drink their
own urine with you?" COMMENTARY ON ISAIAH
11.36.11-21.[17]

36:12 Eat Dung

LISTEN TO THE APOSTLES. CHRYSOSTOM: In
order . . . that both our houses may be continually
open to [the poor] and our ears to [the apostles],
we should purge away the filth from the ears of our
soul. For as filth and mud close up our fleshly ears,
so do the prostitute's songs, worldly talking, debts
and the business of borrowing and paying interest
close up the mind's ear even worse than dirt. Not
only do these things close up the ear, but also they
make it unclean. Those who cause you to listen to
the prostitute's songs[18] put dung in your ears. They
make you endure not just in word but in deeds,
what the barbarian threatened: "You shall eat your
own dung," and what follows. HOMILIES ON THE
GOSPEL OF MATTHEW 37.7.[19]

36:13-20 Do Not Listen to Hezekiah

THE RABSHAKEH'S STRATEGY. JEROME:
Immediately then, he supplemented this threat
with an enticement in order to deceive with
counterpromises and temptations those whom

he had not conquered with terror, saying on
behalf of the king of the Assyrians: "Make peace
with me and come to me," or as we read in the
book of Kings: "Do with me what is useful and
come to me."[20] Both have the same meaning. Do,
he said, what is to your own advantage and it
will accrue to your blessing. In other words:
Bless the king of Assyria and praise him, and
confess him to be your lord that you might
receive a reward. Also, live in your cities and
enjoy your crops until I return from Egypt or
until I restore captured Libnah. After I come, I
will take you to a land much like your own, with
grain and wine and oil. But he did not give a
name for this land because he could not find an
equal to the Promised Land. Yet he promised it
nevertheless, for everyone desires to be in the
land of his birth. Some think the land that he
promised was Media, which has terrain similar
in both location and foliage to that of Judea.
Then he added: "Where is the god of Hamath
and of Arpad and of Sepharvaim? Have they
delivered Samaria from my hand?" This shows
that Samaria will be subject to them for all of its
days and therefore that it should be taken. If, he
said, we were easily victorious over the ten
tribes who had the protection of so many gods,
how much more easily will we conquer you,
even lonely Jerusalem, which has the protection
of only one God? COMMENTARY ON ISAIAH
11.36.11-21.[21]

36:21 They Were Silent

LOYALTY TO HEZEKIAH. JEROME: All of the people remained silent and no one said anything to
him, because they had accepted the instruction of
the king not to respond to him. For because
Hezekiah was a truly righteous man, acting in
complete fidelity and with all counsel, he had
asked that no response be made to the blasphem-

---

[17]CCL 73:433. [18]Chrysostom is preaching against Christians attend-
ing the theater. [19]NPNF 1 10:248**. [20]2 Kings 18:31. [21]CCL
73:433-34.

ing Assyrian, lest it provoke him to even greater blasphemy. Hence it is written: "Do not ignite the coals of a sinner."[22] We also read in the Psalms: "When the sinner stood against me, I was mute and I was humbled and I was silent concerning the good."[23] And again, "Place a guard at my mouth, Lord, and a fortified door over my lips; do not incline my heart toward evil words."[24] COMMENTARY ON ISAIAH 11.36.11-21.[25]

---

[22]Sir 8:10. [23]Cf. Ps 39:2-3 (38:2-3 LXX). [24]Ps 141:3-4 (140:3-4 LXX). [25]CCL 73:433-34.

37:1-38 THE ASSYRIAN ARMY
DESTROYED BY GOD

[1]When King Hezekiah heard it, he rent his clothes, and covered himself with sackcloth, and went into the house of the LORD. [2]And he sent Eliakim, who was over the household, and Shebna the secretary, and the senior priests, clothed with sackcloth, to the prophet Isaiah the son of Amoz. [3]They said to him, "Thus says Hezekiah, 'This day is a day of distress, of rebuke, and of disgrace; children have come to the birth, and there is no strength to bring them forth. [4]It may be that the LORD your God heard the words of the Rabshakeh, whom his master the king of Assyria has sent to mock the living God, and will rebuke the words which the LORD your God has heard; therefore lift up your prayer for the remnant that is left.'"

[5]When the servants of King Hezekiah came to Isaiah, [6]Isaiah said to them, "Say to your master, 'Thus says the LORD: Do not be afraid because of the words that you have heard, with which the servants of the king of Assyria have reviled me. [7]Behold, I will put a spirit in him, so that he shall hear a rumor, and return to his own land; and I will make him fall by the sword in his own land.'"

[8]The Rabshakeh returned, and found the king of Assyria fighting against Libnah; for he had heard that the king had left Lachish. [9]Now the king heard concerning Tirhakah king of Ethiopia, "He has set out to fight against you." And when he heard it, he sent messengers to Hezekiah, saying, [10]"Thus shall you speak to Hezekiah king of Judah: 'Do not let your God on whom you rely deceive you by promising that Jerusalem will not be given into the hand of the king of Assyria. [11]Behold, you have heard what the kings of Assyria have done to all lands, destroying them utterly. And shall you be delivered? [12]Have the gods of the nations delivered them, the nations which my fathers destroyed, Gozan, Haran, Rezeph, and the people of Eden who were in Telassar? [13]Where is the king of Hamath, the king of Arpad, the king of the city of Sepharvaim, the king of Hena, or the king of Ivvah?'"

[14]Hezekiah received the letter from the hand of the messengers, and read it; and Hezekiah went

up to the house of the LORD, and spread it before the LORD. ¹⁵And Hezekiah prayed to the LORD: ¹⁶"O LORD of hosts, God of Israel, who art enthroned above the cherubim, thou art the God, thou alone, of all the kingdoms of the earth; thou hast made heaven and earth. ¹⁷Incline thy ear, O LORD, and hear; open thy eyes, O LORD, and see; and hear all the words of Sennacherib, which he has sent to mock the living God. ¹⁸Of a truth, O LORD, the kings of Assyria have laid waste all the nations and their lands, ¹⁹and have cast their gods into the fire; for they were no gods, but the work of men's hands, wood and stone; therefore they were destroyed. ²⁰So now, O LORD our God, save us from his hand, that all the kingdoms of the earth may know that thou alone art the LORD."

²¹Then Isaiah the son of Amoz sent to Hezekiah, saying, "Thus says the LORD, the God of Israel: Because you have prayed to me concerning Sennacherib king of Assyria, ²²this is the word that the LORD has spoken concerning him:

'She despises you, she scorns you—
    the virgin daughter of Zion;
she wags her head behind you—
    the daughter of Jerusalem.

²³'Whom have you mocked and reviled?
    Against whom have you raised your voice
and haughtily lifted your eyes?
    Against the Holy One of Israel!
²⁴By your servants you have mocked the Lord,
    and you have said, With my many chariots
I have gone up the heights of the mountains,
    to the far recesses of Lebanon;
I felled its tallest cedars,
    its choicest cypresses;
I came to its remotest height,
    its densest forest.
²⁵I dug wells
    and drank waters,
and I dried up with the sole of my foot
    all the streams of Egypt.

²⁶'Have you not heard
    that I determined it long ago?
I planned from days of old
    what now I bring to pass,
that you should make fortified cities
    crash into heaps of ruins,

^{27}*while their inhabitants, shorn of strength,*
are dismayed and confounded,
and have become like plants of the field
and like tender grass,
like grass on the housetops,
blighted^e before it is grown.

^{28}*'I know your sitting down*
and your going out and coming in,
and your raging against me.
^{29}*Because you have raged against me*
and your arrogance has come to my ears,
I will put my hook in your nose
and my bit in your mouth,
and I will turn you back on the way
by which you came.'

^{30}"And this shall be the sign for you: this year eat what grows of itself, and in the second year what springs of the same; then in the third year sow and reap, and plant vineyards, and eat their fruit. ^{31}And the surviving remnant of the house of Judah shall again take root downward, and bear fruit upward; ^{32}for out of Jerusalem shall go forth a remnant, and out of Mount Zion a band of survivors. The zeal of the LORD of hosts will accomplish this.

^{33}"Therefore thus says the LORD concerning the king of Assyria: He shall not come into this city, or shoot an arrow there, or come before it with a shield, or cast up a siege mound against it. ^{34}By the way that he came, by the same he shall return, and he shall not come into this city, says the LORD. ^{35}For I will defend this city to save it, for my own sake and for the sake of my servant David."

^{36}And the angel of the LORD went forth, and slew a hundred and eighty-five thousand in the camp of the Assyrians; and when men arose early in the morning, behold, these were all dead bodies. ^{37}Then Sennacherib king of Assyria departed, and went home and dwelt at Nineveh. ^{38}And as he was worshiping in the house of Nisroch his god, Adrammelech and Sharezer, his sons, slew him with the sword, and escaped into the land of Ararat. And Esar-haddon his son reigned in his stead.

e With 2 Kings 19.26: Heb *field*

OVERVIEW: Hezekiah and the people tore their clothes because of the Rabshakeh's blasphemy. Isaiah did not refer to himself as a prophet, whereas others who wrote about him did.

Hezekiah sent a tactful message to Isaiah, who assured Hezekiah that God will respond to blasphemy by sending an adversarial spirit. When comparing this account in Isaiah with the similar account in Chronicles, one must consider that the book of Isaiah is a mixture of history and prophecy. The Rabshakeh used the defeat of other nations to try to persuade the Israelites that as other gods could not defend other cities, so God could not defend Jerusalem. But Jerusalem was spared, likely because the Assyrian army fell to disease. Hezekiah proclaims through prayer the weakness of idols and the sovereignty of the one true God. In Sennacherib's sentence, Lebanon represents Jerusalem, cedar and fir represent its elders and aristocrats, the height of its summit represents the temple, and waters represent the people conquered by it. Sennacherib's anger and pride turn the tide from his military success, according to God's will, to his failure to capture Jerusalem, also according to God's will (JEROME). Weeping and mourning are the means to forgiveness of sin and strength in virtue (PASCHASIUS OF DUMIUM).

37:1 King Hezekiah Tore His Clothes

RESPONSIBILITY OF THE KING. JEROME: Let us examine those remaining matters whose meaning remains hidden. They tore their garments because they heard the Rabshakeh speaking blasphemy. The king also tore his clothing because he believed that it was due to his sins and the sins of the people that the Rabshakeh came to the gate of Jerusalem and spoke such things against the Lord. Hence, the high priest, because he believed the Savior to have been blasphemed, also cut his garments.[1] Paul and Barnabas, moreover, when the Lycaonians offered to them the worship of God, cut their clothes.[2] COMMENTARY ON ISAIAH 11.37.1-7.[3]

37:2 Isaiah Son of Amoz

ISAIAH DOES NOT CALL HIMSELF A PROPHET. JEROME: For the sake of royal worship, therefore, Hezekiah wrapped himself in sackcloth and, walking from his palace to the temple, sent Eliakim, the high priest, Shebna, the scribe, and

senior priests to the prophet Isaiah son of Amos, an act that must be attributed to the humility and prudence of the king. He proceeded to the temple and sent leaders of the people and senior priests, not draped in priestly stoles but covered in sackcloth, to the prophet Isaiah son of Amos, concerning which we read in the book of Kings: "Himself covered in sackcloth, having entered the house of the Lord, he sent Eliakim, leader of the house, and Shebna the scribe and senior priests, covered with sackcloth, to the prophet Isaiah son of Amos."[4] Because Isaiah was writing a history about himself here in his book, he did not call himself a prophet but the son of a prophet, whereas the passage just quoted does use the title *prophet* because it comes from a different author of the history.[5] Similarly, we read from the Gospel of Matthew that Matthew called himself a publican,[6] whereas other Evangelists refrained from calling him a publican, granting him such apostolic dignity.[7] COMMENTARY ON ISAIAH 11.37.1-7.[8]

37:3-4 Thus Says Hezekiah

HEZEKIAH'S TACTFUL WORDS TO ISAIAH. JEROME: "And they said to him, 'Thus says Hezekiah,'" not "thus says the king," not swelling pridefully with political power. "This is a day of tribulation, of punishment, and a day of blasphemy," of our tribulation, of God's punishment, of the enemies' blasphemy. And he drew an analogy to a woman suffering the pains of childbirth—who has come to the point of delivery but is unable to give birth—to say, "We have conceived from fear of you, Lord, and we suffered, and we gave birth to the spirit of salvation."[9] Hezekiah continues: "Perhaps the Lord your God heard the words of the Rabshakeh." We do not dare to call the Lord of all "our Lord," whereby we would suffer such wrath, but we say "your Lord." And we have confidence in

---

[1]Mt 26:65. [2]Acts 14:13. [3]CCL 73:435. [4]2 Kings 19:1-2. [5]Jerome's text reads *ad Esaiam filium Amos prophetae* ("to Isaiah the son of the prophet Amos"). [6]Mt 9:9-11. [7]The last phrase of the previous sentence is unclear. [8]CCL 73:435. [9]Is 26:18 LXX.

[God's] punishment because the living God is being blasphemed by the worship of idols of the dead. "And they will chastise with the words which the Lord your God heard. Lift up a prayer, therefore, not for all the people who have already perished, but for the remnant who are besieged." COMMENTARY ON ISAIAH 11.37.1-7.[10]

37:5 They Came to Isaiah

ISAIAH'S HUMILITY AND DISCERNMENT. JEROME: "When the servants of King Hezekiah came to Isaiah." . . . Again he does not use the title of prophet, maintaining the humility with which he began. And Isaiah anticipated them, for he had heard of their departure from the king by the same Spirit from which he also learned of future events. Then he tells them what they ought to reply to their master, humbled in fidelity of conscience: "Say to your master, who is your master, that my Lord says this: 'Do not be afraid of the words with which not you but I am blasphemed. I will not foretell everything that I am about to do to the king of Assyria, lest I appear to be throwing my weight around, but the spirit which will be given to them is that of the adversary, not of God.'" COMMENTARY ON ISAIAH 11.37.1-7.[11]

37:8 The Rabshakeh Returns

PROPHECY AND HISTORY. JEROME: Anyone who seeks to know why the history contained in the books of Kings and Chronicles appears to be confused in the book of the prophet should consider that prophecy may be mixed with history in the latter. . . . The liberation of the city and the downfall of Assyria and the reversion of the sun for ten hours[12] and the fifteen years' prolongation[13] . . . belong both to prophecy and to history. COMMENTARY ON ISAIAH 11.37.1-7.[14]

37:10 Do Not Let God Deceive You

THE NATIONS EXEMPLIFY CONQUEST. JEROME: The Rabshakeh, according to the will of the

Lord, abandoned his blockade of Jerusalem and directed himself to his master, whom he knew to be heading to fight Libnah, having either deserted or captured Lachish. Sennacherib himself, hearing that Tirhakah the king of Ethiopia was waging war against him, went out to confront him but nonetheless also sent a messenger with letters to Hezekiah to frighten those men who had not yet begun. And just as he had said to the people, "Do not let Hezekiah seduce you,"[15] so now he speaks the same blasphemy to the king, saying, "Do not let God deceive you." He made an example of the elders: because the gods of other lands were unable to deliver them from his hands, neither will Jerusalem be liberated. But in enumerating the other nations, he includes Hena and Ivvah, whom the Septuagint confused by saying Anavegava, using the Hebrew language to place the conjunction vaw[16] between the two nations Hena and Ivvah, that it might appear to the ignorant to be one nation or city. COMMENTARY ON ISAIAH 11.37.8-13.[17]

37:11 Shall You Be Delivered?

JERUSALEM DELIVERED. JEROME: We are hastening past the obvious, that we would remain with doubts. But Herodotus writes[18] (as does the most prolific Berosus,[19] historian of the Chaldeans, whose faith can be derived from their own books) that Sennacherib the king of the Assyrians fought against the Egyptians and besieged Pelusium. And with mounds already amassed in the city for conquest Tirhakah the king of Ethiopia came to their assistance, and in one night 185 thousand soldiers of Assyria fell to disease near Jerusalem. COMMENTARY ON ISAIAH 11.37.8-13.[20]

37:14-20 Hezekiah's Prayer

---

[10]CCL 73:435-36. [11]CCL 73:436. [12]Is 38:7. [13]Is 38:4. [14]CCL 73:436. [15]Is 36:14. [16]The sixth letter of the Hebrew alphabet. [17]CCL 73:436-37. [18]Herodotus Historiae 2.141. [19]Berosus Antiquitates 10.1.4.20. [20]CCL 73:437.

Only One God. Jerome: Against the blasphemies of King Sennacherib, Hezekiah's customary armory failed. So he goes back to the temple and opens his letter before the Lord. Previously he was silent, for he did not dare to open his mouth in the temple for fear of the Lord, nor to pour out extemporaneous prayers to God. Now, however, because he has already heard Isaiah saying, "Do not be afraid of the words which you hear, with which the sons of the king of the Assyrians have blasphemed me," and so on, he beseeches the Lord boldly and claims that the Lord alone is the living God, through whom we understand idols to be images of the dead.... That these idols weakened their makers is proven by many histories that record that the kings of Persia came to Greece, and subverted and ruined the temple of the Greeks. It also postulates vengeance, that through this opportunity all kingdoms would recognize that there is only one God, who is able to deliver his own from peril. Commentary on Isaiah 11.37.14-20.[21]

37:21-25 Isaiah Sent to Hezekiah

The Sentence on Sennacherib. Jerome: Because Hezekiah prayed to the Lord so boldly and did not send for Isaiah, as he had done previously, the prophet did not visit him in person but sent messengers who spoke to him the words of God: "This is the sentence of the Lord on Sennacherib, against whom you prayed: the virgin of Zion and daughter of Jerusalem"—who is called virgin and daughter because, with all the other nations worshiping the idols of dead men, she alone preserved the purity of the religion of God and the worship of one divinity—"has mocked and despised you. And lest she provoke you to greater blasphemy, she did not respond in your presence, but wagged her head behind you, immune from vengeance, secure from punishment. She also said this: 'It is not against me that you have rebelled but against the Lord. Nor did you do it yourself, but through your servants, that the arrogance of your blasphemy might be greater. For you said that with the multitude of your chariots you would ascend the heights of the mountains and the yokes of Lebanon, and that you would fell the highest of its cedars and firs.'" We should read this metaphorically[22] as concerning all the Gentiles and their princes, or as concerning Jerusalem, which Lebanon represents, such that we would refer her cedars and firs to the rulers and aristocrats but the height of her summit and the forest of her Carmel to the temple.[23] For he had said above: "Have you not heard what the kings of Assyria did to all the earth, destroying it? Therefore, neither can you be liberated." And because he adds: "I dug a well and drank water and dried up with my footsteps all the rivers of Egypt," it can be understood in accordance with history that all the streams ran dry before the multitude of the army, thus making it necessary to dig wells. This means that by means of his army he destroyed all the peoples, who are sometimes known under the name of "waters," as only the Seventy translated:[24] "And I made a bridge and I turned the desert into waters and all the congregations of the waters."[25] None of the nations were impassable to themselves, of course, but he trampled with his foot on all the waters of the people. Commentary on Isaiah 11.37.21-25.[26]

37:26-29 Oracle Against Sennacherib Continued

What God Planned Comes to Pass. Jerome: This is directed from the person of God against the words of Assyria, to whose blasphemy the Lord responds thus: "Do you not know that you did this with my permission? Do you not know that I predict the future and command that certain things be done through you? Hence, what I

---

[21]CCL 73:437-38. [22]Jerome uses the Greek here (*metaphorikōs*) without providing a Latin equivalent. [23]In both the ancient and the modern edition of the Vulgate, Isaiah 37:24 reads *Et introibo altitudinem summitatis eius, saltum Carmeli eius*, but most modern English translations make no reference to Carmel. [24]In the Septuagint. [25]Cf. Ps 107:35 (106:35 LXX); Is 41:18. [26]CCL 73:338-39.

decreed long ago is being fulfilled at this time: that the hills (that is, princes who fight among themselves) and the fortified cities will be shaken and eradicated, and will perish when I withdraw my hand and offer them none of the assistance to which they have grown accustomed. They were also compared not to olive groves and vineyards and fruitful trees but to straw and turf, to roof grass, all of which impede fruitfulness and wither before they reach maturity. In this way I have also foreknown your sitting down and your going out and your coming in, and I predicted through the prophets the insanity with which you would rage against me. Through these I knew long ago that you would say, 'I will ascend to heaven; I will set my throne above the stars of heaven, and I will be like the Most High.'[27] Thus, your anger and your pride have reached my ears, and I will bear you no longer, that you may understand that you are not capable by your own strength but by my will. For the impious Gentiles and the unfruitful trees deserved to be cut down and felled through you, as though you were my axe and saw. Hence, I put a ring or a bit in your nostrils to restrain your verbal blasphemy, that you would dare to speak such things no more. I will also place a bridle on your lips to tame your ferocity and to lead you back to Egypt." Scripture employs the same imagery in

the Psalms against the impious: "Constrain their jaws with a bit and bridle, that they not approach you."[28] COMMENTARY ON ISAIAH 11.37.26-29.[29]

37:36 Death of the Assyrians

FREEDOM FROM SINS. PASCHASIUS OF DUMIUM: A brother asked Antony,[30] "What shall I do for my sins?" He replied, "He who desires to be freed from his sins will be freed from them by tears and weeping. He who wishes to be strengthened in virtues will be strengthened by weeping and tears. The very praise of the Psalms is mourning. Remember the example of Hezekiah, king of Judah, as it is written in the prophet Isaiah, who by weeping not only recovered his health but won an increase of life for fifteen years."[31] By the outpouring of his tears, the strength of the Lord brought to death the advancing army of the enemy, even 185,000. QUESTIONS AND ANSWERS OF THE GREEK FATHERS 38.1.[32]

---

[27]Is 14:14. [28]Ps 32:9 (31:9 LXX). [29]CCL 739-40. [30]The famous desert monk. [31]Is 38:3-9. [32]FC 62:159*.

38:1-22 GOD'S CURSE ON KING HEZEKIAH LIFTED

[1]*In those days Hezekiah became sick and was at the point of death. And Isaiah the prophet the son of Amoz came to him, and said to him, "Thus says the LORD: Set your house in order; for you shall die, you shall not recover." [2]Then Hezekiah turned his face to the wall, and prayed to the LORD, [3]and said, "Remember now, O LORD, I beseech thee, how I have walked before thee in faith-*

*fulness and with a whole heart, and have done what is good in thy sight." And Hezekiah wept bit-
terly.* [4]*Then the word of the Lord came to Isaiah:* [5]*"Go and say to Hezekiah, Thus says the Lord,
the God of David your father: I have heard your prayer, I have seen your tears; behold, I will add
fifteen years to your life.* [6]*I will deliver you and this city out of the hand of the king of Assyria, and
defend this city.*

[7]*"This is the sign to you from the Lord, that the Lord will do this thing that he has promsied:*
[8]*Behold, I will make the shadow cast by the declining sun on the dial of Ahaz turn back ten steps."
So the sun turned back on the dial the ten steps by which it had declined.*[f]

[9]*A writing of Hezekiah king of Judah, after he had been sick and had recovered from his sickness:*
   [10]*I said, In the noontide of my days*
      I must depart;
   *I am consigned to the gates of Sheol**
      for the rest of my years.
   [11]*I said, I shall not see the Lord*
      in the land of the living;
   I shall look upon man no more
      among the inhabitants of the world.
   [12]*My dwelling is plucked up and removed from me*
      like a shepherd's tent;
   like a weaver I have rolled up my life;
      he cuts me off from the loom;
   from day to night thou dost bring me to an end;[g]
     [13]*I cry for help*[h] *until morning;*
   like a lion he breaks all my bones;
      from day to night thou dost bring me to an end.[g]

   [14]*Like a swallow or a crane*[i] *I clamor,*
      I moan like a dove.
   My eyes are weary with looking upward.
      O Lord, I am oppressed; be thou my security!
   [15]*But what can I say? For he has spoken to me,*
      and he himself has done it.
   All my sleep has fled[j]
      because of the bitterness of my soul.
   [16]*O Lord, by these things men live,*
      and in all these is the life of my spirit.[k]
      Oh, restore me to health and make me live!

[17]*Lo, it was for my welfare*
    that I had great bitterness;
but thou hast held back[l] my life
    from the pit of destruction,
for thou hast cast all my sins
    behind thy back.
[18]*For Sheol cannot thank thee,*
    death cannot praise thee;
those who go down to the pit cannot hope
    for thy faithfulness.[†]
[19]*The living, the living, he thanks thee,*
    as I do this day;
the father makes known to the children
    thy faithfulness.

[20]*The Lord will save me,*
    and we will sing to stringed instruments[m]
all the days of our life,
    at the house of the Lord.

[21]*Now Isaiah had said, "Let them take a cake of figs, and apply it to the boil, that he may recover." [22]Hezekiah also had said, "What is the sign that I shall go up to the house of the Lord?"*

f The Hebrew of this verse is obscure   g Heb uncertain   h Cn: Heb obscure   i Heb uncertain   j Cn Compare Syr: Heb *I will walk slowly all my years*   k Heb uncertain   l Cn Compare Gk Vg: Heb *loved*   m Heb *my stringed instruments*   *Vg *I will go to the gates of the nether world*   †LXX *mercy*

Overview: Confession, epitomized by Hezekiah, is a strong weapon of salvation (Cyril of Jerusalem). Hezekiah did not ask for long life but to be permitted to stand before the judgment of God (Jerome). Hezekiah's prayer brought life, but it can also bring death (Sahdona). The addition of fifteen years to Hezekiah's life signifies a perfect life (Cassiodorus). Though the sun turned back for Hezekiah, he cannot match the power of Christ to forgive sins (Cyril of Jerusalem). The lives of the impious are cut short. They await God's mercy in Sheol (Jerome). Only those who live in a godly manner are able to give glory to God (Athanasius). Hezekiah's children did not fulfill his promise that they would announce God's righteousness (Cyril of Alexandria). Hezekiah exemplifies thanksgiving in times of tribulation (Athanasius).

38:3 Remember Me, O Lord

The Power of Repentance. Cyril of Jerusalem: Do you want to know the power of repentance? Do you want to understand this strong weapon of salvation and the might of confession? By confession Hezekiah routed 185,000 of the enemy.[1] That was important, but it was small compared with what else happened. The same king's repentance won the repeal the sentence

[1] Is 37:36.

God had passed on him. When he was sick, Isaiah had said, "Give direction for your household, for you will surely die, and not live."[2] What expectation was left? What hope of recovery was there? The prophet had said, "You will surely die." But Hezekiah remembered what was written: "In the hour that you turn and lament, you will be saved."[3] He turned his face to the wall, and from his bed of pain his mind soared up to heaven (for no wall is so thick as to stifle fervent prayer). He said, "Lord, remember me.". . . He whom the prophet's sentence had forbidden to hope was granted fifteen further years of life, the sun turning back its course as a witness. CATECHETICAL LECTURES 2.15.[4]

HEZEKIAH'S GOOD WORKS. JEROME: Hearing that he was about to die, Hezekiah prayed not that he be granted several more years of life but that he be permitted to stand before the judgment of God, as he wished. For he knew that Solomon pleased God by not asking for a longer life. Preparing to journey to the Lord, therefore, Hezekiah chronicled his works, how he had walked before the Lord in truth and in perfection of heart. Happy is the conscience that remembers good works at a time of affliction: "Blessed are the pure in heart, for they will see God,"[5] or as it is written elsewhere, "Who will glory in the purity of his heart?"[6] This is the explanation: perfection of heart can now be attributed to him because he destroyed idols, overturned the vessels of Baal in the temple,[7] shattered the bronze serpent[8] and did other things that Scripture commemorates. COMMENTARY ON ISAIAH 11.38.1-3.[9]

38:5 Fifteen Years Added to Hezekiah's Life

PRAYER CAN BRING LIFE OR DEATH. SAHDONA: Prayer sometimes brings the dead back to life, but sometimes it may slay the living, as happened with the godly Peter. He brought Tabitha back to life by prayer,[10] but he effected the death of Ananias and Sapphira.[11] . . . The case of Hezekiah was also astonishing. Through prayer

he added to the days of his life as king. He routed the mighty Assyrian army through the agency of a spiritual being.[12] BOOK OF PERFECTION 41.[13]

FIFTEEN REPRESENTS THE PERFECT LIFE. CASSIODORUS: The number seven, as has often been said, denotes the week occasioned by the sabbath of the Old Testament. The number eight signifies the Lord's day, on which he clearly rose again, and this is relevant to the New [Testament]. When joined together, they are seen to make up the number fifteen. . . . Some commentators think that the fifteen additional years accorded to King Hezekiah are related to this parallel, so that the number fifteen is shown to have signified the course of his perfect life. EXPOSITION OF THE PSALMS 119.[14]

38:8 Turning Back the Sun

JESUS GREATER THAN HEZEKIAH. CYRIL OF JERUSALEM: For Hezekiah's sake the sun turned back, but for Christ the sun was eclipsed. The sun did not simply retrace its path for Christ but was completely eclipsed. This shows the difference between Hezekiah and Jesus. The former's prayer resulted in the canceling of God's decree. But does not Jesus forgive sins? Repent, shut your door, and pray to be forgiven. Pray that Christ may remove you from the burning flames, for confession has power even to quench fire, power even to tame lions. CATECHETICAL LECTURES 2.15.[15]

38:10 The Gates of Sheol

THE LENGTH OF ONE'S DAYS. JEROME: "Thus, in desperation I said, 'I will go to the gates of the netherworld,'" referring either to death by the common law of nature or to those gates from which the

---

[2] 2 Kings 20:1. [3] Is 30:15. [4] FC 61:104-5**. [5] Mt 5:8. [6] Prov 20:9. [7] 2 Kings 23:4. [8] 2 Kings 18:4. [9] CCL 73:443. [10] Acts 9:40. [11] Acts 5:3-10. [12] 2 Kings 19:35. [13] CS 101:219*. [14] ACW 53:260-61. [15] NPNF 2 7:12**.

psalmist was liberated and therefore sings, "You who raise me from the gates of death, that I might declare all your praises in the gates of the daughter of Zion."[16] I believe that these are the same gates of the netherworld that did not prevail against Peter,[17] who fell asleep in the fullness of his days. The saints complete their days, like Abraham, who "died full of years at an old age."[18] Sinners and the impious, however, die in the midst of their days, about which the psalmist also speaks: "Men of blood and deception will not complete half of their days."[19] For they neither perform works of virtue nor strive to amend their faults through penance. Hence, they will be led to the netherworld with their lives half finished and in the darkness of error. COMMENTARY ON ISAIAH 11.38.10-13.[20]

38:18-19 The Living Shall Bless You

SHEOL GIVES NO PRAISE. JEROME: For the netherworld and death will neither confess nor praise you, according to what is written: "In the netherworld, who will confess you?"[21] Confession in this instance, moreover, is received not as an act of penance but as an offering of glory and praise, as we read in the Gospel: "I praise you Lord, Father of heaven and earth."[22] He also says: "They who descend to the pit will not hope for your truth," which is better than the Septuagint's "will not hope for your mercy." For he who is in the grave hopes not for the truth of judgment but for the mercy of God, ultimately when the Savior will descend to the netherworld to liberate the captives from it. COMMENTARY ON ISAIAH 11.38.[23]

ONLY THE SAINTS CAN PRAISE. ATHANASIUS: [Those who live in a godly manner] and participate in such goodness are the only ones able to give glory to God, and that is what really constitutes a feast and a holy day. For the feast is not indulging in a lot of food or dressing up in lovely clothes. It is not enjoying days of leisure. It is acknowledging God and offering thanksgiving and songs of praise to him. But this belongs to the saints alone, who live in Christ. . . . That is

the way it was with Hezekiah, who was delivered from death and therefore praised God, saying, "Those who are in hell cannot praise you; the dead cannot bless you; but the living shall bless you, as I do today." FESTAL LETTER 7.3.[24]

THE FAILURE OF HEZEKIAH'S CHILDREN. CYRIL OF ALEXANDRIA: "For from this day I shall beget children who will announce your righteousness." Some say that he promises to institute a choir [chorostasia] and to appoint chanters of psalms with good voices in the temple. Others, who pay attention to more esoteric things, say that Hezekiah, since he thought on a high plane, was of the opinion that he would have a kingdom without end and unceasing life. For he was persuaded that the writings concerning the son of David destined to be the Christ were said about himself. Hence they say, although he was in the fifteenth year of his reign he does not seem to have procreated children. Accordingly, on learning that his end was near, he pays attention to the question of his successors and adds with reference to his children that they will announce the righteousness of the Lord. However, this statement was not verified since Manasseh was wicked and impious. COMMENTARY ON ISAIAH 3.4.38.[25]

38:20 The Lord Is My Salvation

THANKFULNESS IN TRIBULATION. ATHANASIUS: At no time should one freely praise God more than when one has passed through afflictions. Nor again should one at any time give thanks more than when he finds rest from toil and temptations. As Hezekiah, when the Assyrians perished, praised the Lord and gave thanks, saying, "The Lord is my salvation, and I will not cease to bless you with harp all the days of my life, before the house of the Lord." FESTAL LETTER 10.3.[26]

---

[16]Ps 9:14 (9:15 LXX). [17]Mt 16:18. [18]Gen 25:8. [19]Ps 55:23 (54:24 LXX). [20]CCL 73:446. [21]Ps 6:5 (6:6 LXX). [22]Mt 11:25. [23]CCL 73:449. [24]NPNF 2 4:524. [25]SCA 353; PG 70:789. [26]NPNF 2 4:528.

39:1-8 HEZEKIAH AND THE BABYLONIANS

[1]*At that time Merodach-baladan the son of Baladan, king of Babylon, sent envoys with letters and a present to Hezekiah, for he heard that he had been sick and had recovered.* [2]*And Hezekiah welcomed them; and he showed them his treasure house, the silver, the gold, the spices, the precious oil, his whole armory, all that was found in his storehouses. There was nothing in his house or in all his realm that Hezekiah did not show them.* [3]*Then Isaiah the prophet came to King Hezekiah, and said to him, "What did these men say? And whence did they come to you?" Hezekiah said, "They have come to me from a far country, from Babylon."* [4]*He said, "What have they seen in your house?" Hezekiah answered, "They have seen all that is in my house; there is nothing in my storehouses that I did not show them."*

[5]*Then Isaiah said to Hezekiah, "Hear the word of the LORD of hosts:* [6]*Behold, the days are coming, when all that is in your house, and that which your fathers have stored up till this day, shall be carried to Babylon; nothing shall be left, says the LORD.* [7]*And some of your own sons, who are born to you, shall be taken away; and they shall be eunuchs in the palace of the king of Babylon."* [8]*Then said Hezekiah to Isaiah, "The word of the LORD which you have spoken is good." For he thought, "There will be peace and security in my days."*

OVERVIEW: Hezekiah was judged because he envied the Babylonians (TERTULLIAN). The cave in which Christ was born was more glorious than the palaces of Hezekiah (EPHREM THE SYRIAN). By refusing to examine ourselves, we fall into sin (GREGORY THE GREAT). The Babylonians gave gifts to Hezekiah either because they saw him as a man of God or because they wanted to show him friendship in his time of loss (EUSEBIUS). If we are prideful about our possessions, they will be taken from us (APHRAHAT). Hezekiah is not reproved for failing to intercede for those to become eunuchs (JEROME).

39:1-2 Royal Gifts and Treasures

THE VANITY OF HEZEKIAH'S TREASURES. TERTULLIAN: In the parable of the rich man, he flattered himself about the increase of his fields. But God said to him, "Fool! This night your soul is required of you; and the things you have prepared, whose will they be?"[1] It was the same way when King Hezekiah heard from Isaiah the sad doom of his kingdom after he had gloried before the envoys of Babylon in his treasures and the deposits of his precious things. AGAINST MARCION 4.28.[2]

THE BABYLONIANS REDEEMED BY THE MAGI. EPHREM THE SYRIAN: You[3] juxtaposed [events] so that you might not grieve us and that you might save them. Those who had seized our silver brought gold.[4] Those who had wounded our bodies brought myrrh. Those who had burned our sanctuary offered frankincense to your divinity.

The myrrh [of the Magi] intercedes for their swords with which they killed us. Their gold intercedes for our treasures, for they plundered the treasuries of the house of Hezekiah.[5] Their

---

[1]Lk 12:16. [2]ANF 3:397*. [3]This is a hymn of Mary in praise of her son. [4]Mary speaks as a member of the Jewish people, referring to the Assyrian invasions of Israel under Tiglath-pileser III, Shalmaneser, Sargon II and Sennacherib in the late eighth century B.C.; cf. 2 Kings 16—18; Is 5:26-30. [5]2 Kings 18:14-18.

frankincense appeases your divinity, for they had angered your Father. . . .

The Babylonians, too,[6] came up [and] afflicted the children in Judah.[7] By you the children have found peace, for by you the vicious have become worshipers. Those who despised old men honor a Child who is older than all.

Babylon, too, sent offerings to Hezekiah; the envoys who saw his treasures were amazed. What did you show to the Magi? You showed a wonder, for they rendered you homage although you were poor. However great was the ivory palace of the kings of our people,[8] greater and more beautiful is the little cave in which I bore you. HYMNS ON THE NATIVITY 19.3-4, 10-12.[9]

HEZEKIAH'S DISTRACTION LEADS TO SIN. GREGORY THE GREAT: Often the care of government when undertaken distracts the heart in many different directions. The ruler finds himself unequal to the task of dealing with particular things when his mind becomes confused, having its attention diverted by so many different things. . . . When one, because of this, neglects the business of self-examination, that person does not even consider the losses it is suffering or know how great they are. For neither did Hezekiah believe himself to be sinning[10] when he showed to the strangers who came to him his storehouses of spices. He fell under the anger of the judge, however, and his future offspring were condemned because of what he supposed himself to be doing lawfully. Often, when means are abundant and many things can be done for subordinates to admire, the mind exalts itself in thought. But in so doing, it also provokes the anger of the judge, even though the acts of iniquity may have not been overt. For the one who judges us is within, as is that which is judged. When, then, in our hearts we transgress, what we are doing within ourselves is hidden from men. And yet in the eyes of the Judge we sin. PASTORAL CARE 1.4.[11]

TWO ACCOUNTS OF THE EVENTS. EUSEBIUS OF CAESAREA: Now,[12] when the Babylonians heard about Hezekiah's healing from the sickness, they sent ambassadors to him, and not without reason. Indeed, on the day when the sun went backward, one extra hour was added to the duration of the day, which did not elude the Babylonians, who were skilled in their observation of the stars. And as they venerated the sun as divine, they perceived that it was turned back by a superior power. Therefore they were eager to investigate the cause of the phenomenon. Thus driven by curiosity, they learned that the God of the Hebrew people was great and that he was the Creator of the world. When Hezekiah was healed, through which also the miracle of the sun took place, they perceived what happened and strongly desired the friendship of Hezekiah as a man loved by God. That is the story of the Jewish teacher.

However, I grasped that all of the following events happened the same year: the attack of the Assyrians against the Jewish people, the defeat of the Assyrians by the angel of God, Sennacherib's escape, the revolt of his subjects and the death of the son who succeeded him, which is not mentioned in this text. It is likely that the rumor about all those events reached the Babylonian king, who showed friendship toward Hezekiah and sent him gifts, an ambassador and letters. COMMENTARY ON ISAIAH 39.1.[13]

39:7-8 They Shall Be Eunuchs

THE DANGER OF HEZEKIAH'S WEALTH AND PRIDE. APHRAHAT: Be quiet, you who exalt yourself. Do not think you are better than you are! For if your wealth has caused your heart to be proud, it still is not more abundant than that of Hezekiah. He went in and boasted of his wealth

---

[6]Ephrem has previously mentioned the Assyrian conquest. [7]2 Kings 24:10-16; Jer 24:1; 27:20; 28:4. [8]1 Kings 22:39. [9]ESH 167-68*. [10]Cf. 2 Kings 20:13. [11]NPNF 2 12:3-4*. [12]Eusebius brings up a narrative from Jewish tradition that is also mentioned by Jerome. Then he gives his own interpretation, which does not necessarily exclude the Jewish interpretation. Note the resemblance between the Jewish story and the story of the magi in the Nativity narrative of Matthew. [13]PG 24:361-64**.

before the Babylonians, yet it was all carried away to Babylon. And, if you glory in your children, they shall be led away from you to the beast, as the children of King Hezekiah were led away, and became eunuchs in the palace of the King of Babylon. DEMONSTRATION 5.7.[14]

THOSE TO BE MADE EUNUCHS. JEROME: Isaiah offered this thought by the word of God: "Hear the word of the Lord of hosts: 'A time will come when all this that is in your house, not you, but the goods acquired through the labor of your fathers, will be taken to Babylon, and some of your children will be made eunuchs in its royal court.'" From this the Hebrews want Daniel, Ananiah, Mishael, Hazariah (each of them belonging to the royal line, who were without doubt in the service of King Nebuchadnezzar) to be made eunuchs. This is why Hezekiah said, "The word of the Lord which was spoken is good," a statement for which he is reproached by the Hebrews, who ask why he should not have imitated the goodness of Moses, who said to the Lord: "Either forgive them for this crime or, if you will not, then remove me from the book which you have written."[15] Thus also the apostle Paul wished to be anathema to Christ for his brethren who belong to Israel.[16] Hezekiah, therefore, who subsequently said: "Comfort, comfort my people, says your God," is not reproved by this address from God for not interceding that the people be consoled by the Lord's mercy. COMMENTARY ON ISAIAH 11.39.3-8.[17]

---

[14]NPNF 2 13:354*. [15]Ex 32:32. [16]Rom 9:3. [17]CCL 73:452-53

Appendix

Early Christian Writers and the Documents Cited

The following table lists all the early Christian documents cited in this volume by author, if known, or by the title of the work. The English title used in this commentary is followed in parentheses with the Latin designation and, where available, the Thesaurus Linguae Graecae (=TLG) digital references or Cetedoc Clavis numbers. Printed sources of original language versions may be found in the bibliography of works in original languages.

Adamnan

On the Holy Places (*De locis sanctis*) — Cetedoc 2332

Ambrose

Apology on David (*Apologia David altera*)	Cetedoc 0136
Cain and Abel (*De Cain et Abel*)	Cetedoc 0125
Concerning Widows (*De viduis*)	Cetedoc 0146
Death as a Good (*De bono mortis*)	Cetedoc 0129
Duties of the Clergy (*De officiis*)	Cetedoc 0144
Explanation of the Twelve Psalms (*Explanatio psalmorum xii*)	Cetedoc 0140
Exposition of Psalm 118 (*Expositio psalmi cxviii*)	Cetedoc 0141
Exposition of the Gospel of Luke (*Expositio Evangelii secundum Lucam*)	Cetedoc 0143
Flight from the World (*De fuga saeculi*)	Cetedoc 0133
Isaac, or the Soul (*De Isaac vel anima*)	Cetedoc 0128
Jacob and the Happy Life (*De Jacob et vita beata*)	Cetedoc 0130
Joseph (*De Joseph*)	Cetedoc 0131
Letters (*Epistulae; Epistulae extra collectionem traditae*)	Cetedoc 0160
On Helia and Fast (*De Helia et jejunio*)	Cetedoc 0137
On His Brother Satyrus (*De excessu fratris Satyri*)	Cetedoc 0157
On Paradise (*De paradiso*)	Cetedoc 0124
On the Christian Faith (*De fide libri v*)	Cetedoc 0150
On the Holy Spirit (*De spiritu sancto*)	Cetedoc 0151
On the Mysteries (*De mysteriis*)	Cetedoc 0155
On the Patriarchs (*De patriarchis*)	Cetedoc 0132
The Prayer of Job and David (*De interpellatione Job et David*)	Cetedoc 0134
Six Days of Creation (*Exameron*)	Cetedoc 0123

Aphrahat

Demonstrations (*Demonstrationes*)

Aponius (Apponius)

Exposition of Song of Songs (*In Canticum canticorum expositio*) — Cetedoc 0194

Arnobius the Younger
Commentary on the Psalms (*Commentarii in Psalmos*)   Cetedoc 0242

Athanasius
Festal Letters (*Epistulae festalis*)   TLG 2035.014
Four Discourses Against the Arians (*Orationes tres contra Arianos*)   TLG 2035.042
Letters (*Epistula ad Adelphium*)   TLG 2035.050
Life of St. Anthony (*Vita sancti Antonii*)   TLG 2035.047
On the Incarnation (*De incarnatione verbi*)   TLG 2035.002

Augustine
Christian Instruction (*De doctrina christiana*)   Cetedoc 0263
City of God (*De civitate Dei*)   Cetedoc 0313
Enchiridion (*Enchiridion de fide, spe et caritate*)   Cetedoc 0295
Explanations of the Psalms (*Enarrationes in Psalmos*)   Cetedoc 0283
Harmony of the Gospels (*De consensu evangelistarum libri iv*)   Cetedoc 0273
In Answer to the Jews (*Adversus Judaeos*)   Cetedoc 0315
Letter to the Catholics on the Sect of Donatists
  (*Ad catholicos de secta Donatistarum*)   Cetedoc 0334
Letters (*Epistulae*)   Cetedoc 0262
On Faith in Things Unseen (*De fide rerum invisibilium*)   Cetedoc 0292
On Grace and Free Will (*De gratia et libero arbitrio*)   Cetedoc 0352
On Nature and Grace (*De natura et gratia*)   Cetedoc 0344
On the Christian Life (*De vita christiana*)   Cetedoc 0730
On the Spirit and the Letter (*De spiritu et littera*)   Cetedoc 0343
On the Trinity (*De Trinitate*)   Cetedoc 0329
Predestination of the Saints (*De praedestinatione sanctorum*)   Cetedoc 0354
Questions (*De diversis quaestionibus octoginta tribus*)   Cetedoc 0289
Reply to Faustus the Manichaean (*Contra Faustum*)   Cetedoc 0321
Sermon on the Mount (*De sermone Domini in monte*)   Cetedoc 0274
Sermons (*Sermones*)   Cetedoc 0284
Tractates on the Gospel of John (*In Johannis evangelium tractatus*)   Cetedoc 0278

Basil the Great
Commentary on Isaiah (*Enarratio in prophetam Isaiam [Dub.]*)   TLG 2040.009
Homilies on the Hexameron (*Homiliae in hexaemeron*)   TLG 2040.001
Homilies on the Psalms (*Homiliae super Psalmos*)   TLG 2040.018
Letters (*Epistulae*)   TLG 2040.004
The Long Rules (*Asceticon magnum sive Quaestiones [regulae fusius tractatae]*)   TLG 2040.048
Preface on the Judgment of God (*Prologus 7 [De judicio Dei]*)   TLG 2040.043

Bede
Commentary on the Acts of the Apostles (*Expositio actuum apostolorum*)   Cetedoc 1357
Exposition of the Gospel of Luke (*In Lucae evangelium expositio*)   Cetedoc 1356
Exposition on the Gospel of Mark (*In Marci evangelium expositio*)   Cetedoc 1355

Four Books on 1 Samuel (*In primam partem Samuhelis libri iv*)	Cetedoc 1346
Homilies on the Gospels (*Homiliarum evangelii libri ii*)	Cetedoc 1367
On Genesis (*Libri quattuor in principium Genesis usque ad nativitatem Isaac et ejectionem Ismahelis adnotationum*)	Cetedoc 1344
On the Tabernacle (*De tabernaculo et vasis eius ac vestibus sacerdotem libri iii*)	Cetedoc 1345
The Reckoning of Time (*De temporum ratione liber*)	Cetedoc 2320
Six Books on the Song of Songs (*In Cantica canticorum libri vi*)	Cetedoc 1353
Three Books on Ezra and Nehemiah (*In Ezram et Neemiam libri iii*)	Cetedoc 1349
Three Books on the Proverbs of Solomon (*In proverbia Salomonis libri iii*)	Cetedoc 1351
Two Books on the Temple (*De templo libri ii*)	Cetedoc 1348

Caesarius of Arles

Sermons (*Sermones ex integro a Caesario compositi bel ex aliis fontibus hausti*)	Cetedoc 1008

Cassian, John

Conferences (*Collationes xxiv*)	Cetedoc 0512
Institutes (*De institutis coenobiorum et de octo principalium vitiorum remediis*)	Cetedoc 0513
On the Incarnation of the Lord Against Nestorius (*De incarnatione Domini contra Nestorium*)	Cetedoc 0514

Cassiodorus

Exposition of Romans (*Expositio sancti Pauli Epistulae ad Romanos*)	Cetedoc 0902
Exposition of the Psalms (*Expositio Psalmorum*)	Cetedoc 0900

Chromatius of Aquileia

Tractate on Matthew (*Tractatus in Matthaeum*)	Cetedoc 0218

Clement of Alexandria

Christ the Educator (*Paedagogus*)	TLG 0555.002
Stromateis (*Stromata*)	TLG 0555.004

Clement of Rome

1 Clement (*Epistula i ad Corinthios*)	TLG 1271.001

Constitutions of the Holy Apostles (*Constitutiones apostolorum*)   TLG 2894.001

Cyprian

The Dress of Virgins (*De habitu virginum*)	Cetedoc 0040
The Good of Patience (*De bono patientiae*)	Cetedoc 0048
The Lapsed (*De lapsis*)	Cetedoc 0042
Letters (*Epistulae*)	Cetedoc 0050
The Lord's Prayer (*De dominica oratione*)	Cetedoc 0043
To Quirinus: Testimonies Against the Jews (*Ad Quirinum*)	Cetedoc 0039

Cyril of Alexandria
Against Julian (*Contra Julianum imperatorem [fragmenta]*)   TLG 4090.144
Commentary on Isaiah (*Commentarius in Isaiam prophetam*)   TLG 4090.103
Letters (*Concilium universale Ephesenum [Concilia oecumenica]*)   TLG 5000.001
Third Letter to Nestorius (*Concilium universale Ephesenum [Concilia oecumenica]*)   TLG 5000.001

Cyril of Jerusalem
Catechetical Lectures (*Catecheses ad illuminandos 1-18*)   TLG 2110.003

Ephrem the Syrian
Commentary on Tatian's Diatessaron (*In Tatiani Diatessaron*)
Hymns on the Nativity (*Hymni de nativitate*)

Epistle of Barnabas (*Barnabae epistula*)   TLG 1216.001

Eusebius of Caesarea
Commentary on Isaiah (*Commentarius in Isaiam*)   TLG 2018.019
Proof of the Gospel (*Demonstratio evangelica*)   TLG 2018.005

Eusebius of Gaul
Homilies (*Collectio homiliarum*)   Cetedoc 0966

Facundus of Hermiane
To Justinian (*Pro defensione trium capitulorum libri xii. Ad Justinianum*)   Cetedoc 0866

Faustus of Riez
Two Books on the Holy Spirit (*De spiritu sancto libri duo*)   Cetedoc 0962

Firmicus Maternus
Error of the Pagan Religions (*De errore profanarum religionum*)   Cetedoc 0102

Fulgentius of Ruspe
Book to Victor Against the Sermon of Fastidios the Arian
   (*Liber ad Victorem contra sermonem Fastidiosi Ariani*)   Cetedoc 0820
Letters (*Epistulae*)   Cetedoc 0817
On the Forgiveness of Sins (*Ad Euthymium de remissione peccatorum libri II*)   Cetedoc 0821
Three Books to Trasamundus (*Ad Trasamundum libri III*)   Cetedoc 0816
To Peter on the Faith (*De fide ad Petrum seu de regula fidei*)   Cetedoc 0826

Gregory of Elvira
Origen's Tractate on the Books of Holy Scripture
   (*Tractatus Origenis de libris Sanctarum Scripturarum*)   Cetedoc 0546

Gregory of Nazianzus
In Defense of His Flight to Pontus, Oration 2 (*Apologetica*)   TLG 2022.016

The Last Farewell, Oration 42 (*Supremum vale*) — TLG 2022.050
On His Father's Silence, Oration 16 (*In patrem tacentem*) — TLG 2022.029
On Holy Baptism, Oration 40 (*In sanctum baptisma*) — TLG 2022.048
On Pentecost, Oration 41 (*In pentecosten*) — TLG 2022.049
On the Birth of Christ, Oration 38 (*In theophania*) — TLG 2022.046
On the Holy Spirit, Theological Oration 5 (31) (*De spiritu sancto*) — TLG 2022.011
On the Son, Theological Oration 3 (29), (*De filio*) — TLG 2022.009

Gregory of Nyssa
Against Eunomius (*Contra Eunomium*) — TLG 2017.030
On the Baptism of Christ (*In diem luminum [vulgo In baptismum Christi oratio]*) — TLG 2017.014

Gregory the Great
Dialogues (*Dialogorum libri iv*) — Cetedoc 1713
Forty Gospel Homilies (*Homiliarum xl in evangelia libri duo*) — Cetedoc 1711
Homilies on Ezekiel (*Homiliae in Hiezechihelem prophetam*) — Cetedoc 1710
Morals on the Book of Job (*Moralia in Job*) — Cetedoc 1708
Pastoral Care (*Regula pastoralis*) — Cetedoc 1712
Six Books on 1 Kings (*In librum primum Regum expositionum libri vi*) — Cetedoc 1719

Hippolytus
Fragments from Commentary on Daniel 2 (*Commentarium in Danielem*) — TLG 2115.030
On the Antichrist (*De antichristo*) — TLG 2115.003
On the Theophany (*De theophania [dubious]*) — TLG 2115.026

Horsiesi
The Testament of Horsiesi

Ignatius
To the Smyrnaeans (*Epistulae interpolatae et epistulae suppositiciae, Ad Smyrnaeos*) — TLG 1443.002

Irenaeus
Against Heresies (*Adversus haereses*) — Cetedoc 1154

Isaac of Nineveh
Ascetical Homilies (*De perfectione religiosa*)

Isidore of Seville
Three Books of Thoughts (*Sententiarum libri tres*) — Cetedoc 1199

Jerome
Against John of Jerusalem (*Contra Johannem Hierosolymitanum*) — Cetedoc 0612
Against Jovinianus (*Adversus Jovinianum*) — Cetedoc 0610
Against the Pelagians (*Dialogi contra Pelagianos libri iii*) — Cetedoc 0615
Commentary on Daniel (*Commentarii in Danielem*) — Cetedoc 0588

Commentary on Ezekiel (*Commentarii in Ezechielem*)	Cetedoc 0587
Commentary on Isaiah (*Commentarii in Isaiam*)	Cetedoc 0584
Commentary on Jeremiah (*In Hieremiam prophetam libri vi*)	Cetedoc 0586
Commentary on Matthew (*Commentarii in evangelium Matthaei*)	Cetedoc 0590
Commentary on the Minor Prophets (*Commentarii in prophetas minores*)	Cetedoc 0589
Commentary on Titus (*Commentarii in iv epistulas Paulinas*)	Cetedoc 0591
Homilies on the Psalms (*Tractatus lix in psalmos*)	Cetedoc 0592
Homilies on the Psalms, Alternate Series (*Tractatuum in psalmos series altera*)	Cetedoc 0593
Homily on the Nativity (*Homilia de nativitate Domini*)	Cetedoc 0598
Letters (*Epistulae*)	Cetedoc 0620
Preface to Isaiah (*Praefatio in Isaia propheta*)	Cetedoc 0591
Six Books on Jeremiah (*In Hieremiam prophetam libri vi*)	Cetedoc 0586

John Chrysostom

Against the Anomoeans	
1-5 (*Contra Anomoeos homiliae 1-5=De incomprehensibili dei natura*)	TLG 2062.012
7 (*Contra Anomoeos homilia 7=De consubstantiali*)	TLG 2062.015
11 (*Contra Anomoeos homilia 11*)	TLG 2062.019
Baptismal Instructions (*Ad illuminandos catecheses 1-2 [series prima et secunda]*)	TLG 2062.025
(*Catecheses ad illuminandos [series tertia]*)	TLG 2062.382
Commentary on Isaiah (*In Isaiam*)	TLG 2062.497
Demonstration Against the Pagans (*Contra Judaeos et Gentiles, Quod Christus sit Deus*)	TLG 2062.372
Discourses Against Judaizing Christians (*Adversus Judaeos [orationes 1-8]*)	TLG 2062.021
Homilies Concerning the Statues (*Ad populam Antiochenum homiliae [de statuis]*	TLG 2062.024
Homilies on 1 Corinthians (*In epistulam i ad Corinthios [homiliae 1-44]*)	TLG 2062.156
Homilies on 2 Corinthians (*In epistulam ii ad Corinthios[homiliae 1-30]*)	TLG 2062.157
Homilies on Ephesians (*In epistulam ad Ephesios*)	TLG 2062.159
Homilies on Genesis (*In Genesim [homiliae 1-67]*)	TLG 2062.112
Homilies on Lazarus and the Rich Man (*De Lazaro (homiliae 1-7*)	TLG 2062.023
Homilies on Repentance and Almsgiving	
(*De paenitentia [homiliae 1-9]*)	TLG 2062.027
(*De eleemosyna*)	TLG 2062.075
Homilies on Romans (*In epistulam ad Romanos*)	TLG 2062.155
Homilies on the Acts of the Apostles (*Homiliae in Acta apostolorum [homiliae 1-55]*)	TLG 2062.154
Homilies on the Gospel of John (*In Joannem [homiliae 1-88]*)	TLG 2062.153
Homilies on the Gospel of Matthew (*In Matthaeum [homiliae 1-90]*)	TLG 2062.152
Homilies on 1 Timothy (*In epistulam i ad Timotheum*)	TLG 2062.164
Homily on Eutropius (*Homilia de capto Eutropio [Dub.]*)	TLG 2062.142
Letter to the Fallen Theodore (*Ad Theodorum lapsum [lib. 1]*)	TLG 2062.002
On the Epistle to the Hebrews (*In epistulam ad Hebraeos*)	TLG 2062.168

John of Damascus

Barlaam and Joseph (*Vita Barlaam et Joasaph [Sp.]*)	TLG 2934.066
Orthodox Faith (*Expositio fidei*)	TLG 2934.004

Justin Martyr
Dialogue with Trypho *(Dialogus cum Tryphone)*   TLG 0645.003
First Apology *(Apologia)*   TLG 0645.001

Lactantius
Epitome of the Divine Institutes *(Epitome divinarum institutionum)*   Cetedoc 0086

Leander of Seville
Homilies on the Triumph of the Church *(Homilia in laudem ecclesiae)*

Leo the Great
Letters *(Epistulae)*
Sermons *(Tractatus septem et nonaginta)*   Cetedoc 1657

Maximus of Turin
Sermons *(Collectio sermonum antiqua)*   Cetedoc 0219a

Nicetas of Remesiana
Explanation of the Creed *(Explanatio symboli habita ad competentes)*
Vigils of the Saints *(De Vigiliis servorum Dei)*

Novatian
On the Trinity *(De Trinitate)*   Cetedoc 0071

Origen
Against Celsus *(Contra Celsum)*   TLG 2042.001
Commentary on Matthew

    (Commentarium in evangelium Matthaei [lib. 10-11])   TLG 2042.029
    (Commentarium in evangelium Matthaei [lib. 12-17])   TLG 2042.030
Commentary on the Gospel of John
    (Commentarii in evangelium Joannis [lib. 1, 2, 4, 5, 6, 10, 13])   TLG 2042.005
Fragments from the Philocalia *(Philocalia)*   TLG 2042.019
Homilies on Exodus *(Homiliae in Exodum)*   TLG 2042.023
Homilies on Genesis *(Homiliae in Genesim)*   TLG 2042.022
Homilies on Jeremiah
    (In Jeremiam homiliae 1-11)   TLG 2042.009
    (In Jeremiam homiliae 12-20)   TLG 2042.021
Homilies on Leviticus *(In Leviticum homiliae)*   TLG 2042.024
Homilies on the Gospel of Luke *(Homiliae in Lucam)*   TLG 2042.016
On First Principles *(De principiis)*   TLG 2042.002

Pachomius
Instructions *(Catecheses)*
Letters *(In Catecheses)*
Life of Pachomius (Sahidic) *(Vita Pachomii)*

Pacian of Barcelona
On Penitents (*De paenitentibus*)

Paschasius of Dumium
Questions and Answers of the Greek Fathers (*De vitis patrum liber septimus,*
  sive verba seniorum auctore graeco incerto, interprete Paschasio S. R. E. Diacono)

Paulus Orosius
Defense Against the Pelagians (*Liber apologeticus contra Pelagianos*)   Cetedoc 0572

Peter Chrysologus
Sermons (*Collectio sermonum a Felice episcopo parata*
sermonibus extravagantibus adjectis)   Cetedoc 0227+

Primasius
Commentary on the Apocalypse (*Commentarius in Apocalypsin*)   Cetedoc 0873

Pseudo-Clement of Rome
2 Clement (*Epistula ii ad Corinthios [Sp.]*)   TLG 1271.002
Homilies (*Homiliae [Sp.]*)   TLG 1271.006

Pseudo-Cyprian
To Novatian (*Ad Novatianum*)   Cetedoc 0076

Pseudo-Dionysius
Ecclesiastical Hierarchy (*De ecclesiastica hierarchia*)   TLG 2798.002

Quodvultdeus
Against Five Heresies (*Sermo 10: Adversus quinque haereses*)   Cetedoc 0410
The Book of Promises and Predictions of God
  (*Liber promissionum et praedictorum Dei*)   Cetedoc 0413
On the Approach to Grace (*Sermo 8: De accedentibus ad gratiam*)   Cetedoc 0408
On the Creed (*Sermo 2: De symbolo II*)   Cetedoc 0402

Rufinus of Aquileia
Commentary on the Apostles' Creed (*Expositio symboli*)   Cetedoc 0196

Sahdona (Martyrius)
Book of Perfection

Salvian the Presbyter
The Governance of God (*De gubernatione Dei*)   Cetedoc 0485

Tertullian
Against Marcion (*Adversus Marcionem*)   Cetedoc 0014

An Answer to the Jews *(Adversus Judaeos)*   Cetedoc 0033
On Prayer *(De oratione)*   Cetedoc 0007
On the Flesh of Christ *(De carne Christi)*   Cetedoc 0018
On the Resurrection of the Flesh *(De resurrectione mortuorum)*   Cetedoc 0019
Scorpiace *(Scorpiace)*   Cetedoc 0022
To His Wife *(Ad uxorem)*   Cetedoc 0012

Theodore of Tabennesi
Instructions *(Catecheses)*

Theodoret of Cyr
Commentary on Isaiah *(Commentaria in Isaiam)*   TLG 4089.008
Dialogue *(Eranistes)*   TLG 4089.002
Letters *(Ad eos qui in Euphratesia et Osrhoena regione, Syria, Phoeni)*   TLG 4089.034
On Divine Providence *(De providentia orationes decem)*   TLG 4089.032

Theophylact
Explanation of Matthew

Valerian
Homily *(Homilia i. De bono disciplinae)*

Verecundus
Commentary on the Canticle of Deuteronomy
   (Commentarii super cantica ecclesiastica)   Cetedoc 0870
Commentary on the Canticle of Exodus
   (Commentarii super cantica ecclesiastica)   Cetedoc 0870
Commentary on the Canticle of Ezekiel
   (Commentarii super cantica ecclesiastica)   Cetedoc 0870
Commentary on the Canticle of Habakkuk
   (Commentarii super cantica ecclesiastica)   Cetedoc 0870
Commentary on the Canticle of Manasses *(Commentarii super cantica ecclesiastica)*   Cetedoc 0870

Victorinus of Petovium
Commentary of the Apocalypse *(Scholia in Apocalypsin beati Joannis)*

Timeline of Writers of the Patristic Period

Location / Period	British Isles	Gaul	Spain, Portugal	Rome* and Italy	Carthage and Northern Africa
2nd century		Irenaeus of Lyons, c. 135-c. 202 (Greek)		Clement of Rome, fl. c. 92-101 (Greek); *Shepherd of Hermas*, c. 140 (Greek); Justin Martyr (Ephesus, Rome), c. 100/110-165 (Greek); Valentinus the Gnostic (Rome), fl. c. 140 (Greek); Marcion (Rome), fl. 144 (Greek)	
3rd century				Callistus of Rome, regn. 217-222 (Latin); Minucius Felix of Rome, fl. 218-235 (Latin); Hippolytus (Rome, Palestine?), fl. 222-235/245 (Greek); Novatian of Rome, fl. 235-258 (Latin); Victorinus of Petovium, 230-304 (Latin)	Tertullian of Carthage, c. 155/160-c. 225 (Latin); Cyprian of Carthage, fl. 248-258 (Latin)
4th century		Lactantius, c. 260-330 (Latin); Hilary of Poitiers, c. 315-367 (Latin)	Hosius of Cordova, d. 357 (Latin); Potamius of Lisbon, fl. c. 350-360 (Latin); Gregory of Elvira, fl. 359-385 (Latin); Prudentius, c. 348-c. 410 (Latin); Pacian of Barcelona, 4th cent. (Latin)	Firmicus Maternus (Sicily), fl. c. 335 (Latin); Marius Victorinus (Rome), fl. 355-363 (Latin); Eusebius of Vercelli, fl. c. 360 (Latin); Lucifer of Cagliari (Sardinia), d. 370/371 (Latin); Faustinus (Rome), fl. 380 (Latin); Filastrius of Brescia, fl. 380 (Latin); Ambrosiaster (Italy?), fl. c. 366-384 (Latin); Faustus of Riez, fl. c. 380 (Latin); Gaudentius of Brescia, fl. 395 (Latin); Ambrose of Milan, c. 333-397; fl. 374-397 (Latin); Rufinus (Aquileia, Rome), c. 345-411 (Latin); Aponius, fl. 405-415 (Latin)	Paulus Orosius, b. c. 380 (Latin)

*One of the five ancient patriarchates

Alexandria* and Egypt	Constantinople* and Asia Minor, Greece	Antioch* and Syria	Mesopotamia, Persia	Jerusalem* and Palestine	Location Unknown
Philo of Alexandria, c. 20 B.C. – c. A.D. 50 (Greek)				Flavius Josephus (Rome), c. 37-c. 101 (Greek)	
Basilides (Alexandria), 2nd cent. (Greek)	Polycarp of Smyrna, c. 69-155 (Greek)	*Didache* (Egypt?), c. 100 (Greek)			*Second Letter of Clement* (spurious; Corinth, Rome, Alexandria?) (Greek), c. 150
Letter of Barnabas (Syria?), c. 130 (Greek)	Athenagoras (Greece), fl. 176-180 (Greek)	Ignatius of Antioch, c. 35–107/112 (Greek)			
Theodotus the Valentinian, 2nd cent. (Greek)	*Montanist Oracles*, late 2nd cent. (Greek)				
		Theophilus of Antioch, c. late 2nd cent. (Greek)			
Clement of Alexandria, c. 150-215 (Greek)	Gregory Thaumaturgus (Neocaesarea), fl. c. 248-264 (Greek)		Mani (Manichaeans), c. 216-276		Pseudo-Clementines 3rd cent. (Greek)
Sabellius (Egypt), 2nd–3rd cent. (Greek)					
Letter to Diognetus, 3rd cent. (Greek)					
Origen (Alexandria, Caesarea of Palestine), 185-254 (Greek)					
Dionysius of Alexandria, d. 264/5 (Greek)	Methodius of Olympus (Lycia), d. c. 311 (Greek)				
Anthony, c. 251-355 (Coptic /Greek)	Theodore of Heraclea (Thrace), fl. c. 330-355 (Greek)	Eusebius of Emesa, c. 300-c. 359 (Greek)	Aphrahat (Persia) c. 270-350; fl. 337-345 (Syriac)	Eusebius of Caesarea (Palestine), c. 260/263-340 (Greek)	Commodius, c. 3rd or 5th cent. (Latin)
Peter of Alexandria, d. c. 311 (Greek)	Epiphanius of Salamis (Cyprus), c. 315-403 (Greek)	Ephrem the Syrian, c. 306-373 (Syriac)	Jacob of Nisibis, fl. 308-325 (Syriac)	Acacius of Caesarea (Palestine), d. c. 365 (Greek)	
Arius (Alexandria), fl. c. 320 (Greek)	Basil (the Great) of Caesarea, b. c. 330; fl. 357-379 (Greek)	Nemesius of Emesa (Syria), fl. late 4th cent. (Greek)			
Alexander of Alexandria, fl. 312-328 (Greek)	Macrina the Younger, c. 327-379 (Greek)	Diodore of Tarsus, d. c. 394 (Greek)		Cyril of Jerusalem, c. 315-386 (Greek)	
Pachomius, c. 292-347 (Coptic/Greek?)	Apollinaris of Laodicea, 310-c. 392 (Greek)	John Chrysostom (Constantinople), 344/354-407 (Greek)			
Theodore of Tabennesi, d. 368 (Coptic/Greek)	Gregory of Nazianzus, b. 329/330; fl. 372-389 (Greek)	*Apostolic Constitutions*, c. 375-400 (Greek)			
Horsiesi, c. 305-390 (Coptic/Greek)	Gregory of Nyssa, c. 335-394 (Greek)	*Didascalia*, 4th cent. (Syriac)			
Athanasius of Alexandria, c. 295-373; fl. 325-373 (Greek)	Amphilochius of Iconium, c. 340/345- c. 398/404 (Greek)	Theodore of Mopsuestia, c. 350-428 (Greek)			
Macarius of Egypt, c. 300-c. 390 (Greek)	Evagrius of Pontus, 345-399 (Greek)			Diodore of Tarsus, d. c. 394 (Greek)	
Didymus (the Blind) of Alexandria, 313-398 (Greek)	Eunomius of Cyzicus, fl. 360-394 (Greek)			Jerome (Rome, Antioch, Bethlehem), c. 347-420 (Latin)	
	Pseudo-Macarius (Mesopotamia?), late 4th cent. (Greek)				
	Nicetas of Remesiana, d. c. 414 (Latin)				

Timeline of Writers of the Patristic Period

Location / Period	British Isles	Gaul	Spain, Portugal	Rome* and Italy	Carthage and Northern Africa
5th century	Fastidius (Britain), c. 4th-5th cent. (Latin)	Sulpicius Severus (Bordeaux), c. 360-c. 420/425 (Latin)		Chromatius (Aquileia), fl. 400 (Latin)	Quodvultdeus (Carthage), fl. 430 (Latin)
		John Cassian (Palestine, Egypt, Constantinople, Rome, Marseilles), 360-432 (Latin)		Pelagius (Britain, Rome), c. 354-c. 420 (Greek)	Augustine of Hippo, 354-430 (Latin)
		Vincent of Lérins, d. 435 (Latin)		Maximus of Turin, d. 408/423 (Latin)	Luculentius, 5th cent. (Latin)
		Valerian of Cimiez, fl. c. 422-449 (Latin)		Paulinus of Nola, 355-431 (Latin)	
		Eucherius of Lyons, fl. 420-449 (Latin)		Peter Chrysologus (Ravenna), c. 380-450 (Latin)	
		Hilary of Arles, c. 401-449 (Latin)		Julian of Eclanum, 386-454 (Latin)	
		Eusebius of Gaul, 5th cent. (Latin)		Leo the Great (Rome), regn. 440-461 (Latin)	
		Prosper of Aquitaine, d. after 455 (Latin)		Arnobius the Younger (Rome), fl. c. 450 (Latin)	
		Salvian the Presbyter of Marseilles, c. 400-c. 480 (Latin)			
		Gennadius of Marseilles, d. after 496 (Latin)			
6th century		Caesarius of Arles, c. 470-543 (Latin)	Paschasius of Dumium (Portugal), c. 515-c. 580 (Latin)	Epiphanius the Latin, late 5th–early 6th cent. (Latin)	Fulgentius of Ruspe, c. 467-532 (Latin)
			Leander of Seville, c. 545-c. 600 (Latin)	Eugippius, c. 460- c. 533 (Latin)	Verecundus, d. 552 (Latin)
			Martin of Braga, fl. 568-579 (Latin)	Benedict of Nursia, c. 480-547 (Latin)	Facundus of Hermiane, fl. 546-568 (Latin)
				Cassiodorus (Calabria), c. 485-c. 540 (Latin)	
				Gregory the Great (Rome), c. 540-604 (Latin)	
				Gregory of Agrigentium, d. 592 (Greek)	
7th century			Isidore of Seville, c. 560-636 (Latin)	Paterius, 6th/7th cent. (Latin)	
			Braulio of Saragossa, c. 585-651 (Latin)		
	Adamnan, c. 624-704 (Latin)				
8th century	Bede the Venerable, c. 672/673-735 (Latin)				

*One of the five ancient patriarchates

Alexandria* and Egypt	Constantinople* and Asia Minor, Greece	Antioch* and Syria	Mesopotamia, Persia	Jerusalem* and Palestine	Location Unknown
Palladius of Helenopolis (Egypt), c. 365-425 (Greek)	Nestorius (Constantinople), c. 381-c. 451 (Greek)	Book of Steps, c. 400 (Syriac)	Eznik of Kolb, fl. 430-450 (Armenian)	Jerome (Rome, Antioch, Bethlehem), c. 347-419 (Latin)	
Cyril of Alexandria, 375-444 (Greek)	Basil of Seleucia, fl. 440-468 (Greek)	Severian of Gabala, fl. c. 400 (Greek)		Hesychius of Jerusalem, fl. 412-450 (Greek)	
Ammonius of Alexandria, c. 460 (Greek)	Diadochus of Photice (Macedonia), 400-474 (Greek)	Theodoret of Cyr, c. 393-466 (Greek)		Euthymius (Palestine), 377-473 (Greek)	
Poemen, 5th cent. (Greek)	Gennadius of Constantinople, d. 471 (Greek)	Pseudo-Victor of Antioch, 5th cent. (Greek)			
	Oecumenius (Isauria), 6th cent. (Greek)	Philoxenus of Mabbug (Syria), c. 440-523 (Syriac)	Jacob of Sarug, c. 450-520 (Syriac)	Procopius of Gaza (Palestine), c. 465-530 (Greek)	Pseudo-Dionysius the Areopagite, fl. c. 500 (Greek)
		Severus of Antioch, c. 465-538 (Greek)	Babai the Great, c. 550-628 (Syriac)	Dorotheus of Gaza, fl. 525-540 (Greek)	
		Mark the Hermit (Tarsus), c. 6th cent. (4th cent.?) (Greek)		Cyril of Scythopolis, b. c. 525; d. after 557 (Greek)	
	Maximus the Confessor (Constantinople), c. 580-662 (Greek)	Sahdona/Martyrius, fl. 635-640 (Syriac)	Isaac of Nineveh, d. c. 700 (Syriac)		(Pseudo-) Constantius, before 7th cent.? (Greek)
					Andreas, c. 7th cent. (Greek)
	Theophanes (Nicaea), 775-845 (Greek)	John of Damascus (John the Monk), c. 650-750 (Greek)	John the Elder of Qardu (north Iraq), 8th cent. (Syriac)		
	Cassia (Constantinople), c. 805-c. 848/867 (Greek)		Isho'dad of Merv, d. after 852 (Syriac)		
	Symeon the New Theologian (Constantinople), 949-1022 (Greek)				
	Theophylact of Ohrid (Bulgaria), 1050-1126 (Greek)				

BIOGRAPHICAL SKETCHES &
SHORT DESCRIPTIONS
OF SELECT ANONYMOUS WORKS

This listing is cumulative, including all the authors and works cited in this series to date.

Acacius of Caesarea (d. c. 365). Pro-Arian bishop of Caesarea in Palestine, disciple and biographer of Eusebius of Caesarea, the historian. He was a man of great learning and authored a treatise on Ecclesiastes.

Adamnan (c. 624-704). Abbot of Iona, Ireland, and author of the life of St. Columba. He was influential in the process of assimilating the Celtic church into Roman liturgy and church order. He also wrote *On the Holy Sites*, which influenced Bede.

Alexander of Alexandria (fl. 312-328). Bishop of Alexandria and predecessor of Athanasius, on whom he exerted considerable theological influence during the rise of Arianism. Alexander excommunicated Arius, whom he had appointed to the parish of Baucalis, in 319. His teaching regarding the eternal generation and divine substantial union of the Son with the Father was eventually confirmed at the Council of Nicaea (325).

Ambrose of Milan (c. 333-397; fl. 374-397). Bishop of Milan and teacher of Augustine who defended the divinity of the Holy Spirit and the perpetual virginity of Mary.

Ambrosiaster (fl. c. 366-384). Name given by Erasmus to the author of a work once thought to have been composed by Ambrose.

Ammonius (c. fifth century). An Aristotelian commentator and teacher in Alexandria, where he was born and of whose school he became head. Also an exegete of Plato, he enjoyed fame among his contemporaries and successors, although modern critics accuse him of pedantry and banality.

Amphilochius of Iconium (b. c. 340-345, d.c. 398-404). An orator at Constantinople before becoming bishop of Iconium in 373. He was a cousin of Gregory of Nazianzus and active in debates against the Macedonians and Messalians.

Andreas (c. seventh century). Monk who collected commentary from earlier writers to form a catena on various biblical books.

Antony (or Anthony) the Great (c. 251-c. 356). An anchorite of the Egyptian desert and founder of Egyptian monasticism. Athanasius regarded him as the ideal of monastic life, and he has become a model for Christian hagiography.

Aphrahat (c. 270-350 fl. 337-345). "The Persian Sage" and first major Syriac writer whose work survives. He is also known by his Greek name Aphraates.

Apollinaris of Laodicea (310-c. 392). Bishop of Laodicea who was attacked by Gregory of Nazianzus, Gregory of Nyssa and Theodore for denying that Christ had a human mind.

Aponius/Apponius (fourth–fifth century). Author of a remarkable commentary on Song of Solomon (c. 405-415), an important work in the history of exegesis. The work, which was influenced by the commentaries of Origen and Pseudo-Hippolytus, is of theological significance, especially in the area of Christology.

Apostolic Constitutions (c. 381-394). Also known as *Constitutions of the Holy Apostles* and thought to be redacted by Julian of Neapolis. The work is divided into eight books, and is primarily a collection of and expansion on previous works such as the *Didache* (c. 140) and the *Apostolic Traditions*. Book 8 ends with eighty-five canons from various sources and is elsewhere known as the *Apostolic Canons*.

Arius (fl. c. 320). Heretic condemned at the Council of Nicaea (325) for refusing to accept that the Son was not a creature but was God by nature like the Father.

Arnobius the Younger (fifth century). A participant in christological controversies of the fifth century. He composed *Conflictus cum Serapione*, an account of a debate with a monophysite monk in which he attempts to demonstrate harmony between Roman and Alexandrian theology. Some scholars attribute to him a few more works, such as *Commentaries on Psalms*.

Athanasius of Alexandria (c. 295-373; fl. 325-373). Bishop of Alexandria from 328, though often in exile. He wrote his classic polemics against the Arians while most of the eastern bishops were against him.

Athenagoras (fl. 176-180). Early Christian philosopher and apologist from Athens, whose only authenticated writing, *A Plea Regarding Christians*, is addressed to the emperors Marcus Aurelius and Commodius, and defends Christians from the common accusations of atheism, incest and cannibalism.

Augustine of Hippo (354-430). Bishop of Hippo and a voluminous writer on philosophical, exegetical, theological and ecclesiological topics. He formulated the Western doctrines of predestination and original sin in his writings against the Pelagians.

Babai the Great (d. 628). Syriac monk who founded a monastery and school in his region of Beth Zabday and later served as third superior at the Great Convent of Mount Izla during a period of crisis in the Nestorian church.

Basil the Great (b. c. 330; fl. 357-379). One of the Cappadocian fathers, bishop of Caesarea and champion of the teaching on the Trinity propounded at Nicaea in 325. He was a great administrator and founded a monastic rule.

Basil of Seleucia (fl. 444-468). Bishop of Seleucia in Isauria and ecclesiastical writer. He took part in the Synod of Constantinople in 448 for the condemnation of the Eutychian errors and the deposition of their great champion, Dioscurus of Alexandria.

Basilides (fl. second century). Alexandrian heretic of the early second century who is said to have believed that souls migrate from body to body and that we do not sin if we lie to protect the body from martyrdom.

Bede the Venerable (c. 672/673-735). Born in Northumbria, at the age of seven he was put under the care of the Benedictine monks of Saints Peter and Paul at Jarrow and given a broad classical education in the monastic tradition. Considered one of the most learned men of his age, he is the author of *An Ecclesiastical History of the English People*.

Benedict of Nursia (c. 480-547). Considered the most important figure in the history of Western monasticism. Benedict founded many monasteries, the most notable found at Montecassino, but his lasting influence lay in his famous Rule. The Rule outlines the theological and inspirational foundation of the monastic ideal while also legislating the shape and organization of the cenobitic life.

Book of Steps (c. 400). Written by an anonymous Syriac author, this work consists of thirty homilies or discourses which specifically deal with the more advanced stages of growth in the spiritual life.

Braulio of Saragossa (c. 585-651). Bishop of Saragossa (631-651) and noted writer of the Visigothic renaissance. His *Life* of St. Aemilianus is his crowning literary achievement.

Caesarius of Arles (c. 470-543). Bishop of Arles renowned for his attention to his pastoral duties. Among his surviving works the most important is a collection of some 238 sermons that display an ability to preach Christian doctrine to a variety of audiences.

Callistus of Rome (d. 222). Pope (217-222) who excommunicated Sabellius for heresy. It is very probable that he suffered martyrdom.

Cassia (b. c. 805, d. between 848 and 867). Nun, poet and hymnographer who founded a convent in Constantinople.

Cassian, John (360-432). Author of the *Institutes* and the *Conferences,* works purporting to relay the teachings of the Egyptian monastic fathers on the nature of the spiritual life which were highly influential in the development of Western monasticism.

Cassiodorus (c. 485-c. 580). Founder of the monastery of Vivarium, Calabria, where monks transcribed classic sacred and profane texts, Greek and Latin, preserving them for the Western tradition.

Chromatius (fl. 400). Bishop of Aquileia, friend of Rufinus and Jerome and author of tracts and sermons.

Clement of Alexandria (c. 150-215). A highly educated Christian convert from paganism, head of the catechetical school in Alexandria and pioneer of Christian scholarship. His major works, *Protrepticus, Paedagogus* and the *Stromata,* bring Christian doctrine face to face with the ideas and achievements of his time.

Clement of Rome (fl. c. 92-101). Pope whose *Epistle to the Corinthians* is one of the most important documents of subapostolic times.

Commodian (probably third or possibly fifth century). Latin poet of unknown origin (possibly Syrian?) whose two surviving works suggest chiliast and patripassionist tendencies.

Constitutions of the Holy Apostles. See Apostolic Constitutions.

Cyprian of Carthage (fl. 248-258). Martyred bishop of Carthage who maintained that those baptized by schismatics and heretics had no share in the blessings of the church.

Cyril of Alexandria (375-444; fl. 412-444). Patriarch of Alexandria whose extensive exegesis, characterized especially by a strong espousal of the unity of Christ, led to the condemnation of Nestorius in 431.

Cyril of Jerusalem (c. 315-386; fl. c. 348). Bishop of Jerusalem after 350 and author of *Catechetical Homilies.*

Cyril of Scythopolis (b. c. 525; d. after 557). Palestinian monk and author of biographies of famous Palestinian monks. Because of him we have precise knowledge of monastic life in the fifth and sixth centuries and a description of the Origenist crisis and its suppression in the mid-sixth century.

Diadochus of Photice (c. 400-474). Antimonophysite bishop of Epirus Vetus whose work *Discourse on the Ascension of Our Lord Jesus Christ* exerted influence in both the East and West through its Chalcedonian Christology. He is also the subject of the mystical *Vision of St. Diadochus Bishop of Photice in Epirus.*

Didache (c. 140). Of unknown authorship, this text intertwines Jewish ethics with Christian liturgical practice to form a whole discourse on the "way of life." It exerted an enormous amount of influence in the patristic period and was especially used in the training of catechumen.

Didymus the Blind (c. 313-398). Alexandrian exegete who was much influenced by Origen and admired by Jerome.

Diodore of Tarsus (d. c. 394). Bishop of Tarsus and Antiochene theologian. He authored a great scope of exegetical, doctrinal and apologetic works, which come to us mostly in fragments because of his condemnation as the predecessor of Nestorianism. Diodore was a teacher of John Chrysostom and Theodore of Mopsuestia.

Dionysius of Alexandria (d. c. 264). Bishop of Alexandria and student of Origen. Dionysius actively engaged in the theological disputes of his day, opposed Sabellianism, defended himself against accusations of tritheism and wrote the earliest extant Christian refutation of Epicureanism.

His writings have survived mainly in extracts preserved by other early Christian authors.

Dorotheus of Gaza (fl. c. 525-540). Member of Abbot Seridos's monastery and later leader of a monastery where he wrote *Spiritual Instructions.* He also wrote a work on traditions of Palestinian monasticism.

Epiphanius of Salamis (c. 315-403). Bishop of Salamis in Cyprus, author of a refutation of eighty heresies (the *Panarion*) and instrumental in the condemnation of Origen.

Epiphanius the Latin. Author of the late fifth-century or early sixth century Latin text *Interpretation of the Gospels,* with constant references to early patristic commentators. He was possibly a bishop of Benevento or Seville.

Epistle of Barnabas. See Letter of Barnabas.

Ephrem the Syrian (b. c. 306; fl. 363-373). Syrian writer of commentaries and devotional hymns which are sometimes regarded as the greatest specimens of Christian poetry prior to Dante.

Eucherius of Lyons (fl. 420-449). Bishop of Lyons c. 435-449. Born into an aristocratic family, he, along with his wife and sons, joined the monastery at Lérins soon after its founding. He explained difficult Scripture passages by means of a threefold reading of the text: literal, moral and spiritual.

Eugippius (b. 460). Disciple of Severinus and third abbot of the monastic community at Castrum Lucullanum, which was made up of those fleeing from Noricum during the barbarian invasions.

Eunomius (d. 393). Bishop of Cyzicyus who was attacked by Basil and Gregory of Nyssa for maintaining that the Father and the Son were of different natures, one ingenerate, one generate.

Eusebius of Caesarea (c. 260/263-340). Bishop of Caesarea, partisan of the Emperor Constantine and first historian of the Christian church. He argued that the truth of the gospel had been foreshadowed in pagan writings but had to defend his own doctrine against suspicion of Arian sympathies.

Eusebius of Gaul, or Eusebius Gallicanus (c.

fifth century). A conventional name for a collection of seventy-six sermons produced in Gaul and revised in the seventh century. It contains material from different patristic authors and focuses on ethical teaching in the context of the liturgical cycle (days of saints and other feasts).

Eusebius of Emesa (c. 300-c. 359). Bishop of Emesa from c. 339. A biblical exegete and writer on doctrinal subjects, he displays some semi-Arian tendencies of his mentor Eusebius of Caesarea.

Eusebius of Vercelli (fl. c. 360). Bishop of Vercelli who supported the trinitarian teaching of Nicaea (325) when it was being undermined by compromise in the West.

Euthymius (377-473). A native of Melitene and influential monk. He was educated by Bishop Otreius of Melitene, who ordained him priest and placed him in charge of all the monasteries in his diocese. When the Council of Chalcedon (451) condemned the errors of Eutyches, it was greatly due to the authority of Euthymius that most of the Eastern recluses accepted its decrees. The empress Eudoxia returned to Chalcedonian orthodoxy through his efforts.

Evagrius of Pontus (c. 345-399). Disciple and teacher of ascetic life who astutely absorbed and creatively transmitted the spirituality of Egyptian and Palestinian monasticism of the late fourth century. Although Origenist elements of his writings were formally condemned by the Fifth Ecumenical Council (Constantinople II, A.D. 553), his literary corpus continued to influence the tradition of the church.

Eznik of Kolb (early fifth century). A disciple of Mesrob who translated Greek Scriptures into Armenian, so as to become the model of the classical Armenian language. As bishop, he participated in the synod of Astisat (449).

Facundus of Hermiane (fl. 546-568). African bishop who opposed Emperor Justinian's *post mortem* condemnation of Theodore of Mopsuestia, Theodoret of Cyr and Ibas of Ebessa at the fifth ecumenical council. His written defense, known as "To Justinian" or "In Defense of the Three Chapters," avers that ancient theologians should not be blamed for errors tha became obvioust only upon later theological reflection. He continued in the tradition of Chalcedon, although his Christology was supplemented, according to Justinian's decisions, by the theopaschite formula *Unus ex Trinitate passus est* ("Only one of the three suffered").

Fastidius (c. fourth-fifth centuries). British author of *On the Christian Life*. He is believed to have written some works attributed to Pelagius.

Faustinus (fl. 380). A priest in Rome and supporter of Lucifer and author of a treatise on the Trinity.

Faustus of Riez (c. 400-490). A prestigious British monk at Lérins; abbot, then bishop of Riez from 457 to his death. His works include *On the Holy Spirit*, in which he argued against the Macedonians for the divinity of the Holy Spirit, and *On Grace*, in which he argued for a position on salvation that lay between more categorical views of free-will and predestination. Various letters and (pseudonymous) sermons are extant.

The Festal Menaion. Orthodox liturgical text containing the variable parts of the service, including hymns, for fixed days of celebration of the life of Jesus and Mary.

Filastrius (fl. 380). Bishop of Brescia and author of a compilation against all heresies.

Firmicus Maternus (fourth century). An anti-Pagan apologist. Before his conversion to Christianity he wrote a work on astrology (334-337). After his conversion, however, he criticized paganism in *On the Errors of the Profane Religion*.

Fulgentius of Ruspe (c. 467-532). Bishop of Ruspe and author of many orthodox sermons and tracts under the influence of Augustine.

Gaudentius of Brescia (fl. 395). Successor of Filastrius as bishop of Brescia and author of twenty-one Eucharistic sermons.

Gennadius of Constantinople (d. 471). Patriarch of Constantinople, author of numerous commentaries and an opponent of the Christology of Cyril of Alexandria.

Gnostics. Name now given generally to followers of Basilides, Marcion, Valentinus, Mani and others. The characteristic belief is that matter is a prison made for the spirit by an evil or ignorant creator, and that redemption depends on fate, not on free will.

Gregory of Elvira (fl. 359-385). Bishop of Elvira who wrote allegorical treatises in the style of Origen and defended the Nicene faith against the Arians.

Gregory of Nazianzus (b. 329/330; fl. 372-389). Cappadocian father, bishop of Constantinople, friend of Basil the Great and Gregory of Nyssa, and author of theological orations, sermons and poetry.

Gregory of Nyssa (c. 335-394). Bishop of Nyssa and brother of Basil the Great. A Cappadocian father and author of catechetical orations, he was a philosophical theologian of great originality.

Gregory Thaumaturgus (fl. c. 248-264). Bishop of Neocaesarea and a disciple of Origen. There are at least five legendary *Lives* that recount the events and miracles which led to his being called "the wonder worker." His most important work was the *Address of Thanks to Origen*, which is a rhetorically structured panegyric to Origen and an outline of his teaching.

Gregory the Great (c. 540-604). Pope from 590, the fourth and last of the Latin "Doctors of the Church." He was a prolific author and a powerful unifying force within the Latin Church, initiating the liturgical reform that brought about the Gregorian Sacramentary and Gregorian chant.

Hesychius of Jerusalem (fl. 412-450). Presbyter and exegete, thought to have commented on the whole of Scripture.

Hilary of Arles (c. 401-449). Archbishop of Arles and leader of the Semi-Pelagian party. Hilary incurred the wrath of Pope Leo I when he removed a bishop from his see and appointed a new bishop. Leo demoted Arles from a metropolitan see to a bishopric to assert papal power over the church in Gaul.

Hilary of Poitiers (c. 315-367). Bishop of Poitiers and called the "Athanasius of the West" because of his defense (against the Arians) of the common nature of Father and Son.

Hippolytus (fl. 222-245). Recent scholarship places Hippolytus in a Palestinian context, personally familiar with Origen. Though he is known chiefly for *The Refutation of All Heresies,* he was primarily a commentator on Scripture (especially the Old Testament) employing typological exegesis.

Horsiesi (c. 305-c. 390). Pachomius's second successor, after Petronius, as a leader of cenobitic monasticism in Southern Egypt.

Ignatius of Antioch (c. 35-107/112). Bishop of Antioch who wrote several letters to local churches while being taken from Antioch to Rome to be martyred. In the letters, which warn against heresy, he stresses orthodox Christology, the centrality of the Eucharist and unique role of the bishop in preserving the unity of the church.

Irenaeus of Lyons (c. 135-c. 202). Bishop of Lyons who published the most famous and influential refutation of Gnostic thought.

Isaac of Nineveh (d. c. 700). Also known as Isaac the Syrian or Isaac Syrus, this monastic writer served for a short while as bishop of Nineveh before retiring to live a secluded monastic life. His writings on ascetic subjects survive in the form of numerous homilies.

Isho'dad of Merv (fl. c. 850). Nestorian bishop of Hedatta. He wrote commentaries on parts of the Old Testament and all of the New Testament, frequently quoting Syriac fathers.

Isidore of Seville (c. 560-636). Youngest of a family of monks and clerics, including sister Florentina and brothers Leander and Fulgentius. He was an erudite author of comprehensive scale in matters both religious and sacred, including his encyclopedic *Etymologies.*

Jacob of Nisibis (d. 338). Bishop of Nisibis. He was present at the council of Nicaea in 325 and took an active part in the opposition to Arius.

Jacob of Sarug (c. 450-c. 520). Syriac ecclesiastical writer. Jacob received his education at Edessa. At the end of his life he was ordained bishop of Sarug. His principal writing was a long series of metrical homilies, earning him the title "The Flute of the Holy Spirit."

Jerome (c. 347-420). Gifted exegete and exponent of a classical Latin style, now best known as the translator of the Latin Vulgate. He defended the perpetual virginity of Mary, attacked Origen and Pelagius and supported extreme ascetic practices.

John Chrysostom (344/354-407; fl. 386-407). Bishop of Constantinople who was noted for his orthodoxy, his eloquence and his attacks on Christian laxity in high places.

John of Damascus (c. 650-750). Arab monastic and theologian whose writings enjoyed great influence in both the Eastern and Western Churches. His most influential writing was the *Orthodox Faith.*

John the Elder (c. eighth century). A Syriac author who belonged to monastic circles of the Church of the East and lived in the region of Mount Qardu (northern Iraq). His most important writings are twenty-two homilies and a collection of fifty-one short letters in which he describes the mystical life as an anticipatory experience of the resurrection life, the fruit of the sacraments of baptism and the Eucharist.

John the Monk. Traditional name found in *The Festal Menaion,* believed to refer to John of Damascus. *See* John of Damascus.

Josephus, Flavius (c. 37-c. 101). Jewish historian from a distinguished priestly family. Acquainted with the Essenes and Sadducees, he himself became a Pharisee. He joined the great Jewish revolt that broke out in 66 and was chosen by the Sanhedrin at Jerusalem to be commander-in-chief in Galilee. Showing great shrewdness to ingratiate himself with Vespasian by foretelling his elevation and that of his son Titus to the imperial dignity, Josephus was restored his liberty after 69 when Vespasian became emperor.

Julian of Eclanum (c. 385-450). Bishop of Eclanum in 416/417 who was removed from office and exiled in 419 for not officially opposing Pelagianism. In exile, he was accepted by Theodore of Mopsuestia, whose Antiochene exegetical style he followed. Although he was never able to regain his ecclesiastical position, Julian taught in Sicily until his death. His works include commentaries on Job and parts of the Minor Prophets, a translation of Theodore of Mopsuestia's commentary on the Psalms, and various letters. Sympathetic to Pelagius, Julian applied his intellectual acumen and rhetorical training to argue against Augustine on matters such as free will, desire and the locus of evil.

Justin Martyr (c. 100/110-165; fl. c. 148-161). Palestinian philosopher who was converted to Christianity, "the only sure and worthy philosophy." He traveled to Rome where he wrote several apologies against both pagans and Jews, combining Greek philosophy and Christian theology; he was eventually martyred.

Lactantius (c. 260-c. 330). Christian apologist removed from his post as teacher of rhetoric at Nicomedia upon his conversion to Christianity. He was tutor to the son of Constantine and author of *The Divine Institutes*.

Leander (c. 545-c. 600). Latin ecclesiastical writer, of whose works only two survive. He was instrumental in spreading Christianity among the Visigoths, gaining significant historical influence in Spain in his time.

Leo the Great (regn. 440-461). Bishop of Rome whose *Tome to Flavian* helped to strike a balance between Nestorian and Cyrilline positions at the Council of Chalcedon in 451.

Letter of Barnabas (c. 130). An allegorical and typological interpretation of the Old Testament with a decidedly anti-Jewish tone. It was included with other New Testament works as a "Catholic epistle" at least until Eusebius of Caesarea (c. 260/263-340) questioned its authenticity.

Letter to Diognetus (c. third century). A refutation of paganism and an exposition of the Christian life and faith. The author of this letter is unknown, and the exact identity of its recipient, Diognetus, continues to elude patristic scholars.

Lucifer (d. 370/371). Bishop of Cagliari and vigorous supporter of Athanasius and the Nicene Creed. In conflict with the emperor Constantius, he was banished to Palestine and later to Thebaid (Egypt).

Luculentius (fifth century). Unknown author of a group of short commentaries on the New Testa-

ment, especially Pauline passages. His exegesis is mainly literal and relies mostly on earlier authors such as Jerome and Augustine. The content of his writing may place it in the fifth century.

Macarius of Egypt (c. 300-c. 390). One of the Desert Fathers. Accused of supporting Athanasius, Macarius was exiled c. 374 to an island in the Nile by Lucius, the Arian successor of Athanasius. Macarius continued his teaching of monastic theology at Wadi Natrun.

Macrina the Younger (c. 327-379). The elder sister of Basil the Great and Gregory of Nyssa, she is known as "the Younger" to distinguish her from her paternal grandmother. She had a powerful influence on her younger brothers, especially on Gregory, who called her his teacher and relates her teaching in *On the Soul and the Resurrection*.

Manichaeans. A religious movement that originated circa 241 in Persia under the leadership of Mani but was apparently of complex Christian origin. It is said to have denied free will and the universal sovereignty of God, teaching that kingdoms of light and darkness are coeternal and that the redeemed are particles of a spiritual man of light held captive in the darkness of matter (*see* Gnostics).

Marcion (fl. 144). Heretic of the mid-second century who rejected the Old Testament and much of the New Testament, claiming that the Father of Jesus Christ was other than the Old Testament God (*see* Gnostics).

Marius Victorinus (b. c. 280/285; fl. c. 355-363). Grammarian of African origin who taught rhetoric at Rome and translated works of Platonists. After his conversion (c. 355), he wrote against the Arians and commentaries on Paul's letters.

Mark the Hermit (c. sixth century). Monk who lived near Tarsus and produced works on ascetic practices as well as christological issues.

Martin of Braga (fl. c. 568-579). Anti-Arian metropolitan of Braga on the Iberian peninsula. He was highly educated and presided over the provincial council of Braga in 572.

Martyrius. *See* Sahdona.

Maximus of Turin (d. 408/423). Bishop of

Turin. Over one hundred of his sermons survive on Christian festivals, saints and martyrs.

Maximus the Confessor (c. 580-662). Palestinian-born theologian and ascetic writer. Fleeing the Arab invasion of Jerusalem in 614, he took refuge in Constantinople and later Africa. He died near the Black Sea after imprisonment and severe suffering, having his tongue cut off and his right hand mutilated. He taught total preference for God and detachment from all things.

Methodius of Olympus (d. 311). Bishop of Olympus who celebrated virginity in a *Symposium* partly modeled on Plato's dialogue of that name.

Minucius Felix (second or third century). Christian apologist who was an advocate in Rome. His *Octavius* agrees at numerous points with the *Apologeticum* of Tertullian. His birthplace is believed to be in Africa.

Montanist Oracles. Montanism was an apocalyptic and strictly ascetic movement begun in the latter half of the second century by a certain Montanus in Phrygia, who, along with certain of his followers, uttered oracles they claimed were inspired by the Holy Spirit. Little of the authentic oracles remains and most of what is known of Montanism comes from the authors who wrote against the movement. Montanism was formally condemned as a heresy before by Asiatic synods.

Nemesius of Emesa (fl. late fourth century). Bishop of Emesa in Syria whose most important work, *Of the Nature of Man*, draws on several theological and philosophical sources and is the first exposition of a Christian anthropology.

Nestorius (c. 381-c. 451). Patriarch of Constantinople (428-431) who founded the heresy which says that there are two persons, divine and human, rather than one person truly united in the incarnate Christ. He resisted the teaching of *theotokos*, causing Nestorian churches to separate from Constantinople.

Nicetas of Remesiana (fl. second half of fourth century). Bishop of Remesiana in Serbia, whose works affirm the consubstantiality of the Son and the deity of the Holy Spirit.

Novatian of Rome (fl. 235-258). Roman theologian, otherwise orthodox, who formed a schismatic church after failing to become pope. His treatise on the Trinity states the classic western doctrine.

Oecumenius (sixth century). Called the Rhetor or the Philosopher, Oecumenius wrote the earliest extant Greek commentary on Revelation. Scholia by Oecumenius on some of John Chrysostom's commentaries on the Pauline Epistles are still extant.

Origen of Alexandria (b. 185; fl. c. 200-254). Influential exegete and systematic theologian. He was condemned (perhaps unfairly) for maintaining the preexistence of souls while purportedly denying the resurrection of the body. His extensive works of exegesis focus on the spiritual meaning of the text.

Pachomius (c. 292-347). Founder of cenobitic monasticism. A gifted group leader and author of a set of rules, he was defended after his death by Athanasius of Alexandria.

Pacian of Barcelona (c. fourth century). Bishop of Barcelona whose writings polemicize against popular pagan festivals as well as Novatian schismatics.

Palladius of Helenopolis (c. 363/364-c. 431). Bishop of Helenopolis in Bithynia (400-417) and then Aspuna in Galatia. A disciple of Evagrius of Pontus and admirer of Origen, Palladius became a zealous adherent of John Chrysostom and shared his troubles in 403. His *Lausaic History* is the leading source for the history of early monasticism, stressing the spiritual value of the life of the desert.

Paschasius of Dumium (c. 515-c. 580). Translator of sentences of the Desert Fathers from Greek into Latin while a monk in Dumium.

Paterius (c. sixth-seventh century). Disciple of Gregory the Great who is primarily responsible for the transmission of Gregory's works to many later medieval authors.

Paulinus of Nola (355-431). Roman senator and distinguished Latin poet whose frequent encounters with Ambrose of Milan (c. 333-397) led to his eventual conversion and baptism in 389. He eventually renounced his wealth and influential position and took up his pen to write poetry in service of Christ. He also wrote many letters to, among others, Augustine, Jerome and Rufinus.

Paulus Orosius (b. c. 380). An outspoken critic of Pelagius, mentored by Augustine. His *Seven Books of History Against the Pagans* was perhaps the first history of Christianity.

Pelagius (c. 354-c. 420). Contemporary of Augustine whose followers were condemned in 418 and 431 for maintaining that even before Christ these were people who lived wholly without sin and that salvation depended on free will.

Peter of Alexandria (d. c. 311). Bishop of Alexandria. He marked (and very probably initiated) the reaction at Alexandria against extreme doctrines of Origen. During the persecution of Christians in Alexandria, Peter was arrested and beheaded by Roman officials. Eusebius of Caesarea described him as "a model bishop, remarkable for his virtuous life and his ardent study of the Scriptures."

Peter Chrysologus (c. 380-450). Latin archbishop of Ravenna whose teachings included arguments for adherence in matters of faith to the Roman see, and the relationship between grace and Christian living.

Philo of Alexandria (c. 20 B.C.-c. A.D. 50). Jewish-born exegete who greatly influenced Christian patristic interpretation of the Old Testament. Born to a rich family in Alexandria, Philo was a contemporary of Jesus and lived an ascetic and contemplative life that makes some believe he was a rabbi. His interpretation of Scripture based the spiritual sense on the literal. Although influenced by Hellenism, Philo's theology remains thoroughly Jewish.

Philoxenus of Mabbug (c. 440-523). Bishop of Mabbug (Hierapolis) and a leading thinker in the early Syrian Orthodox Church. His extensive writings in Syriac include a set of thirteen *Discourses on the Christian Life*, several works on the incarnation and a number of exegetical works.

Poemen (c. fifth century). One-seventh of the sayings in the *Sayings of the Desert Fathers* are attributed to Poemen, which is Greek for shepherd. Poemen was a common title among early Egyptian desert ascetics, and it is unknown whether all of the sayings come from one person.

Polycarp of Smyrna (c. 69-155). Bishop of Smyrna who vigorously fought heretics such as the Marcionites and Valentinians. He was the leading Christian figure in Roman Asia in the middle of the second century.

Potamius of Lisbon (fl. c. 350-360). Bishop of Lisbon who joined the Arian party in 357, but later returned to the Catholic faith (c. 359?). His works from both periods are concerned with the larger Trinitarian debates of his time.

Procopius of Gaza (c. 465-c. 530). A Christian exegete educated in Alexandria. He wrote numerous theological works and commentaries on Scripture (particularly the Hebrew Bible), the latter marked by the allegorical exegesis for which the Alexandrian school was known.

Prudentius (c. 348-c. 410). Latin poet and hymn-writer who devoted his later life to Christian writing. He wrote didactic poems on the theology of the incarnation, against the heretic Marcion and against the resurgence of paganism.

Pseudo-Clementines (third-fourth century). A series of apocryphal writings pertaining to a conjured life of Clement of Rome. Written in a form of popular legend, the stories from Clement's life, including his opposition to Simon Magus, illustrate and promote articles of Christian teaching. It is likely that the corpus is a derivative of a number of Gnostic and Judeo-Christian writings. Dating the corpus is a complicated issue.

Pseudo-Dionysius the Areopagite (fl. c. 500). Author who assumed the name of Dionysius the Areopagite mentioned in Acts 17:34, and who composed the works known as the *Corpus Areopagiticum* (or *Dionysiacum*). These writings were the foundation of the apophatic school of mysticism in their denial that anything can be truly predicated of God.

Pseudo-Macarius (fl. c. 390). An anonymous writer and ascetic (from Mesopotamia?) active in Antioch whose badly edited works were attributed to Macarius of Egypt. He had keen insight into human nature, prayer and the inner life. His work includes some one hundred discourses and homilies.

Quodvultdeus (fl. 430). Carthaginian bishop and friend of Augustine who endeavored to show at length how the New Testament fulfilled the Old Testament.

Rufinus of Aquileia (c. 345-411). Orthodox Christian thinker and historian who nonetheless translated and preserved the works of Origen, and defended him against the strictures of Jerome and Epiphanius. He lived the ascetic life in Rome, Egypt and Jerusalem (the Mount of Olives).

Sabellius (fl. 200). Allegedly the author of the heresy which maintains that the Father and Son are a single person. The patripassian variant of this heresy states that the Father suffered on the cross.

Sahdona (fl. 635-640). Known in Greek as Martyrius, this Syriac author was bishop of Beth Garmai. He studied in Nisibis and was exiled for his christological ideas. His most important work is the deeply scriptural *Book of Perfection* which ranks as one of the masterpieces of Syriac monastic literature.

Salvian the Presbyter of Marseilles (c. 400-c. 480). An important author for the history of his own time. He saw the fall of Roman civilization to the barbarians as a consequence of the reprehensible conduct of Roman Christians. In *The Governance of God* he developed the theme of divine providence.

Second Letter of Clement (c. 150). The so-called *Second Letter of Clement* is an early Christian sermon probably written by a Corinthian author, though some scholars have assigned it to a Roman or Alexandrian author.

Severian of Gabala (fl. c. 400). A contemporary of John Chrysostom, he was a highly regarded preacher in Constantinople, particularly at the imperial court, and ultimately sided with Chrysostom's accusers. He wrote homilies on Genesis.

Severus of Antioch (fl. 488-538). A monophysite theologian, consecrated bishop of Antioch in 522. Born in Pisidia, he studied in Alexandria and Beirut, taught in Constantinople and was exiled to Egypt.

Shepherd of Hermas (second century). Divided into five *Visions*, twelve *Mandates* and ten *Similitudes*, this Christian apocalypse was written by a former slave and named for the form of the second angel said to have granted him his visions. This work was highly esteemed for its moral value and was used as a textbook for catechumens in the early church.

Sulpicius Severus (c. 360-c. 420). An ecclesiastical writer from Bordeaux born of noble parents. Devoting himself to monastic retirement, he became a personal friend and enthusiastic disciple of St. Martin of Tours.

Symeon the New Theologian (c. 949-1022). Compassionate spiritual leader known for his strict rule. He believed that the divine light could be perceived and received through the practice of mental prayer.

Tertullian of Carthage (c. 155/160-225/250; fl. c. 197-222). Brilliant Carthaginian apologist and polemicist who laid the foundations of Christology and trinitarian orthodoxy in the West, though he himself was later estranged from the catholic tradition due to its laxity.

Theodore of Heraclea (d. c. 355). An anti-Nicene bishop of Thrace. He was part of a team seeking reconciliation between Eastern and Western Christianity. In 343 he was excommunicated at the council of Sardica. His writings focus on a literal interpretation of Scripture.

Theodore of Mopsuestia (c. 350-428). Bishop of Mopsuestia, founder of the Antiochene, or literalistic, school of exegesis. A great man in his day, he was later condemned as a precursor of Nestorius.

Theodore of Tabennesi (d. 368) Vice general of the Pachomian monasteries (c. 350-368) under Horsiesi. Several of his letters are known.

Theodoret of Cyr (c. 393-466). Bishop of Cyr (Cyrrhus), he was an opponent of Cyril who commented extensively on Old Testament texts as a lucid exponent of Antiochene exegesis.

Theodotus the Valentinian (second century). Likely a Montanist who may have been related to the Alexandrian school. Extracts of his work are known through writings of Clement of Alexandria.

Theophanes (775-845). Hymnographer and bishop of Nicaea (842-845). He was persecuted during the second iconoclastic period for his support of the Seventh Council (Second Council of Nicaea, 787). He wrote many hymns in the tradition of the monastery of Mar Sabbas that were used in the *Paraklitiki*.

Theophilus of Antioch (late second century). Bishop of Antioch. His only surviving work is *Ad Autholycum*, where we find the first Christian commentary on Genesis and the first use of the term *Trinity*. Theophilus's apologetic literary heritage had influence on Irenaeus and possibly Tertullian.

Theophylact of Ohrid (c. 1050-c. 1108). Byzantine archbishop of Ohrid (or Achrida) in what is now Bulgaria. Drawing on earlier works, he wrote commentaries on several Old Testament books and all of the New Testament except for Revelation.

Valentinus (fl. c. 140). Alexandrian heretic of the mid-second century who taught that the material world was created by the transgression of God's Wisdom, or Sophia (*see* Gnostics).

Valerian of Cimiez (fl. c. 422-439). Bishop of Cimiez. He participated in the councils of Riez (439) and Vaison (422) with a view to strengthening church discipline. He supported Hilary of Arles in quarrels with Pope Leo I.

Verecundus (d. 552). An African Christian writer, who took an active part in the christological controversies of the sixth century, especially in the debate on Three Chapters. He also wrote allegorical commentaries on the nine liturgical church canticles.

Victorinus of Petovium (d. c. 304). Latin biblical exegete. With multiple works attributed to him, his sole surviving work is the *Commentary on the Apocalypse* and perhaps some fragments from *Commentary on Matthew*. Victorinus expressed strong millenarianism in his writing, though his was less materialistic than the millenarianism of Papias or Irenaeus. In his allegorical approach he could be called a spiritual disciple of Origen. Victorinus died during the first year of Diocletian's persecution, probably in 304.

Vincent of Lérins (d. before 450). Monk who has exerted considerable influence through his writings on orthodox dogmatic theological method, as contrasted with the theological methodologies of the heresies.

Bibliography of Works in Original Languages

This bibliography refers readers to original language sources and supplies Thesaurus Linguae Graecae (=TLG) or Cetedoc Clavis (=Cl.) numbers where available. The edition listed in this bibliography may in some cases differ from the edition found in TLG or Cetedoc databases.

Adamnan. "De locis sanctis." In *Itineraria et alia geographica*. Edited by L. Bieler. CCL 175, pp. 175-234. Turnhout, Belgium: Brepols, 1965. Cl. 2332.

Ambrose. "Apologia David altera (dub)." In *Sancti Ambrosii opera*. Edited by Karl Schenkl. CSEL 32, pt. 2, pp. 357-408. Vienna, Austria: F. Tempsky; Leipzig, Germany: G. Freytag, 1897. Cl. 0136.

———. "De bono mortis." In *Sancti Ambrosii opera*. Edited by Karl Schenkl. CSEL 32, pt. 1, pp. 701-53. Vienna, Austria: F. Tempsky; Leipzig, Germany: G. Freytag, 1897. Cl. 0129.

———. "De Cain et Abel." In *Sancti Ambrosii opera*. Edited by Karl Schenkl. CSEL 32, pt. 1, pp. 337-409. Vienna, Austria: F. Tempsky; Leipzig, Germany: G. Freytag, 1897. Cl. 0125.

———. "De excessu fratris Satyri." In *Sancti Ambrosii opera*. Edited by Otto Faller. CSEL 73, pp. 207-325. Vienna, Austria: Hoelder-Pichler-Tempsky, 1895. Cl. 0157.

———. "De fide libri v." In *Sancti Ambrosii opera*. Edited by Otto Faller. CSEL 78. Vienna, Austria: Hoelder-Pichler-Tempsky, 1962. Cl. 0150.

———. "De fuga saeculi." In *Sancti Ambrosii opera*. Edited by Karl Schenkl. CSEL 32, pt. 2, pp. 161-207. Vienna, Austria: F. Tempsky; Leipzig, Germany: G. Freytag, 1897. Cl. 0133.

———. "De Helia et jejunio." In *Sancti Ambrosii opera*. Edited by Karl Schenkl. CSEL 32, pt. 2, pp. 409-65. Vienna, Austria: F. Tempsky; Leipzig, Germany: G. Freytag, 1897. Cl. 0137.

———. "De interpellatione Job et David." In *Sancti Ambrosii opera*. Edited by Karl Schenkl. CSEL 32, pt. 2, pp. 209-96. Vienna, Austria: F. Tempsky; Leipzig, Germany: G. Freytag, 1897. Cl. 0134.

———. "De Isaac vel anima." In *Sancti Ambrosii opera*. Edited by Karl Schenkl. CSEL 32, pt. 1, pp. 639-700. Vienna, Austria: F. Tempsky; Leipzig, Germany: G. Freytag, 1897. Cl. 0128.

———. "De Jacob et vita beata." In *Sancti Ambrosii opera*. Edited by Karl Schenkl. CSEL 32, pt. 2, pp. 1-70. Vienna, Austria: F. Tempsky; Leipzig, Germany: G. Freytag, 1897. Cl. 0130.

———. "De Joseph." In *Sancti Ambrosii opera*. Edited by Karl Schenkl. CSEL 32, pt. 2, pp. 71-122. Vienna, Austria: F. Tempsky; Leipzig, Germany: G. Freytag, 1897. Cl. 0131.

———. "De mysteriis." In *Sancti Ambrosii opera*. Edited by Otto Faller. CSEL 73, pp. 87-116. Vienna, Austria: Hoelder-Pichler-Tempsky, 1895. Cl. 0155.

———. "De officiis." In *Sancti Ambrosii mediolanensis opera, Pars V*. Edited by Maurice Testard. CCL 15. Turnhout, Belgium: Brepols, 2000. Cl. 0144

———. "De paradiso." In *Sancti Ambrosii opera*. Edited by Karl Schenkl. CSEL 32, pt. 1, pp. 263-336. Vienna, Austria: F. Tempsky; Leipzig, Germany: G. Freytag, 1897. Cl. 0124.

———. "De patriarchis." In *Sancti Ambrosii opera*. Edited by Karl Schenkl. CSEL 32, pt. 2, pp. 123-60. Vienna, Austria: F. Tempsky; Leipzig, Germany: G. Freytag, 1897. Cl. 0132.

———. "De spiritu sancto." In *Sancti Ambrosii opera*. Edited by Otto Faller. CSEL 79, pp. 5-222. Vienna, Austria: Hoelder-Pichler-Tempsky, 1964. Cl. 0151.

————. "De viduis." In *De virginibus: De viduis*. Edited by Franco Gori. Sancti Ambrosii episcopi Mediolanensis opera, vol. 14.1, pp. 243-319. Milan, Italy: Biblioteca Ambrosiana; Rome: Città nuova, 1989. Cl. 0146.

————. "Epistulae; Epistulae extra collectionem traditae." In *Sancti Ambrosii opera*. Edited by Otto Faller and M. Zelzer. CSEL 82. Vienna, Austria: F. Tempsky; Leipzig, Germany: G. Freytag, 1968-1990. Cl. 0160.

————. "Exameron." In *Sancti Ambrosii opera*. Edited by Otto Faller. CSEL 32, pt. 1, pp. 1-261. Vienna, Austria: F. Tempsky; Leipzig, Germany: G. Freytag, 1897. Cl. 0123.

————. "Explanatio psalmorum xii." In *Sancti Ambrosii opera*. Edited by Michael Petschenig. CSEL 64. Vienna, Austria: F. Tempsky; Leipzig, Germany: G. Freytag, 1919. Cl. 0140.

————. "Expositio Evangelii secundum Lucam" In *Sancti Ambrosii mediolanensis opera, Pars IV*. CCL 14, pp. 1-400. Turnhout, Belgium: Brepols, 1957. Cl. 0143.

————. "Expositio psalmi cxviii." In *Sancti Ambrosii opera*. Edited by Michael Petschenig. CSEL 62. Vienna, Austria: F. Tempsky; Leipzig, Germany: G. Freytag, 1913. Cl. 0141.

Aphrahat. "Demonstrationes (IV)." In *Opera omnia*. Edited by R. Graffin. PS 1, cols. 137-82. Paris: Firmin-Didot, 1910.

Aponius [Apponius]. "In Canticum canticorum expositio." In *Apponii: In Canticum Canticorum Expositionem*. Edited by B. de Vregille and L. Neyrand. Turnhout, Belgium: Brepols, 1986. CCL 19. Cl. 0194.

Arnobius the Younger. "Commentarii in Psalmos." In *Arnobii Junioris opera omnia, pt. 1*. Edited by Klaus-D. Daur. CCL 25. Turnhout, Belgium: Brepols, 1990. Cl. 0242.

Athanasius. "De incarnatione verbi." In *Sur l'incarnation du verbe*. Edited by C. Kannengiesser. SC 199, pp. 258-468. Paris: Éditions du Cerf, 1973. TLG 2035.002.

————. "Epistulae festalis." In *Opera omnia*. Edited by J.-P. Migne. PG 26, cols. 1351-444. Paris: Migne, 1887. TLG 2035.014.

————. "Orationes tres contra Arianos." Edited by J.-P. Migne. PG 26, cols. 11-526. Paris: Migne, 1887. TLG 2035.042.

————. "Epistula ad Adelphium." In *Opera omnia*. Edited by J.-P. Migne. PG 26, cols. 1072-84. Paris: Migne, 1887. TLG 2035.050.

————. "Vita sancti Antonii." In *Opera omnia*. Edited by J.-P. Migne. PG 26, cols. 835-976. Paris: Migne, 1857. TLG 2035.047.

Augustine. "Ad catholicos de secta Donatistarum." In *Sancti Aurelii Augustini*. Edited by Michael Petschenig. CSEL 52, pp. 229-322. Vienna, Austria: F. Tempsky; Leipzig, Germany: G. Freytag, 1909. Cl. 0334.

————. "Adversus Judaeos." In *Opera omnia*. Edited by J.-P. Migne. PL 42, cols. 51-64. Paris, Migne, 1861. Cl. 0315.

————. "Contra Faustum." In *Sancti Aurelii Augustini*. Edited by Joseph Zycha. CSEL 25, pp. 249-797. Vienna, Austria: F. Tempsky; Leipzig, Germany: G. Freytag, 1891. Cl. 0321.

————. *De civitate Dei*. In *Aurelii Augustini opera*. Edited by Bernhard Dombart and Alphons Kalb. CCL 47-48. Turnhout, Belgium: Brepols, 1955. Cl. 0313.

————. *De consensu evangelistarum libri iv*. In *Sancti Aurelii Augustini*. Edited by Francis Weihrich. CSEL 43. Vienna, Austria: F. Tempsky; Leipzig, Germany: G. Freytag, 1904. Cl. 0273.

————. "De diversis quaestionibus octoginta tribus." In *Aurelii Augustini opera*. Edited by Almut Mutzenbecher. CCL 44A, pp. 11-249. Turnhout, Belgium: Brepols, 1975. Cl. 0289.

————. "De doctrina christiana." In *Aurelii Augustini opera*. Edited by Joseph Martin. CCL 32, pp. 1-167. Turnhout, Belgium: Brepols, 1962. Cl. 0263.

———. "De fide rerum invisibilium." In *Aurelii Augustini opera*. Edited by M. P. J. van den Hout. CCL 46, pp. 1-19. Turnhout, Belgium: Brepols, 1969. Cl. 0292.

———. "De gratia et libero arbitrio." In *Opera omnia*. Edited by J.-P. Migne. PL 44, cols. 881-912. Paris: Migne, 1861. Cl. 0352.

———. "De natura et gratia." In *Sancti Aurelii Augustini De peccatorum meritis et remissione et de baptismo parvulorum ad Marcellinum libri tres, De spiritu et littera liber unus, De natura et gratia liber unus, De natura et origine animae libri quattuor*. Edited by Karl Franz Urba and Joseph Zycha. CSEL 60, pp. 233-99. Vienna, Austria: F. Tempsky; Leipzig, Germany: G. Freytag, 1913. Cl. 0344.

———. "De praedestinatione sanctorum." In *Opera omnia*. PL 44, cols. 959-92. Edited by J.-P. Migne. Paris: Migne, 1861. Cl. 0354.

———. "De sermone Domini in monte." In *Aurelii Augustini opera*. Edited by Almut Mutzenbecher. CCL 35. Turnhout, Belgium: Brepols, 1967. Cl. 0274.

———. "De spiritu et littera." In *Sancti Aurelii Augustini De peccatorum meritis et remissione et de baptismo parvulorum ad Marcellinum libri tres, De spiritu et littera liber unus, De natura et gratia liber unus, De natura et origine animae libri quattuor*. Edited by Karl Franz Urba and Joseph Zycha. CSEL 60, pp. 155-229. Vienna, Austria: F. Tempsky; Leipzig, Germany: G. Freytag, 1913. Cl. 0343.

———. "De Trinitate." In *Aurelii Augustini opera*. Edited by W. J. Mountain. CCL 50-50A. Turnhout, Belgium: Brepols, 1968. Cl. 0329.

———. "De vita christiana." In *Augustini opera omnia*. Edited by J.-P. Migne. PL 40, cols. 1031-46. Paris: Migne, 1861. Cl. 0730.

———. "Enarrationes in Psalmos." 3 vols. In *Aurelii Augustini opera*. Edited by D. E. Dekkers and John Fraipont. CCL 38, 39 and 40. Turnhout, Belgium: Brepols, 1956. Cl. 0283.

———. "Enchiridion de fide, spe et caritate." In *Aurelii Augustini opera*. Edited by E. Evans. CCL 46, pp. 49-114. Turnhout, Belgium: Brepols, 1969. Cl. 0295.

———. "Epistulae." In *Sancti Aurelii Augustini opera*. Edited by A. Goldbacher. CCL 34, pts. 1, 2; 44; 57; 58. Turnhout, Belgium: Brepols, 1895-1898. Cl. 0262.

———. "In Johannis evangelium tractatus." In *Aurelii Augustini opera*. Edited by R. Willems. CCL 36. Turnhout, Belgium: Brepols, 1954. Cl. 0278.

———. "Sermones." In *Augustini opera omnia*. Edited by J.-P. Migne. PL 38 and 39. Paris: Migne, 1844-1865. Cl. 0284.

"Barnabae epistula." In *Épitre de Barnabé*. Edited by Pierre Prigent and Robert A. Kraft. SC 172, pp. 72-218. Paris: Éditions du Cerf., 1971. TLG 1216.001.

Basil the Great. "Asceticon magnum sive Quaestiones [regulae fusius tractatae]." In *Opera omnia*. Edited by J.-P. Migne. PG 31, cols. 905-1052. Paris: Migne, 1857. TLG 2040.048.

———. "Enarratio in prophetam Isaiam (Dub.). In *San Basilio. Commento al profeta Isaia*, 2 vols. Edited by P. Trevisan. Turin: Societa Editrice Internazionale, 1939. TLG 2040.009.

———. "Epistulae." In *Saint Basil: Lettres*. Edited by Yves Courtonne. Vol. 2, pp. 101-218; vol. 3, pp. 1-229. Paris: Les Belles Lettres, 1961-1966. TLG 2040.004.

———. "Homiliae in hexaemeron." In *Basile de Cesaree. Homélies sur l'hexaéméron*, 2nd ed. Edited by Stanislas Giet. SC 26, pp. 86-522. Paris: Éditions du Cerf, 1968. TLG 2040.001.

———. "Homiliae super Psalmos." In *Opera omnia*. Edited by J.-P. Migne. PG 29, cols. 209-494. Paris: Migne, 1857. TLG 2040.018.

———. "Prologus 7 (De judicio Dei)." In *Opera omnia*. Edited by J.-P. Migne. PG 31, cols. 653-76. Paris: Migne, 1857. TLG 2040.043.

Bede. "De tabernaculo et vasis eius ac vestibus sacerdotum libri iii." In *Opera*. Edited by D. Hurst. CCL 119A, pp. 5-139. Cl. 1345.

———. "De templo libri ii." In *Opera*. Edited by D. Hurst. CCL 119A, pp.140-234. Turnhout, Belgium: Brepols, 1969. Cl. 1348.

———. *De temporum ratione liber*. Edited by W. Jones. CCL 123B. Turnhout, Belgium: Brepols, 1977. Cl. 2320.

———. "Expositio actuum apostolorum." In *Opera*, pp. 1-99. Edited by M. L. W. Laistner. CCL 121. Turnhout, Belgium: Brepols, 1983. Cl. 1357.

———. *Homiliarum evangelii libri ii.* In *Opera*. Edited by D. Hurst. CCL 122. Turnhout, Belgium: Brepols, 1955. Cl. 1367.

———. "In Cantica canticorum libri vi." In *Opera*. Edited by D. Hurst. CCL 119B, pp. 165-375. Turnhout, Belgium: Brepols, 1983. Cl. 1353.

———. "In Ezram et Neemiam libri iii." In *Opera*. Edited by D. Hurst. CCL 119A, pp. 235-392. Turnhout, Belgium: Brepols, 1969. Cl. 1349.

———. "In Lucae evangelium expositio." In *Opera*. Edited by D. Hurst. CCL 120, pp. 1-425. Turnhout, Belgium: Brepols, 1960. Cl. 1356.

———. "In Marci evangelium expositio." In *Opera*. Edited by D. Hurst. CCL 120, pp. 431-648. Turnhout, Belgium: Brepols, 1960. Cl. 1355.

———. "In primam partem Samuhelis libri iv." In *Opera*. Edited by D. Hurst. CCL 119, pp. 1-287. Turnhout, Belgium: Brepols, 1962. Cl. 1346.

———. "In proverbia Salomonis libri iii." In *Opera*. Edited by D. Hurst. CCL 119B, pp. 21-163. Turnhout, Belgium: Brepols, 1983. Cl. 1351.

———. "Libri quatuor in principium Genesis usque ad nativitatem Isaac et ejectionem Ismahelis adnotationum." In *Bedae Venerabilis opera*." Edited by Ch. W. Jones. CCL 118A. Turnhout, Belgium: Brepols, 1967. Cl. 1344.

Caesarius of Arles. *Sermones Caesarii Arelatensis*. 2 vols. Edited by D. Germani and G. Morin. CCL 103 and 104. Turnhout, Belgium: Brepols, 1953. Cl. 1008.

Cassian, John. *Collationes xxiv.* Edited by Michael Petschenig. CSEL 13. Vienna, Austria: F. Tempsky; Leipzig, Germany: G. Freytag, 1886. Cl. 0512.

———."De incarnatione Domini contra Nestorium." In *Johannis Cassiani*. Edited by Michael Petschenig. CSEL 17, pp. 233-391. Vienna, Austria: F. Tempsky; Leipzig, Germany: G. Freytag, 1888. Cl. 0514.

———. "De institutis coenobiorum et de octo principalium vitiorum remediis." In *Johannis Cassiani*. Edited by Michael Petschenig. CSEL 17, pp. 1-231. Vienna, Austria: F. Tempsky; Leipzig, Germany: G. Freytag, 1888. Cl. 0513.

Cassiodorus. *Expositio Psalmorum*, 2 vols. Edited by M. Adriaen. CCL 97 and 98. Turnhout: Brepols, 1958. Cl. 0900.

———. "Expositio sancti Pauli Epistulae ad Romanos." In *Primasii: Opera omnia*. PL 68, cols. 415-506. Edited by J.-P. Migne. Paris: Migne, 1847. Cl. 0902.

Chromatius of Aquileia. "Tractatus in Matthaeum." In *Chromatii Aquileiensis opera*. Edited by R. Étaix and Joseph Lemarié, CCL 9A, pp. 185-489; CCL 9A supplementum, pp. 624-36. Turnhout, Belgium: Brepols, 1974-77. Cl. 0218.

Clement of Alexandria. "Paedagogus." In *Le pédagogue [par] Clement d'Alexandrie*. 3 vols. Translated by Mauguerite Harl, Chantel Matray and Claude Mondésert. Introduction and notes by Henri-Irénée Marrou. SC 70, 108, 158. Paris: Éditions du Cerf, 1960-1970. TLG 0555.002.

———."Stromata." In *Clemens Alexandrinus*, vol. 2 (3rd ed.) and vol. 3 (2nd ed.). Edited by Otto Stählin, Ludwig Früchtel and Ursula Treu. GCS 15 and 17, pp. 1-102. Berlin: Akademie-Verlag, 1960-1970. TLG 0555.004.

Clement of Rome."Epistula i ad Corinthios." In *Clément de Rome: Épître aux Corinthiens*. Edited by Annie

Jaubert. SC 167. Paris: Éditions du Cerf, 1971. TLG 1271.001.

Constitutiones apostolorum. In *Les constitutions apostoliques,* 3 vols. Edited by Marcel Metzger. SC 320, 329, 336. Paris: Éditions du Cerf, 1985-1987. TLG 2894.001.

Cyprian. "Ad Quirinum." In *Sancti Cypriani episcopi opera.* Edited by R. Weber. CCL 3, pp. 3-179. Turnhout, Belgium: Brepols, 1972. Cl. 0039.

―――. "De bono patientiae." In *Sancti Cypriani episcopi opera.* Edited by C. Moreschini. CCL 3A, pp. 118-33. Turnhout, Belgium: Brepols, 1976. Cl. 0048.

―――. "De dominica oratione." In *Sancti Cypriani episcopi opera.* Edited by C. Moreschini. CCL 3A, pp. 87-113. Turnhout, Belgium: Brepols, 1976. Cl. 0043.

―――. "De habitu virginum." In *S. Thasci Caecili Cypriani opera omnia.* Edited by William Hartel. CSEL 3.1, pp. 185-205. Vienna, Austria: Gerold, 1868. Cl. 0040.

―――. "De lapsis." In *Sancti Cypriani episcopi opera.* Edited by R. Weber. CCL 3, pp. 221-42. Turnhout, Belgium: Brepols, 1972. Cl. 0042.

―――. *Epistulae.* Edited by G. F. Diercks. CCL 3B, 3C. Turnhout, Belgium: Brepols, 1994-1996. Cl. 0050.

Cyril of Alexandria. "Commentarius in Isaiam prophetam." In *S. P. N. Cyrilli: Alexandria Archiepiscopi.* Edited by J.-P. Migne. PG 70, cols. 9-1450. Paris: Migne, 1864. TLG 4090.103.

―――. "Contra Julianum imperatorem (fragmenta)." In *Analecta patristica.* Edited by Franz Diekamp. Orientalia Christiana analecta 117, pp. 228-29. Rome: Pontifical Institute for Oriental Studies, 1938. TLG 4090.144.

―――. "Epistulae." In *Acta conciliorum oecumenicorum.* 7 vols. Edited by Eduard Schwartz. Berlin: Walter de Gruyter, 1927-29. TLG 5000.001.

Cyril of Jeruslaem. "Catecheses ad illuminandos 1-18." In *Cyrilli Hierosolymorum archiepiscopi opera quae supersunt omnia.* 2 vols. Edited by W. C. Reischl and J. Rupp. Munich: Lentner, 1860 (reprint, Hildesheim: Olms, 1967). TLG 2110.003.

Ephrem the Syrian. "In Tatiani Diatessaron." In *Saint Éphrem: Commentaire de l'Evangile Concordant—Text Syriaque* (Ms Chester-Beatty 709), Vol. 2. Edited by Louis Leloir. Leuven and Paris: Peeters Press, 1990.

―――. *Hymni de nativitate.* Edited by Edmund Beck. 2 vols. CSCO 186, 187. Louvain: Secretariat du Corpus, 1959.

Eusebius of Caesarea. "Commentarius in Isaiam." In *Eusebius Werke, Band 9: Der Jesajakommentar.* Edited by J. Ziegler. GCS, pp. 3-411. Berlin: Akademie-Verlag, 1975. TLG 2018.019.

―――. "Demonstratio evangelica." In *Eusebius Werke, Band 6: Die Demonstratio evangelica.* GCS 23, pp. 1-492. Leipzig: Hinrichs, 1913. TLG 2018.005.

Eusebius of Gaul. *Collectio homiliarum.* Edited by Francisci Glorie. CCL 101-101A. Turnhout, Belgium: Brepols, 1970-71. Cl. 0966.

Facundus of Hermiane. "Pro defensione trium capitulorum libri xii. Ad Justinianum." In *Opera omnia.* Edited by Johannes-Maria Clémont and Rolandus Vander Plaetse. CCL 90A, 3-398. Turnhout, Belgium: Brepols, 1974. Cl. 0866.

Faustus of Riez. "De spiritu sancto libri duo." In *Fausti Reiensis opera.* Edited by August Engelbrecht. CSEL 21, 99-157. Vienna, Austria: F. Tempsky; Leipzig, Germany: G. Freytag, 1891. Cl. 0962.

Firmicus Maternus. *De errore profanarum religionum.* Edited by Robert Turcan. Paris: Belles letters, 1982. Cl. 0102.

Fulgentius of Ruspe. "Ad Euthymium de remissione peccatorum libri II." In *Opera.* Edited by J. Fraipont. CCL 91A, pp. 649-707. Turnhout, Belgium: Brepols, 1968. Cl. 0821.

―――. "Ad Trasamundum libri III." In *Opera.* Edited by J. Fraipont. CCL 91, pp. 95-185. Turnhout,

Belgium: Brepols, 1968. Cl. 0816.

———. "De fide ad Petrum seu de regula fidei." In *Opera*. Edited by J. Fraipont. CCL 91A, pp. 711-60. Turnhout, Belgium: Brepols, 1968. Cl. 0826.

———. "Epistulae XVIII." In *Opera*. Edited by J. Fraipont. CCL 91, pp. 189-280, 311-12, 359-444; and CCL 91A, 447-57, 551-629. Turnhout, Belgium: Brepols, 1968. Cl. 0817.

———. "Liber ad Victorem contra sermonem Fastidiosi Ariani." In *Opera*. Edited by J. Fraipont. CCL 91, pp. 283-308. Turnhout, Belgium: Brepols, 1968. Cl. 0820.

Gregory of Elvira. "Tractatus Origenis de libris Sanctarum Scripturarum." In *Gregorii Iliberritani episcopi quae supersunt*. Edited by Vincentius Bulhart. CCL 69, pp. 1-146. Turnhout, Belgium: Brepols, 1967. Cl. 0546.

Gregory of Nazianzus. "Apologetica [orat. 2]." In *Opera omnia*. Edited by J.-P. Migne. PG 35, cols. 408-513. Paris: Migne, 1857. TLG 2022.016.

———. "In patrem tacentem [orat. 16]." In *Opera omnia*. Edited by J.-P. Migne. PG 35, cols. 933-64. Paris: Migne, 1857. TLG 2022.029.

———. "In pentecosten [orat. 41]." In *Opera omnia*. Edited by J.-P. Migne.PG 36, cols. 428-52. Paris: Migne, 1858. TLG 2022.049.

———. "In sanctum baptisma [orat. 40]." In *Opera omnia*. Edited by J.-P. Migne. Paris PG 36, cols. 360-425.: Migne, 1858. TLG 2022.048.

———. "In theophania [orat. 38]." In *Opera omnia*. Edited by J.-P. Migne. PG 36, cols. 312-33. Paris: Migne, 1858. TLG 2022.046.

———. "Orationes 29-31." In *Discours 27-31*. Translated by Paul Gallay. SC 250. Paris: Éditions du Cerf, 1978. TLG 2022.009-011.

———. "Supremum vale." In *Opera omnia*. Edited by J.-P. Migne. PG 36, cols. 457-92. Paris: Migne, 1858. TLG 2022.050.

Gregory of Nyssa. "Contra Eunomium." In *Gregorii Nysseni opera*, vol. 1.1, pp. 3-409; vol. 2.2, pp. 3-311. Edited by W. Jaeger. Leiden: Brill, 1960. TLG 2017.030.

———. "In diem luminum (*vulgo* In baptismum Christi oratio)." In *Gregorii Nysseni opera*, vol. 9.1, pp. 221-42. Edited by E. Gebhardt. Leiden: Brill, 1967. TLG 2017.014.

Gregory the Great. "Dialogorum libri iv." In *Dialogues*. 3 vols. Translated by Paul Antin. Introduction and notes by Adalbert de Vogüé. SC 251, 260, 265. Paris: Éditions du Cerf, 1978-1980. Cl. 1713.

———. "Homiliae in Hiezechihelem prophetam." In *Opera*. Edited by Mark Adriaen. CCL 142, pp. 3-398. Turnhout, Belgium: Brepols, 1971. Cl. 1710.

———. "Homiliarum xl in evangelia libri duo." In *Opera omnia*. Edited by J.-P. Migne. PL 76, cols 1075-1312. Paris: Migne, 1857. Cl. 1711.

———. "In librum primum Regum expositionum libri vi (dub)." In *Opera*. Edited by Patrick Verbraken. CCL 144, pp. 47-614. Turnhout, Belgium: Brepols, 1963. Cl. 1719.

———. *Moralia in Job*. Edited by Mark Adriaen. 3 vols. CCL 143, 143A and 143B. Turnhout, Belgium: Typographi Brepols Editores Pontificii, 1979-85. Cl. 1708.

———. *Regula pastoralis*. Edited by Floribert Rommel and R. W. Clement. CCL 141. Turnhout, Belgium: Brepols, 1953. Cl. 1712.

Hippolytus. "Commentarium in Danielem." In *Hippolyte. Commentaire sur Daniel*. Edited by Maurice Lefèvre. SC 14, pp. 70-386. Paris: Éditions du Cerf, 1947. TLG 2115.030.

———. "De antichristo." In *Hippolyt's kleinere exegetische und homiletische Schriften*. Edited by Hans Achelis. GCS 1.2, pp. 1-47. Leipzig: Hinrichs, 1897. TLG 2115.003.

———. "De theophania (dubious)." In *Hippolyt's kleinere exegetische und homiletische Schriften*. Edited by Hans Achelis. GCS 1.2, pp. 257-63. Leipzig: Hinrichs, 1897. TLG 2115.026.

Horsiesi. "Testamentum." In *Pachomiana Latina. Règle et épîtres de s. Pachôme, épître de s. Théodore et 'Liber' de s. Orsiesius*. Edited by Adeline Boon. Texte Latin de s. Jérôme. Bibliothèque de la Revue d'histoire ecclésiastique 7, pp. 109-47. Louvain, 1932.

Ignatius. "Ad Smyrnaeos." In *Epistulae interpolatae et epistulae suppositiciae*. Edited by F. X. Funk and F. Diekamp. *Patres apostolici* 2 (3rd ed.), pp.190-204. Tübingen: Laupp, 1933. TLG 1443.002.

Irenaeus. "Adversus haereses [liber 3]." In *Irénée de Lyon. Contre les heresies, livre 3*, vol. 2. Edited by Adelin. Rousseau and Louis Doutreleau. SC 211. Paris: Cerf, 1974. Cl. 1154.

Isaac of Nineveh. "De perfectione religiosa." In *Mar Isaacus Ninivita. De perfectione Religiosa*, pp. 1-99. Edited by Paul Bedjan. Paris, 1966.

Isidore of Seville. "Sententiarum libri tres." In *Opera omnia*. Edited by J.-P. Migne. PL 83, cols. 537-738. Paris: Migne, 1845. Cl. 1199.

Jerome. "Adversus Jovinianum." In *Opera omnia*. Edited by J.-P. Migne. PL 23, cols. 221-352. Paris: Migne, 1845. Cl. 0610.

———. "Commentarii in Danielem." In *S. Hieronymi presbyteri opera*. Edited by Francisci Glorie. CCL 75A, pp. 769-913. Turnhout, Belgium: Brepols, 1964. Cl. 0588.

———. "Commentarii in evangelium Matthaei." In *S. Hieronymi presbyteri opera*. Edited by D. Hurst and Mark Adriaen. CCL 77. Turnhout, Belgium: Brepols, 1969. Cl. 0590.

———. "Commentarii in Ezechielem." In *Commentariorum in Hiezechielem libri XIV ; Commentariorum in Danielem libri III*. Edited by Francisci Glorie. CCL 75, pp. 1-743. Turnhout, Belgium: Brepols, 1964. Cl. 0587.

———. *Commentarii in Isaiam*. In *S. Hieronymi presbyteri opera*. Edited by Marci Adriaen. CCL 73 and 73A. Turnhout, Belgium: Brepols, 1963. Cl. 0584.

———. "Commentarii in iv epistulas Paulinas." In *Opera omnia*. Edited by J.-P. Migne. PL 26, cols. 307-618. Paris: Migne, 1845. Cl. 0591.

———. *Commentarii in prophetas minores*. 2 vols. Edited by M. Adriaen. CCL 76 and 76A. Turnhout, Belgium: Brepols, 1969-1970. Cl. 0589.

———. "Contra Johannem Hierosolymitanum." Edited by J.-P. Migne. PL 23, cols. 371-412. Paris: Migne, 1845. Cl. 0612.

———. *Dialogus adversus Pelagianos libri iii*. Edited by C. Moreschini. CCL 80. Turnhout, Belgium: Brepols, 1990. Cl. 0615.

———. *Epistulae*. Edited by I. Hilberg. CSEL 54, 55 and 56. Vienna, Austria: F. Tempsky; Leipzig, Germany: G. F. Freytag, 1910-1918. Cl. 0620.

———. "Homilia de nativitate Domini." In *S. Hieronymi presbyteri opera*. Edited by G. Morin. CCL 78, pp. 524-29. Turnhout, Belgium: Brepols, 1958. Cl. 0598.

———. "In Hieremiam prophetam libri vi." In *S. Hieronymi presbyteri opera*. Edited by Sigofredus Reiter. CCL 74. Turnhout, Belgium: Brepols, 1960. Cl. 0586.

———. "Tractatus lix in psalmos." In *S. Hieronymi presbyteri opera*. Edited by G. Morin. CCL 78, pp. 3-352. Turnhout, Belgium: Brepols, 1958. Cl. 0592.

———. "Tractatuum in psalmos series altera." In *S. Hieronymi presbyteri opera*. Edited by G. Morin. CCL 78, pp. 355-446. Turnhout, Belgium: Brepols, 1958. Cl. 0593.

———. "Praefatio in Isaia propheta." Edited by J.-P. Migne. PL 28, cols. 771-74. Paris: Migne, 1846. Cl. 0591.

John Chrysostom. "Add illuminandos catecheses 1-2 (series prima et secunda)." In *Opera omnia*. Edited by J.-P. Migne. PG 49, cols. 223-40. Paris: Migne, 1862. TLG 2062.025.

———. "Ad populam Antiochenum homiliae (de statuis)." In *Opera omnia*. Edited by J.-P. Migne. PG 49, cols. 15-222. Paris: Migne, 1862. TLG 2062.024.

———. "Ad Theodorum lapsum (lib. 1)." In *Jean Chrysostom. A Théodore*. Edited by Jean Dumortier. SC 117. Paris: Éditions du Cerf, 1966. TLG 2062.002.

———. "Adversus Judaeos (orationes 1-8)." In *Opera omnia*. Edited by J.-P. Migne. PG 48, cols. 843-942. Paris: Migne, 1862. TLG 2062.021.

———. "Catecheses ad illuminandos 1-8 (series tertia)." In *Jean Chrysostome. Huit catéchèses baptismales*. 2nd ed. Edited by Antoine Wenger. SC 50. Paris: Éditions du Cerf, 1970. TLG 2062.382.

———. "Contra Anomoeos (homiliae 1-5): De incomprehensibili dei natura." In *Jean Chrysostome. Sur l'incompréhensibilité de Dieu*. Edited by F. Cavallera, J. Daniélou and R. Flaceliere. SC 28. Paris: Cerf, 1951. TLG 2062.012.

———. "Contra Anomoeos (homilia 11)." In *Opera omnia*. Edited by J.-P. Migne. PG 48, cols. 795-802. Paris: Migne, 1862. TLG 2062.019.

———. "Contra Judaeos et Gentiles, Quod Christus sit Deus." In *Opera omnia*. Edited by J.-P. Migne. PG 48, cols. 813-42. Paris: Migne, 1862. TLG 2062.372.

———. "De consubstantiali (Contra Anomoeos, homilia 7)." In *Opera omnia*. Edited by J.-P. Migne. PG 48, cols. 755-68. Paris: Migne, 1862. TLG 2062.015.

———. "De eleemosyna." In *Opera omnia*. Edited by J.-P. Migne. PG 51, cols. 261-72. Paris: Migne, 1862. TLG 2062.075.

———. "De Lazaro (homiliae 1-7)." In *Opera omnia*. Edited by J.-P. Migne. PG 48, cols. 963-1054. Paris: Migne, 1862. TLG 2062.023.

———. "De paenitentia (homiliae 1-9)." In *Opera omnia*. Edited by J.-P. Migne. PG 49, cols. 277-348. Paris: Migne, 1862. TLG 2062.027.

———. "Homilia de capto Eutropio (Dub)." In *Opera omnia*. Edited by J.-P. Migne. PG 52, cols. 395-414. Paris: Migne, 1862. TLG 2062.142.

———. "In Acta apostolorum (homiliae 1-55)." In *Opera omnia*. Edited by J.-P. Migne. PG 60, cols. 13-384. Paris: Migne, 1862. TLG 2062.154.

———. "In epistulam i ad Corinthios (homiliae 1-44)." In *Opera omnia*. Edited by J.-P. Migne. PG 61, cols. 9-382. Paris: Migne, 1862. TLG 2062.156.

———. "In epistulam ii ad Corinthios (homiliae 1-30)." In *Opera omnia*. Edited by J.-P. Migne. PG 61, cols. 381-610. Paris: Migne, 1862. TLG 2062.157.

———. "In epistulam ad Ephesios." In *Opera omnia*. Edited by J.-P. Migne. PG 62, cols. 9-176. Paris: Migne, 1862. TLG 2062.159.

———. "In epistulam ad Hebraeos (homiliae 1-34)." In *Opera omnia*. Edited by J.-P. Migne. PG 63, cols. 9-236. Paris: Migne, 1862. TLG 2062.168.

———. "In epistulam ad Romanos." In *Opera omnia*. Edited by J.-P. Migne. PG 60, cols. 391-682. Paris: Migne, 1862. TLG 2062.155.

———. "In epistulam i ad Timotheum (homiliae 1-18)." In *Opera omnia*. Edited by J.-P. Migne. PG 62, cols. 501-600. Paris: Migne, 1862. TLG 2062.164.

———. *In Genesim (homiliae 1-67)*. In *Opera omnia*. PG 53, 54, cols. 385-580. Edited by J.-P. Migne. Paris: Migne, 1859-1862. TLG 2062.112.

———. "In Isaiam." In *Jean Chrysostome. Commentaire sur Isaie*. Edited by Jean Dumortier. SC 304, pp. 36-356. Éditions du Cerf, 1983. TLG 2062.497.

———. "In Joannem (homiliae 1-88)." Edited by J.-P. Migne. PG 59, cols. 23-482. Paris: Migne, 1862. TLG 2062.153.

———. *In Matthaeum (homiliae 1-90)*. In *Opera omnia*. PG 57-58. Edited by J.-P. Migne. Paris: Migne, 1862. TLG 2062.152.

John of Damascus. "Expositio fidei." In *Die Schriften des Johannes von Damaskos*, vol. 2, pp. 3-239. Edited by B. Kotter. Patristische Texte und Studien 12. Berlin: De Gruyter, 1973. TLG 2934.004.

———. "Vita Barlaam et Joasaph." In *Barlaam and Joasaph*. LCL 34. Edited by G. R. Woodward and H. Mattingly. 1914. Reprint, Cambridge, Mass.: Harvard University Press, 1983. TLG 2934.066.

Justin Martyr. "Apologia." In *Die ältesten Apologeten*, pp. 26-77. Edited by E. J. Goodspeed. Göttingen, Germany: Vandenhoeck & Ruprecht, 1915. TLG 0645.001.

———. "Dialogus cum Tryphone." In *Die ältesten Apologeten*, pp. 90-265. Edited by E.J. Goodspeed. Göttingen, Germany: Vandenhoeck & Ruprecht, 1915. TLG 0645.003.

Lactantius. "Epitome divinarum institutionum." In *L. Caeli Firmiani Lactanti Opera omnia*. Edited by Samuel Brandt. CSEL 19, pp. 673-761. Vienna, Austria: F. Tempsky; Leipzig, Germany: G. Freytag, 1890. Cl. 0086.

Leander of Seville. "Homilia in laudem ecclesiae." In *Pelagii II, Joannis III, Benedicti I summorum pontificum opera omnia*. Edited by J.-P. Migne. PL 72, cols. 893-98. Paris: Migne, 1849.

Leo the Great. "Epistula xxviii." Edited by J.-P. Migne. PL 54, 755-82. Paris: Migne, 1846. Cl. 1657.

———. *Tractatus septem et nonaginta*. Edited by Antonio Chavasse. CCL 138 and 138A. Turnhout, Belgium: Brepols, 1973. Cl. 1657.

Maximus of Turin. "Collectio sermonum antiqua." In *Maximi episcopi Taurinensis sermons*. Edited by Almut Mutzenbecher. CCL 23, pp. 1-364. Turnhout, Belgium: Brepols, 1962. Cl. 0219a.

Nicetas of Remesiana. "De vigiliis servorum Dei." Edited by J.-P. Migne. PL 68, cols. 365-72. Paris: Migne, 1847.

———. "Explanatio symboli habita ad competentes." In *Sancti Petri Chrysologi opera omina: sanctorum Valeriani et Necetae*. Edited by J.-P. Migne. PL 52, cols. 865-74. Paris: Migne, 1859.

Novatian. "De Trinitate." In *Opera*. Edited by G. F. Diercks. CCL 4, pp. 11-78. Turnhout, Belgium: Brepols, 1972. Cl. 0071.

Origen. "Commentarii in evangelium Joannis (lib. 1, 2, 4, 5, 6, 10, 13)." In *Origene. Commentaire sur saint Jean*. 3 vols. Edited by Cécil Blanc. SC 120, 157 and 222. Paris: Éditions du Cerf, 1966-1975. TLG 2042.005.

———. "Commentarium in evangelium Matthaei (lib.10-11)." In *Origène. Commentaire sur l'évangile selon Matthieu*, vol. 1. Edited by R. Girod. SC 162, pp. 140-386. Paris: Cerf, 1970. TLG 2042.029.

———. "Commentarium in evangelium Matthaei [lib.12-17]." In *Origenes Werke*. 2 vols. Vols 10.1 and 10.2. Edited by E. Klostermann. GCS 40.1, pp. 69-304; GCS 40.2, pp. 305-703. Leipzig: Teubner, 1935-1937. TLG 2042.030.

———. "Contra Celsum." In *Origène Contre Celse*. 4 vols. Edited by M. Borret. SC 132, 136, 147 and 150. Paris: Éditions du Cerf, 1967-1969. TLG 2042.001.

———. "De principiis." In *Origenes vier Bücher von den Prinzipien*, pp. 462-560, 668-764. Edited by Herwig Görgemanns and H. Karpp. Darmstadt, Germany: Wissenschaftliche Buchgesellschaft, 1976. TLG 2042.002.

———. "Homiliae in Exodum." In *Origenes Werke*, vol. 6. Edited by W. A. Baehrens. GCS 29, pp. 217-30. Leipzig: Teubner, 1920. Cl. 0198.

———. "Homiliae in Genesim." In *Origenes Werke*, vol. 6. Edited by W. A. Baehrens. GCS 29, pp. 23-30. Leipzig: Teubner, 1920. Cl. 0198.

———. "Homiliae in Leviticum." In *Origenes Werke*, vol. 6. Edited by W. A. Baehrens. GCS 29, pp. 332-34, 395, 402-7, 409-16 Leipzig: Teubner, 1920. TLG 2042.024.

———. "Homiliae in Lucam." In *Opera omnia*. Edited by J.-P. Migne.PG 13, cols. 1799-1902. Paris: Migne, 1862. TLG 2042.016.

———. "In Jeremiam [homiliae 12-20]." In *Origenes Werke*, vol. 3. Edited by E. Klostermann. GCS 6, pp. 85-194. Berlin: Akademie-Verlag, 1901. TLG 2042.021.

———. "Philocalia sive Ecloga de operibus Origenis a Basilio et Gregoria Nazianzeno facta (cap. 1-27)." In *The Philocalia of Origen*. Edited by J. Armitage Robinson. Cambridge: Cambridge University Press, 1893. TLG 2042.019.

Pachomius. "Catecheses." In *Oeuvres de s. Pachôme et de ses disciples*. Edited L. T. Lefort. CSCO 159, pp. 1-26. Louvain: Imprimerie Orientaliste, 1956.

———. "Vita Pachomii." *Le corpus athénien de saint Pachome*, pp. 11-72. Edited by F. Halkin. Cahiers d'Orientalisme 2. Genève: Cramer, 1982.

Pacian of Barcelona. "De paenitentibus." In *Opera omnia*. Edited by J.-P. Migne. PL 13, cols. 1081-90. Paris: Migne, 1845.

Paschasius of Dumium. "De vitis patrum liber septimus, sive verba seniorum auctore graeco incerto, interprete Paschasio S. R. E. Diacono." Edited by J.-P. Migne. PL 73, cols. 1025-62. Paris: Migne, 1860.

Paulus Orosius. "Liber apologeticus contra Pelagianos." In *Pauli Orosii historiarum adversum paganos*. Edited by Karl Zangemeister. CSEL 5, pp. 601-64. Vienna: F. Tempsky, 1882. Cl. 0572.

Peter Chrysologus. *Collectio sermonum a Felice episcopo parata sermonibus extravagantibus adjectis*. 3 vols. In *Sancti Petri Chrysologi*. Edited by Alexander Olivar. CCL 24, 24A and 24B. Turnhout: Brepols, 1975-1982. Cl. 0227+.

Primasius. "Commentarius in Apocalypsin." In *Primasius Episcopus Hadrumetinus*. Edited by A. W. Adams. Turnhout: Brepols, 1985. CCL 92. Cl. 0873.

Pseudo-Clement of Rome. "Epistula ii ad Corinthios (Sp.)" In *Die apostolischen Väter*, pp. 71-81. 3rd ed. Edited by Karl Bihlmeyer and W. Schneemelcher. Tübingen: Mohr, 1970. TLG 1271.002.

———. "Homiliae (Sp.)." In *Die Pseudoklementinen I. Homilien*. 2nd ed. Edited by B. Rehm, J. Irmscher and F. Paschke. GCS 42, pp. 23-281. Berlin: Akademie-Verlag, 1969. TLG 1271.006.

Pseudo-Cyprian. "Ad Novatianum." In *Novatiani Opera*. Edited by G. F. Diercks. CCL 4, pp. 137-52. Turnhout, Belgium: Brepols, 1972. Cl. 0076.

Pseudo-Dionysius. "De ecclesiastica hierarchia." In *Corpus Dionysiacum II*. Edited by Gunter Heil and Adolf Martin Ritter. Patristische Texte und Studien, pp. 61-132. Berlin: de Gruyter, 1991.

Quodvultdeus. *Opera Quodvultdea tribute*. Edited by R. Braun. CCL 60 Turnhout: Brepols, 1976. Cl. 0402, 0408, 0410, 0413.

Rufinus of Aquileia. "Expositio symboli." In *Opera*. Edited by Manlio Simonetti. CCL 20, pp. 125-82. Turnhout, Belgium: Brepols, 1961. Cl. 0196.

Sahdona. "Book of Perfection." In *Martyrius (Sahdona): Oeuvres spirituelles*, part 2. Edited by André de Halleux. CSCO 252 (Scriptores Syri 110). Louvain, Belgium: Secrétariat du Corpus, 1965.

Salvian the Presbyter. "De gubernatione Dei." In *Ouvres*, vol. 2. Edited by Georges LaGarrigue. SC 220. Paris: Éditions du Cerf, 1975. Cl. 0485.

Tertullian. "Ad uxorem." In *Opera*. Edited by E. Kroymann. CCL 1, pp. 371-94. Turnhout, Belgium: Brepols, 1954. Cl. 0012.

———. "Adversus Judaeos." In *Opera*. Edited by E. Kroymann. CCL 2, pp. 1337-96. Turnhout, Belgium: Brepols, 1954. Cl. 0033.

———. "Adversus Marcionem." In *Opera*, vol. 1. Edited by E. Kroymann. CCL 1, pp. 437-726. Turnhout, Belgium: Brepols, 1954. Cl. 0014.

———. "De carne Christi." In *Opera*. Edited by E. Kroymann. CCL 2, pp. 871-917. Turnhout, Belgium: Brepols, 1954. Cl. 0018.

———. "De oratione." In *Opera*. Edited by G. F. Diercks. CCL 1, pp. 255-74. Turnhout, Belgium: Brepols, 1954. Cl. 0007.

———. "De resurrectione mortuorum." In *Opera*. Edited by J. G. Ph. Borleffs. CCL 2, pp. 919-1012. Turnhout, Belgium: Brepols, 1954. Cl. 0019.

———. "Scorpiace." In *Opera*. Edited by A. Reifferscheid and G. Wissowa. CCL 2, pp.1067-97. Turnhout, Belgium: Brepols, 1954. Cl. 0022.

Theodore of Tabennesi. "Catéchèse." In *Oeuvres de S. Pachôme et de ses disciples*. Edited by L. T. Lefort. CSCO 159, pp. 37-60. Louvain, Belgium: Imprimerie Orientaliste 1956.

Theodoret of Cyr. "Ad eos qui in Euphratesia et Osrhoena regione, Syria, Phoeni." Edited by J.-P. Migne. PG 83, cols. 1416-33. Paris: Migne, 1859. TLG 4089.034.

———. *Commentaria in Isaiam*. In *Théodoret de Cyr. Commentaire sur Isaïe*. 3 vols. Edited by J. N. Guinot. SC 276, 295 and 315. Paris: Éditions du Cerf, 1980-84. TLG 4089.008.

———. "De providentia orationes decem." Edited by J.-P. Migne. PG 83, cols. 556-773. Paris: Migne, 1859. TLG 4089.032.

———. "Eranistes." In *Theodoret of Cyrus: Ernaistes*, pp. 61-266. Edited by G. H. Ettlinger. Oxford: Clarendon Press, 1975. TLG 4089.002.

Theophylact. *Ennarratio in Evangelium S. Matthaei*. Edited by J.-P. Migne. PG 123, cols. 143-488. Paris: Migne, 1859.

Valerian. "Homilia i. De bono disciplinae." Edited by J.-P. Migne. PL 52, cols. 691-96. Paris: Migne, 1859.

Verecundus. "Commentarii super cantica ecclesiastica." In *Opera*. Edited by R. Demeulenaere. CCL 93, pp. 1-203. Turnhout, Belgium: Brepols, 1976. Cl. 0870.

Victorinus of Petovium. "Scholia in Apocalypsin beati Joannis." In *Opera omnia*. Edited by J.-P. Migne. PL 5, cols. 317-44. Paris: Migne, 1844.

Bibliography of Works
in English Translation

Ambrose. *Funeral Orations*. Translated by Leo P. McCauley et al. FC 22. Washington, D.C.: The Catholic University of America Press, 1953.

———. *Hexameron, Paradise, and Cain and Abel*. Translated by John J. Savage. FC 42. Washington, D.C.: The Catholic University of America Press, 1961.

———. *Letters*. Translated by Mary Melchior Beyenka. FC 26. Washington, D.C.: The Catholic University of America Press, 1954.

———. *Select Works and Letters*. Translated by H. De Romestin. NPNF 10. Series 2. Edited by Philip Schaff and Henry Wace. 14 vols. 1886-1900. Reprint, Peabody, Mass.: Hendrickson, 1994.

———. "Selections from Ambrose, Letters." In *Early Latin Theology*, pp. 175-278. Translated and edited by S. L. Greenslade. LCC 5. Philadelphia: Westminster Press, 1956.

———. *Seven Exegetical Works*. Translated by Michael P. McHugh. FC 65. Washington, D.C.: The Catholic University of America Press, 1972.

Aphrahat. "Demonstration 4." In *The Syriac Fathers on Prayer and the Spiritual Life*, pp. 1-28. Translated by Sebastian Brock. CS 101. Kalamazoo, Mich.: Cistercian Publications, 1987.

———. "Select Demonstrations." In *Gregory the Great, Ephraim Syrus, Aphrahat*, pp. 345-412. Translated by James Barmby. NPNF 13. Series 2. Edited by Philip Schaff and Henry Wace. 14 vols. 1886-1900. Reprint, Peabody, Mass.: Hendrickson, 1994.

Athanasius. *Selected Works and Letters*. Translated by Archibald Robertson. NPNF 4. Series 2. Edited by Philip Schaff and Henry Wace. 14 vols. 1886-1900. Reprint, Peabody, Mass.: Hendrickson, 1994.

Augustine. *Anti-Pelagian Works*. Translated by Peter Holmes and Robert Ernest Wallis. NPNF 5. Series 1. Edited by Philip Schaff. 14 vols. 1886-1889. Reprint, Peabody, Mass.: Hendrickson, 1994.

———. *City of God, Christian Doctrine*. Translated by Marcus Dods and J. F. Shaw. NPNF 2. Series 1. Edited by Philip Schaff. 14 vols. 1886-1889. Reprint, Peabody, Mass.: Hendrickson, 1994.

———. *The City of God: Books VIII-XVI*. Translated by Gerald G. Walsh and Grace Monahan. FC 14. Washington, D.C.: The Catholic University of America Press, 1952.

———. *The City of God: Books XVII-XXII*. Translated by Gerald G. Walsh and Daniel J. Honan. FC 24. Washington, D.C.: The Catholic University of America Press, 1954.

———. *Commentary on the Lord's Sermon on the Mount with Seventeen Related Sermons*. Translated by Denis J. Kavanagh. FC 11. Washington, D.C.: The Catholic University of America Press, 1951.

———. *Eighty-Three Different Questions*. Translated by David L. Mosher. FC 70. Washington, D.C.: The Catholic University of America Press, 1982.

———. "Enchiridion." In *Christian Instruction; Admonition and Grace; The Christian Combat; Faith, Hope and Charity*, pp. 369-472. Translated by Bernard M. Peebles. FC 2. Washington, D.C.: The Catholic University of America Press, 1947.

———. *Exposition of the Psalms, 33-72*. Translated by Maria Boulding. WSA 16, 17. Part 3. Edited by John E. Rotelle. New York: New City Press, 2000-2001.

———. *Expositions on the Book of Psalms*. Edited and annotated by A. Cleveland Coxe. NPNF 8. Series 1. Edited by Philip Schaff. 14 vols. 1886-1889. Reprint, Peabody, Mass.: Hendrickson, 1994.

———. *Four Anti-Pelagian Writings: On Nature and Grace, On the Proceedings of Pelagius, On the Predestination of the Saints, On the Gift of Perseverance*. Translated by John A. Mourant and William J. Collinge. FC 86. Washington, D.C.: The Catholic University of America Press, 1992.

———. *Letters*. Translated by Sister Wilfrid Parsons. FC 12, 18, 20 and 30. 4 vols. Washington, D.C.: The Catholic University of America Press, 1951-1955.

———. "On Faith in Things Unseen." In *The Immortality of the Soul; The Magnitude of the Soul; On Music; The Advantage of Believing; On Faith in Things Unseen*, pp. 451-69. Translated by Roy Joseph Deferrari. FC 4. Washington, D.C.: The Catholic University of America Press, 1947.

———. "On the Spirit and the Letter." In *Augustine: Later Works*, pp. 182-250. Translated by John Burnaby. LCC 8. London: SCM Press, 1955.

———. "Reply to Faustus the Manichaean." In *The Writings Against the Manichaeans, and Against the Donatists*, pp. 155-345. Translated by J. R. King. NPNF 4. Series 1. Edited by Philip Schaff. 14 vols. 1886-1889. Reprint, Peabody, Mass.: Hendrickson, 1994.

———. *Sermon on the Mount, Harmony of the Gospels, Homilies on the Gospels*. Translated by William Findlay, S. D. F. Salmond and R. G. MacMullen. NPNF 6. Series 1. Edited by Philip Schaff. 14 vols. 1886-1889. Reprint, Peabody, Mass.: Hendrickson, 1994.

———. *Sermons*. 8 vols. Translated by Edmund Hill. WSA 1, 2, 3, 4, 5, 6, 8 and 10. Part 3. Edited by John E. Rotelle. New York: New City Press, 1990-1995.

———. *Sermons on the Liturgical Seasons*. Translated by Mary Sarah Muldowney. FC 38. Washington, D.C.: The Catholic University of America Press, 1959.

———. *The Teacher, The Free Choice of the Will, Grace and Free Will*. Translated by Robert P. Russell. FC 59. Washington, D.C.: The Catholic University of America Press, 1968.

———. *Tractates on the Gospel of John, 28-54*. Translated by John W. Rettig. FC 88. Washington, D.C.: The Catholic University of America Press, 1993.

———. *Treatises on Marriage and Other Subjects*. Translated by Charles T. Wilcox et al. FC 27. Washington, D.C.: The Catholic University of America, 1955.

———. *Treatises on Various Subjects*. Translated by Mary Sarah Muldowney et al. FC 16. Washington, D.C.: The Catholic University of America, 1952.

———. *The Trinity*. Translated by Stephen McKenna. FC 45. Washington, D.C.: The Catholic University of America, 1963.

Basil the Great. *Ascetical Works*. Translated by M. Monica Wagner. FC 9. New York: Fathers of the Church, Inc., 1950.

———. *Commentary on the Prophet Isaiah*. Translated by Nikolai A. Lipatov. TASHT 7. Mandelbachtal/Cambridge: Edition cicero, 2001.

———. *Exegetic Homilies*. Translated by Agnes C. Way. FC 46. Washington, D.C.: The Catholic University of America Press, 1963.

———. *Letters*. Translated by Agnes C. Way. 2 vols. FC 13 and 28. Washington, D.C.: The Catholic University of America Press, 1951, 1955.

———. *Letters and Select Works*. Translated by Blomfield Jackson. NPNF 8. Series 2. Edited by Philip Schaff and Henry Wace. 14 vols. 1886-1900. Reprint, Peabody, Mass.: Hendrickson, 1994.

Bede, the Venerable. *Commentary on the Acts of the Apostles*. Translated by Lawrence T. Martin. CS 117. Kalamazoo, Mich.: Cistercian Publications, 1989.

———. *Homilies on the Gospels*. 2 vols. Translated by Lawrence T. Martin and David Hurst. CS 110-11. Kalamazoo, Mich.: Cistercian Publications, 1991.

———. *On the Tabernacle*. Translated with notes and introduction by Arthur G. Holder. TTH 18. Liverpool: Liverpool University Press, 1994.

———. *The Reckoning of Time*. Translated with introduction, notes and commentary by Faith Wallis. TTH 29. Liverpool: Liverpool University Press, 1999.

Caesarius of Arles. *Sermons*. Translated by Mary Magdeleine Mueller. 3 vols. FC 31, 47 and 66. Washington, D.C.: The Catholic University of America Press, 1956-1973.

Cassian, John. "Conferences." In *Western Asceticism*, pp. 190-289. Translated by Owen Chadwick. LCC 12. Philadelphia: Westminster Press, 1958.

———. *Conferences*. Translated by Colm Luibheid. The Classics of Western Spirituality. New York: Paulist Press, 1985.

———. *The Conferences*. Translated and annotated by Boniface Ramsey. ACW 57. New York: Paulist Press, 1997.

———. "Institutes." In *Sulpitius Severus, Vincent of Lerins, John Cassian*, pp. 201-90. Translated by Edgar C. S. Gibson. NPNF 11. Series 2. Edited by Philip Schaff and Henry Wace. 14 vols. 1886-1900. Reprint, Peabody, Mass.: Hendrickson, 1994.

Cassiodorus. *Explanation of the Psalms*. Translated by P. G. Walsh. 3 vols. ACW 51, 52 and 53. New York: Paulist Press, 1990-1991.

Clement of Alexandria. *Christ the Educator*. Translated by Simon P. Wood. FC 23. Washington, D.C.: The Catholic University of America Press, 1954.

———. *Fathers of the Second Century: Hermas, Tatian, Athenagoras, Theophilus, and Clement of Alexandria*. Translated by F. Crombie et al. ANF 2. Edited by Alexander Roberts and James Donaldson. 10 vols. 1885-1887. Reprint, Peabody, Mass.: Hendrickson, 1994.

———. *Stromateis: Books 1-3*. Translated by John Ferguson. FC 85. Washington, D.C.: The Catholic University of America Press, 1991.

Clement of Rome. "First Letter to the Corinthians." In *The Apostolic Fathers*, pp. 9-58. Translated by Francis X. Glimm et al. FC 1. New York: Christian Heritage, Inc., 1947.

———. "The Letter of the Church of Rome to the Church of Corinth, Commonly Called Clement's First Letter." In *Early Christian Fathers*, pp. 33-73. Translated by Cyril C. Richardson. LCC 1. Philadelphia: The Westminster Press, 1953.

"Constitutions of the Holy Apostles." In *Lactantius, Venantius, Asterius, Victorinus, Dionysius, Apostolic Teaching and Constitutions, 2 Clement, Early Liturgies*, pp. 385-508. Edited by James Donaldson. ANF 7. Edited by Alexander Roberts and James Donaldson. 10 vols. 1885-1887. Reprint, Peabody, Mass.: Hendrickson, 1994.

Cyprian. *Letters 1-81*. Translated by Rose Bernard Donna. FC 51. Washington, D.C.: The Catholic University of America Press, 1964.

———. *Treatises*. Translated and edited by Roy J. Deferrari. FC 36. Washington, D.C.: The Catholic University of America Press, 1958.

Cyril of Alexandria. "Against Julian." Quoted in *Biblical Interpretation*, by Joseph W. Trigg. MFC 9. Wilmington, Del.: Michael Glazier, 1988.

———. "Commentary on Isaiah." In *St. Cyril of Alexandria: Interpreter of the Old Testament*, by Alexander Kerrigan. Analecta Biblica 2. Roma, Italy: Pontificio Istituto Biblico, 1952.

———. *Letters 1-50*. Translated by John I. McEnerney. FC 76. Washington, D.C.: The Catholic University of America Press, 1985.

———. *Commentary on Isaiah*. Selections translated by Robert Louis Wilken in "In Dominico Eloquio: Learning the Lord's Style of Language." Comm. 24.4 (1997): 846-66.

Cyril of Jerusalem. "Catechetical Lectures." In *Cyril of Jerusalem and Nemesius of Emesa*, pp. 64-199. Edited by William Telfer. LCC 4. Philadelphia: Westminster, 1955.

———. "Catechetical Lectures." In *S. Cyril of Jerusalem, S. Gregory Nazianzen*, pp. 1-202. Translated by

Edward Hamilton Gifford et al. NPNF 7. Series 2. Edited by Philip Schaff and Henry Wace. 14 vols. 1886-1900. Reprint, Peabody, Mass.: Hendrickson, 1994.

[Cyril of Jerusalem]. *The Works of Saint Cyril of Jerusalem*. Translated by Leo P. McCauley and Anthony A. Stephenson. 2 vols. FC 61 and 64. Washington, D.C.: The Catholic University of America Press, 1969-1970.

Ephrem the Syrian. *Hymns*. Translated by Kathleen E. McVey. Classics of Western Spirituality. New York: Paulist Press, 1989.

————. "Nineteen Hymns on the Nativity of Christ in the Flesh." In *Part 2: Gregory the Great, Ephraim Syrus, Aphrahat*, pp. 221-62. Translated by J. B. Morris and A. Edward Johnston. NPNF 13. Series 2. Edited by Philip Schaff and Henry Wace. 14 vols. 1886-1900. Reprint, Peabody, Mass.: Hendrickson, 1994.

[Ephrem the Syrian]. *Saint Ephrem's Commentary on Tatian's Diatessaron*. Translated by Carmel McCarthy. Journal of Semitic Studies Supplement 2. Oxford: Oxford University Press, 1993.

Epistle of Barnabas. In *The Apostolic Fathers*, pp. 191-222. Translated by Francis X. Glimm. FC 1. New York: Christian Heritage, Inc., 1947.

————. In *The Apostolic Fathers*, pp. 133-58. Translated by J. B. Lightfoot and J. R. Harmer. Edited by M. W. Holmes. 2nd ed. Grand Rapids, Mich.: Baker, 1989.

————. In *The Apostolic Fathers with Justin Martyr and Irenaeus*, pp. 133-50. ANF 1. Translated by M. Dods. Edited by Alexander Roberts and James Donaldson. 10 vols. 1885-1887. Reprint, Peabody, Mass.: Hendrickson, 1994.

Eusebius of Caesarea. *Proof of the Gospel*. 2 vols. Translated by W. J. Ferrar. London: SPCK, 1920. Reprint, Grand Rapids, Mich.: Baker, 1981.

[Eusebius of Caesarea]. *Eusebius of Caesarea's Commentary on Isaiah: Christian Exegesis in the Age of Constantine*. Translated by M. J. Hollerich Oxford: Clarendon Press, 1999.

Firmicus Maternus. *The Error of the Pagan Religions*. Translated and annotated by Clarence A. Forbes. ACW 37. New York: Newman Press, 1970.

Fulgentius of Ruspe. *Selected Works*. Translated by Robert B. Eno. FC 95. Washington, D.C.: The Catholic University of America Press, 1997.

Gregory of Nazianzus. "Orations" In *Cyril of Jerusalem, Gregory Nazianzen*. Translated by Charles Gordon Browne et al. NPNF 7. Series 2. Edited by Philip Schaff and Henry Wace. 14 vols. 1886-1900. Reprint, Peabody, Mass.: Hendrickson, 1994.

[Gregory of Nyssa]. *Select Writings and Letters of Gregory, Bishop of Nyssa*. Translated by William Moore and Henry Austin Wilson. NPNF 5. Series 2. Edited by Philip Schaff and Henry Wace. 14 vols. 1886-1900. Reprint, Peabody, Mass.: Hendrickson, 1994.

Gregory the Great. *Dialogues*. Translated by Odo John Zimmerman. FC 39. Washington, D.C.: The Catholic University of America Press, 1959.

————. *Forty Gospel Homilies*. Translated by David Hurst. CS 123. Kalamazoo, Mich.: Cistercian, 1990.

————. *Morals on the Book of Job*. Translated by Members of the English Church. 3 vols. LF 18, 21 and 23. Oxford: John Henry Parker, 1844-1850.

————. *Pastoral Care*. Translated by Henry Davis. ACW 11. New York: Newman Press, 1950.

————. *Pastoral Rule and Selected Epistles*. Translated by James Barmby. NPNF 12. Series 2. Edited by Philip Schaff and Henry Wace. 14 vols. 1886-1900. Reprint, Peabody, Mass.: Hendrickson, 1994.

[Gregory the Great]. *The Homilies of St. Gregory the Great on the Book of the Prophet Ezekiel*. Translated by Theodosia Gray. Etna, Calif.: Center for Traditionalist Orthodox Studies, 1990.

[Hippolytus]. "Hippolytus." In *Fathers of the Third Century: Hippolytus, Cyprian, Caius, Novatian, Appendix*, pp. 9-266. Translated by J. H. MacMahonet et al. ANF 5. Edited by Alexander Roberts and James

Donaldson. 10 vols. 1885-1887. Reprint, Peabody, Mass.: Hendrickson, 1994.

[Horsiesi (Horsiesios)]. "The Testament of Horsiesios." In *Pachomian Koinonia: Volume Three, Instructions, Letters, and Other Writings of Saint Pachomius and His Disciples*, pp. 171-224. Translated by Armand Veilleux. CS 47. Kalamazoo, Mich.: Cistercian, 1982.

Ignatius. "Letter to the Smyrnaeans." In *The Apostolic Fathers*, pp. 118-23. Translated by Gerald G. Walsh. FC 1. New York: Christian Heritage, Inc. 1947.

Irenaeus. "Selections from *Against Heresies*." In *Early Christian Fathers*, pp. 343-97. Translated by Edward Rochie Hardy. LCC 1. Philadelphia: The Westminster Press, 1953.

[Isaac of Nineveh]. *The Ascetical Homilies of Saint Isaac the Syrian*. Translated by the Holy Transfiguration Monastery. Boston: Holy Transfiguration Monastery, 1984.

Jerome. *Dogmatic and Polemical Works*. Translated by John N. Hritzu. FC 53. Washington, D.C.: The Catholic University of America Press, 1965.

―――. *Letters and Select Works*. Translated by W.H. Fremantle. NPNF 6. Series 2. Edited by Philip Schaff and Henry Wace. 14 vols. 1886-1900. Reprint, Peabody, Mass.: Hendrickson, 1994.

―――. "Preface to Isaiah." As quoted in "*In Dominico Eloquio*: Learning the Lord's Style of Language," by Robert Louis Wilken. *Comm.* 24.4 (1997): 846-66.

[Jerome]. *The Homilies of Saint Jerome*. Translated by Marie Liguori Ewald. 2 vols. FC 48 and 57. Washington, D.C.: The Catholic University of America Press, 1964, 1966.

―――. *Jerome's Commentary on Daniel*. Translated by Gleason L. Archer, Jr. Grand Rapids, Mich.: Baker Book House, 1958.

John Chrysostom. "Against the Anomoeans." In *On the Incomprehensible Nature of God*. Translated by Paul W. Harkins. FC 72. Washington, D.C.: The Catholic University of America Press, 1984.

―――. *Baptismal Instructions*. Translated by Paul W. Harkins. ACW 31. New York: Newman Press, 1963.

―――. *Commentary on Saint John the Apostle and Evangelist*. 2 vols. Translated by Thomas Aquinas Goggin. FC 33, 41. Washington, D.C.: The Catholic University of America Press, 1957, 1959.

―――. "Demonstration Against the Pagans." In *Apologist*, pp. 153-262. Translated by Paul W. Harkins. FC 73. Washington, D.C.: The Catholic University of America Press, 1985.

―――. *Discourses Against Judaizing Christians*. Translated by Paul W. Harkins. FC 68. Washington, D.C.: The Catholic University of America Press, 1979.

―――. *Homilies on Galatians, Ephesians, Philippians, Colossians, Thessalonians, Timothy, Titus, and Philemon*. Translated by Gross Alexander et al. NPNF 13. Series 1. Edited by Philip Schaff. 14 vols. 1886-1889. Reprint, Peabody, Mass.: Hendrickson, 1994.

―――. *Homilies on Genesis*. Translated by Robert C. Hill. FC 82. Washington, D.C.: The Catholic University of America Press, 1990.

―――. "Homilies on Lazarus and the Rich Man." In *On Wealth and Poverty*. Translated by Catharine P. Roth. New York: St. Vladimir's Seminary Press, 1984.

―――. *Homilies on the Acts of the Apostles and the Epistle to the Romans*. Translated by J. Walker, J. Sheppard and H. Browne. NPNF 11. Series 1. Edited by Philip Schaff. 14 vols. 1886-1889. Reprint, Peabody, Mass.: Hendrickson, 1994.

―――. *Homilies on the Epistles of Paul to the Corinthians*. Translated by Talbot W. Chambers. NPNF 12. Series 1. Edited by Philip Schaff. 14 vols. 1886-1889. Reprint, Peabody, Mass.: Hendrickson, 1994.

―――. *Homilies on the Gospel of Saint Matthew*. The Oxford translation. NPNF 10. Series 1. Edited by Philip Schaff. 14 vols. 1886-1889. Reprint, Peabody, Mass.: Hendrickson, 1994.

―――. *On Repentance and Almsgiving*. Translated by Gus George Christo. FC 96. Washington, D.C.: The Catholic University of America Press, 1998.

————. *On the Priesthood, Ascetic Treatises, Select Homilies and Letters, Homilies on the Statues*. Translated by W. R. W. Stephens et al. NPNF 9. Series 1. Edited by Philip Schaff. 14 vols. 1886-1889. Reprint, Peabody, Mass.: Hendrickson, 1994.

————. "Two Letters to the Fallen Theodore." In *Chrysostom: on the Priesthood, Ascetic Treatises, Select Homilies and Letter, Homilies on the Statues*, pp. 87-116. Translated by W. R. W. Stephens. NPNF 9. Series 1. Edited by Philip Schaff. 14 vols. 1886-1889. Reprint, Peabody, Mass.: Hendrickson, 1994.

John of Damascus. *Barlaam and Ioasaph*. Translated by G. R. Woodward. LCL 34. London: William Heinemann, 1914. Reprint Cambridge, Mass.: Harvard University Press, 1937.

————. "Orthodox Faith." In *Writings*, pp. 165-406. Translated by Frederic H. Chase. FC 37. Washington, D.C.: The Catholic University of America Press, 1958.

Justin Martyr. "Dialogue with Trypho." In *The Apostolic Fathers with Justin Martyr and Irenaeus*, pp. 194-270. Arranged by A. Cleveland Coxe. ANF 1. Edited by Alexander Roberts and James Donaldson. 10 vols. 1885-1887. Reprint, Peabody, Mass.: Hendrickson, 1994.

————. "First Apology." In *Early Christian Fathers*, pp. 242-89. Translated by Edward Rochie Hardy. LCC 1. Edited by Cyril C. Richardson. Philadelphia: Westminster Press, 1953.

————. "First Apology." In *The Apostolic Fathers with Justin Martyr and Irenaeus*, pp. 163-87. Arranged by A. Cleveland Coxe. ANF 1. Edited by Alexander Roberts and James Donaldson. 10 vols. 1885-1887. Reprint, Peabody, Mass.: Hendrickson, 1994.

Lactantius. *The Divine Institutes: Books I-VII*. Translated by Mary Francis McDonald. FC 49. Washington, D.C.: The Catholic University of America Press, 1964.

————. "The Epitome of the Divine Institutes." In *Lactantius, Venantius, Asterius, Victorinus, Dionysius, Apostolic Teaching and Constitutions, 2 Clement, Early Liturgies*, pp. 224-58. Translated by William Fletcher. ANF 7 Edited by Alexander Roberts and James Donaldson. 10 vols. 1885-1887. Reprint, Peabody, Mass.: Hendrickson, 1994.

Leander of Seville. "Sermon on the Triumph of the Church for the Conversion of the Goths." In *Iberian Fathers*, vol. 1, pp. 229-38. Translated by Claude W. Barlow. FC 62. Washington, D.C.: The Catholic University of America Press, 1969.

Leo the Great. *Letters*. Translated by Edmund Hunt. FC 34. Washington, D.C.: The Catholic University of America Press, 1957.

————. *Sermons*. Translated by Jane P. Freeland and Agnes J. Conway. FC 93. Washington, D.C.: The Catholic University of America Press, 1996.

Maximus of Turin. *The Sermons of St. Maximus of Turin*. Translated and annotated by Boniface Ramsey. ACW 50. New York: Newman, 1989.

Niceta of Remesiana. "Writings." In *Niceta of Remesiana, Sulpicius Severus, Vincent of Lerins, Prosper of Aquitaine*, pp. 3-78. Translated by Gerald G. Walsh. FC 7. Washington, D.C.: The Catholic University of America Press, 1949.

Novatian. "Treatise Concerning the Trinity." In *Fathers of the Third Century: Hippolytus, Cyprian, Caius, Novatian, Appendix*," pp. 611-44. Translated by Robert Ernest Wallis. ANF 5. Edited by Alexander Roberts and James Donaldson. 10 vols. 1885-1887. Reprint, Peabody, Mass.: Hendrickson, 1994.

[Novatian]. *Novatian: The Trinity, the Spectacles, Jewish Foods, in Praise of Purity, Letters*. Translated by Russell J. DeSimone. FC 67. Washington, D.C.: The Catholic University of America Press, 1974.

Origen. "Against Celsus." In *Tertullian (IV); Minucius Felix; Commodian; Origen (I and III)*, pp. 395-669. Translated by Frederick Crombie. ANF 4. Edited by Alexander Roberts and James Donaldson. 10 vols. 1885-1887. Reprint, Peabody, Mass.: Hendrickson, 1994.

————. *An Exhortation to Martyrdom, Prayer and Selected Works*. Translated by Rowan A. Greer. The Classics of Western Spirituality. New York: Paulist Press, 1979.

————. *Commentary on the Gospel According to John, Books 13-32.* Translated by Ronald E. Heine. FC 89. Washington, D.C.: The Catholic University of America Press, 1993.

————. "Commentary on the Gospel of Matthew." In *Gospel of Peter, Diatessaron, Testament of Abraham, Epistles of Clement, Origen, Miscellaneous Works,* pp. 411-512. Translated by John Patrick. ANF 9. Edited by Allan Menzies. 10 vols. 1885-1887. Reprint, Peabody, Mass.: Hendrickson, 1994.

————. *Homilies on Genesis and Exodus.* Translated by Ronald E. Heine. FC 71. Washington, D.C.: The Catholic University of America Press, 1982.

————. *Homilies on Jeremiah, Homilies on 1 Kings 28.* Translated by John Clark Smith. FC 97. Washington, D.C.: The Catholic University of America Press, 1998.

————. *Homilies on Leviticus: 1-16.* Translated by Gary Wayne Barkley. FC 83. Washington, D.C.: The Catholic University of America Press, 1990.

————. *Homilies on Luke; Fragments on Luke.* Translated by Joseph T. Lienhard. FC 94. Washington, D.C.: The Catholic University of America Press, 1996.

————. *On First Principles.* Translated by G. W. Butterworth. London: SPCK, 1936; Reprint, Gloucester, Mass.: Peter Smith, 1973.

Pachomius. *Pachomian Koinonia.* Vols. 1 and 3. Translated by Armand Veilleux. 2 vols. CS 45 and 47. Kalamazoo, Mich.: Cistercian Publications, 1980, 1982.

Pacian of Barcelona. "On Penitents." In *Iberian Fathers,* vol 3, pp. 71-86. Translated by Craig L. Hanson. FC 99. Washington, D.C.: The Catholic University of America Press, 1999.

Paschasius of Dumium. "Questions and Answers of the Greek Fathers." In *Iberian Fathers,* vol. 1, pp. 117-74. Translated by Claude W. Barlow. FC 62. Washington, D.C.: The Catholic University of America Press, 1969.

Peter Chrysologus. "Sermons." In *Saint Peter Chrysologus: Selected Sermons and Saint Valerian: Homilies,* pp. 25-282. Translated by George E. Ganss. FC 17. New York: Fathers of the Church, Inc., 1953.

[Pseudo-Clement of Rome]. "2 Clement." In *The Apostolic Fathers,* pp. 65-85. Translated by Francis X. Glimm. FC 1. New York: Christian Heritage, Inc., 1947.

————. "Clementine Homilies." In *The Twelve Patriarchs, Excerpts and Epistles, The Clementina, Apocrypha, Decretals, Memories of Edessa and Syriac Documents, Remains of the First Ages,* pp. 223-46. Translated by William Wilson. ANF 8. Edited by Alexander Roberts and James Donaldson. 10 vols. 1885-1887. Reprint, Peabody, Mass.: Hendrickson, 1994.

[Pseudo-Dionysius]. *Pseudo-Dionysius: The Complete Works.* Translated by Colm Luibheid. The Classics of Western Spirituality. New York: Paulist, 1980.

Rufinus of Aquileia. "Commentary on the Apostles' Creed." In *Theodoret, Jerome, Gennadius, Rufinus: Historical Writings, etc.,* pp. 541-63. Translated by William Henry Fremantle. NPNF 3. Series 2. Edited by Philip Schaff and Henry Wace. 14 vols. 1886-1900. Reprint, Peabody, Mass.: Hendrickson, 1994.

Sahdona (Martyrius). "Book of Perfection." In *The Syriac Fathers on Prayer and the Spiritual Life,* pp. 202-39. Translated by Sebastian Brock. CS 101. Kalamazoo, Mich.: Cistercian Publications, 1987.

[Salvian the Presbyter]. *The Writings of Salvian the Presbyter.* Translated by Jermiah F. O'Sullivan. FC 3. Washington, D.C.: The Catholic University of America Press, 1962.

[Tertullian]. In *Latin Christianity: Its Founder, Tertullian.* Translated by S. Thelwall et al. ANF 3. Edited by Alexander Roberts and James Donaldson. 10 vols. 1885-1887. Reprint, Peabody, Mass.: Hendrickson, 1994.

————. "Tertullian." In *Tertullian (IV); Minucius Felix; Commodian; Origen (I and III),* pp. 5-166. Translated by S. Thelwall. ANF 4. Edited by Alexander Roberts and James Donaldson. 10 vols. 1885-1887. Reprint, Peabody, Mass.: Hendrickson, 1994.

Theodore of Tabennesi. "Instructions." In *Pachomian Koinonia.* Vol. 3, pp. 91-122. Translated by Armand

Veilleux. CS 47. Kalamazoo, Mich.: Cistercian, 1982.

Theodoret of Cyr. *On Divine Providence*. Translated and annotated by Thomas Halton. ACW 49. New York: Newman Press, 1988.

[Thedoret of Cyr]. "Theodoret." In *Theodoret, Jerome, Gennadius, Rufinus: Historical Writings, etc.*, pp. 1-348. Translated by Blomfield Jackson. NPNF 3. Series 2. Edited by Philip Schaff and Henry Wace. 14 vols. 1886-1900. Reprint, Peabody, Mass.: Hendrickson, 1994.

[Theophylact]. *The Explanation by Blessed Theophylact of the Holy Gospel According to St. Matthew*. Introduction by Fr. Christopher Stade. House Springs, Mo.: Chysostom Press, 1992.

Valerian. "Homilies." In *Saint Peter Chrysologus, Selected Sermons, and Saint Valerian, Homilies*, pp. 299-435. Translated by George E. Ganss. FC 17. Washington, D.C.: The Catholic University of America Press, 1962.

[Victorinus of Petovium]. "Victorinus." In *Lactantius, Venantius, Asterius, Victorinus, Dionysius, Apostolic Teaching and Constitutions, 2 Clement, Early Liturgies*, pp. 341-60. Translated by Robert Ernest Wallis. ANF 7. Edited by Alexander Roberts and James Donaldson. 10 vols. 1885-1887. Reprint, Peabody, Mass.: Hendrickson, 1994.

Authors/Writings Index

Subject Index

Aaron, 165
Abel, 80
Abraham
    bosom of, 231
    Christians and, 63
    death of, 263
    descendants (seed) of, 85,
    96
    promise to, xxi
    sees God, 48
    servant of, 96
    testing and obedience of,
    189, 225
abyss, 127
academicians, 111
Acts of Pontius Pilate, 245
Adam, 85, 109, 124, 168, 221
adoption, 4, 9, 16
adornment, 33
advent
    first, 96, 111, 130, 233
    second, 111, 233
adversary, 85
afflicted, the, 216-21
affliction, 188-89. See also trials
    and tribulations
Africa, 145
Ahaz, 60
Alexandria, 139
Alexandrian interpretation, xxii
allegory, 97, 233
almah, 61
alms, almsgiving, 13-14
altar in Egypt, 144

Amos, book of, 129
Ananiah, 266
Ananias and Sapphira, 262
angel, angels
    Christ as, 73-76
    Christ comes with, 35
    of God, 265
    meaning of, 73
    praise with, 49-50
    a vision of, 186
anger, 180, 195
Anna, 136
anointing, 90, 165, 168, 193
antichrist, 67, 104, 111, 130,
    183, 201
Antiochene interpretation, xxii
Antiochus the Great, 144
Antony, 259
apostasy, 46
apostles
    children represent, 105
    church and, 80
    fear of, 207
    as first fruits, 188
    lament of, 149
    mountain represents, 25
    proclaim the cross, 109
    saints and, 40
    salvation of (as remnant),
    xxi, 10, 37, 88-89
Apostles' Creed, 167 n. 35, 196
Aquila, xvii, 10, 39, 130, 159
Arabia, 67, 147-50
Aramaic, 252. See also languages
Arian, 243
Ariel, 199
ark, 183
arrogance, 15
asp, 108. See also serpent
Assyrians
    conversion of, 141-45
    defeat of, 132, 253-59
    oracle against, 140
    rulers of, 91

threat by, 212-16
attention, 199
Augustus, edict of, 36
awe, 50
ax, 86, 91
Baal, 262
Babylon, Babylonians
    Hezekiah and, 264-66
    invasion by, 133
    king of, 119
    oracle concerning, 115-17,
    147-50
    represents sins, 237
    represents the world, 140
Balaam, 126-27
Balak, 126
balm in Gilead, 241
Balthasar, 140
baptism
    confession and, 168
    Holy Spirit and, 100
    prophecy of, 16
    purification and regenera-
    tion by 17-19
    virginity and, 62
    of water and spirit, 37
Barabbas, 44
Barnabas, 256
Bashan, 91
beasts, wild, 105-6
Behemoth, 108
belief, 56
Berosus, 257
Bethsaida, 68, 240
blame, 213-14
blessed, the, 226-27
blessing, blessings, 97-98
blood, 13, 17
book, 201-2, 214
book of judgment, 101
branch, branches, 91, 94, 96-97
bread, 54, 150, 165, 223, 232
bribes, 232
bronze serpent, 262

Cain, 80, 225
calf, 105
Cana, wedding at, 68
Canaan, 143
canon, xvii
Capernaum, 68
captives, 96
captivity, 146
carelessness, 156
Carmel, 211, 240, 258
Carthage, 145
cedars of Lebanon, 91
celestial bodies, 162-65, 220-21,
    265. See also moon; sun.
chalice, 143
chariot, 149, 236
charismata, 98. See also Holy
    Spirit, gifts of
charity, 214. See also love
chastity, 61
cherubim, 49, 52
child, children, 68, 101, 105,
    108
childbirth, 116. See also labor
choir, 263
Chorazin, 68
chrism, 165. See also anointing
Christian, Christians, 63, 75,
    145, 164-65
Christology, xviii
Chronicles, book of, 257
church, churches
    ark represents, 183
    built of stone, 80
    Christ and, 25, 77, 98, 109,
    138, 192
    city represents, 36
    diversity in, 105, 107
    divine protection of, 165-66
    enemies of, 175
    Eve represents, 109
    exaltation of, 166
    exodus represents, 97
    Holy Spirit and, 31, 90

311

wrath, 180
effects of, 43
forgiveness of, 16, 54, 215-16, 218-19, 225, 240, 262
freedom from, 259
ignorance and, 7
incarnation and, 108
Isaiah's confession of, 52-53
law and, 167
and punishment, 177
purification of, 55
remission of, 17, 215
remorse and shame for, 54-55, 158
separates from God, 176
stain of, 37
treatment of, 8
warning to the unrepentant, 20
by word, 54
Sinai, 25-26
sinner, sinners
in darkness, 70
destiny of, 178
destruction of, 116-17
judgment of obstinate, 125
the unrepentant, 8-9
sleep, 201
Sodom (and Gomorrah), 10, 31, 117, 140
soldiers, 214
solitude, 55
Solomon, 76-78, 165
Son
of the Dawn, 121-22
of God, 72
of Man, 111
See also Jesus Christ
song of victory, 169-73
sorrow, 246-47
soul
city represents, 143, 186
cultivation of, 9
desert represents, 240
heart and, 207
purity of, 18
shadows in the, 209
silence and, 226
vineyard represents, 39
wall represents, 186
womb of the, 178
wounds of, 8
spirit of the Lord, 102-3
spiritual growth and maturity, 100, 154, 220, 232, 244
spiritual journey, 247
spiritual warfare, 140
Stephen, 146-47

steps, 101-3
stone, 67-68, 80
straw, 108. See also hay
strong man, 114
stumbling block, 193
stump of Jesse, 93-98, 110-11
suffering, 84, 113. See also pain
sun, 220-21, 262, 265
swaddling clothes, 62
sword (of God), 19-20, 104, 185, 236
Symmachus, xvii
Syro-Phoenicia, 67
tabernacle, 97
Tabitha, 262
table, 149
tablets, 166
Tarshish, 158
teacher, teachers, 9-10, 75, 218-19
teaching, 53, 242, 252
temple, 31, 43, 77, 91-92, 196
temptation, 189
tempter, 121
Ten Commandments, 89, 100, 102
thanksgiving
for blessings, 177
song of, 163-69
in tribulation, 263
Theodotian, xvii, 130
theosis, 54
thieves, 208, 214
thigh, 96
thorns, 237
throne
of Christ, 129-30
of David, 78
of God, 48-49
Tiberias, 68
Tiglath-pileser, 250
time, 140-41, 221
tin, iron and lead, 81
Tirhakah, 257
tomb of Christ, 111, 193, 233
tongue, tongues
gift of, 189-90
as hand, 15
power of, 122-23
of the sea, 111-12
tower of Babel, 80
tradition, apostolic, 152, 210
transfiguration, 139
transformation
through Christ, 105-6
by the gospel, 26-27
of humanity, 61
through love, 107
unexpected, 211

See also regeneration; renewal
tree, trees, 91, 94, 109
tree of life, 70, 248
trials and tribulations
afflictions and, 188-89
efficacy of, 215
enduring, 215, 229
and fear of God, 176
for the present, 236
purification through, 22, 81
thankfulness in, 263
tribes, names of, 31
Trinity
doctrine of, 166
essence of, 51-52
grace of, 71
light of, 149
unity of, 102-3
vision of, 49-51
voice of, 101
trumpet, 136
truth
Christ the, 105
doctrine of, 181
nourishment of, 245-46
and righteousness, 104-5
from shadow to, 14
signs of, 40
streams of, 114
violation of, 232
twelve, 26
Twelve Prophets (writings), 129
twins, 111
two by two, 149
typology, 60
Tyre, 140, 158-59
understanding, 59-60, 195-96, 210
unity, 193-94
urn, 246
Uzziah, 48
values, 42
vanity, 29
veil, 202
Vespasian, 144
vice, 86, 166
victory, God's help and, 173-84
vigils, 171-72
vineyard
destruction of, 127-30
on the holy, 89
parable of, 195
represents the church, 39
represents the soul, 39
song of, 38-40
virgin, xx, 64
virgin birth, xx, 60-64, 94-95, 97

virginity, 62, 197
virtues
Christ and, 71-72
and fullness of life, 230
goodness, the mother of, 19
Holy Spirit and, 99
home of, 237
rejection of, 7
vision(s)
of Daniel, 24
Isaiah's, of God, 47-55
of Israel, 47-55
meaning of, 2-3
visitation, 84
Vulgate, xviii
wailing, 127
wall, 170-71, 186
war, 27
watchman, 149-50
water, 74, 108, 226
weakness, 45
wealth, the wealthy
appropriate attitude toward, 179
danger of, 265-66
genuine, 230
of the people, 85-86
and the poor, 114
and teaching, 114
See also money; possessions
well, 258
wheat, 105
widow, widowhood, 17-18
will
belief and, 56
of Christ, 242
and deeds, 19
of God, 3, 74-75, 125
need for a good, 19
wine, 166, 188, 200
wisdom
dew represents, 181
doctrine of, 181
false, 209-10
from fear to, 100
insufficiency of, 209-10
practical, 225
saving streams of, 139
true, 230
and understanding, 59
wolf, 105-6
women at Christ's resurrection, 186, 214
wonder, 50
wool, 17
word
Christ as, 74
and deed, 42, 205-9

Scripture Index

Old Testament

Genesis
1:4, *45*
1:5, *70*
1:7, *236*
1:26, *84*
1:31, *220*
3:5, *124*
3:8, *221*
3:14, *236*
3:16, *168*
3:17, *108*
3:18, *236*
3:22, *194*
4:3, *80*
5:24, *225*
6:3, *140*
9:22, *80*
11:1, *141*
11:2-9, *80*
11:6, *141*
12:4, *225*
12:6, *89*
13:12, *89*
14:14, *90*
15:5, *88*
15:13, *140*
16:7, *75*
17:8, *94*
18:20, *32*
19:1, *89*
22:1, *189*

22:18, *63, 96*
24:2, *96*
25:8, *263*
27:28, *107*
27:40, *88*
28:10-22, *100, 102*
28:12, *193*
29, *192*
29—30, *205*
32:10, *95*
37:25, *241*
40:9-11, *199*
49:9, *95*
49:10, *67, 94*
49:27, *105*

Exodus
2:15, *89*
3:3, *178*
3:10, *55*
4:10-13, *55*
4:13, *94*
5:2, *123, 137*
5:6, *195*
7:1, *222*
7:3-4, *189*
7:20, *113*
7:22, *195*
9:16, *210*
12:18, *221*
12:22, *17*
15:2, *192*
15:9, *85*
15:10, *85*
17:11, *216*
20:13-16, *89*
20:18, *3*
22:6, *154*
29:42, *13*
29:45, *170*
32:19-20, *166*
32:32, *266*
33:23, *139*
34:7, *177*

Leviticus
2:4, *223*
11:13, *154*
25:9, *13*

Numbers
14:20-21, *51*
17:1-10, *96*
19:9-10, *13*
24:17, *127*
27:18, *129*

Deuteronomy
4:24, *86, 139*
6:16, *60*
17:16-17, *250*
18:15, *95, 189*
25:4, *226*
28:13, *111*
28:44, *111*
28:66, *95*
32:1, *3*
32:2, *181*
32:13, *90*
32:43, *107*

Joshua
1:8, *202*

Judges
6:36-40, *60*
7:5, *89*
13:8-11, *60*

2 Samuel
5:7, *199*
5:9, *199*
6:14, *147*
6:20-22, *147*

1 Kings
1:39, *165*
5, *78*
6:38, *78*

17:22, *244*
19:18, *90*
22:39, *265*

2 Kings
2:11, *137, 236*
4:34-35, *244*
5:14, *244*
6:16, *236*
6:17, *236*
15:17-20, *250*
15:29, *250*
16—18, *264*
17:1-6, *142*
17:3-6, *250*
18—19, *250*
18:4, *262*
18:13, *250*
18:14-18, *264*
18:31, *252*
19:1-2, *256*
19:26, *255*
19:35, *215, 262*
20:1, *215, 262*
20:1-3, *170*
20:2, *215*
20:13, *265*
23:4, *262*
24:10-16, *265*

Nehemiah
12:37, *223*

Job
1:16, *189*
3:8, *185*
4:18, *162*
7:1, *189*
19:10, *81*
19:25-27, *129*
21:10, *179*
25:5, *162*
29:6, *90*
33:15, *171*